ARKANSAS: A CONCISE HISTORY

Arkansas
A CONCISE HISTORY

JEANNIE M. WHAYNE
THOMAS A. DEBLACK
GEORGE SABO III
MORRIS S. ARNOLD

The University of Arkansas Press
Fayetteville
2019

ISBN: 978-1-68226-092-0 (paper)
eISBN: 978-1-61075-661-7

23 22 21 20 19   5 4 3 2 1

Designed by Liz Lester

♾ The paper used in this publication meets the minimum requirements
of the American National Standard for Permanence of Paper for Printed
Library Materials Z39.48–1984.

Library of Congress Cataloging-in-Publication Data

Names: Whayne, Jeannie M., author. | DeBlack, Thomas A., 1951– author. |
    Sabo, George, author. | Arnold, Morris S., author.
Title: Arkansas : a concise history / Jeannie M. Whayne, Thomas A. DeBlack,
    George Sabo III, Morris S. Arnold.
Description: Fayetteville : The University of Arkansas Press, 2019. | Includes
    bibliographical references and index. |
Identifiers: LCCN 2018034081 (print) | LCCN 2018034366 (ebook) | ISBN
    9781610756617 (electronic) | ISBN 9781682260920 (pbk. : alk. paper)
Subjects: LCSH: Arkansas—History.
Classification: LCC F411 (ebook) | LCC F411 .W47 2019 (print) | DDC
    976.7—dc23
LC record available at https://lccn.loc.gov/2018034081

CONTENTS

ARKANSAS: A CONCISE HISTORY

1 A Land "Inferior to None"

Happen! happened in Arkansaw: where else could it have happened, but in the creation State, the finishing-up country—a state where the sile runs down to the center of the 'arth, and the government gives you title to every inch of it? Then its airs—just breathe them, and they will make you snort like a horse. It's a State without fault, it is.

—THOMAS BANGS THORPE, "The Big Bear of Arkansas"

The soil of the Arkansas bottoms is inferior to none in the world.

—ALBERT PIKE, letter to the New England Magazine, 1835

MILLIONS OF YEARS before the first human being set foot there, dynamic forces shaped the land that would become the state of Arkansas, making it one of the most varied and beautiful in the American nation. Some 500 million years ago, all of present-day Arkansas was covered by the waters of what we now know as the Gulf of Mexico. Shallow waters teeming with marine life covered the northern part of the state, and as sea creatures died their shells became incorporated in bottom sediments that later formed into limestone. The tiny fossils that can be found today in that limestone provide a record of this era in the state's geological history. Over time, the land began to emerge from the water, as ancient continents collided to form a supercontinent called Pangea. The first to emerge was the land in the northern and western regions, where the collision of continents gradually thrust the land upward. The land in the southern and eastern parts of Arkansas remained underwater for a much longer period. When the waters finally receded from this region, they left a flat and rolling landscape that resembled the ocean floor it had been for so long.

At the conclusion of this lengthy period of dynamic change (roughly one million years ago), Arkansas assumed the general geologic pattern that exists today. A diagonal line running northeast to southwest divides the state approximately in half, with the areas north and west of the line being characterized by mountainous uplands, while the southern and eastern parts are flat or rolling lowlands.

Pangea: A supercontinent formed by the collision of the other continents about 300 million years ago. This supercontinent persisted throughout Paleozoic and Mesozoic eras until it began to break up some 200 million years ago.

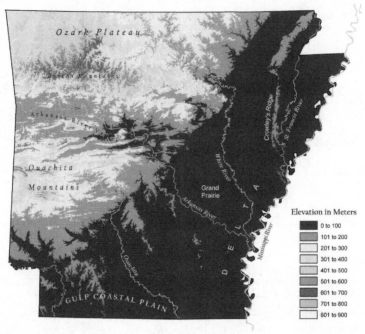

Arkansas Elevation. *Courtesy of Joseph Swain.* (Sources: US Geological Survey, National Elevation Dataset ned.usgs.gov.)

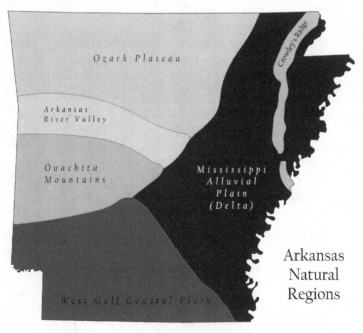

Arkansas Natural Regions. *Courtesy of Joseph Swain.* (Sources: Arkansas Geographic Information Office, *Encyclopedia of Arkansas History & Culture,* US Geological Survey.)

This geologic division would have profound implications for social, economic, and political development in Arkansas. But for all its significance, this division of Arkansas into highlands and lowlands greatly oversimplifies the complex nature of the state's geology. Today geologists recognize six major natural divisions in Arkansas. Three—the Ozark Mountains, the Ouachita Mountains, and the Arkansas River valley—make up the highland region, and three others—the West Gulf Coastal Plain, the Mississippi Alluvial Plain (the Arkansas delta), and Crowley's Ridge—constitute the lowlands.

The Ozark Mountains

Perhaps the most well known of these natural divisions is the Ozark Mountains. Occupying the northwest corner of the state, the Ozarks reach elevations over two thousand feet higher than in the lowlands. Technically, these mountains are actually what geologists call an elevated plateau. After the continental collision forced this land upward, a long process of erosion began that gradually lowered the surface of the land until it reached layers that were resistant to erosion. The result was the creation of a relatively flat, level plateau. Over long periods of time, rivers dissected the Ozark Plateau creating three smaller, discontinuous plateaus separated by valleys and erosional remnants in the shapes of hills and mountains. These plateaus are called the Springfield Plateau, the Salem Plateau, and the Boston Plateau.

Plateau: An area of fairly level high ground.

The Springfield Plateau extends westward from St. Louis, Missouri, to southwest Missouri, northeast Oklahoma, and northwest Arkansas. It is composed largely of highly soluble limestone and a flint-like rock called chert that was an important resource for stone toolmaking American Indians during the prehistoric era. Much of this plateau is forested, but sizable areas of prairie with level land and tillable soil drew early settlers from southern Missouri to the area. Today the cities of Fayetteville and Springdale (Washington County), Rogers (Benton County), and Harrison (Boone County) are located in the Springfield Plateau.

Prairie: A large open area of grassland.

North and east of the Springfield Plateau lies the Salem Plateau. The vast majority of this plateau lies in Missouri, but the southernmost part crosses the border into north-central Arkansas. The soil here is much thinner and poorer than in the Springfield Plateau. Some nineteenth-century accounts described large parts of the region as "barrens." Today, Eureka Springs lies on an escarpment between the Springfield and Salem Plateaus, and the towns of Mammoth Springs (Fulton County), Mountain Home (Baxter County), Calico Rock (Izard County), Cherokee Village (Sharp and Fulton counties), and Yellville (Marion County) are located on the Salem Plateau.

The third plateau, the Boston Plateau (commonly called the Boston Mountains), lies south of the Springfield Plateau. Reaching elevations of up to 2,600 feet above sea level, this plateau is the highest in the Ozarks. The region is characterized by magnificent mountain vistas, but its rugged nature limited transportation and agricultural development, which led to the creation of an isolated, hill-country culture that gave the Ozarks its "hillbilly" image. The Boston Plateau was traditionally the poorest section of a region that was for much of Arkansas history the poorest in the state.

Hardwood forests of oak and hickory dominate the Ozark landscape, and clear, spring-fed rivers like the King, the Spring, the Buffalo, and numerous other streams cut deep valleys through parts of the Ozarks. The best known of these Ozark rivers is the Buffalo. Originating in the Boston Plateau, the Buffalo follows a generally east-to-west course for over 150 miles through present-day Newton, Searcy, and Marion counties before entering the White River in Baxter County. The beautiful bluffs, rapids, and waterfalls created by this river, in addition to the clear water and the abundance of fish, birds, and other wildlife, make the Buffalo one of the most scenic rivers in the nation.

The Ozarks are also home to another of the state's unique features. Water seeping through cracks in the region's limestone base causes the underlying rock to dissolve, creating large caves. The most spectacular of these may be Blanchard Springs Cavern near Mountain View. This massive underground cave contains an underground river, stalactites (formations descending from the cave's ceiling), stalagmites (formations rising from the cavern floor), columns (where stalactites and stalagmites meet), and extensive areas of flowstone (sheet-like calcite deposits formed where water flows down a wall or along the floor). Bats, snails, spiders, and the rare Ozark blind salamander (the first cave-dwelling amphibian found in the United States) find a home in the cavern. Another geological feature—rock shelters eroded into the faces of vertical limestone and sandstone bluffs—was used extensively by prehistoric American Indians for short-term occupation. The dry environments of many rock shelters made them suitable for the storage of nuts and grains.

Travelers to the Ozarks have long been impressed by the region's great natural beauty. The geologist Henry Rowe Schoolcraft left an account of his visit to the Missouri and Arkansas Ozarks in 1819–1820. He wrote, "It is a mixture of forest and plain, of hills and long sloping valleys, where the tall oak forms a striking contrast with the rich foliage of the evergreen cane, or the waving field of prairie-grass. It is an assemblage of beautiful groves, and level prairies, of river alluvion, and high-land precipice, diversified by the devious course of the river, and the distant promontory, forming a scene so novel, yet so harmonious, as to strike the beholder with admiration; and the effect must be greatly heightened, when viewed under the influence of a mild clear atmosphere, and an invigorating sun, such as is said to characterize the region during the spring and summer."

The Ouachita Mountains

The Ouachita Mountains make up the second part of the Arkansas highlands. Lying south of the Ozarks, the Ouachitas extend from eastern Oklahoma to the western edge of present-day Little Rock in central Arkansas. Like the Ozarks, the Ouachitas were created by the collision of continents, but here uplift was only a minimal factor. Rather the collision folded layers of rock over other layers. Riverine erosion accentuated the folds, shaping them into a series of east-west running ridges. Sandstone and shale compose much of the Ouachitas, but the region also has deposits of quartz crystals and novaculite, a hard, dense stone prized for use as a whetstone during historic times and by ancient American Indians as a material for stone toolmaking long before that. Pine forests predominate on the warmer south-facing slopes of the Ouachitas' ridges, while the cooler north-facing ridges tend to favor hardwood forests. The valleys between the ridges are mixtures of pine and hardwood. Streams in the region tend to follow the east-west fold patterns, and rainwater that follows the folds below ground emerges at various points in the region as hot springs, most noticeably at today's Hot Springs National Park.

On his expedition up the Ouachita River with fellow Scottish immigrant George Hunter in 1804–1805, William Dunbar described the land along the Ouachita River just below the hot springs:

> From the river camp for about two miles, the lands are level and of second rate quality, the timber chiefly oak intermixed with others common to the climate and a few scattering pine-trees; further on, the lands on either hand arose into gently swelling hills, clothed chiefly with handsome pine-woods; the road passed along a valley frequently wet, by numerous rills [small brooks] and springs of excellent water which broke from the foot of the hills: as we approached the hot-springs the hills became more elevated and of steep ascent & generally rocky.

The Arkansas River Valley

In 1819 the English-born naturalist Thomas Nuttall traveled up the Arkansas River from Arkansas Post on the river's lower reaches to Fort Smith. As he

Ozark rock shelter. Photo by George Sabo III. *Courtesy of the Arkansas Archeological Survey.*

Ouachita Mountains. Photo by Mary Beth Trubitt. *Courtesy of the Arkansas Archeological Survey.*

passed the point where Little Rock would soon be established, he remarked on the changing nature of the lands that bordered the great river. "After emerging as it were from so vast a tract of alluvial lands, as that through which I had now been traveling for more than three months," he wrote, "it is almost impossible to describe the pleasure which these romantic prospects afford me. Who can be insensible to the beauty of the verdant hill and valley, to the sublimity of the clouded mountain, the fearful precipice, or the torrent of the cataract." This region, where the river passes between the Ozarks and the Ouachitas, is known as the Arkansas River valley. The same geologic forces that caused the Ozarks and the Ouachitas to be uplifted forced the area between them downward into a trough that was carved and sculpted by the Arkansas River. Up to forty miles in width and extending from the Oklahoma border to the Mississippi River, the Arkansas River valley contains characteristics of both the Ozarks and the Ouachitas, with both uplifted plateaus and folded ridges, and pine and hardwood forests. Other features are unique to the region. The wide bottomlands provide fertile farmland and also feature bottomland forests and swamps. Pockets of coal and natural gas are also found in the region.

Trough: A long hollow in the earth's surface.

Three unique features of the river valley are Mount Magazine (Logan County), Mount Nebo (Yell County), and Petit Jean Mountain (Conway County). All are mesas—isolated hills with steep sides and flat tops. Mount Magazine is the highest point in Arkansas, reaching an elevation of 2,753 feet above sea level. The mountain is also famous for its diverse butterfly population. Ninety-four of the 134 species of butterflies in Arkansas can be found there, including the rare Diana fritillary. Petit Jean Mountain contains the greatest concentration of prehistoric American Indian pictographs (rock paintings) in the state. Mount Nebo was an important landmark for navigation along the Arkansas River during the early historic era. The three mountains provide magnificent views of the bottomlands and rolling uplands that characterize most of the Arkansas River valley.

Mesas: Isolated hills with steep sides and flat tops.

Thomas Nuttall reported that he was "amused by the gentle murmurs of a rill and pellucid water, which broke from rock to rock. The acclivity, through a scanty thicket, rather than the usual sombre forest, was already adorned with violets, and occasional clusters of the parti-colored Collinsia. The groves and thickets were whitened with the blossoms of the dogwood (Cornus florida). The lugubrious vocifications of the whip-poor-will, the croaking frogs, chirping crickets, and whoops and halloos of the Indians, broke not disagreeably the silence of a calm and fine evening."

The river itself and its adjacent lowlands have long served as a transportation corridor for both animals and people. Long before highways or railroads, the river was a major artery of commerce for early Arkansans, and some of the state's earliest settlements grew up along its banks. Today Fort Smith, Ozark, Clarksville, Russellville, Morrilton, Conway, and several smaller communities are located in the river valley.

The West Gulf Coastal Plain

Even after most of the water that originally covered Arkansas had receded, much of the southwestern region remained covered by a wide, shallow lagoon that was home to a variety of living things ranging from microorganisms to shellfish to dinosaurs. Near present-day Nashville (Howard County), paleontologists found the tracks of a number of huge dinosaurs that had traversed the area between 150 and 200 million years ago, when the climate was hotter and much more humid than today. Recent investigations led by University of Arkansas geosciences professor Steve Boss have identified numerous species, including *Acrocanthosaurus atokensis*, one of the largest predators ever to roam the earth's surface, as well as gigantic long-necked, plant-eating sauropods. The remains of the shellfish eventually formed a soft version of limestone known as chalk.

Paleontologists: Scientists who study the life of past geological periods through fossil remains.

Because various parts of the Coastal Plain formed at different times, the soil in this natural division varies widely. It ranges from the fertile farmland and bottomland forest of the Red River and the Blackland Prairies in the west to the later (and poorer) sandy pine-covered regions in the east. The varying soils gave rise to varying ways of life. In the western portion of the region, farming and livestock raising predominate, while in the east, timber harvesting is a major economic activity.

Several varieties of minerals are found in the Coastal Plain. Bauxite (used in making aluminum) is found in Saline County, and the discovery of oil and gas near present-day El Dorado and Smackover created a boomtown economy in the early twentieth century. A unique mineral found in the Coastal Plain comes from near present-day Murfreesboro (Pike County). Thousands of diamonds have been found at the site of an ancient volcano that exploded millions of years ago.

The Mississippi Alluvial Plain (the Delta)

The last part of Arkansas to take shape was the southeastern region. As the climate cooled dramatically some 110,000 years ago, thick glacial ice scoured

Nashville dinosaur tracks. © 2011 University Relations, Photo Russell Cothren.

northern parts of the continent. When the last vestiges of the ice sheets began to melt some 11,500 years ago, rivers filled with outwash spread deep sedimentary deposits across the more southerly regions. The Mississippi Alluvial Plain and a remnant-elevated area in eastern Arkansas called Crowley's Ridge were created during this period. The Mississippi Alluvial Plain, better known as the Delta, occupies roughly the eastern third of the state. The most obvious feature of the Delta landscape is its flat, level surface. Maj. Amos Stoddard, a US Army officer who came to the region in 1804, noted that the land "presents an almost perfect level, and . . . is much more elevated on the river than in the rear of it. This vast tract affords a thick growth of large and tall trees, mostly cotton wood and cypress, with extensive cane breaks . . . from fifteen to twenty feet in height . . . All these lands are of an alluvial nature, and extremely fertile." Tupelo trees are also common. For the earliest white settlers, these dense forests, impenetrable canebrakes, and large swamps made travel through the region difficult or impossible.

Alluvial: Deposits of clay, silt, and sand left by flowing floodwater in a river valley or delta.

Ecologist Tom Foti has written that the Delta is "a land of rivers, built by rivers, and defined by rivers." The foremost of these is the Mississippi River, which has carved and sculpted the Delta landscape for millions of years, as it followed an ever-changing path southward to the Gulf of Mexico. Its frequent floods have been a bane to travel and settlement in the region, but those same floods have deposited tons of incredibly fertile soil over the area, making the Mississippi Alluvial Plain one of the richest agricultural regions in the world.

The Arkansas River has also played a major role in creating the Delta. From its headwaters in Colorado, the Arkansas flows east-southeast across Kansas and Oklahoma before entering western Arkansas near Fort Smith (Sebastian County) and continuing southeastwardly through the Arkansas River valley before entering the Mississippi Alluvial Plain near Little Rock. The river continues its southeasterly path through the Delta and enters the Mississippi River in eastern Desha County. At almost fifteen hundred miles in length, the Arkansas is the nation's sixth longest river.

Other major streams have also shaped the Delta landscape. The White River begins its 722-mile journey in northwest Arkansas, flowing north into Missouri before crossing back into Arkansas near Bull Shoals in Marion County. The river continues on a southeasterly course, entering the Mississippi Alluvial Plain near Batesville and proceeding 295 miles through the Delta before entering the Mississippi in Desha County just north of the mouth of the Arkansas. The Black and the Cache rivers flow southward from northeast Arkansas into the White. To the east the L'Anguille and the St. Francis rivers flow southward along opposite sides of Crowley's Ridge. The smaller L'Anguille joins the St. Francis in eastern Lee County, not far from where the St. Francis enters the Mississippi just north of present-day Helena.

In parts of the region, American Indian communities living in the area between ad 900–1600 built large, fortified towns that were supported by an agriculture based on the production of corn, beans, and squash. The first white

settlers subsisted on the abundant game and fish, but later settlers accumulated great wealth by exploiting the fertile land. In the sandy soils along the rivers, cotton became the primary crop, and by the mid-nineteenth century the
region was tied to plantation-style agriculture and to the institution of slavery.

Within this region there exists a subregion consisting of a broad ter-
race covered by wind-blown dust (loess) underlain by a substratum of clay.
Originally covered by tall prairie grass, today the region is
largely covered by croplands. The clay base in the region's **Loess:** A loosely
soil causes it to hold water, making the Grand Prairie compacted deposit
an excellent region for growing rice. This Grand Prairie of wind-blown
extends over half a million acres and covers all or part of sediment.
four counties—White, Lonoke, Prairie, and Arkansas. The
entire Alluvial Plain is a major bird migration corridor in the fall and spring,
and the numerous flooded rice fields in the Grand Prairie annually attract
tens of thousands of migrating ducks, making the area one of the nation's
best duck-hunting regions. Other smaller terraces are common north of the
Arkansas River.

For untold centuries, the region's rivers changed course with almost
every flood, wreaking havoc on settlers and creating a nightmare for anyone
attempting to plot out permanent county or state boundary lines. Improved
flood-control measures that were put in place after the disastrous Mississippi
River flood of 1927 have greatly decreased the danger of flooding and stabi-
lized the course of the Arkansas and the Mississippi rivers.

Crowley's Ridge

Running from north to south through the northern half of the Mississippi
Alluvial Plain is an elevated strip of ground that varies in width from a half
mile to twenty miles and rises up to two hundred feet above the flat Delta land.
This ridge takes its name from Benjamin Crowley, one of the first white settlers
in the region (c. 1820). Crowley's Ridge runs for over 150 miles from extreme
northeast Arkansas to Helena on the Mississippi River in Phillips County,
disappearing briefly just north of present-day Marianna (Lee County). The
ridge, which has its origins near Cape Girardeau, Missouri, is the sixth and
smallest natural division in Arkansas. As elsewhere in the Delta, the receding
waters of the Gulf of Mexico left deposits of sand and marine organisms here.
But unlike in the Delta the rivers did not remove all of this material. Instead,
they left a narrow ridge that was gradually overlain by riverine deposits of
sand and gravel. Originally much lower than it is today, the ridge was built up
to its present height by loess that has accumulated in some places to a depth
of fifty feet. This loess is severely prone to erosion, making landslides a threat.

Thousands of years ago, the Mississippi River actually flowed west of the ridge and the Ohio River flowed to its east, near the path of the modern Mississippi River. Over time, the Ohio retreated north and the Mississippi changed course to flow west of the ridge. Today hardwood forests of oak and hickory trees are found here, as are some of the most valuable gravel deposits in the state.

The heights of Crowley's Ridge provide a spectacular view of the surrounding Delta. The German traveler and sportsman Friedrich Gerstacker, who lived in Arkansas from 1837 to 1843 including for a time on the ridge, described one such vista looking east from the eastern edge of the ridge on a foggy morning. "The thick white fog, through which not a tree was visible, north, south, or east, looked like the sea, and I was prompted to look out for a sail; the glowing red ball of the sun as he worked his way through it, cast a roseate hue over all. As the sun rose higher the fog began to disperse, and the tips of the highest trees appeared. As the fog vanished, it gave place to a boundless extent of green, unbroken by any rise, save that on which we stood. I remained for a long time in silent admiration of the fascinating sight."

Climate

The other major environmental feature that has impacted the development of Arkansas is the climate, which is defined as the general weather conditions that prevail in an area over a long period of time. Climatic changes have a profound impact on the type of vegetation that can exist in a particular region. In Arkansas, the climate, like the land itself, has gone through a dynamic series of changes over time. At the end of the last Ice Age the midcontinental climate was colder than it is today but seasonal variations in temperature and precipitation were much less pronounced. Spruce and jack pine forests extended across the upland parts of Arkansas and much of the Gulf Coastal Plain. Spruce boreal forests covered much of the Mississippi Alluvial Plain, though mixed deciduous woodlands grew along the river bottomlands. Animal life was very different as well: though several familiar species including deer and elk were present, now-extinct species of large mammals roamed the land, including mammoths and mastodons, giant sloths and llamas, peccaries, and large bison.

Boreal: Of, relating to, or comprising the northern biotic area, characterized especially by the dominance of coniferous forests.

Deciduous: Falling off or shed seasonally at a certain stage of the development of the life cycle.

Warming temperatures between 14,000 and 10,000 years ago caused glaciers to retreat and vegetation to expand into newly emerging habitats. Oak and hickory woodlands dominated the northern part of the state, while the south was characterized by oak and hickory mixed with southern pine. Cypress and tupelo trees and a few hardwoods characterized the Mississippi Alluvial Plain. As we have seen, grassland prairies remained in parts of Arkansas, remnants of a drier period in Arkansas's ancient past.

A period of pronounced global warming developed between 8,000 and 5,000 years ago. Climate patterns interacting with topography, soil, and hydrography produced different patterns of vegetation and wildlife in each of Arkansas's major physiographic regions. These changes had important consequences for American Indian communities across the mid-South.

Modern landforms and habitats developed with a return to more temperate and moist conditions after 5,000 years ago. A "blip" in this environmental trajectory occurred between circa ad 1400–1850, the result of another global climate change called the Little Ice Age when cooler conditions prevailed. Protracted episodes of drought were experienced in many parts of Arkansas, with dramatic consequences for animals and plants as well as human settlement patterns and economic activities.

Today Arkansas has what scientists refer to as a humid subtropical climate, defined as a region with a hot summer and no specific dry season. Summers are generally hot and humid with high temperatures in the center of the state averaging around 90 degrees in the summer and 50 degrees during generally mild, drier winter months. When warm, moist gulf air clashes with cool, dry air moving east from the Rocky Mountains, strong thunderstorms are produced. Arkansas has approximately sixty days of thunderstorms. Tornadoes are also common in the state. On average Arkansas experiences 26 tornadoes a year, but 107 tornadoes were recorded in the state during 1999. Thunderstorms and tornadoes are most common in the spring, but they can also occur in the fall and winter. Three of the state's deadliest tornadoes occurred in the months of November, January, and February.

Rainfall averages between forty-five and fifty-five inches per year, but snowfall averages only five inches per year. With fertile soil, adequate rainfall, and over two hundred frost-free days a year, the southeastern part of the state is ideal for plantation-style agriculture.

Arkansas experiences all four seasons of the year, and the state has long been known for its changeable, unpredictable weather. Longtime residents are fond of telling newcomers, "If you don't like the weather in Arkansas, just wait a few minutes and it will change." Change has, in fact, been the operative word in describing the geology and climate of Arkansas. These geologic and climatic factors set the stage upon which human activity in Arkansas would take place, and it continues to influence activity in Arkansas today.

2 Ancient Native Americans

THE ROOTS OF Arkansas history reach back to the end of the last Ice Age, which brought the Pleistocene epoch to a close. Around 28,000 BC, hunters pursuing mammoths, mastodons, and other large animals expanded out of Europe into western Asia. Warmer conditions developing after 18,000 BC made it possible for some groups to reach North America, using boats to navigate from island to island across the north Pacific rim or by crossing Beringia—a thousand-mile-wide land mass connecting Siberia and Alaska. Within only a few hundred years these groups had dispersed throughout the Western Hemisphere.

Archeologists reconstruct the record of human achievement prior to the availability of written accounts in terms of eras or time ranges rather than the calendar dates that comprise the stock-in-trade for historians. We'll examine the earliest events in Arkansas history accordingly, employing archeological periods. Archeologists refer to the first people to reach the Americas as Paleoindians, and their time as the Paleoindian period (ca. 14,500–9,500 BC). Who were these people? How did they reach Arkansas? What did they accomplish after they arrived?

Pleistocene epoch:
The geological era that includes the last series of Ice Ages, from 2,588,000 to 11,700 years before the present (BP). The Pleistocene and (current) Holocene epochs represent the Quaternary Period.

Beringia:
A Pleistocene age land bridge (now inundated by the Bering Strait) that connected eastern Siberia and western Alaska.

Arkansas's First People: Entering Ice Age Landscapes

Ice sheets covering northern North American began to recede about 11,500 BC, opening land routes leading south from Beringia, which was submerged by rising sea levels around 10,000 BC. Descending the Mississippi River basin from the northern Plains, Paleoindians reached the mid-South by 10,500 BC. They entered a land very different from today. Mammoths, mastodons, and giant bison roamed expansive grasslands, caribou grazed scattered tundra zones, and elk and smaller animals sheltered in forests along larger rivers and streams. There were few edible plant foods, and most streams and rivers were too cold to support fish, shellfish, reptiles, or amphibians. Paleoindians relied on land animals as their main source of food, hides, and other materials including antler, bone, and ivory.

Paleoindians hunted with composite spears, made using a technology developed by their Upper Paleolithic ancestors in Europe and Asia. Elegantly flaked stone spear points could be affixed to a bone or ivory foreshaft fitted to the end of a longer main shaft. This weapon could be thrust into an animal from close quarters or hurled from a distance using a throwing stick, or atlatl. Stone cutting blades and blunt-end scrapers hafted onto wood or antler handles provided tools for butchering animal carcasses and cleaning and softening hides.

At sites in Oklahoma and Missouri, Paleoindian weapons and butchering tools occur with the remains of mammoths and mastodons, radiocarbon dated to around 9,500 BC. Smaller game discovered at these and other sites—including deer, rabbit, squirrel, and gopher—provides evidence of a rich environment from which Paleoindians acquired abundant food and other resources.

Radiocarbon date:
A measurement, based on analysis of radioactive carbon isotopes, that indicates the age of organic material (such as charcoal or bone) preserved in archeological or geological contexts.

Holocene epoch:
The current geological period that began after the end of the last Ice Age about 11,700 years ago.

With a lifestyle adapted for tracking large animals across Ice Age landscapes, Paleoindians often erected temporary dwellings including lean-tos and pole-frame tents, covered with hides and warmed by glowing campfires. Paleoindians used finely made antler or ivory needles and sinew thread to sew snug-fitting hide clothing. They located their campsites in areas providing access to fresh water and other raw materials, and a favorable vantage for observing game animals. Domesticated dogs transported tent poles, hide coverings, and other items from one camp to another.

At a site in Oklahoma, archeologists found Paleoindian artifacts in deposits of bison bone representing repeated hunting and butchering episodes. One bison skull had a red zigzag line painted on the frontal bone. The pigment appears to be hematite (or red ochre), a substance widely used by ancient hunters for ritual purposes. Among many modern hunters and gatherers, religious beliefs frame hunting as an interaction with the spirit world in which respect for the soul of the animal is exchanged for the gift of sustenance to support the hunter and his family. Ritual marking of the Oklahoma bison skull may represent an ancient version of these beliefs.

Paleoindian artifacts are thinly distributed across Arkansas, suggesting a population of perhaps only one hundred to one hundred and fifty people at first, organized in small groups each consisting of one or more extended families. Populations increased through time, a testament to their successful adaptation to Ice Age environments. But eventually, those environments changed. The change was sufficiently profound that geologists assign the next era, extending from 8,500 BC to the present, to the Holocene epoch.

The Pleistocene to Holocene Transition

One hallmark of the Pleistocene to Holocene transition is the extinction of large Ice Age animals. Paleoindian hunters shifted their focus to deer, elk, and modern bison. The distribution and habits of these animals are very different, requiring modified hunting strategies coupled with changing patterns of seasonal movement across the landscape. This stimulated a new way of life that archeologists refer to as the Dalton culture. The Dalton culture (ca. 9,500–8,500 BC) represents a transition in Native American lifeways, from Ice Age adaptations to a way of life adjusting to newly emerging Holocene conditions.

Dalton sites are distinguished by different kinds of artifacts, including a new type of spear point. Dalton points (along with other implements in the Dalton tool kit) are made using the same stone-working technology that Paleoindians used, suggesting direct descent. Nonetheless, Dalton people left a very different imprint on the land.

Dalton sites in Arkansas are more numerous and more widely distributed than earlier Paleoindian sites. Increase in site numbers indicates a corresponding increase in population, to perhaps five hundred or more for the entire state.

Paleoindian points (*top*) with artist's reconstruction of a throwing stick and dart assemblage (*bottom*). *Courtesy of the University Museum Collection, University of Arkansas.*

Dalton preform, spear point, and reworked points (*top*); adze blade and reconstructed adze (*bottom*). *Courtesy of the University Museum Collection, University of Arkansas.*

Dalton people developed a more sedentary way of life that gave rise to a different settlement pattern. They occupied base camps for several years at a time, from which they traveled to other nearby places to hunt, fish, collect nuts and other seasonal plant foods, and gather stone for manufacture of tools and weapons. Dalton people invented new kinds of woodworking tools, including stone-bladed adzes and celts, reflecting an increase in the use of wood for making more substantial dwellings.

Sedentary: A pattern in which groups or populations occupy a specific location for an extended time.

The most fascinating Dalton site in Arkansas is the Sloan site, located on the summit of a low sand dune in the northeastern part of the state. Excavations revealed numerous clusters of artifacts, forming alignments consistently oriented parallel to the dune's long axis. Careful sifting of excavated sediments around each cluster produced dozens of small, badly eroded bone fragments, most identified as human. This evidence suggests the site is a cemetery where grave offerings were placed with the dead. Dated at 8,500 BC, the Sloan site is considered the oldest cemetery in the Western Hemisphere.

The Shift to Holocene Lifeways

Archeologists divide Native American history during the Holocene epoch into three periods, called the Archaic, Woodland, and Mississippian. Communities living during each of these periods created distinctive technologies, economies, and settlement patterns.

Throughout the Archaic period (8,500–600 BC), Native Americans in Arkansas and the mid-South refined strategies for harvesting wild animals and plants, developing secure economies that supported increasingly sedentary communities. This led, in time, to the domestication of several native plant species, and the advent of gardening in sedentary base camps. Some communities also built earthen mounds to mark their presence within the lands they inhabited. Most Archaic communities remained small, with only a few dozen members who continued to range across the landscape in pursuit of seasonally available animals and plants.

The Woodland period (600 bc–ad 900) witnessed the expansion of gardening economies and proliferation of mound building associated in part with new uses as burial chambers for community members possessing newly elevated social statuses. New technological innovations included the bow and arrow and manufacture of fired-clay pottery for food storage, preparation, and consumption. Community sizes grew to include regional networks of associated hamlets, some with populations numbering in the hundreds. Trade in food and other commodities became increasingly important as a means to acquire provisions.

During the Mississippi period (ad 900–1541), Native Americans across Arkansas and the mid-South replaced their locally domesticated garden crops with varieties of corn, beans, and squashes originally domesticated in Mexico. These more prolific species made possible the development of large-scale field agriculture that, in some parts of Arkansas, supported populations numbering in the thousands living in well-organized towns. Larger communities were ruled by powerful chiefs and priests, who built their own residences, along with shrines and temples, on top of large earthen platform mounds. Some towns extended political and economic control over neighboring communities, to create networks of civic and ceremonial centers supported by surrounding towns and hamlets.

The Archaic Period and the Origins of Plant Domestication

The Archaic period (8,500–600 BC) was a time of extraordinary development, driven partly in response to climate changes but partly also by an increase in Native American efforts to modify the environment to better suit their needs. The most far-reaching change involved domestication of several native plant species. Over the past quarter century, archeologists and botanists have discovered evidence identifying Arkansas and the mid-South as one of only ten places in the world where local plants were domesticated.

Stone-working technologies used to make hunting weapons and other implements also changed, resulting in tool kits exhibiting greater regional variation. New tools include large chipped and ground stone axes that attest to the importance of tree felling and woodworking for construction of larger

Archaic dart points (*top*), notched pebbles used as net weights (*middle left*), woven bag containing acorns (*middle right*), and bone awls and needles (*bottom*). *Courtesy of the University Museum Collection, University of Arkansas.*

and more permanent dwellings and manufacture of dugout canoes. Milling basins and grinding stones provided a means to produce meal from nuts, seeds, and other plant foods.

Dry rock shelters in the Ozark Highlands preserve artifacts made of perishable, organic materials. Bone fish hooks and harpoon heads attest to development of fishing technology as rivers and streams began to slow down and warm up, providing habitats suitable for fish, shellfish, and turtles. Clothing made of skins sewn with antler needles and deer sinew thread have been found in addition to clothing made from woven plant fibers. Bracelets and necklaces made of marine shell, obtained via long-distance trade, added ornamentation to body and dress. Woven fiber nets, baskets, and other containers have been found, illustrating important nonfood uses for native plants.

Plant and animal remains preserved at many archeological sites increase our understanding of how Archaic Indians expanded their food-producing economies. A diversified economy based on hunting animals and birds, fishing and collecting other aquatic species, and gathering a variety of plant foods including nuts and acorns, wild seeds, fruits, and roots was in place by 6,000

BC. Variations took hold in many regions in relation to locally available foods and group preferences. For example, many Ozark sites attest to the importance of deer hunting and acorn gathering, whereas excavations at sites along the Ouachita River in southwest Arkansas reveal that its inhabitants relied heavily on seasonal harvest of hickory nuts, supplemented by hunting and net fishing.

Most Archaic communities organized their living arrangements around permanent base camps occupied year-round, surrounded by other sites used for hunting and butchering, nut and seed harvesting, stone quarrying, and wood cutting. Dwellings had circular floor plans with bark- or mat-covered, pole-frame walls and roofs. Central hearths provided heat and light, surrounded by benches for sitting, sleeping, and storage of food and equipment.

Archeologists estimate that several thousands of Indians occupied Arkansas by the end of the Archaic period. As populations grew, more communities developed and occupied territories extending to the borders of their neighbors. Consequently, people began to use material objects, including regionally distinctive styles of dart points and a few other high-visibility artifacts, to signal their identities. At first, only a few archeologically recognizable territories existed in Arkansas. By Late Archaic times (3,000–600 BC), stylistic differences in artifacts mark a much larger number of territories. Such displays of social identity helped maintain community boundaries, organize trade relations, and facilitate interactions among groups. Social identities were probably also expressed in clothing and other elements of body presentation, including tattooing and hair styles.

As community sizes increased, so too did needs for larger supplies of food. Greater reliance on plant foods led gradually to domestication of several native species. Some of the best evidence for the domestication of local plants by Archaic Indians in Arkansas and the mid-South comes from University of Arkansas Museum collections of ancient plant remains excavated during the 1930s from dry Ozark rock shelters. Studies of the DNA preserved in these desiccated remains help archeologists reconstruct how plant domestication came about. Clearing vegetation around base camps, cutting down trees to build houses, disposing of refuse by scattering it or burying it in the ground, and foot traffic and other outdoor activities contributed to disturbance of soil habitats around active settlements. Many plant species that prefer disturbed areas open to sunlight invaded the margins of Archaic Indian settlements. These plants include *Chenopodium*, knotweed, marsh elder, maygrass, and little barley, all producing highly nutritious seeds. Archaic Indians learned to manipulate the reproductive cycles of these plants—and a few others, such as sunflower and several species of wild gourds and squashes—by weeding out smaller plants and sowing seeds that had been harvested from larger and more prolific plants. These practices led to the evolution of cultigens, or domesticated plants, that produced more food but now at the cost of manual planting and tending. The overall result, achieved between

2,500–1,500 BC, was significant expansion in gardening. Easily dried for long-term preservation, grain production also led to new storage technologies, including grass-lined pits found both in dry rock shelters and at residential sites. When emptied out, food storage pits were often reused for refuse disposal.

Expansion of food-producing strategies not only supported growing populations but also produced new environmental relationships in which larger communities reshaped landscapes to a much greater extent than before. One consequence of these new land-use practices is seen in the first examples of mound and earthwork construction. The earliest examples east of the Mississippi River date to around 5,000 BC. By 1,200 BC, Indians living in southeastern Arkansas were also building mounds. Mound placement on prominent landforms near local population centers suggests use for community rituals.

The most spectacular example of Late Archaic mound building is attributed to the so-called Poverty Point culture, which began about 2,000 BC. At the famous Poverty Point site in northeast Louisiana, Archaic Indians built numerous earthworks including several artificial mounds, the largest of which is in the shape of a bird. Six sets of concentric earthen embankments, each about six feet high and eighty feet across, form a semicircle measuring four thousand feet in diameter. This was by far the largest Archaic ceremonial center in the Southeast.

A trade network extending from the Poverty Point site drew the participation of dozens of communities throughout the lower Mississippi Valley and Gulf Coastal Plain, including some in southeastern Arkansas. Participants in this network traded a variety of distinctive artifacts, including carved stone beads and figurines of naturalistic and stylized humans, insects, animals, and birds. These objects, in company with the large bird effigy mound, illustrate how Arkansas Indians expanded the use of art to symbolize relationships with animal communities and the spirit world.

Social and economic ties supporting the network of Poverty Point communities also suggest a high level of coordination and cooperation. The impressive earthworks at the Poverty Point site are likewise the product of a well-organized effort. Both phenomena point to the emergence of powerful forms of leadership extending beyond a single community. As effective as these institutions might have been, the Poverty Point network wasn't sustained over the long run. Interaction among groups contracted, the Poverty Point site itself was abandoned around 1,000 BC, and mound building declined across the Southeast. New evidence suggests that global climate changes undermined the subsistence economies of Poverty Point communities. The rise and fall of the Poverty Point culture represents an early but transitory experiment in cultural elaboration, in which many Archaic communities in Arkansas participated.

By the end of the Archaic period, communities across Arkansas had devised new technologies to establish more sedentary patterns of settlement and land use. Small communities lived year-round in base camps and supported themselves by a mix of hunting, gathering, and gardening. The need to maintain more durable ties to the land, now sown with increasing amounts of domesticated crops, led to mound building as a new form of inscribing social identities onto the land. Stylistically distinctive weapons, tools, and clothing also signaled local group identities, and artistically decorated objects grew increasingly important as means to convey religious beliefs. This trajectory witnessed great elaboration during the subsequent Woodland period.

The Woodland Period: Cultivation, Mortuary Ceremonies, and Monumental Earthwork Construction

The Woodland period (600 bc to ad 900) is marked by continued growth of settled communities and increased reliance on domesticated grains. The latter stimulated a container revolution that resulted in the production of many kinds of fired-clay pottery vessels. The invention of the bow and arrow provided a new weapon so superior to the dart and throwing-stick complex that it was quickly and widely adopted as the weapon of choice for hunting as well as for conflict with other human groups. Expansion of gardening—the small-scale production of domesticated plants—led to proliferation of new soil-working tools, including digging sticks and hoe blades made of chipped stone, bone, and shell.

Artistic designs on pottery, woven fabrics and basketry, carved-stone smoking pipes and figurines, and paintings (pictographs) and engravings (petroglyphs) on natural rock surfaces, played increasingly important roles in signaling social identities through local variations in style and composition, and inscribing those identities on inhabited territories.

Woodland Indians in Arkansas and the mid-South maintained the diversified subsistence economy inherited from their Archaic period ancestors. Hunting, fishing, and gathering continued to supply much food, though nut harvesting and gardening grew ever more important. Sometime during the first millennium ad, corn, which had been domesticated in Mexico around 8,000 years ago, made its way into the mid-South where it was gradually incorporated into local diets.

Woodland arrow points (*top*), chipped-stone hoe blade (*bottom left*), and decorated ceramic jar (*bottom right*). *Courtesy of the University Museum Collection, University of Arkansas.*

An example of the impact of gardening on Woodland settlement and land-use strategies is represented at sites along the Buffalo River in northern Arkansas. Sedentary Late Woodland communities supported themselves from ad 600–900 by hunting, fishing, nut and wild fruit gathering, and garden cultivation of *Chenopodium*, little barley, maygrass, knotweed, squash, and small amounts of corn. Analysis of the environmental context of site locations reveals that residential sites are strategically located to provide access— even under periodic flood conditions—to several dispersed and generally small stretches of bottomland habitats containing the only soils in the area capable of supporting garden cultivation. Late Woodland sites also feature more substantial square dwellings with associated food storage pits.

Trade for exotic raw materials and finished ceremonial artifacts linked Woodland communities across eastern North America. During the Middle Woodland period, trade networks helped to export a ceremonial cult developed among Hopewell culture people living in the Ohio River valley around 200 BC. The most distinctive feature of this cult was the practice of burying high-status community leaders beneath conical earthen mounds. Burials are usually accompanied by artifacts made of nonlocal materials, fashioned into elaborately decorated artworks. Hopewell ceremonialism spread to many areas across eastern North America, resulting in construction of many thousands of burial mounds.

One example of Hopewell ceremonialism in Arkansas is seen at the Helena Mound site, near the confluence of the Mississippi and the St. Francis rivers. Excavations revealed several individuals buried in massive log tombs covered by conical earthen mounds. One adolescent female was interred with a copper- and silver-covered panpipe, copper ear spools, a drilled wolf canine and shell bead belt, and pearl and marine shell bead armbands, bracelets, and necklace. A young person buried in such a conspicuous location, before reaching an age sufficient to have made noteworthy accomplishments, suggests the existence of ranked lineages whose members were uniformly accorded great esteem.

Another cultural development is represented at the Toltec Mounds site located near Scott, Arkansas. This site has no ties with Toltec Indians of Mexico, but a nineteenth-century landowner believed that its impressive earthworks were built by ancient Mexican mound builders and so the site came to be known as the "Toltec Mounds." Here, Late Woodland people representing the Plum Bayou culture constructed at least eighteen earthen mounds across a large, flat area surrounded on three sides by a mile-long earthen embankment and ditch complex and on the fourth side by Mound Pond, a relict segment of an earlier Arkansas River channel. Some of the mounds are very large and pyramidal shaped with a flat upper surface—intended not to cover burials but instead to support temples, mortuary houses, and shrines.

Of additional interest is the discovery that several mounds are aligned to form an astronomical observatory for monitoring the rising and setting positions of the sun at seasonal solstices and equinoxes. The Toltec site is not unique in this astronomical function, which became widespread across the mid-South during Woodland and Mississippian times. The ability to construct such an observatory enabled the Plum Bayou people to acquire great prestige by linking earthly affairs—like periodic rituals—with the cyclical movements of astronomical objects like the sun, moon, and certain stars or constellations that Southeastern Indians associate with powerful spirit beings.

Through time, growth of Late Woodland communities—with their agrarian economies, social hierarchies, power centers like the Toltec Mounds site, and associated ritual organization—developed even greater levels of complexity, giving rise to subsequent Mississippian cultures.

The Mississippi Period: Agricultural Ecosystems and Powerful Communities

The Mississippi period (ad 900–1541) represents cultural development in the centuries prior to the arrival of Hernando de Soto's expedition, which produced the first written descriptions of Arkansas lands and its inhabitants.

Population growth, the advent of large-scale agriculture, and the emergence of large communities with powerful leaders and priests are hallmarks of this era.

Arkansas was populated by tens of thousands of Indians living in communities across the state. Three regional cultural traditions emerged, each characterized by distinctive settlement patterns, architecture, and subsistence economies: the Mississippian tradition reflected at archeological sites in the Ozark Highlands and the Mississippi Valley above its confluence with the lower Arkansas River; the Caddoan tradition in the Ouachita Mountains and Gulf Coastal Plains drained by the Ouachita and the Red rivers; and the Plaquemine tradition restricted to a comparatively small area in southeast Arkansas. The core area of the Plaquemine tradition is centered along the lower Mississippi Valley in Louisiana and Mississippi, extending at its northern terminus into southeastern Arkansas below the confluence of the Arkansas and the Mississippi rivers.

Native American communities representing the Mississippian tradition engaged in large-scale field agriculture requiring more specialized tilling implements including large hoe blades, some made of a resilient stone acquired via long-distance trade. Finely made woodworking tools, including a wide variety of axe and celt forms, suggest regular clearing of forests to obtain wood for fuel and construction and to clear large tracts of land for community agriculture. By the sixteenth century, some communities had agricultural fields extending, as one of Soto's chroniclers put it, from one town to the next. Pottery making developed into a specialized craft, in which artisans produced exquisitely decorated vessels in a wide range of forms, some produced specifically for trade and others for use in ceremonial contexts. A proliferation of artworks on other media, including stone, shell, bone, and native copper exhibit regional stylistic variations reflecting social identities and statuses.

From ad 1250 on, intensive production of corn, beans, and squash supported large populations in many parts of Arkansas. Corn, which can yield abundant harvests even with simple, hand-held agricultural technologies, is deficient in lysine, an amino acid that humans require. Meat and fish contain lysine, and so do beans. The Southeastern Indians' "Three Sisters"—corn, beans, and squash—provide a nearly complete complex of nutrients and when planted together create a mutually beneficial habitat that promotes the growth of all three plants.

In some parts of the Mississippi Valley, reliance on field agriculture produced competition over control of fertile lands. This led to violent conflicts between competing groups, so in some areas settlements clustered around large, fortified towns, which offered refuge when violence flared.

Mississippian villagers engaged in specialized production of surplus goods for trade to neighboring communities. Salt, hides, grain, dried meat,

Mississippian chipped-stone hoe (*top left*) and ground-stone celt (*top right*), decorated ceramic vessels (*middle*), and wood and antler mask (*bottom*). *Courtesy of the University Museum Collection, University of Arkansas.*

woven basketry and fabrics, and other utilitarian or ceremonial objects, some crafted from rare and exotic raw materials, are some of the commodities produced specifically for trade.

Community leaders managed profits acquired through such commerce by organizing associated trade networks and controlling the distribution of wealth objects within their own communities. Wealth was represented by consumer goods, including food and utilitarian objects, along with prestige items like ceremonial weapons, whose possession reflected an elevated rank or office. Some communities succeeded better than others in managing their wealth, and the leaders of those communities could extend influence over neighboring communities. This created a settlement landscape comprised of both large and small towns along with a hierarchy of temple mound sites, the latter functioning much like medieval European church and castle towns where the most powerful leaders resided and where officials conducted important ceremonies and festivals attended by community members scattered across the surrounding countryside.

Large, fortified agricultural towns like the Nodena and Parkin communities in northeast Arkansas represent examples of these societies. The main towns contained platform mounds that supported the residences of leaders, shrines dedicated to the memory of ancestors, and temples housing sacred fires that served as focal points for religious activities. Open plazas hosted ceremonies performed to honor peoples' accomplishments, renew and solidify social and political institutions, and celebrate life-sustaining relationships connecting earthly communities with invisible forces of the spirit world. Hundreds of houses sheltered the resident population, which numbered in the thousands. Houses were square, typically measuring about four to six meters on a side, with clay-plastered floors, walls constructed of stout posts driven into the ground or set into excavated wall trenches and covered with woven mats or sheets of bark, and grass-thatched roofs with clay-plastered, central smoke holes. Fortified walls and excavated moats surrounded and protected the main towns. Large, above-ground storage facilities suggest redistribution of agricultural produce by community leaders.

A second type of community organization is represented at sites associated with the late prehistoric Caddoan tradition in the Ouachita and Red River valleys in southwest Arkansas, and adjacent parts of Louisiana, Oklahoma, and Texas. Dispersed farmsteads surrounded centrally located settlements containing temple mounds. There is no evidence of fortification or of community field agriculture. Family farmsteads had their own dwellings, work areas, crop fields, and woodlots. Houses were entirely grass thatched and circular in shape, built on frameworks of tall upright posts drawn together at the top, with smaller cross members woven in between. European eyewitnesses observed that the construction of these houses continued into the seventeenth century, and they described them as resembling tall, grass-covered beehives. Covered work platforms and household grain silos stood nearby. Like their contemporaries in the Mississippi Valley, some Caddoan leaders extended authority over the leaders of neighboring communities. Unlike their Mississippian counterparts, Caddoan leaders did not control economic resources. Individual families controlled essential goods and contributed to the material support of their leaders.

Mississippians and Caddoans both developed elaborate mortuary programs involving specialized disposition of ancestral remains, intended as much to affirm or reorganize relations among the living as to commemorate the departed. One example is represented at the Spiro site in eastern Oklahoma, just a few miles west of Fort Smith. There, religious leaders reburied the remains of individuals and their grave goods, removed from local cemeteries, within a low mound in which a large pit had been excavated to receive the remains. This practice continued for several generations, resulting in an ossuary created as a memorial to the collective memory of ancestors. Later, the ossuary was sealed under a newly added layer of sediments and a shrine was erected over it. The floor of the shrine supported a display of sacred objects, some engraved with elaborate imagery, carefully arranged to celebrate the life-sustaining interaction between humans and important deities.

The level of artistry exhibited on sacred objects from Spiro and many other sites is extraordinary, and some are decorated with highly detailed compositions illustrating important religious beliefs. Artworks featuring amphibians, snakes, and spiders, which among historic Southeastern Indians are symbolically associated with a watery Below World, represent disorder and destruction along with the promise of a hopeful future. Bird motifs and other avian imagery represent the Above World beyond the vault of the sky, symbolizing order and creative power along with ancestral legacies. Combination motifs, such as winged serpents shown with the head of a deer or a panther, represents the possibility of conjoining the antithetical powers of Above and Below Worlds for the benefit of communities inhabiting This World on the earth's surface. Images showing figures dressed in elaborate regalia further suggest that the potentially dangerous prospect of conjoining sacred forces could be accomplished only through appropriate rituals performed by highly trained specialists. These artworks demonstrate that many historic Southeastern Indian religious traditions can be traced back at least to Mississippian times.

The Plaquemine cultural tradition emerged along the lower Mississippi River in Louisiana and Mississippi, extending into southeast Arkansas south of the confluence of the Arkansas and the Mississippi rivers. Plaquemine settlement landscapes resemble those of their Mississippian neighbors to the north, and include large, well-organized communities linked to centers featuring large platform mounds with ceremonial structures, overlooking open plazas used for public gatherings and surrounding residential precincts. Most of the larger centers are in Mississippi and Louisiana, but a few Plaquemine villages have been identified in southeast Arkansas along Bayou Bartholomew and the lower stretches of the Ouachita and the Saline rivers. As with Mississippian and Caddoan people, Plaquemine people produced a series of material objects that display their own unique and distinctive stylistic traditions and religious imagery. Unlike their Mississippian neighbors, Plaquemine communities continued to support themselves with a food-getting economy based mainly on hunting, fishing, and gathering wild plant foods. The garden production of corn, beans, and squash contributed comparatively less to Plaquemine foodways than to Mississippian and Caddoan subsistence. Plaquemine communities also participated in long-distance trade and exchange networks linking them to their Mississippian and Caddoan neighbors.

To sum up, archeologists divide Native American history in Arkansas and the mid-South into four major periods, called the Paleoindian, Archaic, Woodland, and Mississippian. Each is distinguished by different forms of community organization and cultural practices reflected in technology, subsistence, settlement pattern and architecture, social and political organization, and religious beliefs and ceremonies.

The Paleoindian period represents adaptations to Ice Age environments including the pursuit of now-extinct mammoths, mastodons, and other large animals. The Dalton culture, developing from earlier Paleoindian groups, represents a transitional adaptation to newly emerging Holocene environments. During the Archaic period, communities developed new strategies for harvesting wild animals and plants that led, in time, to the domestication of several local plant species and the advent of gardening. The first attempts to transform local landscapes by building earthen mounds also dates to this period. Woodland period communities elaborated on the accomplishments of their Archaic predecessors by expanding gardening, establishing more sedentary settlement patterns organized around permanently occupied hamlets, greatly increasing the numbers of mounds and other earthworks across the landscape, and inventing new technologies including fired-clay pottery and the bow and arrow. Mississippi period communities incorporated new crops from Mexico to develop extensive field agriculture. They lived in large towns, some with populations numbering in the thousands. Civic and ceremonial centers emerged with platform mounds supporting buildings used by powerful leaders and priests whose influence extended across surrounding hinterlands. Three regionally distinctive cultural traditions emerged in Arkansas—the Mississippian, Caddoan, and Plaquemine—each possessing a unique organization of settlement patterns, architecture, and subsistence economy.

3   First Encounters

European Explorers Meet Arkansas Indians

The Spanish Entrada of Hernando de Soto, 1539–1543

The event that most profoundly affected sixteenth-century Mississippian, Caddoan, and Plaquemine Indians in Arkansas and the mid-South was the 1539–1543 exploration of the region by the Spanish conquistador Hernando de Soto. His army of more than six hundred soldiers, accompanied by horses, armored war dogs, and an emergency food larder in the form of droves of live hogs, had a devastating impact on Indian communities across the Southeast. Soto's forces introduced new diseases, enslaved thousands of Indians, pillaged and destroyed villages and agricultural fields, escalated warfare, and disrupted social and economic systems throughout the region.

The consequences of Soto's expedition have long been acknowledged. Southeastern Indians had difficulty repelling the Spaniards' use of wholly unfamiliar warfare strategies. Spanish swords, lances, and crossbows were brutally effective at close quarters. Armored horses and mastiffs added to the terror of Spanish attacks. European military strategy was also designed for killing on a scale unimagined by Southeastern Indians. When Soto demanded food and hostages from communities he visited, Indians generally had two options: comply, or resist and suffer even worse consequences. A third option, available only with foreknowledge of the Spaniards' arrival, was to abandon homeland territories and seek refuge elsewhere until it was safe to return.

Recent studies of climate change add another dimension to the assault on Indian communities. The fourteenth and fifteenth centuries witnessed the onset of what climate scientists call the Little Ice Age, a global event bringing generally cooler and wetter conditions that persisted into the nineteenth century. Opposite effects prevailed in Arkansas and the mid-South, dominated by droughts of protracted length and of a severity unequaled during the past five hundred years. By the sixteenth century, the agricultural economies of Indian communities in many parts of Arkansas had suffered devastating impacts. Soto's expedition added yet another level of stress.

Soto's army reached the Mississippi River in the spring

Little Ice Age: A period of global climate change that brought cooler conditions and drought to many parts of the mid-South coinciding with the arrival of European explorers.

of 1541, after two long years in search of wealthy civilizations like the Aztec and Incan empires defeated by Spanish conquistadores just a few years earlier. Soto, in fact, had taken part in the overthrow of the Inca empire in Peru in 1532. In the Southeast, Soto led his forces into numerous Indian villages, confiscating food and capturing thousands of Indians to serve his army's needs, but finding no valuables comparable to those taken in Mexico and South America. Soto destroyed numerous villages, towns, and crop fields in his battles with Southeastern Indians, but he also lost many men, horses, and equipment, and disenchantment soured the mood of his soldiers.

On May 8, 1541 (in the Old Style or Julian calendar), Soto's army entered the Indian province of Quizquiz, which modern scholars place on the eastern side of the Mississippi River in present-day Mississippi and Tennessee. There the Spaniards received a visit from Aquixo, the leader of a populous community on the opposite side of the river. Aquixo claimed that his province, along with Quizquiz, was subject to an even more powerful leader named Pacaha, who lived farther north on the west side of the Mississippi. Imagining that a wealthy Indian province was finally within reach, the Spaniards built four large rafts, and early on the morning of June 18 they crossed the great river, most likely at a point just south of modern-day Memphis.

Julian calendar: The calendar adopted in 45 BC by Julius Caesar, containing 365 days divided into twelve months with a February leap day added every fourth year. It was replaced by the modern Gregorian calendar, introduced in 1582 by Pope Gregory XIII, which added adjustments to synchronize with the solar year.

On reaching the opposite bank, the Spaniards passed through the empty province of Aquixo, whose residents had fled, and turned north. They entered the province of Casqui after two days of very difficult travel through swampy lands. Upon reaching higher ground, Spanish hopes lifted as they entered a land "well peopled with large towns, two or three of which could be seen from one town."

Fields of corn and groves of nut and fruit trees filled the open spaces between Indian settlements. Soto's forces reached the main town of Casqui on June 24, which modern scholars believe is the Parkin site (now Parkin Archeological State Park) in Cross County, where excavations produced several European artifacts, including sixteenth-century coins, a brass harness bell, and a faceted glass bead of a type produced during the mid-sixteenth century. The Parkin site was also the largest ceremonial center of the Mississippian Parkin Phase community, described in the previous chapter.

The leader of Casqui welcomed the Spaniards on the road leading into the main town. He brought gifts of food and hides and offered to lodge Soto's men in the village. Soto's chroniclers mention that severe drought had parched the Indians' crop fields, and Soto, who proclaimed that he was the "son of the sun," was asked if he could help bring rain. Soto ordered his men

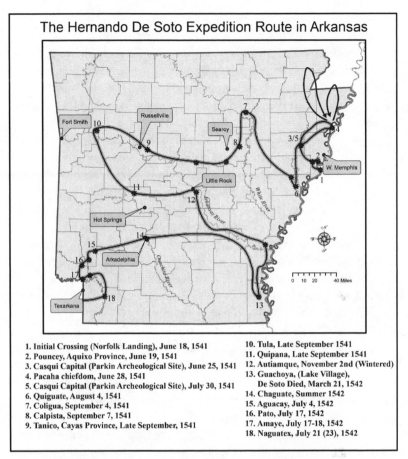

The Hernando De Soto Expedition Route in Arkansas

1. Initial Crossing (Norfolk Landing), June 18, 1541
2. Pouncey, Aquixo Province, June 19, 1541
3. Casqui Capital (Parkin Archeological Site), June 25, 1541
4. Pacaha chiefdom, June 28, 1541
5. Casqui Capital (Parkin Archeological Site), July 30, 1541
6. Quiguate, August 4, 1541
7. Coligua, September 4, 1541
8. Calpista, September 7, 1541
9. Tanico, Cayas Province, Late September, 1541
10. Tula, Late September 1541
11. Quipana, Late September 1541
12. Autiamque, November 2nd (Wintered)
13. Guachoya, (Lake Village),
    De Soto Died, March 21, 1542
14. Chaguate, Summer 1542
15. Aguacay, July 4, 1542
16. Pato, July 17, 1542
17. Amaye, July 17-18, 1542
18. Naguatex, July 21 (23), 1542

Hernando de Soto Route through Arkansas. *Courtesy of Joseph Swain.* (Sources: Arkansas Archeological Survey, Arkansas Geographic Information Office, National Atlas of the United States, Proceedings of the De Soto Symposia.)

to erect a cross on the summit of a large, earthen mound in the center of the village, and on the next day Spanish priests performed a ceremony of adoration. It rained on the following day, convincing the Indians—so say the accounts—that Soto truly was a man of extraordinary power.

Casqui warriors then led the Spaniards to rival Pacaha—the main ceremonial center of Nodena Phase communities—where Soto was led to believe that he might find gold. The village was ransacked, but the Spaniards found no gold. The "sacred metal" revered by the Indians turned out to be copper. Though highly prized by Southeastern Indians, who considered it a gift from the heavens, it was a low-value commodity for Spaniards. Even so, the Spaniards were impressed by other things they saw. Rodrigo Ranjel, Soto's secretary, described the town as "a very good one, thoroughly well stockaded;

walls were furnished with towers and a ditch round about, for the most part full of water which flows in by a canal from the river."

From Pacaha the Spaniards returned to Casqui, then continued south-ward along the St. Francis River to another province called Quiguate. The Spaniards described Quiguate as the largest town they visited in *La Florida*. While there, Soto learned about another province named Coligua, located in mountainous lands to the northwest. Believing that gold and silver most often came from mountainous regions, they spent a week slogging through very swampy, uninhabited terrain to reach the "River of Coligua" (the White River) along the eastern edge of the Ozark Mountains, probably near present-day Batesville. The Spaniards' appearance took the Indians by sur-prise. Soto found many buffalo hides at Coligua, but no gold or silver. With food supplies running short, Soto turned his path to the southwest.

At Calpista farther down the White River, the Spaniards found "an excel-lent salt spring." Palisema, along the Little Red River, contained a few scat-tered houses and only a little corn. At Tutilcoya, probably near Conway, Soto heard about a large province located farther up the "River of Cayas," which modern scholars believe to be the Arkansas River.

The Spaniards arrived at the settlement of Tanico, perhaps near modern-day Russellville, in the province of Cayas on September 16. Though well populated and with plentiful fields of corn, here the Indians lived in scat-tered settlements with no communal food stores. The Spaniards remained in Cayas for three weeks, observing Indians making salt at brackish ponds for trade to distant provinces.

From Tanico, the Spaniards crossed over to lands south of the Arkansas River, and traveled through mountainous terrain to reach the province of Tula. Tula Indians spoke a language that guides from Tanico could not understand. They may have been a Caddoan-speaking group located in the northern Ouachita Mountains south of modern-day Fort Smith. Expedition accounts describe the Tula Indians as expert buffalo hunters who were not intimidated by the Spanish cavalry, as other Indians had been. Using long buffalo hunting lances, Tula warriors killed many Spanish horses and riders.

Finding no gold and little food at Tula, the Spaniards turned back toward the Mississippi Valley, passing through the provinces of Quipana and Quitamaya. Continuing east, they returned to the Arkansas River midway between Little Rock and Pine Bluff, where they spent the winter of 1541–1542 at the main town of the province of Autiamque. Fearing Indian attacks, the Spaniards erected a stockade around part of the town. Winter brought extremely cold weather and snow, so the Spaniards ventured only occasion-ally out of their compound to gather firewood. Juan Ortiz, a survivor from the 1528 Narvaez expedition to Florida, whom Soto had rescued and who thereafter had served as a translator, died that winter. The Spaniards subsequently had considerable difficulty communicating with Indians.

In the spring of 1542, Soto's dwindling army continued down the Arkansas River through the province of Ayays to Anilco, located near the southern tip of Little Prairie in southern Arkansas County. Here the Spaniards found another densely populated agricultural region and hope swelled again as they described the landscape as the richest they had so far observed. But, the Indians had already abandoned the main town and set it afire. Finding the food stores intact, the Spaniards occupied an undamaged part of the town, only to discover Indians returning at night to retrieve their corn.

The Spaniards trudged on to Guachoya, located on the south side of the Arkansas River just upstream from its confluence with the Mississippi. There, Soto intended to remain while sending boats to Cuba for much-needed supplies. He sent a cavalry detachment to determine the shortest route to the coast, but they returned eight days later, having wandered, lost, through boggy and desolate terrain.

Disheartened by this news, alarmed by increasing boldness of the Indians, and growing evermore doubtful about his prospects, Soto sent a final message to Quigualtam, a powerful leader whose province was located several days' travel down the Mississippi. As was his practice, Soto claimed that he was the "son of the sun" and demanded that "in token of love and obedience [Quigualtam] should bring him something of what was most esteemed in [his] land." Soto's fervent hope was the return of a gift of gold from a humbled Indian chief. Instead, Quigualtam replied, a few days later, that it was not his custom to visit anyone; rather, others served and obeyed him. In reply to Soto's claim of being the son of the sun he said, "Let him dry up the great river and he [Quigualtam] would believe him."

Quigualtam's reply enraged Soto, now ill with fever. Fearing imminent attack, he ordered his soldiers to burn the previously visited town of Anilco. The Spaniards attacked with such cruelty that even their own accounts of the battle reflect shame and remorse. They gained nothing from the assault, and on May 21, 1542, Soto died.

Luis Moscoso de Alvarado was elected to take command of the expedition. Soto was quietly buried at Guachoya, but when the Indians found his grave the Spaniards exhumed the corpse, wrapped it in blankets weighted with sand, and sunk it late at night in the Mississippi River. When the leader of Guachoya asked about Soto, Moscoso replied that he had gone to the sky, as he had often done before.

Moscoso and the remaining soldiers, now numbering about three hundred, decided to push on toward Spanish settlements in Mexico. Two routes lay before them: down the Mississippi and along the Gulf Coast, or over land.

The land route was chosen with the hope of finding food at Indian villages along the way. On June 5, the Spaniards headed west.

Traveling up the Arkansas River perhaps as far as Pine Bluff, the army turned southwest and followed the southern edge of the Ouachita Mountains to enter the Caddoan culture area. Passing through the province of Chuguate, the Spaniards reached the Ouachita River between present-day Malvern and Arkadelphia. Continuing southward to the Red River valley, they entered the province of Naguatex where the Indians launched a well-organized attack that divided Spanish forces and nearly succeeded in overwhelming them. An Indian captured by the Spaniards revealed the attack had been a joint effort planned by the leaders of Naguatex, Amaye, and Hacanac. This Indian's further statement that the *cacique* of Naguatex was the "captain and head of all" suggests a large and well-organized network of Caddoan communities subject to a single, powerful leader.

Cacique:
A term used by sixteenth-century Spanish explorers (based on a Nahuatl term) to refer to the leaders of Indian communities.

At Naguatex, where the Spaniards camped for a month, Moscoso sent out a message inviting the esteemed leader to visit him. Two days later messengers returned bearing news that the leader was on his way. The venerable old man soon arrived, "well attended by his men." The Indians approached the Spaniards "one ahead of the other in double file, leaving a lane in the middle through which the cacique came." Moscoso treated the cacique with respect because he knew he would need his help to continue the journey.

After their stay in Naguatex, the Spaniards entered present-day Texas, where they had trouble finding enough food for themselves and their horses. The Spaniards had become used to plundering large Mississippian villages where produce from the surrounding countryside was stored in community granaries. Caddoans of eastern Texas had a different economic organization. Each family stored its own crops at scattered farmsteads. To make matters worse, these Indians, too, began to hide their corn.

Eventually the expedition reached the province of Guasco, where the Spaniards found little corn. They learned of a "River of Daycoa" located ten days' travel toward the west, where a different group of Indians lived. Moscoso sent a detachment of men to investigate. The soldiers found a desolate area occupied only by small groups of hunters and gatherers who spoke a language that the Guasco Indians could not understand.

This was the end of the trail for the Spaniards. They returned to the Mississippi River, where they planned to spend the approaching winter building boats in which to descend to the gulf. Passing back through lands they had plundered, the Spaniards found very little food and Indians hostile to their return.

The Spaniards spent a hard winter at a province named Aminoya, where they melted down their remaining armaments to make spikes for building boats. In one of the few strokes of good luck the Spaniards experienced in Arkansas, the Mississippi River flooded in June 1543, its waters rising to where the newly constructed boats lay. The Spaniards eased the boats into the water on July 2 and began their voyage down the river. Additional losses were suffered when Plaquemine Indian attackers, including some from Quigualtam, came after them in large war canoes. When the beleaguered flotilla finally reached the mouth of the Mississippi River, a lone Indian standing on the bank called out: "If we possessed such large canoes as yours, we would follow you to your own land and conquer it, for we too are men like yourselves."

Sixteenth- and Seventeenth-Century Transformation of Native American Culture and Identity

Soto expedition accounts provide scant information about sixteenth-century native populations and even fewer credible facts about routes traveled and placed visited. Identities of Indians the Spaniards met include names used by the people themselves or names they were called by other people, including native guides or interpreters who spoke other languages. It is often impossible to decide which is the case. Spanish chroniclers also introduced phonetic errors as they translated Indian words into Spanish and Portuguese. These facts complicate efforts to use Spanish accounts to determine the cultural identity of sixteenth-century native communities. Soto's forces traversed Mississippian, Caddoan, and Plaquemine culture areas described in the previous chapter, and observations made by Soto's chroniclers concerning cultural and linguistic barriers correspond reasonably well with archeological data on the boundaries separating different communities. Beyond that, we are left with a mishmash of odd names that imperfectly correspond to native language families and link not at all to tribal identities mentioned in later European accounts.

What happened to those communities in the decades following the departure of Spanish conquistadores? The effects of battle and enslavement at the hands of Soto's army took a horrific toll. Old World diseases against which the Indians had no immunity—smallpox, tuberculosis, plague, typhus, influenza, yellow fever, measles, and possibly malaria and mumps—also reduced many groups. Environmental changes associated with Little Ice Age droughts resulted in further losses. Deaths in disproportionate numbers of elderly people responsible for passing along cultural traditions, and of the young who would inherit those traditions, dealt severe blows both to the heritage of the past and to hopes for the future.

Native cultural landscapes were transformed to an extent making it diffi-cult if not impossible to identify direct lines of descent linking historic Native Americans with specific prehistoric communities reconstructed as archeo-logical phases or cultures. In some parts of Arkansas, remnants of previously existing groups amalgamated to create descendant communities organized along very different lines. In other areas, native immigrants brought different cultural traditions that also changed as their communities took root.

In the Mississippi Valley, the powerful chiefdoms that Soto's chroniclers described at Casqui and Pacaha collapsed; French explorers descending the Mississippi River at the end of the seventeenth century encountered no com-munities in that formerly populous region. Some of their refugees may have migrated farther down the Mississippi into southeastern Arkansas, joining Tunica and Natchez groups—descendants of pre-Columbian Plaquemines— as they consolidated into towns and villages located even farther south in Mississippi and Louisiana.

Quapaws—who had been displaced from Ohio River valley homelands by Iroquois territorial expansion from the northeast—established new com-munities near the confluence of the Arkansas and the Mississippi rivers in the early seventeenth century. Osages relocating from the same homelands moved into southwest Missouri. Farther up the Arkansas River, an early seventeenth-century village in the Carden Bottoms locality was comprised of a multiethnic, amalgam group of families tracing their ancestry to communi-ties along the Mississippi and the lower Arkansas rivers, the central Arkansas River valley, and the Ouachita River in southwest Arkansas. A few Caddoan groups living in the middle Ouachita and Red River valleys in southwest Arkansas appear to be the only communities not forced to relocate in the century following the departure of Soto's army.

In the wake of these dislocations, new Native American cultural tradi-tions emerged, some with no direct links to earlier archeological manifes-tations, but each reflecting adaptation to emerging features of new worlds created by European colonization.

New Traditions for a New World: Seventeenth- and Eighteenth-Century Native Americans in Arkansas

French and Spanish explorers and colonists visiting present-day Arkansas during the seventeenth and eighteenth centuries left valuable accounts of native people they met. Quapaws, Osages, Caddos, Tunicas, and Koroas car-ried into the historic era partial legacies of earlier Mississippian, Caddoan, and Plaquemine traditions. To those earlier traditions, new economic, social, political, and religious practices aligned with the realities of different environments, changing distributions and compositions of indigenous neighbors, and an ever-shifting framework of relationships with "Old World newcomers."

Quapaws

Quapaws are linguistically related to Osage, Omaha, Kansa (Kaw), and Ponca tribes, all of whom speak similar dialects and believe that a supernatural force called *Wakondah* created the world before humans arrived to live upon its surface. As new communities formed, each adopted rituals performed to maintain favorable relationships with spiritual forces responsible for creating and sustaining life.

Wakondah: The creative, universal life force in Osage and Quapaw religious thought.

Upon arriving in Arkansas, Quapaws established three villages—Osotuoy, Tourima, and Tongigua—along the lower Arkansas River and a fourth village, Kappa, located astride the Mississippi. Families related through the male (or father's) line lived in longhouses constructed by driving poles into the ground in parallel rows, then bending and tying the tops of the poles to create an arched framework strengthened by interwoven laths and covered with sheets of bark. Interiors had platforms for sitting and sleeping along inner walls and at the ends. Hearths set along the midline provided each family with heat, light, and a place to cook their meals. Longhouses surrounded an open, central plaza used for ceremonial gatherings. The council house and sacred temple stood close by. Crop fields extended outward from the villages.

Quapaw society was organized by inherited statuses and relationships acquired through marriage. Each individual belonged to a descent group, or clan, traced through his or her father's line. Each clan had a guardian spirit—usually an animal or some element of nature—considered to be spiritual relatives who conferred on clan members the right to perform sacred duties. Clans were divided into two groups, called Sky People and Earth People. Clans representing the Earth People performed rituals that helped sustain community physical and material well-being while clans representing the Sky People performed rituals devoted to maintenance of spiritual affairs.

Clan: A kinship-based social unit in Southeastern Indian communities with various ceremonial responsibilities, with membership determined by line of descent.

Sky People and Earth People divisions also regulated marriage, since a person could only marry someone belonging to certain clans in the opposite division.

Each village had a leader whose office was inherited. Although leaders possessed considerable esteem, their authority rested mainly on powers of persuasion. A council of male elders and clan leaders assisted the village leader at meetings and during various other ceremonies. Village councils made decisions concerning their own affairs; representatives attending inter-village assemblies discussed issues affecting the tribe as a whole.

Ceremonial performances led by priests marked important annual events. Planting ceremonies held in spring honored the efforts of women who sowed and tended crops and offered thanks to creative forces associated with sunshine, rain, and the earth's fertility. A Green Corn ceremony performed later during summer celebrated and gave thanks for successful crop production. Gifts and prayers offered throughout the year helped maintain this cycle of life.

Quapaws based their economy on agricultural production of corn, beans, squash, gourds, melons, and tobacco. They cultivated fruit trees introduced by European colonists, and collected wild plant foods, including fruits, nuts, seeds, and roots. Deer, bear, and buffalo provided meat, hides, tallow, and oil. Turkeys, fish and other aquatic species, and waterfowl added variety to the diet. Quapaws also raised dogs, chickens, and horses.

Quapaw women managed crop production, butchered animals captured in the chase, and prepared hides. They gathered firewood and wild foods, cooked, cared for children, and managed household affairs. Men hunted, fished, waged war, and managed political and religious affairs.

Quapaw women wore deerskin skirts that reached from the waist to the knees. Married women wore their hair loose, while unmarried women wove their hair in braids rolled into coils secured behind the ears and decorated with ornaments. Men wore loincloths during warm seasons, adding leggings, moccasins, and cloth shirts at other times of the year. They decorated themselves with tattoos and strings of beads in their ears and noses. Everybody wore buffalo robes to ward off the cold of winter. For ceremonial occasions, Quapaws painted themselves red and black and wore headdresses, masks, and other ornaments decorated with paint, feathers, buffalo horns, and animal furs.

Relations with other tribes consisted of warfare with enemies or alliances created with friends for purposes of trade or to pursue common interests. War preparations involved elaborate rituals to purify participants and ensure the blessings of spirit beings. Success in military ventures provided a means to achieve elevated social status.

Trade relations, especially with Europeans, grew steadily during the colonial era. Quapaw involvement in the frontier exchange economy, in which crops, meat, hides, and other indigenous products were traded for European goods, had a profound effect on men's and women's economic activities as they devoted increased time and effort to produce goods sought by European merchants. In return, Quapaws and their neighbors gained access to new kinds of food, clothing, tools and utensils, and firearms.

The calumet ceremony was an important rite for securing alliances with other groups, Indian or European. The calumet was a two-piece implement consisting of a decorated wooden stick, about two feet long, attached to a bowl carved of red pipestone, or catlinite. The calumet ceremony was an elaborate affair involving feasting, dancing, gift exchanges, and, of course, passing the calumet for all of the participants to smoke. The ceremony created kinship-like relations between participants so that allies would be bound by the same obligations that family and clan members shared.

The calumet ceremony served as the primary means by which Quapaws interacted with Europeans and Americans. Consequently, obligations and expectations shared by clan members in Quapaw society extended to relations with Europeans and Americans.

Frontier exchange economy: An economic system in colonial Louisiana in which Indian goods (food, hides, other animal products) were exchanged with traders, via face-to-face bartering, for European goods (firearms, cloth, ornaments, tools, etc.).

Calumet: A decorated wooden shaft, attached to a carved stone pipe, that seventeenth-century Indians in the Mississippi Valley used in greeting ceremonies to welcome visitors into their villages.

Osages

Eighteenth-century Osages located their villages on the Missouri and the Osage rivers in southwestern Missouri, but seasonal hunting and trading forays brought them annually into northern Arkansas.

Osages called themselves "Children of the Middle Waters." In the beginning, *Wakondah* separated air, earth, and water from the original middle waters to create a place for people to live. Osages trace their origin to a time long ago when the Sky People descended from the heavens and met the isolated Earth People, whom they joined to create the Osage tribe.

Osages also lived in longhouses, with doors opened to the east in the direction of the rising sun. Houses stood on either side of a main road running east to west, which symbolized the earth's surface between the sky above and the underworld below. Sky People occupied clan neighborhoods on the north side of the road, while Earth People arranged their houses on the south side. In permanent villages, special lodges provided space for council meetings and rituals.

Osages divided their overall population into five major groups, called bands, each of which had its own village. Village life was patterned by customs maintained by a group of religious leaders called Little Old Men, who underwent lengthy periods of training. This group of elders was responsible for establishing standards for appropriate conduct, advising village leaders, making important decisions affecting tribal affairs in times of peace and war, and maintaining sacred knowledge and traditions.

Osage clans held responsibility for rituals and other activities performed on behalf of the entire tribe. Earth People clans assisted Sky People clans in the performance of ritual duties, and vice versa, so that ritual performances reflected an overall solidarity of purpose.

Osage men and women married outside of their clan division and usually outside of their village. A young man's family sent gifts to a prospective bride's family. These were kept if the marriage proposal was accepted and returned if not. Sometimes a man took his first wife's sisters in marriage, and, since inheritance passed through the male line, a man often married his deceased brother's widow so that he could provide for his brother's children.

Hunting, gathering, and gardening produced most of the food and other goods. Men and women cleared fields along river bottoms adjacent to each village during spring. Women tended family plots of corn, beans, squashes, pumpkins, and tobacco until the plants were established. Residents of several villages then gathered into large camps and traveled west during summer, to Kansas and Nebraska, to hunt buffalo. During the hunt, the tribal camping circle reflected the village arrangement of clans and divisions. Men, women, and children took part in the hunt, each playing specific roles coordinated in strict military order. Hunting groups returned to the villages in autumn to harvest ripened crops and to gather nuts, fruits, and other wild plant foods. People from several villages joined together in the fall to hunt buffalo, deer, elk, and other animals. Northern Arkansas was an important hunting ground for Osage groups during early historic times. During winter people moved back to their Missouri villages, surviving on stored garden produce and animals taken locally.

Osage men hunted and waged war, defended their villages against enemies, and managed most economic and political affairs. Men shaved their heads, leaving only a scalp lock or roach extending from the forehead to the back of the neck. Different scalp lock designs identified clan membership. Men wore deerskin loincloths, leggings, and moccasins, with bearskin or buffalo robes added during cold weather. They wore ornaments in their ears and on their arms, and warriors tattooed their upper bodies. Body paint was worn for ceremonial occasions.

Women performed a wide variety of activities in addition to planting and tending crops and preparing meals. Women built houses, along with interior furnishings and utensils. They also worked hides and made clothing, and wove sashes, belts, neckbands, and cords from buffalo hair and nettle weed fibers. Women kept their hair long and loose. They wore deerskin dresses cinched at the waist with woven belts, along with leggings and moccasins. Jewelry consisted of earrings, pendants, and bracelets, and many women decorated their bodies with elaborate tattoos. They donned ceremonial garments for special occasions, with designs conveying social identity and status.

Family, clan, and village all shared in the responsibilities of raising children. Fathers instructed sons in skills of hunting and warfare, while mothers taught daughters how to tend crops and manage domestic affairs. Elders taught values and important social and religious beliefs. Each child was carefully nurtured to sustain Osage traditions through the generations.

Major changes in the Osage way of life came through their involvement in trade with Europeans. Occupying the prairie ecotone connecting woodland environments on the east and plains environments to the west, the Osages found themselves in a geographical position well suited for managing trade relations connecting tribes scattered across a wide area with merchants in St. Louis, the major regional trading center. Consequently, involvement in the frontier exchange economy did much more than affect the economic roles of men and women in Osage communities; it had a profound impact on larger political and military alliances, as other Indian groups challenged Osage control of trade across the prairie-plains borderlands.

Caddos

Several communities dispersed around the Great Bend of the Red River in southwest Arkansas and eastern Texas comprised the Kadohadacho alliance of Caddoan speakers. The Natchitoches Indians lived in several villages in present-day Louisiana. Hasinai villages were located farther west along the upper Angelina and the Neches rivers in east Texas. The Cahinnios, allies of the Kadohadachos in the seventeenth century, lived in the Ouachita River drainage in western Arkansas.

The Kadohadacho, Natchitoches, and Hasinai alliances each consisted of several autonomous communities connected through diplomatic ties. These groups, plus the Cahinnios, represent the southern core of Caddoan-speaking people. Southern Caddos occupied a vast area between the northern borderlands of New Spain and the Mississippi Valley, so they played a pivotal role in the contests for empire between France and Spain.

A Kadohadacho creation story traces origins to a cave in a hill named Chakanina (or "place of crying") out of which came an old man from the underworld bringing fire, a pipe, and a drum. The old man's wife accompanied him, bringing corn and pumpkin seeds. Others followed, both people

Osage traders, by Charles Banks Wilson. *Courtesy of the artist and Nancy Pillsbury Shirley.*

and animals, but before they could all make their escape Wolf closed the cave's entrance, trapping forever those who remained below. The people on the surface wept bitterly for those left behind, before they dispersed across the land to create new homes.

Caddo settlements consisted of family farmsteads dispersed at intervals along major rivers and streams. Extended (multigenerational) families or groups of closely related families occupied an area of sufficient size to build dwellings and clear crop fields. Farmsteads consisted of one or more grass-thatched, circular dwellings plus elevated corncribs and work platforms. Family garden plots and woodlots surrounded the houses. The compound of the village leader, or *caddi*, usually occupied a central place among the scattered farmsteads. The sacred fire temple, managed by priests, was also located nearby.

Caddi: Caddo village leader.

Since several families might occupy a single dwelling, they often were quite large. A hearth fed by four large logs oriented to the cardinal directions occupied the center of each house, lit from an ember brought from the fire in the village's sacred temple. The sense of community that nearby families shared derived in part from common use of the sacred fire to light family hearths, thereby linking each household to the same temple. Family quarters consisted of sleeping platforms made of woven cane mats supported by a pole framework. Buffalo robes covered the mats, and additional mats—some decorated with brightly colored designs—arched over the platforms to create alcoves. Lofts provided storage space for food supplies and equipment. Although each family maintained its own food supplies, the central fire was shared by all. The senior woman of the house prepared meals from contributions made by each family, and supervised most other domestic activities.

Clans provided the building blocks of Caddo social organization. Every person belonged to a clan inherited either from the mother or the father, depending on which parent's clan was regarded as the strongest. An individual from one community could rely upon clan relatives in other communities for shelter and assistance. People chose spouses from a clan other than their own.

Political organization was based on a hierarchy of offices. Leadership at the community level was vested in the office of the *caddi*, who held authority in numerous civic and religious affairs. Upon the death of this leader, the office would pass to the eldest son or closest male heir. Many other officials assisted the *caddi* in directing community affairs, including house construction and preparation of fields. Other specialists performed specific rituals including blessing food and treating illnesses. A head priest known as the *xinesi* possessed authority in both civil and religious affairs that extended across several allied communities. The *xinesi* was a full-time manager, supported by contributions from members of allied communities.

The Caddo world was populated by many spirit beings. The Supreme Being, *Ayo-Caddi-Aymay*, was regarded as the most powerful. His power was represented by the sun in the daytime sky and the sacred fire burning on the community temple mound. This deity had authority over other beings and forces that affected worldly events. Rituals performed throughout the year served to maintain positive relations among seen and unseen components of the Caddo world. The most important ceremonies regulated the agricultural cycle. A forecasting ceremony was held in spring, at which priests contacted spirit beings to obtain information about prospects for the coming year. A planting ceremony served to honor women as they began the sacred task of crop production. A first fruits ceremony was performed later in the summer to bless the crops as they began to ripen. A fall harvest ceremony was the largest celebration, during which the people gave thanks for the year's crops and performed other rites that reinforced community solidarity. Additional rituals served to organize other activities, including house construction, warfare, trade fairs, births, marriages, and deaths.

House construction and the clearing and planting of fields reveal much

Xinesi: The head priest who presided over sacred fire temples in Caddo villages.

Ayo-Caddi-Aymay: The Supreme Being in seventeenth-century Caddo belief.

about the nature and organization of Caddo villages. When a new house had to be constructed or when a crop field needed to be cleared and prepared, the *caddi* set a date for the event and dispatched assistants to assign responsibilities. On the appointed day, the *caddi* arrived at the work site and took his seat in a place of honor. At the call of the individual in charge of the work detail, community members gathered, bringing construction materials, tools, or other contributions. Everyone pitched in to build the house, clear and prepare the field, or perform other necessary tasks. Priests performed blessing ceremonies at the conclusion of the work, and participants shared a feast provided by the host family.

Caddos supplemented agricultural crops with meat from buffalo, deer, and turkey, and wild plant foods including nuts, roots, seeds, and berries.

Caddo men and women manufactured and traded salt and other materials, including bear oil or grease and the wood of the Osage orange tree, prized across the Southeast for the manufacture of bows. Caddo women excelled at making pottery, baskets, woven mats, and dressed skins. Elaborately decorated vessels were created in many shapes, including platters, bowls, jars, and bottles, and these served a variety of food storage, preparation, and consumption needs.

Osage Orange (or, bois d'arc): A highly prized type of wood used for making Indian bows and other implements.

Caddo men kept their hair trimmed short, except for a long lock that was braided or decorated with feathers or shell ornaments. Caddo women wore their long hair braided and tied close to the head. Both men and women had tattoos, and both sexes painted designs on their faces and bodies for religious ceremonies. Clothing made of hides, woven plant fibers, and European cloth, along with painted and tattooed body decorations served as symbolic representations of group membership, status, and personal identity.

Warfare was an important means by which southern Caddos maintained the integrity of their territories against pressures from rival groups. When the leaders of a Caddo community wished to organize a war party, they sent ambassadors to allied communities bearing requests for support. Battle preparations included elaborate ritual performances, along with offerings made to spirit beings to gain their sanction and support.

Funeral ceremonies consisted of a series of rituals conducted by priests, intended to facilitate the travel of a person's soul to the House of Death, located in the Above World. Offerings of food placed on the grave were replenished over the next several days, until the family was certain the soul had completed its journey.

The hierarchical organization of Caddo society provided a framework for interaction with Europeans. When European travelers approached Caddo

Caddo woman, by Gary Simmons. *Courtesy of the artist.*

villages, a contingent sent out from the village met and escorted them to the village where they were seated in a place of honor. The calumet served to create a bond of friendship between the leaders that extended to other members of their respective groups.

The finely honed diplomatic skills of Caddo village leaders came into play throughout the colonial era. Caddo leaders often played important roles, at the request of European and American officials, in negotiating alliances and political arrangements among groups inhabiting the contested borderlands separating northern New Spain on the west and the Louisiana Territory on the east.

Tunicas and Koroas

At the beginning of the seventeenth century, Tunica Indians occupied an area extending along both sides of the Mississippi River in Tennessee, Mississippi, and eastern Arkansas. Later, French explorers and missionaries reported Tunica Indians and closely related Koroa Indians (who probably also spoke a Tunica dialect) living along the Arkansas and the Ouachita rivers and along the Mississippi River south of the Arkansas. By 1699, most Tunicas had relocated their villages along the lower stretch of the Yazoo River in present-day Mississippi. Within a few more years the Koroas were severely reduced and remnants of that tribe also moved to the lower Yazoo. In the aftermath of the Natchez Rebellion of 1729, the few remaining Koroas along with the Natchez joined with Chickasaws, while the Tunicas relocated farther down the Mississippi River.

The Tunicas recognized supernatural powers in many aspects of nature, although they attributed a female identity to the sun—considered male by most other groups—and they recognized fire as a deity in its own right, and not, as many Southeastern Indians believed, as merely a symbol on earth of the sun's power. Each village contained a sacred fire temple in which priests performed community rites. One Frenchman saw small statues of a woman and a frog in one of these temples. The woman may have symbolized the sun or Above World, with the frog symbolizing the watery Below World.

Tunicas built circular houses by setting upright posts in the ground and weaving cane laths through them. Walls were plastered with clay, and grass thatch covered dome-shaped roofs. Small doorways provided the only source of natural light, and the only exit for smoke from small fires that provided additional light and warmth. French witnesses reported that Koroas decorated their houses with "great round plates of shining copper, made like pot covers." Houses also had outdoor cooking fires and above-ground granaries. Dwellings were arranged around an open central plaza with a temple at one end. Tunica temples stood on platform mounds in some villages.

Tunica leaders inherited their offices, and in the eighteenth century some villages had two groups of leaders with separate responsibilities for internal civil affairs and external warfare. Warriors achieved distinction for their exploits, which entitled them to wear special tattoos. One French visitor to a Koroa village wrote that games, dances, and feasts took place in the settlement's open plaza.

Like many other Southeastern Indians, Tunicas grew corn and squash, collected wild plant foods including persimmons and other fruits, berries, nuts, seeds, roots, and herbs and hunted deer, bear, and occasionally buffalo. Unlike many Southeastern Indians, Tunica men, rather than women, tended the crop fields. Tunicas also produced salt at seeps and other natural deposits, some of which they traded to other groups.

Tunica men wore deerskin loincloths during the warm seasons, and like other Southeastern Indians decorated themselves with tattoos, beads, and pendants. Women wore short, fringed skirts of cloth woven from the inner bark of mulberry trees. They also tattooed themselves and further enhanced their appearance with beads, pendants, and earrings. Women kept their hair in a single, long braid that hung down the back or was wrapped about the crown. In cold weather, men and women wore mantles of mulberry cloth, turkey feathers, or muskrat skins.

Pressures felt by the Tunicas stemming from the expanding influence of English traders and their native allies on the eastern side of the Mississippi led them to abandon their settlements along the lower Yazoo in 1706. Moving farther down the Mississippi, the Tunicas established new villages—still arranged according to traditional patterns—at a location across from the mouth of the Red River known as Portage de la Croix. This location put the Tunicas closer to the settlements of their French allies. Veteran traders, the Tunicas sustained themselves through a combination of farming, hunting, and commercial activity and by adopting members of less fortunate tribes.

At the beginning of the sixteenth-century, much of present-day Arkansas was populated by well-established and relatively stable settlements inhabited by numerous Mississippian, Caddoan, and Plaquemine communities. A century later, new cultural landscapes had emerged in many regions, the result of changes internal to sixteenth-century Native American societies, combined with the impacts of external climate changes and damages suffered in relation to Hernando de Soto's *entrada*. In the Red River and the Ouachita River regions of the Gulf Coastal Plain, the descendants of pre-contact Caddoan groups continued to thrive in dispersed family farmsteads linked to temple mound centers occupied by powerful civic and religious leaders. In contrast, Mississippian chiefdoms long established in the Mississippi Valley underwent decline and dispersal. Immigrant Quapaws established new settlement landscapes around the confluence of the Arkansas and the Mississippi rivers. Osages likewise moved into the Ozark Highlands in southwest Missouri, extending their control into northwest Arkansas. Tunicans and Koroas emerged out of the earlier Plaquemine tradition, moved farther down the Mississippi River and out of Arkansas by the end of the seventeenth century. These newly organized Native American groups witnessed the arrival of the next waves of European visitors, including French colonists descending the Mississippi River from nascent Great Lakes settlements and Spanish explorers pushing northward from northern Mexico and the American Southwest.

4
Indians and Colonists in the Arkansas Country, 1686–1803

IN THE SUMMER of 1686, French Canadians established a post on the Arkansas River about twenty miles by water from its confluence with the Mississippi. This *Poste aux Arkansas* (Post at the Arkansas), as the Canadians called their little settlement, served, except for a short hiatus in the early eighteenth century, as a trading and military post during the entire colonial period. Though it survived as a small village well into the twentieth century, it is nevertheless safe to say that Arkansas Post is not particularly well known today, even in Arkansas, partly because it is, as it was in 1686, out in the middle of nowhere. What is more, not even the slightest physical trace of a colonial occupation has survived above the ground. In the neighboring states of Missouri, Louisiana, Mississippi, and Texas (in fact, in parts of each of them barely one hundred miles from Arkansas's border), eighteenth-century buildings and cemeteries serve to stir the imagination and keep alive the memory of a time when France, Spain, and England all vigorously competed for hegemony in the heart of America. In Arkansas, however, all that bears witness to that early struggle are a few French names for places, rivers, and mountains, many now mangled beyond the possibility of easy recognition.

A Peripatetic Settlement

French Canadian traders situated their outpost on the first relatively high ground that they encountered after entering the mouth of the Arkansas River. This place, in Arkansas County near where the little community named Nady is located today, had been occupied for centuries by various Indian groups. When the traders came, the Quapaws were living there. Native Americans had chosen to settle on this little detached part of Grand Prairie because it was near the great Mississippi highway, was out of the floodplain for the most part, had abundant fresh water available from the nearby stream later named Menard Bayou (the Arkansas River was brackish but its water was drinkable in a pinch), and the woods close by provided fuel for fires and material for houses. The French chose the spot because the Quapaws were there, and the French wanted to trade with them and engage them in

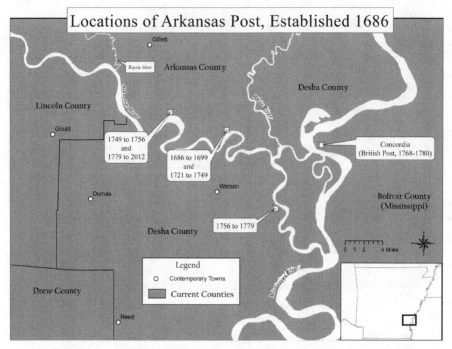

Locations of Arkansas Post, Established 1686. *Courtesy of Joseph Swain.* (Sources: Arkansas Geographic Information Office, Arkansas Post National Memorial, *Encyclopedia of Arkansas History & Culture,* National Atlas of the United States.)

a military alliance against the English of Carolina and their Indian allies, principally the Chickasaws. The environment and the Indians would continue to play important roles in the choices that the Europeans made, but their imperial ambitions also provided significant motives for their activities in the Arkansas region.

The first "owner" (in the minds, that is, of Europeans) of the lower Arkansas River was one Henri de Tonty, an associate of Robert Cavelier de La Salle. King Louis XIV of France had commissioned La Salle to explore the Mississippi and establish alliances with all of the Indian tribes that he encountered. Tonty settled six of his men at the Post. A Frenchman who visited Tonty's settlement only about a year after it was founded reported that its mission was to monopolize the Quapaw trade, serve as a way station for travelers between the Illinois country and the Gulf of Mexico, and establish a presence in the middle of the continent to thwart the western advance of the English colonies. The mission of the Post never really deviated from its original one during the entire colonial epoch.

This first Arkansas Post seems to have been abandoned by 1699, when Jean-Baptiste Le Moyne de Bienville finally established the colony of Louisiana on the Gulf Coast, though the rivers of the region, and especially the Arkansas River, continued to be visited more or less regularly by the *coureurs de bois* (forest rangers) and *voyageurs* (boatmen) who hunted and traded with the Indians of Louisiana and Canada. The English moved quickly to fill the void: A Carolina trader named Thomas Welch had sent goods to the Quapaws in 1698, and an Englishman had by 1700 married into the tribe. The French then established a missionary among the Quapaws named Father Nicholas Foucault. He was Louisiana's first martyr: His Koroa Indian guides murdered him in 1702 after he abandoned his efforts because of a lack of success and some unspecified disagreements with the Quapaws. In 1700, an Englishman had boasted that he would kill the first French priest whom he encountered in the Arkansas region, so it is not impossible that the English had had a hand, directly or indirectly, in the disagreements between Father Foucault and the Quapaws and perhaps even in the missionary's death itself.

Coureurs de bois: Literally "woods runners" or "forest rangers"; a term used to describe unlicensed traders.

Welch evidently maintained some influence among the Quapaws even as late as 1708, for in that year a Quapaw delegation attended a council at the Yazoo River, during a colonial conflict called Queen Anne's War, where Welch tried to engage them in the English effort to destroy the French Louisiana capital at Mobile. Governor Bienville of Louisiana reported, however, that Welch's blandishments fell on deaf ears, and Bienville was probably correct.

In 1720, John Law, a banker from Scotland who was the most famous financier in eighteenth-century France, decided to revive the settlement at the Arkansas. He took a personal interest in the place, made sure that his company granted him a huge tract of land on the lower Arkansas River, and set about recruiting colonists to settle there. A few thousand people did migrate to Louisiana under his auspices, many of them German peasants from the Alsace region of France, some of whom were destined for the Arkansas; but large numbers of these colonists perished *en route* and on the Gulf Coast after arrival, and none of the Germans made it to Law's projected settlement on the Arkansas River. Although a few French indentured servants (*engagés*) of the company did arrive at the old site of Tonty's Post in 1721, Germans assigned to Law's Arkansas concession settled instead in the lower part of the colony, principally at a place called then and now the German Coast, where these peasant farmers soon became the main suppliers of vegetables and other foodstuffs to the growing population of New Orleans. A military garrison was first assigned to the Arkansas in 1721, to provide security for Law's colonists, but it was recalled a few years later.

Engagés: "Employees"; people who usually worked for a trader or merchant.

Once it was reestablished in 1731 or 1732, there was a military presence on the Arkansas throughout the colonial period.

One of the circumstances on which the government of Louisiana kept a wary eye was the mood of the Chickasaw nation, ancient foes of the Quapaws and much attached to the English, who lived to the east in what is now the state of Mississippi. During the 1730s and 1740s, the Quapaws joined in various French military efforts to destroy the Chickasaws, and they frequently raided the Chickasaw villages, bringing back scalps and prisoners to be burned alive or adopted. A truly splendid scene that a Quapaw artist painted on a buffalo hide in about 1750, which survives in a Paris museum, probably records one of these raids. During the 1740s, the colony of Louisiana got drawn into a general conflict between the French and the English known as King George's War, and in 1749 the Chickasaws (with perhaps a few Choctaws and Creeks) launched a full-scale attack on the Post. Their scout, according to one report, was a drummer who had deserted from the French garrison. Though the French repulsed the attack, it was not without a considerable loss: A number of men were killed, and several women and children were captured and taken as prisoners to the Chickasaw towns.

This English and Chickasaw success greatly alarmed the French government in New Orleans, and it ordered the Post moved and rebuilt about six miles upriver by land to a place in what is now Arkansas County that the French called *Écores Rouges* (Red Bluffs), where the Arkansas Post National Memorial is now located. The Quapaws had moved there shortly before the attack because of devastating floods, and their absence was probably a main reason that the Chickasaw siege had enjoyed so much success. The French, not surprisingly, had resolved to rejoin their Quapaw allies for defensive purposes. Environment and geography had again forced a choice on the French and the Quapaws. A rather large investment was made in a new fort and settlement at the new site, but in 1756, the outpost moved yet again, this time downriver, to a site in what is now Desha County about ten miles by river from the Mississippi River. It is likely that the need to be close to that main artery during the Seven Years' War, so the Post could be of service to the French convoys that plied the great river, provided the impetus for this change of location.

Geography had again influenced the activities of the French, and environment would dictate what kind of settlement, if any, was going to gather around the little isolated military outpost that was created at the new location. This third Arkansas Post was across from Big Island, in the middle of a vast alluvial plain, where annual floodwaters made agriculture virtually impossible, the soil was sandy, and the insects frequently devoured what few crops managed somehow to survive. Every spring, the inhabitants braced

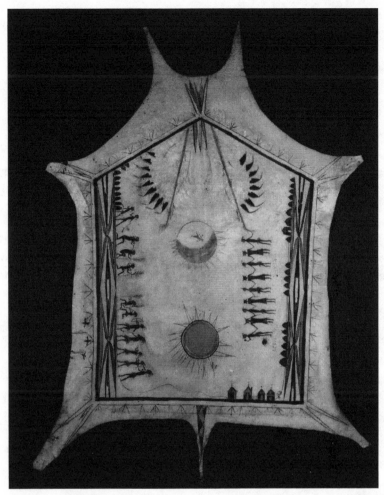

Robe of the Three Villages, Quapaw painted buffalo hide, circa 1750, showing the Quapaw villages, Arkansas Post, and a battle between the Quapaws and the Chickasaws. *Courtesy Musée du quai Branly, Paris.*

themselves for the Mississippi floods that would overwhelm the waters of the White River, roar through a cutoff between it and the Arkansas, rush down the chute on the western edge of Big Island, and overrun the little French *Poste aux Arkansas.* The topography in the environs of the Post thus made it impossible to attract farmers to the place in any numbers. If there was going to be a settlement there at all, it would have to be a trading and hunting community. But it proved impossible to attract many people to settle at the Post, and by 1777, almost a century after its founding, there were only fifty-one civilians, white and black, at this most remote of Louisiana's outposts of empire.

The few traders and merchants at the Post were drawn to this sink not so much to trade with the Quapaws as to outfit the numerous hunters who had been attracted to the Arkansas region to exploit the abundant wildlife that flourished there because the region was virtually empty of people. The Quapaws, who numbered about ten thousand when Marquette and Jolliet first visited them in 1673, had been decimated by smallpox in the 1690s. By 1700, their population was probably no more than a thousand, and later epidemic episodes had reduced them to around seven hundred souls by 1770. The only substantial group of Indians that regularly ventured into the Arkansas region during the period to exploit the animal life were the Osages, who claimed much of the northern and western part of the state as their hunting territory. There were small groups of other tribes who occasionally migrated into the area in search of game. Chief among these were some Illinois (Miamis and Kaskaskias), many of whom were taken in by the Quapaws, and a group of Abenakis (Delawares). Very late in the colonial period a significant number of Cherokees, and roving bands of Choctaws and Chickasaws, were driven across the Mississippi to hunt by the expanding frontier of American settlement.

In 1779, Capt. Balthazar de Villiers finally succeeded in getting the governor's permission to move his town and fort out of the floodplain, this time for the last time, back upriver to the high land at *Écores Rouges*. Here his prospects for creating an ordered, agrarian community were a good deal brighter, and conditions at the Post improved measurably in its new location. By 1790, a gristmill or two had appeared there (they would have been horse powered), a sawmill was erected around 1802 and soon after the Louisiana Purchase a cotton gin was built. By the late 1790s, the population had steadily grown to almost four hundred people, white and black, a parish had finally been created, and priests were at least sporadically instructing the young in elementary matters.

The Post also achieved a kind of architectural maturity in its waning years as a colonial outpost. By the middle of the 1790s, many of the houses there were constructed in the distinctive creole style typical of the other settlements of Louisiana. These houses were built of upright logs and had double-pitch hipped roofs, wide galleries all around (onto which the interior rooms opened), casement windows with shutters, French doors, and frequently a double fireplace in the center. They usually had just two rooms and contained only about four hundred square feet; the largest on record was around one thousand square feet. But the covered galleries could effectively double the amount of living space available to occupants and were frequently used as sleeping porches.

Despite the significant improvements that were wrought, the colonial Post did not achieve the agrarian respectability that Villiers and his successors had hoped for. There were never more than a few true farmers there, eight or ten at the most. Most of the farmers supplemented their income by trading and hunting, and the Post was not self-sufficient: To the very end of the colonial period, the Spanish garrison sometimes had to depend on flour from the Illinois country, or from Ohio, to sustain itself.

Arkansas Post was the only real settlement ever established during the colonial period in what would become the state of Arkansas. It is true that events during the American Revolution spurred the Spanish to establish a command on the Ouachita River in 1782, at first at a place called *Écore à Fabri* (modern-day Camden, Arkansas), where Capt. Jean Filhiol attempted to coax the dispersed hunters of the region into a militia unit and sedentary life. But an utter lack of success at *Écore à Fabri* soon required Filhiol to abandon the post there and refocus his efforts farther down the river, where he founded Ouachita Post, present-day Monroe, Louisiana. In 1797, a little fort was built on the Mississippi River across from Memphis at what the Spanish called Campo del Esperanza (the Field of Hope). But no real town sprang up there until the American period was well under way (it was called Hopefield), and the river had claimed the fort itself by 1810. A number of hunters occupied the White River and the Black River regions sporadically from the middle of the eighteenth century, but the settlements made there were temporary camps and corresponded only to the hunters' peripatetic style of life.

In 1719, Jean-Baptiste Bénard de La Harpe established an outpost at a Caddo village on the Red River, not many miles northwest of Texarkana. The Caddos, a sedentary agricultural people, were looking for protection from Osage raids that had greatly reduced their population and virtually destroyed some of their villages. The official moniker of La Harpe's post was St. Louis des Caddodoches, which makes it sound rather grand, but its population never exceeded seventy or eighty. Like Arkansas Post, it attracted a small number of traders and farmers, and a tiny garrison of perhaps six soldiers sometimes occupied the fort there.

Economy, Government, and Religion

The Arkansas region fairly teemed with game animals, and products of the hunt formed the chief exports of the Arkansas country. There were some deerskins, otter pelts, beaver pelts, bearskins, and bobcat skins shipped from the Post, but the skin and fur trade was not a very significant part of the economic activity there until the very late eighteenth and early nineteenth century. The exports that were the most important for most of the colonial period were salted buffalo meat, buffalo tallow, and bear's oil.

Huge canebrakes in the river bottoms and in extensive lowlands provided buffalo with a congenial forage, as did Little Prairie, the Grand Prairie, and the smaller prairies with which Arkansas was dotted at the time. The residents of New Orleans consumed large quantities of Arkansas buffalo meat, as did soldiers garrisoned throughout Louisiana. An Arkansas commandant who wanted to ingratiate himself with his governor in New Orleans would send him a couple of dozen salted buffalo tongues, along with pecans from the St. Francis River region, as a present.

Commandant: The military officer who was the head of the government at Arkansas Post.

Tallow, the rendered fat of the buffalo, was used for a number of purposes, such as burning in lamps and making candles. In the 1770s, François Ménard, a Post merchant who became in time the richest man in colonial Arkansas, contracted with the Spanish government to furnish ten thousand pounds of buffalo tallow to the Havana shipyards for caulking boats and other purposes. But bear's oil was the most versatile of Arkansas's eighteenth-century products. One principal use was for illumination: The government bought great amounts of it for lamps in its buildings and, late in the colonial period, for use in the New Orleans streetlight system. It was also used as a base for face paint by the Indians, as a mosquito repellant, as a drink, as cooking oil, and even as salad dressing. Some colonial Louisianans claimed that it was as good as the best olive oil in Europe. In the winter, the oil solidified into a white lard and was spread on bread like butter.

Since money was scarce in colonial Arkansas, most products were traded for goods. For hunting and war, traders offered guns, wadpullers, flints, powder, and balls; for clothing, they provided blankets of various quality, trade shirts, shoes, Limbourg (a lightweight woolen cloth, often of red or blue), twilled woolen serge, beads, and wool ribbon; and some trade inventories even mention white and blue paint that Indians used for decorating their faces and bodies. In 1758, the king's warehouse at the Post contained breechclouts, awls, strike-a-lights, folding knives, and butcher knives. One could even buy candles, flour, biscuit (hardtack), and four kinds of nails at this government store, along with rum and brandy.

Governing the Arkansas in the colonial period proved more than a little difficult, because of its remoteness and the nature of its population, and because neither the French nor the Spanish (who took over Louisiana in 1766) ever made much of an investment in government there. Lieutenant Governor Athanase de Mézières, who lived in Natchitoches, once described some of the denizens of the Arkansas River as "the most wicked men, without doubt, in all of the Indies," and this was not an isolated opinion.

The commandant was always a military officer, usually a lieutenant or a captain, who was posted to Arkansas for a few years and would then be sent to a command elsewhere in the colony. He was a marine during the French period, and while the Spanish were in possession of the country he was an army officer in the Fixed Infantry Regiment of Louisiana. Besides being commander-in-chief of the forces stationed at the Post, the commandant was also the sole civil and military judge for the entire region and ambassador to the Indian nations. He carried out the judgments of the New Orleans courts, and acted as the Post's notary, a nonforensic lawyer, drafting, executing, and recording legal documents. (Forensic lawyers, that is, lawyers who appeared in court, were not tolerated in French Louisiana, for, as an early ordinance excluding them from the colony had explained, such pettifoggers stirred up and maintained unnecessary quarrels.)

The commandant, in other words, was the government. He was, of course, expected to exercise his authority according to law, and French and Spanish law, each in its turn, was put in place and enforced to a degree at the Post. As early as 1712, for instance, the Custom of Paris, a legal code that governed certain civil relations, including marital property, was adopted as the law of Louisiana, and the gentry of the Post followed this code in their marriage contracts. Early in the Spanish period, the *Leyes de las Indias* (Laws of the Indies) were made applicable to Louisiana. Though there was, therefore, a lot of law that nominally bound him, the commandant possessed a great deal of residual authority at remote forest settlements like Arkansas Post, and he regularly laid down local police regulations.

Since there was only one person with real power and authority in the Arkansas country, the costs of governing the region were, to say the least, minimal. But providing government there was even less expensive than at first might appear, for officers' salaries were very low. The expectation was that the commandant would be a trader and a merchant during his sojourn at the Post; indeed, the great bulk of his income was typically derived from his private enterprises, not his public emolument. This could sometimes involve the commandant in a conflict of interest. Several commandants were called upon to judge cases involving their business competitors, many of whom they cordially despised.

While a functioning, even-handed government had a difficult time gaining a purchase in the Arkansas country, at least there was always someone there who was nominally in charge of it. The church, however, struggled even to maintain a presence. The church was a full partner in the state's imperial ambitions, and traders, soldiers, and priests were the vanguard of the

European expansionist effort. The church's main objects were to convert the native peoples and minister to the French residents, but its priests understood and quietly accepted their political role as the government's eyes and ears in the Indian villages, where the native people often called them "Black chiefs" because of the robes they wore. (A missionary also frequently carried medicines to his station, and helped residents draft legal documents, so he operated literally as a doctor, lawyer, and Indian chief.)

In fact, only a year or two after he founded Arkansas Post, Henri de Tonty set his mind to developing what he called his French quarter at his new settlement and asked the Jesuits to establish a priest there. These large plans came to naught, however, for the Jesuits never sent a missionary to Tonty's Post. And while the Seminarians of Canada aspired to settle among the Quapaws in the waning years of the seventeenth century, it was not until 1701 that Nicholas Foucault was able to establish himself there, and, as we saw, he became Louisiana's first martyr only a little more than a year later. Unfortunately, the priest destined for Law's colony in 1721 died on his way upriver. The Jesuit Father Du Poisson established himself at the Arkansas six years later, and was enjoying some success in his effort to learn the Quapaw tongue; but in 1729 the Natchez Indians killed him while, according to one report, he was standing at the altar celebrating mass in the church at Natchez.

The only priest who sojourned long enough in the Arkansas region during the French period to have had much influence was Louis Carette, a Jesuit who came to the Post in 1750 or 1751 and followed it in its peregrinations up and down the Arkansas River. He did his best to bring order to the place, but in 1758 he resigned in dismay because of the sacrilegious character of his flock, and no priest took up residence at the Post again until the 1790s. It was not until 1796 that the first canonical parish was created at the Post. In that year, Father Pierre Janin, who had fled the French Revolution and landed in Philadelphia in 1794, had made the mistake of telling the bishop of Louisiana and the Floridas that he did not like big cities; so the bishop had indulged Father Janin's preferences and named him the first parish priest at Arkansas Post. When he was called away three years later to minister to the more important congregation in St. Louis, the little parish at Arkansas failed and was never revived.

One upshot of all this was that whatever influence the church could have brought to bear as a partner of the civil government at the Post was very much attenuated. The church had found itself unable to sustain a presence in the region because the Post was so tiny and remote. The episodic attempts to establish a mission among the Quapaws were too short lived to have had a significant effect on the native belief system, and the efforts of the priests who ministered to the Post's French populace had usually proved no more rewarding than had the work among the Indians.

The church did enjoy some initial success in protecting its religious monopoly in the province. Protestants were at first excluded altogether, but late in the colonial period the Spanish were forced to let them immigrate to the colony without adopting the Roman Catholic religion. They were not, however, allowed to worship publicly. Jews, too, were excluded from Louisiana early on but Jewish merchants began to settle in New Orleans around 1757. Why these Jewish merchants were allowed to remain in the colony is not altogether clear: Some critics of the governor unkindly suggested that he had been bribed. Although Governor Alexander O'Reilly expelled most Jews from Louisiana in 1769, a number of them returned in rather short order, and they do not seem to have been officially molested thereafter.

It appears that there were no Jews living in Arkansas during the colonial period. Arkansas colonial residents did, however, have dealings with Jews. For instance, Etienne Layssard, who was the king's storekeeper at the Post in the 1750s, was at an earlier time evidently the New Orleans correspondent for the Jewish businessman Josue Henriques Jr., who was a resident of Curaçao. The famous Jewish merchant Isaac Monsanto, who lived in New Orleans, had business dealings with all the Mississippi towns, and there is evidence that François Ménard of Arkansas Post was one of his customers. We know more certainly that Monsanto sold goods on credit to a "Mr. Devidiers" (probably Balthazar de Villiers) who lived at Arkansas Post, and when Monsanto died, the governor instructed the Arkansas commandant to help Monsanto's executor collect debts that the denizens of Arkansas owed the estate.

What kind of reception Monsanto and his coreligionists might have been accorded at the Post and elsewhere in Louisiana is a question that does not have an obvious answer. Monsanto's expulsion from the colony in 1769, along with other Jewish residents of Louisiana, was perhaps not attributable so much to his religion as to his business success. (A number of English merchants were turned out of the colony at the same time.) Jean-Bernard Bossu, a French officer who claimed to have visited Arkansas Post three times, maintained that the French merchants of New Orleans were "enemies of the Jews on account of competition."

Society and Social Life

Though the Post was remote and the life there was rugged (one disgruntled commandant dubbed it "the most disagreeable hole in the universe"), there was an active social life there. There were numerous *cabarets* (bars) and a billiard parlor or two at which liquor, coffee, sugar, tobacco, and other luxury items were available. Card playing was a favorite pastime, and frequent balls, some lasting all night, provided needed diversion. In fact, Sunday afternoon following Mass (if any) was a favorite time for dances; and, after the Louisiana Purchase, Protestant preachers at the Post were scandalized when French ladies appeared dressed in their ball gowns in the back of the church, listened curiously to the sermon for a few minutes, and then unceremoniously stole away to attend the afternoon's festivities.

One difficult but important question about life at the Post is the extent to which the French and the Quapaws socialized together. When mixed-blood marriage ceremonies took place in the Quapaw villages, there were surely attendant celebrations in which both Indians and whites participated. Quapaw chiefs often dined with the Post commandant at his table in his house, especially on the day when the government delivered the annual present to the Quapaws. Such occasions were sometimes the scene of general celebrations in which hundreds of Indians and whites took part, consuming great amounts of meat, corn, and liquor.

Sometimes, medals were presented to the Quapaw chiefs at these events in the presence of a large assembly of Quapaws, Frenchmen, and Spanish soldiers, and the commandant personally placed the medals around the necks of the honorees while the garrison's drum rolled and the fort's cannons thundered. A Spanish commandant in the 1770s once purposely timed a volley from his cannons to coincide with the moment that the Quapaw chiefs sat down at his table to dine: The resulting reverberation knocked the dishes from the walls of the commandant's *salle* (dining room), and this, so the commandant reported at least, greatly impressed the assembled Indian dignitaries with the might of the Spanish king. Post residents also regularly attended annual fairs at one of the Quapaw villages, probably at a time that coincided with the Indians' green corn festival in early June.

The letters of commandants and the reports of European visitors to Arkansas are full of detailed descriptions of society at the Post; and even when one discounts them properly for the inevitable class bias of the people who wrote them, it is plain that the class structure at the Post was skewed toward the lower orders and that among them lawlessness and poverty was a not uncommon feature. The dangers and difficulties of the hunting life made it more or less inevitable that the white *voyageurs* and hunters drawn to the region would be among the most economically desperate men of the colony. The commandants at the Post despised most of them, calling them vagabonds, debauchees, bankrupts, riffraff, and professional drunks who valued lead more than silver or gold, owned nothing but their guns, and knew nothing except how to shoot them. Many of these hunters, in their turn, were deeply unhappy with the treatment that the merchants, including the commandants, afforded them. At least one disgruntled hunter, and probably more, joined in the English effort to take the Post during the Revolutionary War because of trade disputes with the commandant. Because the hunters were penniless for the most part, the merchant class was forced to outfit them on credit and wring whatever payment they could from them after they had completed their hunt.

While numerous *voyageurs* and hunters congregated at and around the Post, and constituted the largest part of its population, there were, nevertheless, representatives there of almost all the classes of which colonial Louisiana could boast. Though no titled nobleman ever made his home in Arkansas, the Post did give shelter to a few gentry with high-sounding names containing the particle "de," a highly reliable indication of gentle birth. Jean-François Tisserant de Montcharvaux, Marie-Françoise Petit de Coulange, and her son, Charles Melchior de Vilemont, provide excellent examples of these. Almost all the ladies and gentlemen of the Post were associated with the military. Just below these on the social scale were the substantial merchants, like François Ménard. He may have had a university education, for he first appears in the Arkansas in 1770 as a surgeon attached to the Spanish garrison. He was a highly successful merchant whose main business was supplying hunters for their annual campaign, trading with Indians, and exporting peltries, buffalo meat, tallow, and bear's oil to New Orleans and elsewhere. In addition, Ménard was a habitant, that is, a farmer, as some other merchants were. The number of serious farmers at the Post was very small, though, perhaps no more than ten or twelve at any one time.

Women married early, and during the time of their "coverture," as their marital condition was called, they suffered from certain civil disabilities: They could not bring lawsuits in their own name, and their husbands had the power to manage and control the community property. Although a wife could retain the property that she brought to a marriage, and could inherit other property that would not become part of the community, she could not deal with this separate estate without her husband's participation. It is true, though, that a married woman in Louisiana could become a *marchande* (merchant) and contract and own the property associated with her business the same as if she were single. It would be a mistake, moreover, to think that the civil disabilities visited on married women rendered them dependent and powerless. For instance, Madame Villiers, wife of Post commandant Balthazar de Villiers, was very active in her husband's mercantile affairs, and traveled constantly between the Post and New Orleans, transacting his business and dealing with New Orleans merchants and with the governor on commercial and governmental matters, acting essentially as her husband's partner.

There is reason to think that women were prime movers in the various efforts to establish a church at the Post, and actively sought the services of a priest to minister to the people and instruct the young. Women encouraged religious observance at the Post in other ways as well. For instance, in 1770, Madame DeClouet, wife of Post commandant Alexandre Chevalier DeClouet, left certain undescribed ornaments as a gift for the little chapel at the Post when she and her husband departed for New Orleans upon the expiration of his tour of duty at the Arkansas. Traditional female activities of a nurturing character also earned the women of the Post respect and gratitude. For example, in 1769 our same Madame DeClouet set the example for the other women at the Arkansas by nursing the victims of an epidemic that had struck the Post.

Widows, it is important to note, could be powerful people, and since many women outlived their husbands, there were frequent opportunities for them to enjoy full civil emancipation. Colonial Arkansas produced a number of these enfranchised widows. Marie-Françoise Petit de Coulange, for instance, who was born at Arkansas Post in 1732, had survived three husbands, all of them quite well-to-do, by the time she was thirty-nine. She did not thereafter remarry, and she became one of the richest people in the entire colony. (Her son, Charles de Vilemont, served as commandant of the Post from 1794 to 1802, and a town in Chicot County once bore his name.) François Ménard's relict was probably the richest person in the 1793 census of Arkansas Post: She owned nine slaves and on François's death she had succeeded to his very considerable mercantile business.

Women nevertheless frequently appear in the records in highly distressed circumstances. For instance, Indian slaves were common throughout colonial Louisiana and most of them were women. Many of these enslaved women toiled as concubines and laborers for hunters and trappers in the Arkansas country, and, as we would expect, some were subject to shocking abuse. A Spanish priest, for example, reported that in 1770 a Frenchman at La Harpe's post on the Red River was keeping five captive Indian women of various nations at his house "for the infamous traffic of the flesh." In other words, these women were forced into prostitution. The priest made unsuccessful attempts to rescue them.

Throughout the eighteenth century, Comanches abducted numerous Spanish and mixed-blood women from communities in northern New Mexico. Many of these women were physically and sexually abused by their captors and a number of them were sold as slaves to the Wichitas (the French called this tribe the Panis), who lived high up the Arkansas River in Oklahoma and on the Red River in Oklahoma. In the 1780s, the Arkansas commandant reported that there were a number of captive white women

Marie-Françoise Petit de Coulange de Vilemont, born at Arkansas Post in 1732. *Courtesy of Mrs. Elmire Villere Dracken, New Orleans.*

Capt. Charles Melchior de Vilemont, commandant of Arkansas Post from 1794 to 1802. *Historic Arkansas Museum, Little Rock.*

for sale in the Wichita village, and some of them were redeemed by French hunters who claimed them as their slaves.

In 1780, María Banancia, one of these enslaved women, wrote a pitiable letter from *Écores Rouges* to Governor Gálvez, begging him to free her from the clutches of a brutal, drunken hunter with the suggestively truculent nickname of La Bombard ("The Mortar"). She said that La Bombard frequently beat her, claimed that she was his property because she had cost him good money, and threatened to resell her "into the forests" where she would never be heard of again if she complained of his ill treatment. In a later legal proceeding against La Bombard, he freely confessed to beating her, but, in a revealing admission, said that he did so because she had stolen something from the Wichitas when she was in their village. It appears that La Bombard believed that he had a perfect right to punish her physically for this transgression. One of his companions accused him of raping María, a charge that he denied.

Althanase de Mézières, the lieutenant governor stationed at Natchitoches on the Red River, who had reasonably frequent contact with and news from the Wichita tribe, believed that captive white women among the tribe often suffered sexual abuse from their captors. But, in a classic case of blaming the victim, he said the women would never be accepted if they were released because of the "well-merited shame which they would suffer among Christians for their infamous inchastity."

White women were sometimes captured and abducted by Indian raiders even at the Post itself. In 1749, a number of French women and children were taken during the attack by the Chickasaws. Most of them, if not all, were later ransomed at Charleston and Mobile, but not before undergoing a harrowing ordeal. Enemies located on the plains or across the Mississippi were not the only ones who could inspire terror in the women of Arkansas. In the early 1770s, when the Quapaws were being held in only the most tenuous way to the Spanish alliance, a large party of them caused such an alarm at the Post that all the women and children had crowded into the commandant's bedroom, where they had huddled together, holding one another and crying.

The black population of the Arkansas region, including the Post, was never large: Even as late as 1798 the Post census listed only about sixty slaves, all black or mulatto, in a total population of almost four hundred. They spoke a French dialect sometimes called Afro/creole and perhaps an African language or two as well. A number of these slaves would have been engaged in agricultural work: Most of the French farmers in late eighteenth-century Arkansas had a few slaves to help them in their fields, but no one, so far as the record goes, ever owned more than the eleven whom Joseph Bougy claimed in 1794.

Although some of the slaves of the Arkansas worked at agriculture, captive Africans engaged in a wide variety of activities there in the colonial period. In 1789, for instance, Capt. Joseph Vallière's household servants served dinner to an American visitor, and it is probable that his servants were black slaves. Four years later, when Capt. Pierre Rousseau put in at the Post to have the rudder of his Spanish war vessel inspected, Captain Vallière supplied him with an old black artisan who soon had him on his way with newly manufactured parts for his ships. Since Rousseau paid the artisan directly with a draft on the treasury in New Orleans, it is possible that the old man was a free person of color, acting on his own account, but slaves often served as the trusted agents of their masters and conducted business for them without direct supervision. For instance, in the 1770s a merchant at Concordia left his trading post in the hands of his black clerks when he embarked on a brief trip. Most interestingly, at least one of these slaves was literate, for when they found it necessary to abandon the store they left behind a note in English explaining why they had done so. Many Africans in the Arkansas region showed other signs of assimilation into the white culture. For example, in 1793 some of François Ménard's slaves requested Father Gibault, the local priest, to say four Masses for Ménard when he died. They paid for the church services with tobacco, grown on plots given over to them for their own use and profit, as was the custom throughout Louisiana.

Marie-Félicité de Vallière Vaugine, 1770–1806. Daughter of Joseph Vallière. *Historic Arkansas Museum, Little Rock.*

Blacks also worked as laborers for merchants, dressing and packing hides, preparing other exports for shipment, and loading carts and boats. In 1793, for example, the widow Ménard had nine slaves at Arkansas Post, but she produced no crop, and the census lists her as a merchant, not a farmer. There were also a few, a very few, identifiable free black men at the Arkansas, some of whom engaged in farming on a small scale; and the 1790 census reveals the presence of two free mulatto women, both of whom occupied themselves as seamstresses.

Cruel penalties were inflicted on slaves convicted of committing crimes against whites. In 1742 a runaway slave of the Sango nation (from the Congo region), who belonged to Madame Lepine of Arkansas Post, attacked and seriously injured a French soldier bent on returning him to his mistress. He was originally sentenced to death, but, probably because he was too valuable to execute, his sentence was commuted. He was flogged for a number of days running at the crossroads of New Orleans, his right ear was cut off, and he was condemned to wear a six-pound weight on his foot for the rest of his life. Despite the dreadful punishment that often awaited recaptured fugitive slaves (*marons*), bondsmen ran away with some frequency. Three or four slaves belonging to Post merchant François Ménard found sanctuary among

Marons:
Runaway slaves.

Métis: Descendants
of mixed French/
Indian alliances or
marriages.

the Choctaws in the late eighteenth century, and it seems likely that they were never recovered.

In 1781, the French-Quapaw *métis* named Chalmet, while hunting on the Bayou Bartholomew between Arkansas Post and Ouachita Post, encountered and captured a young black runaway whom he had found sitting with a gun near a little campfire. Chalmet had resolved to keep the slave, but Captain Villiers intended to make him give the young man up and return him to his master. This is the only indication that the Quapaws possessed any black slaves in the colonial period, though it would not be surprising if they owned a few.

Fugitive slaves who were captured were imprisoned until the commandant could determine who their masters were. In 1783, for instance, *engagés* of François Ménard seized a black slave on an island in the Mississippi. The Arkansas commandant believed that the runaway belonged to one James Sullivan of Louisville, but he nevertheless drafted a notice that he sent to New Orleans, evidently for circulation to the other towns and posts of Louisiana, and perhaps also to some of the constituent republics of that new country called the United States. That same year, Captain DuBreuil reported that on his arrival at Arkansas Post he had found a *maron* in the Post jail who had fled from Natchez where his New Orleans master had sent him to work. No one had wanted to take charge of the runaway, so DuBreuil, feeling an obligation to shelter him from the cold, had taken him in. The slave had begged DuBreuil to ask his master for mercy, and DuBreuil had written the governor requesting him to use his good offices to intercede.

The white residents of colonial Louisiana, who were greatly outnumbered by their slaves in the lower part of the colony, were always alert to the possibility of a slave uprising; and when the slave conspiracy was uncovered in 1795 in Pointe Coupée, the government executed twenty-three slaves implicated in the plot and exiled thirty-one others to hard labor outside the province. Eighteenth-century revolutionary ideas about equality and the rights of man had penetrated even so remote a colony as Louisiana. Though there is no evidence of slave conspiracies at the Arkansas, in 1778 Captain Villiers complained that "vagabonds" and fugitive slaves were leading forays against the French hunters of the Arkansas River, pillaging and even killing them. Perhaps there was at least the beginnings of a *maron* community on the Arkansas River, in which some whites cooperated, though the fugitive slaves to whom Villiers had made reference may well have been Indians, or mainly so.

However that may be, it appears that the few farmers and gentry who owned slaves at Arkansas Post felt themselves attached by class and economic interest to the distant planters of lower Louisiana. Proof of this comes from a revealing event that occurred in the wake of the abortive Pointe Coupée rebellion. Governor Carondelet wrote to Captain Vilemont asking him to prevail on the Post slave owners to contribute voluntarily to a fund to compensate the owners of the slaves who had been executed or exiled for their part in the conspiracy. The aim was to raise $15,000 from the province as a whole, and the slaveholders of the Post, save one lonely holdout, answered the call by donating the requested six *reales* (seventy-five cents) for each slave that they owned. The effort raised a grand total of $34.75 from the denizens of Arkansas Post.

European and Quapaw Relations

Probably the most interesting aspect of life in colonial Arkansas, perhaps even the Post's real and most important story, has to do with the ways in which Quapaws and the Europeans who lived there found to coexist.

A number of visitors to Arkansas in the early nineteenth century maintained that intermarriage between the Quapaws and their French neighbors had been common, but the matter is somewhat controversial. An important cultural datum, though, that can serve as a useful starting point for considering this question, is that the Quapaws sometimes used marriage as a way to establish ties between their tribe and its trade allies. So, as early as 1700, when English traders were attempting to gain a foothold in the Arkansas country, one of them married a daughter (maybe two) of an important Quapaw headman. Similar alliances occurred about seventy years later when the English took possession of the east bank of the Mississippi River following the end of the Seven Years' War: An English trade mission boldly intruded up the Arkansas River and established itself in a Quapaw village, and one of its number promptly married a chief's daughter.

It would be odd if the Quapaws did not forge these kinds of bonds with the colonial French as well, given the closeness of the relationship between them for upwards of 120 years. It is true that the colonial sacramental records reveal only one or two such unions. But these records are sporadic and incomplete, and in any case largely irrelevant, because diplomatic trade marriages would have taken place in the Quapaw villages according to Indian custom. These connections quite obviously would not have left a trace in any church records. In addition, there are numerous contemporaneous histories and reports, some of them evidently independent of each other, that assert that the French residents of Arkansas intermarried with the Quapaws from very early times and in some numbers. Sometimes, though, European observers mistakenly assumed that the *métis* whom they saw in and around the Post had Quapaw origins, when instead they owed their lineage to marriages between French hunters and their Indian slaves from other tribes. So the extent to which Frenchmen and Quapaws entered into marital arrangements is probably not determinable to any very certain degree on the basis of this equivocal record.

While conjugal relationships, whether formal or not, may provide examples of the closeness that the two very disparate peoples inhabiting the Arkansas region achieved, in other ways the native Americans remained quite distinct from the European colonists. For example, the French and Spanish had scant success in applying their laws to the Quapaws because the Quapaws insisted on maintaining their sovereignty and refused to cede jurisdiction over members of their tribe to foreign nations. Quapaws exhibited their independence and individuality both internally within the tribe and collectively in their external dealings with their European allies. Father Vitry cautioned his readers, for example, that the Quapaws reserved the right to abandon a military venture at any time without the permission of its French commander: He also remarked on another highly important feature of Quapaw society, namely, that chiefs did not have the power to order their warriors into battle. That was a matter for persuasion and consensus.

Events that occurred when the Spanish took formal possession of Arkansas in October of 1769 reveal rather clearly how the Quapaws had conceptualized their political relationship with the French and how they intended to continue to view it with their new European ally. In that year, the Quapaw great chief Cossenonpoint put his mark to a document that he and Captain DeClouet, who commanded at the Post for Spain, had prepared together. The instrument said that Cossenonpoint, as chief of the great medal and great chief of all the Quapaw warriors, promised to recognize the new Spanish governor, Alexander O'Reilly, as his father and to listen to everything that DeClouet told him on O'Reilly's behalf. It is important to note, first of all, that the recognition of the governor as a "father" did not, in the Indian culture and idiom, come outfitted with the same patriarchal freight that such an undertaking would carry in European societies. Quapaw fathers were generous providers as much as disciplinarians, and in Quapaw society the primary duty of protection and care fell to them. The assumption of the father role by the French and Spanish governments placed heavy duties of support on the Europeans, but did not give them significantly extensive rights over the Indians and their behavior.

The Quapaws' retention of the essential aspects of their sovereignty is even more evident in Cossenonpoint's undertaking to "listen to" what DeClouet told him. In this highly important phrase, the parties adopted a familiar Indian idiom that was used to describe a well-respected and influential chief: The Spanish commandants at the Post not infrequently evaluated the various Indian leaders in their bailiwick for the governor, and those whom they believed to be particularly useful and dependable they described as "much listened to." So what Cossenonpoint was saying to the Spanish was that he would regard the Spanish governor as a "chief," that is, as an important leader, worthy of being listened to; but this was, in Quapaw society, a long way from accepting the governor as a European-style commander-in-chief. The governor, in other words, had to be content with being Indianized.

A comparison of Cossenonpoint's promise with the oath of allegiance that the French of the Arkansas took the same day to the Spanish monarchy makes the Quapaws' reservation of sovereignty, and the delicacy and tenuousness of their ties to the general Spanish interest, even more evident. The Frenchmen at the Post pledged fidelity to the Catholic Spanish king, swore that from that moment on they recognized him "as master of [their] life and property," and dedicated themselves "to his supreme royal will." The contrast could hardly be greater: The Quapaws promised to listen respectfully, an activity that falls somewhere between hearing and heeding; the French swore abjectly to obey.

The single exception of record to the Quapaws' refusal to submit to European law occurred in 1778, when Captain Vallière cajoled the Quapaws into executing one of their number who had killed an American hunter without provocation. But even in this instance it seems that the Quapaws achieved a partial cultural victory, for the commandant had originally demanded that a second Quapaw be executed as well because he had participated in the slaying. Under European law, of course, both perpetrators stood liable to forfeit their lives because both had guilty minds and both had acted: European law, under the influence of Christian thinking and teaching, concentrated on punishing the intentionally bad acts of all individuals. Quapaw law, however, in the case of a homicide, demanded only that the death be avenged ("covered," as the Indians said) by another death, and thus required that only one life be forfeited. Since that is precisely what happened in this instance, it appears that the Quapaws had persuaded the commandant to recognize their legal customs and not to exact the more stringent European penalty.

On many other occasions, Europeans were simply unable to apply their law to Indians at all. For instance, when a Quapaw chief struck at a Spanish commandant with a hatchet during a drunken confrontation, the officer was powerless to do anything about it, despite the condign punishment that would have awaited a white person who had dared to offer such an insult to the representative of His Catholic Majesty. Sometimes the Quapaws were influential enough even to have their own legal customs applied to Frenchmen when those customs were directly contrary to European law. An example occurred in 1754 when the Quapaws succeeded in prying pardons from the Louisiana governor for six soldiers who had deserted from the Post garrison and were subject to the death penalty under military law for doing so. Guedetonguay, a Quapaw chief, argued vigorously and successfully that the soldiers were entitled to clemency because they had sought refuge in the Quapaws' *cabanne de valeur* (house of valor) where religious rites were practiced, and under Quapaw sanctuary law this provided them with an immunity from punishment. The Quapaws were such important allies that the governor felt obliged to grant their request.

Cabanne de valeur: A French term used in reference to Indian (specifically, Quapaw) sacred temples.

The French and Spanish authorities worked hard to nurture and maintain the Quapaws' allegiance, and they forged some significant institutional connections with them that were designed to carry out their undertaking to be the Quapaws' "father." To uphold their end of the bargain, for instance, the Spanish provided the Quapaws with a gunsmith to keep their weapons in good repair and with an interpreter (who was sometimes a *métis*) who acted as a kind of Indian agent for the Europeans. The centerpiece of the European effort, however, was the annual present to the tribe, which included, in addition to the trade goods already mentioned, kettles, hoes, pipes, bells, and even silver-braided longcoats and trousers.

During the Spanish period, the principal impediment to European expansion in the Arkansas region was the mighty Osage nation, which, while it lived most of the year in villages in what is now Missouri, claimed northern and western Arkansas as its hunting territory, and thus often interfered with French hunters operating on the Arkansas River west of Little Rock. It appears that Arkansas hunters preferred to work the upper reaches of this river between Little Rock and Fort Smith, and they even ventured well into Oklahoma. Between 1770 and 1800 alone, the Osages killed more than fifty hunters on the Arkansas River, some under extremely gruesome circumstances.

The Quapaws occasionally retaliated against these Osage depredations, but the usual Spanish policy was to try to negotiate with the Osages and bring them to terms. There was, in any case, little practical hope of ever subduing the mighty Osage nation, since the meager Spanish forces, even taking the militia into account, were simply not up to anything like a successful campaign against them. The sad truth was, as well, that Spanish officials in New Orleans regarded the deaths on the Arkansas as unfortunate but not sufficiently important to avenge, because that might inconvenience the merchant class of St. Louis, who had an oligopoly on trade with the Osages and depended heavily on the tribe for their living. This attitude on the part of the New Orleans and St. Louis grandees enraged Commandant Villiers at the Arkansas, and he demanded to know whether commerce was to be cemented with the blood of innocents. The Osages continued to harry the hunters of the Arkansas until the end of the colonial epoch.

The Quapaws were more than a little amazed by the nonchalance of the Spanish government's reaction to the killing of its own people in such substantial numbers, and they were inclined to regard the Spanish government as pusillanimous. Spanish equivocation and impotence may, in part, have accounted for the attitude of the Quapaws toward the American Revolution. The Quapaws had, from about 1768, frequented an English trading village called Concordia that was established after the Seven Years' War across the Mississippi from the mouth of the White River. The English there were always spreading sedition among the tribe, ridiculing the Spanish army, its ordnance, and its fort at the Arkansas, and they predicted that Spain would soon be swept from Louisiana for good. Much of what the English said, especially about the ludicrously dilapidated condition of the Spanish fort and the weakness of the garrison at the Post, corresponded with what the Quapaws already knew from their own observation and experience.

So when the Spanish declared war against the British during the American Revolution, it is not surprising that the Quapaws were less than enthusiastic about committing themselves to the enterprise. When the English attacked the Post with a Chickasaw force in 1783, the Quapaw tribe remained aloof and refrained from helping the Spanish. As one village chief put it, only the great chief Angaska had the authority to commit the tribe to a white man's war, and he had not given the word. Some Spaniards fumed that Angaska had actively connived in the British effort to destroy the Post, but there is no real evidence for this. Four members of the tribe joined with some Spanish soldiers in a daring sally from the fort that routed the invaders and turned the day in the Spaniards' favor. But these Quapaws were acting as individuals who happened to have been in the fort when the attack had come in the wee hours of the morning. One of them was a French-Quapaw *métis* named Saracen, whose rescue of an officer's children from the Chickasaws after the battle was later commemorated in a church window in Pine Bluff.

While trade with the Quapaws was not especially remunerative, one aspect of it, the provision of liquor (brandy and rum) to the Indians, was of concern throughout the colonial era. French and Spanish authorities, depending on the perceived needs of the moment, blew hot and cold on prohibiting the liquor trade with the Quapaws. On the one hand, liquor caused considerable havoc: Inebriated white hunters and Indians alike made for forgetful debtors and unreliable warriors. On the other hand, liquor was very much in demand, frequently in preference to any other good. In the 1760s for instance, Comdt. Alexandre DeClouet allowed that the Quapaw alliance simply could not be held together without liquor, and the English across the Mississippi at Concordia constantly importuned the Quapaws with it in an effort to undermine their attachment to the Spaniards. The French residents of the Arkansas, moreover, were occasionally in such dire straits that they were forced to trade liquor with the Quapaws for corn.

DeClouet eventually prohibited the liquor trade with the Quapaws, but later commandants resorted merely to licensing liquor traders in an attempt to control the flow of spirits into the Indian nation. This kind of restriction did not at first sit well with the tribe: Quapaw leaders complained that every other kind of trade was free and open, and argued that the regulation of the liquor trade with them constituted an irritating and insulting discrimination. When Captain Villiers, a vocal devotee of the free market, resolved to open this trade to everyone, some of the *habitants* and merchants of the Post became alarmed and petitioned the governor to prevent it: "A wiser decision," they believed, would be to establish "a single place . . . where drink would be distributed to [the Indians] in an orderly and proper manner." Villiers's original decision with respect to trading liquor at the Post, he explained to the governor, had been to license only one cabaret for selling liquor by the glass (*en detail*), "to prevent the disorders that a free distribution might generate" on account of "the Indians by whom we are surrounded." He had, however, allowed any merchant to sell liquor, even *en detail*, for consumption off premises.

> **Habitants:**
> "Farmers"; sometimes "inhabitants."

The Quapaws' attachment to the virtues of free enterprise was not long lived. In 1786, three Quapaw chiefs asked the governor to prohibit the liquor trade with their tribe altogether because of widespread alcohol dependence in their nation. The governor temporized, and, during a three-month period alone, five Quapaws died in alcohol-related brawls. Finally, in 1787, after a minor Quapaw chief was killed during yet another drunken altercation, and his mutilated body was thrown into the Arkansas River, the governor forbade the sale of liquor to the tribe entirely. "All traffic of drink with the Indians" must cease, the governor ordered, "because of the consequences" that had flowed from that trade. Violators of the ban, the order warned, would have their goods confiscated and would be imprisoned for an indefinite term.

This prohibitionist effort, as we would have expected, was not successful, or at least not entirely so, for late in the colonial period Captain Vilemont complained to the governor about "the great influx of Indians [no doubt Choctaws and Chickasaws] who are difficult to contain when they drink." Since the small population of the Post would be unable to protect itself from the disasters that Vilemont predicted, he asked the governor to forbid the importation of rum to the Post completely except for the use of the *voyageurs* and sailors who worked the rivers. A short time later, a petition from some leading citizens at the Arkansas seconded Vilemont's request, and they pointedly noted not only that liquor had had a pernicious effect on the behavior of the Indians, but also that the French hunters' immoderate use of it had made debt collection more difficult.

Despite these and other occasional conflicts, conditions in the colonial Arkansas country had virtually conspired to optimize prospects for peaceful coexistence and cooperation between the Quapaws and the Europeans who lived there. Around 1700, the Caddos who had lived in Arkansas retreated south, some to join the Caddodoches on the great bend of the Red River in east Texas, others to positions lower down the river in Louisiana. This left the Quapaws as the only tribe permanently residing in the region. So even a very generous estimate of the number of people occupying Arkansas in the late eighteenth century yields a population density there of only about one person (Indian, white, and black) to every five square miles. (Present-day Western Sahara has a population density ten times as great.) There was therefore no real competition between the Europeans and the Quapaws for either land or animal resources in the territory that the tribe claimed. Because there was plenty to go around, a frequent source of friction between colonists and native people was eliminated.

In addition, the European population consisted for the most part of highly individualistic hunters, who proved unreliable militiamen, and the French and Spanish garrisons were small and its soldiers often unseasoned and undisciplined; all of this added greatly to the military usefulness of the Quapaws. This helps explain why the French and the Quapaws joined together in the 1770s to build a road connecting their settlements, the first road construction project of record in the state.

It is also significant that the French, and then the Spanish in imitation of them, never attempted to cajole, coax, or force the Quapaws into becoming mission farmers; indeed, the Spanish did not proselytize the Indians at all. Nor did the European powers that claimed to hold sway over the Arkansas country try to incorporate the Indians into their legal systems in any significant way. It is well known that proselytizing was a significant cause of strife between whites and Indians, but it needs saying that the same would be true of attempts at legal assimilation. The respect that colonial Louisiana officials showed to indigenous legal and religious traditions no doubt did a great deal to ingratiate them with the Quapaws' political and religious leaders.

Whatever may have been the case elsewhere in North America, therefore, it would seem right to characterize the small number of Europeans who came to Arkansas during its colonial epoch as more like immigrants than invaders. It is true that immigrants do not typically claim sovereignty, build forts, and establish garrisons. But French and Spanish claims to sovereignty over Arkansas were basically hollow: The Indians did not consider themselves subjects, and the Europeans did not even pretend that they were. This was hegemony writ small.

End of an Era

In 1800, Spain, under a secret treaty, retroceded the colony of Louisiana to France, but France did not move to retake possession of the province until late in 1803. By then, France had already found it necessary to sell Louisiana to the United States, and the French interregnum lasted only twenty days, after which, on December 20, 1803, the American government took possession of the colony.

An American lieutenant named James Many did not venture up the Arkansas River until March of 1804 to receive the fort at the Post of Arkansas on behalf of his nation. There he found Capt. Caso y Luengo commanding a Spanish force already reduced to three soldiers. The settlement that Many entered comprised about four hundred souls; and the dilapidated fort that he occupied for the United States was worth, so its appraisers reckoned, only 631 dollars, a small enough sum for one hundred and twenty years of imperial effort.

Civil government was slow in coming to the Post. For a few years, Lieutenant Many and his successors imitated, no doubt to the great relief of Post residents, the military government of the previous French and Spanish regimes, judging and settling disputes and recording documents themselves. It would not be long, however, before a new republican machinery was put in place, and the old colonial residents of Arkansas soon found their mores and themselves rudely shoved aside. New arrivals from the United States were not slow to criticize the French creoles whom they encountered, damning them wholesale as a lazy and superstitious lot, excluding them from government offices and from jury service, ridiculing their religious practices and even the way that they built their houses. The French language languished, too: The only item that the *Arkansas Gazette*, a weekly newspaper established at the Post in 1819, ever published in French was a small, four-line notice for a local political candidate who was evidently plumping for the creole vote.

The Post itself soon received an official snub. It served as the Arkansas territorial capital from 1819 to 1821, but with the creation of Little Rock in the latter year the seat of government was moved there. About a decade later, Washington Irving used the two towns to contrast the idle creoles of Louisiana with the bustling American immigrants, hard after the main chance, who were soon to engulf them for good. He pictured the Post as the paradigmatic creaky creole village, inhabited by an amiable collection of indolent Frenchmen; Little Rock he filled with lawyers, banks, newspapers, and electioneering candidates, all engaged in a furious competition. Irving was deliberately caricaturing both the French and the Americans to a degree, but he was certainly right about the complete substitution of cultures that had rapidly occurred in the Arkansas country.

With the removal of the capital to Little Rock, the Post gradually declined. The old French houses that survived, with their tall chimneys and their distinctive galleries all around, succumbed to the drubbing that Union gunboats gave the town in 1863. Though a small settlement managed to struggle on, and the United States Government stoutly maintained a post office called Arkansas Post until 1941, today there is nothing left of the first European settlement in what became Jefferson's Louisiana. The federal government, however, some decades ago established the Arkansas Post National Memorial at the old town site, with a fine visitors' center that features exhibits and a film outlining Arkansas's colonial history. And a considerable amount of archeology has been undertaken at two of the former locations of the village: There have been important discoveries, including the probable site of Tonty's first outpost.

5 The Turbulent Path to Statehood

 Arkansas Territory, 1803–1836

THE PERIOD BETWEEN 1803 and 1836 marked an important formative era in the history of the United States and of the territory of Arkansas. The young United States fought for and established its territorial integrity, devised and began to carry out a draconian Indian policy, and reinvented its political party system. All of these developments would have their parallels in Arkansas. The territory began its integration into the national political economy almost immediately after the Louisiana Purchase of 1803. Within fifteen years it became a staging ground for the removal of Indian groups from east of the Mississippi River, and it began the process of dispossessing its own native population. The two dominant national political parties, the Whigs and Democrats, both found adherents in the state, but the Democratic Party emerged as the dominant political force. Finally, by the 1830s parts of the territory's agricultural economy began to resemble that of the older Southern slave states, with a small plantation elite playing a disproportionate role in the territory's politics and economy.

The Louisiana Purchase

The Arkansas region came into the possession of the United States by virtue of the Louisiana Purchase of 1803, an altogether unexpected and monumental real estate transaction. What had started as an attempt by the fledgling United States to buy New Orleans from France and thus secure unfettered access for Western farmers to the Gulf of Mexico and the Atlantic Ocean turned into something much bigger when the French emperor Napoleon offered for sale not only New Orleans but all of the Louisiana Territory, approximately 828,000 square miles. Surprised at the proposal but recognizing the implications, the American emissaries pursued the offer, and on April 30, 1803, they completed a treaty giving the United States ownership of the Louisiana Territory for the price of $15 million.

The extraordinary purchase more than doubled the size of the United States, and it also enhanced the young country's potential as a world power, but its immediate impact on the region that would become Arkansas was small. It was not until March of 1804 that Lt. James Many arrived at Arkansas Post to accept the transfer of Arkansas Post from Spanish authorities, and American settlers were slow to arrive in the region. Three days after Lieutenant Many's arrival, Congress divided Louisiana along the thirty-third parallel (the present boundary between Arkansas and Louisiana), creating the Territory of Orleans south of that line and the District of Louisiana north of it. This arrangement lasted only until the following March, when the District of Louisiana became the Louisiana Territory with its capital at St. Louis.

Historian Charles Bolton has noted that the first official use of the name Arkansas came in 1806 when the southern portion of New Madrid County was designated as the District of Arkansas. In 1812 when the Orleans Territory entered the Union as the state of Louisiana, the Louisiana Territory became the Missouri Territory, and the following year the Missouri territorial legislature created a separate Arkansas County with Arkansas Post as the county seat. These administrative changes notwithstanding, Arkansas remained, in Bolton's words, "remote and restless," largely underappreciated by the Missouri territorial government located at New Madrid (in present-day Missouri), a 250-mile trip upriver from Arkansas Post. The residents at the Post and surrounding regions thus were subject to little government, and remained under military authority longer than any other place in Louisiana.

Exploring the Territory

The first American attempt to explore the Arkansas region took place in the winter of 1804–1805, when President Thomas Jefferson selected two Scottish immigrants—William Dunbar and Dr. George Hunter—to lead an expedition up the Ouachita River to the hot springs, a site that had been sought out by a few whites for their purported medicinal powers and accompanying economic benefits. Dunbar was a noted scientist and wealthy Mississippi planter, while Hunter was an apothecary and physician who had established himself in Philadelphia as a chemist and entrepreneur. The expedition was originally intended to ascend the Red River as part of Jefferson's goal of establishing the precise boundaries of the Louisiana Purchase. But because of Spanish hostility to an expedition that would skirt Spanish territory and also because of fear of the Osage Indians along the Arkansas River, it was changed to an exploration of the Ouachita.

The expedition, consisting of the two Scotsmen, two of Dunbar's slaves, one of his servants, Hunter's teenage son, and thirteen soldiers set out on October 16, 1804, from a spot about fifteen miles below Natchez, near Dunbar's plantation, "The Forest." They descended the Mississippi to the mouth of the Red River and then ascended the Red and the Black riv-

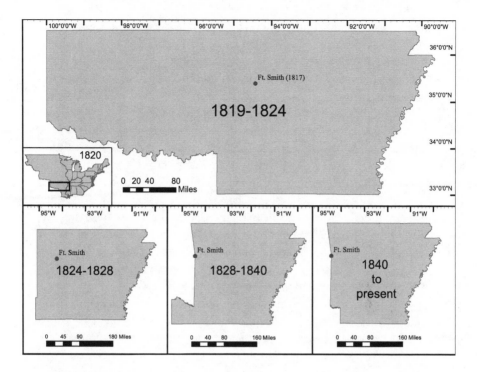

Arkansas land subdivision and boundary changes. *Courtesy of Joseph Swain (Source: Newberry Library, Chicago, Dr. William M. Scholl Center for American History and Culture [Atlas of Historical County Boundaries, https:// publications.newberry.org/ahcbp/downloads/united_states.html]).*

ers to the mouth of the Ouachita. On October 23 they began the ascent of the Ouachita and arrived at the Post of Ouachita or Fort Miro (present-day Monroe, Louisiana) on November 6. There they took on a guide and swapped the unwieldy Chinese-style scow that Hunter had designed for the expedition for a flat-bottomed barge more suited for river travel. They resumed their journey on November 11, and four days later crossed thirty-three degrees north latitude (the present-day boundary between Louisiana and Arkansas).

In early December the expedition reached the hot springs. Dunbar and Hunter conducted experiments on the waters there, looking for any evidence of its medicinal properties. They found none, nor did they find any evidence of substantial salt deposits or valuable minerals. The expedition began the return voyage on January 8, 1805, and reached Natchez on January 27.

Dunbar's and Hunter's reports, filed separately and widely published, were the first to provide a glimpse into the new territory after the purchase. While they had entered what most whites considered an isolated wilderness, the expedition almost daily encountered white or Indian hunters or evidence of their recent passage. Perhaps the greatest contribution of the reports was their description of the complex and fluid sociopolitical situation along the Ouachita in which Indian and white politics and economics were intertwined.

The period before and immediately after the Louisiana Purchase represented what historian Richard White has termed the "middle ground," where whites and Indians borrowed from each other culturally and collaborated in their economic activity. Historian Kathleen DuVal argues in *The Native Ground* that Indians in Arkansas held their own, retaining their cultural identity. However, the middle-ground hypothesis provides a useful way to understand the accommodation of whites and Indians to each other in the period before the beginning of white settlement after the Louisiana Purchase. This accommodation continued into the territorial era but eroded rapidly as new white settlers, desiring to acquire land to grow cash crops for an expanding market, began to demand the removal of the Indians.

Middle ground: The collaboration and cultural exchange between Native Americans and Europeans who encountered each other on the frontier.

Native ground: A phrase coined by Kathleen DuVal that posits an alternative to the middle-ground collaboration and highlights the persistence of Native ways in the face of European incursions.

One of the most important revelations concerning Indians and white hunters appears in Hunter's account of events occurring on November 21, 1804. On that date the expedition noticed a pictograph on a tree near their breakfast encampment. The pictographer had removed some bark from the tree and painted a scene depicting a man on horseback with one hand pointing toward the river and the other toward the woods. Two other figures, one of them wearing a round hat, a typical Indian symbol for a European, were apparently shaking hands. This seems to represent an expression of friendship. When Hunter took a party into the woods in the direction the horseman was pointing, they found a hunter's camp and fourteen deerskins tied in a bundle on a pole. Just as they arrived at the camp, however, another white man, by the name of Campbell, appeared. Campbell, a carpenter who was taking a consumptive man to the hot springs, had encamped near the expedition the evening before and had apparently left his boat to hunt in the woods. He claimed that he had placed the skins there a year before for an Indian chief by the name of Habitant, but Hunter doubted his story, concluded that the skins belonged to a Choctaw Indian, and took possession of them, determined to locate the rightful owner or deposit them at the Post on the way back down river for safekeeping. Hunter believed that if he left the skins in place, Campbell would take them, and the expedition might be blamed. Perhaps he feared retaliation for violating the custom and thought that if he had possession of the skins he could surrender them in exchange for safe passage.

Whether Campbell had made an agreement with an Indian by the name of Habitant or not, the assertion that he had done so suggests the cooperation that existed between white hunters and Indians. Hunter's disbelief did not necessarily represent an ignorance of this kind of cooperation, but rather his distrust of Campbell. It may well have been that Campbell was truly a scoundrel violating a long-held custom. But neither Dunbar nor Hunter was predisposed to trust a man of Campbell's social standing. Just as they routinely denigrated the soldiers, they also dismissed their own pilot as a man who was "not remarkable either for his judgment or veracity."

They seemed to place white hunters, however, in a separate category. From hunters they could secure essential information about the terrain and about conditions up river. For example, from an "old Dutch hunter," named Paltz, they received intelligence about hostilities among the Osages and the Chickasaws, Choctaws, and certain other "Indian nations." They encountered Paltz and his three sons on November 29. Having lived for forty years on the Ouachita and before having traversed the White, the St. Francis, and the Arkansas rivers, Paltz provided them with valuable information about the interior of Arkansas. His information about the Arkansas River was of particular interest to Dunbar and Hunter, for they were anticipating an important expedition up that river. That expedition never occurred, and the one that did take place was led by Lt. James Wilkinson, who, unfortunately, devoted only a few pages in his diary to Arkansas. The Dunbar-Hunter accounts would serve as the only substantive information by expeditioners in the early territorial period. Fortunately, Dunbar and Hunter wrote copiously and revealed much about the area.

Settlement

At the time of the Louisiana Purchase only about five hundred white people resided in what is now Arkansas, the majority of them French. A few years later the census of 1810 counted only slightly over a thousand, clustered mainly in settlements across the Mississippi River from present-day Memphis and along the lower reaches of the Arkansas River.

Many of those settlers were dramatically impacted by a natural disaster in late 1811. Events of the following year did little to encourage immigration into Arkansas. At approximately 2:00 a.m. on December 16, 1811, an earthquake rated as one of the twenty greatest to occur anywhere in the world and the worst to hit North America, struck the region. The quake was centered in northeastern Arkansas but was named for the town of New Madrid in southeastern Missouri, which, with 103 villagers, was one of the most densely populated places in the stricken area.

The first shock was followed five hours later by an even more powerful one, which destroyed the few brick buildings in New Madrid and knocked down log and frame houses throughout the earthquake zone. Two additional severe shocks occurred on January 23 and on February 7, 1812, but hundreds of aftershocks punctuated the larger ones and the tremors and shocks lasted for at least a year. One chronicler counted 1,874 shocks between December 16 and March 8, and he classified 18 of them as either violent or very severe.

While the largest shocks could be felt in an area covering approximately one million square miles, their force brought devastation to parts of southeastern Missouri and northeastern Arkansas. New lakes were created and old ones went dry. Sinks and sand blows replaced forests and farmlands. Travelers on the river reported the disappearance of whole islands, and some people foolish enough to place structures close to the river watched them disappear or disappeared with them as the riverbank collapsed, sometimes burying flatboats carrying cargo, crew, and passengers unlucky enough to have tied to the shore there. White settlers and Indians along the St. Francis River took the brunt of the earthquake in Arkansas, and many of them, Indian and white alike, abandoned their homes, never to return.

The quake created the Arkansas "sunk lands," an area that became swampy and subject to complete inundation every spring. The existence of the sunk lands retarded settlement in northeastern Arkansas for another century. But the earthquake also resulted in an Act of Congress in 1815 that encouraged white settlement elsewhere in Arkansas. On February 17, 1815, Congress passed the New Madrid Act providing certificates, which came to be known as New Madrid Certificates, to individuals who had owned or had claims to land destroyed or made relatively worthless by the earthquake.

New Madrid Act: An act of Congress that provided land certificates in Arkansas to those settlers in Missouri whose land was damaged by the New Madrid earthquakes of 1811 and 1812.

Bolstered in part by those certificates and by additional grants given to veterans of the War of 1812, the number of non-Indian settlers in Arkansas increased significantly in the years between 1810 and 1820. The pattern of settlement changed as well. Many of the new arrivals avoided the swampy and disease-ridden lowlands of eastern Arkansas, choosing instead to follow the Southwest Trail, a route that ran southwesterly along the eastern edge of the Ozark and the Ouachita highlands from Ste. Genevieve, Missouri, on the Mississippi River to the Spanish province of Texas. It was the first road in Arkansas to be improved after the Louisiana Purchase, and President Andrew Jackson later designated it as a military road, giving it priority on maintenance and improvements.

Wherever the trail crossed a major stream, a settlement sprang up—Poke Bayou (present-day Batesville) developed where the trail crossed the White

River, Blakeleytown (present-day Arkadelphia) where it crossed the Ouachita River, and Fulton where it crossed the Red River. Between Blakeleytown and Fulton, Washington grew up as a major stopping point along the trail, even without the benefit of a river. By 1820 the population of the territory had grown to 14,255, a thirteen-fold increase from 1810. Ten years later, it reached 30,388.

Political and Economic Development

As the region's population grew, momentous political affairs were also underway. When citizens in the northern part of the Missouri Territory began to petition Congress for statehood in 1818, they excluded the area located below thirty-six degrees thirty minutes. That included the southern portion of Lawrence County and four other counties that had been created out of the old District of Arkansas in the period between 1812 and 1818—Clark, Hempstead, Pulaski, and Arkansas. Missouri's petition opened the way for the creation of Arkansas Territory.

Petitions to admit the new state of Missouri and to create Arkansas Territory, however, stimulated a congressional debate over the issue of slavery. When the Missouri Enabling Act (which authorized the inhabitants of Missouri to create a constitution and form a state government preparatory to being admitted to the Union) was introduced on February 13, 1819, New York representative James Tallmadge proposed an amendment that would bar the further introduction of slaves to Missouri and provide freedom at age twenty-five to those slaves born after the territory's admission as a state. The House of Representatives approved the Tallmadge amendment, but the Senate promptly rejected it.

Meanwhile, on February 16 the House began consideration of the Arkansas Territory bill. This time, it was another representative from New York, John Taylor, who introduced amendments similar to those that Tallmadge had proposed regarding Missouri. The supporters of slavery, however, having been alerted by the Tallmadge amendment, marshaled their forces and presented a powerful challenge to the Taylor amendment. The House defeated the Taylor amendment by a narrow margin.

Representative Taylor subsequently offered three other amendments designed to restrict slavery in the Arkansas Territory, but they were also defeated. In his third effort, he introduced a motion proposing that a dividing line be established at thirty-six degrees thirty minutes north latitude with slavery excluded from all territory north of that line. Although Taylor was defeated in this, his final attempt to impose prohibitions on slavery in the proposed territory of Arkansas, the thirty-six degrees thirty minutes dividing line would become a crucial factor in the famous Missouri Compromise (1820), which allowed Missouri to enter the Union as a slave state (balanced by the admission of Maine as a free state) but prohibiting slavery in any other part of the Louisiana Purchase territory north of the line.

In the process leading up to Missouri statehood, the border in extreme southeast Missouri was dropped to 36 degrees from the Mississippi River to the St. Francis River. The reasons for this remain the subject of conjecture. Missouri historian Perry McCandless has noted, "There seems to be no clear explanation for the inclusion of the southeast Bootheel in the new state of Missouri. According to tradition, John Hardeman Walker, a significant land-owner in the area, led the effort to get the Panhandle into the proposed state of Missouri and successfully enlisted John Scott and other political figures from the Jackson area to support its inclusion." In that same year, a treaty gave a piece of the territory on Arkansas's southwestern corner to Spain, ending a long struggle over the international border. Arkansas lost a segment lying below the Red River, but still its western border extended to approximately 100 degrees west longitude, encompassing most of present-day Oklahoma.

President James Monroe signed the act creating Arkansas Territory on March 2, 1819. The next day he appointed Brig. Gen. James Miller of New Hampshire as territorial governor and twenty-two-year-old Robert Crittenden, the scion of a prominent Kentucky family, as territorial secretary. Miller was a hero of the War of 1812, but skill on the battlefield did not trans-late into effective leadership in administering the new territory's affairs. Less than enthusiastic about his new position, Miller did not arrive at Arkansas Post until the day after Christmas.

Crittenden had no such qualms. The act creating the territory provided that it begin operations on July 4, 1819, and the young secretary was already in the territory when that date arrived. In Miller's absence, Crittenden, by law, became the acting governor. Described by a contemporary as "a man of fine presence and handsome face (light hair, blue eyes, under medium height, rather stockily built)," Crittenden soon became the major power in the new territory. He waited for Miller until July 28 and then called the newly appointed three judges—Robert P. Letcher, Charles Jouett, and Andrew W. Scott—together as Arkansas's first legislative body.

In addition to declaring in force all the laws applicable to the Territory of Missouri, they provided for the judicial and financial mechanisms under which Arkansas could be governed. They divided the territory into two judi-cial districts, each to have its own circuit judge, and established the offices of auditor and treasurer. Finally, they passed an act to raise public funds to pay for the territory's administrative expenses. On August 3 they disbanded, and the three justices left the territory to Crittenden's care.

Judge Scott later returned with his family, but Jouett and Letcher abandoned their appointments and were replaced. One of those replacements, Benjamin Johnson, was a member of a politically powerful Kentucky family. His brother, Richard M. Johnson, was credited with killing the great Shawnee leader Tecumseh in the War of 1812 and would use the fame gained in that conflict to become vice president of the United States under Martin Van Buren. Benjamin Johnson and his son, Robert Ward Johnson, would become major figures in Arkansas politics.

Crittenden quickly developed a group of loyal supporters. On November 20, 1819, voters selected one of those supporters, James Woodson Bates, as a delegate to Congress. They also elected a five-member legislative council representing the five counties, and a nine-member house of representatives.

That same day a twenty-four-year-old New York–born printer named William Woodruff published the first edition of the *Arkansas Gazette*, the territory's first newspaper. Woodruff had worked for a time for a newspaper in Nashville, Tennessee, but when the Arkansas Territory was created, his editor had encouraged him to go there. Woodruff bought a small stock of printing materials and a second-hand press and set off by boat for Arkansas Post, arriving at the end of October 1819. He announced that his paper would be nonpartisan, a promise that he would not be able to keep.

In early 1820 Secretary Crittenden and the recently arrived Governor Miller became involved in a controversy over a new location of the territorial capital. Few people seriously disputed that the ill-placed Arkansas Post, with its frequent flooding and unhealthy climate, was an inappropriate location for the capital of the new territory. The question was where to relocate, and two major contenders arose. One was the small village of Cadron, located approximately 250 miles upriver from Arkansas Post at a spot where Cadron Creek entered the Arkansas River. Another likely choice was the area near the "little rock," about thirty-five miles downriver from Cadron. In 1722 the French explorer Bernard de la Harpe, on an expedition to explore the Arkansas River, had recommended the placement of a trading post there. No such trading post was established by the French or later by the Spanish during their occupation of the territory.

Sometime during the second decade of the nineteenth century, a white hunter and trapper, William Lewis, lived at the "little rock" site with his family in a rude shack that they occupied only briefly during every year. After securing a preemption certificate that gave him title to the land and shack in 1814, he sold it in the fall of that year and then disappeared from the historical record. The title changed hands several times before being acquired by William Russell, a St. Louis land speculator.

Russell's title to the land was not clear, however. A rival group (including a young Stephen F. Austin) held four New Madrid certificates, granted to compensate those who had lost land in the famous earthquake of 1811–1812, which, they claimed, gave them legal title to the site. They enlisted Governor Miller and a recently arrived New York attorney named Chester Ashley to press their case.

In February 1820 Russell made a compact with Townsend Dickinson, also an attorney from New York whom he met at Arkansas Post, to help lobby the territorial delegates to relocate the capital to the "little rock" site. But the legislators were unable to decide between that location and Cadron and postponed the matter to the October session. In March 1820 a post office was established at the site, taking the name Little Rock. Between the February and October sessions of the legislature, a number of legislators and influential men, including Crittenden, purchased "lots" at Little Rock. Dickinson acted as agent in the transactions, while Russell lobbied the legislators. On October 10, 1820, the bill to remove the capital to Little Rock passed by a vote of six to three.

In the spring of 1821, with the title to the site still in dispute, the capital was officially moved to Little Rock. One of the relocated government's first actions was a decision by the superior court affirming the Russell faction's claim to the land. Outraged, the New Madrid claimants removed or destroyed the buildings they had constructed on the site. In November the two rival groups reached a compromise, whereby they would combine their interests and support each other's legal rights to the land. The settlement helped make Chester Ashley one of the wealthiest men in the territory and a major force in territorial politics. He soon opened a law partnership in Little Rock with Robert Crittenden.

Political machinations aside, Little Rock was well situated at a point where the Southwest Trail crossed the Arkansas River and where the landscape began the transition from the lowlands of the southeast to the highlands of the northwest. By 1828 it would be the western terminus of the first "military road" constructed in Arkansas, linking it to Memphis.

As the capital controversy was coming to a close, a new political force was emerging. In 1823, after supporting James Bates for two terms as territorial delegate, Crittenden threw his support to Henry Conway, a member of a prominent Tennessee family. With Crittenden's help, Conway won the election and was reelected in 1825 and 1827.

In late 1824, Governor Miller, citing health concerns, announced that he would resign the governorship effective December 31. He subsequently accepted a position as collector for the Post of Salem, Massachusetts, and left Arkansas for good. Historian Charles Bolton has noted that, with his late arrival and his frequent trips home to New Hampshire, Miller was actually in Arkansas less than half the time he was governor.

With Miller's departure, Crittenden hoped to gain actual title to the position that he had administered for much of the preceding five years. Delegate Henry Conway and congressional delegations from Kentucky, Tennessee, and Illinois supported Crittenden for the position but to no avail. President James Monroe, who was then finishing out his second term in office, appointed George Izard, a Federalist and the son of a successful diplomat, politician, and planter from South Carolina, to be the state's second territorial governor.

Izard had been educated in military schools in England and France and had taken his university degree in Edinburgh. He achieved the rank of major general during the War of 1812. Having developed a cosmopolitan background from time spent in England, France, and Spain, as well as residence in Philadelphia and Charleston, South Carolina, Izard had to be persuaded to accept the governorship of the Arkansas Territory. His appointment was confirmed by the Senate on March 3, 1825. Although he was Monroe's choice, President John Quincy Adams sanctioned the appointment after his inauguration in March 1825.

Unlike his predecessor, Izard was unwilling to allow Crittenden to run the territory. He called the secretary back from Washington, where he had the territorial papers in his possession—a common practice in that period—and began to administer affairs. Izard regularized certain functions of government, including reorganizing the territorial militia.

One of the most significant events of Izard's tenure as governor was one in which he was not directly involved. In April 1827, territorial delegate Henry Conway announced that he would seek reelection to a third term. A week later, Robert Oden, a Little Rock attorney, announced that he would also seek the office. In addition to being perhaps the first licensed lawyer in Little Rock, Oden was known primarily for having killed William Allen, a territorial legislator and commander of the territorial militia, in a duel in March 1820.

In the campaign that followed, Oden charged that Conway had misappropriated $600 out of a sum of $7,000 entrusted to him by the secretary of war to deliver to Crittenden for treating with the Quapaw Indians. Conway did not deny taking the money but contended that he had done so with Crittenden's express permission, a contention that Crittenden denied. Charges and countercharges ensued until Crittenden, angered by what he perceived as an attack on his integrity, deserted Conway and threw his support behind Oden. For the first time since arriving in the territory in 1819, Woodruff abandoned his neutral stance and used the *Gazette* to support

Conway. When voters in the state's thirteen counties went to the polls on August 6, 1827, Conway won an overwhelming victory, polling 2,427 votes to Oden's 856.

Conway's victory did not end the personal invective that had characterized the campaign. Eleven days after the election, Conway published a letter in the *Gazette* stating that he was convinced that Crittenden did "willfully and intentionally state what he knew to be false for the purpose of injuring my election" and was "destitute of principle." Crittenden's response was to challenge Conway to a duel.

Since dueling was against the law in the territory, the two men met on the east side of the Mississippi River on October 29, 1827, and fought with pistols. They fired almost simultaneously. Conway's volley shot the button off Crittenden's coat but did not injure him. Crittenden's shot hit Conway in the chest, the force of the ball blunted slightly by a toothbrush that Conway was carrying in his coat pocket. The wounded Conway was taken to the home of William Montgomery near the mouth of the White River. His surgeon announced that the wound was "severe, but not dangerous" and predicted that he would be able to resume activities in two or three weeks. That prognosis proved to be overly optimistic. Conway died of complications of his wound at Montgomery's home on November 9.

At a special election in December, Conway's cousin Ambrose Sevier, a former speaker of the Arkansas Territorial House of Representatives, was chosen to fill the position of territorial delegate. Sevier, James and Elias Conway (brothers of Henry Conway), and territorial judge Benjamin Johnson formed the nucleus of a political "Dynasty," also known as "the Family," which would dominate Arkansas politics until the Civil War. Sevier had solidified the familial nature of the alliance by marrying Benjamin Johnson's daughter Juliette in September 1827.

Though he had survived unscathed, the duel tarnished Crittenden's reputation. When Governor Izard died in November 1828, Crittenden asked Secretary of State Henry Clay to appoint him to the position. But territorial delegate Sevier told Clay that he believed that the new governor should be someone from outside the state who would have no ties to either political faction in Arkansas. He left no doubt as to his feelings regarding the territorial secretary. "I have an unconquerable hatred for Mr. Crittenden," he wrote, "and the same aversion exists with two thirds of our citizens . . . His hands are stained with our lamented Conway's blood."

"The Family":
"The Family" was a powerful alliance that dominated the Arkansas Democratic Party and state politics in the years between statehood and the Civil War. Many of its members were related by blood or by marriage. Principal members included Ambrose Sevier, James and Elias Conway, Benjamin Johnson, Robert Ward Johnson, and Chester Ashley. Also known as "the Dynasty."

Painting of Robert
Crittenden by L. E.
Yandell, ASA Photo
G4543.15, Arkansas
State Archives.

The outgoing president, John Quincy Adams, who had been defeated in his bid for reelection, submitted a nomination for the position, but the Senate refused to confirm the nomination, opting to leave that decision to incoming president Andrew Jackson. Jackson's election was the death knell for Crittenden's ambitions, as his bitter enemies, "the Family," were staunch Jacksonian Democrats. Shortly after taking office in March 1829, Jackson appointed John Pope to be the third territorial governor.

A native of Virginia, Pope had moved to Kentucky with his family, where he attended school and studied law. He served in the Kentucky legislature and as a United States senator before his opposition to the War of 1812 cost him his political career. He left the Senate after his term expired and practiced law until his support for Jackson in 1828 improved his political prospects..

A few weeks after Pope's appointment, Jackson compounded Crittenden's problems by removing him as territorial secretary and appointing William Fulton in his place. Fulton was born in Maryland in 1795, served in the War of 1812, and had been Jackson's private secretary in the Seminole Wars. He moved to Tennessee and later Alabama, where he practiced law.

In the same month that Jackson appointed Pope to be territorial governor, Ambrose Sevier announced for reelection as territorial delegate. In his brief tenure, Sevier had done much to enhance his standing in the territory. He had fought successfully to add an additional superior court judge for the territory, had persuaded the federal government to provide compensation for members of the territorial legislature, and had secured passage of an act providing for popular elections of most civil and military officers. Given those accomplishments and the backing of "the Family," the election was surprisingly close. Sevier won by only 308 votes out of 3,820 cast.

Though deprived of any position in the territorial government, Crittenden did not go away quietly. In 1830 he financially backed the creation of the *Arkansas Advocate* newspaper to combat Woodruff's *Gazette*, which had, since 1827, strongly supported "the Family." The *Advocate* was owned and published by Crittenden's brother-in-law, Charles Bertrand, and later by the accomplished writer and Arkansas politician Albert Pike. It was the mouthpiece of the Crittenden faction in the state. That faction gained control of the legislature in 1831, and awarded the state's printing contract to the *Advocate*.

Crittenden was soon involved in another controversy. For most of the territorial period the state legislature had met in a run-down two-room log cabin that one observer described as a "wretched, decayed, unfinished old frame . . . devoid of a solitary comfort, not even a fire-place." When the federal government allocated ten sections of land to finance the construction of a building to house the territorial legislature, Crittenden offered to exchange his recently constructed mansion in Little Rock for the ten sections. His faction in the legislature secured the votes to approve the transaction, but Governor Pope believed that the building was worth far less than the ten sections and vetoed the bill.

Ten Sections controversy: Originated when Robert Crittenden offered to exchange a building he owned for ten sections of land Congress had awarded the territory in order to build a statehouse.

The issue of what to do with the ten sections remained unresolved until April 1832 when delegate Sevier submitted a proposal to Congress signed by 110 Arkansans asking that the governor be authorized to select the land. Congress complied, and Pope eventually sold the land for an amount significantly higher than the value of the building and property Crittenden had offered.

Undeterred, Crittenden made one final bid to regain some measure of the power and influence he had once enjoyed. He challenged Sevier for territorial delegate in 1833. The election results showed the growing power of the "Family" and the depths to which Crittenden's fortunes had fallen. Sevier won by a vote of 4,476 to 2,520, running strongly in all sections of the territory and carrying eighteen of the territory's twenty-three counties. A dejected Crittenden threw himself full-time into his law practice. Historian Farrar Newberry has noted, "Very soon he was representing clients over the entire Territory, associating with the most distinguished members of the bar, and was engaged by litigants in other states."

In December 1834, Crittenden was trying a case before the western division of the Mississippi Supreme Court, sitting at Vicksburg. He had just completed a seven-hour argument when the court asked him to explain some points. As he rose to speak, he collapsed and was taken to his hotel room where he remained for several days. When word reached him that he had won his case, he returned to the courtroom but collapsed again and died a few days later. The local newspaper listed the cause of death as pleurisy. He was only thirty-seven years old. In the years that followed, his followers would make up the Whig Party in Arkansas, and Albert Pike would become its leader.

Crittenden's death ended the career of Arkansas's first political superstar, but it did not put an end to the conflict that had characterized the relationship between the territorial governor and the territorial secretary since the earliest days of the territory's existence. A disagreement between Governor Pope and Secretary Fulton arose over the always controversial ten-sections bill and intensified when Fulton challenged the governor's authority to supervise the building of the state capitol. The specifics of the issue notwithstanding, Fulton had the ear of President Jackson, and Pope did not. In 1835, Jackson declined to reappoint Pope, nominating Fulton in his stead.

Accommodation, Resistance, and Removal

Neither the influx of white settlers nor the creation of a territorial government worked to the advantage of the Indians of the region. At the same time that the white population was increasing, the American government was instituting a removal policy that brought thousands of Indians to parts of Arkansas. It is estimated that about one thousand Cherokees were living along the St. Francis and the White rivers by 1805, but beginning in 1812, the Cherokees moved to the north side of the Arkansas River, locating themselves between the present-day cities of Morrilton and Fort Smith. A treaty negotiated in 1817 called for some Cherokees east of the Mississippi River to exchange their lands there for lands near those already settled along the Arkansas River. This placed them in direct contact with the Osages, who had expanded their hunting territory in western Arkansas during the last years of the eighteenth century, driving the Caddos in southwest Arkansas into present-day Texas and posing a threat to hunters and travelers who ventured into the upper reaches of the Red and the Arkansas rivers.

The Cherokee presence was the catalyst for no fewer than five wars that broke out between the Cherokees and the Osages. The first of these occurred in 1817 and was largely responsible for the creation of Fort Smith. The fort was located at Belle Point, a bluff on the Arkansas River just north of its juncture with the Poteau River and was intended to ameliorate hostilities between the two tribes. A small settlement soon grew up around the fort. The army abandoned the fort in 1824 and moved the garrison eighty miles to the west where they established Fort Gibson. But the settlement survived the move, and in the 1830s the army reestablished a presence there.

The superintendent of Indian affairs in the territory, William Clark, picked up on efforts initiated by William Lovely in 1816 and, in negotiations with the Osages conducted in St. Louis in 1818, purchased a tract of land north of the Arkansas River. That triangular tract, which came to be known as Lovely's Purchase, was intended to serve as a buffer zone between the Osages and the Cherokees. The effort to establish peace between the two groups failed, however, and hostilities between the two tribes continued. In 1825 a final treaty with the Osages called for the removal of the tribe to the Three Forks area of what is today northeastern Oklahoma.

Lovely's Purchase: Negotiated in 1818, this purchase of a triangular tract of land north of the Arkansas River was intended to provide a buffer between the Osage and the Cherokee, then engaged in an intense struggle.

The Osages, other long-standing enemies, the Choctaws, would soon meet a similar fate. The Choctaws had begun to move into Arkansas in the late eighteenth century and had established at least one village on the Arkansas River by 1819. On more than one occasion they had warred against the Osages, and when in 1820 a treaty was signed providing for the removal of Choctaws from Mississippi and Alabama to a reservation in Arkansas contiguous to the Osages, war threatened once more.

But the Osages were not the least of the problems confronting the Choctaws. Three thousand white settlers, who lived in the area ceded to the Choctaws, threatened to make war against them and circulated petitions in protest. The Arkansas General Assembly sided with the settlers, in part because many legislators regarded plans to resettle eastern Indians in Arkansas as a direct threat to their own interests. The general assembly petitioned Congress to reconsider the decision to relocate the Choctaws to Arkansas, and by 1825 a new settlement was reached that provided for the removal of all Choctaws to the southeast part of present-day Oklahoma.

The Cherokees attempted to avoid the fate that had befallen the Osages and Choctaws by assimilating into white culture. By almost any objective standard, they had succeeded. Thomas Nuttall, a botanist who traveled the Arkansas territory in 1819, remarked favorably upon their "civilized" ways. In

Arkansas, these so-called "Western Cherokees" built homes and established prosperous farms along the St. Francis River (and later along the Arkansas River). Some owned slaves.

Thanks to the efforts of a remarkable half-Cherokee, half-Anglo-European man named Sequoyah (George Guess), they had even developed their own written language and soon their own newspaper. Many also adopted the Christian religion. In 1818 these Arkansas Cherokees invited a Protestant mission board to send missionaries to attend them. Cephas Washburn and Alfred Finney subsequently established Dwight Mission in 1820 near present-day Russellville, where they founded the first school in Arkansas.

In the end it availed the Cherokees nothing. Pressure by the federal government and white settlers in Arkansas led to the Treaty of Washington (May 1828) in which the Cherokees ceded their lands in Arkansas and accepted removal to present-day Oklahoma. Most tragically of all, perhaps, given their historical ties to the earliest Europeans who came to Arkansas, were the Quapaws. The process of cultural blending, which had been encouraged by the economic ties to the French and Spanish, had serious consequences for the Quapaws. The growing economic dependence upon European goods—steel axes, brass kettles, and so on—and their reliance on the annuity system had bound them to the French and then the Spanish. But nothing that occurred in the eighteenth century prepared the Quapaws for the coming of the Americans after the Louisiana Purchase. The assault on Quapaw habitation of Arkansas began because of their occupation of valuable lands along the Mississippi and the Arkansas rivers, land that was clearly suited for plantation agriculture. Initially the American government protected the rights of the Quapaws to their lands but soon found that it could not effectively prohibit white settlement on Indian lands. By 1818 certain white settlers, territorial politicians, and newspapermen in Arkansas dedicated themselves to appropriating Quapaw land. It is perhaps no coincidence that this occurred just when John C. Calhoun, an avid expansionist and no friend to the Indians, became secretary of war in the first year of James Monroe's presidency (1817). Calhoun believed that America's defense depended on the existence of white settlements on the perimeter, and thus he had no qualms about removing any Indians who inhibited the settlement of whites in the territory. He instructed the governor of the territory to secure a land cession from the Quapaws. The Quapaws were eager for an alliance with the Americans and considered the treaty they signed on August 24, 1818, as an opportunity to secure it. The generous annuities promised at the meeting seemed to both seal the alliance and end years of uncertainty with regard to the receipt of annuities.

The terms demanded by the Americans, moreover, appeared entirely reasonable. The Americans recognized Quapaw ownership of two million acres and required only that they forfeit ownership of approximately thirty million acres of land in south and southeastern Arkansas that the Quapaws used only for hunting. Since the Americans granted them perpetual hunting rights in those lands, the Quapaws believed they were striking a good bargain and securing valued allies in the Americans.

However, territorial secretary Robert Crittenden, who frequently acted as superintendent of Indian affairs in the absence of territorial governor James Miller, was determined to rid the territory of the Quapaws. He was not alone in this position. Prominent white men and many ordinary white settlers simply wanted Indian lands, and both groups began to urge the relocation of the Quapaws so that their valuable acreage in southeastern Arkansas could be opened for white settlement.

The departure of Governor Miller in 1824 and the arrival of the new territorial governor, George Izard, did not work to the advantage of the Quapaws. By the time Izard arrived, Crittenden and others had engaged in a public campaign to discredit the Quapaws, referring to them as indolent and worthless savages, and had convinced the secretary of war, John C. Calhoun, that the Quapaws actually desired removal to the Caddo reservation along the Red River in Louisiana. Although this was patently false, a treaty was forced on the Quapaws on November 15, 1824, which required not only their removal but their amalgamation with the Caddos. In return, they were promised a small allotment and were allowed to remain in Arkansas through the winter of 1824–1825. Chief Heckaton appealed to the new territorial governor in June 1825 to postpone the removal further, but Izard merely suggested that the chief send representatives to Louisiana to examine the site, and he agreed to allow Antoine Barraque, a Frenchman who traded with the Quapaws and who had their confidence, to accompany the delegation.

What Barraque and the delegation of Quapaws found in Louisiana was most unpromising. The Caddos were unenthusiastic if not hostile to the newcomers. Nevertheless, with Barraque in charge, the Quapaws began their march to the Red River in early January 1826. They settled on land adjacent to the river and planted their crops, only to have them flooded and ruined twice in the spring. That summer, sixty of them died as destitution set in, and some, under the leadership of Saracen, a Quapaw with French blood, returned to Arkansas. Others drifted back as well and took up residence in remote, swampy areas that they believed white settlers were least likely to desire. The federal government allowed them to remain, allocated one-fourth of the tribe's annuity to those in Arkansas, and urged them to amalgamate with the Cherokees.

The next few years saw further deterioration of the Quapaws' position in Louisiana and a worsening of their treatment in Arkansas, where white settlers began to roughly remove them from the shacks they occupied. But the situation in Louisiana was worse than that in Arkansas, and by November 1830 all of the Quapaws had returned to Arkansas. Although this heralded the reunification of the tribe, something that Chief Heckaton, who had been practically the last Quapaw to leave Louisiana, was committed to, their troubles were far from over. The lion's share of their annuities was still going to Louisiana, and their ability to provide for themselves was seriously undermined by both their residence in the swamp and their tenuous hold on even those inadequate lands. They were now more than ever dependent upon annuities, but bureaucratic delays prevented their dispersal even after the federal government permitted them to be distributed in Arkansas. Even when they were finally resumed, they were not regularly allocated and were periodically suspended.

The appointment of John Pope in March 1829 after Izard's death in late 1828 resulted in the arrival of a man more sympathetic to the plight facing the Quapaws. Although a Jackson appointee, he deviated from the callous Jacksonian attitude toward Indians. Meanwhile, even some citizens in Arkansas began to temper their strong language and call for more humane treatment of the Quapaws. In December 1830 Chief Heckaton accompanied Ambrose H. Sevier, Arkansas's territorial delegate, to Washington, DC, to seek an audience with President Jackson. Although it is unlikely that Heckaton was successful in his effort to see the president, he did begin correspondence with Jackson's secretary of war, John Eaton, concerning the assignment of tribal lands in the vicinity of Arkansas Post. More significantly, perhaps, was his plea to Eaton to allow the Quapaws to live as American citizens and to permit the apportionment of some of their annuity for the education of young Quapaws at the Choctaw Academy in Kentucky. In other words, Heckaton, who had for so long attempted to keep the tribe together and retain its cultural identity, was now himself suggesting assimilation.

Secretary Eaton apportioned almost half the tribal annuity for educational purposes, but he refused to sanction the purchase of land in Arkansas for the Quapaws. Thus they remained in a vulnerable situation. A decision to suspend all annuities, issued by a new commissioner of Indian affairs in January 1832, put the Quapaws in an impossible position. Their situation became so desperate that Governor Pope gave official sanction to Heckaton's earlier plea for the purchase of Arkansas land for the Quapaws by making the recommendation himself. His unusual recommendation prompted a reassessment of their situation and a hearing before the Stokes Commission, a commission appointed to reexamine the government's Indian removal policy with regard to eastern Indians.

Meanwhile, leading politicians and newspapers renewed their attack on the Quapaws, once again referring to them as worthless savages, but a new subagent, Richard Hannon, began to press for their relief. On May 13, 1833, the Quapaws reluctantly agreed to their final removal from Arkansas, this time to Indian Territory in present-day Oklahoma. Although they were to be assigned their own reservation, many Quapaws were no longer willing to trust the federal government and failed to accompany the trek that began in September 1834. Some returned to the Red River, some went to Texas, and some even joined the Choctaws, temporarily at least, in the southern part of the Indian Territory. Saracen and a few others remained in Arkansas. Government policy had finally achieved what Heckaton had so long sought to prevent: the partial dissolution of the tribe.

The removal of Indian tribes from Arkansas was part of the larger national tragedy that characterized the nation's relationship with native peoples. But Arkansas would also pay a heavy price for white Americans' greed for Indian land. In 1824, to accommodate the tribes removed to the west, the federal government separated the westernmost portion of Arkansas Territory (which included all of present-day Oklahoma except the three Panhandle counties in the west and a small strip of land in the east) from the remainder of the territory, moving the western boundary from approximately 100 degrees west longitude to a point forty-five miles west of Fort Smith. While the act drastically reduced the size of the territory, it still placed Arkansas's western boundary well within the borders of present-day Oklahoma, where members of the Cherokee and Choctaw tribes had begun to settle. The two Indian nations strenuously objected, and both proved to be skilled negotiators. By 1828, in separate treaties with the Choctaws and the Cherokees, the line was pushed some forty-five miles farther east to the approximate location of Arkansas's present-day western border. In return, both tribes gave up their claims to land east of the new border. As a result of these adjustments, Arkansas Territory lost approximately half of its total size to what would soon be called the Indian Territory, and, though no one could know it at the time, it lost uncounted millions of dollars from the oil that now lay under the surface of the future state of Oklahoma. In addition, the presence of the large numbers of Indians on its western border destroyed any hope that Arkansas would become a major jumping-off point for Americans heading west.

Free Men and Slaves

As the number of Indians in the territory declined through removal, the number of slaves increased. The resolution of the Arkansas Territory bill virtually guaranteed the expansion of plantation slavery in the new territory. However, during the territorial period, the number of slaves was small, and the percentage increase in the slave population did not keep pace with the general growth in population. Although the slave population between 1810 and 1820 had increased from fewer than 200 to more than 1,600, this represented a percentage decline of the total population. The number of slaves rose to 4,576, by 1830, but that still represented only 15 percent of the total population of 30,388. The decade of the 1830s, however, would see a dramatic increase not only in the number of slaves but in the percentage of slaves in the total population. By 1840, the state's population had more than tripled to 97,574, but the number of slaves had grown more than fourfold to 19,935.

Despite this dramatic increase in population and the greater reliance on slavery, certain impediments to growth existed. First, claims to possession of Spanish land grants, necessitating the creation of a land commission, left the title to tens of thousands of acres of Arkansas lands in question. Second, the issuance of New Madrid certificates, designed to resettle persons displaced by the great earthquake of 1811 and 1812, created numerous disputes in Arkansas over title to land claimed by those holding preemption certificates and those holding the New Madrid certificates. Preemption certificates were secured by those who had squatted on land and subsequently made a claim of ownership.

As the plantation system grew in the 1830s, black slavery became a major demographic feature in southeastern Arkansas. Northeastern Arkansas, heavily damaged by the New Madrid earthquakes, remained too swampy for easy access and for agricultural development. While there were slaveholders in northwestern Arkansas, they were generally fewer in number and held far fewer slaves, though Washington County remained one of the top ten counties in slave population as late as 1840. Some northwestern Arkansas slave owners held a sufficient number of slaves to work them in gangs and produce a cash crop, but the soil was not fertile enough to devote much acreage to cotton, so they grew wheat and corn.

Transportation was inadequate but sufficient enough to move their crops to markets—south to Fort Smith and north to Missouri. Rivers were important but, aside from the White River, which flowed north into Missouri before reentering northeastern Arkansas, they were inadequate to the task of transportation, so roads, which were little more than improved Indian trails, were relied upon. The Carrollton Road was the most "improved" road running out of northwest Arkansas in the territorial era, and it ran east, linking up with the Southwest Trail in northeast Arkansas.

The vast majority of the white population in northwest Arkansas did not own slaves—or owned only one or two—and occupied themselves in small farming enterprises, mainly of the subsistence variety. Most settlers came from mountainous areas in Kentucky, Tennessee, North Carolina, and Virginia (later

West Virginia), and they replicated the economic system with which they were familiar. They grew some corn, but they were principally occupied in raising livestock, and they depended upon the open range. Just as they imported an economic system they knew and understood, they brought with them certain egalitarian ideas and had a special attachment to social, economic, and political independence. While they were not opposed to the institution of slavery, they were suspicious of the wealthy planters of southeastern Arkansas.

Many of the planters of southeastern Arkansas were the sons and nephews of planters in the lowlands of Kentucky, North Carolina, and Virginia. They were part of the vanguard of southerners who led the expansion of the plantation system westward. They were few in number during the territorial period, but they grew wealthy as cotton production increased. They relied heavily on rivers—the Arkansas and especially the Mississippi—to get their crops to market in Memphis and St. Louis to the north and, particularly, to New Orleans to the south. Consequently, most settlement was along the rivers, but as roads were improved, settlement away from the rivers increased. Gradually other roads were improved, linking the southeastern Arkansas planters to Little Rock and to points in Louisiana. The importance of these connections would be brought into sharp relief when delegates gathered to create a state constitution in early 1836. Indeed, the differences between the northwest and southeast would become a major feature of the debate over the creation of that document.

The Statehood Movement

The statehood question first arose in the early 1830s, and while the northwest and southeast did not appear to be divided over the issue, Arkansas's two political factions were not initially in agreement over the question. Charles Bolton's *Arkansas: Remote and Restless, 1800–1860*, provides a cogent summary of the agitation for statehood and an analysis of the argument outlined by the editor of the *Arkansas Advocate*, which represented the Crittenden faction. In 1830 editor Charles Bertrand argued that "the Census of 1830 would show that the territory had grown substantially and was ready to end what he called its 'territorial vassalage.'" A subsequent letter to the editor from "Aristides" suggested that statehood "would lead to a dramatic increase in population," and thus would result in greater economic development. That writer also expressed concern about the federal government's alleged plans to relocate the Chickasaw Indians to Arkansas and seemed to believe that achieving statehood would give Arkansas greater leverage in deciding that question.

The *Arkansas Gazette*, which continued to represent "the Family" position, published a letter from "Henry" that focused attention on the financial burden that would accompany statehood. The federal government paid for much of the cost of territorial administration, and in the absence of those funds, taxes would have to be imposed on the citizens of Arkansas. "Henry" also suggested "that the Chickasaws could not legally be located in an existing territory and that it was foolish to talk about statehood until Arkansas had the necessary population."

Ambrose Sevier, territorial delegate and Family member, adopted the *Gazette*'s position when he ran for reelection in 1831, but certain developments were taking shape that would cause him, the Family, and the *Gazette*, to reconsider. Sevier was motivated by at least three factors. First, as Jack B. Scroggs has noted in his thorough analysis of the statehood question published in the *Arkansas Historical Quarterly*, Family considerations were a significant factor. Richard M. Johnson of Kentucky, who was brother to Benjamin Johnson, was preparing for a possible run for the vice presidency in 1836, and his Arkansas relatives hoped to be in a position to assist him. Benjamin Johnson was a territorial superior court judge but, more important, he was father-in-law to Ambrose Sevier and one of the most prominent members of the Family.

A second factor motivating Sevier and the Family was the desire to support Andrew Jackson in his battle with the ever-strengthening Whig Party. The territories held some of Jackson's strongest supporters, and many territorial officials were Jackson appointees. A third factor, however, proved to be the one that led most directly to action on the statehood question. By 1834 it became clear that the free territory of Michigan was intending to apply for statehood, and Sevier and others with slaveholding interests became alarmed about the possibility of disturbing the balance of power between slaveholding and non-slaveholding states in the Senate. The principle of pairing a slave territory and a free territory motivated Sevier to take action abruptly during the 1834 session of Congress. He had no opportunity to prepare his constituents for his change in position on the issue of statehood, for the Michigan petition was circulating, and the delegate from Florida, the only other southern territory that might apply for statehood, was absent from Congress. Sevier saw his opportunity and did not hesitate to grasp it. On December 17, 1834, he presented a resolution to Congress asking that the Committee on Territories consider the question of statehood for Arkansas Territory.

Sevier's constituents back in Arkansas were caught by surprise, but the *Arkansas Gazette* supported his new position. Aside from criticizing the fact that Sevier acted without consulting his constituents, the *Advocate* also supported his actions. Only the *Arkansas Times,* a third Little Rock newspaper, objected. Their objections echoed in one respect those first advanced by the *Gazette* in 1831, expressing concern about the financial burden of statehood.

But the *Times* also suggested that the drive for statehood was one led by planters and for planters and that it would create a greater financial burden for non-slaveholders, a burden not worth bearing.

Despite the qualms expressed in the *Times*, momentum for statehood continued to grow in Arkansas, but Whigs in Congress were actively involved in attempting to block the effort. They recognized that both territories would support their archenemy, Andrew Jackson, and they hoped to stall the drive for statehood, at least until after the election of 1836. Ultimately, Arkansas and Michigan were each required to hold a special census to ascertain whether they had the required population, but neither was authorized to draft state constitutions. When Michigan's lawmakers began to draft a constitution without authorization, planning to present the finished document to Congress as a *fait accompli*, Arkansas determined to do the same. Governor Fulton was initially opposed to this maneuver and did not lend his support to the effort until he was certain it had President Jackson's backing.

The drive for statehood was given an additional boost when the special census conducted in Arkansas revealed that the territory had a total of 52,240 individuals, easily surpassing the 40,000 required for admission as a state. With the census behind them, the territorial legislature began to debate the calling of a constitutional convention. Such a convention required the election of delegates, and difficulties arose almost immediately. Those representing the interests of southeastern planters hoped to establish a formula whereby they would be able to send more delegates to the convention than their free white population might otherwise allow. As Bolton points out, "the lowland south and east in this division had only three-fourths as many white people as did the highland north and west, but it had twice as many slaves." The southeastern delegates hoped to adopt the three-fifths rule, a method of counting each slave as three-fifths of a person for purposes of determining representation. It was familiar to most because it was the formula used in the United States Constitution.

David Walker, a Whig from Fayetteville, led the northwest Arkansas faction in the battle to adhere to a count of the free white population only. Unsuccessful in securing the three-fifths formula, the planters successfully maneuvered for apportionment by districts rather than by population, with each geographic district electing an equal number of delegates: twenty-six for the northwest and twenty-six for the southeast.

The battle over apportionment resumed when the elected delegates met in Little Rock in January 1836. Under an admonition to act quickly in order to present the proposed state constitution to Congress in time for it to be considered along with Michigan's constitution and petition, the delegates nevertheless engaged in heated debate over representation. In the end, they agreed to the district representation scheme but identified three rather than two districts: the southeast, the northwest, and a middle district made up of Pulaski, Saline, and White counties. Pulaski, within which Little Rock was located, was by far the largest of the three counties, and everyone understood that the capital city's ties to the southeast would have significant political ramifications. Under this scheme, eight delegates each were apportioned to the southeast and northwest and one delegate was apportioned for the middle district. Despite the concerted opposition of David Walker and twenty-one other delegates from the northwest, it passed by six votes.

The thorny issue of representation notwithstanding, the new constitution was, by the standards of the day, a democratic document. Voting was limited to free white adult males, but there were no property requirements either for voting or for holding office and poll taxes were prohibited except as a device to raise funds for counties. The governor, the state legislators, and almost all local officials were to be popularly elected. The governor would have a four-year term but was limited to serving only eight years in any twelve. State representatives had terms of two years, state senators four, and there was no limit on the number of terms either could serve. The legislature was clearly the dominant branch of state government. It not only chose the state's US senators but also all supreme court and circuit judges, the secretary of state, the state auditor, the state treasurer, and the circuit attorneys. It could also override the governor's veto by a simple majority vote.

The Arkansas convention completed its deliberations and finalized the constitution on January 30, 1836. Convention delegate Charles F. M. Noland was given the honor of conveying the document to Washington, but he took a circuitous route as a precaution against winter storms, and by the time he arrived in the capital on March 8, the US mail had already delivered a copy of a special edition of the *Arkansas Gazette* containing a complete draft of the Arkansas constitution.

The ultimate success of the effort to secure statehood for Arkansas was not assured, however, and the forces for and against admission prepared to engage each other in debate in Congress. The Whigs sought to delay consideration of statehood for the two territories until after the 1836 elections. Meanwhile, some northern congressmen opposed statehood for Arkansas on the basis of its status as a slave state. As Jack Scroggs notes, "A continuous stormy session of twenty-five hours duration marked the final effort of the Whigs to delay the bills, with administration forces facing the recurrent problem of maintaining a quorum. Acrimonious debate characterized the struggle, with several members being called to order for caustic comments." Ultimately, however, the Democrats prevailed and both bills passed on June 13, 1836. The president signed the bill creating the state of Arkansas on June 15, 1836.

In less than three decades, from the time of the Louisiana Purchase until Arkansas became the twenty-fifth state of the Union, the "remote and restless" territory passed through a monumental transformation. It moved from a small European outpost of little real importance and even less economic and political activity, to full membership in a new and potentially powerful nation. Native Americans struggled, vainly, to maintain a place on the territory's stage, for the interests of white settlers and citizens prevailed over Indian hopes and dreams and over bargains they made with US officials. By the 1820s, removal was in full swing, orchestrated by a group of self-interested politicians who made the territory their home, their place to realize the opportunity for economic and political gain. The debate over the expansion of slavery positioned Arkansas to play a small role in the great Missouri Compromise, the first time since the constitutional debates that the nation faced the implications of slavery.

The young men who occupied positions of political power in Arkansas were not all of one accord, however, and by the early 1830s had divided as Democrats and Whigs, and had gone beyond mere invective in settling their disputes. They largely united, however uneasily, in the drive for statehood, seizing the opportunity to assume a more purposeful and important role in the nation.

6 "The Rights and Rank to Which We Are Entitled"

Arkansas in the Early Statehood Period

AFTER A LENGTHY and often tedious struggle, Arkansas was admitted to the Union as the twenty-fifth state in June 1836. Six years previously the editor of the Little Rock-based *Arkansas Advocate* had proclaimed that statehood would give Arkansas "the rights and rank to which we are entitled," and most Arkansans probably agreed that the action validated Arkansas's position in the Union. But events of the early statehood period confirmed many of the worst fears of those who had thought the move premature. The new state's meager resources proved inadequate to fill the void created by the loss of federal revenues, and the first attempt to address those financial problems ended disastrously, saddling the state with chronic financial instability. Those who hoped that statehood would improve Arkansas's image as a violent and lawless frontier found instead that subsequent events confirmed rather than refuted that image. In the years between 1836 and 1850, statehood would prove to be a very mixed blessing.

Government in the Early Statehood Era

The first state elections in Arkansas were held in August 1836, and they demonstrated conclusively the dominance of the Democratic Party in the state and the power of the political alliance known as "the Family." Arkansas voters elected James S. Conway the state's first governor; the new state legislature chose Ambrose Sevier and former territorial governor William Fulton to be the state's first two US senators; and Benjamin Johnson was appointed to be the first federal district judge for Arkansas. The Family's influence extended to the national level where Johnson's brother, Senator Richard M. Johnson of Kentucky, was the Democratic candidate for vice president on a ticket with Martin Van Buren.

Archibald Yell was elected to be the new state's lone congressman. Yell had come to Arkansas in 1834 and had quickly become a leading proponent of statehood. Like the Conways and Sevier, Yell came from Tennessee, and he shared their devotion to Jacksonian politics. But though he enjoyed Family support in his race for Congress in 1836 and in his successful race for governor in 1840, Yell pursued an independent course. A personal friend of President Jackson with a strong base of personal support in northwest Arkansas, Yell was less dependent on the Family than many other Arkansas office seekers. In addition, he was a gifted politician who, contemporaries observed, could "out-talk, out-drink, out-shoot, and out-pray" any opponent.

In the years following the death of longtime territorial secretary and Family opponent Robert Crittenden, the political faction he had led would align itself with the national Whig Party. The Whigs' chief unifying principle was opposition to Andrew Jackson, but the party also supported an economic program that called for protective tariffs, federally funded internal improvements, and a second Bank of the United States. Led on the national level by Henry Clay of Kentucky, the party had great appeal to those business interests involved in the emerging market economy and drew to its ranks men of wealth and privilege, including many large planters.

Whig Party: The Whig Party was a national political party whose chief organizing principle was opposition to Andrew Jackson. They also favored an economic program that included protective tariffs, federally funded internal improvements, and a second Bank of the United States.

Under the leadership of Crittenden's handpicked successor, Albert Pike, the Whig Party in Arkansas provided the state with a number of capable men, and Pike himself was the intellectual and oratorical equal of anyone in the state. Little Rock would be a Whig stronghold in Arkansas throughout the state's early years, but the Whigs never exerted enough popular appeal in the state to wrest control of the reins of government from the Family. They remained a minority party in Arkansas until the slavery controversy destroyed the national party in the 1850s. Throughout the first quarter century of the state's existence, the Democrats controlled all the major state offices and a majority of the seats in the state legislature.

The first state legislature that assembled in September 1836 in the unfinished statehouse faced major problems. The financial concerns that had made many Arkansans reluctant to pursue statehood proved to be well founded. With low tax rates on real estate (the principal source of tax revenue), few assets to sell, and fewer government services for which to charge licenses and fees, the money the state took in was barely sufficient to maintain the most basic governmental operations.

The absence of banking institutions in Arkansas meant that those funds the state government did derive went to banks outside the state. It also meant that there were no lending institutions capable of stimulating economic development. To address this deficiency the state constitution specifically empowered the legislature to charter two banks, and the first state assembly wasted little time in doing so. It created the Bank of Arkansas (also known as the State Bank), a state agency whose directors were appointed by the legislature. Headquartered in Little Rock, the bank had branches in Fayetteville, Batesville, Arkansas Post, and Washington. The State Bank was to serve as the repository of all state funds, and it could issue bank notes (paper money) that could be used to pay debts owed to the state. Additionally, it was allowed to sell bonds backed by the state government and to use the proceeds for operating funds. The bank would then lend money to attract and promote business, using the interest from those loans to repay the state, which would in turn pay the bondholders.

While the State Bank was at least nominally a state agency and was designed to promote business activity throughout the state, the Real Estate Bank of Arkansas was a creation of, by, and for the state's planter interests. The bank's headquarters were in Little Rock, but three of its four branches were in the southern and eastern lowlands.

Like the State Bank, its operating capital came from the sale of state bonds, but unlike the State Bank, the Real Estate Bank also sold stock, which could be purchased with land or crops. Shareholders were permitted to borrow up to one-half the value of their shares. Also unlike the State Bank, the governor appointed only two of the nine directors of each branch bank with the stockholders choosing the other seven. The directors of each branch then chose two of their members (one of whom was required to be a gubernatorial appointee) to be members of a central board. The state thus pledged itself to back the financial transactions of an entity over which it had little actual control.

State Bank of Arkansas: The State Bank of Arkansas was chartered by the first state legislature. It was designed to serve as a repository for all state funds and to promote business activity throughout the state. Through corruption, mismanagement, and a national economic downturn, the bank was declared insolvent in 1843.

Real Estate Bank: The Real Estate Bank was chartered by the first state legislature. It was designed to promote the interests of the state's planters. The bank issued loans on inflated land valuations, and by 1841 it was insolvent.

Though fraught with the potential for abuse, with favorable economic conditions and careful management, the banks might have succeeded. Absent either, they were doomed to failure. Both banks opened in December 1838, and initially redeemed their notes in specie (gold and silver). But like many unregulated banks throughout the country, the banks issued paper money far in excess of their specie reserves. To compound the problem, both made questionable loans without adequate securities. The Real Estate Bank, in particular, made loans based on inflated land valuations. Rumors of unfair appraisals and complaints of favoritism in the dispensing of its stock dogged the bank almost from its inception.

The State Bank also suffered from corruption. The books of the Fayetteville branch bank were stolen, and when they were recovered, several pages of cash transactions had been ripped out. The bank's cashier soon fled to Texas. The banks also suffered from poor timing. They went into operation one year after the beginning of the Panic of 1837, a severe national economic downturn brought on by a host of factors including a depression in England, falling cotton prices, and the failure of the domestic wheat crop.

The situation was exacerbated by the short-sighted policies of the Jackson administration. Jackson's destruction of the Second Bank of the United States in the early 1830s removed the last vestige of federal regulation of state banks, resulting in the kind of financial irresponsibility demonstrated by the two Arkansas banks and dozens of others across the nation.

In 1836 Jackson attempted to halt the wild speculation by issuing the Specie Circular, which required land payments to be made in specie. The act destroyed public confidence in paper money and brought ruin to many financial institutions across the country. The effects were first felt in the East, but by 1839 the shock waves reached the Old Southwest where land specula- tion and easy money had run rampant. Land and crop prices plummeted. By 1839 both Arkansas banks were in trouble. The Real Estate Bank ceased oper- ations in July 1841. Acting under the bank's charter, the directors appointed themselves as receivers and refused to turn over the books to the legislature. Receiver Albert Pike built a magnificent Greek Revival mansion in Little Rock, but the receivers did nothing to repay the money owed the state. Two years later, the State Bank was declared insolvent.

The banking fiasco left the state with a debt of over three million dollars. It brought financial ruin to many Arkansans, resulted in hundreds of lawsuits, left the state's credit in shambles, and fostered a distrust of banking. The fact that both Democrats and Whigs were deeply involved prevented either of the major parties from using the issue for partisan purposes, but certain individuals, including Ambrose Sevier, were tarred by their involvement with the banks.

In 1844 the legislature overreacted and adopted the first amendment to the state constitution, which stated that "No bank or banking institution shall be hereafter incorporated, or established in the state." It was a classic example of throwing the baby out with the bath water. Arkansas had needed a sound banking system in 1836, and it still needed such a system in 1844. Now, economic progress, if it came, would have to do so without the aid of state government.

The banking debacle also led to the most infamous event in the history of the Arkansas legislature. In a special session in the fall of 1837 (the first session in the new state capitol), house speaker and Real Estate Bank pres-

Arkansas's first state capitol as it appeared circa 1842, looking from Markham Street toward the Arkansas River, by artist Ken Oberste (1991). *Courtesy of the Old State House Museum.*

ident John Wilson got into a verbal sparring match on the house floor with state representative Joseph J. Anthony, one of the bank's staunchest critics. When Anthony refused Wilson's order to take his seat, Wilson charged down from the speaker's chair and physically assaulted Anthony. In the struggle that followed both men drew knives, and Wilson fatally stabbed Anthony.

Wilson was subsequently tried and acquitted of murder but was expelled from the legislature. His constituents reelected him in 1840. Wilson eventually defaulted on his Real Estate Bank loan and disappeared into the wilds of Texas.

Wilson's actions highlighted another of the young state's persistent problems—its image. The Arkansas Territory had developed a reputation as a refuge for the fringe elements of society. The English traveler George Featherstonhaugh, who passed through the territory in 1834, referred to the "criminals, gamblers, speculators, and men of broken fortunes, with no law to restrain them, no obligation to conceal their vices, no motive to induce them to appear devout or to act with sobriety." An early Arkansas political figure (who lived to regret the remark) was more blunt, "[E]very man left his honesty and every woman her chastity on the other side of the Mississippi, on moving to Arkansas."

The violence that characterized early Arkansas was not limited to outlaws and the fringe elements common to every frontier. In the same year that territorial secretary Robert Crittenden mortally wounded territorial delegate Henry Conway, Ambrose Sevier fought a bloodless duel with future Whig congressman Thomas Newton. The Anthony-Wilson affair quickly squashed any hopes that statehood would bring an end to such violence.

"The Arkansas Traveler": "The Arkansas Traveler" was the name of a story and a song based on an incident in the 1840 campaign in which a sophisticated Arkansas planter had a humorous encounter with an unlettered but clever squatter. Later appropriators of the image and dialogue made the traveler an outsider, leaving the squatter and his family to represent Arkansas and making Arkansas the butt of the joke.

The new state's reputation was compounded by a lingering image of Arkansas as the home of the poor and the shiftless. One of the most enduring examples of that image is *The Arkansas Traveler*. Originally the *Traveler* was the story of the passing of the frontier, when squatters were beginning to fade from the scene. Based on an incident that occurred during an 1840 campaign trip through a remote region of the state, the image and accompanying dialogue provide a humorous glance at a squatter whose humble lifestyle and recalcitrant ways contrast nicely with Sandford Faulkner, a sophisticated Arkansas plantation owner and politician trying to find his way back to civilization. Faulkner told the story to many an appreciative audience. However, later appropriators of the image and dialogue made the character of the traveler an outsider, leaving the squatter and his family to represent Arkansas. With this change, Arkansas became the butt of the joke, a fact that left many in the state unhappy with the *Traveler* and the damage it caused the state's reputation.

Arkansas Society, 1836–1850

But if many Americans viewed Arkansas as a place of violence, lawlessness, and poverty, others saw it in a different light. Massachusetts native Albert Pike traveled widely as a young man and wrote accounts of his travels as well as poetry and some satirical pieces. But it was perhaps his descriptions of the richness and promise of Arkansas's land that most affected the region's image. Arriving in the territory in 1832, Pike settled in Pope County where he taught school. In 1835 he proclaimed himself "a citizen of Arkansas for life," and began to write glowing accounts of the region to skeptical and often condescending friends back East. In 1835 he wrote to the *New England Magazine*:

> The soil of the Arkansas bottoms is inferior to none in the world; and the facilities offered a man for making a living and a fortune there, are nowhere equaled. A poor man comes here, whose necessities have driven him from the States. He has not a cent in the world—nothing but his axe and his rifle. He goes into the Arkansas

A lithographic print of "The Arkansas Traveler" (1859), hand colored after an original painting by Edward Payson Washbourne. Leopold Grozilier, lithographer, J. H. Buford, printer. The original caption reads, "Designed by one of the natives and dedicated to Col. S. C. Faulkner." "The Arkansas Traveler" became nationally popular in the last half of the nineteenth century. It was reproduced by both J. H. Bufford and Currier and Ives. The dialogue provided many an entertainer with usable material, and the music is still played today. *Courtesy of the Historic Arkansas Museum, Little Rock.*

> bottom, cuts a few logs, and his neighbors help him raise a hut, with a wooden chimney, daubed with mud . . . In four or five years that man will raise twenty bales of cotton and a thousand bushels of corn, and be steadily enlarging his crop and increasing his income.

In the early statehood period, thousands of settlers came to Arkansas to share in the opportunities that Pike described. Many of these emigrants sought lands that were similar to the ones that they were leaving. Accordingly, those from the highlands of the upper South tended to prefer the mountainous regions of Arkansas, while those from the Deep South favored the lowlands. They often came in groups composed of extended families, following other family members who had come previously.

Both the state and the federal government encouraged the immigration of families by generous grants of land. Under the terms of the "Donation Law" of 1840, settlers could obtain tax-forfeited lands by agreeing to pay the future taxes. In 1850 the law was amended to permit a family to obtain a 160-acre plot for every member of the immediate family regardless of age or gender. In 1841 the federal government turned over 500,000 acres to the state, which then offered it to the public at $1.25 an acre, with the proceeds going to finance internal improvements. Two years later the state received the right to sell the sixteenth section of each township to fund schools, making over 900,000 additional acres available. In 1850 the national government began turning over to the state over seven and a half million acres of "swamp and overflow" land, and by 1859 the state had disposed of over three and half million of these acres. Despite these opportunities to buy land, many immigrants to Arkansas in the antebellum period simply "squatted" on unsurveyed tracts of federal land, a policy that the federal government encouraged through "preemption laws," which gave the squatters the right to purchase 160 acres where they had settled for the minimum price.

Antebellum: Occurring or existing before a war, especially the American Civil War.

By 1840 the state's population stood at 97,574, a three-fold increase over 1830 and almost twice the figure at the time of statehood only four years earlier. But despite these gains, Arkansas in 1840 remained very much a frontier state with an average of fewer than two people per square mile. Its population was six times smaller than Alabama, and almost four times smaller than the neighboring states of Mississippi and Louisiana.

In *Arkansas, 1800–1860: Remote and Restless*, Charles Bolton provides a good portrait of Arkansas settlers of this period. Almost all Arkansans were farmers, approximately one-third of whom owned their own land while the rest "squatted" on government land that they hoped one day to purchase. Livestock were ubiquitous. There were twice as many cattle and four times as many hogs in the state as there were people, and a typical Arkansan ate about four times as much pork as beef. Corn was grown statewide and was the basis of the subsistence agriculture that characterized much of the state.

The log cabin remained the dominant style of housing. The simplest was the so-called single-pen variety, a one-room structure, sixteen- to eighteen-foot square, made from oak logs. The more elaborate "dogtrot house" or "double pen" consisted of two cabins built side by side under a common roof with an open area in between. Since the average Arkansas family contained six people, privacy was at a minimum, and eating, sleeping, and cooking all occurred in one or two rooms. Travelers to the region noted little difference between the houses of the poor and those of the more well-to-do.

Early Arkansas had few amenities of civilization and was a particularly hard place for women. Consequently in 1840 men outnumbered women in Arkansas by three to two, and women of child-bearing age made up only about 17 percent of the white population, the lowest in the nation. Those women who did come to Arkansas proved to be extremely prolific, however. The birth rate for Arkansas women was the highest in the nation, 43 percent higher than the national average. Women married early and began bearing children almost immediately. Large families were seen as a distinct economic advantage on the frontier where land was plentiful but labor was in short supply. The hardships involved in bearing and raising such large numbers of children, however, were staggering.

In addition to her responsibilities as a mother, an Arkansas woman had to slaughter animals for food, cook the meals, tend to the house, care for the sick, assist her husband in the fields at planting and harvest time, and, when requested, offer advice on economic matters. Yet despite the contributions women made to the care and maintenance of the family, Arkansas society remained highly patriarchal. Women had no political rights, and educational and occupational opportunities outside the home were almost nonexistent.

Adding to these hardships was the lack of social opportunities. In a sparsely populated state where homesteads were often far from the nearest neighbor, Arkansas women frequently suffered from intense loneliness. Many found in evangelical Christianity not only religious nurturing but also the chance for interaction with and mutual support from other women.

Arkansas would later come to be considered a part of the so-called Bible Belt, but in the early antebellum period it was largely an irreligious place, and travelers to the region commented on the appalling conditions they found there. One early missionary who passed through the Arkansas delta noted, "It is painful to witness the deplorable state of morals in this place. The Sabbath is awfully profaned; idleness, drinking, swearing, and gambling almost universally prevail."

By the second decade of the nineteenth century, a hardy group of Protestant preachers, fired by the religious revivalism known as the Second Great Awakening, attempted to transform the situation. A Baptist preacher, George Gill, delivered a sermon at the Mount Olive community along the White River in northeast Arkansas on Christmas Day in 1814, and four years later the first Baptist church in what would become the Arkansas Territory was founded on the Fourche-a-Thomas River in northeast Arkansas. By 1840 there were thirty-seven Baptist churches in the state.

The Baptist contribution was significant, but as Charles Bolton has noted, "It was the Methodists who brought southern evangelicalism into Arkansas." As early as 1814 Methodist preacher William Stevenson had conducted religious services for isolated settlers along the Southwest Trail. In the tradition of early American Methodism, Stevenson sought to create a "circuit," a regularly traveled route served by an itinerant preacher on horseback. The primitive conditions of travel in frontier Arkansas made such efforts a daunting task, but those hardships notwithstanding, Methodist circuit riders became a regular feature of life on the Arkansas frontier. "If you hear something lumberin' through the canebrake," went one common saying, "it's either a bear or a Methodist preacher, and either one's bound to be hungry!"

These early ministers utilized any available structure to conduct services, and they also organized "camp meetings," outdoor religious gatherings that lasted for several days. Camp meetings drew people of all denominations or no denomination at all from the surrounding countryside to a central location for preaching and singing and served a social as well as a religious function.

Presbyterians (regular and Cumberland), Disciples of Christ, Episcopalians, and other denominations entered the state's religious scene in the years before the Civil War, but Methodist and Baptist churches far outnumbered the combined total of all other Christian denominations. After a slow start, the number of churches increased dramatically in the 1840s and 1850s. By 1850 there were 168 Methodist and 114 Baptist churches in the state, and by 1860 those numbers increased to 505 and 281, respectively. While many Arkansans attended religious services, church membership in the antebellum period remained relatively small. Probably fewer than one in five Arkansans was formally affiliated with a church in 1860.

Public education also struggled to establish a foothold in the state. From its inception, the state lagged behind much of the rest of the nation in the education of its citizens. While there was no public taxation to support the creation and operation of schools, the federal government subsidized education in the state by setting aside the sixteenth section of every township for the support of local schools and two townships for the creation and support of a university. But the revenue generated from leasing these lands proved insufficient to support a public school system, and the problem was compounded by a haphazard system of organization and administration.

The effort to establish a viable school system was further hampered by what one state official described as "the indifference that pervades the public mind on the subject of education." As a result, no viable system of public education was established, and no public university was founded in the state before the Civil War. Many wealthy Arkansans employed private tutors for their children and opposed the use of tax money for public education. Many poorer Arkansans had neither the time, the money, nor the inclination to pay for their children's education, through taxes or otherwise. Thus, for the majority of the state's citizens, the education system remained a hodge-podge of public schools and private academies manned by underpaid and often incompetent teachers. About half of Arkansas's school-age children did not attend any school at all. Most of the rest attended only sporadically.

In spite of these handicaps, several Arkansas communities developed reputations as centers of learning. Private academies flourished in northwest Arkansas at Fayetteville and nearby Cane Hill, in central Arkansas at Little Rock, in southwest Arkansas at Springhill and Washington, and in south-central Arkansas at Tulip and Princeton. These academies or "subscription schools," taught by an itinerant schoolmaster who charged a set price per pupil, were almost always segregated by gender and usually operated for two to three months a year. As these communities grew, the length of the term increased, and teachers became more permanent.

Higher education was rare indeed, but northwest Arkansas had two institutions of higher learning in operation by 1852—Cane Hill College (supported by the Cumberland Presbyterian Church) and Arkansas College at Fayetteville. St. John's Masonic College opened its doors in Little Rock in 1859. Despite the efforts of these early institutions, however, formal education remained beyond the reach of most Arkansans. Perhaps as many as one in four adult Arkansans could neither read nor write and thus remained largely ignorant of events outside their own locality. The lack of a system of public education deepened Arkansas's isolation from the rest of the nation.

That isolation was further compounded by the abysmal state of transportation. In the 1820s Congress provided funds for the construction of a "Military Road" from Memphis to the Indian Territory via Little Rock and Fort Smith. The road, intended to facilitate defense of the frontier and constructed, in part, by US Army engineers, reached Little Rock in 1827 and Fort Smith the following year. A second military road stretched from southern Missouri through Little Rock to Fulton on the Red River. Federal specifications called for the roads to be "opened 16 feet wide and entirely cleared; all brush and saplings 6 inches in diameter to be cut even with the ground; all trees between 6 and 12 inches in diameter, within 4 inches of the ground; and all trees over 12 inches within 8 inches of the ground; the stumps to be well trimmed."

In the late territorial period the federal government contributed over a quarter of a million dollars to improve the condition of the road from Memphis to Little Rock, but parts of the route that passed through the lowlands of eastern Arkansas were often underwater, and other portions were covered with rocks and fallen trees. Federal funds to complete the project dried up after Arkansas achieved statehood in 1836, and little progress was made in road building throughout the remainder of the antebellum era.

Regular stagecoach service began on a crude road between Little Rock and Hot Springs in the late territorial period, and by the early statehood era coaches made a tri-weekly run between Little Rock and Washington, Arkansas. But even on "good" roads, overland travel was slow and uncomfortable at best, dangerous at worst. On other roads, actually little more than trails, it was often impossible. The trip from Little Rock to Hot Springs (a distance of fifty-four miles) took nineteen and a half hours, while the journey from Little Rock to Washington (slightly over a hundred miles) took fifty hours. Prior to 1850 there was not one mile of railroad track in the state, and no bridges crossed any of the state's major rivers. River travel remained the safest and most efficient form of transportation throughout the antebellum period.

The Mexican War, the Gold Rush, and Westward Migration

In November 1835 former Tennessee congressman David Crockett, whose exploits were already legendary, made a brief stop in Little Rock on his way to the Mexican province of Texas, where rumors of a revolt against the Mexican government were rampant. When Crockett and his party departed down the Southwest Trail for Texas, a few impressionable young Arkansans may have joined him.

Many Arkansans shared Crockett's fascination with Texas. Events there were followed closely by the Arkansas press, and several of the major figures of the Texas Revolution of 1836 had ties to Arkansas. Stephen F. Austin had speculated in Arkansas land and served for a time as a territorial judge. James Bowie and his brothers had claims to thousands of acres of land in Arkansas, almost all of them fraudulent. Sam Houston spent time at both Little Rock and Washington and was instrumental in helping the Cherokees settle in the territory. At least two Arkansans died with Crockett and Bowie at the Alamo in March 1836.

Arkansans were ambivalent about their large neighbor to the southwest. As early as the 1820s Arkansans had worried that the lure of cheap land in Texas robbed Arkansas of immigrants and lowered land values in the territory, and that fear continued after Texas won its independence from Mexico in 1836. Yet Ambrose Sevier and other prominent Arkansas political figures supported the notion of westward expansion and "Manifest Destiny" and felt that Texas annexation would not only increase the size of the country but would add to the power of the slave South. That reasoning was not lost on Northern "free soilers," and Texas soon became caught up in the growing controversy over slavery. Fears of exacerbating that dispute precluded any attempt by the United States to annex Texas for almost a decade.

The Texas question was a pivotal issue in the presidential election of 1844. Democratic candidate James K. Polk of Tennessee, a strong proponent of the annexation of Texas, was opposed by longtime Whig leader Henry Clay of Kentucky. The 1844 election was also significant in Arkansas. Historian Michael Dougan has called it "the highwater mark of the two-party system" in the state. Both presidential candidates had strong followings in Arkansas, and both parties fielded strong state tickets. In the end, Arkansas gave its electoral votes to Polk, and elected Thomas Drew, the Family-backed Democratic candidate, governor.

The death of Senator Fulton in August of 1844 provided an added incentive for aspiring politicians. Archibald Yell eyed the vacant seat with great interest as did the prominent Little Rock attorney Chester Ashley. Ashley had amassed a small fortune through a series of lucrative, if sometimes questionable, land transactions. He had been active in the movement to relocate the capital to Little Rock (where he owned a considerable amount of land) and later built one of the city's first great houses there. Ashley had at one time been a law partner of Robert Crittenden but had dissolved the partnership and become a prominent member of the Family-dominated Democratic Party. By the mid-1840s, however, Ashley's influence in the party had waned, and he was often at odds with his former allies. Still he was a man of acknowledged talent and considerable influence, and the legislature chose him to fill out the remaining two years of Fulton's term. Ashley took his seat in the Senate in March of 1845 and shortly thereafter made a powerful speech in support of the annexation of Texas.

When the United States did annex Texas in March 1845 it brought tensions with Mexico to the boiling point. Mexico had never recognized the independence of its former province and viewed the American action as a virtual declaration of war. After Texas was formally admitted to the Union in December 1845, an American army under Gen. Zachary Taylor was dispatched to the Rio Grande, the traditional boundary of the American claim. Mexico insisted that the boundary was at the Nueces River farther to the north and thus viewed the American presence on the Rio Grande as an invasion of Mexican territory. In late April 1846, Mexican forces crossed the river and attacked the American positions. Shortly thereafter, claiming that Mexico had invaded American territory and "shed American blood on American soil," the president asked for a declaration of war, and Congress responded in early May, authorizing Polk to call up fifty thousand volunteers.

The secretary of war requested that Governor Drew organize one regiment of cavalry and one battalion of infantry. The cavalry regiment was to assemble at Washington in southwest Arkansas, while the infantry was to report to Fort Smith to serve as replacements for the regular army troops there who had been ordered to the Rio Grande. While there was little interest in frontier duty on the state's western border, there was great enthusiasm for service in Mexico. Young men eager for glory and adventure and aspiring politicians eager to pad their resumes rushed to enlist. By July, 44 officers and 749 men organized into ten companies had assembled at Washington.

The officers of the companies were allowed to choose the regimental officers, including the top position of regimental colonel. The only prominent Arkansan with any significant military experience was former governor Archibald Yell, who had fought in the Creek War (1813–1814), had served with Andrew Jackson in the epic American victory at New Orleans in January 1815, and later fought in the First Seminole War (1818). One historian has noted that, including his service in the Mexican War, Yell had "fought the Indians, the Spanish, the British, and the Mexicans in all the wars that occurred during those four decades when the young and lusty United States was expanding from one coast to the other."

Yell was serving in Congress and was considering a run for the US Senate seat then occupied by Chester Ashley when the war broke out. Without resigning his seat in Congress, he rushed back to Arkansas to enlist as a private. In addition to his military experience and the support of President Polk, Yell was a skilled and beloved politician and possessed great personal courage. It was little wonder that he was elected to lead the Arkansas regiment as its colonel.

The only other prominent Arkansan with military experience was Albert Pike. Pike had been involved in military affairs almost since the time of his arrival in Arkansas in 1832. He commanded the First Company of Arkansas Artillery, which had formed in the fall of 1836 to protect the citizens of Little Rock against the attacks from Indian tribes passing through Arkansas on their way to the Indian Territory. Such attacks were highly unlikely given the peaceful nature and scarce resources of these tribes, and "Pike's Artillery," as the company was soon known, saw action mainly in parades and other ceremonial occasions. Nonetheless, Pike drilled his men in infantry and artillery tactics and developed a reputation as a competent officer and a strong disciplinarian.

If Pike's military credentials recommended him for a high position, however, his Whig political affiliation weighed against him. The majority of the company's officers, like the majority of Arkansas officeholders, were Democrats, and their political loyalties carried over into their military service. They chose Solon Borland, the volatile doctor, politician, and editor of the state's major Democratic Party newspaper, as major, and John Seldon Roane, an ambitious young attorney and Democratic politician, as lieutenant colonel. Pike had to content himself with the role of company commander.

The Arkansas regiment left Washington in mid-July 1846 and arrived in San Antonio in late August. The regiment was soon at war not with the Mexicans but with Gen. John Wool, the overall commander of the American forces at San Antonio. On his first inspection of the regiment shortly after its arrival, Wool found the Arkansas encampment poorly organized, unsanitary, and generally undisciplined. He soon took to referring to them as "Yell's Mounted Devils." The record of Arkansas's participation in the Mexican War was decidedly mixed. Some Arkansas soldiers performed admirably (Yell was killed in close-order fighting with Mexican lancers), but others killed innocent Mexican civilians whom they believed (erroneously) had killed an Arkansas soldier.

The significance of the American victory in the war, finalized by the signing of the Treaty of Guadalupe Hidalgo in February 1848, was immense. The Mexican Cession gave the United States over 500,000 square miles of new territory (more than a million square miles counting Texas), and the newly acquired territory was not long in paying dividends. In late January 1848, gold was discovered at Sutter's Mill in California (near present-day Sacramento). Reports of easy wealth to be found in the west reached Arkansas in the late summer and early fall of that year, and many Arkansans, like thousands of other Americans, quickly fell victim to "gold fever." Citizens of Fort Smith and Van Buren, on opposite banks of the Arkansas River near the border with the Indian Territory, quickly began to promote their towns as ideal jumping-off points for the journey to the gold fields. In March 1849 a Fort Smith reporter noted, "The streets are literally crowded with California wagons and teams."

Numerous Arkansas companies began organizing for the trip to the gold fields, and they were joined by others from twenty-five states and at least four foreign countries. One estimate placed the number of "forty-niners" who chose the Arkansas route at three thousand. The five miles of river-bank between Fort Smith and Van Buren were crammed with people, and the economies of the two towns boomed as the demand for supplies exploded. The population of Fort Smith doubled, and a Van Buren resident estimated that local merchants took in at least sixty thousand dollars. Mules, horses, oxen, corn, and a host of other supplies were at a premium. Downriver, Little Rock also experienced a boom as emigrants passed through the city on their way to the jumping-off points.

The principal Arkansas route passed through the Indian Territory and the Texas Panhandle, then on to the halfway point at Santa Fe or Albuquerque in the New Mexico Territory. Here the trail turned south and crossed southern Arizona Territory to San Diego on the southern California coast before turning north toward San Francisco and the gold fields, a total distance of about twenty-three hundred miles.

Companies were composed largely of males (often as much as 90 percent) and were organized along military lines with specific instructions regarding the nature of supplies to be taken and the maximum weight allowed. The requirements of one company, the Little Rock and California Association, were typical. They stipulated, "Every member of the association binds himself to provide the following articles and be with them at Fort Smith, on the last day of March, 1849, to wit: 100 lbs. bacon, 125 lbs. flour, 25 lbs. coffee, salt, pepper, etc., in proportion . . . He shall also provide 5 lbs. of powder and 12 lbs. shot; one rifle or shot gun; pistols and knife." In addition, every member was to provide "a good substantial wagon with four good mules; and this wagon shall not carry over 2,000 lbs."

Most companies tried to depart in late March or early April in order to ensure that their livestock would find an adequate supply of grass on the prairies. Wagon trains hoped to make fifteen to twenty miles a day, allowing them to complete the journey in under six months. For most travelers, that proved to be an overly optimistic projection. The spring of 1849 was unusually wet, and the combination of inexperienced travelers, overloaded wagons, and roads rendered nearly impassable by rains slowed travel and dampened spirits. More than a few travelers reported that they "had seen the elephant" (had seen what they set out to see) and returned home.

Others persevered. Those who made it as far as Santa Fe found the frontier town to be a den of drinking, gambling, and prostitution. The town was violent, even by Arkansas standards. "I think it was a little of the hardest place I was ever in," one Arkansan noted. "Men shoot one another for past time. Not a day without the enactment of a bloody tragedy." Prices were astronomical. A bushel of corn that cost 35–40 cents in Fort Smith cost $2.50 in Santa Fe or Albuquerque. Still some found the cultural dissonance intriguing and wrote home glowingly of the Mexican *fandangoes* and the beautiful Hispanic women they encountered.

On the next part of the journey, the problem was not too much water but too little. Across the arid southwest, grass grew scarce and tempers short. Internal dissension threatened many companies, and it was not uncommon to see larger groups split into smaller units either to avoid further strife or to better facilitate grazing their animals. In this climate, animals faltered, and wagons had to be abandoned. Rivers were a welcome sight for weary travelers, but crossing the swift Rio Grande and the Colorado River held hazards all their own.

Rather than the predicted six months, most trips took seven or eight. A few of those hardy souls who made the journey found the fabled wealth they had sought. Most did not. What they did find were harsh conditions in the mining camps, disease, homesickness, and, again, exorbitant prices. Bacon, which sold for 4–6 cents a pound in Fort Smith, cost $1.25; flour, which went for 3 cents a pound in Arkansas, sold for 56 cents a pound. Perhaps most galling to some Arkansans, whiskey, which could be had back home for 35 cents a *gallon*, sold in the gold fields for 25 cents a *glass*.

Some Arkansans found wealth in California not by prospecting for the elusive golden nuggets but by providing services and supplies to those who did. Teamsters could make from $300 to $400 a month hauling supplies to the camps and mines, and enterprising Arkansans soon found other ways to profit from the rush. Kirkbride Potts left a wife and eight children at his home at the foot of Crow Mountain on Galla Creek (near present-day Russellville) to seek his fortune in the gold fields. Like so many others, he failed to find it. He did, however, find a tremendous demand for beef, and in 1851 he returned to California where, his daughter reported, he was "merchandising in Sacramento City." She does not mention what he was "merchandising," but five years later he was back in California herding over three hundred head of cattle.

The boom continued in 1850, leading some to fear that the gold rush fever was depopulating the state and depressing land values. Such fears proved to be unfounded. Unfavorable reports from the gold fields soon helped stem the tide. A letter from one disillusioned emigrant to the *Fort Smith Herald,* written in late January 1851, noted, "Not a single Arkansas man who came to this country either last year or this year, has made 1/10 part of his anticipation," and closed by advising the readers to "stay home & not come to California." Many heeded his advice, and traffic along the overland trails fell off dramatically in 1851.

It swelled again the following year, but the new emigrants were predominantly settlers seeking land and a permanent home in the West. Women and children now joined with their husbands in making the journey. More clearly marked routes and lighter wagons enabled them to complete the journey in shorter time, but like the forty-niners who preceded them, this second wave of emigrants faced innumerable hardships, disappointments, and misfortunes in their search for a better life. One such group became involved in one of the greatest tragedies of the entire westward movement.

In mid-April 1857, a party composed largely of prosperous farmers from northwest Arkansas set out from near present-day Harrison bound for a new life in California's central valley. Of the approximately 135 members of the company, at least 15 were women (mostly young mothers), and 60 were dependent children. A large herd of cattle estimated at anywhere between three hundred and a thousand head accompanied the party on its way west.

The caravan of thirty to forty wagons was led by fifty-two-year-old George Baker and forty-five-year-old Alexander Fancher, both veterans of earlier trips to California in the gold rush days. The route Baker and Fancher chose was the Cherokee Trail, which had been opened in 1849 by members of the Cherokee Nation and a group of whites from northwest Arkansas (possibly including Baker). Because it was less traveled than some other western trails, the route offered ample grazing for cattle.

The trail led through Kansas into Colorado Territory where it turned north into southern Wyoming. Proceeding west again it linked up with the Oregon-California-Mormon Trail at Fort Bridger. From there it turned south along the Mormon Trail into the Salt Lake Valley in northern Utah. By August 3, the party reached Salt Lake City. Countless others had followed this trail in the preceding eight years to reach California, and the Baker-Fancher party anticipated no major problems. They were tragically mistaken. As one recent historian notes, the party "had come to the wrong place at the wrong time."

The Utah Territory was home and sanctuary to a religious sect that called itself the Church of Jesus Christ of Latter-day Saints but was more commonly known as the Mormons. Founded by Joseph Smith in New York in 1830, the movement grew rapidly, but Mormon religious beliefs and their attempts to institute a form of government based on those beliefs had brought them into repeated conflict with their non-Mormon neighbors. Driven successively from New York, Ohio, and Missouri, they moved in 1839 to Illinois where they established a settlement called Nauvoo on the banks of the Mississippi River. Once again they fell into serious disputes with non-Mormons, and in 1844 a mob killed Smith and his brother. Faced with extermination if they remained in Illinois, the Mormons, under the leadership of Brigham Young, decided to relocate to the far West where they would be outside the jurisdiction of the United States and isolated from hostile neighbors.

In the summer of 1847 they established themselves in the barren valley of the Great Salt Lake, and Mormon settlements soon spread throughout the territory. But their dreams of an isolated kingdom soon disappeared. The United States acquired the territory from Mexico in 1848, and the gold rush of the following year sent thousands of Americans streaming through Mormon territory on their way to California. Relations between the United States and the territorial government had been strained from the beginning, with non-Mormon territorial officials complaining of constant interference and harassment by Mormon officials loyal to Brigham Young, who was now the territorial governor.

The situation deteriorated to the point that President James Buchanan ordered the US Army to the region in the spring of 1857. When news of the president's order reached the Mormons, they determined to resist. Mormon preachers harangued crowds to prepare themselves for an invasion, and suspicion and hostility toward outsiders grew.

It was into this tense environment that the Fancher-Baker party entered in the summer of 1857. Their situation was compounded by another, unrelated event. In May of that year a popular Mormon elder named Parley Pratt had been brutally stabbed to death near Fort Smith by the angry husband of a woman whom Pratt had taken as his tenth wife. The fact that the Baker-

Fancher party was from the same region of the state as Pratt's murderer only served to increase the enmity that the Mormons felt for the company.

The Arkansans were probably unaware of the events surrounding Pratt's murder, but the party had encountered elements of the US Army on its way to Utah and were likely to have been informed of the unrest there. Baker and Fancher apparently felt that these events posed no threat to them for they chose the southern route across Utah rather than a northern route that would have taken them more quickly out of the territory. As they moved south from Salt Lake City, however, evidence of Mormon hostility soon became apparent. At settlements along the way Mormons, under strict orders from Brigham Young not to provide "one kernal" of grain to the enemy, refused to sell the party the flour and other provisions it badly needed. When the party's large herd of cattle grazed on Mormon land, tensions increased.

On Sunday, September 6, the Arkansans made camp in a spring-fed valley called Mountain Meadows in the southwestern corner of the territory. The valley provided abundant grass and water, but it was a poor choice for a defense if attacked. Before sunrise the following morning the party was surrounded and attacked by a party of about three hundred Indians and Mormons disguised as Indians. The attackers' initial volley killed several of the Baker-Fancher party, but the rest quickly formed the wagons into a circle and returned the fire.

The siege continued until Friday morning, when John Lee and another Mormon leader drove two wagons into the besieged camp under a flag of truce. It was apparent that the party had lost many animals and was running low on ammunition. The Mormon emissaries convinced the Arkansans that their only hope was to give up their arms, turn over their cattle and supplies to the Indians, and put themselves under the protection of the Mormon militia.

The Arkansans, who had few alternatives, agreed. The members of the company were placed in separate groups according to age and gender. The first wagon that left the encampment carried children under six years old. Lee walked behind this wagon, and behind him followed a second wagon containing two or three wounded men and one woman. At some distance behind the second wagon, the women and older children followed on foot. About a quarter of a mile farther to the rear marched the remaining men of the party, each escorted by an armed Mormon guard.

When the women and children reached a narrow passage between surrounding hills, a mounted Mormon officer ordered a halt and commanded his men to "Do your duty." The command was a signal for each of the Mormons guarding the Arkansas men to shoot his prisoner. Most did. That firing was the predetermined signal for the Indians and some of their Mormon allies who swarmed out of the brush and butchered the women and older children with hatchets and knives.

Accurate casualty figures for what came to be called the Mountain Meadows Massacre are impossible to determine. One recent historian places the number at 120, including about 50 men, 20 women, and approximately 50 children between the ages of seven and eighteen. "Measured in lives lost," historian David Bigler notes, "the massacre at Mountain Meadows was the second worst tragedy during America's westward migration during the nineteenth century."

Mountain Meadows Massacre: Incident that occurred in 1857 when a party of 135 Arkansans headed for California was attacked in southern Utah by a combination of Paiute Indians and Mormons. After surrendering to the Mormons under a promise of protection, over a hundred members of the party, including men, women, and children, were massacred.

Seventeen children under six years of age were spared and placed in Mormon homes. In 1859 all seventeen were reclaimed and returned to family members in Arkansas. The Mormons billed the US government several thousand dollars for boarding and sheltering the children in the interval. At least fifty Mormons took part in the massacre, and many more attempted to cover up the outrage by placing the blame solely on the Indians. The degree of Brigham Young's involvement in the massacre is still debated, though he clearly participated in the cover-up and took no action to punish the perpetrators.

The killing was too massive and involved too many people for the truth to stay hidden for long, however. In 1859 the US Army, at the urging of the victims' Arkansas relatives, launched an investigation of the massacre. Their report placed the blame squarely on the Mormons. As the truth of the story leaked out, pressure for punishment of the responsible parties grew within the Mormon community as well. In the end, John Lee was chosen to bear the guilt for all involved. He was excommunicated by the church in 1870 and twice tried for murder. The second trial resulted in a guilty verdict, and, in March 1877, Lee was taken back to Mountain Meadows and shot by a firing squad.

In many ways, Mountain Meadows marked a tragic end to the brief and colorful episode in Arkansas history that began with the gold rush of 1849. In the years that followed, Texas, not California, continued to be the destination of choice for many Arkansans, and Arkansas never became the major jumping-off point for the westward movement that some of the state's leaders had hoped. But the turbulent years of the Mexican War and the gold rush did witness dramatic and far-reaching changes in the economic, social, and political course of the state's history.

7 Prosperity and Peril

Arkansas in the Late Antebellum Period

THE FIRST DECADE and a half following statehood gave little indication that Arkansas was prepared to shed its reputation as a poor, frontier society. In the 1840s frontier conditions still prevailed, and many Arkansans, particularly those living in the highland regions, remained tied to subsistence agriculture. But by the 1850s significant changes were underway that would transform the state's economy and positively impact the lives of many of its citizens. Growing numbers of Arkansans were becoming involved in the emerging market economy, and a cotton-based plantation-style agriculture had taken firm root in the fertile lands of southern and eastern Arkansas. By the late antebellum period Arkansas stood on the verge of a prosperity unknown in its history. But at the core of that prosperity lay the seeds of its dissolution.

The Arkansas Economy in the Late Antebellum Period

In his analysis of the US Census records for Pope County in west-central Arkansas in 1850, historian Ted Worley provides a revealing portrait of an Arkansas county that, in many ways, resembled the state as a whole. Pope County was a geographically diverse region, containing both the highlands of the Ozark Plateau to the north and lowlands along the Arkansas River to the south. The county's white population stood at 695 families with an average family size of 6.1. It was a young society with 62 percent of its white population under fifteen years of age and only eighty-eight people over sixty.

The citizens of the county had come from twenty-four states and four foreign countries, but 95 percent had been born in a slave state. A hundred families owned slaves, but only nine owned ten or more, and only three of these owned twenty or more. There were no free blacks in the county. The county had 11 one-teacher schools enrolling a total of 326 pupils and operating on an income of $3,892 ($12/student) per year, none of it from taxes.

More than 80 percent of the population made a living by farming and raising cattle. The remainder were carpenters, blacksmiths, lumber men, tanners, and wagon makers with a few of what would today be called professional people—lawyers, doctors, teachers, and preachers. The average family owned fifteen head of cattle, thirty-three hogs, and four milk cows. Despite these rather meager holdings, Pope County residents were largely self-sufficient. Farmers grew enough corn to feed both people and animals, and enough cotton, when combined with wool from the county's abundant sheep herds, to provide adequate material for clothing. But this was not merely a "hog and hominy" existence. Pope County farmers also grew oats, wheat, sweet potatoes, Irish potatoes, peas, beans, flax, hops, and tobacco.

Equally important, Pope County residents possessed a wide variety of skills necessary to self-sufficiency. Worley notes:

> The average farmer could build a house, make his fences of rails, construct an ash-hopper, gather tannin from bark and tan hides, mould bullets, make plows, churns, and shoes, including the pegs that held them together. He could find a bee-tree, hit a squirrel's head with a rifle, or make a gig for taking fish. His wife could spin, weave, make clothing, quilts, soap, candles, and even medicine. She knew how to render lard, what greens were good to eat; she could cook on an open fireplace, do the washing in the creek, and in a pinch could help worm tobacco, tie up fodder, or grit new corn for bread.

In these early communities, family and kinship networks played a large role, often determining the economic, social, and political viability of an individual or group. But what the individual or family could not do alone, they did with the help of the community at large. "It cannot be emphasized too strongly," Worley writes, "that the self-sufficiency of the pioneer was only in part due to individual effort; the welfare of every family was the concern of the neighborhood."

Despite the fact that both the county and the state as a whole remained largely societies of self-sufficient farmers, signs of an economic transformation were apparent. In Pope County there were thirteen sawmills (two of which were steam powered), two tanneries, and one cotton factory. One county resident operated a tar kiln (which extracted tar from pine knots) and sent the tar by flatboat to New Orleans.

In the county and throughout the state hundreds of artisans practiced their trades. Gunsmiths, cabinetmakers, potters, and silversmiths made a living and produced a rich material legacy even while competing with eastern manufacturers. Some rejected the factory system with its strict division of labor for the freedom of running their own shops on the Arkansas frontier. Blacksmith James Black, who had apprenticed to a silverplater in Philadelphia, ended up in Washington, Arkansas, producing what is likely the

Artisan:
A skilled craftsman.

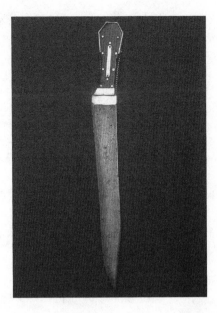

The thirteen-inch knife known as "Bowie No. 1" because of an engraving on the escutcheon plate, possibly the original bowie knife. *Historic Arkansas Museum, Little Rock.*

earliest form of the bowie knife, a form copied by cutlers as far away as Sheffield, England. Gunsmith John Pearson had been the mechanic for Samuel Colt (the maker of the first revolver) before taking his trade to Fort Smith. Women in the antebellum period had fewer opportunities for creative expression, but many excelled in the textile arts.

While these Arkansans practiced their crafts, commercial centers were springing up along the state's rivers. Little Rock, strategically located in the center of the state at the point where the Southwest Trail crossed the Arkansas River, was bustling with business activity, and, as the state capital, also exerted great political influence in the state. But as Charles Bolton has pointed out, the state's river system created a decentralized market that allowed other settlements to develop into regional commercial centers.

Along the Arkansas River in northwest Arkansas, Fort Smith flourished. In the 1850s the army guaranteed the fort's status as a permanent post by designating it a quartermaster depot, and local merchants carried on a brisk trade with Native Americans being resettled in the Indian Territory to the west and with troops stationed at the forts there. Roads led from the town to Texas and California, and in 1858 Fort Smith became a station on the Overland Mail Company route. In extreme northwest Arkansas, Fayetteville

Bowie knife: The bowie knife was a large knife specifically designed for use in personal combat. Named for Jim Bowie, a member of a pioneer family who settled in early Arkansas and Louisiana, the first knife was produced by blacksmith James Black at Washington, Arkansas, in the 1820s.

became a leading center of commerce even without the benefit of a river as large numbers of settlers moved into the region in the 1830s. Along the White River in north-central Arkansas, Batesville and later Jacksonport became centers of commercial activity. The same was true of Helena and Napoleon on the Mississippi River. The towns of Fulton, situated along the Red River, and Washington, located on the Southwest Trail near the Red River, served the needs of Arkansans in the southwestern part of the state, while Camden on the Ouachita River dominated commerce in south-central Arkansas.

If rivers were the highways of commerce, steamboats were its vehicles. The boats that plied Arkansas waters and those of other western rivers were largely the creation of Henry M. Shreve, a famous riverboatman whose broad, shallow-draft vessels were well suited to shallow, fast-moving rivers like the Mississippi, the Arkansas, and other rivers in the state.

In March 1822, the *Eagle* became the first steamboat to reach Little Rock, and the *Robert Thompson* reached Fort Smith the following month. The steamboat *Waverly* reached Batesville on the White River in January 1831, and boats were soon in operation on all the state's major rivers. The *Eagle* displaced slightly over a hundred tons and took seventeen days to make the trip upriver from New Orleans to the capital. By the mid-1830s, however, larger steamboats like the *Arkansas* were operating on the Arkansas River. The *Arkansas* was over 150 feet long and displaced well over two hundred tons. It had a spacious, well-lighted cabin with fifteen staterooms for male passengers and another cabin for female passengers containing four staterooms. More importantly, by 1836 boats of this type could make the roundtrip from New Orleans to Little Rock and back in sixteen days.

Wherever they went, steamboats caused great excitement. Not only were the boats mechanical wonders, but they also connected Arkansas to the wider world, bringing passengers from other parts of the country, eastern and regional newspapers, and merchandise from New Orleans, Cincinnati, St. Louis, and other cities. They were also especially important in promoting the expansion of large-scale cotton production in the state.

Since Eli Whitney's invention of the cotton gin in 1793, the production of short-staple cotton had skyrocketed throughout the South, and in the early 1800s the center of that production had moved from the Carolinas and Georgia to the fertile lands of the Old Southwest. In the river bottoms of Arkansas's southern and eastern lowlands, planters and farmers grew a variety of crops, including corn, peas, beans, and potatoes, but as early as the 1820s cotton had become the territory's leading staple crop. To a large extent, the cotton planter's entire year's schedule revolved around preparing the ground, planting, cultivating, and picking cotton.

Cotton was a fickle crop. Too much or too little rain could prove fatal, and an early frost would cause a plant to stop producing. Diseases and insects could devastate a crop. Even good crops could fall victim to falling prices.

Despite these pitfalls and unpredictable fluctuations in price, cotton production nationwide steadily increased throughout the nineteenth century. Arkansas produced over 6 million pounds (approximately twelve thousand 500-pound bales) of cotton in 1840, a trifling amount when compared to Louisiana's 152 million pounds or Mississippi's 193 million pounds. By 1850, however, Arkansas produced over 26 million pounds (roughly fifty-two thousand bales), the majority of it in the Delta, and the expansion continued throughout the next decade.

The growth of slavery in Arkansas was inexorably linked to this expansion. The majority of white Arkansans owned no slaves, and Arkansas ranked near the bottom of all slave states (thirteenth of fourteen) in total number of slaves in both 1840 and 1850. But while the state's slave population lagged behind those of other slave states, the percentage of increase in slaves in Arkansas far exceeded that of any other state. Between 1830 and 1840, the number of slaves increased by 335 percent, and from 1840 to 1850 by 136 percent. By 1860 Arkansas would be home to over 111,000 slaves and over eleven thousand slave owners.

In 1840 slavery existed in almost every county in the state, and the census conducted in that year reported that Washington County in extreme northwest Arkansas was still one of the top ten counties in the state in terms of slave population. Historian Gary Battershell has pointed out that slavery remained an important fact of life for the residents of much of the Arkansas upcountry until the time of the Civil War. This was particularly true for counties like Pope and Johnson that contained rich bottomland along the Arkansas River. Battershell notes that while the percentage of upcountry slaveholders in the total population declined from 1840 to 1850, the actual number of slaves and slaveholders both increased. Further, while slaveholdings were smaller in this region, slaveholders enjoyed great social and political prominence.

The small slaveholders of the highlands were more the norm than the exception among Arkansas slaveholders. Orville W. Taylor, the great historian of slavery in Arkansas, has noted that as late as 1860, 5,806 (51 percent) of Arkansas's 11,481 slave owners held no more than four slaves; 4,312 (37 percent) held between five and nineteen slaves; and only 1,363 (12 percent) owned twenty or more slaves, enough to be considered "planters." But this small group of wealthy slaveholders possessed a disproportionate share of the state's wealth. In dispelling the myth of economic equality on the frontier,

"Old Southwest": The name given to the southwestern frontier territories from the Revolutionary War era through the early nineteenth century. It included the future states of Alabama, Arkansas, Louisiana, Mississippi, Missouri, and Texas, as well as parts of Kentucky and Tennessee and the panhandle region of Florida.

Charles Bolton has pointed out that, between 1840 and 1860, the wealthiest 10 percent of taxpayers owned more than 70 percent of the taxable wealth in the state. "In terms of the distribution of wealth," he writes, "Arkansas was a very unequal society." And in an agricultural society that measured a man's status largely by the amount of land and slaves he owned, the planter class also exerted an influence in social and political affairs far out of proportion to their actual numbers.

Planter: Term generally applied to a slave owner who owned twenty or more slaves.

By the 1830s, a slave-based, plantation-style agriculture was rapidly developing along the rivers of the state's southern and eastern lowlands—the Mississippi, the Arkansas, the Red, and the Ouachita. As cotton production soared in the Arkansas delta in the late antebellum period, the slave population expanded rapidly. In 1830 Chicot County in the southeastern corner of the state had a total population of 1,165 of whom 888 (76 percent) were free white, 270 (23 percent) were black slaves, and seven (.6 percent) were free persons of color. Slave owners were a minority of the county's population, and almost all of those who did own slaves owned only a few. Only two men in the county owned twenty or more slaves.

By 1850 the county's population had reached 5,115. Whites made up only 1,122 (22 percent) of that total, while the slave population rose to 3,984 (78 percent). Chicot County exceeded any other county in the state in proportion of slaves to total population and was second only to Union County in total number of slaves. Sixty planters owned 20 or more slaves, thirty-three owned 50 or more, and eight owned 100 or more. The largest slave owner in the county, Horace Walsworth, owned 230 slaves. One historian noted, "With its flat, fertile fields along the Mississippi and preponderance of large plantations and slaveholders, Chicot County was more nearly representative of the idealized Southern plantation country than any other Arkansas county."

Slavery in Arkansas

By 1860 there were 111,115 slaves in Arkansas, constituting 25.5 percent of the state's total population of 435,450. The southern and eastern lowlands contained at least three-quarters of the state's slave population, and the majority of slaves in Arkansas lived on larger holdings. On those large planta- tions, slaves generally worked in gangs under the direction of a white overseer or a black "driver." During harvest times, slaves rose before dawn and often worked until after sun- down. Picking cotton was a back-breaking task. Slaves were given a large sack with a strap that fastened over the neck and held the mouth of the sack breast high while the bot-

Overseer: Person charged with the day-to-day manage- ment of the slave labor force on a plantation.

tom reached nearly to the ground. Pickers went down the long rows stooped over for hours on end, repeatedly filling and emptying it into large baskets at the ends of the rows. A skilled picker could pick well over two hundred pounds of cotton a day.

In Arkansas and the other states of the Old Southwest, the abundance of cheap, fertile land maximized the potential for profit on well-run plantations and made slaves an extremely valuable commodity. By the late antebellum period the economy of this region was booming, and slave prices in Arkansas were among the highest in the South.

Laws regulating slavery in Arkansas in the early nineteenth century had been enacted by the legislature of the Louisiana Territory in October 1804. While whipping remained an acceptable form of punishment, the Louisiana code had eliminated some of the harsher features of previous slave codes such as branding and the cutting off of ears, reforms that nineteenth-century slave owners proudly pointed to as evidence of the increasingly humanitarian nature of the institution.

As Arkansas changed in status and jurisdiction over the course of the next three decades, additional laws were added, but the restrictions on slaves' activities generally were the same as they had been since the introduction of slavery by the French and Spanish. Slaves were forbidden to carry guns, to assemble in large groups, to leave the plantation without a pass, or to buy or sell any commodity. The various laws concerning slavery were incorporated in the first digest of Arkansas laws, compiled under the direction of territorial governor John Pope in 1835.

The actual treatment of slaves varied from one plantation or slave owner to another. Fanny Johnson, who was born a slave on the Woodfork plantation near Grand Lake in southern Chicot County in the 1850s, recounted her own experience and those of her grandmother to a Federal Writers' Project interviewer in 1936. Her master was an absentee owner who owned several plantations and maintained a residence in Nashville, Tennessee. Johnson recalled, "The Woodfork colored folks was always treated good . . . We had plenty to wear and lots to eat and good cabins to live in . . . He [Woodfork] didn't believe in separating families. He didn't believe in dividing mother from her baby."

But a Union County slave recalled that his master was "a right mean man" who "whipped his slaves a lot" and "would whip the women the same as he would the men." Some planters and overseers used the whip to prod slaves to pick a certain amount of cotton. A Chicot County slave remembered hearing her mother say that "lots of times she would pick cotton and give it to others that couldn't keep up so that they wouldn't be punished. She had a brother they used to whip all the time because he didn't keep up."

There were factors that mitigated against overuse of the whip. "Throughout the South," one historian commented, "publicists denounced as un-Christian masters who mistreated those placed under their authority, and stressed the need for 'moderate,' predictable punishment for offenses that were clearly spelled out." Fear of public disapproval or the master's own deeply held religious convictions also served to prevent harsh treatment. Many antebellum ministers placed great emphasis on the master's duty to treat his slaves fairly and humanely.

On a more practical level, planters realized that slaves scarred by the whip were worth less on the auction block, and experience taught them that extreme or arbitrary punishment was counterproductive. Consequently, many masters attempted to use rewards as well as the threat of punishment to maintain order and maximize output on the plantation. But the slave narratives clearly indicate that use of the whip was commonplace in Arkansas and throughout the slave South, and even on those plantations where it was used infrequently, the whip was an omnipresent threat.

Slaves had little recourse to such abuse. Whites usually outnumbered blacks and were well armed, factors that severely limited opportunities for large-scale resistance. Accordingly, American slaves attempted only a few such revolts, and those that did occur were quickly suppressed. Still, slaves did find ways to resist. They deliberately worked slowly and inefficiently, faked illness or injury, intentionally destroyed farm tools, and stole from the master.

Others simply ran away. Rather than trying to reach freedom in the faraway North, most runaway slaves remained in the vicinity of their own plantations, often hiding in nearby woods before returning after a few days to face his master's ire. Slave owners seldom advertised or hired slave catchers for those runaways thought to be in the immediate area. Most owners came to accept these temporary absences as a part of the normal routine and generally punished such slaves mildly when they returned.

For many years, historians of the institution believed that the physical and psychological horrors of slavery and the frequent separation of family members by sale precluded the formation of a strong sense of community in slave society. Revisionist studies of the 1970s challenged this assumption, arguing that a true slave community, based on a foundation of slave Christianity and strong, relatively stable, two-parent families, did exist. Farsighted slave owners understood the importance of family in the slave community and were hesitant to break it up.

Recent studies have indicated that the two-parent nuclear family was less common in Arkansas than in the older slave states. Historian Carl Moneyhon has noted a correlation between the size of a slaveholding and a slave family's stability. Because larger slaveholding operations provided a more stable economic environment and a greater opportunity for a slave to find a suitable mate, the two-parent nuclear family was more likely to exist and survive on a larger holding than on a smaller one.

Slaves on both large and small holdings had certain basic expectations of slave masters, including adequate food, housing, and clothes. But they also expected a certain degree of autonomy from whites and occasional time off from work to enjoy the company of friends and family within the slave community and to practice their religion. Slave religion, a combination of African and Christian religious traditions, was a particularly important issue for slaves and a particularly difficult one for masters. As a result of the great evangelical crusades of the early nineteenth century, Christianity made vast inroads among American slaves and became a major factor in shaping the black community. Slave religious experiences varied greatly. Some masters permitted their slaves no religious services at all. Others hired white preachers who constantly stressed the notion of obedience and urged slaves to refrain from stealing from the master.

But there was another aspect to slave religion. "Regular Sunday worship in the local church was paralleled by illicit, or at least informal, prayer meetings on weeknights in the slave cabins," historian Albert Raboteau writes. "Preachers licensed by the church and hired by the master were supplemented by slave preachers licensed only by the spirit." In the so-called invisible institution of slave Christianity, meetings were often conducted in secret, and the theological themes were very different from those espoused by white preachers. A major theme was deliverance from oppression and the equality of all men before the Lord.

Another important aspect of slave society is less frequently discussed in the literature of the period—sexual relationships between white masters and female slaves. Miscegenation, historian Eugene Genovese notes, generally "occurred with single girls under circumstances that varied from seduction to rape and typically fell between the two," and "manifested itself in acts of love in the best cases, sadistic violence in the worst, and ostensible seduction and imposed lust in the typical."

Miscegenation was only the most extreme example of the complex series of relationships between white masters and black slaves. The fact that the vast majority of American slave masters were resident rather than absentee owners assured that they would not only be more actively involved in the management of the plantation, but also more actively involved with the personal lives of their slaves.

An early white resident of the county no doubt overstated the case when she described an idyllic situation in which the slaves were "protected by their owners, whom they loved and obeyed. Free from care, no thought of food nor clothes; they knew they had comfortable homes and would be cared for in times of sickness or distress." But a recent historian of American slavery has concluded that, while former slaves remembered slavery as "a barbaric institution" and "had bitter memories of particular injustices they had endured," many "tempered their overall condemnation of slavery with fond recollections of particular experiences and sympathetic portrayals of particular owners, and testified to the pervasive nature of slave-owner paternalism." The slave narratives abound with references to "our white folks." Whites in turn often spoke of their slaves as "our black family" and treated them as such.

Existing side by side with the slaveholders' genuine affection was a strong sense that slavery was a mixed blessing, often more of an unpleasant duty than an asset. Chicot County resident Miriam Hilliard wrote, "Negroes are nothing but a tax & annoyance to their owners." By June 1850, she concluded, "When we change our residence, I cast my vote for a free state."

But the Hilliards did not give up their plantation or their slaves. Like many other Arkansas slaveholders, they found slavery was simply too profitable to relinquish. By 1860, Arkansas produced 367,393 bales of cotton. Cotton prices remained relatively low throughout the first half of the 1850s. But in 1856, prices rose by over 3 cents to 12.4 cents per pound, the highest price since 1838. Throughout the remainder of the decade, the price only once dipped below 11 cents per pound. In May of 1857, a writer to the *Arkansas State Gazette and Democrat* remarked, "If cotton will only hold present prices for five years, Arkansas planters will be as rich as cream a foot thick." It seemed entirely possible that he was correct. The economic gains of the 1850s far surpassed anything in the young state's history. Agricultural production was up dramatically statewide. The cash value of farms in Arkansas increased almost sixfold between 1850 and 1860.

Signs of economic development were also beginning to appear in other areas. The troubled Cairo and Fulton Railroad, long supported by the Family, had begun to move south from St. Louis toward the Arkansas border, the Memphis and Little Rock line had actually laid thirty-eight miles of track in the state, and the Mississippi, Ouachita, and Red River line had laid about twenty-seven. Arkansas in 1860 still had less railroad mileage than any state in the Union except Oregon, but despite these shortcomings, industry, particularly in the western and northwestern sections of the state, was growing. By 1860 manufactured items were valued at almost three million dollars. In terms of real estate and personal wealth per capita, Arkansas ranked sixteenth of the nation's thirty-three states, and the states of the Old Southwest constituted the fastest-growing economic region of the country. After a slow and clumsy beginning, Arkansas seemed to be on the verge of a promising economic future.

This photograph showing young Harriet Ashley, the granddaughter of Chester Ashley, being held by her slave nurse is illustrative of the complex relationships between slaves and masters in the antebellum period. *From the Collection of Mr. and Mrs. Sterling Cockrill.*

While the prosperity of the 1850s was a statewide phenomenon, the economic gains were particularly pronounced in the slaveholding regions of the state. Orville Taylor has observed that while the cash value of farms in six northwestern counties with few slaves increased fourfold between 1850 and 1860, in the six lowland counties with the highest concentration of slaves the cash value of farms increased more than sixfold. The growing concentration of slaves in the southern and eastern sections of the state, combined with immigration to the lowlands from Deep South states, forged closer economic and cultural bonds between those regions while it exacerbated the sectional differences within Arkansas. Thus, as Arkansas's economy experienced unparalleled growth in the 1850s, the social, economic, and political dissonance between highland and lowlands increased.

Politics in the Late Antebellum Period

The last years of the 1840s also witnessed a dramatic shakeup in the state's political leadership. Archibald Yell's death at Buena Vista in early 1847 cut short a political career that included two stints in the US Congress and one term as governor. In April 1848 US senator Chester Ashley contracted a fever during the Senate session of 1848 and died within a week.

The previous month President James Polk appointed the state's other US senator, Ambrose Sevier, as minister to Mexico for the purpose of concluding peace negotiations. Forced to resign his Senate seat, Sevier hoped for the appointment of a political ally who would step aside and allow him to reclaim the seat in 1848. But Governor Thomas Drew, a Democrat who had enjoyed Family backing but who also had support among independents, broke with the Family shortly after his renomination for a second term earlier in the year and appointed Solon Borland, a rising political star, to serve out the remainder of the term. In November the Democratic-controlled general assembly chose Borland to serve the full term. Disheartened and possibly weakened by an illness contracted in Mexico, Sevier died on December 31, 1848, at his plantation home near Little Rock. In October of that year, Judge Benjamin Johnson, one of the founding members of the Family, died at the age of sixty-five. James Conway, another Dynasty stalwart and the state's first governor, died in March of 1855.

The deaths of Yell, Ashley, Sevier, Benjamin Johnson, and Conway marked the passing of the first generation of Arkansas's political leadership. Their demise prepared the way for the rise of a new generation of young politicians. Solon Borland was one such man. Another was John Seldon Roane, who had gained some notoriety, if not renown, for his service in Mexico and his subsequent duel with Albert Pike. Governor Drew's abrupt resignation in January 1849 gave Roane the political opening he was waiting for. A compromise candidate of a divided Democratic caucus, Roane went on to narrowly defeat his Whig challenger in a March 1849 special gubernatorial election that was widely ignored by Arkansas voters. In an election in which only 6,518 people cast votes, Roane won by a margin of 62 votes.

The Dynasty was also experiencing significant changes. The deaths of several of its founding members, the lingering taint of the banking fiasco, and a growing dissension within the Democratic Party created the greatest challenge to Family dominance since statehood. Robert Ward Johnson soon emerged as the acknowledged leader of the second generation of Family politicians. The eldest son of Judge Benjamin Johnson, Robert had accompanied his parents to Arkansas, but returned to Kentucky for his formal education before moving on to Yale University where he studied law.

Even as a young man, Johnson evidenced a strong inclination to carry on two important Family traditions—politics and dueling. In 1833, he sought retribution against three men who had tried to bring impeachment charges against his father, attacking one with a walking stick on a Little Rock street,

Robert Ward Johnson, leader of
the second generation of "Family"
politicians. *Courtesy of the Arkansas
History Commission.*

fighting a duel with another, and threatening to horsewhip the third. When he
was not engaged in fighting duels or otherwise defending the family honor,
Johnson won a reputation as a fearless prosecuting attorney in the district
around Little Rock and later served as attorney general of the state before
being elected to Congress in 1846. In Congress, Johnson quickly developed
a reputation as a supporter of John C. Calhoun, an outspoken advocate of
"Southern rights," a term that encompassed a traditional Southern aversion
to the centralized power of the federal government (especially when that
power was not used to the South's benefit) and a defense of the rights of the
individual states to decide for themselves on such issues as economic development, moral reform, and especially the maintenance of slavery.

The Missouri Compromise of 1820, which had laid the groundwork
for Arkansas's admission to the Union as a slave state, kept the lid on the
slavery issue for a quarter of a century by balancing the admission of slave
and free states, but events of the late 1840s again stirred the controversy
over slavery. The rush to California following the discovery of gold swelled
that territory's population far beyond that required for statehood, and in
1849 California requested admission to the Union as a free state. California's
admission threatened to undo the carefully crafted balance between slave and
free states in the US Senate.

In January of 1850, Senator Henry Clay of Kentucky brought forward a series of resolutions that he hoped would solve the problem. Clay proposed to admit California as a free state, organize the remainder of the Mexican Cession without restrictions as to slavery, abolish the slave trade (though not slavery itself) in the District of Columbia, and adopt a more effective fugitive slave law. Debate raged over the provisions for the next nine months, but Congressman Robert W. Johnson did not take long to make up his mind.

The same month that Clay introduced his compromise proposals, Johnson issued an "Address to the People of Arkansas" in which he proclaimed that "the Union of the Northern and Southern States, under a Common Government for a period beyond this Congress is a matter that may be seriously questioned . . . The South," he proclaimed, "will present to the world one united brotherhood and will move in one column under a banner—EQUALITY OR INDEPENDENCE, OUR RIGHTS UNDER THE CONSTITUTION WITHIN OR WITHOUT THE UNION! ! !" Governor John Seldon Roane was also a strong spokesman for Southern rights, as were both of the state's US senators, William Sebastian and Solon Borland.

In their extreme zeal, however, Johnson and his fellow Southern radicals had dramatically miscalculated the mood of their constituents. While the great majority in 1850 supported Southern rights, most continued to hope for compromise within the Union. One of the state's most influential Democratic newspapers, William Woodruff's *Arkansas State Gazette and Democrat,* chided Johnson for his "peculiar views" and noted, "Our people do not believe that the time has yet come when they are to be called upon to assist in dismembering the Confederacy. It is the universal sentiment that the Union must be preserved; and the universal belief is that it cannot be dissolved." It also condemned Johnson's "wholesale denunciation of those of his constituents who do not choose to endorse his views."

A correspondent to the paper from Chicot County, in the heart of the state's cotton-producing region, proclaimed himself to be a strong supporter of slavery and Southern rights but also "a Union man" and a friend of compromise. He condemned Robert Johnson's views and added that a tour of the state satisfied him "that Arkansas is still American, altogether American, in hope, thought, and feeling." Whig leader Albert Pike declared that he was "for the Union, the whole Union, and nothing less than the Union."

Senator Borland returned to Little Rock in the summer of 1850 and quickly began to soften his rhetoric, declaring in Little Rock in July his great love for the Union. He never returned to Washington to vote against the compromise he had so roundly condemned. In September, the various individual bills that collectively came to be called the Compromise of 1850 passed both houses of Congress after nine months of contentious debate. Most Arkansans, like most other Americans, were relieved that the crisis had passed.

Despite the best efforts of their political leaders, Arkansans failed to rally to the cause of Southern rights in 1850. Why was this so? Historian James Woods has provided several answers to this question. To begin with, Arkansans had only been in the Union for fourteen years when the controversy over California came to the fore, and many Arkansans still needed federal protection and federal aid. Citizens of western Arkansas, bordered by the Indian Territory, wanted the protection and economic benefits that the presence of federal troops supplied. Delta residents were beginning to derive substantial profits from cotton and stood to benefit further from a federal swampland reclamation project begun in 1850. It is also important to remember that slaveholders and their families accounted for less than 20 percent of Arkansas's population in 1850. And, as previously noted, most Arkansans were too preoccupied with their own survival on this frontier society to worry too much about the threat to slavery.

Following the passage of the compromise, a disheartened Robert Ward Johnson, stung by harsh criticism from much of the state press and many of his constituents, announced that he would not be a candidate for reelection. But in April 1851 the state Democratic convention "drafted" Johnson as its candidate for Congress citing his "fidelity to southern rights and public success." His "fidelity to southern rights" notwithstanding, Johnson had learned his lesson, and he tempered his fire-eating rhetoric. Campaigning in northwest Arkansas, he assured his audience that he was "the truest and best friend of Unionism" and did not propose secession as the remedy to the South's ills. He was reelected with over 57 percent of the vote.

Johnson's reelection gave clear evidence that, while the Dynasty had failed to convince Arkansans of the immediacy of the Southern rights cause, it did continue to dominate the state's politics. It received an additional boost when Elias Conway received the Democratic Party's nomination for governor. The youngest of Thomas and Ann Rector Conway's seven sons and the younger brother of former territorial delegate Henry Conway and former governor James Conway, Elias Conway had served as state auditor from 1836 to 1848 and had been active in Family politics.

In the presidential election of 1852, Arkansans continued their Democratic tradition by voting for Franklin Pierce over Whig candidate Winfield Scott, a hero of the Mexican War. Even Whig leader Albert Pike thought Scott to be "soft on slavery." Elias Conway was elected governor. When Solon Borland resigned his Senate seat in 1853, Governor Conway appointed Robert Johnson to fill the position. The state legislature unanimously elected Johnson to a full term in 1854, further strengthening the Family's grip on the major state offices.

In the years following the election of 1852, the national Whig Party divided over the issue of slavery and ceased to be a major factor in Arkansas or national politics. The new political parties that sprang up to fill the void had little appeal in Arkansas. This was particularly true for the new Republican Party, which first fielded a candidate for president in the election of 1856. The Republican platform favored homesteads, protective tariffs, and internal improvements, but staunchly opposed the extension of slavery into the territories, a development that many Southerners considered essential to the survival of the institution. Accordingly, the new party had almost no adherents in the slaveholding states.

The other new party to develop in the 1850s was the American Party. Originally organized in secret fraternal lodges, the party became commonly known as the Know-Nothings because its members answered, "I know nothing," to inquiries about the party's composition and goals. Its founding principle was opposition to foreign immigrants, particularly Roman Catholics. The Know-Nothings showed strength in New England, the Mid-Atlantic states, and parts of the South, but for obvious reasons the party's appeal in Arkansas was limited. The state simply had too few foreign immigrants and Catholics in the state to arouse much enthusiasm, and in the election of 1856, the Know-Nothings polled less than 40 percent of the popular vote in Arkansas, its poorest showing in any Southern state.

Thus, it appeared that by the middle of the 1850s the Dynasty was without serious challengers. Ironically, the greatest challenge to Family hegemony would come from within the Democratic Party and would be led by a man who shared the Southern rights sentiments of its leaders. Thomas Carmichael Hindman was the diminutive (barely five feet tall), hot-tempered son of a prominent Mississippi planter who had served in the Mexican War and in the Mississippi legislature. One acquaintance opined that Hindman had "a wonderful talent for getting into fusses" and another thought that he gave the appearance of being "perpetually anxious to have a duel."

Hindman moved to Helena in 1854 and married the daughter of a wealthy land speculator. A lawyer by profession but a born politician, he soon immersed himself in the politics of his new state. Intelligent and a gifted orator, Hindman initially ingratiated himself to the Family by holding a three-day political rally at his Helena home in November 1855 at which he castigated the Know-Nothings and expressed his belief that "[t]he purpose of any real Southern party is to protect slavery." In the gubernatorial elections of the following year, Elias Conway easily defeated Know-Nothing candidate James Yell (nephew of Archibald) with 65 percent of the vote, and the state gave its support to Democrat James Buchanan for president.

But if Hindman and the leaders of the Family were concerned with the protection of slavery, most Arkansans were not, and the growing national crisis kindled little interest in the state. By the mid-1850s cotton prices had increased to their highest level since 1838, and while Kansas was engulfed in civil war over slavery, a Camden newspaper urged its readers to "Forget about Kansas and rejoice in our glorious wealth, delightful showers, and abundant crops."

In 1858 the Family rewarded Hindman for his service by supporting him in a successful race for the congressional seat in the northern district. He was thirty years old and had been a resident of the state for only four years, yet in that brief time he had made a socially and economically successful marriage and had become a major player in state politics. For the average man, this meteoric rise would have been immensely satisfying. But Hindman was not the average man. As one chronicler noted, he was "a man who regarded Arkansas as an empire of which he should be emperor."

Dynasty leaders had thrown him a large bone that they felt would assuage his appetite, but for Thomas Hindman, it was not enough. He desperately wanted William Sebastian's US Senate seat when the term expired in late 1858. When the Dynasty supported Sebastian for reelection, Hindman was furious. He turned against the Family and established his own newspaper, the *Old Line Democrat*, in Little Rock and by the following year was at war with his former allies.

Hindman proved to be the most potent challenger to the Dynasty in the state's history. Unmatched as a public speaker, he became a rallying point for dissident Democrats who had long chafed under the Dynasty's domination of the state's politics. As the individual county conventions met in early 1860 to choose delegates to the state Democratic convention, it became clear that the Hindman forces would mount a serious challenge to the Family's hegemony.

Despite that challenge, the Dynasty secured the party's gubernatorial nomination for Robert Ward Johnson's younger brother, Richard H. Johnson. They also managed to control the writing of the party platform and to secure the selection of six of its members to the eight-man delegation to the Democratic national convention to be held later that month in Charleston, South Carolina. The platform rejected popular sovereignty and insisted on the federal protection of slavery in the territories.

Arkansas delegates shared the hostility felt by most southern Democrats for Illinois senator Stephen Douglas, who had alienated them with his "Freeport Doctrine" of 1858, which suggested that territories could evade the terms of the *Dred Scott* decision simply by refusing to provide the police powers necessary to enforce slavery. (In the 1857 case of *Dred Scott v. Sandford*, the Supreme Court ruled that Congress could not ban slavery from the territories.)

Events of late 1859 dramatically increased the tension nationwide. In

October of that year, the fanatical abolitionist John Brown led nineteen men in a raid on the federal arsenal at Harper's Ferry, Virginia, for the purpose of arming the slaves he believed would rush to join him. Brown and his men were overwhelmed by a detachment of US Marines, and before the month was out, a Virginia court convicted Brown of treason and conspiracy to incite insurrection. On December 2, he and six co-conspirators were hanged.

The shock waves from Brown's raid swept across the South and helped to further polarize the nation. Throughout the winter of 1859–1860 rumors of slave insurrections abounded in the Southern states, and Southerners became more determined than ever to resist those who threatened the survival of their "peculiar institution." Many ceased to distinguish between the abolitionists who wished to destroy slavery and others, like the new Republican Party, who wished only to restrict its spread. John Brown was still very much on the minds and tongues of Southern delegates as they prepared to assemble for the national convention in Charleston, South Carolina, in April 1860.

The convention was rent apart by the issue of slavery. When free state delegates refused to accede to Southern demands for federal protection of slavery in the territories, delegates from seven Southern states walked out of the convention. Six of the eight Arkansas delegates ignored the instructions of the state convention and joined the walkout.

With further progress impossible, the convention agreed to reassemble in Baltimore in mid-June and adjourned without nominating a candidate. The Baltimore convention, however, proved no more amenable to compromise than had the Charleston assembly. Once again Deep South delegates walked out, this time followed by delegates from the upper South. What remained of the convention nominated Stephen Douglas for president. The Southern delegates hastily assembled their own convention and nominated John C. Breckinridge of Kentucky, the sitting vice president of the United States, as their candidate for president on a platform pledging federal protection for slavery.

But while much of the country was riveted to the explosive events on the national political scene, Arkansans were preoccupied with events at home. In the interval between the demise of the Charleston convention and the convening of the Baltimore convention, another political bombshell exploded back in Arkansas.

Thomas Hindman secured his renomination for Congress from the northern congressional district, but it seemed that no serious rival would appear to challenge Richard Johnson for governor. Then in May, Henry Rector, a forty-four-year-old planter and attorney from Saline County who had served as a state representative, a US marshal, and a justice on the state supreme court, announced his candidacy for governor as an Independent Democrat. Rector was Governor Elias Conway's first cousin and a longtime member of the Family, but his relationship with his kinsmen had been a rocky one.

The gubernatorial campaign of 1860 was, one historian noted, a "fratricidal war." The Dynasty had thrived for over a quarter century by portraying itself as the party of Andrew Jackson and the common man. Now, adopting the tactics successfully employed by the Whigs in the presidential election of 1840, the Hindman press set out to cast Rector as the true champion of the common man and the Dynasty as aristocratic and corrupt. Rector, a longtime political insider and, since 1854, a prominent Little Rock attorney, was portrayed as a "poor, honest farmer of Saline County, who toils at the plow handles to provide bread, meat, and raiment for his wife and children." Meanwhile, from the stump, Hindman charged, "Of all the unholy alliances and corrupt political influences that ever crushed the energy of a free people, that of Johnsonianism was the most blighting, withering and corrupt."

The charges struck home. Not only did dissident Democrats and former Whigs flock to the Rector camp, many members of the lower echelons of the Dynasty itself joined the anti-Family crusade. They could identify with the frustrations felt by both Hindman and Rector at the overbearing dominance of Family leaders. On the major issues of the day—Southern rights and the expansion of slavery—the opposing factions were in complete agreement. Both strongly supported the expansion of slavery into the territories and held out the possibility of secession as a final remedy. Ironically, at a time when national politics was at its most sectionally polarized, sectional divisions in Arkansas were almost nonexistent. Both candidates campaigned in and drew support from all quarters of the state. Arkansas voters went to the polls on August 6, but it took two weeks to tabulate the final vote. The results marked the end of a political era. Rector received 31,948 votes to Johnson's 28,487. To compound the Family's fiasco, Hindman was reelected to Congress from the northern congressional district and a Hindman ally, Edward Gantt, was chosen to represent the southern district.

Historians have long debated the reasons for this turn of events. James Woods has suggested that the greatest factor may well have been Hindman's organizational, oratorical, and political skills. Unlike previous challengers, Hindman was able to bypass the Dynasty-dominated Democratic Party machinery and appeal directly to the voters. Unlike the Whigs, he was able to disassociate the Dynasty from its image as the party of the common man and to portray it instead as a group of wealthy aristocrats. In Rector, the Family's opponents had a candidate who could appeal to many different groups. To the poor and disaffected, he was the rebel challenging the entrenched aristocratic governing class. To Delta slave owners, he was a staunch defender of slavery. To the former Whigs, he was a member of the Little Rock elite who shared many of their economic ideas.

Behind it all lay the political genius of Thomas Carmichael Hindman. While Richard Johnson had inherited the bloodlines of the Family, it was Thomas Hindman who embodied the political and oratorical skills that were the true legacy of Ambrose Sevier. The defeat of the Family was a landmark event in the state's history and seemed to presage the rise of a new political alignment in Arkansas. But the new political landscape was not as clearly defined as it might first have appeared. For one thing, though Rector owed his election in no small measure to Hindman, he was in no sense Hindman's puppet. Rather, the man Arkansans had chosen to guide the state during this critical period was an eccentric maverick determined to steer his own course.

The Road to Secession

Four men sought the presidency in 1860, but only three found support in Arkansas. Abraham Lincoln of Illinois, the candidate of the Republican Party and a staunch opponent of the expansion of slavery, was not a factor in the race. Of the three remaining candidates, Stephen Douglas, the candidate of the northern wing of the now-sundered Democratic Party, enjoyed the least support in the state. Opposed by both the Family and the Hindman camp, Douglas forces had few newspapers to champion their cause and also lacked the financial resources to sponsor the rallies and barbecues so necessary to political campaigns in the mid-nineteenth century.

Those problems did not plague the supporters of the new Constitutional Union Party. Organized largely by former Whigs in the border states in early May, the party was intent on keeping the Union together. Its candidate, a wealthy Tennessee slaveholder named John Bell, found great support among former Whigs, including many of the wealthy planters of the southern and eastern parts of the state. Accordingly, there was plenty of money to conduct a full campaign. Press support was also abundant, including the powerful *Arkansas Gazette*, which tried diligently to portray John C. Breckinridge, the nominee of the Southern wing of the Democratic Party, as the candidate of extremism, disunion, and treason.

These aspersions notwithstanding, Breckinridge remained the most formidable candidate in Arkansas. He enjoyed the support of the vast majority of the state's newspapers as well as the backing of both rival Democratic factions in the state. The presidential campaign forced the Dynasty and Hindman's followers into an uneasy alliance that was made more difficult by the fact that they were still warring vigorously over state politics.

Breckinridge also gained support from an unlikely source. Longtime Family opponent Albert Pike had foregone participation in national politics since withdrawing from the American (Know-Nothing) Party in 1856. But the political crisis of 1860 brought him once more into the fray. Pike produced a lengthy and reasoned letter that defended the "state rights" theory and the *Dred Scott* decision and challenged the doctrine of popular sovereignty.

Whatever their political persuasion, Arkansans realized the critical nature of the election to the future of their state and nation. On election day, November 6, 1860, Camden attorney John Brown wrote in his diary, "This is the most important day to the United States and, perhaps, to mankind since July 4, 1776." Almost 80 percent of the state's eligible voters went to the polls, the highest percentage turnout in the state's history. The final returns showed a clear, if modest, victory for Breckenridge. The Kentuckian received 28,783 votes (53 percent), to Bell's 20,094 (37 percent), and Douglas's 5,227 (9 percent).

An analysis of the vote reveals that Bell did best in those parts of the state where the Whigs had traditionally done well—among the wealthy planters of the Delta and in the business-oriented urban areas where voters feared a disruption of commerce. Breckinridge ran strongest in the traditionally Democratic northwest and among the farmers and small slave owners of south and southwest Arkansas who hoped to rise to planter status. It may seem strange that the candidate most identified with slavery and states' rights found such great support in an area where slavery was least important. But the northwest part of the state had always been staunchly Democratic, and the best explanation may be that these voters were influenced more by party loyalty than by the overheated rhetoric about slavery.

In addition to Arkansas, Breckinridge carried all the Deep South and Gulf South states, garnering almost 850,000 popular votes and 72 electoral votes. Douglas received almost 1.4 million popular votes, but carried only one state (Missouri) and 12 electoral votes. Bell received almost 600,000 popular votes and carried the border states of Virginia, Kentucky, and Tennessee. None of this was enough to offset Lincoln's sweep of the more populous free states. Final national returns gave the Republican candidate over 1.8 million popular votes and more importantly 180 electoral votes. Though he received slightly less than 40 percent of the total popular vote, his electoral vote total easily surpassed the total of his three rivals.

In Arkansas, reaction to Lincoln's election was generally mild. On November 17 the *Gazette* editorialized, "Lincoln is elected in the manner prescribed by the law and by the majority prescribed by the Constitution. Let him be inaugurated, let not steps be taken against this administration until he has committed an overt act, which cannot be remedied by law." Even the

Democratic press seemed to take the result in stride and urged caution and restraint. The Family-controlled Fayetteville *Arkansian* advised its readers to "wait until after his [Lincoln's] inaugural and see what course he will pursue." Only the Hindman press spoke of secession.

In mid-November, only days after the election, the Arkansas General Assembly convened for its biennial session. On November 15, Henry Rector was inaugurated as the state's sixth governor and the first from outside the ruling Dynasty. Rector had a reputation as something of a fire-eater, but he was also largely an unknown quantity. Legislators and common citizens eagerly awaited his inaugural address to see what position he would take on the major issue of the day. Acknowledging "the bare possibility that the North may still be induced to retrace her steps, and award to the southern states the rights guaranteed to them by the constitution," the governor stated that he could not "counsel precipitate or hasty action, having for its object a final separation of the States, and breaking up of the Union." But he also spoke of the "fanaticism of the North" and "the irrepressible conflict" between slave and free states and warned that "the states stand tremblingly upon the verge of dissolution." Near the conclusion of his remarks, he cut through the ambiguities of "states' rights" and "Southern rights" and went directly to the heart of the matter. "The issue," he proclaimed, "is the Union without slavery, or slavery without the Union."

Key members of the state's congressional delegation pushed hard for secession. Both Hindman and Congressman-elect Edward Gantt gave inflammatory addresses to the general assembly in late November. Senator Robert Johnson soon joined in, publishing an open letter to his constituents that reached the state in mid-December. He said that he regarded the secession of the Southern states as a fact and that "Arkansas must go with them." Governor Rector added his voice to the growing clamor in a written address to the legislature on December 11, noting, "The Union of States may no longer be regarded as an existing fact" and warning Arkansans to "gird her loins for the conflict" he felt certain was to come.

These appeals notwithstanding, the legislature refused to be stampeded into a hasty action. It began the task of selecting a replacement for the retiring Senator Johnson, a clear sign that legislators did not feel that secession was imminent. On December 20, South Carolina voted an Ordinance of Secession dissolving its union with the other states. This action, coming only six weeks after Lincoln's election and over two months before his inauguration, caught many Arkansas Unionists and even some secessionists by surprise, and it hastened the demise of the old political alignments.

The following day Senator Johnson and Congressman Hindman, temporarily putting aside the bitterness of the 1860 gubernatorial campaign, collaborated on a joint statement calling for a state convention to consider secession. It was clear that the same unlikely political alliance that had carried the state for Breckinridge was now united behind secession. The old political alignments dissolved as the issue of secession polarized the state along sectional lines. Unionist sentiment was strongest in the upland counties of northern and western Arkansas. Secession forces were greatest in the southern and eastern parts of the state where many former Whigs joined lowland Democrats to form a common front.

On December 22, the state house of representatives called for a state convention to consider the issue, although the more conservative state senate did not concur until January 15. By the terms of the measure, voters would go to the polls on February 18 to decide whether or not to call a convention and to elect delegates. Unionist candidates had the unenviable task of asking voters to reject the convention while at the same time soliciting their votes as a delegate to the convention.

The Unionist dilemma was compounded by events of early 1861. Between January 9 and February 1, six more Deep South and Gulf South states left the Union, including the neighboring states of Mississippi, Louisiana, and Texas. Local affairs also contributed to the secession frenzy. In January a rumor spread that the sixty-five soldiers of the Second US Artillery Regiment who occupied the federal arsenal at Little Rock were about to be reinforced. The rumor spread by telegraph from Little Rock to Memphis and then downriver to the secessionist stronghold of Helena. Firebrands there demanded that the governor seize the arsenal.

Such a precipitate and illegal action was too much for Governor Rector. He replied that while Arkansas was still in the Union, the governor of the state had no right to seize federal property. But, as always, Rector was not content with a clear and unambiguous statement. He went on to say that any attempt to reinforce the arsenal would be an act of war. By the time his adjutant general (who was also his brother-in-law) reworded and released the statement, it appeared that the governor was encouraging a spontaneous action on the part of the people to seize the arsenal. By the end of January over a thousand "volunteers" from the Delta had arrived in the capital. In Pine Bluff a group of secessionists fired on the USS Tucker as it was heading up the Arkansas River in the mistaken belief that the ship was carrying federal reinforcements to Little Rock.

In the capital city, the governor tried to disavow any call to arms, but the hastily assembled volunteers were in no mood to listen. With the situation spiraling out of control, Rector took a gamble. On February 6 he called on the federal commander at the arsenal, Little Rock native James Totten, to peacefully surrender the post. Outnumbered and without any orders from

Washington, Totten agreed to the governor's demands. The federal troops evacuated the arsenal on February 8 and marched through a jeering crowd to Fletcher's Landing just downstream from the city, where they made camp and waited for a steamboat to take them out of the state.

On the surface, the bloodless seizure of the arsenal seemed to be a great triumph for the governor. In fact, however, the opposite was true. Far from being a hero, Rector was seriously damaged by the affair. Arkansas Unionists denounced him for precipitating a crisis where none existed, and even secessionists sensed that the governor had lost control of the situation.

On February 18, 1861, in Montgomery, Alabama, Jefferson Davis of Mississippi took the oath of office as president of the new Confederate States of America. That same day Arkansans went to the polls to vote on whether to hold a convention to consider secession. The results reflected the ambivalence most Arkansans felt about the issue of secession. An overwhelming majority of Arkansas voters favored the convention (27,412 to 15,826), but the majority of the delegates elected to attend the convention opposed secession. Clearly while Arkansans were willing to consider the possibility of secession, many were in no hurry to secede.

On March 4, 1861, Abraham Lincoln assumed the office of President of the United States. In his inaugural address, Lincoln expressed his belief that the union of states was perpetual, and he pledged to enforce the laws and hold federal property. At the same time, he insisted that he had no intention of interfering with slavery where it already existed.

That same day, the Arkansas convention assembled to take up the question of whether to secede. The make-up of the delegates, like the vote itself, reflected the clear geographic division in the state. Unionists from the northern and western portions of the state enjoyed a narrow majority of the seventy-seven delegates. In a key early vote to select the president of the convention, Unionist and former Whig David Walker of Fayetteville narrowly defeated a secessionist candidate by a vote of forty to thirty-five. It was indicative of the course the convention would take. While the Arkansas Unionists majority never exceeded five votes, it was enough to decide all the major questions.

The secessionist press thundered for disunion, secessionist delegates gave impassioned speeches, delegates from the seceded states of South Carolina and Georgia addressed the convention, Confederate president Jefferson Davis sent his own representative, and both Governor Rector and Senator Johnson made personal appeals. The ascension of Lincoln to the presidency, Johnson argued, would lead to "the extinction of four million dollars of southern property, and the freedom, and the equality with us of the four millions of negroes now in the South."

Still, the Unionist majority was unmoved. In two weeks of intense deliberation, the convention rebuffed every attempt to pass an ordinance of secession or even to allow a popular referendum on the issue. Finally, fearing that southern and eastern Arkansas might attempt to secede from the rest of the state or that Rector would attempt to bypass the assembly by taking the issue directly to the state legislature, the Unionists agreed to a referendum to be held on the first Monday of August in which Arkansans would vote either "for secession" or "for cooperation."

Arkansas secessionists pilloried the Unionist delegates, but the Crawford County town of Van Buren fired a thirty-nine-gun salute in honor of the thirty-nine delegates who had held firm against secession and the town's two returning delegates were greeted by a cheering crowd and a brass band. Both sides prepared for a four-month-long campaign leading up to the August referendum.

Despite the heated words and animosities that characterized the March convention, Unionists and secessionists were in agreement on several major issues. Both were committed to the protection of slavery, and both agreed that any attempt to coerce the seceded states back into the Union would be legitimate grounds for the state to secede. Such an action, the delegates had declared, would be "resisted by Arkansas to the last extremity." This was the Achilles' heel of the Unionist position and put them at the mercy of events over which they had no control. Events in South Carolina would soon alter the political balance in Arkansas and bring the state to a critical juncture.

Confederate authorities in South Carolina had demanded the surrender of Fort Sumter in Charleston harbor and made it clear that any attempt by the federal government to resupply the fort would be considered a hostile act. Lincoln had pledged in his inaugural address to "hold, occupy, and possess" federal property. On April 11, Confederate authorities in Charleston demanded the federal garrison's surrender. The demand was refused. At 4:30 on the following morning, April 12, 1861, Confederate gunners opened fire on Fort Sumter. The fort sustained a continual bombardment for thirty hours without the loss of a single life, but further resistance was clearly futile. The federal garrison surrendered the fort on April 14.

The following day, President Lincoln called for a force of 75,000 men to suppress the rebellion, including 780 men from Arkansas. Governor Rector's response came one week later. "In answer to your requisition for troops from Arkansas to subjugate the Southern States, I have to say that none will be furnished . . . The people of this state are freemen, not slaves, and will defend to the last extremity, their honor, lives and property against Northern mendacity and usurpation."

For secessionists, the attack on Fort Sumter and the president's response were political godsends, and even the cautious Unionists of March now felt compelled to move into the secessionists' camp. *Gazette* editor Christopher Danley, a longtime opponent of secession, noted, "Now that the overt act has been committed we should I think draw the sword, and not sheath it until we can have a guarantee of all of our rights, or such standards as will be honorable in the South."

Governor Rector wasted no time in seizing the initiative. Though Arkansas had not formally left the Union, he ordered former senator Solon Borland to take command of the state militia and seize the federal outpost at Fort Smith. A thousand men boarded three steamboats for the trip up the Arkansas River. Crowds cheered the men at every town and landing along the way. The militia reached Fort Smith on April 23 only to find that the federal garrison had withdrawn into the Indian Territory with all its equipment and supplies. The militia's return trip downriver to Little Rock was a triumphal procession as crowds again lined the riverbank to cheer the great "victory" over federal forces.

In late April, chairman David Walker reluctantly called for the state convention to reassemble at Little Rock on May 6 to once again consider the question of secession. Walker had been under extreme pressure since the attack on Sumter, and he was now convinced that Missouri and the other border states would soon secede. The convention assembled at ten in the morning before packed galleries. A motion was quickly made to prepare an ordinance of secession. The document was ready by three o'clock, and the delegates reassembled to vote. The outcome was a foregone conclusion. A last desperate attempt by a few die-hard Unionists to submit the question to the people was overwhelmingly defeated, and the roll call proceeded in the tense and hushed chamber.

In stark contrast to the vote of two months earlier, only five of the seventy delegates voted to remain in the Union. In response to the chairman's appeal for a unanimous vote, four of these added their names to the ordinance of secession. Only Isaac Murphy of Madison County refused to join the secessionists' bandwagon. "I have cast my vote after mature reflection and have considered the consequences," Murphy stated, "and I cannot conscientiously change it."

In the end, Murphy's principled stand made no difference. Shortly after four in the afternoon on May 6, 1861, Arkansas declared that it had severed its bonds with the Union that it had so eagerly joined only twenty-five years earlier. The state now faced the greatest crisis in its history.

8 "Between the Hawk & Buzzard"

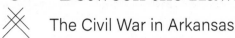

The Civil War in Arkansas

THE CIVIL WAR was the most divisive and destructive event in Arkansas history. The war exacerbated sectional and cultural divisions and engendered personal animosities that continued long after the fighting had ended. While slavery was the underlying cause of the conflict, Arkansans went to war for a variety of reason—to fight for what they saw as the "Southern way of life," to defend homes and families, to affirm their manhood, to seek excitement away from the often-dreary routine of farm or small-town life, or, in the case of black Arkansans, to fight for their freedom. Initially most went because they wanted to; because war was the great adventure for a young man in the nineteenth century. Most had never been in battle before, and many had never ventured more than a few miles from the place where they were born. They shared a romanticized view of war that would quickly be shattered by the boredom and disease of camp life and the horrors of the battlefield. What began with parades and stirring speeches in 1861 would end in injury and death for thousands of young Arkansas men and unimaginable hardships for those parents, sweethearts, wives, and children who remained at home.

A Call to Arms: The War in 1861

The Arkansas secession convention remained in session through June 3. Many old-line Whigs, who had composed the Unionist element before Sumter, joined with their former enemies, the Family Democrats, to ensure that radical secessionist elements did not take control of the convention. *Gazette* editor Danley had written to a friend, "I think the conservative men of the convention should take charge of the affairs of the state and prevent the wild secessionists from taking us to the Devil." The five-man Arkansas delegation to the Confederate Congress was headed by Family stalwart Robert Ward Johnson, but the other four men had been Unionists before Sumter. The convention pointedly rejected Hindman's attempt to join the Confederate congress. As James Woods has noted, "The Whig-Dynasty leaders simply did not want change to get out of hand, so they took control of the new government. Thus the revolution against the Union would not become a revolution at home."

A serious challenge to state unity arose in the mountainous regions in the north-central part of the state. By late 1861 some citizens from Searcy, Izard, Carroll, Fulton, Marion, and Van Buren counties formed what may have been the first organized resistance group in the Confederacy. The Arkansas Peace Society was a clandestine organization whose members pledged to resist the war effort. Local citizens or Confederate authorities quickly rounded up many members of the society. Seventy-eight were chained together in pairs and marched under guard to Little Rock where they were given the choice of enlisting in the Confederate army for the duration of the war or being tried for treason. Most chose the former, but opposition to Confederate authority continued in the region throughout the war. Other Arkansans chose to openly oppose the Confederacy by enlisting in the Union army at the first opportunity. Despite having the third smallest white population of any Confederate state, Arkansas provided more troops for the Federal army than any other Confederate state except Tennessee.

Arkansas Peace Society: The Arkansas Peace Society was a clandestine organization in north-central Arkansas whose members were opposed to the Confederate government and the war. Many members of the group were arrested and given the choice of serving in the Confederate army or being tried for treason. Most chose the former but later deserted and fought for the Union.

Outside of the northern and western regions of the state, however, many Arkansans greeted secession with a burst of enthusiasm. A Little Rock volunteer artillery company fired a salute from the statehouse grounds, and thousands of young men from around the state rushed to enlist. Many came as a unit from local communities, armed only with old flintlocks, squirrel guns, or shotguns, and with a prominent local citizen in command. Their unit names were designed to reflect their hometowns or home counties as well as their courage and enthusiasm—the Camden Knights, Hempstead Hornets, Polk County Invincibles, Chicot Rebels.

Historian James Willis has written that no other state had a larger proportion of military age men fight for the Confederacy than Arkansas. Helena, whose 1860 white population numbered slightly over a thousand, contributed six generals to the Confederate cause including Patrick Cleburne, generally considered to be one of the best divisional commanders in the Confederate service. Before the conflict ended, Arkansas soldiers would take part in most of the war's major engagements including the battles of Shiloh, Vicksburg, Gettysburg, Chickamauga, Atlanta, and Franklin.

Many of the new enlistees thought that the war would be glorious, brief, and victorious. Adoring crowds cheered the young warriors as they marched, and local leaders made stirring orations. Unfortunately, cheering crowds and stirring orations could not hide the Arkansans' lack of experience or knowledge of the military arts. An officer sent to the state to evaluate military preparedness and training reported to the Confederate secretary of war, "Arkansas has less the appearance of a military organization than any people I ever yet knew." The enthusiasm of enlistment soon gave way to the boredom of camp life and drill, and something more sinister. As the young men from isolated communities gathered in large numbers, disease ravaged their ranks. Hundreds died of measles, mumps, typhoid fever, pneumonia, or diarrhea long before they ever had a chance to fire a shot in anger.

Strategically, Arkansas was critical to the Confederate war effort in the Trans-Mississippi, especially as a base of operations in any attempt to claim the critical slave state of Missouri for the Confederacy. But that fact seemed to be lost on the Confederate high command in Richmond, which viewed Arkansas primarily as a source of men and material for fighting east of the Mississippi. Arkansas's security, in turn, depended in part on the cooperation of the various tribes in the Indian Territory, particularly the so-called Five Civilized Tribes (Cherokees, Choctaws, Chickasaws, Creeks, and Seminoles). In May 1861, the Confederate government sent Albert Pike as special agent to secure an alliance with these tribes.

Trans-Mississippi Theater: The area of Civil War operations west of the Mississippi River.

Five Civilized Tribes: Name given by whites to the Cherokees, Choctaws, Chickasaws, Creeks, and Seminoles. Their cooperation with the Confederacy was considered critical to the defense of the Indian Territory.

By August 1, 1861, Pike had concluded treaties with the Choctaws, Chickasaws, Creeks, and Seminoles that cemented an alliance between the tribes and the Confederacy, provided for the raising of Indian troops for Confederate service, and guaranteed that all money due them under laws and treaties with the United States would be paid by the Confederate government. The treaties also specified that Indian troops would not be asked to serve outside the Indian Territory without their consent.

The only group that Pike had failed to win over also happened to be the most powerful of the five tribes—the Cherokees. Tribal politics made such negotiations difficult. In December 1835, a small group who advocated removal west of the Mississippi had signed the Treaty of Echota with the federal government, surrendering claims to tribal land in the southeast. The majority of the tribe opposed removal, and the action created a serious division between them and the members of the so-called Treaty Party. Over ten years of bitterness and violence followed, but in 1846 the two factions had signed a treaty that recognized one government for the Cherokee Nation, with John Ross, the leading opponent of removal, as the tribe's principal chief.

Ross clung to a policy of neutrality, steadfastly resisting Pike's offers of an alliance with the Confederacy. But another group of Cherokees led by Stand Watie, a member of the Treaty Party, signed on to fight for the Confederacy.

In addition to Watie's Cherokees, by the fall of 1861 the Confederacy had a force of fourteen hundred mounted Indian warriors from the Choctaw, Chickasaw, Creek, and Seminole tribes in the field, supported by five hundred white soldiers.

As summer drifted into fall, the pressure on Ross grew. He and his Cherokee followers were increasingly isolated in the Indian Territory, surrounded by Indian soldiers from the other tribes who had sworn allegiance to the Confederacy. Events in Missouri would soon help convince him to change his mind.

Confederate forces in the Indian Territory were commanded by Brig. Gen. Ben McCulloch, a former Texas Ranger. McCulloch assembled a fighting force composed of Texas, Louisiana, and Arkansas troops. His orders were to remain on Confederate soil and adopt a defensive stance. But in August 1861 McCulloch decided to move his command into southwest Missouri to join a force of Missouri Confederates under the command of former Missouri governor Sterling Price. Price was being fiercely pursued by a Federal army under the command of Brig. Gen. Nathaniel Lyon. When McCulloch's reinforcements swelled Price's army to almost eleven thousand men, he turned to meet his pursuer.

The two armies met at Wilson's Creek, twelve miles below Springfield, on the morning of August 10. The resulting battle was one of the bloodiest small battles of the war. Federal forces suffered over twelve hundred casualties; the aggressive General Lyon, one of the early Union heroes of the war, was killed; and the Federals were forced to retreat back toward their supply base at Rolla, Missouri. The battle had also been costly for the Confederates. Of the eleven thousand Rebels engaged, twelve hundred were killed, wounded, or missing.

The victory at Wilson's Creek, combined with the news of the Rebel victory at Manassas, Virginia, in July and continued pressure from within the Indian Territory, persuaded Cherokee principal chief John Ross to enter into a treaty of alliance with the Confederacy. Despite the treaties, however, the allegiance of the members of the Five Civilized Tribes would remain divided throughout the war. Eventually over twelve thousand Native Americans would serve in the Confederate army, while another six thousand would fight with Federal forces.

The victorious Confederate commanders at Wilson's Creek had developed an intense dislike for one another, and to Price's consternation, McCulloch withdrew his command into northwest Arkansas after the battle. For many of the two thousand Arkansas soldiers involved, Wilson's Creek ended forever the notion of war as a romantic endeavor. When they returned to northwest Arkansas, whole companies disbanded and went home.

Confederate authorities in Richmond, Virginia, soon reached the conclusion that relations between McCulloch and Price had deteriorated to the point where neither could effectively serve under the other. They sent Earl Van Dorn, a Mississippian and a longtime friend of Jefferson Davis, to take command over both in what was to be styled the Military District of the Trans-Mississippi. Van Dorn had West Point credentials, but he was reckless, and he lacked a real understanding of the situation in the Trans-Mississippi. He established his headquarters at Pocahontas in northeast Arkansas because he intended to launch an invasion of southeast Missouri in the spring of 1862. Events in northwest Arkansas soon forced Van Dorn to alter his plans.

From Pea Ridge to Prairie Grove: The War in 1862

Following his victory at Wilson's Creek, Price went on the offensive in Missouri, but more than half of his army soon left him either to return home to harvest their crops or to act as bushwhackers. The popular uprising he had hoped for never materialized, and, short of men and supplies, Price began a retreat back toward the southwest corner of the state, with twelve thousand Federal troops under Brig. Gen. Samuel Curtis hot on his trail. Curtis was a fifty-six-year-old West Point graduate and Mexican War veteran who had worked as a civil engineer and railroad promoter in civilian life. He had helped found the Republican Party in Iowa and in 1856 was elected to Congress where he was a strong supporter of Abraham Lincoln and a staunch opponent of slavery and secession. His limited experience notwithstanding, he would become the most successful Union field commander west of the Mississippi River.

Despite freezing winter weather, Curtis relentlessly pursued the retreating Rebels, and advance elements of his army skirmished repeatedly with Price's rearguard. On February 17, the Union army invaded Arkansas, its band blaring patriotic music. It was barely nine months since the vote for secession. The Confederates fell back before the Federals' advance, ransacking and burning much of Fayetteville before finally halting in the Boston Mountains. Curtis, his supply lines dangerously extended, halted his pursuit and dispersed his forces into two large camps—one just west of Bentonville and the other at Cross Hollow (between the present-day towns of Springdale and Rogers).

Meanwhile, Earl Van Dorn hastened to the Boston Mountains to take personal command of Confederate forces, reaching there on March 2. He wanted to regain the initiative as soon as possible and quickly planned a surprise attack on Curtis. He sent a message to Albert Pike in the Indian Territory ordering him to move with his Indian troops to a rendezvous point at Bentonville, and on March 4 Van Dorn's army, some sixteen thousand strong and supported by sixty-five cannon, moved out of the

Boston Mountains and headed north. It was, historian William Shea notes, "the largest and best-equipped Confederate military force ever assembled in the Trans-Mississippi," enjoying a numerical advantage over Union forces in both men and guns. Van Dorn hoped to interpose himself between Curtis's divided forces and defeat them in detail. If he could score a decisive victory, the road to Missouri would be wide open. But by the time his troops arrived at Bentonville on March 6, Curtis had been alerted to the Rebel advance and had concentrated his army in a strong defensive position on high ground overlooking Little Sugar Creek.

Van Dorn now faced a dilemma. The three-day march in freezing weather had exhausted his army, and a straight frontal assault against such a strongly defended position would be suicidal. But a retreat would cost him the initiative and render his proposed invasion of Missouri untenable. He decided on a bold plan. He would send his army on a night march around the Federals' right flank and behind a rocky hill called Big Mountain to reappear along the Telegraph Road in the Federal rear. Curtis would be cut off from his lines of supply and his strong position rendered useless. On paper the plan was a good one, but the harsh winter weather and the deplorable condition of his men squandered much of the tactical advantage that Van Dorn had sought. Hundreds of exhausted, hungry soldiers fell by the wayside during the night. By morning on March 7, Price's division had reached the Telegraph Road, but much of McCulloch's command was strung out all the way back to Little Sugar Creek, its progress slowed by barricades of trees that Curtis's troops had felled across the roadway.

Fearful that the remainder of his command would not reach Telegraph Road in time, Van Dorn ordered McCulloch's division to take a shortcut around the front of Big Mountain. The two elements would unite around noon at a stagecoach stop named Elkhorn Tavern along a broad plateau called Pea Ridge. Unfortunately for the Rebels, Federal patrols detected the Confederate movement. Curtis launched separate attacks on the two converging wings of the Confederate force, one on each side of Big Mountain. Meanwhile, he began the Herculean task of turning his army 180 degrees to face the threat from the rear.

Sharp engagements soon broke out along both ends of Big Mountain. To the southwest, McCulloch's men had the better of the early fighting, as his cavalry quickly overran the small force that Curtis had sent against him. Pike's Cherokees drove off two isolated companies of Federal cavalry, and a few of the Indians killed, scalped, and mutilated some of the Union soldiers before being driven off by Federal artillery. Though he was not responsible for the atrocities by his Indian troops, Pike received the blame, and the incident left a blemish on his reputation for the remainder of his life.

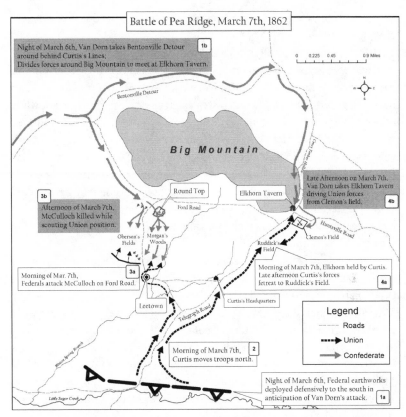

Inside the map:

Battle of Pea Ridge, March 7th, 1862

1b Night of March 6th, Van Dorn takes Bentonville Detour around behind Curtis's Lines; Divides forces around Big Mountain to meet at Elkhorn Tavern.

Bentonville Detour

0 0.225 0.45   0.9 Miles

Big Mountain

Round Top

Ford Road

Elkhorn Tavern

4b Late Afternoon on March 7th, Van Dorn takes Elkhorn Tavern driving Union forces from Clemon's field.

3b Afternoon of March 7th, McCulloch killed while scouting Union position.

Oberson's Fields   Morgan's Woods

Huntsville Road

Clemon's Field

Ruddick's Field

3a Morning of Mar. 7th, Federals attack McCulloch on Ford Road.

4a Morning of March 7th, Elkhorn held by Curtis. Late afternoon Curtis's forces retreat to Ruddick's Field.

Leetown

Curtis's Headquarters

Telegraph Road

Legend
- - - - Roads
▪▪▪▪► Union
➤ Confederate

2 Morning of March 7th, Curtis moves troops north.

1a Night of March 6th, Federal earthworks deployed defensively to the south in anticipation of Van Dorn's attack.

Little Sugar Creek

Battle of Pea Ridge, the first day, March 7, 1862. *Courtesy of Joseph Swain.* (Sources: Pea Ridge National Military Park, Arkansas Geographic Information Office.)

Despite their early success, events soon took a disastrous turn for the Rebels. The disaster began when McCulloch was killed by a volley fired by a company of Federal infantry as he rode forward to survey the field during a brief lull in the fighting. Before the day was over, a second Confederate general was killed and a third captured. The leaderless Rebels drifted away from the battlefield. To the southeast of Big Mountain, Van Dorn and Price pressed the outnumbered Federals hard but were driven back by artillery and the fierce determination of Curtis's soldiers. During the night of March 7–8, both sides consolidated their forces. A portion of McCulloch's command joined Price and Van Dorn near Elkhorn Tavern, while to the south, Curtis gathered his forces along Telegraph Road. On the morning of March 8, Curtis waited for Van Dorn to renew his attack of the previous evening. But it soon became obvious that the Rebels were not coming. Van Dorn was dangerously low on ammunition, and his supply train was still at Little Sugar Creek over ten miles away.

Curtis now seized the initiative. For two hours he pounded the Rebel lines with twenty-seven cannon. Then at ten o'clock he sent ten thousand troops toward Elkhorn Tavern. Van Dorn realized that he could not hold and ordered a general retreat. He led the retreat himself, fleeing to the east while large numbers of his soldiers were still engaged and most of his wounded still lay on the field. The victorious Federals converged on Elkhorn Tavern where their commander saluted them, waving his hat and shouting "Victory! Victory!" Van Dorn had frittered away his splendid opportunity and suffered at least two thousand casualties in the process. Union losses numbered almost fourteen hundred killed, wounded, and missing. In the days following the battle, hundreds of starving Confederate soldiers drifted away from the army and went home.

The Battle of Pea Ridge was one of the most significant battles in the entire Civil War, and it marked a dramatic turning point in the war in Arkansas. Missouri remained securely in Union hands, and the Confederacy in Arkansas suffered a defeat from which it would never fully recover. For Arkansas Confederates, the aftermath of the battle was even more disastrous than the battle itself. Van Dorn transferred the remainder of his army across the Mississippi River to Corinth, Mississippi, taking not only the bulk of able-bodied soldiers, but also animals, equipment, arms, and ammunition. His actions left Arkansas virtually defenseless, and Union forces soon took advantage of the situation.

Curtis had fallen back to Missouri until it was clear that Van Dorn's destination was Mississippi and not Missouri. On April 29, he reentered Arkansas near Salem, reaching Batesville on May 2. On May 4, a separate Federal force occupied Jacksonport about twenty-five miles to the southeast. The two Federal forces combined and began to move toward Little Rock, one hundred miles to the south. An alarmed and outraged Governor Rector packed up the state archives and fled to Hot Springs. From there he fired off an angry letter to President Davis, pleading for immediate assistance and threatening to secede from the Confederacy if help was not forthcoming.

Unbeknown to Rector and other Arkansas Confederates, however, the steam was quickly going out of the Federal offensive. Curtis had been ordered to send ten regiments east of the Mississippi to join Federal forces in southern Tennessee, reducing his infantry force by half, and his supply line back to his base at Rolla, Missouri, was stretched dangerously thin. Though Curtis could not know it, Texas cavalry units were arriving in the Little Rock area. The Texans were on their way to duty east of the Mississippi, but they were

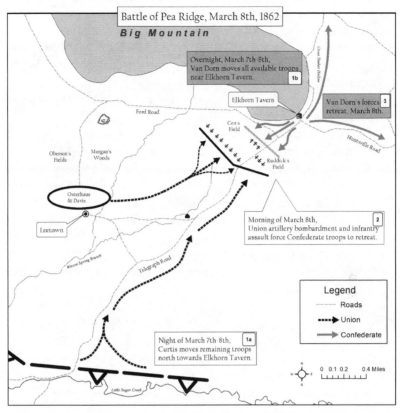

Battle of Pea Ridge, March 8, 1863. *Courtesy of Joseph Swain.* (Sources: Pea Ridge National Military Park, Arkansas Geographic Information Office.)

quickly commandeered by Confederate authorities and sent north to oppose the Federal advance.

By mid-May, Rebel units were attacking Federal foraging parties. The Federal commander realized that his situation was deteriorating and decided to abandon his plans to seize Little Rock. Instead, he marched his army down the north bank of the White River to meet a relief flotilla that had been dispatched from Memphis via the Mississippi, the Arkansas, and the White rivers to meet him. When Curtis failed to make contact with the supply ships at Clarendon, he turned his army eastward toward the Mississippi River town of Helena.

As the Federal army moved, it altered the nature of the war in Arkansas, transforming it from a contest of army against army into a "total war" designed to destroy anything that might be of use to the Rebels and to weaken civilian morale. Completely cut off from its base of supply, the army was totally dependent on forage and provisions from the surrounding countryside. Federal soldiers plundered barns and private residences, seizing livestock, food, and anything else they needed or wanted. They burned public buildings and private homes, bringing the horrors of war home to the civilian population. "I am roaming the wilds of Arkansas, and desolating the country as we pass," one Yankee soldier wrote.

The Union army's march transformed the war in another way as well. As the blue-clad soldiers moved through the Delta, slaves fled from nearby plantations to follow them. The Emancipation Proclamation was still months away, but black Arkansans along the line of march were not inclined to wait for an official proclamation. The Union army was their ticket to freedom, and thousands rushed to embrace it. Unlike most Federal commanders in other theaters, Curtis made no effort to return them to their masters.

Total war: Strategy of warfare that was designed to consume or destroy anything that might be of use to the enemy and to weaken civilian morale by bringing the war home to noncombatants as well as the enemy army.

His midwestern soldiers felt that they were fighting to preserve the Union rather than to end slavery, and some, if not most, had been sympathetic to slavery when the war began. For many, however, their first face-to-face encounter with the institution changed their thinking. An Illinois officer wrote home, "Now I have witnessed the unnaturalness of slavery with my own eyes and with disgust." Another noted, "I am not yet quite an Abolitionist, but am fast becoming one."

With the Federal threat to the capital at least temporarily removed, the governor returned to Little Rock in late May. Meanwhile, in an attempt to bolster its sagging fortunes in Arkansas, Confederate authorities sent Thomas Hindman back to the state as commander of the Military District of the Trans-Mississippi. Early in May Hindman had been promoted to major general, completing a meteoric rise from the rank of colonel in less than a year. His courage, organizational ability, and zeal were unquestioned, but all the talents he possessed would be tested in his new command. "I found here almost nothing," Hindman remarked on reaching Little Rock at the end of May. "Nearly everything of value was taken away by General Van Dorn."

What he lacked in men and material, however, Hindman made up in fanatical devotion to the cause. In the weeks that followed his appointment, Hindman assumed dictatorial powers, declaring martial law and strictly enforcing the conscription act. In an attempt to slow the advance of the Federal army, he ordered Arkansans along the Yankees' line of march to burn their cotton and other crops, drive off their livestock, and poison their wells. In addition, he authorized the use of so-called partisan rangers, bands of guerrillas whose purpose was ostensibly to stage hit-and-run raids on detached Federal units and harass its lines of supply.

Hindman's order gave legal sanction to a brutal and merciless guerrilla conflict that historian Daniel Sutherland has called "the real war" in Arkansas. Some of the "partisan rangers" were legitimate guerrilla fighters, strongly dedicated to defending the state against the Northern invaders. Their actions seriously disrupted Federal operations in Arkansas, tied down large numbers of enemy troops, and compelled Union forces to employ harsh countermeasures. But many of the "partisans" were little more than armed bandits whose only causes were self-aggrandizement and the settling of personal grudges. They preyed not only on the Yankees but also on civilians of all political persuasions and contributed greatly to the breakdown of law and order in the state.

Guerrilla warfare: A type of irregular warfare in which small bands of combatants confront a larger force by using greater mobility and employing tactics such as ambushes and hit-and-run raids.

Hindman's tactics failed to halt the progress of Curtis's army, but they did help keep Little Rock out of Federal hands for another year. The Federal army entered Helena without opposition on July 12, followed by thousands of former slaves (known to the Union soldiers as "contraband"), and the river town quickly became a Union supply base and a port for the Federal riverine fleet.

In his brief stint as overall commander of the Trans-Mississippi, Hindman's draconian actions had three major effects—they created a viable fighting force almost out of thin air; they prevented, at least for the time being, the capture of the capital; and they earned Hindman an enmity from many of his fellow Arkansans that they had previously reserved only for the Yankees. Camden's John Brown condemned Hindman's "tyrannical acts of military power" and "military despotism," and Albert Pike railed against Hindman's "substitution of despotism" for constitutional government. So great was the outcry against Hindman that Confederate president Jefferson Davis was forced to demote him and reorganize the department.

Contraband: Name given to former slaves who left their plantations and farms to follow the Union army to freedom as it marched through their region.

The political situation was about to change as well. After taking Arkansas out of the Union, the secession convention had rewritten the state's constitution, including a provision reducing the governor's term from four years to two. Governor Rector realized that this action was little more than an attempt by his enemies in the Family to punish him. After attempting unsuccessfully to have the state supreme court set aside the provision, Rector announced as a candidate for reelection.

His chief opposition was Harris Flanagin, an attorney and a former Whig from Clark County. Flanagin had been a delegate to the March and

Thomas Carmichael Hindman, Arkansas politician and military leader. *Walter J. Lemke Paper, Series 3, Box 3. Number 483. Special Collections Division, University of Arkansas Libraries, Fayetteville.*

May state secession conventions and had voted in favor of secession at both. After the ordinance of secession was passed, he left the convention to accept command of Company E of the Second Arkansas Mounted Rifles. In the reorganization that followed Pea Ridge, Flanagin was elected regimental colonel, and the Second Arkansas was transferred east of the Mississippi River where it became part of the Army of Tennessee. His candidacy for governor was backed by an unlikely coalition of prewar enemies including Thomas Hindman and the Family's Elias Conway.

Since Flanagin was serving in the army outside the state, it was impossible for him to campaign, and historians still debate whether or not he even wanted the position. But it also made it difficult for Governor Rector to attack him. In the October election, Flanagin received 18,187 votes to Rector's 7,419 and was inaugurated as Arkansas's seventh governor on November 14, 1862.

Though he tried to address some of the serious issues confronting the state, the absence of money precluded any significant action. Most of the major decisions in the state would devolve on the military authorities. Unfortunately for Arkansas, the military leaders sent to the state by the Richmond government were unequal to the task.

In the summer of 1862 Confederate president Davis sent his old friend Maj. Gen. Theophilus Holmes to take command in Arkansas. Holmes was a fifty-eight-year-old North Carolinian and West Point graduate who had compiled a distinguished record in the Mexican War. His Civil War service, however, was marred by controversy and failure. He had been so ineffective in the eastern theater that he was relieved of command, and he had requested to be dismissed from the service. But instead Davis put him in charge of one of the most difficult theaters of the war. Holmes lacked the manpower, animals, and supplies to effectively operate in such a far-reaching theater; Richmond was constantly requesting that he send additional troops east of the river to assist in the defense of Vicksburg; and, to compound his problems, he was now in charge of Hindman.

Perhaps nowhere in the entire war did two such disparate personalities attempt to forge a working relationship. Hindman was belligerent, impulsive, and decisive, and he believed that the best way to defend Arkansas was to take the war to the enemy. Holmes was timid, indecisive, and so plagued by poor health and premature old age that his troops soon gave him the unflattering nickname of "Granny." Remarkably, despite their differences and the adverse conditions, they soon had another viable fighting force in the field.

In late 1862, Holmes placed roughly half his troops at various locations along the Arkansas and the White rivers to counter any Federal invasion coming from Helena or elsewhere along the Mississippi River. The remainder he placed in northwest Arkansas to deter any Federal invasion coming out of southwest Missouri. These latter troops were under Hindman's personal direction, and the fiery commander wasted little time in lobbying his new superior officer for permission to use them against the Federals.

In October 1862, three divisions of Federal troops invaded northwest Arkansas and briefly occupied Fayetteville and Bentonville. In early November, two of the three divisions returned to Springfield leaving only one division under Brig. Gen. James Blunt in northwest Arkansas. The aptly named Blunt was an aggressive, no-nonsense amateur soldier from Kansas whose zeal for the offensive matched that of Hindman. That very aggressiveness had left him deep in northwest Arkansas and dangerously isolated from the remainder of his army.

By early December, Blunt was at Cane Hill, nearly one hundred miles from Springfield but only about thirty miles from Hindman. The opportunity was too great for the aggressive Hindman to pass up. He believed that if he moved quickly and with stealth, he could overwhelm Blunt's smaller force before Federal reinforcements could arrive from Springfield. The road to Missouri would then be open to him. The ever-cautious Holmes initially rejected the plan but relented when Hindman assured him that he would return to Fort Smith as soon as the operation was concluded.

Hindman sent a small cavalry detachment across the Boston Mountains as a diversion and on December 3 the main body of eleven thousand men and twenty-two cannon moved out and proceeded slowly northward. Hindman hoped to swing undetected around Blunt's left flank and strike him from the east. His army was composed largely of raw recruits and reluctant conscripts and was short of ammunition and rations, but it was still a potent force. The fact that there was any army at all was a tribute to Hindman's brilliance as an organizer, recruiter, and administrator. In these areas, he had few peers on either side anywhere in the war.

Blunt was aware of his own vulnerable position, but retreat was not in his nature. Rather than fall back to the safety of Missouri, he took a strong defensive position at Cane Hill, and, on December 2, he telegraphed the two divisions at Springfield to march immediately to join him. On December 6, Hindman successfully slipped undetected to the east of Cane Hill only to learn that night that more Federal troops were moving toward him down the Telegraph Road from Springfield. The command of these two Federal divisions had passed to Francis J. Herron, who earlier had been wounded and captured while making a courageous stand against Rebel infantry at Pea Ridge (an action for which he won the Medal of Honor). In a truly incredible feat, about half of Herron's seven thousand troops covered the 110 miles from Springfield to Fayetteville in only three days, arriving on December 6 and clashing with advance elements of Hindman's cavalry.

Hindman realized that he was in a dangerous position, caught between two Federal forces whose combined strength roughly equaled his own. If he attacked Blunt as he had planned, he exposed his rear to an attack from Herron. If he turned and attacked Herron, he suffered the same danger from Blunt. After weighing his options, he moved to high ground beyond the Illinois River about ten miles west of Fayetteville, established a defensive position near the Prairie Grove Presbyterian Church, and waited for the Yankees to make the next move. He did not have to wait long.

Herron had less than half as many men as Hindman, and his troops were exhausted from their long march. Still he did not hesitate. The Federal soldiers crossed the Illinois River on the morning of December 7 and opened an artillery barrage on the Confederate position with twenty-four rifled cannon. Around noon, Herron ordered a portion of his troops to assault the Confederate right, where his artillery had done its greatest damage and where it appeared the Rebels were retreating. The blue-clad soldiers charged forward and crested the hill but were met by a withering barrage of Rebel rifle fire that decimated their ranks and sent the survivors scurrying back down the slope. A Confederate counterattack was driven back by Federal artillery.

The stalemate continued until the early afternoon when Hindman decided to take advantage of his numerical superiority and longer lines to sweep down the hill and envelop the Federal right. A decisive Confederate victory loomed when Blunt, alerted by the rumble of artillery, arrived from Cane Hill. His arrival extended the Federal line, equalized the odds, and continued the stalemate. Despite intense fighting that lasted until dark, neither side could dislodge the other or gain any significant advantage. Because they still held their position atop the hill when the fighting ended, the Battle of Prairie Grove was a tactical victory for the Confederates. But during the night of December 7–8, Hindman, his ammunition depleted, withdrew his hungry and exhausted soldiers from the field and began a long, slow retreat to Van Buren, and then on down the Arkansas River to Little Rock. A Federal officer later recalled, "For forces engaged, there was no more stubborn fight and no greater casualties in any battle of the war than at Prairie Grove, Arkansas." Each side suffered over 1,250 casualties, and Confederate losses were compounded by widespread desertions.

The sights and smells of the battlefield etched themselves indelibly in the minds of all who fought there. Wounded men, too weak to reach the safety of their own lines, crawled into bales of hay for warmth. When the firing ignited the bales, many were too weak to crawl out and burned to death. The day after the battle, hogs from area farms feasted on the carcasses of dead soldiers. Wounded Confederate soldiers were taken to Cane Hill, wounded Federals to Fayetteville. A prominent Fayetteville citizen, William Baxter, visited one of the town's makeshift hospitals where, he reported,

> the entire floor was so thickly covered with mangled and bleeding men that it was difficult to thread my way among them; some were mortally wounded, the life fast escaping through a ghastly hole in the breast; the limbs of others were shattered and useless, the faces of others so disfigured as to seem scarcely human; the bloody bandages, hair clotted, and garments stained with blood, and all these with but little covering, and no other couch than the straw, with which the floor was strewed, made up a scene more pitiable and horrible than I had ever conceived possible before.

Baxter noted that twenty other buildings offered similar scenes.

The Federal invasion also disrupted the day-to-day operations of government and society. William Shea has noted, "Dozens of county and local governments ceased to function as judges, sheriffs, clerks, and other officeholders fled or failed to carry out their duties. Taxes went uncollected, lawsuits went unheard, and complaints went unanswered. With courts closed and jails open, the thin veneer of civilization quickly eroded. Incidents of murder, torture, rape, theft, and wanton destruction increased dramatically."

Poor harvests in both 1861 and 1862 further exacerbated the hardships for those who remained at home. For the next two and a half years, the citizens of the state who lived north of the Arkansas River would experience the horrors of civil war to an extent matched by few other Americans. For many the struggle to preserve slavery and the Southern way of life would quickly be overshadowed by a struggle merely to survive.

The Union Triumphant: The War in 1863

As the year 1863 began, the nature of the conflict was dramatically altered. Shortly after the Battle of Antietam (Maryland) in September 1862, President Lincoln issued his preliminary Emancipation Proclamation, which declared that slaves in those states still in rebellion on January 1, 1863, would be "then, thenceforward, and forever free." Neither Arkansas nor any other Confederate state took advantage of the president's three-month window to give up the rebellion and thus maintain the institution of slavery, but the proclamation transformed the Civil War into a crusade to end slavery as well as to preserve the Union, and it severely dimmed the prospect of European intervention on the side of the Confederacy.

In Arkansas the enthusiasm that had greeted the outbreak of the war, had, by the war's second winter, given way to a widespread disenchantment. Holmes had taken note of this, writing in a December 1862 letter to Confederate president Jefferson Davis of "the growing disaffection to the war among the people." By late 1862 and 1863 the disaffection was strongest in southwest Arkansas, especially in the region south and west of the Saline River. Holmes attributed this disaffection to a variety of factors including a food shortage brought on by a drought the previous summer, spiraling inflation, the failure to pay or adequately provision the soldiers, and discontent with the Confederacy's conscription laws, particularly the provision that exempted one white man on each plantation for every twenty slaves. He informed the president that he could not control the situation without imposing martial law. In late January 1863, President Davis agreed to suspend the writ of *habeas corpus*, and Holmes declared martial law on February 9. He further authorized the raising of local partisan ranger units to round up deserters and enforce the conscription laws and sent some regular army units to assist in the task.

This internal dissent ate away at the state's morale and caused Confederate authorities to detach badly needed troops to deal with the situation. In the meantime, the military situation in the state was deteriorating. In January, Camden resident John Brown noted in his diary, "The enemy destroying with fire and sword as they go in the vicinity of the Mis[sissippi] river & the people moving their negroes & stock as fast as possible." He closed his entry by remarking sarcastically, "What a beautiful thing this *peaceable* secession is!!"

In January 1863, Richmond appointed Edmund Kirby Smith to replace the much-maligned Theophilus Holmes as commander of the Department of the Trans-Mississippi but left Holmes in charge of Arkansas. For all his shortcomings (and they were many), Holmes understood the importance of defending the river approach up the Arkansas to Little Rock. In late 1862, he ordered the construction of an earthen fort approximately 120 miles downriver from the capital at the small village of Arkansas Post.

The site selected for the Confederate fort was on high ground at the head of a horseshoe bend with a commanding view of the river for over a mile in either direction. Fort Hindman, as it was known, was diamond shaped, three hundred feet on each side, and armed with three heavy and eight smaller cannon. A line of rifle pits extended westward from the fort for about a mile to a stream called Post Bayou. The garrison of approximately five thousand troops from Texas, Arkansas, and Louisiana was commanded by Brig. Gen. Thomas Churchill, a Kentuckian and Mexican War veteran, whose marriage to Ambrose Sevier's daughter, Anne, had assured him a place in the state's political elite.

Churchill determined to use the Post both to protect the river approaches to Little Rock and to serve as a base of operations for harassing Union communication and supply lines on the Mississippi River. In late December, Confederate forces operating out of the Post captured an unarmed Union supply ship on the Mississippi eight miles below Napoleon and towed it back to Fort Hindman. This Rebel triumph attracted the attention of Union forces downriver near Vicksburg. Unable to crack the defenses of that "Confederate Gibraltar," Union commanders decided to deal with the threat posed by the Post.

On January 8, 1863, Union major general John McClernand loaded thirty-two thousand infantry, one thousand cavalry, and forty pieces of artillery on board sixty transports and started upriver from Vicksburg, escorted by a small flotilla of rams and gunboats under the command of Adm. David D. Porter. At 5 p.m. on January 9, the Federal troops began disembarking at Nortrebe's farm about three miles below Fort Hindman. Late the following day, McClernand sent the gunboats upriver to engage the fort's guns, while he began moving his troops to a plateau north of the fort. After a fierce exchange, the gunboats succeeded in silencing most of the fort's artillery. Union troops continued moving into position during the frigid night of January 10–11.

That same night Churchill received a telegraphic dispatch from Holmes in Little Rock ordering him to "hold out till help arrived or all dead." Against such odds and with the possibility of help remote, such an order was absurd. Nonetheless, Churchill determined to do all he could to see the order carried out or at least to hold out until nightfall when his command might cut its way through the Union lines to safety.

At 1 p.m. on January 11, the Federal gunboats once again moved upriver, pounding the fort from close range and lobbing explosive shells over the walls. Shortly after the bombardment commenced, soldiers on the far right of the Union line under the command of William Tecumseh Sherman moved forward to attack the Rebel rifle pits. Soon the whole Union line was in motion. Heavy small arms fire from the entrenched defenders staggered and halted the advancing blue line, but by 3 p.m., Federal troops on the Union right had reached to within one hundred yards of the rifle pits, while those on the left had reached the ditch that surrounded the fort.

As Federal troops prepared for a final assault, white flags of surrender appeared along part of the Confederate line. This astonished and outraged Churchill, who had not given the order to surrender, but Union troops quickly crowded into the area where the white flags had appeared, making any further resistance futile. Reluctantly, Churchill ordered the remainder of his command to lay down their arms. He had suffered sixty killed and seventy-five to eighty wounded. His remaining 4,793 men were taken prisoner. In addition, the Confederates lost vast quantities of sorely needed arms, ammunition, and supplies. The victory had not come cheaply for the Northern army. Over a thousand men were killed, wounded, or missing. McClernand ordered the destruction of Fort Hindman and steamed with his command back to Milliken's Bend near Vicksburg.

Despite the fact that their ability to defend the state was increasingly being called into question, some Confederate commanders in Arkansas continued to think in terms of the offensive and continued to view the conquest of Missouri as their main goal. On April 16, 1863, Brig. Gen. William Cabell, a thirty-six-year-old Virginian and West Point graduate, led nine hundred Confederate cavalry north from Ozark to attack the Federal garrison occupying Fayetteville.

Two days later Cabell's cavalry charged "with wild and deafening shouts" up Dickson Street toward the Federal commander's headquarters. For four hours an intense firefight raged around the headquarters house. Around 9 a.m. the Rebels launched a desperate charge against the Union right only to run into "a galling crossfire . . . piling rebel men and horses in heaps" in front of the Federals' ordnance office on College Avenue. Unable to advance any farther, the Confederates slowly withdrew, leaving approximately seventy-five men killed, wounded, or missing.

Two days after the battle, the Federal commander received orders to move his troops to Springfield, Missouri, and, shortly thereafter, Cabell's command returned to occupy peacefully the town they had failed to take by storm. The town changed hands several times during the course of the war, and perhaps no community in the state suffered more from the ravages of war. William Baxter noted how the war had disrupted the normal patterns of life. "Schools and institutions of learning all broken up, churches abandoned, the Sabbath unnoted, every thing around, indeed, denoting a rapid lapse into barbarism, all trade at an end, nearly all travel suspended, the comforts of life nearly all gone, the absolute necessities difficult to be obtained."

At the same time that Cabell was leaving to attack Fayetteville, another Confederate commander was preparing to embark on a more ambitious raid. John Sappington Marmaduke, the twenty-nine-year-old son of a politically prominent Missouri family, had studied at Harvard and Yale before graduating from West Point in 1857. Beginning the war as a colonel in the Missouri militia, he had, by the beginning of 1863, risen to the rank of brigadier general. Marmaduke was in many ways the very embodiment of the Southern cavalier, his unquestioned courage matched only by his inflated sense of personal honor. Both characteristics would strongly affect the course of his career in Arkansas during the war.

Marmaduke convinced Holmes that a Missouri raid would rally Confederate sympathizers there, replenish Confederate supplies, and relieve the Federal pressure on Arkansas and, perhaps, Vicksburg as well. Marmaduke left from the Eleven Points River north of Batesville on April 17 with over five thousand men, but almost twelve hundred of these had no weapons, and nine hundred had no horses. The ever-optimistic Marmaduke hoped to equip them from captured Federal supplies. After several scattered skirmishes, the Federals withdrew to the fortified Union supply base at Cape Girardeau on the Mississippi River. As Marmaduke waited outside the town, unwilling to risk an assault on this strong position, his status soon changed from the hunter to the hunted. Federal soldiers steamed down the Mississippi to reinforce the garrison at Cape Girardeau, and a second Union army moved quickly from the west to support them.

Marmaduke began a hasty retreat along the military road atop Crowley's Ridge, an elevated strip of land extending south from Cape Girardeau to Helena. As he did so, two Federal armies with a combined strength of eight thousand united to pursue him. He sent a construction party ahead to build a bridge across the St. Francis River, the dividing line between Arkansas and Missouri in the "bootheel" of southeast Missouri.

During the night of May 1–2, the raiders crossed single file over the bobbing, rickety bridge and ascended the heights along the Arkansas bank known as Chalk Bluff. The horses were too heavy for the makeshift structure and were forced to attempt to swim the fast-moving stream. Many of the exhausted animals could not make it. Area residents reported that a large number of dead horses floated downstream to an old mill drift. The Confederate rearguard crossed back into Arkansas near dawn on May 2, cut the bridge supports, and watched the bridge break in two and float downstream. The Federals showed no desire to follow the raiders back into Arkansas.

Marmaduke's raid failed to reverse the Rebels' sagging fortunes in Arkansas. As spring gave way to summer, it became increasingly clear that if the Confederacy in Arkansas were to survive, it would require more than bold, ambitious failures; it would require a decisive victory, and soon. In June, General Holmes met with Sterling Price to plan for what they hoped would be just such a victory.

The object of their discussion was Helena, the Mississippi River port city located at the point where Crowley's Ridge meets the river. In 1860 Helena was a busy agricultural and commercial center 70 miles downriver from Memphis and 230 miles above Vicksburg, with a population of 1,024 white citizens and 527 black slaves. After the Union occupation in July 1862, it had become a jumping-off point for Union forces operating against Vicksburg, and its population had exploded with the addition of twenty thousand Federal troops and additional thousands of former slaves who had followed the Union army to freedom. Health and sanitary conditions were so deplorable and disease so rampant that some Union soldiers had rechristened the town "Hell-in Arkansas." But while Helena was anathema to white Union soldiers, for some former slaves, it was the starting point on the road to freedom. In April 1863 three companies of black men were inducted into the Union army, forming the First Arkansas Volunteer Infantry Regiment (African Descent). By June a second such regiment had been formed.

For Confederate leaders in Arkansas, Helena was seen as the key to retaking the initiative in the state. If the town could be recaptured, the disastrous course of the war in Arkansas might be reversed, and Federal troops might have to be diverted to Helena from the ever-tightening Federal siege of Vicksburg. Should Vicksburg fall, Helena could provide the Confederacy with a much-needed strategic position on the river. When scouts informed Holmes that the departure of large numbers of Union troops for Vicksburg had seriously depleted the Federal garrison at Helena, the Confederate commander decided to attack.

But Holmes had failed to carry out any serious reconnaissance of Helena's defenses. When his army arrived outside the town, he quickly surmised that, despite its reduced garrison (roughly four thousand effective men), Helena would not be an easy conquest. The Federal commander, Benjamin M. Prentiss, had utilized the steep hills and deeply thicketed ravines around the town to great advantage. He fortified the four large hills that formed a rough semicircle around the town with artillery protected by rifle pits. Closer to town stood Fort Curtis, an earthen bastion astride the major east-west road into Helena. Finally, the gunboat *USS Tyler* lay offshore, ready to move quickly to support any threatened position.

Despite serious misgivings, Holmes decided to order the attack. At a council of war on the evening of July 3, he drew up a plan for a three-pronged, coordinated advance by over 6,000 men on the following morning. General Marmaduke with 1,750 men would attack from the northwest, Gen. James Fagan, a former Arkansas legislator, would strike from the southwest with 1,300 men, and Price would lead the main body of 3,000 men against the center of the Union defenses. Holmes told his commanders to begin the attack "at daylight."

Coordinated attacks were difficult under the best of circumstances, and conditions on this Fourth of July were far from ideal. Marmaduke's attack was stalled by Federal fire coming from the levee to his left. On the Rebel right, a communications problem hindered the assault. Fagan had interpreted Holmes's order to attack "at daylight" to mean first light, and he sent his men in accordingly. But when he looked to his left, Price was nowhere to be seen. The Missourian had interpreted "at daylight" to mean sunrise, and thus the main Confederate assault did not begin for another hour. The failure to coordinate the attacks allowed the Federals to concentrate their fire against individual Rebel units.

The Confederates fought with a desperate bravery, marching uphill one noted, "amid the leaden rain and iron hail." Price's attack against the center of the Federal line temporarily captured one of the hilltop strong points, but confusion, the July heat, and a withering Federal fire that seemed to come from all directions compelled Holmes to order a retreat. Before noon, the Battle of Helena was over. The Rebels retreated, leaving hundreds of dead and wounded men littering the hills around the town. They had suffered over 1,600 casualties and gained nothing. Federal casualties totaled only 239. A Wisconsin soldier summed up the battle in a letter to his father: "The general opinion here is that the enemy fought desperately and with a bravery and determination worthy of a better cause."

The devastating Confederate defeat at Helena was compounded by the news that Confederate general Robert E. Lee had been repulsed at Gettysburg, Pennsylvania, on July 3 and was retreating with heavy casualties into Virginia. Even more ominous for Arkansas Confederates was the news that the South's Mississippi River stronghold at Vicksburg had surrendered to Gen. Ulysses Grant on July 4.

Residents of the capital were well aware of the implications of the fall of Vicksburg for their city. A local editor wrote that "Any head, with a thimble full of brains, ought to know that should that city be captured . . . the state of Arkansas falls an easy prey to the combined and various columns of the enemy." Before the month of July was out, those fears proved to be well founded.

Union major general Fredrick Steele, a New Yorker and a West Point classmate of Grant's, arrived in Helena to take command of all Federal forces in the state and quickly set about preparing to capture Little Rock. On August 10 and 11, 1863, Steele's infantry, some six thousand strong, left Helena and headed for Clarendon on the White River where they would link up with a like number of Federal cavalry moving south from Missouri.

In Little Rock, one of Theophilus Holmes's chronic illnesses gave Sterling Price another chance to command, although this particular command at this particular time was a dubious honor. There were only eight thousand men present for duty, and many Arkansans believed that Confederate authorities in the Trans-Mississippi had written off the further defense of Arkansas in favor of establishing a new defensive line along the Red River.

While Price was under no illusions about his ability to hold Little Rock against a strong enemy force, he tackled his new job with enthusiasm, ordering out cavalry units to scout and harass the Federals, constructing a strong defensive position on the north side of the Arkansas River, and issuing an appeal to the citizens of Little Rock to rally to the city's defense. The appeal drew little response. A Confederate surgeon in Little Rock noted, "[T]he dangers now menacing her [Little Rock] kindles no patriotic fire to blaze forth and consume the invader . . . Her chivalry has long since gone from her shores."

At sunrise on August 25, advance elements of the Federal cavalry collided with Confederate cavalry at Brownsville (near present-day Lonoke). After a brisk exchange, the outnumbered Rebels withdrew. Two days later, the two sides clashed again at Reed's Bridge on Bayou Meto twelve miles northeast of Little Rock. Again the Rebels slowed the Federal advance, but again they withdrew, this time to the outskirts of the city. The main Federal force, reinforced to a strength of 14,500, followed in the cavalry's wake and reached the Arkansas River downstream from the capital at Ashley's Mill (near present-day Scott) on September 7.

As the Federal army prepared to cross the river, the Confederates suffered a self-inflicted wound. Enmity between two of Price's top generals, John Marmaduke and L. M. Walker, had been building since July when Marmaduke questioned Walker's competence and his courage at the Battle of Helena. It had increased when Marmaduke was assigned to serve under Walker in the Little Rock campaign. On September 6 the two men and their seconds met on the Godfrey Le Fevre plantation seven miles below Little Rock to settle the matter with pistols at ten paces. Their first shots missed, but

Marmaduke's second shot struck Walker in the side, mortally wounding him. The encounter was one of the last recorded duels in Arkansas history, and it spread dissension through the Confederate ranks at a critical time.

On the morning of September 10, Steele sent his cavalry across a pontoon bridge over the Arkansas River and began to move his infantry up the north bank of the river toward Little Rock. Price's worst fears had been realized. He had concentrated his defenses on the north bank in the hope that the Federal commander would attack him head on. But he knew that the Arkansas River was fordable at several points downstream from the capital, and once the Federals got across it and moved on the city from the south bank, his position was untenable. He began to withdraw his troops from their positions north of the river, crossing them back into Little Rock on a pontoon bridge and sending them southwest toward Arkadelphia.

South of the river, another group of Rebels made a brief stand at Fourche Bayou before they too fell back toward the city and joined the retreat. The last Confederate defender left Little Rock around 5 p.m. Federal cavalry entered the city shortly thereafter, and at 7 p.m. Little Rock's civil authorities formally surrendered the city. It had been one month since Steele set out from Helena, and now, at a cost of only 137 casualties, his forces had seized the state capital and recaptured the arsenal that Capt. James Totten had surrendered some two and a half years earlier. The Confederates also abandoned Pine Bluff, and on September 14, Steele sent a detachment of cavalry to the town.

Many central Arkansas residents now found themselves at the mercy of the Yankees. Susan Fletcher was left alone on her Pulaski County plantation after her husband enlisted in the Confederate service. Following the fall of Little Rock, she recalled,

> After we were visited by the first half dozen squads of blue coats, we knew what civil war was when it was brought to your door. They first demanded water, then feed, after which they began to look around to see what could be carried away or destroyed.

However, many central Arkansas residents benefited from the Federal occupation, as Little Rock businesses experienced a revival. A local editor wrote that "the streets are filled with a restless, quick-motioned business people . . . [E]very store and storehouse is full, drays and wagons crowd the streets; two theaters are in full blast and all is bustle and business."

In mid-September Steele sent additional cavalrymen to garrison Pine Bluff, bringing the total Federal strength there to 550 men. The troops were commanded by Col. Powell Clayton, a Kansas officer who had fought at Wilson's Creek, Helena, and in the Little Rock campaign. Many Arkansas Confederates considered Clayton to be the best Union cavalry officer west

Major Civil War Battles in Arkansas

Battle Dates
1. March 7-8, 1862
2. June 17, 1862
3. July 7, 1862
4. November 28, 1862
5. December 7, 1862
6. January 9-11, 1863
7. April 18, 1863
8. May 1-2, 1863
9. July 4, 1863
10. August 27, 1863
11. September 1, 1863
12. September 10, 1863
13. October 25, 1863
14. April 3-4, 1864
15. April 10-12, 1864
16. April 18, 1864
17. April 25, 1864
18. April 30, 1864
19. June 6, 1864

Counties feature 1860 boundaries.

0   15   30   60 Miles

Major Civil War Battles in Arkansas. *Courtesy of Joseph Swain.* (Source: Encyclopedia of Arkansas History & Culture.)

of the Mississippi River, and even some Confederate sympathizers in Pine Bluff were impressed by him.

White Union soldiers were not the only ones coming to Pine Bluff. Large numbers of former slaves swarmed into the city. A white female resident noted, "They came pouring in by the 100's—every ones servants ran off to P. Bluff, there is scarcely a house here that has a servant left. They came in such numbers that they [Federal authorities] did not know what to do with them." To handle this massive influx of former slaves, Clayton established large camps east and west of the city.

While Steele was consolidating his hold on Little Rock and Clayton was establishing a Federal presence in Pine Bluff, Sterling Price was withdrawing the bulk of the Confederate infantry to Camden on the Ouachita River. The ever-aggressive Marmaduke held the Rebel cavalry at Princeton (Dallas County), and despite the reverses of the previous nine months, he was determined to take the war to the enemy. Little Rock was too strongly defended, but the smaller Federal garrison at Pine Bluff seemed vulnerable, particularly if the Rebels had the element of surprise.

On Saturday, October 24, 1863, Marmaduke led over two thousand cavalry supported by twelve pieces of artillery across the Saline River and through the soggy bottomlands toward Pine Bluff, reaching a point just outside the town after daylight on Sunday morning. Here he divided his command into three columns to approach the town from the southeast, southwest, and northwest. A cannon shot from his artillery would signal the start of the attack. The element of surprise was lost around 8 a.m. when one of Marmaduke's advancing columns encountered a Federal patrol. Shots were exchanged, and a Federal courier raced back to town to warn Clayton of the impending attack.

Clayton wasted no time after he learned of the Rebel advance. He sent skirmishers out in all directions, placed cannon to command the main approaches to the square, and set his contraband force to work barricading the streets leading into the square with cotton bales from a nearby warehouse. The former slaves accomplished the task in less than half an hour.

The Confederate attack began around 9 a.m. Despite failing to catch the Federals totally by surprise, Marmaduke still enjoyed a manpower advantage of four to one, and the Rebels quickly drove the Federal skirmishers back into the courthouse square. Throughout the remainder of the morning and into the early afternoon, the Rebels blasted away at the barricaded Yankees with artillery and small arms fire, trapping many Pine Bluff civilians in the middle of the fighting.

The Rebels set fire to over six hundred bales of cotton and inflicted heavy damage on the town, but they could not penetrate the Federals' inner defense ring. Around 2 p.m. Marmaduke ordered a retreat, taking some three hundred of the former slaves with him as prisoners, as well as some 250 horses and mules. "The Federals," he wrote in his official report, "fought like devils."

Clayton's leadership at Pine Bluff against superior odds added to his already considerable reputation. He praised the courage of his troops and particularly singled out the former slaves, noting, "The negroes did me excellent service . . . and deserve much therefore." A Federal soldier concurred, writing that the African Americans "worked patiently, and with an unselfish devotion to our cause that goes far to remove the jaundiced prejudice of color." Ironically, white cotton and black labor, so essential to the Southern way of life, had saved the Union army on this Sunday morning.

By the end of 1863, Confederate authority was largely confined to the southwest corner of the state. After the fall of Little Rock, the Confederate capital was moved to Washington in southwest Arkansas, and the Confederate military forces were encamped there and at Murfreesboro, Camden, and Springhill. As historian Michael Dougan has noted, "Only bad roads, burned out houses, and abandoned fields separated Confederate from Union Arkansas. In the vast no-man's land which constituted three fourths of the state, both armies foraged, and bushwhacker bands, with and without legal sanction, operated."

Confederate Resurgence and Collapse: The War in 1864 and 1865

If 1863 had been a disastrous year for Arkansas Confederates, 1864 began on an equally ominous note. In late December 1863, seventeen-year-old David Dodd was returning to Camden after attending to some family business in Little Rock when he was detained by a Union patrol along the Benton Road some twenty miles south of the capital. A search revealed that Dodd, who had previously served as a telegrapher for the Confederate army in Louisiana, carried a Morse-coded message detailing the disposition of part of the Federal defenses in Little Rock.

On January 5, 1864, a military commission in Little Rock found him guilty of spying and sentenced him to be hanged. Residents of the capital made several appeals to General Steele to spare Dodd's life, but the Federal commander refused to intervene. Dodd was hanged on January 8 on the grounds of St. John's Masonic School, where he had once attended classes. Though Dodd was almost certainly guilty, his youth, his refusal to implicate others, and the calm dignity with which he faced his death earned him an enduring place in Arkansas history as "the boy martyr of the Confederacy."

The Dodd affair notwithstanding, Frederick Steele pursued a conciliatory policy toward Arkansas Confederates. In accord with President Lincoln's "Ten Percent Plan" (which permitted a state to form a loyal government and be recognized by the president whenever 10 percent of the state's voters took an oath affirming loyalty to the Union and support for emancipation), Steele had begun to administer the amnesty oath, and, in January 1864, he called for a constitutional convention and the election of a provisional Unionist governor.

In March, while Unionist voters were going to the polls to approve the constitution and elect officials for the provisional government, Federal forces prepared to embark on an ambitious military venture. The Red River expedition, as it was styled, was a prelude to a grand Union design that would see Federal armies move simultaneously against Mobile, Richmond, and Atlanta, the object being to tie down Confederate defenders in all theaters, thereby preventing them from reinforcing one another. The Trans-Mississippi aspect of this grand strategy called for Steele to march southwest from Little Rock while another Federal army of 30,000 men under Nathaniel P. Banks would move up from New Orleans and ascend the Red River. The two armies would converge on and seize Shreveport, Louisiana, the Confederate headquarters in the Trans-Mississippi, and then move on to invade Texas. If successful, the operation would render the *coup de grace* to Confederate forces in southern Arkansas and northern Louisiana, would lead to the reassertion of Federal authority in Texas, and would result in the seizure of millions of dollars' worth of Confederate cotton and other supplies.

Steele had serious misgivings about the operation, but he obeyed his orders and left Little Rock on March 23 with 8,500 men. At Arkadelphia, seventy miles to the southwest, he was supposed to rendezvous with Brig. Gen. John M. Thayer's Frontier Division, which was moving southeast from Fort Smith. A week later, the Federals reached Arkadelphia, having encountered neither the Rebels nor Thayer. As Steele pressed on toward Washington, Confederate cavalry began to snap at his column.

When the Federal columns reached the Little Missouri River at Elkins Ferry, Price, who was under orders to prevent Steele from linking up with Banks, led his Confederates out of Camden and moved to meet them. Price's force had been seriously weakened when two of his infantry divisions were ordered to Louisiana to oppose Banks. Nonetheless, the Confederates took up positions along Steele's line of march at Prairie D'Ane (near present-day Prescott). On April 9, Thayer's division finally caught up with Steele's main body a few miles south of the Little Missouri River, but the newcomers brought few supplies and thus served to further deplete Steele's already scarce provisions. Price was also reinforced by fifteen hundred men in two mounted brigades from the Indian Territory, one composed of Texans and another of Choctaw Indians.

By April 10, Steele's columns had moved to within a mile of the Confederate entrenchments at Prairie D'Ane, where they stopped and constructed earthworks. Neither army seemed eager to directly confront the other. On April 12, Price withdrew to near Washington. His path to Camden now clear, Steele turned his army to the east and made for the Ouachita River town some forty miles away. Price took up pursuit, and Rebel cavalry again slashed at the front and rear of the Federal column, but the Yankees reached the safety of Camden's fortifications on April 15.

Price established his headquarters a few miles outside town. Outnumbered two to one, he could not attack Camden, but he instructed his cavalry to watch the roads leading from the town for Federal patrols or foraging parties. Steele had ordered supplies to be rushed to Camden from Little Rock and Pine Bluff. When they did not arrive by April 17, he sent a large foraging party west from the town along the Washington-Camden Road. The party consisted of almost two hundred wagons escorted by over a thousand cavalry and infantry (including four hundred black soldiers from the First Kansas Colored Infantry) and four cannon.

Alerted by their patrols, about 3,600 Confederate cavalry (composed of Marmaduke's Arkansans and the Texas and Choctaw brigades from the Indian Territory) backed by twelve cannon took a position between the returning supply train and Camden along high ground at Poison Spring fourteen miles west of the town. The Federals detected the presence of the Confederates in time to form a defensive position, but the Rebels soon overwhelmed them. The First Kansas bore the brunt of the attack. For many Rebel soldiers, the rules of warfare did not apply to black troops, whom they regarded as no more than runaway slaves. At Poison Spring, the Rebels shot wounded black soldiers as they lay helpless on the ground, gunned down others as they tried to surrender, and deliberately drove the captured wagons over the bodies of wounded blacks. The First Kansas lost 117 killed and 65 wounded in the engagement.

As the survivors of the Federal column staggered into Camden, the full extent of the defeat became apparent. Total Federal casualties at Poison Spring were 204 killed and 97 wounded. In addition, the Federals lost 170 wagons and over 1,200 mules. The Confederates suffered only 13 killed and fewer than 100 total casualties.

For Steele, the debacle at Poison Spring was compounded by the news of Banks's defeat and subsequent retreat in Louisiana, which freed thousands of additional Confederates to concentrate against his embattled command at Camden. On April 20, a supply train reached Camden from Pine Bluff carrying ten days' worth of provisions. Two days later, Steele sent the 240-wagon train back to Pine Bluff for additional provisions, escorted by 1,400 troops and accompanied by a large number of civilians eager to leave the town and about three hundred former slaves. Three days out of Camden the train approached a series of gristmills owned by Hastings Marks. Four thousand Confederate cavalry waited along the road. At 8 a.m. when the Federal advance guard came into view, the Rebels attacked.

After five hours of intense fighting, the Federal commander surrendered. Remarkably he had suffered only about a hundred men killed, but the Rebels took thirteen hundred prisoners and seized all the wagons. Finding few supplies in the wagons, the Confederates robbed many of the prisoners, and reports surfaced that many of the unarmed freedmen had been shot down in cold blood. Total Confederate casualties were fewer than three hundred. A Federal soldier later acknowledged that the little-known Battle of Marks' Mill "was one of the most substantial successes gained by the western Confederates during the war."

For Steele, it was the final straw. With supplies rapidly dwindling and the Confederate forces outside Camden growing, he had no choice but to attempt to get back to Little Rock. The Federals quietly stole out of Camden before dawn on April 26 and headed toward the capital, two rivers and a hundred miles to the north. It was the chance the Confederates had been waiting for, but for once their cavalry patrols let them down. By the time the Rebels realized that the Federals were gone, Steele's forces were well on their way.

On April 29 twenty-two miles north of Princeton, the Union army reached the Saline River crossing at Jenkins' Ferry (about twelve miles southwest of present-day Sheridan and a little over forty miles from Little Rock), and Steele's engineers quickly began construction of a pontoon bridge. As soon as the bridge was in place, Steele began crossing his men to the north bank. It was a slow process under the best of conditions, and a driving rain made it even more so. The riverbank soon became "a sea of mud." Wagons sank to their axles and mules lost their footing.

At 8:00 on the following morning, while the Federal wagon train still stretched back two miles down the road toward Princeton, the main body of the pursuing Confederate army reached the ferry and attacked the retreating Yankees. The return of Price's two divisions from Louisiana increased Confederate strength to about four thousand men, but Federal forces benefited from the weather and the terrain of the battlefield. From the point where the attack began, the terrain sloped down to the riverbank funneling the attacking force into an area only about a quarter mile across. With a swamp to one side and a hill to the other, flanking movements were impossible, and the Confederates were unable to deploy their entire force at one time. Rain-softened ground slowed the attackers, and smoke and mist obscured much of the field. Time and again the Confederates charged, only to be driven back with heavy losses.

The Second Kansas Colored Infantry Regiment fought with particular ferocity at Jenkins' Ferry. The regiment was the companion unit to the First Kansas, and the memory of Poison Spring was fresh on their minds. Before leaving Camden, the officers of the regiment had agreed "that in the future the regiment would take no prisoners so long as the Rebels continued to murder our men." At Jenkins' Ferry the Second Kansas put that philosophy into practice. The regiment overran a Confederate battery and bayoneted every Confederate gunner, including three who were attempting to surrender. Later in the day, as they were covering the retreat of the last elements of Steele's army, the Second Kansas searched the battlefield for wounded Union soldiers. While assisting their own wounded, however, they slit the throats and otherwise mutilated the bodies of wounded Rebels. For the duration of the conflict, the war between Confederates and black Union soldiers would be one of "no quarter."

Around 12:30 in the afternoon the exhausted Rebels called off the attack, and by 3 p.m. the entire Federal army was safely on the north bank of the river. Steele ordered the pontoon bridge destroyed to prevent further pursuit, and the bespattered Federal columns sloshed on toward Little Rock. They reached the capital on May 3, looking, one observer noted, "as if they had been rolled in the mud." The Camden Expedition (as the Arkansas part of the Red River campaign came to be called) was the greatest Federal disaster of the Civil War in Arkansas. Union forces lost over 2,500 men killed, wounded, or missing, hundreds of wagons, thousands of livestock, and gained not one inch of ground.

The failure of the Federals' Camden Expedition breathed new life into Arkansas Confederates. Confederate guerrillas, encouraged by the Federal debacle, raided federally leased plantations around Helena and tore up stretches of railroad track between DeValls Bluff and Little Rock. In Chicot County in late May and early June 1864, Rebel cavalry operating along the levee so disrupted Federal shipping on the Mississippi River that six thousand Federal troops, headed upriver to Memphis, were ordered to disembark briefly in southeast Arkansas to disperse them. The Confederates took up positions behind a slow-moving stream called Ditch Bayou that flowed into nearby Lake Chicot. From midmorning until midafternoon on June 6, six hundred Confederates, protected from a direct assault by the bayou, held off three thousand Yankees, inflicting over 150 casualties while losing only 4 killed and 33 wounded. Finally, their artillery ammunition exhausted, the Rebels withdrew. The remainder of the Federal force—wet, weary, and angry—moved on to Lake Village where they burned several buildings before reembarking the following morning for Memphis.

Like their fellow citizens in northwest Arkansas, the residents of the southeastern part of the state suffered greatly from the depredations of both armies and from outlaw gangs. In 1864 a Chicot County resident wrote to a friend, "We have been tossed and tumbled about considerably by the Feds and our own soldiers and then by bands of independent marauders calling themselves 'guerillas' and having authority from almost any or every general in the Confederacy or out of it." Citizens of the county were trapped, he noted, "between the Hawk & Buzzard." The same statement could have been made by residents of other regions of the state.

"For the ordinary Arkansas civilian caught in the storm of war, legitimate economic activity had practically come to a standstill by the summer of 1864," Dan Sutherland notes. "Nearly all industry had ceased. Cotton and woolen factories, gristmills, sawmills, saltpeter works, and most craft shops had been closed or destroyed. Financial inflation had made any manufactured articles and most other product incredibly expensive." At Little Rock and the other few places firmly in Federal control, conditions were much better. But at isolated outposts, unreliable transportation and the activities of guerrillas and outlaws made everyday life both difficult and dangerous.

For the Federal garrison at Fort Smith, Confederate Indian guerrillas led by Stand Watie were a constant thorn in the side of Union forces. Watie, the talented Cherokee leader, had risen to the rank of brigadier general in the Confederate army. Acting in conjunction with white guerrillas and Chickasaw and Choctaw cavalry units, Watie's forces disrupted supplies and harassed Federal forces at Fort Smith so severely throughout the summer and fall that government authorities in Washington, DC, decided in early December 1864 to abandon the post altogether. The Federal garrison had actually started for Little Rock when Gen. Ulysses Grant ordered the evacuation halted and the fort maintained.

It seemed that the Confederate commanders in Arkansas had at last found a formula that might, at best, win back the state or, at worst, confine Federal influence to Little Rock and a handful of strongly garrisoned towns. But it was not to be. Price, another native son of the "Show Me" state, saw a chance to realize the dream of a triumphant return to Missouri that he had harbored ever since his ignominious retreat from that state in February 1862.

On September 19, 1864, he led twelve thousand men (four thousand of them without weapons and a thousand with no horses) across the Missouri line and headed for St. Louis. Over the course of the next four and a half weeks, he recruited new soldiers, lost others, burned some towns, tore up bridges and railroads, overran several smaller Federal garrisons, threatened (though he did not capture) both St. Louis and Jefferson City, criss-crossed the state from east to west all the way into Kansas, and generally caused such an uproar that Federal authorities dispatched over twenty thousand troops to deal with him. The two main armies clashed in and around Westport, Missouri (near present-day Kansas City) on October 22 and 23 in the largest Civil War battle (in terms of the number of men engaged) fought west of the Mississippi. The Confederates lost at least fifteen hundred men killed and wounded, and another two thousand were taken prisoner.

Price turned his defeated army southward, but ten days later Federal forces caught up with him at Mine Creek in Kansas and inflicted another 1,200 casualties. By the time he returned to Arkansas on October 30, Price had only 4,000 survivors. With this ragged remnant, he moved briefly into the Indian Territory and Texas, before returning to southwest Arkansas with 3,500 men, the majority of them unarmed. In a little over two months, Price had squandered the momentum that had been won the previous spring and in the process had destroyed the high esteem in which he had been held by many of his troops. "Men are greatly demoralized and we present a pitiable forlorn aspect," one Rebel veteran grumbled. "God damn Old Price."

In late 1864, events on the national political scene were also trending against the Confederacy. On Tuesday, November 8, voters in the North reelected Lincoln to a second term as president. Lincoln's election dashed any hope in the South for a negotiated peace. While Lincoln celebrated his victory in Washington, DC, the Confederate government at Washington, Arkansas, had all but ceased to function. Price's removal of so much of the Confederate military presence in south Arkansas had led to the further deterioration of law and order south of the Arkansas River. His Missouri raid did claim one major casualty among Arkansas Federals, however. Frederick Steele had conquered Little Rock, reasserted Federal authority, and established a new Unionist government in the state, but his conciliatory policy toward Arkansas Confederates had always been too conciliatory for some Arkansas Unionists. Blamed for the failure of the disastrous Camden expedition and for allowing Price to raid Missouri, he was replaced in December by Gen. Joseph J. Reynolds.

In 1864, while much of the Confederacy was coming apart, Arkansas Confederates had enjoyed their most successful year of the entire war. But, in the end, it availed them nothing. In aptly summarizing the tumultuous events of that year, Daniel Sutherland has written, "The Federals, through miscalculation, poor generalship, and lack of initiative, had nearly lost Arkansas in 1864; only at the last minute, and as a result of poor judgment by the Confederates, were they able to steal it back."

With the failure of Price's raid, Union forces in Arkansas once again gained the upper hand, but events east of the Mississippi soon robbed them of their advantage. Federal reinforcements were needed in Georgia and the Carolinas, where Sherman relentlessly pursued Confederate forces under Joseph Johnston, and along the gulf coast at Mobile.

By early 1865, the antagonists in Arkansas, prevented by lack of numbers from conducting major offensive operations, adopted defensive stances. The Federals strengthened their line of supply from Helena through DeValls Bluff to Little Rock and maintained a tenuous hold on Fort Smith and smaller towns upriver from the capital. Many of the Federal troops now garrisoning the state were themselves Arkansans, either prewar Unionists or former slaves. Confederate forces fell back behind the line of the Ouachita River in southwest Arkansas.

A few Confederate sympathizers continued to find hope in rumors of European intervention (the chances of which had long since passed) or of decisive Rebel victories against Grant or Sherman (which did not occur). But for most Arkansas Confederates, the harsh reality of defeat was beginning to set in. "Our armies have all been defeated and scattered, our resources nearly exhausted, our men dispirited and demoralized," a Phillips County woman recorded in her diary. "My God! What is to become of us?"

The news of the surrender of Confederate generals Robert E. Lee on April 9 and Joseph Johnston on April 26 accelerated the collapse of Confederate Arkansas. Desertions multiplied, illicit trading with the enemy proliferated, famine threatened. A Federal spy in southwest Arkansas reported, "Arkansas is starved out."

As the Confederate army dissolved, the last vestiges of law and social stability evaporated. In May a group of women stormed the Confederate commissary in Lewisville (Lafayette County), demanding and receiving food for the town's hungry civilians. Confederate officers stole army supplies only to be themselves robbed by their own men. "We are experiencing a state of perfect anarchy," John Brown wrote from Camden in late May. "We have no Government, military or civil, a condition most to be dreaded of all others." The formal surrender of Confederate forces in the Trans-Mississippi did not take place until June 2, 1865, but by that time, the Confederacy in Arkansas had already ceased to exist.

The Civil War was the greatest disaster in Arkansas history. By some estimates, as many as ten thousand Arkansans lost their lives in the struggle. Each death represented a life cut short, a dream unfulfilled, a family deprived of a father, a son, or a brother. Countless other men who survived the war were scarred for life, both physically and emotionally. Property losses were staggering. For slave owners, the losses in slaves alone totaled over a hundred million dollars. Land values declined by almost thirty-four million dollars. The number of horses dropped by 50 percent, mules and cattle by almost as much.

The hardships and suffering these losses inflicted on the residents of the state are impossible to quantify, but are clearly revealed in the remembrances of those who lived through them. Susan Fletcher, returning from Washington, Arkansas, to her home near Little Rock at the end of the war described the conditions she saw in Saline and Pulaski counties. "Desolation met our gaze," she wrote, "abandoned and burned homes; cultivated land, overgrown with bushes; half starved women and children; gaunt, ragged men, stumbling along the road, just mustered out of the army, trying to find their families and friends and wondering if they had a home left. We found our home burned to the ground, but went to the home of a relative until we could collect our thoughts and decide what was best to be done." Not surprisingly, the war left a legacy of bitterness that would take many years to assuage.

But for the former slaves, the war marked the coming of freedom—the "year of jubilo," so long hoped for. A Chicot County slave remembered the arrival of Federal troops on her plantation. "I heard them tell all the slaves they were free," she later told an interviewer. "A man . . . called for the three near-by plantations to meet at our place. Then he got up on a platform with

Year of Jubilo:
African American corruption of the biblical term "Year of Jubilee," it refers to the coming of freedom to the slaves. In the Book of Leviticus (Old Testament), the Year of Jubilee is said to occur once in every fifty years. In that year, all slaves are set free, all debts are forgiven, and the glories and mercy of God are particularly manifest.

another man beside him and declared peace and freedom. He p'inted to a colored man and yelled, 'You're as free as I am.' Old colored folks . . . that was on sticks, threwed them sticks away and shouted." After generations of bondage and hopelessness, African Americans in Arkansas had, in a very brief period, made the transition from slaves to contraband and then to freedmen and freedwomen. What that freedom would mean remained to be seen. As the fires of war subsided, Arkansans of all colors and political persuasions looked toward an uncertain future with a mixture of hope and apprehension.

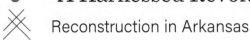

9 "A Harnessed Revolution"

Reconstruction in Arkansas

THE ERA OF Reconstruction that followed the Civil War was one of the most tumultuous and controversial periods in the history of the state and the nation. The term *Reconstruction* actually applies to several distinct but related aspects of the immediate post–Civil War period. Political Reconstruction dealt with the process of determining how the seceded states would resume their place in a reunited nation and who would control the political fortunes of those states. Economic Reconstruction concerned the attempt by white Southerners to recover economically from the devastation of the war, by black Southerners to establish their economic viability in the free labor system, and by the Reconstruction governments to reshape the South in the economic image of the North. Social Reconstruction involved the process of determining how the former slaves and former masters would interact in the new social arrangements brought on by the war and emancipation. The overlapping and intertwining of these various aspects made Reconstruction a complex and confusing era.

Arkansas under Presidential Reconstruction

Though generally considered to have begun with the surrender of the Southern armies in 1865, Reconstruction actually began well before the war ended. The Presidential Reconstruction plan put forward by Abraham Lincoln in his annual message to Congress on December 8, 1863, was one of the most lenient policies ever applied by a victorious government to defeated insurrectionists. The president offered a "full pardon . . . with restoration of all rights of property, except as to slaves" to all Rebels who would take an oath of future loyalty to the Constitution and agree to abide by acts of Congress and presidential proclamations regarding slavery. Only high-ranking Confederate leaders were excluded from this policy, and they could apply for pardons to the president on an individual basis. When the number of people taking the oath reached 10 percent of those who had voted in the election of 1860, those citizens could form a new state government, which the president would recognize. In the case of Arkansas, that meant that the process of forming a new state government could begin when only slightly over 5,400 persons took the oath. Shortly after Federal forces seized Little Rock in September 1863, Maj. Gen. Frederick Steele, the commander of Union forces in Arkansas and *de facto* military governor of the state, began the process of reestablishing a loyal state government.

Following the announcement of the president's plan in December, Arkansas Unionists began taking the required oath, and, by early January 1864, the 10 percent requirement had been met. That same month, Arkansas Unionists from twenty-four of the state's fifty-seven counties assembled in Little Rock to draft a new constitution. The new document was similar to the state's first constitution of 1836, except for a provision abolishing slavery. The convention also chose a provisional slate of officers. The document and slate of officials were submitted to the voters in March of 1864.

The election was in no way a truly statewide or representative process. Confederate forces still controlled portions of southern and southwestern Arkansas, and much of the state outside of the major population centers was still a virtual no-man's land. With only slightly more than twelve thousand Arkansans casting ballots, the document was overwhelmingly approved, a slate of provisional state officials chosen, and a new state legislature elected. Fittingly, Isaac Murphy, the lone holdout against secession in the state convention of 1861 and a man whose devotion to the Union had not wavered during the trying months and years thereafter, was elected governor.

That new legislature chose Elisha Baxter and William Fishback to be the state's United States senators. But Baxter and Fishback soon became part of the developing struggle between the president and Congress over control of Reconstruction. When the two men presented their credentials in Washington, the US Senate, uncomfortable with Lincoln's lenient policies, refused to seat them.

This refusal confirmed the tenuous legal nature of the Murphy government, recognized by the president but not by Congress. The problems facing the new administration were staggering. As Murphy noted in his inaugural address, the loyal state government began "under very embarrassing surroundings; without money power, without military power."

The end of the war in April 1865 created additional problems. The assassination of President Lincoln removed the architect of the lenient plan of Reconstruction and destroyed the South's best hope for peaceful reunification. While his successor, Andrew Johnson of Tennessee, pursued a plan very similar to that proposed by the slain president—repudiation of secession and the Confederate debt, abolition of slavery, and ratification of the Thirteenth Amendment—he lacked Lincoln's stature and political skills and soon found himself at war with congressional Republicans.

The return of Confederate troops who had fought east of the Mississippi River threatened to add to the opposition that the Unionist state government faced. The previous year, in an attempt to head off this threat, the Unionist state legislature had passed a law requiring a second loyalty oath as a prerequisite for voting. To be eligible, a person had to swear that he had not supported the Confederacy since the establishment of the loyal state government in March 1864. With this provision in place, the Murphy government felt confident enough to call for congressional elections in October 1865.

With many former Confederates disqualified, fewer than seven thousand voters cast ballots. Still, the opposition party, composed largely of prewar Democrats and some former Whigs and styling itself as the Conservatives, made a surprisingly strong showing. The administration soon received an additional dose of bad news. First the national Congress, citing the low voter turnout, refused to seat the newly elected congressmen. Then, in the case of *Rison et al v. Farr*, the state supreme court struck down the state's loyalty oath as unconstitutional.

Conservatives: Political faction composed of prewar Democrats and some former Whigs who opposed the Republican Party's plans for Reconstruction.

Thus encouraged, Conservatives began to prepare an all-out effort for the next election in August 1866. Intimidation and violence against blacks and Unionists were commonplace. The results of this first postwar election conducted without restrictions on the former Confederates bore out the worst fears of Arkansas Unionists. Conservative candidates swept away almost the entire Unionist ticket elected in 1864. Only Governor Murphy and the secretary of state, both of whom had four-year terms and were not up for reelection, survived, and Conservatives seemed certain to recapture those two offices in 1868. Former Confederates were also returned to power in many counties.

The new state legislature, which assembled in November, included many of the state's antebellum ruling elite, several of whom had served in the Confederate Congress or the Rebel army. The general assembly enacted laws (over Governor Murphy's veto) legitimizing Confederate debts and making only Confederate veterans eligible for state pensions, and even considered a resolution commending former Confederate president Jefferson Davis.

The new legislature passed no restrictive labor laws such as the infamous Mississippi "Black Codes," which severely restricted the economic rights of the freedpeople, but neither did it permit African Americans to vote, hold office, serve on juries, marry whites, or have access to public education. It did, however, choose two ex-Confederates, including former Confederate senator Augustus Garland, to represent the state in the US Senate. That body refused to seat Garland or any other senator from the former Confederate states. That refusal notwithstanding, it seemed that, despite the devastation, death, and dislocation of the war, many of the same men who had dominated Arkansas politics in the antebellum years were rapidly returning to power.

Many members of that class were also engaged in trying to restore their prewar economic status. Arkansans of all classes had been hit hard by the war, and some of the state's wealthiest citizens had seen their fortunes wiped out and their antebellum lifestyle destroyed. But as historian Carl Moneyhon has noted in a recent study, wealthy individuals generally survived the war years and maintained control over their property better than their poorer neighbors. "The loss of their slaves had a major economic impact," he notes, "but they were still in a better position than others to reestablish their lives and fortunes. Poorer individuals and families did not have as much to lose, but their losses were more disastrous, often involving everything."

The ability to maintain control of the land was particularly important. Land was the major form of wealth in the state and the commodity on which economic, social, and political power were based. For planters in the southern and eastern parts of the state, the key to economic survival lay in maintaining control of the land and reasserting control over the labor force. For the freedmen, on the other hand, the challenge was to use their freedom to enhance their political, economic, and social independence from the planters. Many left the plantations to seek opportunities in the towns and cities. But such opportunities were few and far between. The majority remained on the land and sought to gain for themselves a share of the state's agricultural bounty to which their labor had for so long contributed.

These freedmen and women rightly concluded that ownership of land was critical to attaining their goals. Many hoped and expected that the federal government would redistribute land after the war (the oft-heard rumors of "forty acres and a mule"), and Gen. E. O. C. Ord, head of the military district that included Arkansas, proposed using confiscated lands to provide homesteads for freedmen. But Congress and the president refused to support the idea, insisting that confiscated lands be returned to their previous owners once they received a presidential pardon.

By and large the planters managed to maintain ownership of their land and thus were in a strong bargaining position with the freedmen. Still, without a labor force, the land was of little value, and planters now had to negotiate with their former slaves for their services. In the months following the end of the war, labor relations were in flux, and a wide variety of arrangements between planters and laborers emerged. One Arkansas planter noted that "on twenty plantations around me, there are ten different styles of contracts."

Over time, sharecropping became the dominant arrangement. Under this system a landowner rented a plot of land to an individual family to farm independently and furnished them everything necessary to make a crop. The owner would then receive a share of the crop as rent. If the cropper provided his own tools and/or animals, he could retain a larger share of the crop. Freedmen preferred this system because it gave them more autonomy and held out the hope that, with good weather and good prices, a sharecropper could eventually save enough to purchase his own land and become an independent farmer.

The task of supervising the contractual arrangements between planters and laborers fell to the Bureau of Refugees, Freedmen, and Abandoned Lands, more commonly known as the Freedmen's Bureau. Created by Congress in March 1865, the bureau was under the overall leadership of Maj. Gen. Oliver O. Howard and assistant commissioners in the various Southern states. In Arkansas, three Union officers served as assistant commissioners between March 1865 and May 1869, reporting directly to General Howard and supervising the work of seventy-nine local agents.

These agents (thirty-six civilians and forty-three army officers) were assigned to thirty-six locations centered primarily in thirty towns south, east, and west of Little Rock, the sites determined by the proximity of major rivers, large black populations, and cotton plantations. In addition to supervising labor contracts, the bureau's mission was to provide food, shelter, and medical care for the former slaves, to provide for their education, to help protect their legal rights, and to ease the transition from slavery to free labor.

The success or failure of the Freedmen's Bureau in Arkansas was determined largely by the mindset and actions of these local agents. For most Arkansans, black and white, the local agent was the Freedmen's Bureau. As historian Randy Finley has noted in his recent study of the bureau in Arkansas, "Agents' racial attitudes and ideologies—ranging from humanitarianism and paternalism to racism—critically shaped the workings of the bureau in Arkansas." Some agents worked diligently and often at great personal risk to secure rights for those freedmen and freedwomen under their supervision, while others acted as little more than labor agents for the planters.

With their ability to regain control of the state legislature, to retain their land, and to secure their labor, Arkansas's planter elite seemed on the verge of reclaiming their prewar status and of returning Arkansas society to something closely resembling its antebellum arrangement. But economic and political developments soon dramatically altered the direction of affairs in Arkansas.

Agricultural activity quickened with the end of the fighting. In 1865 returning Arkansas soldiers tended crops already sown, planted late crops of cotton and corn, and looked expectantly to 1866 as they prepared to resume and expand their operations in the first full year of peace. High cotton prices in the immediate postwar period encouraged many Arkansans to plant more cotton and less corn in the spring of 1866, risking self-sufficiency in an attempt to recoup wartime losses. The revival of agricultural activity spurred a corresponding growth in commercial activity in Arkansas towns and created a great demand for labor that boded well for the freedmen.

It seemed that a good crop season in 1866 could lead to a rapid return to the prosperity that had characterized the late 1850s, and, in so doing, help assuage the bitterness of the war and ease the transition from a slave-based to a free labor society. But heavy rains in the late spring of 1866 caused severe flooding along the state's major rivers. The floods were followed by a midsummer drought. In late summer, the heavy rains returned, accompanied in some areas by army worms that stripped cotton plants bare. The fall harvest was well below expectations. The pattern repeated itself the following year, resulting in another small harvest. In the fall, Arkansas farmers were dealt another blow when cotton prices collapsed, falling to about one-half of their 1866 level.

As with the war, those at the bottom of the economic scale were hit hardest by the crop failures. For the freedmen, hardships brought on by natural forces were compounded by human factors. Merchants charged them exorbitant prices and usurious interest; planters failed to fulfill contractual obligations, refused to let literate freedmen examine the books, and cheated those who could neither read nor add. Other planters waited until the harvest was completed, then drove freedmen from the land without settling their accounts. Freedmen's Bureau agents were inundated with complaints.

White yeomen farmers were also in trouble. Deeply in debt after two years of poor harvests, most found credit still available, but with a stipulation. Despite the short crops and the dramatic fall in prices, merchants and other creditors still looked to cotton as the best collateral. When cotton prices remained low, farmers found themselves in an ever-deepening cycle of debt that would continue well into the next century.

The planter class survived the economic downturn better than their poorer neighbors, but many were hard hit, and almost all soon came to realize that the golden years were over. Even before the disastrous season of 1867, the editor of the *Arkansas Gazette* had written, "The day of making sudden fortunes in agricultural pursuits has passed."

Lycurgus Johnson of Lakeport plantation in Chicot County survived somewhat better than many other planters. He managed to hold on to the majority of his 4,600 prewar acres and much of his labor force and accom-

Lakeport plantation. Built in the late 1850s by Chicot County planter Lycurgus Johnson, the seventeen-room Lakeport plantation house was a showplace of the state's cotton aristocracy. By 1860 Johnson owned over four thousand acres of rich delta land and 155 slaves, and the plantation produced thirteen hundred bales of cotton and ten thousand bushels of corn. *Photo courtesy of Lakeport Plantation, Arkansas State University Heritage Site.*

modated himself better than most planters to the new system of free labor. A local Freedmen's Bureau agent reported that Johnson did his one hundred hands "the fullest justice" and referred to him as a "model man of Chicot County." Still the total value of Johnson's taxable property fell from $171,581 in 1860 to $18,556 in 1865. In 1860, Lakeport had produced 1,300 bales of cotton, which ranked Johnson fifth among Chicot County planters. In 1870, Lakeport's 600 bales made Johnson the largest producer in the county. That Johnson was a postwar "success story" is a clear indication that even those cotton aristocrats who survived the twin scourges of war and poor harvests ruled over a greatly diminished realm.

The decision to concentrate on cotton in the immediate postwar period when prices were high was an understandable one, but Arkansans of all economic classes paid a severe penalty for that decision. As Carl Moneyhon has noted, "Nature and the price of cotton were critical factors in the state's postwar economic life, but the decision of Arkansans in 1866 to emphasize cotton helped tie their farms to a crop that languished for the next hundred years and left Arkansas a legacy of poverty."

As the antebellum elites struggled to maintain their economic viability, other events were threatening their political hegemony. In April 1866 Congress enacted, over the president's veto, a Civil Rights Act that defined all persons born in the United States as citizens and provided a federal guarantee for the "full and equal benefit of all laws and proceedings for the security of person and property" regardless of race. A short time later, to remove all doubt about the constitutionality of the Civil Rights Act, Congress approved the Fourteenth Amendment. It reaffirmed state and federal citizenship for persons born or naturalized in the United States and forbade any state to abridge the "privileges and immunities" of citizens or to deprive any person of life, liberty, or property without "due process of law" or to deny to any person "the equal protection of the laws." It voided all Confederate debts, provided for a reduction in congressional representation for those states that denied the vote to any adult male, and prohibited any person from holding a state or federal office who had at any time taken an oath to support the Constitution and subsequently supported the rebellion.

Only one former Confederate state (Tennessee) ratified the amendment. Both houses of the Conservative-dominated Arkansas legislature overwhelmingly rejected the proposal, and they were supported in this action by President Johnson, who was now engaged in a fierce struggle with the Radical elements in Congress for control of the Reconstruction process. The actions of the Arkansas legislature were mirrored in numerous other state legislatures across the South. The failure to guarantee the political and civil rights of the freedmen, the insistence on returning to positions of power in both the state and national government those who had only recently taken up arms against the United States, and the violence directed against freedmen and Unionists combined with the president's combative intransigence to provoke an understandably sharp reaction among Northern moderates and to tilt the political balance of power in the Radicals' favor. In so doing, it doomed to failure the lenient plans of Presidential Reconstruction and the conciliatory policies of Governor Murphy.

Radicals: Republicans who favored a harsh Reconstruction policy toward the former Confederate states.

Three months after Conservative-Democratic elements regained control of the Arkansas legislature, Republicans easily gained over two-thirds of the seats in both the US Senate and the House of Representatives, assuring them of the ability to override presidential vetoes. The views of the Radical element of the Republican Party, which had previously been in the minority, were now clearly the dominant sentiment. The fighting between the weakened president and an emboldened Congress continued throughout 1867.

In March of 1868, the House brought charges of impeachment against the president. The charges were more political than substantive, and the

Senate narrowly failed to convict Johnson, but what remained of his power and influence were effectively destroyed. Arkansas and the rest of the former Confederate states, having missed an opportunity to adopt a conciliatory approach and perhaps reenter the Union under the lenient plan of Presidential Reconstruction, now would have to contend with a much harsher plan.

Congressional Reconstruction and the "Gospel of Prosperity"

The plan for Congressional Reconstruction was embodied in the Military Reconstruction Act, and passed, over the president's veto, in March of 1867. The act divided the former Confederate states into five military districts, each under the control of a military officer authorized to keep order, to protect the rights of the freedmen, and to utilize military tribunals in place of civil courts where necessary. The act further specified that new state constitutions providing for universal male suffrage be drafted, approved by a majority of the state's voters, and accepted by Congress. In addition, state legislatures were required to ratify the Fourteenth Amendment. Only those persons who could swear an "ironclad oath" that they had not aided or abetted the Confederacy were permitted to participate in the process. A Second Reconstruction Act in late March specifically directed the military commanders to register all adult males who could take the oath. A Third Reconstruction Act followed in July, empowering the military commanders to replace state or local officials.

Arkansas and Mississippi constituted the Fourth Military District under the command of Gen. E. O. C. Ord, a former assistant commissioner of the Freedmen's Bureau in Arkansas. Ord advised the state legislature, then in recess, not to reconvene and restricted the authority and jurisdiction of the state courts, especially as it pertained to relations between blacks and whites. Governor Murphy was allowed to remain in office and worked closely with Ord for the remainder of his term, albeit in a clearly subservient position. Under Ord's direction, registration began for the November election on whether to call for a constitutional convention. The Third Reconstruction Act placed great power in the hands of those officials who registered voters, enabling them to disqualify not only those who clearly fell under the prohibitions of the Fourteenth Amendment but also many who were only suspected of disloyalty.

In the November election, 27,576 Arkansans voted for the convention, while 13,558 opposed. Seventy delegates chosen in that election assembled in the hall of the house of representatives in Little Rock in early January 1868. Throughout the South, critics referred to these biracial, Republican-dominated assemblies as "Black and Tan" conventions, and the hostile *Arkansas Gazette* described the Arkansas convention as "a bastard collection whose putridity stinks in the nostrils of all decency." The delegates were a diverse group, but contrary to the *Gazette*'s description, the assembly contained some very capable members. Approximately two-thirds of the delegates were Radical Republicans, the remainder Conservatives or unaligned.

The Radicals fell into three categories—the first (and, in Arkansas, the most politically powerful) group was composed of Northerners who had come to Arkansas during or after the war. Derided as "carpetbaggers" by conservative whites who saw them as political opportunists, most had actually come South to pursue economic gain and to help transform the region into a free labor economy like that of the North. Others were teachers, missionaries, or Freedmen's Bureau agents who had come South to assist the former slaves in the difficult transition to freedom.

Carpetbaggers: Derisive name given by Southerners to Northerners who came to the South after the war for economic or political gain.

Scalawags: Derisive name given by Southerners to white Southerners who collaborated with Northern Republicans during Reconstruction.

The second group consisted of Southerners who had been Unionists before the war or had gone over to the Union side during or after the war. In Arkansas they included prewar Whigs, mountain Unionists, and converted rebels. Many white Southerners viewed these "scalawags" as traitors to their own people and despised them even more than the carpetbaggers.

African Americans composed the third element of the Radical coalition. Eight blacks were delegates to the constitutional convention. Delegate William H. Grey, a minister familiar with parliamentary procedure, was active in the debates and was considered to be one of the most eloquent orators at the convention. Delegate James Mason, the mulatto son of wealthy Chicot County planter Elisha Worthington and one of his slaves, had been educated at Oberlin College and at the French Military Academy.

The constitution produced by the convention gave African American males the right to vote, serve on juries, hold office, and serve in the militia. It provided for the first system of free public schools in Arkansas for citizens of both races and for the establishment of a state university. The new constitution also redrew legislative districts to give greater representation to the Delta and the southwestern regions of the state and strengthened the power of the executive, giving the governor a four-year term and vastly expanded powers, including wide-ranging appointive powers. It disfranchised anyone who had taken an oath of allegiance to the United States government and then served or aided the Confederacy as well as anyone "who during the late rebellion violated the rules of civilized warfare."

The major issue in the ratification campaign was the granting of full civil and political rights to black male Arkansans. Many Conservative elements viewed this as an attempt not only to radically transform Arkansas society but also to ensure the political ascendancy of the Republican Party through black suffrage. The Conservative-Democratic coalition expressed its intent to maintain "a WHITE MAN'S government in a WHITE MAN'S COUNTRY."

Black Arkansans were eager to begin actively participating in the political process, and many joined political societies, like the Union League, whose principal goal was to raise the political consciousness of African Americans and to encourage them to vote. Thanks in no small part to the efforts of the Union League, 22,000 black male Arkansans registered to vote between May and November of 1868. A popular vote on ratification and the election of new state officials was scheduled for mid-March.

Union League: Originally a Northern white, middle-class, patriotic organization during the Civil War years, the league became a political vehicle for the freedmen in the early postwar period. Its principal goal was to raise the consciousness of African Americans and to encourage black males to vote.

The election was marred by irregularities in voting, but the majority of eligible voters approved the charter. Gen. A. C. Gillem, who had succeeded General Ord as commander of the Fourth Military District, certified the results and the slate of officers elected at the same time, and the US Congress accepted them, again over the president's veto. The new state legislature quickly ratified the Fourteenth Amendment, and having thus satisfied the conditions set down by the Reconstruction Acts, Arkansas reentered the Union on June 22, 1868.

The governor elected under the new state constitution of 1868 was thirty-four-year-old Powell Clayton, a former Federal cavalry officer from Kansas who had established a reputation among many Arkansas Confederates as the best Federal cavalry commander west of the Mississippi River. Even before the war ended, Clayton purchased a cotton plantation near Pine Bluff where he settled after the war. Clayton had been a Democrat before the war, but the growing hostility and violence directed against African Americans and Unionists in the immediate postwar period had caused him to turn against his former party. By 1867, he was active in the creation of the Republican Party in Arkansas.

Unlike his conciliatory predecessor, Clayton viewed Reconstruction as little more than a continuation of the war (which in many ways it was), and he employed many of the same aggressive tactics he had used in that conflict. He also used the governor's vastly expanded appointive powers and the Republican-dominated state legislature to build a loyal base of supporters throughout the state.

Clayton and the Republican-dominated legislature hoped to accomplish four major objectives—to put an end to the widespread violence in the state, to implement the Republican program of protection of the civil and political rights of black Arkansans, to rebuild and restructure the state's economy, and to build a viable and lasting Republican Party in Arkansas. The governor also moved to address the question of economic development, modeled along the lines of what came to be called the "gospel of prosperity." Anticipating the New South movement of the late nineteenth century, Republican leaders sought to transform the South into a diversified economy along the lines of the free labor system of the North. As historian Eric Foner notes, "With the aid of the state, they believed, the backward South could be transformed into a society of booming factories, bustling towns, a diversified agriculture freed from the plantation's dominance, and abundant employment opportunities for black and white alike."

To pay for this economic development and for expanded government services, the legislature raised property tax rates and ordered the reassessment of real estate at market value. Historians have disagreed over the extent of the increase and the degree to which the new revenues helped the state. Historian Carl Moneyhon has contended, "The increases were not as outrageous as the Republicans' opponents charged, and most of the money went to actual improvements." Nevertheless, as Moneyhon notes, the new assessments, coming on the heels of two bad crop seasons and falling cotton prices, were particularly hard on large landowners and gave the Democrats a powerful political issue. Republican leaders hoped that in the long run their economic plan would draw support from a wide range of Southerners—former Whigs, entrepreneurs, merchants, and working-class people of both races—thereby reshaping Southern politics and establishing a solid base of Republican support.

The central element of the Republicans' economic plan was railroad construction, one of the few areas on which they and their Conservative-Democrat opponents agreed. Only about sixty-five miles of track were in operation in the state when the Civil War began, and none had been added in the intervening years. Clayton and the Republican-dominated legislature put forward a plan for government assistance to railroad companies that the voters overwhelmingly approved. The plan proposed to pay selected companies $10,000 per mile of track laid for railroads receiving federal land grants and $15,000 per mile for others. The large amounts of money involved made the prospect of railroad building extremely appealing to ambitious entrepreneurs and unscrupulous politicians, many of whom were prominent figures in the new companies' boards of directors.

Eventually eighty-six companies were chartered, though some smaller companies later consolidated. Only five railroads whose routes followed the state's main arteries of commerce received state credit in bonds. By the end of Reconstruction, an additional 662 miles of track had been laid at a cost to the

Considered by many to be the best Union cavalry officer west of the Mississippi during the war, Powell Clayton became the first Republican governor of Arkansas after the war's end. *Courtesy of J. N. Heiskell Collection/UALR Archives and Special Collections.*

state of about $90,000,000. One scholarly examination of railroad building in the state concluded that "the Arkansas case is one in which the mileage actually constructed under state aid approached very closely the mileage for which [state] assistance was intended."

Still, the railroad-building boom was far from an unqualified success. The Arkansas economy was not developed enough to support even a few railroads, much less eighty-six. All companies receiving state money eventually went bankrupt, many of them without ever laying any track. These defaults added to an already severe debt problem including over $3,000,000 remaining from the collapse of the State Bank and the Real Estate Bank that the Republicans had hoped to retire.

White Terror and Martial Law

An even more pressing problem for Clayton was the persistence of widespread violence in the state. Some Conservative elements, barred from participation in the political process by the Military Reconstruction Act, were determined to use any and all means to oppose the new government. One of those means was the Ku Klux Klan. Founded by Confederate veterans as a secretive social fraternity in Pulaski, Tennessee, in the spring of 1866, the

Ku Klux Klan:
Secretive orga-
nization founded
originally as a
social fraternity
by Confederate
veterans in Pulaski,
Tennessee, in
1866. The Klan
became a terroristic
organization that
functioned as the
paramilitary arm of
the Conservative-
Democratic
Party during the
Reconstruction era,
attacking freedmen,
government officials,
and Republicans.

Klan soon evolved into a vigilante organization dedicated to the preservation of white supremacy. To accomplish this goal, the Klan employed terroristic tactics to intimidate or kill African Americans, Republicans, and other Unionists throughout the South. In Arkansas, the rise of the Klan coincided with the beginning of a massive campaign of terror and violence in all but the northwestern counties of the state in 1868. Historian Allen Trelease has estimated that more than two hundred Arkansans were murdered on the eve of the 1868 presidential election. In August of that year, Clayton began to organize the state militia, but he refused numerous requests for troops from voter registration officials around the state.

Despite numerous threats against his life, including what was in all probability an aborted assassination attempt in the fall of 1868, Governor Clayton acted decisively and with great personal courage to stem the violence. Along with moderate Conservative leader and former Confederate senator Augustus Garland, he personally intervened to try to end racial and political strife in Conway County, one of the state's most troubled regions in the postwar years. In addition, Clayton employed a dozen undercover agents to infiltrate the Klan and report on its activities. One of the agents was murdered when his true identity was revealed.

The federal government, however, neither matched nor supported the governor's actions. An appeal for federal troops to supplement the small force remaining in Arkansas was rejected, as was a subsequent request to use the arms stored in the federal arsenal at Little Rock. Finally, Clayton sent agents to purchase guns in the North. In October 1868, the guns were delivered to Memphis, but the steamer *Hesper*, chartered to deliver the weapons to Little Rock, was run aground by another vessel on the Mississippi River below Memphis. Masked men boarded the vessel and seized its cargo, confiscating some and dumping the rest into the river.

The Election of 1868

Despite these setbacks, Clayton managed to hold the state for the Republican ticket. Citing violence against voter registration officials that caused the registrars to resign their posts, he rejected the registration in Ashley, Bradley, Columbia, Craighead, Greene, Hot Spring, Lafayette, Mississippi, Randolph, Sevier, Sharp, and Woodruff counties, effectively excluding them from the election. In addition, there was no registration in Lawrence County and no returns from Fulton County. Of these fourteen counties only two had recorded majorities for the constitution the previous April. The results from the November 3 balloting showed 22,112 votes for Republican presidential candidate Ulysses Grant to 19,078 for Democrat Horatio Seymour of New York. (Arkansas's five electoral votes contributed to Grant's 214 to 80 electoral vote majority.) The Republicans also retained all three of the state's congressional seats. Democrats charged that voters in the counties whose registrations had been rejected would have provided the margin of victory for their candidates, but it is impossible to determine whether the number of potential Democratic voters who were unable to cast ballots would have offset the number of Republican voters who were intimidated away from the polls by the Klan.

The day after the election, Clayton declared martial law in Ashley, Bradley, Columbia, Lafayette, Mississippi, Woodruff, Craighead, Greene, Sevier, and Little River counties, proclaiming them to be "in a state of insurrection" with the civil authorities "utterly powerless to preserve order and to protect the lives of the citizens." He later extended it to include Conway, Crittenden, Drew, and Fulton counties. Since membership was limited to eligible voters, the militia was composed largely of blacks and white Unionists. The state was then divided into four military districts, although little attention was paid to the northwest part of the state where Klan support was minimal and Republican support was strongest. Three Unionist state legislators were placed in charge of the remaining three districts, and the various units of the state militia were ordered to rendezvous at designated points around the state.

Martial law: The imposition of military government over a designated area, usually for a temporary period during an emergency situation when the civilian government is unable or unwilling to maintain order or provide essential services.

The declaration of martial law and the subsequent activities of the militia constitute one of the most controversial aspects of Reconstruction in Arkansas. Over the course of the next five months, violent clashes between the militia and the Klan and Klan sympathizers took place in the southeast, southwest, and northeast regions of the state. From the inception of the so-called Militia War, Clayton was bombarded by complaints of theft, rape, and other abuses by the militia forces. While it is clear that many of the charges lodged against the militia were exaggerated or, in some cases, totally fabricated, the evidence of depredations by the militia is so widespread and so pervasive that it cannot be discounted. Clayton appointed his own adjutant general to investigate some of the charges. His report concluded, "It would be impossible anywhere to call into existence a force as this has been, for temporary purposes, and not have violations of order and military law." In at least two instances, black militiamen were tried and convicted of rape and executed by firing squads. These depredations notwithstanding, Clayton refused to end martial law in a county until he was convinced that law and order had been restored there. Civilian authority was restored in the southwest district in mid-January 1869, in the southeast district in early February, and in the remainder of the state in late March.

Clayton's declaration of martial law and deployment of the militia, combined with the desire of many law-abiding Arkansans of all political persuasions for a return to law and order, contributed to the rapid decline of the Arkansas Klan and the restoration of some semblance of civility. Historian Eric Foner has noted, "Scores of suspected Klansmen were arrested; three were executed after trials by military courts, and numerous others fled the state. By early 1869, order had been restored and the Klan destroyed." While it is an overstatement to say that the Klan had been destroyed in the state, it is possible to argue, as Allen Trelease does, that Clayton "accomplished more than any other Southern governor in suppressing the Ku Klux conspiracy." But if Clayton's actions were effective in suppressing Klan violence, they also left a legacy of bitterness with many white Arkansans that severely undermined his attempts to build support for the Republican Party in Arkansas. Clayton had other political troubles as well. Martial law had scarcely ended when the governor faced a revolt from within his own party.

Republican Schism and Conservative Resurgence

In April 1869 Lieutenant-Governor James Johnson and a group of Republican state legislators met to organize opposition to the Clayton regime. The new faction, which styled itself the "Liberals," advocated an end to corruption, greater economy in government, the curtailing of the governor's powers, and an immediate end to all restrictions on voting rights for former Confederates. Identified with the national Liberal Republican movement that opposed the administration of President Grant, the Liberal Party in Arkansas charged Clayton with extravagance, mismanagement, corruption, and abuse of his power, particularly as it related to his role as commander-in-chief of the militia.

These charges aside, much of the opposition was personal rather than ideological. Johnson, a Madison County resident who had served as an officer in the Union army during the war, and other native Arkansas Unionists had chafed at the dominance of the Republican Party and of state government by "outsiders" like Clayton and at the governor's domineering nature. Clayton clearly understood the importance of patronage in maintaining his political hold on the state government and of the Republican Party. The governor had used the vast patronage power that the new constitution had bestowed on him to appoint men who were loyal not only to the party but also to him personally.

The breach widened in the summer of 1869 when Clayton went to New York to arrange for the American Exchange National Bank to act as the fiscal agent for financing the state debt. Perhaps fearing what actions Johnson might take in his absence, Clayton did not inform the lieutenant governor of his departure. But some of Johnson's supporters got word of the governor's absence and urged Johnson to leave his northwest Arkansas home and come to Little Rock to assume power. Johnson did come to Little Rock, though exactly what he intended to do when he arrived is unclear. It was a moot point because Clayton hastened back to the capital, arriving before Johnson. The lieutenant governor made a public speech condemning Clayton, before, in the governor's words, "sneak[ing] back to his mountain home."

Johnson returned to Little Rock in October, however, to help formally organize the insurgent Republicans. Meanwhile, with an election year approaching and his administration under attack both from within and without the Republican Party, Clayton shifted tactics. In an unusually conciliatory address, the governor co-opted most of the Liberals' platform, advocating lower taxes and the removal of voting disabilities from former Confederates and urged his listeners to "let bygones be bygones; help neighbors, avoid jealousy; let us as one man and one voice strike hands together to build up the fallen fortunes of Arkansas." Longtime observers might well have wondered what had come over the governor in his abbreviated trip to New York. Clayton spent the remaining months prior to the 1870 election attempting to mend fences in his own party and solidifying his control over county organizations, while the Conservative-Democrats vigorously pursued a voter registration campaign.

Liberal gains in the 1870 elections were held to a minimum, but despite disfranchisement, the governor's control of the election machinery, and widespread fraud, the Conservative-Democrats reemerged as a legitimate force in both houses of the state legislature. It was clear to Governor Clayton and other Republicans that the end of voting disabilities on former Confederates would place the Republican Party in Arkansas in dire straits. In the January session of the new legislature, Clayton pursued the US Senate seat that was up for election. He was overwhelmingly elected, garnering not only the votes of his Republican supporters but also those of Conservative-Democrats who wanted him out of the state. But while Clayton was ready to assume the Senate seat, he was unwilling to turn the governor's office over to Lieutenant-Governor Johnson.

Pro-Clayton forces tried to have Johnson impeached. When this failed, a coalition of Democrats and Liberal Republicans succeeded in having the

Ohio native Joseph Brooks was a Methodist preacher who served as a chaplain in the Union army during the war. He later became the leader of a faction in the state Republican Party that was opposed to Governor Powell Clayton. *Courtesy of the Arkansas History Commission.*

house pass articles of impeachment against Clayton. Arkansas law provided that the governor would be suspended when the house informed the senate of its action. Pro-Clayton senators refused to enter the chamber thereby denying the house managers a quorum. Johnson formally demanded that Clayton surrender the office but was rebuffed. Rumors of violence swept the capital.

The end of the crisis came when Clayton persuaded the secretary of state to resign his office and offered the vacant position to the lieutenant governor. Amazingly, Johnson accepted the offer. With the lieutenant governor's position vacant, the line of succession passed to the president of the senate, Ozra Hadley, a devoted Clayton ally. Hadley served out the remainder of the term in a caretaker capacity. Clayton took his seat in the US Senate in March 1871. But while Clayton was gone, he saw to it that he was not forgotten. He remained a powerful figure in Arkansas and national Republican politics until his death in 1914.

With both Clayton and his main challenger within the party now out of the picture, a fierce new battle soon developed for political ascendancy in Arkansas. The man who came to lead the insurgent wing of the Republican Party, Joseph Brooks, was a former Methodist minister from Iowa with a voice "like a brindle-tail bull." Brooks had been the dominant figure at the constitutional convention of 1868 and had supported Governor Clayton's employment of the militia in 1869 before later falling out with the governor. In 1871 Brooks announced his intention to seek the governorship in the 1872 election. He was a formidable candidate. His strong record on civil rights drew support from black Arkansans, and his platform of "Universal suffrage,

Elisha Baxter came to Arkansas in 1852 while in his mid-twenties. A leader of the "Minstrel" faction of the state Republican Party, he was declared the winner of the disputed election of 1872. *Courtesy of J. N. Heiskell Collection/UALR Archives and Special Collections.*

universal amnesty, and honest men in office" combined with his opposition to Clayton gave him strong appeal to many Democrats and other Conservatives.

Without the services of their longtime leader and confronted by a candidate with wide appeal and great political skills, the Regular (pro-Clayton) Republicans faced the greatest challenge in their brief history. Meeting in convention in August, they dumped the colorless Hadley and nominated in his place the Batesville merchant and lawyer Elisha Baxter. Baxter was a native of North Carolina who had moved to Batesville in 1852 and served two terms in the state legislature in the 1850s. His exact political position before the war is difficult to determine. Purported to be a Whig, he had supported Thomas Hindman in the elections of 1858 and 1860 but had opposed secession.

Baxter's wartime experiences were the stuff of adventure novels. When Federal forces occupied Batesville in 1862, he was offered a commission in the Union army but declined. When Confederate forces reoccupied the area, Baxter fled to Missouri where he took a job as a schoolteacher. In 1863, he was captured by a Confederate raiding party led by Col. Robert C. Newton and returned to Arkansas to stand trial for treason. Friends in Little Rock helped him to escape, and he began a long and dangerous flight to Union lines in Missouri, surviving on little more than corn and berries. Arriving in Springfield, he recruited a mounted infantry regiment and became its colonel.

After Little Rock fell to Union forces, Baxter served the Murphy government as a member of the state supreme court and was later elected by the Unionist legislature to the US Senate, though the Radical-controlled body refused to seat him. Governor Clayton later appointed him as judge of the Third Judicial District. The platform of the Regular Republicans (often referred to as "Minstrels" after the previous occupation of one of their leaders) differed little from that of Brooks's "Brindletail" faction.

The nomination of Brooks and Baxter by the opposing factions within the Republican Party initiated the "Brooks-Baxter War," one of the most confused and confusing episodes in all of Arkansas history. As Michael Dougan has noted, "That carpetbagger Brooks ran with Democratic and scalawag support against a scalawag nominated by a Party composed almost exclusively of carpetbaggers was enough to bewilder most voters as well as the modern student." Brooks's oratorical skills gave him a great advantage, but Baxter had an advantage of his own; namely, control of the election machinery. In the final analysis, it proved decisive.

The election in early November 1872 was marred by the now all-too-familiar pattern of fraud, intimidation, and stuffed ballot boxes. Returns from four counties were declared invalid and thrown out. "Official" returns revealed that Baxter had won by a vote of 41,681 to 38,415. Brooks's partisans fiercely contested the results, but were frustrated in their attempts to have the election overturned. The legislature, dominated by Regular Republicans, failed to grant Brooks a hearing. Thus frustrated in the legislature, the Brooks forces turned to the courts. In June 1873, the state attorney general initiated a *quo warranto* proceeding against Baxter, requiring the governor to prove the validity of his claim to the office. The Brooks forces hoped for a favorable ruling from the state supreme court, which was headed by Chief Justice John McClure, a former Clayton ally and appointee and a Brooks supporter. The court denied the writ over McClure's dissent.

That same month, Brooks filed a complaint against Baxter in Pulaski Circuit Court claiming that Baxter had usurped the governor's office without authority. In response, Baxter filed a *demurrer* (a pleading that asserts that, even if the charges of the other party are true, they are insufficient to constitute a cause of action) and no further action was taken for a time. The Regular Republicans also retained control of the legislature, and Arkansas gave its eight electoral votes to President Grant.

In his brief inaugural, Baxter expressed the hope that his election would "mark the commencement of a new era of peace and good feeling in the history of Arkansas." He advocated "the immediate enfranchisement of those persons who are now denied a voice in the selection of their rulers," and he moved quickly to make good that pledge. An amendment restoring the vote was put to the voters in March 1873 and passed overwhelmingly. Thus, Arkansas became the last state to remove voting disabilities on former Confederates.

The new governor appointed Conservative-Democrats and Liberals as well as Regular Republicans to government positions. After the legislature adjourned in April, a combination of gubernatorial appointments and resignations resulted in almost forty legislative vacancies, necessitating a special election in November 1873. The results reflected the changes wrought by the recent passage of the new franchise amendment. Democrats were elected to fill practically all the legislative vacancies, giving them control of the state legislature for the first time since the advent of Congressional Reconstruction.

Baxter continued to broaden his appeal to all factions, but in so doing he began to alienate his own base. Particularly offensive to Republicans of all stripes was the appointment of former Confederate colonel Robert Newton to head the state militia (the same Robert Newton who had arrested Baxter for treason in 1863). But despite their disapproval of many of his actions, Clayton and fellow US senator Stephen F. Dorsey continued to support Baxter.

The following year, however, a major schism occurred that severely threatened the future of the Baxter administration. Democratic success in the special election gave rise to a call for a special convention to draft a new constitution more in line with Conservative-Democratic principles. The prospect of a new charter that threatened to undo all that Republicans had worked for since 1868 sent shock waves through Republican ranks. When it became apparent that Baxter favored the calling of a convention, Senators Clayton and Dorsey hastened to Little Rock to attempt to exert their influence on the governor.

That same month, Baxter announced that all the railroad bonds that had been issued by the Reconstruction government (including apparently $400,000 worth that had been issued by him personally) had been issued in violation of the constitution and indicated that he would not issue any more such bonds. One of the railroad companies affected by this order was closely associated with Senator Dorsey. Even more significantly, this action by the governor threatened to undermine the very foundation of the Republicans' plan for economic Reconstruction as well as the state's credit. For Dorsey and Clayton, this was the last straw. Deserting Baxter, they allied themselves with Brooks and persuaded a friendly Pulaski County circuit judge to bring up the case of *Brooks v. Baxter* (filed ten months previously) and, on April 15, 1874, the judge declared Brooks the legal governor of Arkansas.

Brooks was sworn in by Chief Justice McClure, and shortly thereafter Brooks and over a dozen armed men marched to the statehouse and forced the startled Baxter to vacate the governor's office. Baxter and his supporters established themselves at the Anthony House, a local hotel located less than three blocks east of the capitol near the intersection of Markham and Scott streets. There they laid plans to retake the office. Main Street became the dividing line between the two opposing forces, and federal troops served as a peacekeeping force in attempting to keep the two sides apart. The surreal nature of the situation increased when both sides organized militias, each commanded by a former Confederate officer.

The schism in Republican ranks also divided other political constituencies in Arkansas. Some Democrats and other Conservatives had supported Brooks in the election as the best hope of unseating the hated Regular Republicans, and they welcomed his *coup d'état*. Others, including prominent Little Rock attorneys Augustus Garland and U. M. Rose, remembered Brooks's staunch radicalism in the early days of the Clayton regime and feared his ascension to the governor's chair. Garland, a prewar Whig and former Confederate senator, understood that the Conservative-Democratic element in the state could be a critical swing vote in the struggle between opposing factions in the Republican Party and that Baxter could be the instrument of the state's deliverance from Reconstruction. He and Baxter had become friends, and the embattled governor sought to bolster his position through Garland's standing in the community and his keen legal mind.

For Baxter, Garland was a major weapon in his struggle to retain his office, but for Garland, Baxter was only a means to an end. In a revealing letter to former Confederate governor Harris Flanagin, Garland candidly admitted, "It is small moment really who is Govr. of these two, but it is of great moment to settle these troubles and get a government by & from the people." These sentiments were shared by Robert Ward Johnson and Albert Pike, now residents of Washington, DC, who supported Baxter's cause in the nation's capital.

African Americans were also divided over the issue. When the call for volunteers went out from the rival militias, black Arkansans rallied to both camps. On the last day of April, a predominantly black force of two hundred Baxter supporters led by a charismatic ex-Confederate soldier named Hercules King Cannon White steamed downriver from Pine Bluff to New Gascony, about twenty-five miles below the town, where they surprised and routed a black company of Brooks supporters, killing seven and wounding thirty. A week later two hundred Brooks men ambushed a steamboat carrying forty Baxter supporters near the point where Palarm Creek enters the Arkansas River upstream from Little Rock, killing or wounding half of them and disabling the boat.

Skirmishes between rival factions broke out throughout the state, but Little Rock remained the center of the controversy. Volunteers for both sides flooded into the city until the number of armed men reached about three thousand with each faction seeking desperately to secure weapons and ammunition. Scattered incidents of gunfire erupted, resulting in a few casualties on both sides, and the potential for widespread bloodshed increased with each passing day.

Many Arkansans cared less about who occupied the governor's office than they did about the restoration of stability and order to state government. They joined the warring factions in appealing to President Grant to intervene. Finally, on May 15, 1874, one month to the day after the crisis began, the president, convinced that serious violence was imminent, telegraphed his support for Baxter and ordered the Brooks forces to disband. He cushioned the blow by appointing Brooks to the position of postmaster at Little Rock.

The following month, voters went to the polls to decide whether to hold a convention to write a new constitution and to choose delegates to that convention. This first statewide election since the end of restrictions on former Confederates gave clear evidence of a new day in Arkansas politics. The convention was approved by margin of almost ten to one (80,259 to 8,547), and Conservative-Democrats won over seventy of the ninety-one delegate positions. Historian Thomas Staples has noted, "The Democratic members were elected and came together under the impression that they were to be the chief actors in a work of reform. That reform, as they understood it, was to be the undoing of the work of the Republican Party in Arkansas as far as the state constitution was concerned."

The convention assembled on July 14, 1874, and remained in session until early September. The document it produced provided for the civil and political rights of all citizens regardless of race (a necessary concession to prevent the possibility of federal intervention), but otherwise it undid many of the most significant measures the Republicans had written into the constitution of 1868. The governor's term was shortened to two years, his powers were dramatically reduced, and his salary, along with those of other state officials, kept very low. Gubernatorial vetoes could be overridden by a simple majority vote. Whereas the constitution of 1868 had given the governor the power to appoint many state officials, the new document made all major government offices subject to popular election.

In addition, the convention placed severe restraints on the taxing powers of both state and local governments by imposing low maximum rates. As a result, public education and other government services would be chronically underfunded. Many of the powers that had been assumed by the state during Reconstruction were returned to county and municipal governments, entities that were almost always dominated by local landed and business elites. In the final analysis, the constitution of 1874 largely succeeded in accomplishing most of the "reforms" that the Conservative-Democrats had sought, which is to say that it precluded the kind of strong executive leadership and activist government that Powell Clayton and the Republicans had pursued.

On October 13, 1874, the voters went to the polls to vote for or against ratification of the proposed constitution and to elect officials to serve under the new document if adopted. Arkansas Republicans, their hopes for maintaining their hold on power tied to the increasingly unlikely prospect of federal intervention, did not put forward candidates for state offices. In the largest voter turnout in Arkansas history to that time, the Conservative-Democrats not only won control of those offices but also returned overwhelming majorities in the state legislature (thirty-one Democrats to two Republicans in the senate, eighty Democrats to ten Republicans in the house) and elected Augustus H. Garland governor.

A prominent Whig attorney in the antebellum period, Garland had supported John Bell of the Constitutional Union Party for president in 1860. Elected to represent Pulaski County in the secession convention of 1861, he had opposed secession until President Lincoln's call for troops. Through a combination of personal magnetism and ability, he had risen rapidly through the ranks of the Confederate government, serving first as representative and later as senator in the Confederate congress.

Disfranchised by the Fourteenth Amendment, he had, through the influence of powerful friends, obtained a pardon from President Johnson in July 1865, only seventeen days after submitting his request. Garland then returned to his law practice. Though he had been admitted to the bar of the US Supreme Court in 1860, his inability to take the "ironclad oath" that he had never born arms against the United States nor held office in a government hostile to it prevented him from arguing cases before the court. In the case of *Ex Parte Garland* (1866), he successfully challenged the prohibition as unconstitutional and regained the right to appear before the court. When Governor Baxter declined the Democratic Party's nomination for governor in 1874, the convention turned to Garland, and he won easy nomination and election.

The new legislature that assembled in November 1874 wasted little time in completing the unraveling of the constitution of 1868 by placing the assessment of property in the hands of locally elected assessors rather than officials appointed by the governor. This measure made it possible for politically powerful propertied interests to control the assessment process, and it ensured the continued economic hegemony of the state's landed interests.

Only the long-anticipated report of a special committee of the US House of Representatives charged with investigating the Brooks-Baxter controversy stood between the Conservative-Democrats and their goal of reclaiming control of the state government. The committee's majority report, submitted in early February 1875, concluded that the federal government should not interfere with the existing state government. The full House officially accepted the report on March 2. Three days later, Senator Clayton, who had labored diligently to overturn the Baxter government, conceded defeat, telling his followers, "The action of Congress on Arkansas affairs is conclusive.

The validity of the new constitution and the government established thereunder ought no longer to be questioned. It is the duty of Republicans to accept the verdict, and render the same acquiescence which we would have demanded had the case been reversed." Reconstruction in Arkansas was over.

The Legacy of Reconstruction

The Republican Reconstruction governments could take credit for some significant accomplishments, including dramatically expanding the amount of railroad mileage in the state, providing for the first state-supported institutions for the blind and deaf, and establishing the state's first system of free public education. In addition, the legislature, in March 1871, established the first state university, the Arkansas Industrial University (now the University of Arkansas at Fayetteville). Two years later, the state established a normal school for African Americans at Pine Bluff (now the University of Arkansas at Pine Bluff). In other areas, such as economic diversification, penal reform, and the development of a viable second party, Reconstruction fell far short of what its proponents had hoped.

For black Arkansans, Reconstruction proved a mixed blessing. The Freedmen's Bureau enjoyed notable success in establishing schools for the former slaves, but in other areas it was less successful. Many of the gains made by African Americans in this period were the results of their own efforts. As Randy Finley has noted, "Freedpersons tested their freedom in many ways— by assuming new names, searching for lost family members, moving to new residences, working to provide for their families, learning to read and write, forming and attending their own churches, creating their own histories and myths, struggling to obtain land, and establishing different nuances in race, gender, and class."

For almost a quarter century after the end of the war, relations between the races were more ambiguous, fluid, and flexible than they had been previously or would be after the full flowering of "Jim Crow" segregation in the 1890s. While racial hostility and discrimination still existed, African Americans exercised a degree of political, social, and economic autonomy that would have been unthinkable in 1860. Under Republican rule, blacks played prominent roles in state politics. African Americans served as delegates to the constitutional conventions of 1868 and 1874, were represented in every general assembly between 1868 and 1893, and, particularly in areas with heavy black populations, held numerous offices at the county and local level.

Even the return of the Conservative-Democrats to power in 1874 did not lead to an immediate deterioration of the status of black Arkansans. In his inaugural address, Governor Garland struck a conciliatory tone, noting that while the laws should be rigidly enforced, "no man living under them should be unjustly or illegally deprived of one iota of his rights; and let no man be put in fear or injured, or denied any right on account of race, color or previous condition of servitude." His successor, William Miller, continued this moderate approach, and throughout the remainder of the decade the Democratic Party openly courted the black vote.

In the aftermath of emancipation, Arkansas planters, desperate for laborers, actively recruited workers from surrounding states. While most African Americans continued to be employed in agriculture, others found new opportunities in the state's urban areas, particularly Little Rock and Pine Bluff. In these more heterogeneous settings, blacks served on city councils and school boards; owned and operated boardinghouses, barbershops, saloons, and restaurants; entered the professions as teachers, clergymen, lawyers, and doctors; and formed their own religious and fraternal organizations. Arkansas soon acquired a reputation as a place where African Americans might enjoy a better life. "Arkansas is destined to be the great Negro state of the country," remarked Henry Turner, a bishop of the African Methodist Episcopal Church. "The meagre [sic] prejudice compared to some states, and opportunity to acquire wealth, all conspire to make it inviting to the colored man." The message resonated with many African Americans, and between 1870 and 1890 the black population of the state more than doubled.

In the end, however, the promise that Arkansas had held out for African Americans went largely unfulfilled. The failure of the federal government to provide them with land prevented most black Arkansans from obtaining true independence. Tenancy and declining crop prices kept them in a position of economic and social inferiority, and the advent of Jim Crow in the 1890s closed the brief window of political, social, and economic opportunity that many had enjoyed. At the turn of the century, most black Arkansans remained second-class citizens, condemned to a grinding cycle of poverty and political powerlessness whose effects are still being felt. Though the gains made during Reconstruction laid the foundation for the civil rights movement of the next century, it remained, in Eric Foner's words, an "unfinished revolution."

Some of the reasons for the failure of Reconstruction to achieve its goals were beyond the control of any faction within the state or the region. The bad weather conditions of 1866 and 1867, the steep decline in the price of cotton, and the economic depression of the 1870s all contributed to problems faced by Reconstruction governments. But if the actions of former Confederates in the months following the end of the war destroyed any hope of a lenient Reconstruction, the actions of Republicans in the years between 1867 and 1874 helped assure the failure of Radical Reconstruction. Part of the blame lay with the Northern Republicans who, by the end of the Reconstruction era, had simply lost the will to carry through on their commitment to restructuring Southern society and guaranteeing civil rights for African Americans. But Arkansas Republicans must also take a large measure of responsibility.

The Militia War and the denial of the vote to ex-Confederates engendered a hatred for the Republican Party among many Arkansans that the passage of a hundred years would not assuage. High taxes turned many Arkansans against the Reconstruction regime. To be sure, taxes in the antebellum period had been exceedingly low and government services almost nonexistent. But for many Arkansans the higher taxes exacerbated an already tenuous economic condition, and the new revenues often failed to achieve the promised results. In some Arkansas counties, the property tax assessments increased by sevenfold during Reconstruction, with little to show in return. Despite the increase in taxes, the state debt soared. When Isaac Murphy turned over the reins of government to Powell Clayton in 1868, the state had a surplus of $122,587. Six years later, when the Conservative-Democrats reclaimed control of the government, the state was over ten million dollars in debt.

Widespread corruption also eroded support for the Republican regime. While it is undoubtedly true that much of the alleged corruption was exaggerated by opposition politicians and newspapers, real extravagance and corruption were all too common. Radical legislators submitted grossly inflated requests for travel reimbursement, appropriated funds to provide every member with ten daily newspapers (a virtual subsidy for Radical newspapers that had very little other support), and staffed the legislature with an assortment of functionaries in a thinly disguised effort to provide jobs for their supporters at the public expense.

Republican partisans who obtained the state penitentiary lease were accused of selling furniture in the penitentiary cells to the state for more than five times its original cost. Two of the lessees were alleged to have replaced the penitentiary roof needlessly at state expense while they used the old roof on their private homes. Corruption also tainted federal officials in the state. The federal judge for the Western District of Arkansas, William Story, resigned while under investigation on charges of bribery, and three United States marshals were dismissed after being charged with submitting false accounts and defrauding the government.

Revisionists have argued that such practices have accompanied almost every political organization and have noted that corruption in this period was a national rather than a peculiarly Southern problem. But as Eric Foner has pointed out, "Corruption may be ubiquitous in American history, but it thrived in the Reconstruction South because of the specific circumstances of Republican rule." The disfranchisement of many Arkansans meant that public officials were not responsible to the people they purported to represent.

The expansion of government services, the larger state budgets, the unprecedented amounts of money available to government officials, the corporations (particularly railroads) competing for government assistance, and the tenuous political and economic circumstances of many Republican officeholders combined to create an atmosphere conducive to corruption on a large scale.

For all these reasons, Republicans were never able to gain sufficient support among white Arkansans to maintain themselves as a legitimate and viable second party. All of these factors, combined with its inability to maintain a united political front, doomed the party's efforts to permanently alter the direction of Southern society and allowed Conservative forces to reclaim control of the state government.

Democrats and other Conservative forces liked to refer to their return to power as "Redemption." Their triumph in the elections of 1874 marked the climax of a remarkable political resurgence by Arkansas's prewar elite that matched or exceeded their economic revival. Relegated to the political sidelines by the advent of Congressional Reconstruction, they had employed both fair and foul means to maintain their political viability and bided their time until the split in Republican ranks in 1872 and the subsequent restoration of voting rights to former Confederates enabled them to regain their political dominance. The planter class emerged from the struggles of the Reconstruction era weaker and poorer than before the war, but with their dominant position in Arkansas society restored. Nowhere was this more apparent than in the election of Augustus Garland and the men who followed him to the governor's office in the next two decades. William Miller (1877–1881) had been the Confederate state auditor, Thomas Churchill (1881–1883) a major general in the Confederate army, James Berry (1883–1885) a second lieutenant, Simon Hughes (1885–1889) and James Eagle (1889–1893) lieutenant colonels.

Even had these men been disposed to assume an activist, progressive stance, the new constitution's reduction in the powers of the governor and the strict limits on the ability to raise taxes thwarted any serious attempt to promote the general welfare of the people through government action. Limited government and low property taxes would well serve the interests of the state's landed elite far into the next century. Change would come to Arkansas in the last quarter of the nineteenth century, but it would often come in spite of rather than because of the efforts of the state government.

The war, emancipation, and Reconstruction had been truly revolutionary experiences for the state and the region. But the return to power of the antebellum elites ensured that Reconstruction would remain, in the words of Mississippi planter James Alcorn, a "harnessed revolution."

10 Arkansas in the New South, 1880–1900

ARKANSAS BEGAN TO recover from the devastation of the Civil War in the last two decades of the nineteenth century and embraced the process of reintegration into the national economy and culture. It did so within a southern context, however, and even though sectional reconciliation accompanied this period of transition, certain repressive institutions and a virulent racism also emerged. Many of the state's leaders adopted the New South ideal outlined by Georgia's Henry Grady, particularly its emphasis on attracting northern capital in order to rebuild Arkansas. However, they eventually eschewed his notion of moderate race relations in favor of segregation and disfranchisement and the relegation of blacks into a rigid caste structure. Even here they found kindred spirits in the North, as voters disfranchised and denigrated eastern European immigrants flocking to that region's cities. Conciliation between the sections failed to fully obscure continuing differences, but the eager and enthusiastic participation of two regiments of Arkansas soldiers in the Spanish American War symbolized the distance traveled between 1865 and 1898.

Railroads, the Timber Industry, and Mining

Although the "new" in the New South had its limitations, Arkansas experienced considerable growth and some industrial advancement in the last twenty-five years of the nineteenth century. Most of the industries that came to Arkansas during the so-called "gilded age" were extractive in nature and orchestrated by out-of-state investors who had limited interest in promoting local development. Some home-grown entrepreneurs, however, capitalized on the demand for Arkansas agricultural and lumber resources and made fortunes for themselves. Scott Bond (1852–1933), a former slave who began renting acreage and farming it after the Civil War, later opened a mercantile establishment and began purchasing land. He skillfully negotiated the hyper racism of the era and eventually amassed a 12,000-acre plantation in St. Francis County. Lee Wilson (1865–1933), the son of a former slave owner, capitalized on the demand for lumber and parlayed a 400-acre inheritance into a 50,000-acre plantation empire in Mississippi County. But Bond and Wilson were relatively rare. Few Arkansans were able to accumulate sufficient capital to allow them to profit significantly from the two principle new industries that fueled Arkansas's limited growth: lumber and mining.

The railroad played the dual role of bringing northern investors into Arkansas and opening up the state to the larger market. The plans and schemes of both Democrats and Republicans alike in the years immediately following the war yielded a network of rail lines, but at a greater cost than the state could afford. During the 1880s and 1890s, eastern capitalists like Jay Gould, who had an eye on Arkansas's forests, appropriated or purchased various lines, infused the effort with considerable capital, and dramatically expanded the state's railroad infrastructure. By the end of the century, more than two thousand miles of rail lines stretched into all four corners of the state.

While the railroad began to transform the landscape in significant ways, not merely by the creation of hundreds of new towns but also by the terracing of roadbeds that cut across the state, the lumber industry dramatically altered the landscape and provided tens of thousands of new jobs. Lumber workers flooded to towns in northeastern Arkansas, like Marked Tree and Paragould, the latter at the conjunction of two railroads owned by J. W. Paramore and Jay Gould. Men hungry for work swarmed into Ouachita Mountain communities in southwest Arkansas like Plainview, Mauldin, and Graysonia. Other young men went south from Little Rock to Grant County and found jobs in Sheridan. Large lumber mills producing millions of board feet of lumber a day dominated the towns in which they were located, both in terms of the physical space they occupied and in terms of the number of townspeople they employed. Relatively inexpensive temporary or roving mills, often operated by small landowners taking advantage of the market for lumber or by entrepreneurs who would "cut and run" whether they owned the land or not, were located in previously isolated places. While the railroads were crucial to the industry, roughnecks rafting logs down the Buffalo River in northwest Arkansas or the St. Frances River in eastern Arkansas utilized a more traditional method of transportation. The larger concerns typically located along rivers to take advantage of those waterways.

The cutting of old growth timber across the state created opportunities for both small and large concerns. Indeed, just as the railroads brought prosperity to older towns and created many new ones, the lumber industry flooded these towns with workers who spent, and sometimes squandered, their earnings in local establishments. Although far from all of such laborers were wild and reckless, they had that reputation. The railroad and the accompanying lumber industries stimulated the economy, but the workers (regardless of origin) that accompanied their arrival were not always wel-

Log camp in the woods, circa 1912. *Abbott Family Photographs.*

come. As Ken Smith suggests in his important book on lumbering in the Ozarks, *Sawmill,* the wild and reckless behavior of unattached young men caused leaders of some older towns, particularly those that were thriving commercial centers for agricultural producers, to refuse to allow lumber mills to be established within their limits.

On the western side of the state, Fort Smith, which was founded earlier in the century as a military post, played out a similar scenario. Although more settled and longer lived, Fort Smith's population was dominated by sawmill, railroad, and mine workers, and noisy saloons and brothels were commonplace. Judge Isaac Parker presided over the federal court for the Western District of Arkansas located in Fort Smith, and he had his hands full. Appointed in 1875 by President U. S. Grant, Parker served until his death in 1896. He had been a Union army officer and as a Grant appointee represented Reconstruction government. His federal prosecutor was William Clayton, another former Union army officer and, moreover, brother to the former Republican governor of Arkansas, Powell Clayton. While Parker presided over the court, William Clayton ably prosecuted the outlaws brought to Fort Smith from western Arkansas and, particularly, from Indian Territory where a host of notorious outlaws staged their nefarious operations. A group of sometimes suspect and often fearless deputy marshals were responsible for apprehending the criminals. Among them was Bass Reeves, a former slave born in Crawford County, Arkansas, who gained a reputation for honesty and efficiency. Parker's tenure on the court ended in 1896, the same year that his bench lost jurisdiction over affairs in Indian Territory. By that time, Fort Smith's reputation for lawlessness was no longer entirely deserved, but respectable townspeople found it difficult to throw off the notoriety associated with the town's past. The location of the federal district court for western Arkansas there actually had done little to aid them in establishing a new identity for Fort Smith. Indeed, "hanging judge" Parker's rough justice drew attention to the worst elements of the western district's population. But even his reputation was exaggerated. Of the 168 men sentenced to death during his twenty-one-year tenure as judge, only 88 actually stepped up to the gallows.

Far more than the administration of justice in Parker's court was taking place in Fort Smith in the late nineteenth century. The railroad facilitated the development of the New South timber industry in the state and opened up the coal mines of western Arkansas to larger markets. These markets included those states located to the north (Missouri, Nebraska, Minnesota, Kansas, and Iowa), and acted as yet another mechanism for transcending the boundaries of section and promoting reintegration into the larger economy. Small-scale mining operations dated back to the 1840s, but full-scale exploitation of the area's coal deposits had to wait for the completion of the Little Rock to Fort Smith branch of the Cairo and Fulton Railroad in 1879. A mixed agriculture had dominated the region's economy until then. Corn, wheat, dairy, apples, strawberries, and even some cotton were the predominant crops. The arrival of the railroad and the large-scale coal-mining operations like the Missouri, Kansas, and Texas Coal Company contributed to a significant increase in the population. The mine workers came from a variety of backgrounds, and many of them were immigrants from Italy, Ireland, and Germany. The coal companies were not immune to the labor strife that marked the end of the nineteenth century across the country. Miners in Huntington, Arkansas, for example, went out on strike in support of their compatriots in Pennsylvania and West Virginia in 1894, and the United Mine Workers attracted many members working the mines of western Arkansas.

Union members and rowdy mine workers were not the kind of immigrants that the Arkansas Bureau of Immigration, founded in 1888, had in mind. Working in concert with railroads that offered excursion fares into Arkansas and speaking the language of the "New South" of Henry Grady's imagination, the Bureau of Immigration was endorsed by Democrats and Republicans alike, signaling an important reconciliation within Arkansas. Governor Simon P. Hughes, a Confederate veteran who converted from the

Whig to the Democratic Party during the Civil War, was the featured speaker at the grand opening of the Immigration Convention in early 1888. The convention selected Logan Roots, a Union veteran who settled in the state following the Civil War and founded the Little Rock Oil Company in 1875, as their first president. They designated H. L. Remmel, a leader in the Republican Party, as secretary. Initial backers included such diverse elements of the political structure as Little Rock banker and leading Democrat W. B. Worthen; the Republican boss of Arkansas, Powell Clayton; and a

Bureau of Immigration: An organization established in 1888 to attract the "right kind" of immigrant to the state, immigrants who would promote economic development.

Democratic outsider who would later become governor, William Fishback. In conjunction with the land departments of railroads like the St. Louis, Iron Mountain, and Southern, the bureau sponsored an exhibit at the St. Louis Exposition in 1888, and again in the famous Chicago World's Fair (also known as the World's Columbian Exhibition) in 1892–1893. There Arkansas created a pavilion meant to advertise its accomplishments and prospects. While the bureau declared that it wanted immigrants "without regard to politics, creed, birthplace or profession," some newspapers, like the *Walnut Ridge Telepleane*, proclaimed that it dared not be so liberal: "We don't want any anarchists in politics, we don't want any Mormons in religion, and we don't want any tramps by profession."

Solving the State's Debt Problem

Governor Hughes and others understood that the state had to resolve its chronic debt problem in order to realize its goal of attracting the most desirable immigrants, particularly those with money to invest. But even more was at stake, for the need for investment capital was paramount in order to rebuild Arkansas, and most of that would have to come from outside the South. The failure of the real estate and the state banks in the early 1840s had saddled Arkansas with a poor reputation among potential investors. The debt accruing from the banking fiasco was compounded by debt incurred by Reconstruction legislators eager to expand the state's railroad infrastructure and to repair and expand the levees of eastern Arkansas. Many Confederate veterans and Democrats had supported both endeavors, particularly eastern Arkansas planters, but mismanagement, fraud, and the national depression that began in the early 1870s, doomed these efforts.

Other Southern states faced a similar crisis arising out of damage to their states from the war and from ill-fated attempts to invest in infrastructure. Many turned to an unorthodox solution, particularly in the years after Reconstruction was overthrown. In addition to Arkansas, the states of

Alabama, Florida, Georgia, Louisiana, Tennessee, Virginia, and both Carolinas struggled to distinguish the "honest debt" from the "unjust debt." They eventually repudiated, scaled down, or adjusted the latter. William Meade Fishback led the forces of "repudiation" in Arkansas and identified the unjust debt as either fraudulently incurred or unfairly imposed on the people of the state by Reconstruction legislators. This was unfair and disingenuous, of course, for Democrats had supported and, in some cases, led efforts to expand the railroad network during Reconstruction. Although unorthodox, repudiation was a maneuver designed to resolve a growing economic crisis and to saddle the Republicans with the blame for postwar programs many Democrats had embraced. Fishback first voiced the idea of repudiation of the unjust debt as a delegate to the 1874 constitutional convention, when he attempted to insert repudiation into the document hammered out by delegates. This effort failed, but he was elected to the Arkansas General Assembly in 1876 and again in 1878 and continued to press the issue vigorously.

Repudiation:
A process used to "repudiate" the so-called unjust debt accrued during Reconstruction.

Conservative Democrats like Governor August Garland (1874–1877) regarded Fishback's repudiation scheme as fiscally irresponsible, however. Garland feared that repudiation would further ruin the state's credit standing and threaten chances of attracting out-of-state investors. Garland had wrangled with the debt problem during his own term as governor, when he faced a dire situation. By the time he came into office, the state owed over $17 million, approximately $13 million accrued during Reconstruction. By the time he left office, he had presided over a significant reduction of the debt, but as the state's revenues stagnated with the hard times of the late 1870s and early 1880s, repudiation became much more popular. Still, William Read Miller, elected governor in 1876, joined Garland and U. M. Rose, a prominent Little Rock attorney, in opposing a repudiation amendment Fishback presented to the legislature, which was narrowly defeated in 1880. Their success in fighting off the Fishback amendment, which would forbid the use of state money to repay the "unjust" debt, was only temporary, however. During Thomas James Churchill's governorship (1881–1883), the legislature moved closer to repudiation by passing an act providing that the "unjust" debt go unreported in the biennial reports of the state auditor and the state treasurer. Although Churchill did not endorse it, he allowed the act to become law without his signature. The next governor, James Henderson Berry (1883–1885), capitulated completely to the forces of repudiation by urging submission of the Fishback amendment to voters. It was ratified in 1884.

Agricultural Reorganization and Crisis

Arkansans were initially optimistic about the prospects of recovery of the cotton economy in the years immediately following the Civil War, and they welcomed the arrival of the railroad as the herald of progress. It facilitated the spread of the cotton kingdom to areas in eastern and parts of southern Arkansas, which were being rapidly deforested, by providing a new and more efficient way of sending goods to market. However, significant dangers accompanied these new opportunities. Greater exposure to the marketplace meant increased vulnerability to market forces, and this was especially problematic because agricultural prices declined almost steadily during the fifty years following the Civil War. Thus, some farmers who had engaged in only a nominal connection to the market prior to the coming of the railroad were being drawn into it at the worst possible time.

Even before the arrival of the railroad, however, farmers throughout Arkansas had been producing more cash crops. The Civil War brought such devastation to so many areas that farmers had to borrow to restore their farms to full operation, and many of them pledged to creditors to grow cash crops like cotton in order to secure advances. Cotton prices reached fifty cents a pound in the post–Civil War boom years of 1865 and 1866, which encouraged many farmers to expand cotton production at the expense of other crops, particularly corn. The percentage of those who owned their own farms declined steadily in the last two decades of the nineteenth century, particularly in the areas dominated by cotton cultivation. More and more men were farming on acres owned by others, but the proliferation of small farms suggested to some reading the agricultural census that the plantation was disappearing. In fact, most of these small farming operations were operated by tenants and sharecroppers and signaled the concentration of landowner-ship into fewer hands. The plantation model of development had survived the Civil War and adapted to the loss of slave labor. The tenancy and share-cropping system, in fact, perpetuated the plantation model of development that included an impoverished workforce and that inhibited modernization. Arkansas farmers, like those in the rest of the South, failed to adopt new farm technologies and remained wedded to its repressive labor system.

The sharecropping system had emerged in the years immediately following the Civil War after the contract labor system proved impractical. Contract labor had been employed during the war in order to keep the plantation system afloat and to provide a means of putting slaves back to work. In the postwar period, however, conflicts arose between the freed people and the planters. Freedmen wanted to own their own land but had no means to do so and plantation owners had too little cash income to pay wages.

The emergence of sharecropping gave each something of what they wanted. Without capital, former slaves had little hope of landownership, but sharecropping allowed them to move out of the old slave quarters, finally, and onto twenty- to thirty-acre parcels that they operated semi-independently. Landowners "paid" them at the end of the year out of the proceeds of the crop rather than weekly or monthly as stipulated under the contract labor system. Sharecroppers typically received one-third of the cotton crop in return for a year's work. The system might have seemed a prudent arrangement, but it soon became corrupted by the commissary system. Sharecroppers required advances of supplies and foodstuffs in order to survive to the end of the year. Merchants in small towns often filled that need but eventually planters themselves opened commissaries and supplied their own sharecroppers. In order to maximize their profits, they charged exorbitant interest for credit purchases and soon sharecroppers became seriously indebted, so much so that the amount owed them at the end of the year for the crop they produced often fell short of the amount they were obligated to pay at the plantation commissary.

Even as freed people were becoming ensnared in the sharecropping system, many landless whites were gravitating to plantation jobs in the share-tenancy system. Some of these men had once owned farms and lost them to repossession. Many of them retained their tools and mules left over from a happier time and thus brought more to the bargaining table with planters. By this means they were able to secure one-half of the crop in return for their services. The law soon defined them as "owning the crop they produced" so they had standing in court should a dispute arise between the tenant and the landowner. It is doubtful, however, that many exercised that right. Planters achieved so much political power and social standing in local communities that any challenge to them from a relatively poor landless farmer would be in vain. And, meanwhile, tenants found it necessary to secure advances from merchants or from plantation commissaries and thus, like sharecroppers, became indebted. The divide between the sharecroppers and tenants was real, often marked by both class and race, but the differences were actually minimal. While most sharecroppers were black and most tenants were whites, they shared impoverishment and exploitation.

Regardless of status, all farmers endured the burden of a precipitous decline in cotton prices in the late nineteenth century. In 1867 cotton prices dropped from fifty cents a pound to seventeen or eighteen cents, and then ranged between twelve and eighteen cents until 1874 when prices dropped again, this time to eleven cents a pound. From that point until the 1890s farmers received no more than seven to eleven cents a pound, but worse was to come in the 1890s. In 1894 the price of cotton dropped below a nickel a pound. Added to this decline in prices was an increase in railroad rates. When farmers began to address their economic problems by forming the Agricultural Wheel in 1882, they identified high railroad rates as one of their chief complaints.

The Agricultural Wheel

Agricultural Wheel: An organization founded in Prairie County in 1882 by farmers dissatisfied with the state's response to problems in the agricultural sector.

On February 15, 1882, nine men who owned small farms met at a schoolhouse in Prairie County to discuss their common problems and agreed to form a farmers' organization. Initially the club was little more than an improvement association designed to disseminate information, but from the beginning the organizers expressed disillusionment with political leaders. All were themselves Democrats, but they were disgruntled and unhappy about the circumstances facing them and the apparent unwillingness of politicians to address their problems. Within a month of the first meeting, they named their organization the Agricultural Wheel, arguing that "no machinery can be run without a great drive wheel, and as that wheel moves and governs the entire machinery, however complex, so agriculture is the great wheel or power that controls the entire machinery of the world's industries." By this time the membership of the organization had tripled, and within a year the organization expanded to include five hundred members and had formed the State Agricultural Wheel, drawing members from throughout Arkansas. Three years later the Wheel had extended into several other states, and its name was changed to the National Agricultural Wheel.

Many farmers drawn to the Agricultural Wheel felt particular antipathy toward railroads because their owners were identified as among the "middlemen" who appropriated the profits farmers should have been receiving for their crops. Many resented the rate differentials that carriers charged farmers who lived in remote areas off the more heavily traveled lines. Other grievances against the railroad included favorable land grants and generous tax exemptions granted to them by a state government eager for railroad construction. The practice of extending free passes to legislators and other state government officials raised suspicions of collusion. But most of the complaints aired by the Wheelers only peripherally concerned the railroad. Indeed, their problems were far more complicated, and the solutions would prove to be elusive.

The difficulties faced by farmers in Arkansas were shared by farmers elsewhere, particularly those in the South and the Midwest. Overproduction in an age of declining farm prices, rising indebtedness, and an increasing rate of farm foreclosures plagued all farmers, but Southern farmers also faced the infamous anaconda mortgage, whereby they were obliged to pledge their future crops in order to receive an advance. Many creditors demanded that specific crops, like cotton, be grown, and farmers were in no position to argue. While this had serious consequences for small landowning farmers, it had a particularly pernicious effect on the landless. Planters typically required their tenants and sharecroppers to sign crop lien mortgages and if the tenant owned mules and implements, they were also included in the document. Planters and local law enforcement officials believed that lien laws made it illegal for a tenant or sharecropper to leave a planter to whom he owed a debt, creating a situation known as debt peonage. Local law enforcement officials frequently arrested and returned absconding tenants and sharecroppers, essentially acting as the plantation owner's de facto police force.

Added to these structural problems were the perennial natural disasters that have always afflicted farmers everywhere. The year before the founding of the Agricultural Wheel, Prairie County farmers suffered a severe drought that ruined the 1881 harvest. This was followed by a severe flood that threatened to interfere with spring 1882 planting. Farmers did not expect politicians to prevent natural disasters, but those who joined the Wheel believed that there were governmental remedies for some of their problems if only their political leaders would act. They wanted a reduction in taxes, a suspension of tax payments until after the crisis passed, and their homesteads exempted from farm foreclosures. They believed that their own economic problems were exacerbated by the corruption of state and local officials and the greed of merchants, bankers, and other creditors. They resented the favorable treatment received by railroads, particularly given their own struggles. They viewed land speculators who purchased undeveloped land and held on to it, paying little or no taxes, as parasites.

Farmers elsewhere had expressed concerns similar to these and formed organizations to address their grievances. The Patrons of Husbandry, also known as the Grange, had been founded immediately after the Civil War and spread throughout the North, South, and West. By the mid-1870s there were approximately twenty thousand Grangers in Arkansas alone, and in 1875 John Thompson Jones, who was the Arkansas Grange's "Worthy Master," as its leader was called, was elected Worthy Master of the National Grange. By the late 1870s the Grange had been weakened in the South by the politics of Reconstruction, and, further, the organization was undermined because it admitted to membership men who were not farmers. The merchants, bankers, and brokers who had diluted the Grange were not admitted to membership in the Agricultural Wheel. Wheelers were determined to focus on the problems confronting those who actually farmed and went so far as to exclude from membership anyone who lived within the boundaries of a town or city.

The Agricultural Wheel was not the only organization of farmers to emerge in the wake of the Grange, and plenty of overlap existed among the various groups. Even before farmers in Prairie County met to form their association, farmers in Texas had created the Texas Farmers Alliance in 1878, and at the time the Agricultural Wheel was founded in 1882, the Farmers Alliance was beginning to spread into surrounding states, including Arkansas. In 1887 the Agricultural Wheel secured the support of the National Farmers Alliance, and for a time the local alliances were subordinate to the Wheel. This relationship strained to the breaking point when the Agricultural Wheel became politicized. Leaders of the Arkansas Agricultural Wheel attempted to work within the system by electing Democrats but had been disappointed in the results. In Arkansas and other Southern states, the conservative Democrats had control over who secured the Democratic nominations for local, state, and federal offices, but these men rarely broke with the party line once elected. Arkansas farmers soon began to field Wheelers as candidates for political office and had some success at the local level. In 1886 their gubernatorial candidate, Charles E. Cunningham, ran a poor third behind the Democratic and Republican candidates, but a more formidable challenge was in the wind for 1888 despite internal dissension within the Wheel.

The Wheel had actually violated its constitution in 1886 when it ran its own gubernatorial candidate, and many members were resistant to doing so again. Most of them were lifelong Democrats and were vulnerable to the skillful manipulation of conservative Democrats who could claim that defections from the party might lead to the restoration of Republican and black rule. While the Wheel struggled with this debate within its own ranks, another organization, the Union Labor Party, was gaining a following among both farmers and laborers. The Union Labor Party, which began in Wisconsin and was made up primarily of urban laborers, reshaped itself to match different constituencies as it moved south. In Arkansas it attracted disaffected farmers across the state and workers in the few industries that existed in Arkansas. Cunningham, the failed gubernatorial candidate in 1886, was both a Union Labor and a Wheel man. By 1888, after the Union Labor Party had united agrarian and labor organizations behind its banner, Cunningham was designated as its vice-presidential candidate.

Trouble was on the horizon, however. At the Union Labor Party convention in Arkansas in April 1888, Isaac McCracken, president of the Arkansas Wheel and the

Union Labor Party: A political party created by the Agricultural Wheel and the Knights of Labor, which ran candidates in 1886 and 1888, putting pressure on the Democratic Party of Arkansas.

National Agricultural Wheel, served as chairman. McCracken presided over a convention that selected a former state senator, C. M. Norwood, as its gubernatorial candidate. When the Union Labor Party fashioned a platform clearly meant to attract Wheelers, the Democratic press suggested that the Republicans were behind the party, and the Republican Party's endorsement of the Union Labor candidate (in the interest of broadening the opposition to the Democrats) gave credence to this accusation. At the Wheel convention, which met in May, delegates shied away from endorsing Norwood and instead passed a resolution that simply thanked the Union Labor Party for a platform that addressed the Wheel's concerns. Some Wheelers left the convention unhappy that the organization had not fully repudiated the Union Labor Party and, by implication, the Republicans with whom they were supposedly in cahoots, and burned their membership cards ceremoniously. They renewed their fidelity to the Democratic Party and decried the "bolters" that would return the state to Republican/black rule.

The Democrats, at their own convention that met May 31 to June 5, rejected proposals supported by Wheelers and nominated a candidate for governor, James P. Eagle, who indicated in his acceptance speech that the state of Arkansas had never been more prosperous. Such remarks in the face of the continuing decline in agricultural prices, together with the failure of the Democrats to address Wheeler demands, made it impossible for many farmers to support the Democratic candidate, despite their concerns about the taint of Republican connivance with the Union Labor Party.

Election results attest to the fact that many farmers supported the Union Labor candidate against the Democrat. The election that took place on September 3, 1888, was marked by fraud and intimidation, but Norwood secured majorities in a number of Delta counties with large numbers of black Republicans as well as predominantly white hill-country counties in south Arkansas and in the southwest. He came within 15,002 votes of winning. Eagle won 99,214 votes to Norwood's 84,213. Norwood challenged the vote and only backed down when the legislature demanded of him a $40,000 bond before opening an investigation. Historians generally agree that Norwood almost certainly won the election but was denied the governorship because of out-and-out fraud. Neither the Wheel nor the Union Labor Party recovered from the 1888 election and many former Wheelers aligned with the newly politicized Populist Party. The Farmers Alliance had finally come to the conclusion that some Wheelers reached in 1886: fielding their own candidates was their only option. By this time, however, the Democratic Party was taking steps to shore up its dominant position in Arkansas—and in the South generally.

Challenges to African Americans

Because black farmers had joined with whites in voting for the Union Labor Party candidates in both the 1888 and 1890 elections, Democrats determined that the surest way to maintain their political control was to eliminate the threat from below. In 1891 the legislature passed an act, under the guise of election reform, which effectively disfranchised a large part of the black electorate and denied the ballot to a smaller percentage of the white electorate. According to historian J. Morgan Kousser, 21 percent of black voters and 7 percent of white voters in Arkansas ceased to cast ballots after the 1891 election law. It gave greater authority to local white election officials and provided that they alone could mark the ballots of illiterate voters. Prior to that time illiterates could secure the assistance of friends or bring premarked ballots to the polls with them. After passage of the new election law, not only would they face personal embarrassment and perhaps the ridicule of elections officials, they could not be sure whether those officials marked their ballots as instructed. With 56 percent of black and 13 percent of white voters illiterate, the results were predictable. The Democrats secured their largest margin of victory in the 1892 election since the beginning of the challenge from discontented farmers. The number of voters dropped from 191,458 in 1890 to 156,186 in 1892.

Disfranchisement: Disfranchisement consisted of measures to prevent certain persons, particularly African Americans, from voting in elections.

Ironically, it was in that year that the Farmers Alliance finally realized the futility of working within the existing party structure and created the Populist or People's Party. The organizers of the Arkansas Union Labor Party reconstituted themselves as Populists, as members of the People's Party came to be known, and fielded J. P. Carnahan as their gubernatorial candidate. This time, however, the state's Republicans failed to endorse the agrarian candidate and ran one of their own, William G. Whipple, who would later go on to have a career as a federal prosecutor in Arkansas. But in 1892 neither the Republican nor the Populist candidates for governor came close to unseating the Democrat. The vote was 90,115 for Fishback, 31,117 for Carnahan, and 33,644 for Whipple. The remaining votes went to a Prohibition Party candidate.

Another disfranchising measure followed the 1891 election law. The electorate, reduced in number because of the 1891 legislation affecting illiterates, approved a poll tax amendment that required the payment of a fee prior to voting. Although 75,847 voters cast ballots in favor of the poll tax amendment while 56,589 voted against it, controversy emerged after the election because the Arkansas constitution required that the majority of voters casting ballots in an election must approve a constitutional amendment, and in this case many voters had failed to mark their ballots on the poll tax question. Only 132,436 of 156,186 persons voting in the election voted on that issue, so the 75,847 votes in favor fell short of being a majority. However, the speaker of the house certified the election results as valid, and the poll tax was implemented. As historian John Graves has argued, the individuals most likely to vote against such a measure—the poorest of both races—had been effectively disfranchised by the 1891 election law. The poll tax served to further discourage other poor voters, and then the legislature again contributed to the decline in voter turnout by passing an enforcement measure in 1895 that required potential voters to pay their poll tax months before an election. Only the most committed voters, only those who were not already intimidated by the requirements concerning illiterate voters, would remain active participants in the election process. It particularly impacted poor farmers, such as the growing number of tenants and sharecroppers, some of whom moved from one plantation to another every year and rarely maintained records, thus making it difficult for them to fulfill residency requirements. J. Morgan Kousser's figures indicate that the poll tax deterred 15 percent of the remaining black voters and from 9 to 12 percent of the remaining white voters from exercising the franchise.

The White Primary rule implemented by the Democratic Party was the last disfranchising measure passed in Arkansas. This was even more obviously connected to agrarian discontent as it was designed in part to appease discontented Democrats on the local level by preventing the black vote from being used against them by party rivals. Democratic Party primaries, whereby Democrats competed with one another for the Democratic slot on the fall general election ballot, dated back to the 1870s, but had not completely replaced the old method of having local candidates selected at state conventions. The primary process allowed party members at the local level much greater control over the selection of their own candidates. In 1898 the State Democratic Central Committee required that all counties begin holding primary elections, and in 1906 it excluded black voters from participation in those elections. Since Arkansas and the rest of the South was thoroughly Democratic by that time, the Democratic candidate was guaranteed of success in the fall election, thus the selection of the Democratic candidate in the primary was crucially important to voters who wanted alternatives. Exclusion from participation in the primary election therefore amounted to another form of disfranchisement. As political scientist Diane D. Blair has suggested, the black and white poor alike might reasonably be assumed to be acting prudently in deciding not to waste what little they had to pay poll taxes simply for the privilege of voting for a Democratic candidate who did not represent their interests or a Republican candidate who had no hope of winning the election.

The disfranchising measures adopted in Arkansas had the same intention as those being fashioned to exclude foreign immigrants in the north—except that there they included English-language requirements unnecessary in the South. But Arkansas statutes more particularly resembled such measures passed elsewhere in the South, as were its Jim Crow (segregation) statutes. Jim Crow emerged first and foremost in urban areas, swelled in the last decades of the nineteenth century by blacks looking for opportunities unavailable in rural areas. Arkansas's segregation statutes dated back to the same legislative session that passed the election reform law. In passing the "separate coach law" of 1891, the Arkansas legislature was acting in concert with other Southern states that also witnessed an unprecedented degree of urbanization.

In fact, the disfranchising and segregation statutes were only the legal arm of a new assault against African Americans. Mob violence aimed at African Americans rose dramatically in the 1890s, with lynchings of blacks accused of various crimes reaching its peak in that decade. Whites generally justified the lynchings as necessary to protect white womanhood, claiming that most lynching victims were rapists, but historians have discovered that very few of the black men lynched had actually assaulted a white woman. Many were lynched for petty crimes or for attempting to defend themselves against white violence. Mob action went hand-in-glove with the new legal strictures, which limited black opportunity and challenged black civil rights. Some African Americans, so disillusioned with the deteriorating circumstances confronting them, participated in the "back to Africa" movement. One very prominent black Arkansan, John Gray Lucas, a state legislator who had denounced the 1891 legislation in passionate terms, departed for Chicago, where he became that city's first black millionaire.

Other prominent blacks held their ground and achieved a measure of success, even in the more hostile environment prevailing in Arkansas. Ninth Street in Little Rock became a commercial and social focal point and a haven of safety (for the most part) for the black community. William Grant Still, who lived in Little Rock as a child, reported fond memories of his years there. Still's family left the state, and he grew up to become a prominent composer and was recognized as one of the talented African Americans who fostered the Harlem Renaissance. In Little Rock, meanwhile, John E. Bush founded the Mosaic Templars and Scipio Jones practiced law. Indeed, Little Rock was home to a small but distinguished group of African American professionals and businessmen who made up what Willard Gatewood calls a "black aristocracy." Like elite blacks in other cities—both North and South—

Little Rock's black aristocracy was made up of African Americans who had been privileged slaves or were the descendants of privileged slaves. Some of them had been fathered by white slave masters and had been educated at Oberlin or in Europe. Others had been free in the antebellum period or were the children of such free people of color. Whatever their origins, they accumulated property and achieved considerable status within the black community. Some of them became prominent Republicans and engaged in "fusion" with Democrats until the 1890s when Democrats decided to end that arrangement. Those who remained politically active after the end of fusion typically relied on appointments to federal offices when Republicans held the presidency. John E. Bush, for example, was receiver of the United States land office in Little Rock. Bush had founded the Mosaic Templars, a burial and insurance agency, in 1882. According to historian John Graves, by 1913 the Mosaic Templars also operated "a building and loan association, a hospital in Hot Springs, and owned a two-hundred-thousand-dollar headquarters building at Ninth and Broadway streets in Little Rock; there were eighty thousand dues-paying members in twenty-six states, Central and South America, the Canal Zone, and the West Indies." Bush was closely allied with Booker T. Washington, who considered Bush as among the most prominent Southern blacks, and was founder of the Little Rock chapter of the National Negro Business League.

Mosaic Templars:
A burial and insurance agency for African Americans, which, by the early twentieth century, included a hospital and building and loan association.

While blacks in Little Rock found safety in numbers, blacks in the Arkansas countryside remained relatively isolated and vulnerable. Although groups of blacks occasionally resisted whitecapping activities visited upon them, they found local law enforcement officials unsympathetic to their attempts to defend themselves. Whitecapping, which emerged in the 1890s, was a phenomenon connected to competition between whites and blacks for places on the area's expanding plantations. Some whites, determined to secure plantation jobs, took matters into their own hands and sought to drive out black labor by force. Planters preferred black to white labor, for black laborers were cheaper and, because of disfranchising and segregation measures, more vulnerable. Ironically, some planters emerged as defenders of black sharecroppers in the face of the whitecapping activities of landless whites. Many watched in horror as black labor departed, disillusioned with the laws aimed at relegating them to a second-class status. Some went to Kansas, others to Africa, but no matter where they went, they left planters in desperate need of another source of cheap labor.

The reign of terror against blacks together with the imposition of segregation and disfranchisement created problems for Arkansas planters, but by defeating the populist challenge and erecting a legal structure that effectively relegated blacks to an inferior position, the Democratic Party guaranteed its ability to hold on to power in Arkansas for another seventy-five years. Yet at least the last two governors of the nineteenth century, James Clarke and Daniel Jones, had embraced some of the populist platform, particularly that stressing the monetization of silver, so that they constituted a shift from the conservative Democrats to a new kind of Arkansas Democrat. In holding on to power, the conservative Democrats had departed from the party line and ultimately made room for a politician who spoke the language of populism. Jeff Davis, who became governor in 1901, was clearly a renegade Democrat who was able to secure election precisely because of the primary election process that democratized the selection of candidates. As an outsider identified with populism, he would never have won the Democratic nomination under the old system, dominated as it was by cronyism. He was able to build on the continuing ferment among Arkansas's discontented white farmers by striking out at the old clique of Democratic Party politicians and what he termed the "high collared roosters of Little Rock." He also engaged in a virulent racist rhetoric representative of the extreme view of certain whites toward African Americans, and he carried that point of view into the twentieth century, perpetuating it and elaborating upon it.

Religion

The predominantly Methodist and Baptist denominations within the South worked hand-in-hand with the government to enforce conformity to the notion of white supremacy and to the dominant economic, political, societal, and religious orthodoxy. In Arkansas, this connection was embodied in Governor James P. Eagle (1889–1893), himself a Baptist minister. He served as president of the Arkansas Baptist Convention from 1880 to 1904. In 1902, he was elected president of the Southern Baptist Convention and was subsequently twice reelected.

Baptists and Methodists far outnumbered other Protestant denominations, but Presbyterians and the Disciples of Christ (or one of its offshoots) worshiped in every county of the state by the end of the nineteenth century. Despite sometimes intense denominational disputes among the various churches, there was unanimity among Southern Protestants concerning the literal interpretation of the Bible and the omnipresence of God in the affairs of men. Because they were profoundly conservative in orientation and dedicated to the preservation of the status quo, Protestant churches often avoided addressing the problems confronted by labor, blacks, or the poor. A given church might organize aid to its own poor, but rarely sought to aid the poor in general. Many believed that the poor had no one but themselves to blame for their poverty. They viewed labor agitation as a direct threat to the established order and thus a serious danger. They believed that maintaining racial subordination of African Americans was ordained by God.

While African Americans shared many of the same assumptions about God and religion as whites, they hardly accepted the notion of God having ordained their subordination. Like whites, blacks largely embraced the Baptist and Methodist faiths, although in the years following the Civil War, blacks removed themselves from white churches they had attended during slavery and established their own churches. In addition to the African Methodist Episcopal Church, they flocked to various Baptist churches, and in smaller numbers they attended the Church of Divine Christ, the Church of God in Christ, and the Disciples of Christ. Although theirs too was a "civil religion," in that they saw a connection between church and state, they embraced a notion of racial uplift and cast their charitable nets beyond their own congregations. Increasingly cut off from political participation and treated as second-class citizens by state and local government officials, blacks congregated in their own churches for political and economic reasons as well as for religious and social purposes.

Although religion supported and even celebrated the patriarchy, women—both white and black—found the church to be one arena of activity that was open to them. This was true in the antebellum period too, when women were barred from participation in many community organizations and prevented from establishing their own associations. In this context, they found it possible to begin organizing themselves into groups within their respective churches. They formed sewing circles, ladies aid societies, benevolent associations for widows and orphans, and in the late nineteenth century, district and state women's missionary organizations.

While most Arkansans worshiped in Protestant denominations, individuals with other religious orientations also established churches and temples in Arkansas. By the end of the nineteenth century, the typical Jewish immigrant, like those elsewhere in the nation, was of eastern European origins, and a small but prosperous Jewish community developed in Little Rock. Smaller communities existed in Pine Bluff and Fort Smith. Prominent among the post–Civil War Jewish families was that of young Jacob Trieber, who was a teenager at the time his family settled in Helena, Arkansas, in 1868. As an adult he aligned with the Republican Party, became a prominent lawyer, and was appointed the federal judge for the eastern district of Arkansas by President William McKinley in 1900. The first Jew in the nation to occupy a federal judgeship, he rendered some crucial decisions concerning rights for African Americans. He eventually took up residence in Little Rock and became active in that city's Jewish community. Still heavily German in ethnic identity, Little Rock's Jews established Congregation B'Nai Israel in 1870, and the fact that the local newspaper frequently printed the rabbi's sermons suggests that they enjoyed some level of acceptance within the dominant Christian culture. Certainly, Jacob Trieber successfully negotiated Arkansas's political and social landscape. He became president of the Arkansas Bar Association and the Masonic Grand Master of Arkansas. He also became a member of Little Rock's exclusive XV Club, an all-male dinner and lecture club with no more than fifteen men who met fifteen times a year to discuss the political problems of the day and to dine sumptuously. The club drew members from different religious and political persuasions who had achieved a notable measure of success and respect within the city's community.

Those of the Catholic faith had a much longer history in the state, stretching back to June 25, 1541, when Hernando de Soto held a ceremony at the Indian village of Casqui near present-day Helena and erected a cross. But the Soto party was only passing through, made no actual converts, and left no priests to proselyte among the Indians. Subsequent French and Spanish "occupation" of the territory failed to convert the Indian population to Catholicism and established little European Catholic community. With the Louisiana Purchase in 1803, the protestant Anglo-Americans almost completely overwhelmed the Catholic influence. Nevertheless, in the nineteenth century, monks and nuns established monasteries and convents—in Little Rock, Pine Bluff, and Fort Smith—and Catholic communities began to grow in size and influence. By the end of the nineteenth century, several prominent Catholic families practiced their faith in many of Arkansas's towns. Indeed, historian Carl Moneyhon points out that in Little Rock, the largest single "denomination in 1900 was not even Protestant, it was Roman Catholic" with "over 23 percent of the citizens who stated a religious preference" claiming to be Catholic. Of course, that means all the Protestant denominations put together made the Protestant persuasion clearly dominant.

Religion occupied a central place in the lives of most Arkansans, and politicians, who were almost always members of a Baptist or Methodist denomination, frequently seasoned their political speeches with religious references, evoking the gospel in order to win votes. Indeed, they were skilled in the language of religion and understood how to reach the Arkansas electorate. In the early years, it was not uncommon for church services to be held in the county courthouse or some other public building until funds could be secured to construct a proper church building. Every aspect of life involved the church—birth, marriage, and death. The birth of a child was cause for comment from the preacher and celebration among the congregants, a marriage was a religious and a social occasion, and a death brought a community of worshipers together to grieve and celebrate the passage of a soul to glory. Membership in a church, moreover, offered something beyond spiritual sustenance, especially in isolated rural areas where there were few opportunities for entertainment. Some rural women only left their homes to attend church on Sundays or Wednesday evenings. Others might attend the "preaching" (religious service) and participate in "Sunday school" (Bible study), in addition to joining in with other women to plan picnics that took place on the church grounds. Suppers prepared by the church women provided a safe atmosphere for young people to meet and mingle under the watchful eye of their elders. Indeed, marrying within the family's denomination was often mandatory, and many a child faced censure for choosing a mate from outside the fold. Arkansans were serious about their religion, and it ran deep in their consciousness.

Women's Activism

Historians have argued that women's involvement in church organizations led eventually to movement into associations not directly connected to the church, particularly those involving issues that spoke to the health of the family. Thus, many women gravitated toward the temperance movement, recognizing that excessive alcohol consumption by husbands and fathers endangered the family. They found a particularly effective venue for their concerns about alcohol once the Woman's Christian Temperance Union was founded in 1873 in Ohio. Arkansas women organized their own state chapter in 1878. From the beginning, WCTU activists in Arkansas supported the "local option" approach to controlling alcohol consumption. Local option allowed voters in communities and rural areas to vote on whether to permit the licensing of saloons. If the voters approved, citizens wishing to establish a saloon had to circulate a petition to be presented to the county judge. If the petition contained the signatures of a majority of the registered voters in a particular town or township, the judge had to honor it.

Woman's Christian Temperance Union: An organization founded in Ohio in 1873 to encourage "temperance" in the consumption of alcohol.

Local option: An initiative placed on the ballot in order to provide local area residents with the option of voting against the licensing of saloons in their communities.

Most members of the WCTU were middle-class white women, although separate chapters were organized by middle-class black women. The movement provided public forums from which to speak, including the *Arkansas Ladies' Journal* and the *Woman's Chronicle*. The newsletter of the national organization, the *White Ribboner*, was widely subscribed to. Wearing the WCTU's trademark white ribbons and carrying the organization's banner, Arkansas women began to attend state and national meetings of the WCTU in the 1880s in order to map strategy. By the mid-1880s, however, a coalition of men's prohibition and temperance groups combined to create the Arkansas Prohibition Alliance and deliberately excluded the WCTU and women activists. That organization helped create the state's Prohibition Party, which ran a candidate for governor in 1892. The snub left a lasting legacy of distrust between the WCTU and another men's prohibition group founded in the 1890s, the Anti-Saloon League, and highlighted once again the second-class status of women in Arkansas.

Excluded from politics and from participation in organizations like the Arkansas Prohibition Alliance and the Anti-Saloon League, women found ways to work within the system to make their influence felt. They became actively involved in auxiliary associations connected to fraternal organizations, and they also formed their own patriotic organizations. The Grand Chapter Order of the Eastern Star of the State of Arkansas was organized October 2, 1876; other sister orders in Arkansas included Kings' Daughters, Ladies of the Maccabees, and Pythian sisters. One black fraternal order that originated in Arkansas, the Mosaic Templars of America, chartered on May 24, 1883, included women but in separate "lady chambers . . . under the special watch-care and guardianship of the Grand Mosaic Master." State and local chapters of the Daughters of the American Revolution, United Daughters of the Confederacy, Southern Memorial Association, and other patriotic societies provided Arkansas women with avenues for establishing memorials, preserving battlefields, and marking burial sites of soldiers. These groups also undertook a wide range of civic improvements, including beautification of parks and roadways, health and safety campaigns, hospital assistance, relief to crippled and needy children, and contributions to libraries. They also sponsored history essay contests and raised funds for student loans.

The women's club movement was launched in the 1890s and allowed women with moderate and nonmilitant inclinations to express themselves through literary and aesthetic clubs. The clubs served as vehicles for personal, domestic, and community improvement. The General Federation of Women's Clubs organized on the national level in 1890, and in 1897 the Arkansas Federation of Women's Clubs joined the national federation.

Although refraining from espousing an activist agenda in the nineteenth century, the women's club movement schooled women in a variety of ways for the role they would soon embrace. Participation in a club offered opportunities to broaden their horizons by challenging women to refine critical thinking skills, to engage in debate and speaking exercises, and to become knowledgeable in a wide range of fields. Many clubs emphasized study, reading, and discussion, and some chose to limit their work to those areas.

Charlotte Andrews Stephens, first black teacher in Little Rock, Arkansas. *Courtesy of the Arkansas History Commission.*

The practice of segregation barred black women from participation in clubs organized by white women so black women chartered their own organizations. In 1896, they founded the National Association of Colored Women's Clubs. The first NACW federated club in the state was established in Little Rock in 1897. Charlotte Andrews Stephens, the first black teacher hired in the city public schools, was a charter member. Black women founded literary clubs in Little Rock, Newport, Brinkley, and Searcy, among other places. Like the clubs created by white women, black women's clubs became more numerous and activist in orientation in the Progressive Era of the twentieth century.

Both black and white women's clubs supported public education, and some women, like Little Rock's Charlotte Stephens, found employment opportunities because of the proliferation of public schools after the Civil War. In 1869 white teachers in Arkansas organized the State Teachers Association, and Ida Jo Brooks, daughter of would-be Republican governor Joseph Brooks, became in 1877 the first woman to serve as its president, as well as the first woman to serve as president of any state teachers association in the United States. Black teachers organized the State Colored Teachers Association in 1898. Salaries were low for both black and white teachers, however, and many, particularly in rural areas, found it necessary to board in some household in the neighborhood.

Although some women worked as teachers, it was not an entirely female profession. The teachers' associations were of enormous importance to women, however, for it was the only avenue through which they could hope to exercise influence over the direction education was taking in the state. Reconstruction governments made public education a priority, and the number of schools in the state, though chronically underfunded, greatly expanded. The public school hierarchy was entirely male, and legislators and governors looked to those men to implement policy. Women were often on the receiving end only of policy changes, but in the 1890s one development in particular likely accrued to their benefit: teacher institutes. When Josiah H. Shinn became superintendent of public instruction in 1890, he launched a series of teacher institutes that reached into communities across the state. In the first year alone, 2,242 teachers attended the seventy-six institutes he organized for the purpose of improving the quality of the teachers and thus raising the level of instruction. Grants from the Peabody Fund together with appropriations from the Arkansas legislature ensured the continuation of these institutes even after Shinn left his position in 1894. In 1899, when the legislature ceased appropriating funds for them, the Peabody Fund subsidized sixty-five institutes for white teachers and fifty-two for black teachers in 1899–1900. Thereafter, funds for teacher institutes dried up completely. Education and teacher education would become a major issue for the progressive governors of the early twentieth century.

Aside from teaching, few other employment opportunities existed for women. Midwifery was a profession long associated with women, but with the spread of doctors in the state in the late nineteenth century, that opportunity was slowly eroding. A woman might work as a clerk in a store or assist her husband in running his business, but most white women were confined to the home, and the expansion of jobs considered appropriate to women occurred principally in the next century. Black women might find work as a teacher in the black school system, if they were fortunate, but most worked as household servants or washerwomen at the same time they often assisted their husbands in fieldwork.

The fact that most professions were closed to women inspired some Arkansas women to join the suffrage movement. Women's suffrage in Arkansas was actually launched in 1868 when women packed the legislative gallery to listen to and applaud a proposal to extend suffrage to women in the proposed new state constitution. Some legislators ridiculed the notion that women were intellectually equipped to vote and others suggested that they were too refined for the rough-and-tumble business of politics. The measure failed, but Arkansas women continued to press for suffrage. Two women's journals were founded in the 1880s, both espousing suffrage for women. In 1884 Little Rock's Mrs. Mary W. Loughborough launched the *Arkansas Ladies' Journal*, which, though not solely dedicated to that one issue, called for women's suffrage. In 1888 three other women—Catherine Campbell Cunningham, Mrs. Mary Burt Brooks, and Mrs. William Cahoon—began publishing the *Woman's Chronicle*, which went further than Mrs. Loughborough's *Arkansas Ladies' Journal* in promoting suffrage for women. In fact, it soon became the chief organ for the women's suffrage movement in the South. It ceased publication in 1889, however, because of Cunningham's ill health. Despite the episodic nature of their journals, Arkansas women continued to host suffrage society meetings and speak out on the issue throughout the 1890s. Small auxiliary societies periodically sprang up in towns all over the state, but most of them were short lived. Arkansas suffragists were affiliated with Susan B. Anthony's National American Woman Suffrage Association (NAWSA), filed annual reports with that organization, and sent delegates to national meetings. NAWSA combined in 1890 two previous organizations, the American Woman Suffrage Association and the National Woman Suffrage Association,

National American Woman Suffrage Association (NAWSA): An organization of women who advocated for suffrage for women through state constitutional amendments rather than a federal amendment to the Constitution.

who differed over tactics. NAWSA championed state-by-state woman suffrage amendments rather than a federal constitutional amendment. This was the approach that would be promoted by Arkansas suffragists in the twentieth century. The nineteenth century closed out with the nascent women's suffrage movement growing in strength in Arkansas, laying the groundwork for a successful campaign in the next decade and a half.

For all the things that worked to bring Arkansas back into the mainstream of American politics and culture, the state remained distinctly Southern. The railroad, lumber, and mining industries represented opportunities to link with the national marketplace but at a time when the country faced a series of economic crises, and Arkansas's fragile economy had greater difficulty weathering those particular storms. Lumber, mining, and agriculture were the primary growth industries, but they were largely extractive in nature and much of the wealth of the state was exported elsewhere; that is, the raw products stripped from the forests reserves, dug from the coal mines, and harvested from the farms. Challenges to a Democratic Party unresponsive to the problems facing agriculturalists united, for a time, farmers across racial and sectional lines, but the Democratic Party responded with an aggressive campaign to eliminate the threat from below by disfranchising a segment of the population: blacks and poor whites. White women achieved some gains, fighting for the right to vote and joining the crusade for prohibition, but they also reasserted their devotion to the Southern cause by erecting memorials to Confederate veterans and otherwise demonstrating adherence to racial segregation. Although Southern partisanship influenced both men and women in Arkansas, reconciliation with the North was equally potent and symbolized by the Arkansas exhibition at the Columbian exposition in 1892–1893 and, most dramatically, by the state's eager participation in the Spanish American War in 1898. The solution to the state's debt problem worked through by Governor Clarke in 1898 seemed to position Arkansas to assume equal status with other states. Although it would face a series of unexpected challenges in the next century, Arkansas would also embrace many progressive reforms—including women's suffrage and prohibition—that swept the rest of the nation and thus continue the process of reintegration even as it held on to its Southern distinctiveness.

11 A Light in the Darkness

Limits of Progressive Reform, 1900–1932

Although Arkansas embraced certain elements of the nation's progressive reform movement of the early twentieth century, it did so in a strictly Southern context. Historian Jack Kirby's book, *Darkness at the Dawning*, emphasizes the rise of a virulent new racism during the Progressive Era, and certainly Arkansas's version of reform remained anchored in its repressive racial system, one largely enacted in the last decade of the nineteenth century. Another legacy of the previous century involved the state's tradition of minimal taxation and its fragile economic situation. Nevertheless, Arkansas made an effort to assume the activist role inspired by the progressive impulse sweeping the nation. The need to create new regulatory agencies, expand and reform the state's educational system, and extend the transportation network all required an unprecedented expenditure of funds, and the need to finance these enterprises often collided with the state's inability and unwillingness to raise sufficient tax revenue. Arkansas's low population provided for an inadequate tax base, and a fierce opposition to raising taxes among Arkansas's citizenry and politicians further complicated matters. In order to move beyond the bottom tier of states in various economic and social indices, Arkansas had to fund reform at an unrealistically high level. While the state managed to make some progress in spite of these obstacles, it did so without challenging elite interests and, in fact, often served them. Despite all of the genuine progress made in the first two decades of the twentieth century, a substantial minority of the population enjoyed few of the benefits and actually experienced repression and violence. The imposition of the White Primary in 1906, the last of three measures used to disfranchise black voters, and a massacre of blacks in Phillips County in 1919 demonstrated the state's continuing legacy of racism.

The Impulse for Progressive Reform

The progressive movement began just after the turn of the century and marked an attempt by various interests to come to terms with a society in the midst of a dramatic transformation. The industrial revolution, urbanization, and the emergence of giant corporations seemed to threaten order and stability, and people throughout the country reacted by attempting numerous reforms. Not surprisingly, the reforms generated by Southerners were often peculiar to the South and the rural experience, although many mirrored reforms occurring in the cities. Voting qualifications for immigrants in northern cities, for example, were not so very different from disfranchisement mechanisms applied to blacks. Indeed, many of the reforms passed during this era were repressive; that is, they limited the opportunities or the behavior of certain groups in American society, and they failed to gain the support of all who might term themselves progressives.

African American leaders and their white allies were not unmindful of the new racist ideology and grew concerned enough to form the National Association for the Advancement of Colored People (NAACP) in 1909. Within a decade after its founding, black membership in the NAACP expanded as chapters were chartered in states, counties, cities, and towns. The organization was slow to develop in the South, however, until after Booker T. Washington's death in 1915. Washington had been hostile to the NAACP, largely because its agenda and strategy was diametrically opposed to his own. Washington preached economic self-help, foreswore political involvement, and essentially espoused acceptance of a racial status quo that included the political and social subordination of the black population. The NAACP directly challenged both segregation and disfranchisement and became intimately involved in certain high-profile criminal cases involving poor and often illiterate African Americans.

While Washington was alive, relatively few blacks, south or north, were willing to risk involvement with the NAACP, but once he died, the Southern black elite often became the leaders in establishing branches of the organization. Little Rock's black aristocracy was no exception. In November 1918, some of the leading black businessmen and professionals in the city founded a local chapter of the NAACP. Like many other Southern chapters, however, the Little Rock NAACP served principally as a social club rather than as a black activist organization. The black elite there was an insular group existing within a small city that had hardly outgrown its "frontier" status. They had carved out a comfortable existence for themselves, lived in fine homes in integrated neighborhoods, and enjoyed privileges that most other blacks did not have access to. Many of them had imbibed enough of the Washington accommodationist message to preclude any very activist agenda, and while other individuals within the organization were more militant, most were loath to risk what they had secured for the sake of pursuing the NAACP's goals of achieving civil and political rights for the black population as a whole. Some among the African American elite in Little Rock, however, would grow weary of the passive role the city's NAACP chapter adopted and pursue a more activist agenda, but this would not occur until the 1920s.

Among the many laudable progressive reforms occurring in Arkansas was that involving the conservation of the environment. In 1907 the nation's first national forest was created in southwest Arkansas when a large portion of the Ouachita Mountains was designated as such. Eight years later, Big Lake National Wildlife Refuge was created to protect a sizable swamp in northeast Arkansas that constituted an important point in the great North American flyway for ducks and birds heading south from Canada for the winter. Conservation was only one among many reforms pursued by progressives, particularly regulations on railroads and corporations. But proponents of progressivism in Arkansas differed from those in northern cities in certain key areas. For example, prohibition, heavily supported by Southerners, was opposed by urban bosses.

Jeff Davis, who became governor in 1901, was the first to stake out a claim as a progressive governor in Arkansas. He also positioned himself as a progressive and a trust buster, interpreting the Rector Antitrust Act, passed in 1899, as prohibiting any kind of trust from doing business in Arkansas without regard to where it had been organized. Suits he filed while attorney general of Arkansas against fire insurance companies operating in Arkansas in 1899 resulted in widespread controversy, with many of the companies threatening to cancel policies. The state supreme court overruled him, but Davis had established himself as spokesman for the common people, a man facing off against privilege, and the people loved him. The state Democratic machine, however, was far from enamored of him. Despite being ridiculed by the press and branded as a renegade by his opponents in his 1900 run for governor, he swept into office and promised to continue forcefully interpreting the Rector Antitrust Act.

Other issues soon came to the fore as well: convict leasing and prohibition. He was sincerely horrified by the conditions in the state prisons and in the largely unregulated convict lease camps. His association with the liquor interests, however, came to cloud his credentials as a Southern progressive and his long-standing battle against the state Democratic establishment made it impossible for him to secure support for elimination of the convict leasing system. Throughout all his travails, the public continued to vote for him in large numbers, and in his last run for the governorship in 1904, he carried pro-Davis legislators into office as well.

Part of Davis's appeal to white voters in the state hinged on his rabid race-baiting. Like many other Southern states, Arkansas implemented a statewide primary system restricted to white males and reaffirmed the poll tax, but Davis also began to champion a segregation of school taxes, in which only tax revenues collected from black citizens would fund black education. Since most blacks were mired in poverty so complete that they did not have to pay even the minimum taxes, the measure would have literally doomed black education. But that seemed to be Davis's point. He declared that educating blacks merely spoiled good field hands. The pro-Davis legislators who swept into office on his coattails in 1904, however, were to disappoint him on this, and other issues. He initiated and lobbied for the passage of the Burgess School tax segregation bill, but the 1905 session of the legislature failed to pass the measure.

Burgess School Tax Segregation Bill: A bill that would have segregated local property tax revenues by race and effectively further undermined funding to black schools in the state.

Davis's third term was consumed primarily by his run for the Senate. He won that race and left the state in the hands of his handpicked predecessor, John Sebastian Little. When Little succumbed to a serious illness after only one month in office, Davis's long-standing enemy, Xenophon Overton Pindall, who was the incoming president pro tempore of the senate, soon took over. Pindall served until the general election in 1909, and earned some credentials as a progressive when he secured passage of a pure food and drug law, but his tenure in office—one year and seven months—was as "acting" governor, providing him with an insufficient base from which to launch a movement, and there is small indication that he had much impulse to do so.

George Washington Donaghey, who took office in 1909, was the first governor of Arkansas who could indisputably be labeled a progressive. Yet he, too, was squarely within the Southern progressive tradition. Although he renovated the tax structure to allow for more public spending, in keeping with the demands of the progressive spirit, he supported reforms that did not fundamentally challenge Arkansas elites. He sponsored initiatives in education and public health, and because of Donaghey, Arkansas was the only Southern state to pass both the initiative and referendum that provided citizens with the means of playing a more direct role in fashioning the state's laws. He even brought William Jennings Bryan, the famous populist, to the state to help campaign for these reforms. The initiative process allowed voters to circulate a petition to get a measure on the ballot so that citizens could "initiate" legislation. The referendum allowed voters to pass judgment on a measure already passed by the legislature. Using the petition process to place an act of the legislature on the ballot, the people could affirm or reject it. Thus, ironically, just as the state was finalizing its disfranchisement of African Americans, it was passing impressive political reforms that essentially democratized legislation. As "democratic" as these reforms were, they were used in a manner that reflected the conservatism of the state's progressive spirit. For example, one of the first major initiatives launched in Arkansas was that involving prohibition. The Anti-Saloon League secured enough signatures to place a prohibition statute on the ballot in 1912, and although it went down to defeat, voters later used the referendum to validate a legislative act passed in 1915 that prohibited alcohol: In 1917 citizens circulated a petition to call for a popular vote on the statute, and this time Arkansans voted in favor of prohibition.

Convict Leasing

Perhaps Donaghey's most celebrated accomplishment was in finishing one battle Jeff Davis had waged, that against convict leasing. Conditions were primitive, brutal, and often deadly in convict camps. Because the greatest majority of convicts were African American, the system gained a reputation for imposing "slavery by another name" but many whites were ensnared as well, and it is perhaps as appropriate to identify it as a system that victimized the poor of both races. Upon his election to the governor's office, Donaghey proposed that the legislature censure convict leasing, but the legislature balked. Frustrated in his efforts to end convict leasing, Donaghey moved toward a radical solution. In early 1912, he began to talk about pardoning convicts in county camps if abuses did not stop. In December 1912, he attended a governor's conference and heard Governor Cole Blease of South Carolina reveal that he had pardoned convicts there in order to dramatize the abuse of prisoners. Donaghey returned to the state, sent aides out to gather data on the prisoners (type of crime, length of term in prison, etc.) and then on December 17 pardoned 360 convicts, 44 in county farms and 316 of the 850 convicts in the penitentiary. Most of those pardoned were serving short sentences for relatively minor crimes and had served over half their sentences. This effectively ended convict leasing in the state because it made it impossible for the state to supply convicts to those who wished to lease them.

When newly elected governor Joseph T. Robinson attended his first meeting of the penitentiary board after taking the oath of office in early 1913, he called for the abolition of convict leasing. It passed unanimously. On the same day, a bill was introduced in the legislature that both called for the appointment of a three-person board of penitentiary commissioners (to be appointed by the governor) and outlawed convict leasing. It easily passed both the house and the senate and was signed by Robinson on February 21, 1913. Abuses continued but convict leasing was over.

Political "Infighting" within the Democratic Party

Joseph Robinson's election to the governor's office occurred within the context of a struggle for power within the Democratic Party. Although Robinson would align with some of the most reactionary forces in Arkansas to capture the governor's chair—the old Jeff Davis machine—he established a solid progressive record during his brief tenure in that office. He served as governor less than two months, but he played an active role in directing a legislative session that passed a corrupt-practices act and created three state agencies: a state banking department, a bureau of labor and statistics, and a highway commission. Perhaps had he remained governor, Robinson's progressive legacy would have been greater, but he aspired to higher office, and the opportunity to capture the Senate seat upon Jeff Davis's untimely death was too tempting. Robinson would go on to have a distinguished career in the Senate, running as the vice-presidential candidate with Al Smith in 1928, and becoming a crucial figure in the southern wing of President Franklin Delano Roosevelt's New Deal coalition.

George Hays, an old Davis crony, won a special election to take Robinson's place in the governor's office at a time when public sentiment favored reform, but Hays concerned himself more with building a political constituency than providing progressive leadership. Nevertheless, Hays acquiesced in the legislature's ambitious progressive reform agenda. The Alexander Road Improvement Act allowed counties to create road improvement districts with the power to issue bonds; state elections, which had been held in September, were moved to coincide with federal elections in November; and a law protecting investors from stock and bond fraud was passed. Finally, a measure designed as protection for working women, a nine-hour maximum, six-day maximum week, was enacted. While some historians have suggested that this law actually discriminated against women by limiting their opportunities, others have argued that this was a first step to regulating the hours of all workers. It merely started with women and children because legislators could be convinced more easily by the rationale of protecting women.

Women's Activism—Suffrage and Prohibition

Since late in the nineteenth century, Arkansas women had been organizing in more public ways and agitating for various reforms. By the time that Hays was elected governor, there was sufficient support in the legislature to secure passage of legislation granting married women the right to enter into contracts and own property separate from that of their husbands. The Arkansas women's suffrage movement was revived in 1911 when a new Arkansas suffrage association was organized and began to lobby the legislature heavily to give women the right to vote in primary elections, which, by then, were limited to white participation. Arkansas suffragists were middle-class white women associated with the more conservative National American Women's

Suffrage Association rather than the National Woman's Party founded by the more radical Alice Paul. The Arkansas association's conservative identity likely made it more acceptable to women like Anne Brough, whose husband would become governor in 1917. It was in that year that Mrs. Brough appeared on the steps of the new state capitol at a suffrage rally, and it was in that year that the legislature voted to allow women to vote in Arkansas primary elections. Encouraged by this victory, Arkansas suffragists then began to work tirelessly for a suffrage amendment to the state constitution and were successful in placing such a measure on the 1920 ballot. However, before that election could take place, the United States Congress passed the Nineteenth Amendment in 1919. Arkansas suffragists greeted its passage with optimism, believing that it would have no difficulty being ratified. They successfully lobbied the state legislature to make Arkansas the twelfth state in the union and the second in the South to ratify the Susan B. Anthony amendment on July 20, 1919.

Another issue that involved women and captured even greater attention across the state was prohibition. Although women had found themselves largely excluded from the male-dominated Prohibition Party and from the Anti-Saloon League in the late nineteenth century, they continued to work through the Arkansas branch of the Women's Christian Temperance Union. The WCTU expanded rapidly in the first decade of the twentieth century with many Arkansas counties organizing branches, establishing firm foundations on the local level, and sending representatives to state and national meetings.

Organizations like the WCTU and the Anti-Saloon League were not alone in waging war against demon rum. As Ben Johnson persuasively argues in his book, *John Barleycorn Must Die*, the campaign to curtail alcohol consumption was a colorful and complex phenomenon. The prohibition drive brought together certain disparate groups with little in common beyond that one issue. For some progressives, prohibition made perfect sense as a reform measure because they perceived the very real connection between alcohol abuse and both criminality and disease. Some religions forbade the consumption of alcohol as a matter of course, and other religious leaders merely believed that sober men made better Christians. Manufacturers desired a stable workforce of sober working men who were believed to be less likely than drinkers to break expensive equipment, to injure themselves or their coworkers, or to miss many hours or days of work due to drunkenness. Women, of course, supported the movement because they wished to bring stability to families struggling with husbands and fathers who wasted precious resources on alcohol and sometimes abused their wives and children. Other Arkansans saw a danger in the commingling of the races in saloons

Women's suffrage delegation on the steps of the capitol with Governor Charles Hillman Brough, summer 1919, holding rally in support of the women's suffrage amendment to the constitution. Mrs. Brough appears on the far left (in dark jumper and hat with flower). *Courtesy of the Arkansas History Commission.*

and honkytonks, and thus linked the issue of prohibition with an opportunity to remedy violations of segregation sensibilities. Prohibition forces turned to the legislature itself to achieve their goals and influenced the legislature to pass a "Bone Dry" law in February 1915, a law that was to take effect on January 1, 1916. It was in that year that Charles Hillman Brough, who strongly supported prohibition, was elected governor. Active in the Southern Sociological Congress, he believed that society had a responsibility to solve social problems. When yet another initiated measure appeared on the ballot in 1917, this one intended to overturn the Bone Dry law by resurrecting the local option approach, he campaigned against it, and voters went the way of prohibition, voting to maintain the statute.

Women who sought to test certain occupational boundaries, however, found themselves thwarted and frustrated. Ida Jo Brooks, who had surmounted obstacles in the past—she was the first woman president of the Arkansas Teachers Association (1883–1887)—was stung by rejection in 1887 when she attempted to attend the University of Arkansas Medical School. She was prominent in the Little Rock social scene, having been a member of every elite women's club in Little Rock and active in the WCTU, but her determination to become a physician led her to leave the state to attend medical school in Boston after her own state's medical education establishment deemed her unworthy solely on the basis of her gender. After nine years practicing homeopathic medicine in the northeast, she returned to Little Rock in 1900 and specialized in the treatment of children's diseases. Growing concerned about mental illness among women, she returned to Massachusetts in 1903 to join the staff of Middleborough Mental Hospital where she specialized in psychiatry. By 1906 she was back in Little Rock practicing psychiatry, became assistant medical inspector for the Little Rock School District in 1907, and was appointed an associate professor at the Arkansas Medical School in 1914, thus finally entering a door that had previously been closed to her. She was to find, however, that rejection on the basis of gender would still frustrate her goals. In 1920 the Republican Party nominated her for state superintendent of public instruction, but the attorney general ruled that while women could vote, they could not hold office and thus her name was removed from the ballot. Other women would challenge this decision in the years to come and begin to hold various political offices, from the lowliest county-level position to the United States Senate.

Reforms in Education

From the point of view of progressives, the educational system represented one of the most chaotically organized and undisciplined institutions in the state. At the beginning of the century, there was no state board of education, only a superintendent of instruction who merely reported statistics. Teachers were abysmally trained, with few of them having college degrees and many of them having only eighth-grade educations. With no compulsory attendance laws, less than half of school-age children attended and most of them for less than half the term. Of the nearly five thousand school districts, five hundred enrolled under twenty pupils, and some occupied buildings that were so badly in need of repair that they were simply abandoned during the winter months. This, perhaps, partly accounted for the fact that the state had the lowest average number of days of school in the region. Few high schools existed and of those that did exist, almost none outside of the larger towns and cities were accredited.

In 1902 the state superintendent of public instruction abruptly broke with the precedent of simply reporting statistics and began to criticize the disorganized nature of the educational system in the state. He suggested that the schools within each county be unified under the direction of a single county supervisor who would report to him. The Arkansas Teachers Association also began to press for reform and prompted the creation of the Arkansas Education Commission in 1908. Still, systematic organization of the school system eluded reformers. The commission's report in 1911 outlined a comprehensive plan for improving the state's schools and was instrumental in influencing the creation of a high school board that year, which provided some means of bringing order to secondary education. That board was given the authority to classify high schools and to determine curriculum. It was also given the authority to distribute funds for teacher education. It performed as the only administrative educational unit in the state until the formation of the State Board of Education later that year, which provided state aid for high schools.

The high school board's authority to distribute aid for teacher education spoke to another pressing need in Arkansas. When the legislature ended expenditures for state normal schools in 1899, after almost a decade of extending such aid, the state became ineligible for matching funds from the Peabody Foundation. Teachers, who were notoriously underpaid, had to undertake teacher training courses at their own expense. In 1903 the legislature mandated more stringent examination and licensing procedures for teachers and in 1907 required teachers to attend summer normal institutes. The state superintendent of public instruction sponsored the institutes, and within a very few years fully 90 percent of the state's teachers were participating. Also in 1907, the State Teachers Association, together with the Farmers Union, convinced the state legislature to create a normal school at Conway, and by 1910 both that school and the University of Arkansas were offering summer terms for teachers.

One problem that would defy solution until certain other developments took shape involved the existence of far too many small school districts, many of them with one teacher providing instruction on the whole range of subjects to all the students enrolled. This huge number of districts made for great variation both in the quality of instruction and the resources communities could bring to bear on education. Yet local communities and their legislators were determined to maintain these schools, and the road system, in any case, was so inadequate that little could be accomplished until it was significantly improved and extended. As the roads improved and the population began to shift in mid-century, particularly during World War II, the consolidation movement gained momentum. In 1900 there were 4,903 school districts. By 1920 that number had increased to 5,118, reflecting the emergence of new communities in certain parts of the state in the early twentieth century. Because of the concerted efforts on the part of educators and certain public figures, the number of districts began to decline in the 1920s. By 1930 the number of districts had declined to 3,478; by 1940 it had dropped to 2,920 districts; and in 1948, before the legislature passed a school consolidation bill eliminating those schools with under 350 students, there were 1,589 schools. The law reduced the number of districts to 424.

During this entire period of reform, black schools functioned at a level far below that of white schools, and most white reformers were content to allow that situation to remain unchanged. Black leaders took an interest in the schools within their towns and cities, but the majority of black youngsters resided in the rural areas of the Delta, and those schools proved beyond any doubt that the doctrine of "separate but equal" as established in the 1896 *Plessy v. Ferguson* decision bore no resemblance to reality. Facilities were inferior, school books were often ragged hand-me-downs from white schools, and black teachers were even more poorly trained and underpaid than whites. Black children were less likely than white children to attend school and more likely to be illiterate. The sentiments of Jeff Davis and other white leaders toward black education was shared by the vast majority of whites and acted as a significant obstacle to improvement. Yet the black educational system provided an important institutional arena for black teachers and citizens, principally in towns and cities, and played a significant role in the lives of the black adults and children. Becoming a teacher was a signal accomplishment for a black man or woman, and even though black teachers were less likely than white teachers to be college trained, they took pride in their occupations, cared deeply for their schools, and played an important role in the black community.

Whatever shortcoming existed in black education, some improvement in the overall educational infrastructure occurred in the 1920s. Indeed, even after many improvements had been implemented, Arkansas faced a crisis in education by the time Thomas McRae took office in 1921. According to a report arising out of a federal survey conducted in 1921–1922, Arkansas's children received an education that would put them at a distinct disadvantage later in life, an education that did not prepare them for the modern world. The school system remained seriously underfunded, and although the figures for school attendance had improved, the average school term of six months was the shortest in the country. Few teachers, especially in the rural districts, had received college educations, and many had not completed high school. In fact, high school attendance was the second lowest in the country.

McRae was sincere in his efforts to improve the educational system in Arkansas, but he faced a reluctant legislature and his tenure in office corresponded with the beginnings of the economic crisis in the state. His only success in the area of education during his first term involved instituting a millage basis for continued funding of higher education. The millage system meant that higher education funding would no longer be dependent upon legislative appropriations but would be built into the tax structure in a more fundamental way. During his second term McRae's accomplishments were more substantial. In order to address the serious shortcomings in Arkansas's education system, Governor McRae understood that an even more aggressive funding strategy had to be adopted, and he believed that the tax structure needed revising. The legislature responded by passing a severance tax with all proceeds accruing to public education, but an income tax—and later a tobacco tax—also earmarked for education, were declared unconstitutional. Before he left office, however, McRae persuaded the legislature to restructure the tobacco tax in a way that passed muster with the Arkansas Supreme Court.

McRae was aided in his education campaign by an alliance of educators and urban progressives located in the state's largest towns. The alliance would last beyond McRae's term in office. In order to fund education in the poor rural districts where property taxes did not provide enough revenue to support schools, it was necessary to revise the tax structure to require businesses and corporations located in urban areas like Little Rock to share the burden. Governor Harvey Parnell, who took office in 1928, viewed establishing a more equitable system of taxation as crucial to achieving his goals in education and roads. He was able to secure passage of the Hall Net Income Tax Law in February 1929, which established a system of equitable taxation on incomes, a system of taxation that did not place most of the burden on rural Arkansans. It was also under his leadership that some rural schools were consolidated, a school bus system was inaugurated, and the school term was lengthened.

Reforms in the Health System

Efforts to improve the educational system in Arkansas coincided with a drive to improve the health of the state's citizens. Arkansas created a permanent State Board of Health in 1913, although the State Board of Health initially had only minimal authority. Its responsibilities expanded in the few years after its creation, but it continued to struggle to fulfill its mission with insufficient funding. Working in cooperation with private agencies such as the Rockefeller Sanitary Commission, the federal government and, sometimes, the Arkansas Federation of Women's Clubs, it carried out a variety of health initiatives. In addition to collecting vital statistics and supervising health inspections of public eating establishments, the board made recommendations for improvement in water and sewer systems across the state. When an embarrassingly large number of potential servicemen were denied enlistment during World War I because of a high incidence of venereal disease, the board laid plans to launch an extensive education campaign in 1919 to raise public awareness of the disease and its consequences. In the 1920s the board helped improve the health of infants and mothers by utilizing federal funds made available through the Sheppard-Towner Act. As a result, infant mortality rates dropped and life expectancy increased.

Largely because of the efforts of the state and private organizations, considerable progress was made in combating a number of diseases. Blacks as well as whites were the beneficiaries of programs to eliminate hookworm, programs sponsored by the Rockefeller Sanitary Commission. Although the problem in Arkansas was not as severe as in most other Southern states, the commission found that 25 percent of the state's schoolchildren suffered from hookworm, and in some isolated rural districts, the incidence of the disease reached 65 percent. Another initiative sponsored by that commission addressed the malaria problem in the Delta, and a campaign to eradicate mosquitos in Crossett, Arkansas, in 1916, was so successful it was to serve as a model for other such efforts. Another agency, the American Red Cross, concentrated on a problem that was endemic in the Delta. The flood of 1912–1913 brought that agency to the state, and its relief workers identified pellagra, a dietary deficiency that could be deadly, as a major problem. While some success was had during the progressive years in educating the public about this serious illness, the Red Cross would again report a high incidence of pellagra when the flood of 1927 brought them back to the Arkansas delta.

If hookworm and malaria were not entirely wiped out, they were greatly reduced. In a number of towns and cities, water supplies were purified and the incidence of typhoid fever dropped as a result. The State Board of Health instituted a policy in 1916 requiring that all schoolchildren, teachers, and school staff be inoculated against smallpox, thus ensuring a dramatic decline in that disease. A tuberculosis sanitarium was founded in Booneville in 1910, providing a safe and comfortable place for sufferers to live in quarantine until the disease ran its course. It served only white patients, however, and it was not until 1931 that a sanitarium for black patients was opened near Little Rock.

Road Development in Arkansas

Arkansans embraced the age of the automobile with as much enthusiasm as other Americans but soon discovered that the narrow, unpaved, and often deeply rutted roads, easily maneuvered by horses and wagons, were simply impassable by automobile. Many who purchased automobiles did so for reasons unconnected to their livelihoods, but for traveling salesmen, delivery men, and, particularly, farmers who wanted a faster way to get their crops to market, the necessity of improving the state's roads had a special urgency to it. Thus, a wide variety of citizens supported improvements to the road system, and as early as 1907, the state legislature passed an act allowing citizens to form local road improvement districts, sell bonds to fund construction, and tax themselves to pay off the bonds. A state highway commission was established in 1913, but it had little control or oversight over the widely scattered road improvement districts. The Alexander Road Improvement law, passed in 1915, further intensified the localized nature of road construction, but the state was able to qualify for federal aid to roads in 1917.

Alexander Road Improvement Act: This act, passed in 1915, allowed counties to sell bonds to fund road construction, which led to an explosion of road construction but made it difficult for the state to manage.

World War I constituted a watershed in both the use of the automobile and the recognition of the value of good roads. Wartime Arkansans could easily understand the importance of an adequate transportation system, whereby troops could be moved rapidly wherever they were needed. Intensified interest in road building and wartime prosperity allowed a larger segment of the population to purchase automobiles. A legislature eager to promote roads and please their constituents passed hundreds of road improvement laws in 1919, laws that accelerated the construction of roads. Governor Brough had hoped to include a provision for greater supervision on the part of the state, but acquiesced in the passage of legislation that gave even greater autonomy to county officials administering the road improvement districts. When Thomas McRae took office in 1921, an "Arkansas Roads Scandal" was already on the horizon. The legislators who sponsored the Alexander Road Improvement Act in the previous decade had intended to facilitate the expansion of the road system in the state but secured support for the act by placing funding and administration in local hands. While this approach had its advantages, most of which were political, it was an abysmal failure. Counties were allowed to issue bonds to fund construction of roads, bonds that were to be paid by taxing landowners. Those few counties that administered the improvement districts responsibly built roads that all but ended at the county line, where rough tracks trailed off into fields that turned into mud bogs during the rainy season. Many road improvement districts did little more than incur debts that taxpayers were responsible for discharging even though roads failed to materialize.

By 1921 the road system was in such disarray in Arkansas that the state's ability to take part in a federal program of road construction, whereby matching funds could be received, was in jeopardy. When the federal government threatened to withhold highway funds unless the state centralized road construction in the state highway department, the governor and a forty-member commission appointed to study the roads scandal urged the legislature to abolish the road improvement districts and put the highway department in charge. When the legislature rejected his proposal, federal funds were withdrawn, and many of the road improvement districts faced bankruptcy. Only then did the legislature pass the Harrelson Road Act in October 1923. Even though the state highway commission secured supervisory control over construction and maintenance of the state's roads under this act, the legislation by no means solved the problem. The separate road districts continued to exist, and the supervisory role of the state highway commission was so modest that it did little to mitigate the abuses of the individual road districts.

Harrelson Road Act: An act passed in 1923 in an attempt to provide a more rational management of the state highway system and to secure federal funds.

By the time that John E. Martineau became governor in 1927, the county road districts were either bankrupt or very close to it. Martineau secured legislation that allowed the state to assume the debts and responsibilities of the road improvement districts and launched the Martineau road plan, an ambitious state highway construction program. After Martineau's surprise appointment to the federal judiciary in 1928, his successor in office, Harvey Parnell, secured passage of legislation authorizing $18 million in bonds to continue the expansion of the Martineau road program and additional legislation permitting the sale of $7.5 million in bonds to finance a highway toll-bridge construction program. However, Parnell's ambitious plans for expansion of the highway system in Arkansas were largely undermined by the deteriorating economic situation and the drought of 1930–1931.

The Great War and Its Aftermath: Reaction and Repression

World War I is recognized as an interruption to progressive reforms in the nation and in Arkansas. Indeed, much of Governor Charles Brough's first term in office was taken up with the war effort. He not only organized the state in support of the war, he also took to the road and delivered more than six hundred speeches. A veteran Chautauqua lecturer, his speeches helped raise funds for the Red Cross and the Liberty Loan campaigns, and although his language was more moderate than some promoters of the war, he equated support for the war with true patriotism and dissent against the war as the voice of the traitor. After several years of asking Americans to remain neutral with regard to the war in Europe, President Woodrow Wilson, who had, in fact, always been pro-British, initiated an intemperate campaign to promote the war. Wilson created a Committee on Public Information (CPI), which was largely a propaganda agency, and the Council of National Defense, which was to coordinate the industries and resources of the country toward the purpose of supporting the war effort. The CPI launched a campaign that was so successful in promoting the war that any dissent was labeled treasonous. As a result, historians have catalogued massive violations of civil liberties during the war that spilled over into even more inexcusable infringements after the war as "one hundred percent Americanism" prevailed as the catch phrase of the immediate postwar period. Governor Brough created the Arkansas State Council of Defense, which was designed to organize the state's industries and resources for the war effort, and also to promote the war, thus assuming the Committee on Public Information's role as propaganda agency. Like elsewhere in the country, German Americans encountered discrimination, and draft evaders, known as slackers, incurred the wrath of super patriots, or at least those acting under the guise of patriotism.

The super patriotism inspired by the war spilled over into the postwar period, and likely played a role in slowing if not destroying the impulse for progressive reforms. One disappointment that Governor Brough endured was the failure of the Arkansas voter to approve a new constitution, one that was a progressive document compared to the 1874 Confederate constitution that continues to serve as the state's instrument of government. Brough had fought hard to convene the constitutional convention, but the document hammered out by that convention did not receive a sufficient number of popular votes to pass in 1918.

The most telling blot upon Governor Brough's progressive credentials, however, involved the thorny issue of race. Prior to his governorship he had served as chairman of the University Commission on the Southern Race Question, and although he fully supported segregation and believed that African Americans were inherently inferior, he also acknowledged that they had certain basic rights. In short, he was a paternalistic racist, possessing a merely more enlightened view than many whites of his generation. When the Elaine Race Riot occurred in Phillips County in the fall of 1919, Brough arranged with the secretary of war to dispatch federal troops to the area to restore order. While he later accepted the white version of events, he appointed a special commission made up of prominent whites and blacks to encourage more harmonious relations between the races.

The events in Elaine, near Helena, certainly indicated that harmony between the races was lacking, but they epitomized far more than simply racism. Black farmers in the area had founded the Farmers and Household Union of America and were planning to file suit against planters over settlement of the crop. Sharecroppers, who worked twenty- to forty-acre farmsteads for planters, marketed their crops through the planter and depended upon him to deduct the "furnish" (supplies extended during the crop year) and pay them the difference. Because of high interest rates in plantation commissaries and because some planters manipulated their books, there was rarely much left for the typical sharecropper after the crop was marketed and the furnish deducted. Increased demand and higher prices for cotton during World War I raised the expectations of delta blacks in general and black sharecroppers in particular. The return of black veterans who had experienced conditions in the army far superior to anything they had enjoyed previously in the Delta, coupled with the demands of black sharecroppers there for a greater share of the farm profits made during the war, created an explosive situation, especially given the precipitous drop in prices for agricultural commodities that followed the war.

Farmers and Household Union of America: A union of black sharecroppers formed in eastern Arkansas in order to secure better settlement with the planters for whom they labored.

The causes of the Elaine conflict were embedded deep within the social and economic structure of the area and signaled a clash between the planter class and black sharecroppers. Because of the large black population, race overshadowed economics in the minds of most who participated in or observed the crisis. Certainly, racial violence had long prevailed in the Delta. Although lynchings had declined in the first two decades of the twentieth century, incidents of nightriding or "whitecapping" against African Americans had become more visible. These incidents were related to a vast expansion of the plantation system, due in part to extensive drainage enterprises, in eastern Arkansas and pitted black sharecroppers against white tenants. Both hoped to secure a tenancy on the new plantations, and organized bands of whitecappers sought to drive African Americans away. Some of the earliest reported incidents occurred in Phillips County, and in 1898 the local newspaper characterized the whitecappers as lawless and irresponsible.

Whitecapping: The term used to describe nightriders who concealed their identity and attacked blacks.

Some blacks chose to leave the Arkansas delta rather than endure the debt, the violence, and the intimidation they encountered there. Indeed, the term *debt peonage* came to be identified with the situation confronting both black and white sharecroppers who owed more to the planters, allegedly, than they earned. Laws had been put into place that made it illegal for indebted

Debt peonage: The process whereby tenants and share-croppers became inextricably indebted to the planters for whom they worked.

sharecroppers and tenants to leave the employment of the planters for whom they worked if they owed them a debt. In this context, the exodus of African Americans from the Delta actually began in the late nineteenth century. Most went to other parts of the United States but some headed "back to Africa," a phenomenon that Ken Barnes writes eloquently about. Although a massive black migration from the South would begin during World War I, many African Americans had as much attachment to the South as did white Southerners and were loath to stray far from their birthplaces. The blacks who founded the Progressive Farmers and Household Union of America were among those who chose to attempt to remain in place and make the system work more equitably.

As recent studies by Grif Stockley, Nan Woodruff, and Robert Whitaker have demonstrated, the African Americans who organized the Progressive Farmers and Household Union of America were taking on a formidable system. As blacks began to organize their union, word drifted back to planters who either honestly or deliberately misinterpreted their intentions. They believed that blacks were organizing an insurrection and were planning to seize their lands and murder them. In fact, the union leaders had hired U. S. Bratton, a prominent Little Rock attorney and former federal prosecutor, to represent them in suits they hoped to file for fair settlement of the crop, and they were attempting to keep their plans secret for fear that planters would devise a legal strategy against them. When gunfire was exchanged outside a rural church near Hoop Spur, where a union meeting was underway, the white community sprang into action to put down what they characterized as a racial revolution. Armed whites hunted down and shot innocent blacks by the dozens, perhaps by the hundreds. Local authorities finally asked Governor Brough to arrange for federal troops to intervene when it appeared that incarcerated blacks and a white attorney representing them might be lynched. Planters later appealed to authorities to release many of the blacks who had been arrested for fear their cotton crop would not be harvested on schedule. Twelve blacks were subsequently condemned to death, largely on the basis of coerced testimony in trials that lasted only minutes. The NAACP launched an investigation and pursued a series of appeals that eventually resulted in their release. Scipio Jones, a prominent black attorney in Little Rock, played a major role in representing the "Elaine twelve" and many other black Arkansans contributed to the cost of the appeals.

With the agricultural crisis driving even prominent planters close to bankruptcy, the tendency was to wring what profits could be realized from the most vulnerable partner in the plantation enterprise: the black sharecropper. The emergence of a revitalized Ku Klux Klan during and immediately following the war gave institutionalized racism an added legitimacy, although, to be sure, the new KKK was not only racist but also anti-Semitic, anti-Catholic, and anti-foreign. It also saw itself as the moral arbiter of the communities it functioned within, addressing the evils of illicit liquor distilling, prostitution, and wife beating. Regardless of its claims to serving as a necessary check to such abuses, the KKK functioned as the unofficial military arm of a planter class growing anxious about the exodus of agricultural labor and weary of a deepening crisis in the agricultural economy. Although some Klan groups were town-based organizations that appealed largely to the new business class, others had distinctly rural orientations. Klan groups even formed in the Ozark Mountains, although they tended to be oriented toward issues other than race.

The KKK became so prominent in Arkansas that some politicians valued their support during the election cycle. Thomas McRae was not among them. Governor McRae's background provided him with impeccable credentials as a "Southerner"—as a boy he had been a courier for Confederate forces in Washington, Arkansas—and allowed him to speak out against extreme racism without fear of being labeled "soft" on the "negro" question. His long and distinguished service as a state legislator and as a US congressman gave him additional stature and respectability. He was elected governor in 1920 at a time when the Republican Party itself was divided on the race question, fielding two candidates, a Lily White and a Black and Tan. The Lily Whites feared that black Republicans kept the Republican Party from recruiting white members, thus they shunned blacks. The Black and Tan Republicans, on the other hand, made some effort to attract blacks to the party, believing that they could be of more benefit than harm, that the ballots they cast for Republicans candidates would outnumber the white ballots their inclusion might discourage. In any case, McRae remained above the question of race during his campaign. In his bid for reelection in 1922, the Little Rock chapter of the KKK supported him, although he had not sought their endorsement, while the state chapter threw their support to his opponent. Still, McRae had no trouble winning reelection. While Brough might have been expected to act on behalf of racial moderation because of his connection to the Southern Sociological Conference, it was McRae who in 1925 released the last of the twelve black men sentenced to death in the Elaine Race Riot, although, to be sure, by that time the case against the men had become so hopeless that only token resistance to the pardoning arose. McRae's position on race remained that of a southern conservative Democrat, paternalistic and protective. He was no spokesman for equality, integration, or voting rights.

Lynchings of black men were in decline in the South in the twentieth

Elaine Twelve. *Courtesy of the Arkansas State Archives.*

century, having reached their peak in the 1890s. Governor McRae and other state and local officials in Arkansas were determined in the 1920s to end that kind of lawlessness altogether, but several highly publicized lynchings occurred despite their best efforts. Most white Southerners who attempted to justify lynchings did so on the basis that they were the appropriate punishment for the sexual attacks of depraved black men on white women. The record, however, does not bear out that point of view. Few lynchings in Arkansas or elsewhere in the South were the outcome of sexual attacks on white women. Some were connected to disputes between planters and share-croppers. Others were the result of battles between whites and blacks over "opportunities" to work the plantation. Some were in response to crimes like murder or arson. Whatever their real motivations, in the post–World War I era, they also reflected a population of whites that was itself apprehensive in the face of the turmoil caused by the economic recession following World War I, a turmoil that made the emergence of a revitalized KKK possible. In fact, a KKK initiation occurred in 1923, on the very site where black share-cropper Henry Lowery was lynched in 1921, and the next year, a new school erected for African Americans in nearby Wilson was destroyed by fire in the early morning hours on the day it was to be dedicated.

Henry Lowery, who was engaged in a dispute over settlement of the crop with the planter for whom he worked, killed two whites during a confronta-tion on Christmas Day in 1920. He had escaped to Texas and when he was apprehended there, Governor McRae guaranteed that he would be given a fair trial in Little Rock and ordered his return to that capital city. Instead, he was taken from train in Mississippi in route to Memphis—an unlikely route to Little Rock—and returned to Mississippi County where he was burned to death in front of an audience reported to have been about six hundred in number. The governor, who had run on a law-and-order platform was livid, but he was to find that there was little he could do in the face of mob action and law enforcement complicity. Despite a concerted campaign on his part and that of a few other leading lawmakers in the state to eliminate mob justice in the 1920s, another lynching occurred in May 1927 that spoke to the deepest fears of the white community. John Carter, who was described in some reports as "simple minded," had attacked allegedly two white women, a mother and daughter, on a road south of Little Rock. The women fought him off, escaped, and alerted authorities. Carter was apprehended, and there the incident might have ended in a law-abiding fashion. But his attack on the white women had been preceded by the rape and murder of a white child at the hands of a black youth who, through the careful actions of the Little Rock chief of police, was spirited out of town and away from the clutches of an angry white crowd. In a sense, the mob that took Carter, riddled him with bullets, and then rioted for three hours in the heart of the black business district was avenging the child's death. But the crowd also attacked innocent blacks who happened to be on the street and ransacked black businesses, delivering a chilling message to the black community. Like most lynchings, it was a very public affair that served notice to blacks to stay within their inferior station in life and to refrain from challenging the white community.

The violence facing the black community stirred some African American leaders to action. Dr. John M. Robinson, one of the founders of Little Rock's chapter of the NAACP in 1918 who had grown weary of its timidity in addressing the political handicaps facing blacks, launched a campaign to end the White Primary in 1928. He was chagrined when the New York office of the NAACP refused his request to support his effort on the grounds that the black elite in Arkansas had not been supportive of the NAACP. He knew that Little Rock's black elites had contributed to the NAACP-led defense of the twelve black men sentenced to death for their involvement in the Elaine Race Riot in 1919. Indeed, a prominent black attorney representing the Elaine Twelve, Scipio Jones, was part of the Little Rock black establishment. Given the contributions blacks in Little Rock had made to the defense of the Elaine Twelve, the NAACP's denial of funds on the grounds that Little Rock's blacks had not been forthcoming enough seems specious indeed. The fact is that in 1928 the NAACP was supporting similar cases challeng- ing the White Primary in Virginia, Florida, and Texas and likely wanted to avoid spreading resources too thin by including yet another case from yet another state. Still, the NAACP did make decisions about distribution of funds based on the amount of support it received from the various states. Dr. Robinson was left to pursue his initiatives on his own. In the same year that Robinson sought support from the NAACP, he founded the Arkansas Negro Democratic Association (ANDA), and it was through this organization that he hoped to challenge the White Primary. He pursued the suit even without NAACP support, but in 1930 the Arkansas Supreme Court upheld the white-only Democratic primary in *Robinson v. Holman*. Dr. Robinson's organization remained alive but became inactive during the difficult 1930s, and he left it to a later generation of African American leaders to launch the next phase of black activism in Arkansas.

Arkansas Negro Democratic Association: Founded in 1928 in an unsuccessful attempt to overturn the use of the White Primary, which kept blacks from voting in primary elections.

Natural Disasters

Floods along the Mississippi and the Arkansas rivers and their tributaries were nothing new to Arkansans, but the great flood of 1927 was in a category all its own. It was the greatest natural disaster to hit the state since the New Madrid earthquakes of 1811–1812. It would have diverted any governor's attention from the normal course of business, but John E. Martineau's election to head the Tri-State Flood Commission, made up of the states of Arkansas, Mississippi, and Louisiana, required him to make several trips to Washington, DC, to work closely with Herbert Hoover, who had been appointed by President Coolidge to head relief efforts. His appointment was a testament to the fact that of the eight states affected—Illinois, Missouri, Kentucky, Arkansas, Tennessee, Mississippi, Louisiana, and Oklahoma—Arkansas was the hardest hit. Over 5 million acres were flooded in the state, and over 2 million of those acres were normally devoted to agriculture. Louisiana and Mississippi were also seriously inundated with floodwaters, but Arkansas had almost as many agricultural acres flooded as Louisiana and Mississippi combined (Arkansas, 2,024,210; Louisiana, 1,167,522; and Mississippi, 976,905).

The flood began in the late spring and extended nearly one thousand miles from Cairo, Illinois, to the Gulf of Mexico. In Arkansas most of the damage occurred in counties along the Mississippi River, which suffered thirteen breaks in its levees, but some interior counties were also seriously affected. There were twenty-six breaks on the Arkansas River, sixty-seven on the White River, and twelve on the St. Francis. Hundreds of thousands of acres were flooded along these and other interior waterways in Arkansas. Although the number of deaths was relatively low, over fifty-five thousand homes in Arkansas were inundated with floodwaters, and the American Red

Cross extended emergency aid to over two hundred thousand Arkansans. Because the flood came after weeks of rain and the newspapers had repeatedly reported the increasing likelihood of disaster, many farmers had time to remove their livestock before the waters reached them. Still, it was projected to take twenty-five to thirty carloads of oil to burn the more than twenty-five thousand carcasses of horses, cows, mules, and hogs not moved to safety in time. As slow as the water was to move onto the Arkansas landscape, it was even slower in moving off. Hundreds of thousands of acres remained flooded well into the summer, beyond the time when crops might have been planted.

The first response of the Red Cross was to rescue flood refugees and place them in camps. For the first time in a natural disaster, the radio was used to coordinate rescue efforts and airplanes were used to locate refugees clinging to tree limbs or gathered on rooftops or levees. A variety of watercraft —rowboats, motorboats, barges, towboats, and flatboats—nearly two thousand of them—were then dispatched to rescue the victims in Arkansas. They were then transported, usually by train, to one of eighty camps in the state, ranging in size from a few hundred in camps like that located at Selma (Drew County) to over fifteen thousand in Forrest City. The quick response on the part of the Red Cross and private citizens, who participated in the rescue effort, was one reason why so few deaths were reported in Arkansas.

The danger of disease was of great concern to the agency. As one medical doctor in Arkansas reported to the Red Cross after the worst of the flood was over, the most pressing matter to consider after rescuing people from tree limbs and rooftops was the spread of disease. The crowded conditions at the Red Cross camps, where displaced persons were housed, stimulated fears of epidemic. As the floodwaters subsided, stagnant pools of water, sometimes laden with the carcasses of dead animals, provided the perfect breeding ground for mosquitoes, which could carry disease. The three major health concerns were typhoid, malaria, and dysentery, but the Red Cross also worried about smallpox and launched a massive effort to prevent an outbreak of epidemic diseases that frequently accompanied natural disaster.

But the greatest health problem came as something of a surprise to Red Cross officials, and for a short time they debated the appropriateness of any effort to combat it. The debate within Red Cross circles revealed their reluctance to intervene in a situation having its origins more in local social and economic arrangements than in natural disaster. Pellagra, which had showed its face to Red Cross officials during the 1912–1913 floods, became an even more public affair after the 1927 disaster. A dietary deficiency that could lead to death, it was most frequently manifested in skin rashes and lethargy. Health officials had only recently become cognizant of the causes of the disease—a B3 deficiency—but had discovered that a concentrated form

Pellagra: A disease that stemmed from a dietary deficiency (lack of fresh vegetables) and led to a variety of debilitating symptoms such as skin rashes, lethargy and, in extreme cases, death.

of pure yeast, administered on a regular basis for up to six weeks, restored most patients to health. The critical issue was a lack of fresh vegetables, and planters typically forbid or discouraged their tenants and sharecroppers from devoting valuable agricultural acreage to the production of vegetables. The crucial question for Red Cross officials was whether the high incidence of the disease was a consequence of the flood or a preexisting condition. They were authorized to distribute aid to flood sufferers, not to address the human costs of the plantation system in eastern Arkansas. They understood that the disease was prevalent in the Mississippi Valley region, and particularly in eastern Arkansas, and that the diet was connected to the poor economic conditions of plantation laborers. Incidences of the disease rose and fell with the farm economy. Too often without kitchen gardens that provided vegetables and without cows that furnished milk, the Delta residents experienced a high incidence of the disease, but when economic conditions were good, they could purchase fresh vegetables in the summer, and they could afford to keep a cow. Ultimately the Red Cross determined that the flood had worsened the condition by destroying gardens that otherwise provided green vegetables to people on the verge of the disease. Thus, the Red Cross rationalized its effort to address the problem and began an impressive campaign to distribute yeast throughout the affected area.

The primitive state of public health in Arkansas made extending medical care to the flood sufferers distinctly problematic, however. The state health department was a poorly organized and underfunded affair with limited responsibility and expertise. Red Cross officials reviewing the incidences of typhoid, smallpox, and pellagra over the previous five years, in an effort to establish a base-line comparison, concluded that the morbidity reports produced by the state were worthless and provided no reliable information. Red Cross funds had to be dispersed to place public health nurses in various counties to dispense yeast to fight pellagra and quinine to address the symptoms of malaria. They also vaccinated people against smallpox, and offered advice on screening homes to prevent malaria. Local doctors and pharmacists were called into service to assist the nurses but in some cases disputes arose, disputes that were sometimes the result of professional jealousy and sometimes reflected real differences of opinion about treatment.

The problem between the public health nurses and some local medical care providers remained a largely internal problem that the state and the Red Cross worked out on an individual basis. But another controversy emerged in the months after the flood that gained national attention. Planters became concerned that black sharecroppers housed in the various Red Cross camps scattered over eastern Arkansas would not return to the plantations from which they had come and thus would not honor the debts they had incurred at the plantation commissaries prior to the flood. In addition, some planters still hoped to plant a crop, perhaps only a crop of corn or hay, but they needed agricultural labor in order to do so. In an era when blacks were moving from the South to the North, the prospect of a further reduction in this labor force caused great concern among planters. In order to avoid causing additional strain on the agricultural economy of the region, the Red Cross agreed to release black sharecroppers from its camps only after their respective planters called for them. The spectacle of hapless flood sufferers confined to camps made for poor publicity for the Red Cross and threatened to interrupt the flow of charitable dollars. Nevertheless, the agency continued in its policy, fearing the consequences of a massive shift in population that could cripple the plantation system and inhibit economic recovery after the flood. Indeed, perhaps the most lasting legacy of the Red Cross was the message planters received that interference from this outside agency did not disrupt its relations with tenants and sharecroppers. Together the farm agents and the Red Cross officials demonstrated that planters need not be afraid of outside forces working with their tenants and sharecroppers, that they did not pose a threat. The lessons learned during the flood of 1927 would have a chance to be tested again during the drought of 1930–1931.

The drought was a different kind of disaster, but it was equally devastating. When it struck in 1930, Arkansans had barely recovered from the flood of 1927 and were confronting a deepening crisis in its agricultural economy. As crops wilted in the fields and livestock weakened and died, the Red Cross was finally prevailed upon to recognize the drought as a disaster and stepped in to render aid, just as it had during the flood. No one had to be rescued from treetops, but many had to be fed and provided with replacement livestock, feed, and seed. This relief effort was also plagued by controversy, however.

The first controversy to emerge involved the failure of relief forms to be distributed in England, Arkansas, in January 1931, resulting in a delay of relief supplies to farmers in need. Although referred to as a "riot," it was little more than a gathering of angry farmers demanding that the proper forms be dispensed so they could apply for relief. It passed quickly enough when the necessity for the forms was waived and the relief dispensed. But another controversy passed more slowly. When it became known that some planters were requiring their tenants and sharecroppers to work in exchange for relief supplies, the national headquarters of the Red Cross issued an order condemning the practice. Planters complained bitterly, believing that relief given too freely threatened their labor supply, but they ceased their labor program in the face of the demands of Red Cross officials who themselves feared the cessation of donations to their organization.

The last two years of the 1920s was a particularly challenging time for the nation and for Arkansas. Arkansas—and other rural areas across the country—had never fully recovered from the agricultural depression that set in after World War I. Between the flood of 1927 and the drought of 1930–1931, a devastating stock market crash in 1929 only made matters worse. It was impossible for Governor Parnell to gain much traction in the reforms he hoped to implement. To complicate matters, much of his time and attention in 1928, his first year in office, was taken up with the presidential race, which required him to explain to Arkansas's rural—and Protestant—constituency why they would vote for a Catholic New Yorker for president of the United States. Al Smith was running on the Democratic ticket, but a prominent Arkansan, Joseph T. Robinson, was running as his vice-presidential candidate. Parnell stumped the state for the Smith-Robinson ticket and held Arkansas in the Democratic fold while many other southern states backed Herbert Hoover, the Republican candidate. Smith's Catholicism and his identification as a "wet" on the issue of prohibition rankled many Arkansans, but the majority voted for him, either out of loyalty to the party or affection for Joe Robinson. The vote reflected no ideological differences between Arkansas and its southern neighbors, however. In the same election, they also approved a measure banning the teaching of evolution in Arkansas schools.

However laudable Parnell's road construction and education initiatives were, by 1930 the state treasury was considerably depleted, and his opponent in the governor's race that year, Brooks Hays, declared that any further bond issues would bankrupt the state. But the expansion of the road system was popular with voters and Parnell won the election. Over the next two years he presided over a state stricken with economic collapse and facing yet another natural disaster, the drought of 1930–1931.

By the early 1930s, Governor Parnell's progressive agenda was facing extinction. His laudable but expensive road construction and educational programs had exhausted the state's coffers, particularly because many taxpayers had engaged in a silent but potent tax revolt. They had simply ceased paying their road, drainage, real estate, and personal property taxes. By 1930 millions of acres were subject to confiscation by the state, but officials preferred payment of taxes to confiscation—land values had dropped drastically and there were few buyers even in that market—and, while resorting to strong warnings, they provided for tax extensions, hoping to receive some revenues. With falling revenues and an agricultural economy reeling from another natural disaster in 1931, Parnell was moved to cut state expenditures, despite his belief that recovery was imminent.

Just as some Americans blamed President Hoover for the Great Depression, some Arkansans branded Parnell the architect of the disastrous economic situation facing the state, particularly those in agriculture. Departing drastically from his previous commitment to promoting agribusiness, Parnell began to trumpet the "back to the land movement," suggesting that farmers diversify and strive for self-sufficiency rather than produce crops for a market that was rapidly vanishing. Agricultural extension agents throughout the state had been calling for diversification for more than a decade and many, even in the cotton-dependent delta, were beginning to urge the production of food crops so that farmers could at least feed their families in an era when the price they were receiving for cotton was below the cost of production. Parnell stopped short, however, of calling for any specific measures designed to force diversification. It was the legislature that passed an act calling for a reduction in cotton acreage, but it was too little, too late, and they had no enforcement mechanism in place.

By 1932 no segment of the state's economy could warrant optimism. Farm incomes had plummeted, and nearly 40 percent of the labor force was unemployed. Bank deposits dwindled, and a record number of banks closed across the state as anxious depositors rushed to try to withdraw what they could. Private charities had long been exhausted, and the needs of the state were so great that Arkansas was the recipient of more Reconstruction Finance Corporation (RFC) loans than any other single state. As the situation went from bad to worse, Parnell became the scapegoat. The legislature passed a resolution condemning him as having presided over the most corrupt administration since Reconstruction. They rescinded the resolution a few days later, but they had made their point. The perception was that the Progressive Era governor had ruined the state's finances with profligate spending, particularly on the highway program (which was, in fact, riddled with corruption). Notwithstanding the fact that the legislature and the citizens of Arkansas had strongly supported, even demanded, the extension of the highway system, they blamed the governor for having launched a program that the state could ill afford in the face of a Great Depression of unprecedented proportions. It was as a result of the disillusionment with Parnell and his so-called excessive and profligate spending that the Democrats of Arkansas nominated and elected Junius Marion Futrell in 1932 on the promise of returning the state to solvency.

12 Darker Forces on the Horizon

 The Great Depression and World War II, 1932–1945

AS ARKANSAS BEGAN to embrace new innovations in transportation and communication in the third and fourth decades of the twentieth century, it remained shackled to its rural past and hampered by unprecedented economic challenges. As the Great Depression fastened its grip on the nation, Arkansas stumbled into the New Deal with a governor who foreswore the activist state and with a president who prescribed a federal remedy for the country's ills. This would turn out to be an important contrast. As the state withdrew from its previous progressive commitment, its people turned toward the federal government to solve their problems. The federal role was expanded further during World War II, a war that rivaled the Civil War in terms of the changes it would bring. Indeed, historian Morton Sosna declared in his presidential address to the Southern Historical Association in 1982 that "World War II rather than the Civil War is the crucial event of southern history." Scholars who focus their studies on the devastation of the Civil War and the challenges that followed it might be characterized as appropriately skeptical. Nevertheless, in narrowing his definition of "crucial" to mean whether significant changes occurred, Sosna was on solid ground. By the time he made his provocative observation, scholars had already demonstrated that the antebellum elite survived the Civil War intact and in control, that the status of African Americans only briefly improved, and that the labor-intensive plantation economy survived the devastation of war and defeat. Not until World War II, Sosna argues, was the South truly made to change and then largely because of massive infusions of capital in the form of military spending. Perhaps a bit overeager to prove his point, Sosna dismisses too readily the impact of New Deal programs when, in fact, they caused a shift in crops and the stirrings of mechanization that began the process of radically altering labor systems in the South. Nevertheless, World War II marked a dramatic and important moment in Southern and in Arkansas history. The $300 million spent on military bases and war-related industries in Arkansas resulted in unprecedented prosperity for some, but a massive demographic shift led to enormous challenges during and after the war. Arkansas weathered the darker forces of economic depression and world war but was a different state as a result of them.

Junius Marion Futrell and the Conservative Resurgence

At the very moment that the Great Depression appeared to be at its worst, the state elected its most conservative governor in decades. Governor Junius Marion Futrell, of the northeastern Arkansas delta, came from a plantation background. At first blush, it seems ironic that in the same year Arkansas citizens voted overwhelmingly for Franklin Delano Roosevelt as president, a man who would move the country to accept a much more activist federal government, they also selected a man to fill the governor's chair who repudiated an activist state government. In fact, the two men shared only one thing in common. They acknowledged the existence of a crisis and claimed to have a solution. That Roosevelt's solution would take the country in one direction while Futrell's would take the state in another could not have been foreseen by the average voter. While Roosevelt had not been very specific about his plans, Futrell had campaigned on a platform of retrenchment. He fulfilled his pledge to reduce state expenditures and return the state to a cash basis. Significantly, however, had the federal government not engaged in massive relief programs and launched a plan to rescue agriculture—both of which would pump massive amounts of money into the state—Futrell's severe retrenchment would have brought widespread hardship to the state's people.

By the time that Futrell assumed the governorship, the state's highway debt had reached the staggering sum of $146,000,000, and he identified paying off that debt as his first priority. But he also had in mind devising a new strategy for funding the highway system. He wanted to consolidate all the highway debts into one, a scheme that was not to the liking of many out-of-state bond holders, and the legislature first balked at the governor's plan. They did agree to his proposal to increase fees for truck and automobile licenses and for commercial vehicles as well as increased taxes on the sale of oil and gas. Futrell called a special session in 1934 and pushed his Highway Refunding Act through.

Rather than blame Governor Parnell for the fiscal crisis facing the state, Futrell believed that the highway debt problem was the result of profligate spending on the part of the legislature. He proposed two amendments to the state constitution that severely restricted the taxing and spending power of the legislature—and of the state in general—and marked a dramatic departure from the direction that progressive governors had been taking the state in the previous two decades. Futrell, a fiscal conservative who believed fervently that the state should play a very small role in the affairs of its citizens, thought the state was merely to allow them to pursue life, liberty, and the pursuit of happiness, but otherwise stay out of their business. Thus, he proposed the Nineteenth Amendment, which limited legislative appropriations to a fixed amount and required a three-fourths vote in each house of the legislature, or approval of voters in a general election, before taxes could be increased. The Twentieth Amendment required voter approval before the state could issue new bonds. Voters approved both amendments in a subsequent election.

Convinced that poverty and unemployment resulted from a lack of individual initiative, Futrell was unsympathetic to direct relief programs. Believing that education beyond the primary grades was unnecessary, he reduced expenditures to high schools. Both of these attitudes reflected Futrell's northeastern Arkansas delta background. He had been raised in a socioeconomic system that needed a large underclass of laborers who planters believed needed to be forced to work. They feared relief programs that might offer their tenants and sharecroppers an alternative. No friend to industrialization, which constituted yet another challenge to the plantation economy, Futrell represented a throwback to the period before the progressive governors of the early twentieth century and even the New South advocates of the late nineteenth century.

Futrell's attitudes toward direct relief and education led to a showdown between the state and the Federal Emergency Relief Administration in 1934. Created in March 1933, the FERA, under the leadership of Harry Hopkins, devised a two-pronged program providing for both works projects and direct relief. The states were expected to share the costs of the programs. Given Futrell's attitude toward direct relief and toward education, he was content to divert a greater share of federal funds toward those programs than seemed appropriate to Hopkins. When the Arkansas legislature's 1934 property tax relief package made it clear that the state would rely on the FERA dollars to fund education at an even higher level, Hopkins's patience with Futrell was exhausted. Hopkins notified the governor that all federal aid to Arkansas— including that extended through the agricultural programs—would cease as of March 1, 1935, unless Arkansas raised state funding for education and appropriated $1.5 million for public welfare.

Hopkins's threat to cease funding all federal programs in Arkansas captured the attention of delta planters who began pressuring Futrell to resolve the situation before federal dollars were cut off from programs they needed. In response, Futrell began to fashion measures to meet the expense of providing matching funds for the FERA programs. The state's cost was projected to be $1,500,000. His solution was yet another example of his conservatism and yet another rejection of Progressive Era reforms. He called for the repeal of prohibition so liquor sales could be taxed. He supported the legalization of gambling, providing for the opening of a dog track in West Memphis and a horse racing track in Hot Springs, both of which would be subject to taxation. He initially refused to endorse a tax on retail sales but eventually urged passage of it when it became clear that his endorsement was necessary to get the measure through the state senate. This package of legislation was not completed until after the March 1, 1935, deadline had come and gone and federal funds were lost. The loss of those funds encouraged the legislature to enact all three measures.

The Agricultural Adjustment Administration

Whatever his attitude about the FERA, Futrell supported federal programs designed to aid agriculture. Indeed, prominent planters in Arkansas and in the South heavily influenced the formation and management of the agency charged with revitalizing the farming sector, the Agricultural Adjustment Administration (AAA). By the time that Roosevelt was inaugurated and his advisors had successfully devised a program for the farming sector, farmers and planters had their crops in the ground and were looking forward to a banner production year, notwithstanding the low prices they were likely to receive. Arkansas senator Joseph Robinson and representative William Driver helped fashion legislation calling for a plow-up of up to 30 percent of those crops and laid the groundwork for an acreage restriction program that would take shape in the next year. Although many planters by the end of the decade would grow weary of the restrictions on raising certain crops, they embraced the AAA program in 1933 when they were teetering on the edge of bankruptcy. By that time farmers in Arkansas and elsewhere had endured more than a decade of collapsing farm prices. Cotton was selling for five cents per pound, and the cost of producing the crop was far more than the return farmers realized. Credit facilities had almost completely dried up, mortgage indebtedness was at an all-time high, and some of the most prominent planters in the state turned to the Reconstruction Finance Corporation (RFC), a creature of President Herbert Hoover's administration, for relief. Although some farmers in the state refused to participate in the plow-up campaign, most were eager to secure federal funds for bankruptcy was often the only alternative.

The rationale behind the plow-up and subsequent crop-reduction program was to reduce the amount of certain overproduced crops and thus raise prices. In funneling money into the hands of farmers and planters in

Agricultural Adjustment Administration: An act of Congress designed to revitalize the country's agricultural sector by providing for a means of production control.

exchange for reducing such crops, the program meant to provide immediate relief. For landowners, it was a bonanza but it had a negative impact on tenants and sharecroppers who, as it turns out, were not consistently reimbursed for their share of the crop reduction. In fact, many planters simply fired tenants and sharecroppers, throwing them onto the labor market at a time when there was no work available.

Landless men in Alabama formed a Sharecroppers Union while those in northeastern Arkansas organized the Southern Tenant Farmers Union (STFU) to fight evictions and seek a share of the crop.

The Southern Tenant Farmers Union

In July 1934 tenants and sharecroppers banded together in Poinsett County and formed the STFU. Clay East, a local businessman and member of a well-respected farm family, together with H. L. Mitchell, another small businessman, influenced the founding of the organization. Mitchell had converted East to socialism, and they subsequently hosted a visit to Poinsett County by Norman Thomas, the leader of the Socialist Party of America and perennial candidate for president. The organization they founded was avowedly interracial, and its initial goals were to stop evictions from plantations in the area and to force planters to share the crop subsidy payments with those still on plantations. Later they added securing higher wages for agricultural laborers, such as those picking or hoeing cotton, to their goals, and carried out some successful strikes. Some in the Agricultural Adjustment Administration in Washington, DC, were sympathetic to their demands, but President Roosevelt, desperate to hang on to conservative Southern Democrats in Congress, turned a deaf ear to the pleas of STFU representatives, and in 1935 those in charge of the AAA fired those within the agency who were sympathetic to the STFU. In Arkansas, Oklahoma, and Missouri, which together had about 35,000 STFU members, planters and local officials practiced a more traditional method of discouraging the union. Nightriders, commonly believed to be plantation thugs, routinely broke up union meetings. Constables and sheriff's deputies disrupted others, sometimes arresting the STFU members, particularly those leading the meetings. Shots were fired into the homes of suspected union members and even the attorney representing the union. Finally, enemies of the STFU played to the racism of the white members of the union with some success.

Although the integration within the STFU has been somewhat exaggerated, it is nevertheless true that interracial cooperation existed in many STFU

Southern Tenant Farmers Union: Founded in 1934 in Poinsett County by sharecroppers and tenants (both black and white) because planters were not only not sharing AAA crop subsidy payments with them, they were also often evicting them from plantations.

locals and marked a dramatic departure from earlier attempts by farmers to organize. In the late nineteenth century, the Agricultural Wheel, made up of small farm owners and some few tenants, operated separate white and black Wheels. Although some blacks were allowed to attend a state meeting, white and black Wheelers had little contact. But even that distant relationship left the Wheel vulnerable to charges that it was the tool of blacks and Republicans and probably cost them dearly at the polls. The goals of the Wheel, meanwhile, were quite different from those of the STFU, and the membership of the two organizations best illustrates that point. Although some tenants belonged to the Wheel, it was principally made up of small farm owners who wanted mortgage debt relief, regulation of railroads, and a more flexible monetary system. Three decades later, the Farmers and Household Union of America (FHUA), an organization of black sharecroppers, banded together to hire attorneys to represent them in suits they planned to file against the planters for whom they worked. Their efforts were misinterpreted, either deliberately or innocently, and a major race riot occurred at Elaine. In any event, the FHUA's organizing efforts provided its enemies with a potent weapon against such unions: the use of violent racism.

In fact, one of the founding members of the STFU was Isaac Shaw, who had been a member of the ill-fated Farmers and Household Union of America. In July 1934, at the first meeting of the organization that would become the STFU, Shaw argued that blacks and whites should organize together. He drew explicitly upon his earlier experience, and the six other black men and the eleven whites gathered at that meeting agreed that since they shared similar problems and oppressors, they should organize as one union. Shrewdly, however, the STFU leadership determined that each STFU local should decide the issue of whether to be interracial or segregated on their own, and this policy probably greatly facilitated the expansion of the union. Elected officials in the national STFU office always included blacks and whites. Eventually, planters would play to the racism of a white president who would turn over the union's membership records to them. Although he later recanted, the damage had been done, and the union was seriously weakened. A brief flirtation with Commonwealth College, a socialist institution near Mena, Arkansas, which proved to have ties with the Communist Party, also discredited the union.

Yet the STFU could claim some measure of success. H. L. Mitchell and other union representatives created significant problems for one of the largest cotton planters in the South, Lee Wilson & Company, when it alleged to a *Washington Post* reporter that the three largest recipients of AAA payments in 1934 and 1935, Lee Wilson & Company of Mississippi County, Chapman and Dewey Land Company of Poinsett County, and Delta Pine & Land

Arkansas farmworkers at union meeting. *Courtesy Louise Boyle.*

Company located in the state of Mississippi, were refusing to share subsidies and evicting tenants and sharecroppers wholesale, throwing them onto relief rolls. While it investigated the matter, the AAA suspended payments to Lee Wilson & Company in 1936, a suspension that continued into the early 1940s. In 1941, however, their payments, at least back to 1938, were restored. Perhaps more important to landless farmers in Arkansas, the publicity surrounding the violent attacks on union members, together with the agitation of the union's leadership in Washington, DC, forced Governor Futrell to establish a state commission to study the situation. But among those appointed to the committee were two employees of Lee Wilson & Company and the company's attorney. Although it included STFU representation, it was loaded with those hostile to the union. Before its report could be issued, however, President Roosevelt appointed a Farm Tenancy Commission, and its report, unlike that eventually issued by the state commission, was unsparing in its criticisms of the farm tenancy system. Congress finally responded in 1937 by passing the Bankhead-Jones Farm Tenancy Act, which, among other things, established the Farm Security Administration (FSA), an agency designed to put displaced tenants on their own farms. The FSA absorbed what remained of the Resettlement Administration, which had established some resettlement communities in Arkansas.

The most famous resettlement community was created in Mississippi County in 1934 and named for the state FERA director, William R. Dyess. The most well-known resident of the colony was singer Johnny Cash, whose family moved there in 1936 when he was a young child. William Dyess, a native of Mississippi County, was from a plantation family and held many of Governor Futrell's reservations about direct relief. The Dyess Colony settlement was touted as a model, but the publicity photographs, which showed rows of whitewashed houses and smiling farmers and their wives working in the community canning facility, could not long disguise the fact that considerable unrest and dissatisfaction existed there. An STFU chapter was established there, for example. The community was run much like a plantation and the farmers, many of whom had been farm owners prior to the depression, found themselves under the authority of the local FERA director and the farm extension agent. Planters had never been enthusiastic about the Resettlement Administration, but they had exercised some influence with it, particularly on the local level. They had little influence, however, with the FSA, which absorbed the resettlement communities like Dyess colony. The FSA became particularly unpopular with planters, who saw it competing with them for valuable agricultural acreage, and, in any case, actually helped few tenants and sharecroppers, since most of those placed on the camps were failed farm owners. The FSA communities were accused of being socialistic and were eventually abolished by a less friendly Congress in 1944. By that time, a massive transformation of southern agriculture was fully underway, a transformation that eventually eliminated the farm tenancy system altogether.

Other New Deal Programs

Another federal agency also led to significant changes and secured the cooperation of the state's most prominent citizens: the Works Progress Administration (WPA). The WPA was essentially a successor to the FERA's Civil Works Administration (CWA). The CWA had been charged with putting the able-bodied unemployed to work. Direct relief was administered only to the unemployable poor and women with dependent children. The CWA, and later the WPA, put people to work on building roads, digging drainage ditches, and erecting public buildings, among other things. One significant difference between the WPA and the CWA was the role that local communities played. Communities pledged 50 per-

Works Progress Administration: The Works Progress Administration put people to work in a variety of jobs but worked in concert with local communities to locate projects there.

Mississippi County, resettled family, Dyess Colony. *Courtesy of the Arkansas History Commission.*

cent of the funds for road improvements, for example, and received grants from the WPA for the remainder. Together with the Civilian Conservation Corps (CCC), which employed single young men and engaged in conservation measures, the WPA gave thousands of men gainful employment and helped transform the state in significant ways. CCC workers terraced lands to prevent erosion and planted trees; the WPA significantly improved the state's transportation network through the construction of roads and left a lasting legacy in the way of public buildings, such as libraries, courthouses, and schools. Not only did CCC workers develop outdoor parks like those at Petit Jean in Conway County and at Devil's Den in Washington County, they built Mather Lodge at the former and several cabins at the latter. Many WPA workers engaged in "writers' projects," and created a valuable archive of county histories, church histories, and the famous slave narratives. Many women and some African Americans were employed in these endeavors.

While the AAA had its greatest impact in the Delta, the federal programs that first penetrated the Ozarks and the Ouachitas were the WPA and the CCC. Farmers in those areas were typically more self-reliant and less dependent upon marketing their crops outside their own communities. The collapse of the cotton market hardly mattered to them, for cotton was not a crop they grew. Accustomed to barter and to a cash-scarce economy, many hardly knew that a depression existed, and the CCC and WPA jobs provided some with the first cash wages they had ever known. Those wages opened a whole new world of goods and services to previously isolated communities, and together with WPA projects that funded the construction of schools and libraries, generated a new appreciation of the world outside their isolated farmsteads.

Rural Electrification

Another important New Deal–era program that challenged the isolation of country people was rural electrification. The Rural Electrification Administration (REA), created in 1935, began to operate in Arkansas in 1937, making loans to rural electric cooperatives in order to expand electric service to rural areas. It was slow to grow in many parts of rural America, largely because of the hostility of existing power companies. Arkansas Power and Light (AP&L) was not enthusiastic about the expenditure of federal funds to subsidize competitors for the rural market, but like power companies in other states, AP&L had largely ignored that market and had focused instead on expanding services in towns and cities. Private power companies, like AP&L, were necessarily dedicated to securing returns for their stockholders, and they understood that exploiting the easiest to reach areas first guaranteed the quickest return on investment. Yet the rural market had potential, and Harvey Couch, founder and director of AP&L, devised an "Arkansas plan," which he submitted to the REA. The plan would have funneled REA loans through AP&L, which would then extend loans and supply the power to the rural cooperatives. It was clearly an attempt to make sure AP&L profited from the extension of power to rural populations, and the REA rejected the plan. Although AP&L remained hostile to the funding of competitors in the form of rural electric cooperatives, powerful countervailing forces operated to mediate that entity's hostility. Planters in eastern Arkansas, for example, supported the expansion of electrification and promoted some joint efforts between AP&L and local cooperatives in the extension of electrical service to rural areas. After a fitful start, electrification accelerated during and immediately after World War II.

The extension of electrical service to rural Arkansas transformed the lives of the state's farm families. Townspeople and city folk had been enjoying the benefits of the modern conveniences electricity made possible for two or three decades by the time the REA was created, but country people still worked or read by the kerosene lamp, hauled water from wells or creeks, and

Rural Electrification Administration: Founded in 1935, the Rural Electrification Administration provided federal funds to help create rural electric cooperatives.

depended upon the wood stove to cook their meals and heat their homes. In other words, they lived much as their grandparents had lived in the nineteenth century. Whether wealthy delta planter or poor sharecropper, whether prosperous hill-country farmer or simple backwoodsman, life without electricity meant a much harder and cruder existence.

By allowing indoor plumbing and more reliable means of illumination, refrigeration, and climate control, electricity clearly improved the quality of life for farm families and made country schools safer and more comfortable. Electrical service also greatly augmented certain farming operations. Dairy farmers who had struggled for generations with the problem of milk going sour before reaching the dairy processing facility could now purchase storage tanks cooled by electrical power. Milking usually began at 3:30 or 4:00 a.m., and for the first hour or so (depending upon time of year) farmers had to milk their cows in relative darkness. The kerosene lamps used by most Arkansans provided only about twenty-five watts of light, and many farmers were fearful of using them in their barns in any case because one spark fallen on a bed of straw could send the whole edifice up in flames. Farmers could also invest in milking machines that reduced their labor needs and increased the number of cows that could be milked. Those farmers who grew their own grain to feed their livestock could now use electric grinders, greatly reducing the amount of labor required. As Robert Caro describes the situation in Texas, without an electric grinder, the farmer would "get the corn kernels for his mules and horses by sticking ears of corn—hundreds of ears of corn—one by one into a corn sheller and cranking it for hours." For those who grew cotton, the use of the electric motor was essential. Without one, the farmer "had to unload cotton seed by hand, and then shovel it into the barn by hand; to saw wood by hand, by swinging an axe or riding one end of a ripsaw." For farmers who produced chickens, the availability of electricity made possible the use of cooling fans as well as electrically powered incubators, which were a virtual revolution in the industry.

Political Infighting among Democrats

By the time that Governor Futrell left office in 1937, recovery in the farming sector was well underway, despite the disruption of the tenancy system. While he had initially obstructed some federal programs, such as the FERA, the threatened loss of federal funds forced him to cooperate. Had the federal programs not been implemented in Arkansas, Futrell's severe retrenchment program might have led to much greater hardship among at least some of the state's population. He had greatly reduced state services, laid off state workers and forced others to take salary cuts, and encouraged the passage of two amendments that seriously curtailed the funding of state government expenditures. When Futrell left office, the state was operating on a cash basis and actually enjoyed a treasury surplus. But because of the curtailment of state government services and because of the AAA, the FERA, the WPA, and the CCC, people were more oriented toward the federal government than ever before.

The great irony of Carl Edward Bailey's governorship (1937–1941) was that he was a great supporter of the New Deal, but he was at odds with many of the Arkansans who ran the New Deal agencies both inside and outside the state. A political outsider, he first won elective office in 1930 as state prosecuting attorney in the Sixth Judicial District (Pulaski and Perry counties) and, as fate would have it, prosecuted a case in 1930 that would earn him a formidable enemy, Senator Joseph T. Robinson. Robinson would later influence the selection of many who served in federal agencies, people who would have been the natural allies of Bailey but who owed their positions to Robinson. The trial that pitted Robinson against Bailey involved A. B. Banks, who presided over a banking empire that included the American Exchange Trust Company of Little Rock. When it collapsed in 1930, sixty-six other Arkansas banks, scattered throughout the state, also failed. Bailey charged Banks with accepting deposits in these banks despite the fact that he knew they were about to fail. Robinson represented Banks and believed that he was being made a scapegoat. Bailey secured a conviction, and although Banks was pardoned before beginning his prison sentence, Bailey was widely applauded for having pursued Banks. Despite the feelings of many citizens in Arkansas regarding the matter, Robinson and other prominent Old Guard Democrats were bitter in their contempt for Bailey, who had, essentially, attacked one of their own in his prosecution of Banks.

Rather than work to build a relationship with the Old Guard Democrats, Bailey formed an alliance with Brooks Hays, another political outsider who had gained a reputation as an opponent of the existing power structure. He supported Hays in his unsuccessful run for the Fifth Congressional District seat in 1933 against David D. Terry. Terry had the support of Senator Robinson, Governor Futrell, and Internal Revenue collector Homer Adkins. This marked the beginning of a political rivalry between Bailey and Adkins that would last for the next decade and a half, but, in the meantime, Bailey would stand against yet another Old Guard Democrat, Hal Norwood, in the race for attorney general in 1934. Riding on the publicity of the Banks trial, Bailey bested Norwood, who was the incumbent, in a narrow victory.

The differences between his humanitarian philosophy and that of Governor Futrell became evident very early in Bailey's tenure as attorney general. Bailey was unswerving in his dedication to New Deal programs that provided for direct relief to "unemployables," in other words, women, children, the elderly, or the infirm. Futrell believed that the poor had no one but themselves to blame and that the state should not, in any case, assume the role of dispensing direct relief. Despite his sentiments in favor of such programs, Bailey revealed another aspect of his character once Futrell was forced into creating a Department of Public Welfare or risk losing federal funds. Bailey's own political ambitions led him to fear that the governor would use the creation of the agency as a way to bolster the political establishment. The governor, on the other hand, who appreciated Bailey's ambitious streak, attempted to prevent him from assuming any of the credit for the creation of the agency. Despite his misgivings about Bailey, Futrell found himself in the unenviable position of having to approve an action of Bailey's that gained his enemy much popular press. A New York gangster, Charles "Lucky" Luciano, had fled to Arkansas to escape prosecution and set up house in Hot Springs. When Bailey ordered his arrest and extradition, despite a $50,000 bribe offer from one of the gangster's friends, Futrell approved the order, but it was Bailey who received the lion's share of publicity over the affair. Much to the chagrin of the political establishment in Arkansas, Bailey was able to use the matter to catapult himself into the governor's office.

As governor, Bailey fashioned a state civil service system, arguing that appointments to crucial state positions should be on a merit basis rather than on a political basis. In fact, he was hoping to replace the old system by which Democratic Party stalwarts awarded positions for party loyalty. He understood that most people in office in the state owed allegiance to his political enemies. He came to appreciate, however, that in order to build his own political constituency, he needed to be able to appoint people in his own right rather than rely on a merit system. When the unpopular measure came up for reconsideration during his second term in office, he allowed a bill repealing it to become law without his signature.

One casualty of Bailey's battle with the Democratic Party machine and the federal officeholders was his efforts to refund the highway debt. During his first term he secured legislative approval to sell new highway bonds, but a depression in the bond market in 1937 scuttled the effort, and when he sponsored new measures in 1939, his political enemies, led chiefly by Homer Adkins, sabotaged the scheme. Understanding that his enemies had powerful friends in crucial positions in New Deal agencies, Bailey made a decision to replace some of them, and he probably believed that once Robinson died in 1937 that he would be able to do so with impunity. Before launching a battle to oust some of these officeholders, however, Bailey first attempted to secure Robinson's Senate seat by using his domination of the Democratic state committee to have himself nominated rather than hold a Democratic primary. This seemed out of keeping with his consistent attacks against such manipulations and his opponents made sure the public recognized that fact. He still had to win a special election in the fall, and the Old Guard, led by Homer Adkins, convinced John E. Miller to run as an independent in the special election and many New Deal officeholders, in fear of losing their own jobs if someone like Bailey were in such an important patronage position, campaigned for Miller. Miller defeated him easily.

Bailey was bitter and vulnerable in the 1938 reelection campaign for governor. He took nothing for granted, admitted having made mistakes and, with Adkins preoccupied with campaigning for Hattie Caraway's reelection against John McClellan, he was able to secure election to the customary second term. Realizing more than ever the obstacle that the federal officeholders in the state represented, Bailey began to remove some of them from office and attack others. He fired W. A. Rooksbery, director of unemployment compensation, but one of the most highly publicized contests was that between the governor and WPA director Floyd Sharp. Bailey accused Sharp of using WPA workers in a political battle against him, and the governor's friends in the legislature attempted to investigate the unrest at Dyess Colony, the FSA community in Mississippi County, as a way to embarrass and weaken Sharp. The old party machine was still very much alive, however, and closed ranks in the legislature.

The sudden death of the president of the university, John C. Futrall, in an automobile accident in September 1939, gave Bailey another opportunity to appoint a man who would be loyal to him and to court an important political ally in northwest Arkansas. He had almost no constituency in that part of the state, and after his loss to Miller in the run for the Senate seat in 1938, he was determined to build a political organization there. He focused much of his efforts on securing the allegiance of the *Northwest Arkansas Times*, run by Roberta Fulbright, a formidable and noteworthy newspaperwoman. When Futrall died, Bailey recognized an opportunity to solidify this alliance and appointed James William Fulbright, Roberta's son, to the top administrative position at the university. This caused considerable consternation among the faculty, who assumed they had a role to play in the selection of their own president and who had doubts about Fulbright's qualifications. Although a Rhodes scholar and an attorney, he had no academic credentials of any substance, having published no articles or books and having been on the faculty—at the Law School—for only one year at the time of his appointment. Nevertheless, he proved to be an energetic spokesperson for the university and understood that the university played an important role in preparing the state's future political and economic leaders.

But Fulbright would have little time to demonstrate his mastery of the job at hand. His appointment became an issue during the gubernatorial election in 1940, and his fate was sealed by the outcome of that election. Despite Bailey's efforts to court the Delta vote and build a constituency in northwest Arkansas, he discovered when he ran for the almost unprecedented third term that he had failed to build a political following capable of sustaining him. Homer Adkins, on the other hand, had the backing of the federal officeholders in the state and the entire Arkansas congressional delegation. He put Bailey on the defensive on the third-term issue and on the failed highway refinancing plan. Adkins defeated Bailey and subsequently launched his own refinancing plan, but one of his first acts as governor was to fire Fulbright at his earliest opportunity, a meeting of the board of trustees on June 9, 1941—the first meeting after Adkins's inauguration—which happened to be commencement day.

World War II

Governor Adkins's attention would soon be consumed by the nation's entry into World War II, and, indeed, the state would find its resources stretched beyond its limits in the next few years. When the surprise attack by the Japanese occurred on Pearl Harbor on December 7, 1941, it stunned America and brought the nation into the conflagration known as World War II. Although some Arkansans were aware of the possibility of America's involvement in the war in Europe, like most Americans, they were surprised by the avenue through which the United States entered the conflict brewing abroad. The state's newspapers had been featuring stories on Hitler's rise to power and Germany's military expansion since the early 1930s. Germany's sudden invasion of Poland in 1939, which ended England's policy of appeasement and hurled Europe toward another devastating war, riveted the American population. Arkansas newspapers regularly featured events as France collapsed and British, French, and Belgium soldiers were evacuated from Dunkirk in 1940. Many Americans—Arkansans among them—began to abandon their isolationist sentiments and inch toward support for intervention or, at the very least, efforts to aid the British. While Japanese expansion in the Pacific captured some attention, most newspapers focused on the dramatic events taking shape in Europe. The day following the attack on Pearl Harbor, President Franklin Roosevelt gave his famous "a date which will live in infamy" speech asking Congress to declare war against Japan—a request almost all members of Congress were eager to approve. Given Japan's tripartite pact with Germany and Italy, Roosevelt and Congress understood that it would be only a matter of days before both Germany and Italy entered the war against the United States. Arkansans responded much like other Americans. Men rushing to enlist overwhelmed recruiting offices, and local communities eagerly embraced every opportunity to demonstrate their support for the war effort. The fears that Arkansas's economy would be stressed due to the war's impact were tempered by the hope that the war economy would boost industrial development. Meanwhile, a new militancy on the part of a younger generation of African American activists emerged and began to challenge the racial status quo. The absence of male figures in households and the movement of women and young people into the workforce disrupted the family structure. While the Civil War might occupy an important place in the imaginations of Arkansans today, World War II contributed to vast changes in the way Arkansans lived and worked. The region and the state would never be the same.

Arkansas on the Home Front

In one way or another, everyone participated in the war effort, whether they themselves served in the military or stayed at home, whether they had a loved one on the front or no family member or friend in harm's way. At a minimum the war's impact was felt through rationing demands that severely limited certain goods. Sales of some products, such as canned meat and fish, were for a while entirely frozen while purchases of others, like sugar, important in rural communities to preserve fruits, were closely rationed. Typically, the government issued coupon books to families, who could then use the limited number of certificates to purchase rationed items. One of the first coupon books, for example, contained twenty-eight certificates, and it took eight to accompany the purchase of a pound of sugar. By the end of the first full year of the war, coffee was added to the list, and in early 1943 sales of butter and fats was briefly halted until a rationing regimen could be established.

Rationing: The rationing of items (such as sugar, coffee, butter, and tires) during World War II.

While rationing food products altered the dietary habits of virtually every Arkansan, the rationing of tires and gasoline made it necessary to limit travel and to find alternative means of sending goods to market. County farm and home demonstration agents, who typically traveled extensively within their respective areas, had to alter their method of operation and seriously curtail outreach programs, just when farmers and their wives needed advice about how to incorporate the rationing of necessary items into their operations. Because farmers were expected to produce as much for the war effort as possible, the government selectively reduced rationing of gasoline for producing farmers, but many other individuals who depended upon travel to reach customers suffered loss of income, and most people found it necessary to curtail travel for purely social purposes. Thus, the livelihoods of many were threatened and social patterns were altered.

Arkansans who stayed at home also actively supported the war effort in a number of ways. Communities met and exceeded quotas on the amount they were to raise for the Red Cross relief effort. So many Arkansans contributed to war loan and war bond drives that Arkansas ranked twelfth among all the states in money raised, despite its near bottom ranking in per capita income. While many Arkansans opened their pocketbooks, others donated their time by collecting scrap metal and rubber. Even as the first draftees/enlistees were leaving their homes, plans to launch scrap-metal campaigns were being laid. Farmers brought metal objects to town or piled them on the roadside for committee members to pick up and deliver to central locations. Women whose sons, husbands, brothers, or fathers were away at war contributed in this effort. They also often worked in the Red Cross surgical dressing rooms, rolling bandages to send to the front. So successful was this Red Cross endeavor that the quotas were frequently met and work suspended periodically, only to be suddenly resumed when a major offensive required a new supply of bandages. The reopening of the Red Cross dressing room served as a grim reminder of the tragic news that might come to any one of the women working there. As they rolled bandages for some unknown soldier or sailor, they must have wondered whether their own loved ones would need such a bandage, but by being active, they relieved their sense of helplessness.

Those responsible for organizing farm and industrial production for the war faced particularly serious challenges. In the years immediately preceding the war, a farm labor surplus had developed but with the outbreak of hostilities, the more customary labor shortage reemerged. Because it was connected to a national emergency, the government was willing to play a more active role in attempting to solve the problem. In fact, the Department of Agriculture had been anticipating a labor shortage since October 1939 when a report generated by the Bureau of Agricultural Economics began to circulate. The Army Industrial College had asked the bureau to project how excess farm labor might be transferred to industrial production in the event of war, and the report generated on October 12, 1939, created some anxiety. It revealed that if the industrial sector absorbed all the excess farm labor, a shortfall of 695,000 workers would remain. This report assumed that farm laborers, who had been experiencing a declining standard of living and a lack of protective legislation in the 1930s, would abandon the farms in great numbers, but the report also revealed what should have been obvious: While the transfer of farm labor would not fully satisfy the needs of the industrial sector, it would lead to a farm labor crisis of enormous proportions.

In the face of these staggering statistics, the Department of Agriculture was directed to take aggressive steps. Aside from fashioning some policies to ameliorate the condition of farm laborers to make remaining in the rural environment more attractive, the department understood that farmers and planters would need to resort to more unusual sources of labor. By early 1942 farm leaders throughout Arkansas and elsewhere began holding meetings to develop plans to deal with the situation, and by the fall of that year they publicized a "work, fight, or go to jail" campaign. County farm agents in the Delta coordinated with farmers to recruit labor from the hill counties and from towns. Retired and marginally handicapped people were recruited. They also looked beyond the border to Mexican nationals and to German and Italian prisoners of war. An agreement signed between the United States and the Mexican government in June 1942 outlined a set of provisions governing the importation of Mexican nationals, known as braceros, to various sections of the country. The prospective employers were made responsible for transportation costs and housing, and a minimum wage level was established. Over the next few years, thousands of braceros were placed in Arkansas, principally in the plantation areas.

German and Italian prisoners of war (POWs) were also used to address the labor shortage in agriculture. Although the United States was initially reluctant to bring captured enemy soldiers to the United States, overcrowding in Britain and the recognition that the prisoners could play an important role in addressing the labor shortage convinced policy makers to reconsider the security concerns they first entertained. Approximately twenty-three thousand prisoners of war were relocated to Arkansas by fall of 1943, many of them captured when the Axis forces surrendered after the success of the allies' North Africa campaign in May 1943. The vast majority of POWs placed in camps in Arkansas were German, and they assisted in virtually every aspect of the agricultural process, and some worked in the timber industry. Three principle centers existed in the state: Camp Robinson in North Little Rock, Camp Chaffee in Fort Smith, and Camp Dermott in Dermott. A number of branch camps, particularly in the Delta, were erected in order to place the prisoners closer to the farmers needing labor.

POW labor: German and Italian prisoners of war used in Arkansas to help with agricultural labor.

The local farm labor clerk, a person attached to the county farm agent's office after the war began, assisted farmers and planters in filling out the paperwork to apply for POW branch camps. The local farmers and the businessmen in agricultural communities identified appropriate local sites for these camps, hired construction crews to erect the barracks and guard houses, and provided facilities for military personnel assigned to security. The army transported the prisoners to the branch camps and then it was the responsibility of the farm labor clerk to work with those in need of labor. Farmers would transport their allotment of prisoners to and from the camps, and despite the fact that they did so without a military guard, there were few escape attempts in Arkansas. The interior location of the state made flight more difficult and the good conditions within the camps dampened enthusiasm for escape.

Another response to the labor shortage was a renewed interest in mechanization. Farm agents established committees to encourage the purchase and sharing of farm equipment, and the number of tractors on Arkansas farms more than doubled, from 12,564 to 26,537 between 1940 and 1945. Meanwhile, farmers and planters in the Delta became more intensely interested in experiments with mechanical cotton harvesters. As Don Holly has ably demonstrated, versions of a mechanical cotton harvester had been showcased by the Rust brothers as early as the mid-1930s. John D. Rust and his brother, Mack, lacked the funds to go into production of the machine, however, and given the existing labor surplus, planters and farmers needed more convincing to abandon their old methods. World War II proved to be the watershed. The labor shortage that accompanied the war played a major role in encouraging the mechanization of agriculture, a phenomenon that would have significant long-term ramifications for Arkansas, the South, and the nation.

A migration from the South to the North and the West, which had begun to take shape during and immediately following World War I and was given impetus by New Deal programs, accelerated during World War II. Aside from the labor crisis in agriculture, another serious consequence of the demographic shift was its impact on the educational infrastructure in the state. Teachers left for the military or to take significantly higher-paying jobs in industry, leading to a severe shortage. With close to 50 percent of the state's teachers abandoning their jobs in the educational system for other opportunities, many schools failed to open in the fall of 1942. The trend toward school consolidation, a phenomenon encouraged by the state but long resisted on the local level, accelerated as a result of the teacher shortage. Some federal aid was made available for schools near defense industries, but southern congressmen—often supported by southern governors like Arkansas's Homer Adkins—blocked wide-scale federal aid to schools, largely because the program under consideration would have allocated proportional funds to white and black schools, challenging the practice of southern states to apportion school funds unequally and thus implicitly challenging white supremacy.

Adkins squandered an opportunity to ease the crisis in education in order to maintain segregation, but he did not hesitate to pursue all opportunities open to him in order to promote industrial development. Despite the governor's efforts and those of Arkansas's congressional delegation, the state was not as successful as others in attracting war industries, largely because of Arkansas's poor infrastructure and undereducated population. Although some Arkansans found jobs in war-related industries within the state, most went elsewhere to pursue these opportunities. Nevertheless, six military ordnance plants were located in various locations: Camden, El Dorado, Hope, Jacksonville, Marche, and Pine Bluff. The twenty-five thousand workers—mostly women—produced explosive materials, detonators, fuses, and explosive primers at five of these six plants. The sixth facility, located at Hope, served as a proving ground for testing ordnance.

Because shorter winters made Arkansas a desirable location for the placement of military training bases, a number of them were established around the state and tended to have a largely positive impact on the local economy. They hired some civilians for a variety of purposes, and the trainees spent their money in nearby communities. North Little Rock saw the largest number of army recruits, where nearly three quarters of a million trainees passed through Camp Robinson. The camp had been created in 1917 and was originally named Camp Pike after General Zebulon Montgomery Pike. It was renamed after Senator Joseph T. Robinson in 1937 and vastly expanded during World War II, serving as a basic training camp and as a facility to prepare army medics. Although far fewer trainees passed through the army air bases established in Blytheville, Walnut Ridge, Newport, and Stuttgart, the presence of military personnel and the availability of a limited number of civilian positions impacted those towns as well. The state's insular location worked against the location of navy bases, but navy installations could be found in a number of locations, including an Army and Navy General Hospital in Hot Springs, a navy ordnance plant at Shumaker, and several administrative and recruiting offices in Little Rock and elsewhere.

Perhaps the most controversial "war-related" facilities in the state were the Japanese internment camps in southeastern Arkansas. Arkansas officials initially resisted the relocation of Japanese Americans from the West Coast to Arkansas, a resistance based largely on racism and suspicion. The forced relocation of Japanese Americans, most of them American born, reflected widespread sentiment that they were loyal to the emperor of Japan and posed a potential military threat. But racism also lay behind the arguments that led to presidential order 9102 on March 18, 1942, calling for the removal of approximately 120,000 people of Japanese descent from the West Coast to ten camps in seven interior states, principally in the west.

Japanese internment camps: Camps established in western states and in Arkansas to house Japanese Americans removed from the West Coast in 1942.

Two camps were placed in Arkansas, one at Jerome, near Dermott, where 8,497 Japanese American families were interned; and the other at Rohwer, near McGehee, where a larger number, approximately 16,000, were incarcerated. The tax-delinquent lands had been acquired by the Farm Security Administration through a trust agreement with the state in the late

1930s. The undeveloped and heavily wooded land was poorly drained, and the FSA had wisely refrained from establishing communities there. In 1942 the War Relocation Board acquired it for the purpose of placing the Japanese Americans on it. Unenthusiastic about the establishment of the camps in Arkansas in the first place, Governor Adkins refused to allow Japanese Americans to be used as farm laborers, despite the fact that planters in eastern Arkansas wished to recruit them. Adkins also denied Japanese American children admission to the state's schools, rationalizing that it would place too great a burden on an already overextended school system. Not to be outdone by the governor, the legislature barred Japanese Americans from purchasing property in the state. That measure was later declared unconstitutional.

Women took the brunt of the home-front disruption, often laboring under contradictory demands placed upon them. If they remained within the household and eschewed employment, they were expected to grow victory gardens, work in Red Cross dressing rooms, and assume other various and sundry duties associated with winning the war. They assumed these new obligations at the same time that they shouldered sole responsibility for maintaining the household and oversight of their children. Few resources existed to aid them. Women who chose to work—or who were forced to work given economic exigencies—were doubly burdened. The hostility toward women in the workforce that peaked during the Great Depression, a hostility based upon the often-mistaken notion that women were taking jobs that men might have otherwise occupied, eased considerably during World War II but was by no means altogether absent. Given that it was desirable for women to contribute in some tangible way toward the war effort, certain jobs previously closed to women became available. Still, most women labored in unskilled or traditional clerical positions, and married women particularly found themselves the object of criticism for the lack of supervision over their children.

Although nationwide figures show that between 1940 and 1945 most women who entered the labor force were young and single, the percentage of married women working increased from 13.9 to 22.5 percent. Given that Arkansas was not as successful in securing industry during the war, the figures are probably less for the state. Nevertheless, juvenile delinquency rates rose sharply in Arkansas and, as historian Calvin Smith has noted, social workers, the press, and even the state legislature recognized it as a crisis in the family and often blamed working mothers for it. In fact, juvenile delinquency rates always increase during wartime—in the United States and across the world—and the problems are much more complex than the failure of mothers to supervise their children. Blaming working mothers for the problem reflects the continuing prejudice against married women in the workforce, a hangover from the Great Depression.

Regardless of its causes, increasing cases of juvenile delinquency and a sharp rise in venereal disease rates among young women preoccupied social workers and policy makers during World War II. Most of the experienced and more qualified social workers had departed for war or higher-paying jobs elsewhere, however, and analysis of the problem was often shallow and based on prejudice. A few instances of married women who flagrantly evaded their responsibilities to their children were used as evidence of a widespread trend. In fact, the problem was systemic and reflected a number of factors that should have been obvious. The absence of male authority figures, whether fathers, older brothers, or male teachers, certainly played a role. The preoccupation of married women—whether they worked or not—with a new set of responsibilities was also a factor. But the move to towns and cities introduced teenagers to new temptations, some of which could be fulfilled because of the availability of a variety jobs for them. Although many of them dutifully surrendered their earnings to their mothers (and fathers if they were present), others indulged in a variety of new pastimes, some of which presented them with certain new temptations leading to encounters with the law.

The state of Arkansas responded by attempting to enact legislation meant to strengthen the family. The measures they pursued appear to be a rather round-about way of addressing some very immediate problems, but the state was not accustomed to being involved in legislating social behavior. It did, however, have authority over marriage and divorce laws, and that is where their attention focused. The first bills to appear involved an effort to eliminate the "90-day divorce" and to require waiting periods and physical examinations before issuing marriage licenses. The divorce law had been passed in 1931 providing for a ninety-day residency, possibly in an effort to capitalize on the market for the lucrative divorce business, something that Hot Springs subsequently became particularly notorious for. Although evidence suggested that a large percentage of the divorces were secured by temporary transplants, particularly from border states, lawmakers pursued, without success, measures to revoke it. A Little Rock legislator, meanwhile, introduced a bill requiring physical and mental examinations fifteen days prior to applications for marriage licenses. This measure also failed to pass. Closer to the issue of juvenile delinquency, perhaps, was an effort to raise the legal age of marriage, a measure meant to discourage premarital sex and, presumably, venereal disease. The only measure to pass was one meant to prevent "gin marriages" (those contracted while the parties were intoxicated) by imposing a three-day waiting period prior to issuance of a marriage license, but county court clerks were allowed to waive the requirement on an individual basis so its effectiveness was questionable.

In the final analysis, nothing the legislature considered—or possibly could have considered—truly addressed the issues facing the family structure during the war. Once the war was over, the public and law makers no longer concerned themselves with such matters. Women, whether married or not and whether they wanted to or not, were forced from the workplace and back into households; and children and teenagers were subjected to greater supervision by male authority figures whether at home or in school. Calvin Smith suggests, however, that the patriarchal structure was not fully restored and the postwar period would witness the further erosion of the traditional family. Certainly, growing opportunities for women and teenagers in the workforce, a trend that actually began much earlier in the century in accordance with the demands of the growing consumer society, set in motion forces that could not be turned back by legislative edict.

Civil Rights Activism

Like blacks elsewhere in the United States, African Americans in Arkansas believed they were fighting two wars, one against fascism abroad and another against racism at home. They referred to it as the "Double V" campaign and believed that the sacrifices they made during the war would establish their rights to full citizenship. African Americans contributed heavily to the Red Cross and war bond drives, and they participated in the campaign to collect scrap metal. Many joined the military or were drafted, particularly after A. Philips Randolph, a black activist on the national level, lobbied the president to make certain that blacks were drafted according to their percentage of the population. He had observed that white planters in the South were using their control over the local selective service offices to maintain a plentiful supply of black labor. Randolph understood this control over the draft as another means by which southern planters exercised their hegemony over African Americans, the most impoverished and vulnerable population of laborers in the South. The edict establishing a rubric that made certain that African Americans were drafted at a representative rate and this provided an avenue of escape from a life of toil and servitude. President Roosevelt's Executive Order 8802, which stipulated that there was to be no discrimination of employment in industries securing government contracts, provided another escape route for African Americans, one that beckoned them to war industries in southern, northern, and western cities.

Executive Order 8802: An order issued by President Franklin Roosevelt in 1942 forbidding discrimination of employment by defense industries.

Even before the war began, a new generation of black leaders in Arkansas pressed for a more assertive campaign for black rights. Harold Flowers, an attorney in Pine Bluff, formed the Committee on Negro Organizations (CNO) in 1940 to bring black organizations in Arkansas together to challenge the white-only policy of the state's Democratic Party. He had grown particularly impatient with the failure of Dr. John Robinson's organization, the Arkansas Negro Democratic Association (ANDA), to rebound from its defeat in 1930 when the Arkansas Supreme Court ruled against Robinson in the case he had filed against the White Primary in 1928. In 1942, ANDA renewed its efforts and appealed to US attorney general Francis Biddle to intercede on their behalf and rule the White Primary illegal. When Attorney General Biddle rebuffed ANDA's 1942 appeal, its members attempted to vote in that year's election. Though unsuccessful in that effort, they did not have long to wait for justice. Black Texans—with the help of NAACP attorneys—had taken their case to the Supreme Court, which ruled in *Smith v. Allwright* in 1944 that the White Primary violated the Fifteenth Amendment. Governor Adkins, angered by the decision, charged that it usurped states' rights, and he encouraged other southern governors to challenge it. Democratic Party officials across the South implemented measures designed to continue limiting black voting and office holding. For example, black voters were hampered by a new invention, the double primary. They were allowed to vote in a special primary election held to select federal officeholders but continued to be barred from that held for state offices.

Perhaps it was evidence of interest and activity in Arkansas that inspired the NAACP to come to the support of a lawsuit initiated in 1942, a lawsuit inspired by the efforts of black educators in Little Rock to equalize the salaries of black teachers with those of white teachers. The Little Rock Classroom Teachers Association (CTA) united black teachers and was an affiliate of the Arkansas Teachers Association, a white organization. The CTA appealed to the white school board in the spring of 1942 requesting that they equalize salaries. When the board refused their request, black teachers and principals assembled and agreed unanimously to approach the NAACP to secure their support in bringing a lawsuit against the school board. The association sent Thurgood Marshall to Arkansas to assist in the case. Marshall was destined to play a crucial role in the 1954 *Brown v. Board of Education* decision and to become the first black on the United States Supreme Court, but in 1942 he was a relatively young attorney, eager to be of assistance but willing to allow black attorneys in Little Rock to take the lead: J. R. Booker, Myles Hibbler, and Scipio Jones, the attorney who had represented the Elaine Twelve in 1919. It was the last case the old warrior would take on. Jones died in 1943. Sue

Little Rock Classroom Teachers Association: An organization of black schoolteachers that filed a lawsuit against the Little Rock School Board for equalization of black and white teacher salaries in 1942.

Brown v. Board of Education: A US Supreme Court decision rendered in 1954, which ruled that the doctrine of "separate but equal" established under *Plessy v. Ferguson* in 1896 was unconstitutional.

Morris (aka Sue Cowan Williams), who was chair of the English department at Dunbar High, served as the complainant in the suit. The US District Court ruled against the black teachers in the fall of 1942, and Sue Morris was fired from her position at the end of the 1942–1943 school year. John H. Lewis, the principal of Dunbar High School, who testified in court that the salaries were unfair, was asked to resign.

The CTA and the NAACP appealed the case to the US Eighth Circuit Court of Appeals in the fall of 1943. In June 1945, the Eighth Circuit overturned the decision and ordered Little Rock to equalize the salaries of black teachers, but the school board merely established a complicated new formula for calculating raises for the city's teachers. Part of that formula involved an evaluation of the colleges the teachers had secured their degrees from. Under the rubric, no black college, regardless of reputation, was highly rated. Meanwhile, Lewis became president of Philander Smith College in Little Rock until 1944 when he moved to Wilberforce, Ohio, to become the dean of the School of Theology attached to Wilberforce University. He never returned to Arkansas. Sue Morris secured a job in the Pine Bluff Arsenal after she was fired and then had to turn to domestic work in the postwar period. She was reinstated in 1952, but only after she wrote a letter of apology for having filed the suit.

Among those who championed Sue Morris's suit was L. C. Bates, publisher of the *State Press*, a black newspaper in Little Rock. Trained as a journalist, L. C. Bates had worked for newspapers in California, Colorado, Missouri, and Tennessee before coming to Arkansas to sell insurance. He longed to return to the newspaper business, however, and understood that if he owned his own newspaper he would be able to advocate freely for equal opportunity for African Americans. In 1941 L. C. and Daisy Bates invested their savings and purchased the *Twin City Press*, a black newspaper in Little Rock, which they renamed the *Arkansas State Press*, and began immediately to write editorials covering a wide range of issues confronting blacks. He decried discrimination in employment, police brutality against blacks, and the White Primary system; and he called for repeal of the poll tax.

Between 1942 and 1945, Bates ran stories on the suit against the Little Rock School Board as it made its way from the lower courts to the Eighth Circuit, and reported extensively on other matters of concern to Arkansas's black citizens. When a black serviceman was beaten to death by a white police officer on Ninth Street in Little Rock on March 22, 1942, L. C. Bates wrote strong editorials, calling for a federal investigation after the police officer was acquitted. A federal grand jury convened but failed to indict him. Still, Little Rock authorities were forced to address the situation and assigned eight black officers to Ninth Street. Although it was a meager victory given the gravity of the offense, it energized the young activists. Bates had also championed Harold Flowers's efforts and that of ANDA in restarting the long struggle over the White Primary. Indeed, Bates and his wife, Daisy, would become leaders in a new faction of black civil rights activists in Arkansas. Weary of the status quo and energized after the war by returning black veterans, these black activists would play a crucial role in the civil rights movement that was soon to emerge.

Arkansas on the Battlefields

The 194,645 Arkansans who fought in the war served in every branch of the military and in virtually every theater of war. They held the ground in the Aleutian Islands in Alaska against an attempt by the Japanese to establish staging areas there, which they might have used to launch attacks on the United States. Others from the state joined in battle on the Pacific Islands like Okinawa and Iowa Jima as the American navy led the drive toward the Japanese homeland. Still others landed in North Africa and on the beaches of Normandy, fighting and, too often, dying in the war against Italy and Germany. In the end, 3,519 Arkansans lost their lives. Many were highly decorated for courage under fire and for significant contributions to the war effort. Eight Arkansas men won the Congressional Medal of Honor (MOH)—counting one who enlisted in Michigan after failing his physical exam in Arkansas. They included four graduates of the University of Arkansas: Maurice "Footsie" Britt, Nathan Green Gordon, Edgar Harold Loyd, and Seymour W. Terry. Two of the four would survive the war, return to the state, and become prominent in Arkansas society and politics. Nathan Green Gordon, a navy pilot, won his MOH for risking his life under enemy fire in a daring air-sea rescue in a harbor off Papua, New Guinea, on February 15, 1944. A native of Morrilton, he entered politics after the war and became the longest-running lieutenant governor in the history of the state, serving from 1947 to 1967. His successor in that political position was none other than Footsie Britt, a fellow student at the university and also a winner of the Medal of Honor. While serving as an officer in the Third Infantry Division, Britt participated in the battle to take Rome and was awarded the MOH for his heroism on November 10, 1943. He saved his battalion from certain defeat by taking a small unit of men into an intense firefight and in a close combat situation repulsed a determined force of Germans. Britt returned to Fort Smith after the war and went on to have a distinguished career in business and politics, serving two terms as lieutenant governor.

Two other University of Arkansas graduates who won the Medal of Honor died in different theaters of the war, one in France fighting the

Germans and the other in Okinawa fighting the Japanese. Second Lt. Edgar Harold Loyd, a Mississippi County native, was serving as a rifle platoon leader under Patton's Third Army and was scheduled to receive the medal for heroism he exhibited during a battle to expel the Germans from the Moselle River in France in September 1944. Before he could receive the award, however, he was killed by sniper fire near Limey, France, on November 16, 1944. The final university recipient of the medal, 1st Lt. Seymour W. Terry from Little Rock, was cited for bravery for conducting an assault under heavy enemy fire during the battle to take Zebra Hill on Okinawa on March 6, 1944. He died two days later of his injuries and was subsequently promoted to captain and posthumously awarded the Medal of Honor.

The other winners of the military's highest award were more typical of the Arkansas demographic. Jack Williams of Harrison, Arkansas, graduated high school and bypassed a college education to enlist in the navy. He became a pharmacist mate first class and was killed in action in the battle to take Iwo Jima on March 3, 1945. Under heavy fire, Williams had gone to the aid of a seriously injured man, shielding the soldier's body with his own as enemy fire rained down. Although Williams himself was shot, he paused only long enough to dress his own wounds, and then continued to doctor others hit by gunfire. He was returning to the rear to seek treatment of his injuries when he was killed by sniper fire. James R. Hendrix was the son of a sharecropper from Lepanto, Arkansas, who was drafted into the army at age eighteen. He was serving with Patton's Third Army as a private in Assenois, Belgium, during the Battle of the Bulge when he displayed acts of heroism—capturing two German artillery gun crews, rescuing a comrade from a burning vehicle, and holding off enemy fire enabling others to pull other wounded Americans to safety—which won him the MOH. His unit was attempting to reach Bastogne, a besieged garrison under heavy attack, a garrison famous for having played a crucial role in stopping the German's last desperate offensive against the allied advance toward Berlin. William H. Thomas of Wynne, Arkansas, was working on his father's farm when the war broke out. He was initially rejected for service because of a heart defect, but he was determined to serve so he went to Ypsilanti, Michigan, where he enlisted in 1944. A private first class, he died of wounds suffered in a battle to retake the Philippines on April 22, 1945. Finally, William Watson, who apparently moved with his family to Arkansas from Alabama as a child, had only seven years of grade school and worked on his father's farm until he enlisted in the marines in 1942. He was shot seven times during a battle on Iowa Jima, February 26–27, 1945, died of his wounds, and was posthumously awarded the Medal of Honor.

Another Arkansan, Paul Page Douglas Jr. of Paragould, was twice recommended for the Medal of Honor. A fighter pilot who helped develop tactical strategies connected to the Republic P-47 Thunderbolt fighter plane, Douglas won the Distinguished Service Cross for his heroism in destroying German V-1 rockets aimed at England during the fall 1944 blitz. Two other Arkansans were also recognized for their service to the country: Charles "Savvy" Cooke from Fort Smith and Corydon McAlmont Wassell from Little Rock. Cooke was a University of Arkansas and Naval Academy graduate (1910) who received the Distinguished Service Medal for developing the two-ocean naval strategy during the war. Wassell was one of the first Americans during World War II to receive hero status after he refused to leave his severely injured men upon the evacuation of Java in the Netherlands East Indies (now Indonesia) in the spring of 1942. A physician, he managed to move his patients to safety by convincing a British army convoy to transport them 150 miles over jungle roads to the coast where he persuaded the captain of a Dutch ship to take them to Australia. He received the Navy Cross and was made famous in a 1944 movie—*The Story of Dr. Wassell*—starring Gary Cooper.

Winners of medals for heroism would be the first to say that many of their comrades-in-arms deserved recognition for their own heroism and sacrifice. Few who served in World War II became famous or received much attention for their valorous service. Among those who endured a particularly grueling war were the members of the 206th Coast Artillery Regiment of the Arkansas National Guard, units attached to Arkansas Tech University in Russellville. They had been federalized in August 1941, four months before the Japanese attack on Pearl Harbor, and by early January 1942 they were preparing to depart for training at Fort Bliss, Texas. Among the 104 young men were "twenty-five members of the football team . . . every basketball letter man but one" and "the entire track team." They also included "eleven of 14 student councilmen and the president of the student body." The president of the university hosted a farewell dinner, followed by a heavily attended dance at which the Choral Club sang "God Bless America" in their honor. Like many such young men, they expected to do battle against the nation's foes, but after a year's training in Texas, they were sent to Dutch Harbor on Amaknak Island in Alaska. Their duty was to hold the island against a Japanese advance. Aside from bombing raids by the Japanese in 1942, however, the worst aspect of service there for the Arkansans was the weather. The average annual temperature was 38 degrees (F) and even in summer could dip to a low of 30 degrees. The sky was almost always overcast, the fog omnipresent, the winter days short, and the nights long. It also rained constantly with an average of 250 rainy days per year, the most of any location in the United States. A freakish weather phenomenon called "williwaw" further complicated life there. According to Donald M. Goldstein and Katherine V. Dillon, authors of *The Williwaw War*, the men of the 206th "fought blinding, waist deep snow; sleet that struck as from a sandblaster; fogs so thick and persistent that fliers claimed it was clear enough for takeoff if they could see their copilots; the williwaw, that incredible wind that seemed to blow from every direction at once, and that blew away anything not fastened down." Three members of the 206th died of exposure within days of their arrival. They endured a harsh existence in a cruel environment that nothing in their lives had prepared them for. Their Arkansas backgrounds hardly conditioned them for the climate, and their training in the National Guard and later at Fort Bliss had equipped them for battle, not for boredom and the bitter, bleak existence at Dutch Harbor.

Arkansas women who served in the armed services during the war were banned from armed combat and were initially restricted to noncombat zones. They often faced the derision of some of the public and even, occasionally, the media, presumably because of their temerity in assuming a male prerogative. At first regular army enlistment was not open to women. Instead, military authorities, recognizing the need, consented to the creation of the Women's Auxiliary Army Corps (WAAC). There women performed essential functions that allowed male military members to redeploy to combat zones. On July 1, 1943, however, the Women's Army Corps (WAC) was created as part of the regular army and some of these women found themselves in harm's way. Among them was Lucille Babcock of Little Rock, who was deployed to Italy and the Middle East. She was injured while driving her ambulance, which was over-turned when a German "screaming Mimi" landed close by. But most Arkansans became more familiar with the home-front activities of the Women's Auxiliary Army Corps, which eventu-ally opened several recruitment facilities and performed duties at a variety of training camps around the state. They worked in the Pine Bluff Arsenal; they performed clerical tasks thus freeing men for overseas duty; and when the military, in desperate need of men, began accepting illiterates, the WAACs also became tutors to bring the men up to a minimal standard of literacy.

Women's Auxiliary Army Corps: An organization that allowed women to take on clerical and other tasks so that military men could be deployed overseas.

Whether male or female, whether on the front lines fighting the enemy or serving in some other important way, the men and women of the armed services were being exposed to different worlds and vastly varying experi-ences that altered their perspectives and, in many cases, transformed them into different people. Some young men came back from the war ready to challenge the political establishment. Many women enjoyed new freedoms during the war that they were loath to give up. And African Americans believed they had earned the right to full citizenship. White citizens, however, remained devoted to the idea of white supremacy, and both those in uniform and those on the home front believed that *they* had earned the right to a continuation of that particular status quo. This would lead to confrontations and challenges both during and after the war.

The twin challenges of the Great Depression and World War II resulted in a transformed Arkansas, even as it remained plagued by many of the problems the state inherited from the past. The Great Depression led to federal expenditures and state retrenchment. It resulted in massive relief programs that introduced a transformation of agriculture that was furthered by labor shortages during World War II. While the war brought certain problems, it also opened up opportunities for men to serve in war abroad and in home-front industries both in Arkansas and elsewhere in the nation. A renewed activism emerged in the African American community and, as Morton Sosna suggested, Arkansas would never be the same.

13 From World War to New Era, 1945–1960

WORLD WAR II brought many changes to the state, but one that marked a particularly meaningful departure from the past was the transformation of the plantation system. Indeed, Arkansas's plantation sector moved into a significant new phase after World War II, undergoing a transition from labor-intensive to capital-intensive agriculture, one that necessitated a depopulation of the countryside and supposedly liberated its labor force from certain pervasive social, economic, and political constraints. Powerful countervailing forces limited the extent to which either the transformation or the liberation occurred, however. Remnants of the plantation culture and economy persisted both in the old plantation areas and in the state's capital city. The civil rights movement struck a blow against the traditional white elite and though the state's conservative legislature and Governor Orval Faubus reeled, they recovered their footing and remained in charge of the apparatus that oversaw the limited integration that occurred. While tens of thousands moved from rural sectors in Arkansas to Little Rock or left the state entirely, many remained and Arkansas continued to have some of the poorest counties in the country. Those who moved into Little Rock or other towns found little to employ them and, indeed, Arkansas, like much of the South, struggled to maintain a seriously underemployed population. The small towns that managed to survive the demographic catastrophe that depopulation represented, struggled to find small industries that would keep their storefronts from being shuttered, but the old plantation mentality died hard, and planters, who sat on local economic development committees, were often distinctly cool to industrial development. What industry they attracted, or permitted, paid low wages, little or no taxes, and made such a small investment in Arkansas that they easily abandoned the state at the first promising opportunity, moving away in search of cheaper labor and a better deal elsewhere. The old rural elite would lose their economic edge in this period as new actors—such as Sam Walton and his retail enterprise and Don Tyson and his chicken empire—dislodged them, but these new economic powerbrokers adapted the low-age, low-skill workforce to their needs. The plantation mentality remained alive and well in Arkansas, influencing the direction of economic development and undermining the process of integration at every turn.

Economic Changes in the Early Postwar Period

Despite the rhetoric of Arkansas's New South advocates in the late nineteenth century and over fifty years of efforts to promote economic development and expand industrial production in the state since then, little industrial base of significance had been established. Although strides made during World War II provided a basis upon which to build, the war industries closed down and jobs melted away. The dearth of dense population centers and an undereducated population placed Arkansas at a disadvantage in the competition to attract manufacturing enterprises to the state. In part in response to these and other challenges, the state's governors focused on the reorganization of Arkansas's administrative apparatus and its orientation to business and finance. The demographic shifts that accelerated during World War II necessitated changes in the way the state carried on its business, and Governor Benjamin Laney, who took office in 1945, was determined to make government more efficient. Thus, a measure he presented to the legislature in February 1945 was designed to create a single general fund and consolidate agencies with overlapping responsibilities. He planned to pay off the state's non-highway debt, and at the same time reduce taxes. Buried within his package was also a deficit-spending prohibition that became a permanent fixture in Arkansas government. The main features of the Revenue Stabilization Act remain intact today. Prior to the act, the state deposited funds into over one hundred separate accounts, making it all but impossible to shift money when necessary. With a single general fund, the state could carry on its routine business in a much more efficient manner. Another strategy for ensuring efficiency involved consolidation of a number of agencies into new boards or commissions having broader responsibilities. For example, the Corporation Commission and the Utilities Commission were consolidated into the Public Service Commission. Ten existing boards and commissions were reorganized under the new Fiscal Control Board.

Laney focused particular attention on encouraging industrial development. He combined several offices and created a new agency, the Arkansas Resources and Development Commission (ARDC). The ARDC served as the centerpiece to Laney's "Arkansas Plan," which was to promote coordination among science, business, government, and citizens to encourage development. To persuade industry to settle in the state by keeping wages low, he sponsored a "Right to Work" law, which discouraged collective bargaining by prohibiting the "closed" union shop, thus straining his relationship with organized labor in the state. The measure led to a confrontation between L. C. and Daisy Bates and Judge Lawrence C. Auten in 1946. Although their attention was focused on the ramifications of the law as it pertained to black workers, they were the first to focus on the implications of laws that placed workers at a disadvantageous position with regard to management. Other southern states were passing similar laws. It would eventually become clear that low-wage industries resulted in limited economic growth and blunted interest in further- ing the educational accomplishments of the state's citizens. At the time, however, the focus of most southern politicians, including those in Arkansas, was on promoting industrial development at all costs.

Arkansas Resources and Development Commission: Created by the leg- islature to promote economic and indus- trial development in the state; it was soon renamed the Arkansas Industrial Development Commission.

Laney also sponsored a major tax revision that increased certain sales taxes and the state income tax but lowered inheritance taxes, and he eliminated the state ad valorem property tax, reasoning that it should be apportioned on the local level. These measures were squarely within the southern conserva- tive position regarding low and regressive taxation, sparing the wealthy and placing the burden on the working and middle classes. He stopped short of advocating additional taxes on gasoline that might have been earmarked for improvements to the highway system, believing that voters would not sup- port it, even though he knew that it would eventually be necessary to pass another highway bond issue. That was a sensitive issue, given the fact that the state had defaulted on its highway bonds during the difficult 1930s and had only refunded those bonds during the Adkins administration.

Governor Sidney Sanders McMath, who took office in 1949, seized the opportunity to improve the road system in Arkansas. Under his leadership the legislature passed a special bond issue to revamp and expand the state's highway system. Voters later approved it by a four to one margin. More miles of highway were built and improved upon during his tenure in office than under any other governor in the state's history. Although no impropriety on McMath's part was ever proven, political contributions from contractors cast suspicion on him, and the governor's enemies, which included the Arkansas Power and Light Company and big business, took advantage of the allegations of wrongdoing. His strong advocacy of rural electric cooperatives had angered AP&L's executives and earned him their undying enmity. His support for labor, including an increased minimum wage law and augmented industrial safety codes, had hardly endeared him to the conservative business community.

Francis Adams Cherry defeated McMath in 1952, largely because he secured the support of the conservative business community by running on a platform of business efficiency, and once in office, he restructured the

Fiscal Control Board by centralizing budget control under one office. The new entity was renamed the Department of Finance and Administration. Prior to his governorship and in response to the scandal in the highway department, the legislature had already mandated a restructuring of the Highway Commission. Cherry promoted additional reforms, however, in an effort to insulate the commission from political pressures, but the highway situation remained controversial. A major issue was the power exercised by the commission, which many legislators sought to curtail. Cherry had successfully encouraged the passage of legislation that favored localities that awarded right of way without cost to the state. Many legislators had second thoughts about this and about the power of the commission, and these two questions would figure prominently in Cherry's run for reelection. Cherry was ultimately defeated in his effort to secure a second term, but the highway controversy was only one issue that plagued him. The biggest problem was that he had no political organization when he entered office and he failed to create one.

The *Brown v. Board of Education* decision, which called for an end to the dual education system, was announced while Francis Cherry was running for reelection, and although he believed that this was an issue that should be decided on the local level, he was also convinced that the Supreme Court had spoken and should be obeyed. His position in this regard, however, did not seem to play a role in his defeat in his bid in the Democratic primary for a second term. His opponent, a political unknown from Madison County, Orval Faubus, briefly attempted to identify desegregation as the main issue in the primary campaign, but backed off once editorials in the *Arkansas Gazette* criticized his attempt to pander to racial fears in his campaign. Faubus believed that desegregation was the province of local government but implied that it could be delayed until some unspecified time in the future. Faubus once again raised the desegregation matter in the fall election against his Republican opponent, and this should have served as a sign of his true sentiments on the subject. His election to the office of governor against a Republican opponent was assured; he need not have raised such a divisive issue.

In part in response to newly elected governor Orval Faubus, the Arkansas legislature created the Arkansas Industrial Development Commission, which subsumed Laney's Arkansas Resources and Development Commission, in 1955. Soon renamed the Arkansas Economic Development Commission (AEDC), it was designed to promote economic and industrial development in Arkansas. To direct the new agency, Faubus appointed Winthrop Rockefeller, a New Yorker from a prominent Republican Party family who had settled in Arkansas in 1953. Rockefeller approached the job with enthusiasm. He served as chairman of the AEDC for nine years and oversaw an impressive expansion of the industrial sector. The kind of industrial plants that settled in Arkansas, however, were of a character that did not significantly challenge the dominance of agricultural interests. While more than six hundred new industrial plants were established in the state during Rockefeller's tenure on the AEDC, providing over ninety thousand new jobs, those factories paid low wages to largely unskilled workers. Indeed, factories tended to move from the unionized north to southern states like Arkansas precisely because of the antiunion laws and low wages. But paying low wages meant that workers had little taxable—and spendable—income, and many of the plants were attracted by the fact that they would not be required to pay much, if any, taxes themselves. Sometimes they were provided land on which to build their plants. In other words, they made a minimum investment and paid low wages, thus the communities received questionable dividends from their presence. To add insult to injury, by the mid-1960s it was clear that Arkansas was serving as a way station for those industries on a trek south in search of lower wages. Towns that secured factories in 1955 would likely be looking for replacement factories a decade later.

The willingness of small towns to provide tax breaks and other incentives to these factories reveals the enormity of the challenges confronting them. With the rural population departing in ever-increasing numbers, the old agricultural-centered towns seemed destined for decline, and small businessmen and merchants became increasingly desperate. The undereducated population and a legacy of impoverishment that made any wage seem acceptable provided a ready employment base for low-skill, low-wage factories. Rockefeller encouraged the development of town economic development commissions, but many of them were dominated or heavily influenced by farmers and planters, some of whom were ambivalent about industrial development. With the transition from labor-intensive to capital-intensive agriculture unfolding only slowly, they feared the competition that employment opportunities in industry might present, and they sometimes acted as a check to the work of the committees. But they need not have been overly concerned. Many of the industrial jobs were taken by women whose husbands worked as seasonal farm laborers. The wives provided the year-round income, while the husbands worked only sporadically, searching, often in vain, for other employment when none was available in the farming sector.

According to Charles Aiken, author of *The Cotton Plantation South since the Civil War*, the towns that were most effective at attracting and maintaining small factories, however limited they were in the types of employment they provided, were those that boasted the most farsighted leadership. They also tended to be the towns that best negotiated the civil rights movement and integrated their schools with a minimum of controversy. Nevertheless, as historian Ben Johnson has noted, the first new factories to respond to the opportunities in Arkansas in the 1950s were to locate in areas with few African American residents, and a number of scholars have suggested that the peaceful desegregation of schools in Charleston and Fayetteville owed much to racial demographics. Certainly, the existence of turmoil within certain delta towns discouraged companies from locating industrial plants there. Companies sought to place their factories in quiet, moderate communities that were relatively free from controversy and strife, whether racial or otherwise.

Another crucial factor in a company's decision to place a factory in a particular town was a sufficient supply of labor, and sometimes they were in need of something other than the wives of seasonal farmworkers. Ironically, it was often a town's ability to maintain a significant proportion of its black population that made a difference. Typically, those towns that had a substantial black middle class, some of whose members exerted leadership and partnered with white leaders, retained a significant black population. It required exceptional leadership, both from the white and the black communities, to make the adjustments necessary to survive in the decades after World War II. Towns like Osceola, Pine Bluff, and Forrest City, which also enjoyed better access to major highways, serve as examples. This is not to suggest that they did not have difficulties, both economically and with race relations, but they surmounted the most significant challenges and were positioned to move beyond the past and establish a new legacy. The next few decades, however, would reveal that even there the struggle to overcome the past would challenge the most heroic efforts.

While the AEDC was attempting to promote economic development and attract industry to Arkansas, two dynamic enterprises were emerging on their own, one in Little Rock and the other in Bentonville: W. R. Stephens Investment Company and Wal-mart Stores, Inc. (now known simply as Walmart, Inc.). Both of these companies would become prominent players in state, national, and international business. Wilton Robert "Witt" Stephens, born in Prattsville in 1907, began trading municipal bonds in 1932. Two years later he founded W. R. Stephens, Inc., and built a thriving investment company on the basis of buying and selling Arkansas highway, road, school, levee, and improvement district bonds. He laid the foundation of his empire during the Great Depression when bonds were selling for ten cents on the dollar. Calculating that the Reconstruction Finance Corporation would make certain that government bonds were redeemed, he purchased them and made a fortune doing so. The ratification of an amendment raising the maximum millage on school taxes, which he lobbied for in 1948, permitted schools to market bonds to fund construction projects. Stephens became the largest underwriter of such bonds. He broadened his own holdings to include banks, railroads, and coal and gold mines, but the most important investment he made was in gas production and distribution, particularly the purchase of Arkansas Louisiana Gas Company (Arkla) in 1954. Within two years he turned an unprofitable business into a moneymaker. By that time he was widely regarded as a "king maker" in Arkansas economics and politics, and on a first-name basis with governors, congressmen, and senators.

Sam Walton, World War II veteran, took another path to business innovation, one that not only transformed one corner of the state but reshaped the retail business worldwide. Born in Kingfisher, Oklahoma, in 1918, he earned a business degree at the University of Oklahoma in 1940 and went to work for J.C. Penney before being inducted into the army in 1942. After the war he purchased a Ben Franklin five-and-dime store in Newport, Arkansas, and built it into a highly successful enterprise. His landlord there was so impressed with his success that he refused to renew Walton's lease and turned the property over to his son. In 1950 Sam Walton opened Walton's 5 & 10, another Ben Franklin store, in Bentonville. He was the first in the state to feature self-service shopping. Soon he opened stores in other small towns in the area but broke with Ben Franklin when they refused to countenance his desire to engage in aggressive discount marketing. He opened his first Walmart store in Rogers in 1962. Working now with his brother, Bud, the Waltons were destined over the next decades to shape Walmart into the most innovative and influential company in the world.

A third entrepreneur arose out of the agricultural sector. Just as plantation agriculture was maturing into agri-business in the 1950s and 1960s, poultry farming was developing into an industry. John Tyson and his son, Don, were the most successful practitioners, but it all began inauspiciously enough as a result of the collapse of the fruit industry in northwest Arkansas in the late 1920s. Poultry farming began to take shape at that time, and John Tyson started hauling chickens, as well as other produce, to Kansas City, Missouri, and soon opened his own hatchery. By the eve of World War II, he was trucking poultry to Cincinnati, Cleveland, and Detroit. The rationing of beef during the war was accompanied by subsidies to chicken farmers that significantly benefited those most positioned to take advantage of it. Greatly enriched by the expansion of demand during the war, Tyson survived the postwar period when difficulties with disease and fluctuations in prices drove others into bankruptcy. The company began to buy out other producers and by the mid-1950s built its first processing plant. They contracted with local growers who were characterized as independent contractors but who essentially served the company's interests and at the company's discretion. Ironically, some analysts have described the relationship as a form of sharecropping, even as that kind of arrangement was disappearing in the Delta. By the mid-1960s chicken farming had become big business in northwest

Arkansas, and the Tyson enterprise would soon spread well beyond Arkansas and the Midwest.

Witt Stephens, Sam Walton, and John Tyson depended upon and championed the expansion of Arkansas's transportation network. Witt Stephens understood that there was money to be made by the proposition and positioned himself to market road bonds to accomplish the task. Sam Walton, who learned to fly an airplane so he could visit and oversee his various franchises, dealt with the inferior road system in an unusual way, but better roads were essential to the long-term interests of Walmart, Inc. John Tyson was more intimately familiar with the inadequacies of the roads than either Stephens or Walton, and as his enterprise expanded, so did his support for improvements to roads and highways. As late as 1959, the Arkansas Highway Department oversaw 11,022.12 miles of state highways, but 2,415.25 miles of them were unpaved gravel roads. More than half the county roads in the state were unpaved and some of them little more than dirt paths. John Tyson, who by then was in partnership with his son Don, found accessing his poultry producers under these circumstances to be far from ideal.

While the Arkansas Highway Department worked toward improving the state's road system, the agency also aggressively pursued federal funds to participate in the expansion of the nation's interstate highway system, an expansion promoted heavily by President Dwight D. Eisenhower upon taking office in 1955. As a young West Point graduate during World War I, Eisenhower had crossed over the nation's inadequate highways and later, as Supreme Allied Commander in Europe during World War II, he came to appreciate the impressive German autobahn system. From his perspective, roads and highways were essential to national defense and, indeed, the 1956 act was officially called the Dwight D. Eisenhower National System of Interstate and Defense Highways. The federal government had been sharing the cost of constructing its highways across the country since the early 1920s, but the 1956 act raised the level of contributions from 60/40, established in 1954, to 90/10, a rate calculated to more rapidly accomplish the task that Eisenhower deemed necessary.

The state's first interstate consisted of a stretch of bypass in West Memphis begun in 1952 under an older cost-sharing rubric of 50/50. In 1954, under the newly established 60/40 formula, the southbound lanes of I-30 between Little Rock and Benton were completed. But the passage of the 1956 act, with 90 percent of the funds coming from the federal government, energized the department and encouraged a more aggressive campaign to extend the state's interstate highway system. A plan prepared by the department and approved in 1958 called for 525 miles of interstate along three major corridors: I-30 from the Texas state line at Texarkana to Little Rock; I-40 from the Oklahoma state line near Fort Smith through Little Rock and thence to Memphis; and I-55 from Memphis through West Memphis and then north to the Missouri border near Blytheville. Two smaller corridors were also approved: I-540 around Fort Smith connecting to I-40; and an I-430 loop to the west of Little Rock that included a new bridge over the Arkansas River. All but 9 percent of the routes were entirely new—in other words, not over existing roadways. Once constructed, 77 percent of the state's population would be within fifty miles of an interstate highway.

The improvements in the state's highway system and the construction of interstates across Arkansas worked together with industrial and economic development to bring substantial change to the state. Although efforts at convincing industrial plants to come to Arkansas met with limited results and the transformation of agriculture, both in the Delta and in the hills, included a certain new set of challenges, the roads and highways opened a new world of opportunities to the state's citizens. Some of them would choose to leave the state for better prospects elsewhere, given the limited kinds of development that actually occurred in Arkansas. Thousands left in search of employment in the expanding industrial sector in other parts of the country; thousands of others secured college educations and found little to keep them in Arkansas. The labor and "brain" drain would soon come to preoccupy officials and policy makers.

Agricultural Transformation

Policy makers during World War II began to predict the rise of "scientific agriculture"; that is, the development of agricultural processes that would involve mechanization and the use of chemicals, processes that would result in a dramatic reduction in the need for farm labor. While they foresaw this major reorganization of agriculture in the postwar period, they failed to fully anticipate the social and economic implications. A Post War Planning Commission, operating out of Washington, DC, during the war, established state and local postwar planning committees, which reported their opinions about the direction that agriculture would take after the war. Although there was some disagreement, they generally concurred that farms would increase in size and that mechanization and the use of new chemicals (fertilizers, pesticides, etc.) would play an important role in making agriculture a far more capital-intensive enterprise. They foresaw that the need for farm labor, particularly in southern states like Arkansas, would decline dramatically. They understood that there

Scientific agriculture: A term used to describe the capital-intensive agricultural enterprise that uses machines and chemicals and that arose in the South in the post-World War II period.

would be an inevitable demographic shift, but refrained from suggesting policies that might have addressed the social and economic consequences of that shift. Arkansas planters and farmers were well represented on the postwar planning committees and believed that such consequences should take their natural course and be dealt with as they presented themselves.

The herald of change came in the form of a cumbersome-looking machine. Although planters in eastern Arkansas had experimented with mechanical cotton harvesters in the 1930s, the labor surplus that resulted from the evictions of tenants and sharecroppers because of the AAA program served as a disincentive to an abandonment of their traditional means of harvesting the crop. Labor was still cheap and the mechanical pickers being marketed seemed an unnecessary expense. In addition, as historian James Street argues, the mechanization of the cotton crop awaited the mass production of a marketable machine and that did not occur until after World War II. Even though the first dozen mechanical cotton pickers rolled off International Harvester's assembly line in 1943, the transition occurred slowly. The trash the new pickers stripped from the cotton stalks gummed up the gin works and caused costly delays. The old gins simply could not do a satisfactory job of removing the additional debris that the mechanical cotton harvesters necessarily produced. Cotton gins had to be retooled or new ones constructed in order to more adequately process machine-picked cotton.

While the new cotton gins solved the problems of debris-laden machine-picked cotton, another problem had to be overcome before full mechanization could occur. The labor of picking the cotton—whether by machines or humans—was only one part of the process. Until chemicals could be developed to cut down on the growth of weeds, a two-stage process of "chopping" the cotton had to be employed. In the first stage, usually during May and June, teams of cotton choppers walked the rows with hoes in hand and thinned the cotton to promote the healthy growth of plants that would produce an ample number of cotton bowls. Later in the summer, usually in July, a second stage of chopping took place when weeds were removed. No matter how many mechanical cotton harvesters planters purchased, until the development of weed-killing chemicals, they would still have to recruit labor to chop the cotton.

Finally, in order to embrace scientific agriculture, planters had to overcome an institutional constraint. They had to abandon the use of mules and invest in tractors. The purchase of tractors had been growing in the South since New Deal AAA programs funneled cash into the hands of planters and introduced them to new crops, like soybeans, that required mechanical harvesters. Mule power was insufficient to pull these newfangled harvesters but with a labor surplus developing because of the dispossession of tenants and sharecroppers, there was little incentive for a full-scale transition to tractors. Besides, the breeding and marketing of mules had a long tradition in Arkansas, and many planters had invested heavily not only in the animals but also in the barns and equipment that were essential to their care and use. For small land-owners and those tenants who remained on the land, mules and implements served as collateral for loans that kept them in business, reflecting established networks of finance and commerce. There was also a cultural attachment to mules that, by modern standards, seems almost inexplicable. Songs and stories of the stubborn and cantankerous mule abounded in the folklore of the South. Given the cultural and other constraints involved in the transition to tractors and thus mechanized agriculture, it is no wonder that Arkansas planters and farmers would be slow to fully embrace scientific agriculture.

Perhaps the most revolutionary aspect of the transformation in agriculture was its impact on farm labor. The transition to capital-intensive agriculture put additional stress on the sharecropping and tenancy system. The tenancy system had been undergoing challenges since the mass evictions stimulated by New Deal programs, but World War II sounded its death knell. As sharecroppers and tenants abandoned the plantations to work in war industries or enlist in the military, German and Italian prisoners of war took their places. At the war's end, many sharecroppers and tenants were neither inclined nor encouraged to return to the countryside. The promise of jobs in the industrial sector in the north and on the West Coast provided them with economic opportunities undreamed of at home in Arkansas. Meanwhile, other young men who in another age might have been interested in purchasing their own farms were more attracted to different career paths, in part because the GI bill offered them college educations that were not meant to prepare them for farmwork. And even had they been interested in farming as a livelihood, the price of land was rising in tandem with the cost of the expensive new machinery, and government loan programs were not sufficient to provide them with the opportunity to purchase land. With the Post War Planning Commission reporting that the small farm was not going to be cost effective in the future, they promulgated very tight loan policies designed to discourage applications from veterans.

America's entry into a conflict in Korea in 1950 provided an opportunity for planters and farmers to place their labor needs into the context of yet another national emergency. While most Arkansans were riveted by the news of war and worried because Arkansas National Guard units were being called up for service, planters were pleased when President Truman established a commission on migratory labor to address the needs of agriculturalists. The commission held hearings across the country and heard from no fewer than sixty-six farmworkers and labor representatives who urged a cessation of the bracero program, arguing that a sufficient supply of domestic farm labor existed. The bracero program had originated in 1942 as a war labor arrangement between the United States and the Mexican government, but Arkansas did not take advantage of the program until after the war. Braceros were brought into Arkansas until the end of the program in 1964. George Stith, a former STFU member from Arkansas who became a vice president of the National Farm Labor Union, an affiliate of the American Federation of Labor, argued before President Truman's commission in 1952 that the bracero program, which had the effect of reducing the cost of labor, would ensure the continued unemployment and underemployment of native southerners. There is probably some truth to his claims, but he was preaching to a tone-deaf choir. Reducing the cost of labor probably seemed a good idea to policy makers, and the Department of Agriculture persisted in its support of the bracero program. One advantage of the presence of the Mexicans in small towns throughout the state was that it enabled many small merchants to remain in business, even as much of the long-established rural population departed the region. With their traditional customers gone, many businesspeople hired bilingual clerks to handle the Saturday trade with the Mexicans. Although planters remained dedicated to the perpetuation of the program despite the protestations of representatives of the American Federation of Labor, the program faced formidable new foes in the figures of two successive secretaries of agriculture. Arthur Goldberg, who served under John F. Kennedy (1961–1962), and Willard Wirtz, who served under both Kennedy and Lyndon Baines Johnson, were driven by concern for the plight of the nation's farmworkers. Despite the efforts of Arkansas's congressional delegation—especially Congressman E. C. "Took" Gathings, both Goldberg and Wirtz challenged agriculture's exemption from minimum wage laws and assumed a role for the secretary of labor in the administration of the bracero program. While they expressed concerns about the wages and conditions braceros faced on farms and plantations, they were apparently as influenced by the AFL's assertion that cheap bracero labor displaced local labor and native migrant labor. The program's demise in 1964 occurred in this context.

The transition in agriculture that began during the New Deal and accelerated during World War II reached its inevitable outcome by the mid-1960s. This led to what historian Jack Kirby called the emergence of the "neo-plantation," signaling the concentration of landownership into larger

Bracero program: Involved the use of Mexican nationals in the chopping and harvesting of the cotton crop from World War II to the mid-1960s.

units and fewer owners and, especially, a dependence on the use of chemicals and machinery. The tenant farming system crumbled so rapidly that by 1960, sharecropping was no longer listed as a separate category on the agricultural census, and tenant farmers had a relatively small presence in farming areas. Seasonal wage labor became the norm. The bracero program continued to play an important role in solving the plantation's labor issues in the 1950s, but as cotton planters struggled to manage the transition from handpicked to machine-picked cotton and maintain a cheap supply of labor, another threat emerged. New synthetic fabrics that had been developed during World War II were capturing an ever-larger share of the clothing market. Cotton was falling out of favor with many consumers and thus the demand for it began to drop. Cotton planters launched campaigns to encourage people to continue purchasing cotton products, but they were waging a losing battle. When in 1957 the Arkansas Education Department instituted a program promoting the use of synthetic fibers, fourteen Farm Bureau leaders visited Governor Orval Faubus to request that the department cease spending public tax money on promoting a product that threatened the economic well-being of cotton farmers. On another front, planters lobbied successfully for a textile labeling law requiring manufacturers to list the materials used in various garments, enabling the public to determine whether a garment was made from cotton or synthetics.

Neo-plantation: The neo-plantation is a term used by historian Jack Kirby to describe the capital-intensive plantation that arose in the post-World War II period.

With demand for cotton declining, delta farmers and planters began to devote more acreage to soybean production. County farm agents had been encouraging this development since the 1920s, but it was initially promoted principally as a soil-building crop, and its commercial value was uncertain. To planters and farmers accustomed to cotton production and, furthermore, with an economic infrastructure in place in which planters secured crop financing through advances from cotton factors, soybean production was slow to expand. No significant increase in acreage devoted to soybeans took place until New Deal programs imposed acreage restrictions on cotton production in the 1930s. In part because those same programs put cash in the hands of many planters, the crop financing system began to loosen up. With an accompanying breakdown of the tenancy system, all that remained to inhibit a transition to another crop was a landscape of cotton gins and a romantic attachment to King Cotton. The need to reconstruct gins to meet the needs of the mechanical harvester made many small gins no longer viable, and the romance with cotton faded as the economic demands of the 1950s required planters and farmers to make some hard choices. By the 1980s, the Memphis Cotton Carnival, an annual event that drew many Arkansans, changed its name to Carnival Memphis, signifying the extent to which cotton had fallen in favor.

Soybean production, like the new method of cultivating and harvesting cotton, was a capital-intensive rather than labor-intensive endeavor, and thus it contributed to the depopulation of the countryside. Between 1940 and 1970, the population in the Delta declined by 14.2 percent. In this same period, the population in the southwest section of the state experienced a 20.9 percent decline. Indeed, a fundamental demographic shift within the state was underway. The most dramatic population growth occurred in Pulaski County, home to Arkansas's capital city. A less dramatic but important shift in population patterns was occurring in northern and western Arkansas, both of which lost population in the 1940s and 1950s, but reversed that trend in the 1960s. For the Delta and the southwest, however, there would be no reversal of fortune. The consequences for many small-town merchants in those areas were catastrophic. The presence of Mexican nationals for a few months during the chopping and harvesting season hardly compensated for the profound demographic change taking place. By the early 1960s, the bracero program was dropped, in part because their labor was no longer needed and in part because the Mexican government had negotiated increasingly costly requirements (better pay, housing, etc.) for their nationals. Even as the use of braceros became less common, the native black and white population departed in increasing numbers. The expansion of the road system contributed to this. In an earlier era, it had been a boon to planters and merchants in small-town Arkansas, but it worked a different result in the 1950s. It now took potential customers to more urbanized locations, and the growth of chain stores, which tended to be clustered in more densely populated towns and cities, only accentuated this trend.

A different kind of transformation in agriculture had long been underway in northwest Arkansas, but it was in this period that it reached a certain level of sophistication. While the transition in plantation agriculture was nearly complete by 1970, the hill-country farmers were still finding their way through the advent of the chicken industry. In the Delta, the use of expensive machinery and chemicals transformed farm operations from labor-intensive to capital-intensive enterprises, but concern for the environmental consequences of the use of chemicals did not arise until the late 1960s. The sharecropping system had virtually vanished; and a new set of "renters," who farmed up to a thousand acres each, worked the land with wage laborers. Meanwhile, the small upcountry farmers were turning more and more toward poultry farming and forming business relationships with operations like Tyson Foods that did not always work to their advantage. Both the neo-plantations of the Delta and the poultry farms of the hill country would continue to develop along these lines for the rest of the century.

Postwar Civil Rights

The demographic revolution taking place as a result of World War II played a role in the development of the civil rights movement in southern cities during the postwar period. As African American agricultural laborers crowded into southern cities in the postwar period, they began to form the critical mass necessary to propel a civil rights protest movement. The war had provided civil rights activists with a new energy and enthusiasm, partly because African Americans made significant contributions to the war effort and expected to be rewarded for it. Daisy Bates would become the most famous of Arkansas activists in the postwar period, though her husband, L. C. Bates, had the larger profile during and immediately after the war years. Founder of the *State Press*, an African American newspaper in Little Rock, L. C. served black readers across the state. In 1946, however, while he was away on a trip and his wife, Daisy, was in charge of the newspaper, she wrote a highly critical article after a black picket was killed during a strike called by his CIO union at the Southern Cotton Oil Mill in Little Rock. Historian Grif Stockley summarized the circumstances as follows: "In typical southern fashion, after a [black] picket named Walter Campbell was killed by his replacement, three other [black] pickets were arrested and found guilty of violating Arkansas's right-to-work law and sentenced to a year's imprisonment." L. C. reviewed the story Daisy wrote about the convictions after his return to Little Rock, and although he had misgivings about it, he endorsed its publication. The article focused on Judge Lawrence C. Auten's charge to the jury "that the pickets could be found guilty if they aided or assisted, or just stood idly by while violence occurred." The charge was not inconsistent with the new anti-union law, the so-called "right to work law," and the judge, who was unused to criticism of any sort, bristled at the temerity of the black press and had both L. C. and Daisy arrested. Allowed to post bond after being fingerprinted and photographed, they secured the services of the CIO union's attorneys and returned to court on April 29 when they were sentenced to a $100 fine and ten days in jail. When Judge Auten denied them bail, the union's attorneys took the case to the state supreme court the same day and secured their release. The Bateses then filed an appeal of their conviction and in November the state's highest court exonerated them, citing freedom of the press.

Daisy Bates would go on to play a pivotal role in the civil rights struggle that emerged in Little Rock in the mid-1950s, but the political establishment in Arkansas generally held to the pro-segregationist position. With only one

L. C. and Daisy Bates with Hugh Patterson, publisher, *Arkansas Gazette*. The Theta Sigma chapter of Sigma Gamma Rho Sorority was honoring L. C. Bates at the Camelot Inn in Little Rock on February 19, 1977. *Daisy Bates Collection, Special Collections Division, University of Arkansas Libraries, Fayetteville.*

notable exception—Governor Sidney Sanders McMath (1948–1952)—the men who occupied the governorship clung to white supremacy ideology. Benjamin Laney recognized that blacks had been unfairly treated and personally believed that changes would come, but he was convinced they should evolve slowly and from within the South. When President Harry Truman, in response to a report by his Civil Rights Committee, declared his support for an end to the poll tax, Laney and other southern governors screamed "states' rights," a term that became synonymous with maintaining the white supremacy status quo in the South. They were equally opposed to a federal statute against lynching, which would have allowed federal officers and courts to prosecute such extralegal mob actions. Governor Laney professed to understand the dark side of racial subordination of blacks in the South and said he regretted it, but he was unwilling to support any federal measures designed to remedy the situation, and he became so prominent among states' rights southern Democrats that they named him the national chairman of the Dixiecrat Party (States Rights Democratic Party). Southern politicians who opposed Truman in the 1948 presidential election were the architects of the new party. Although Laney's loyalty to the Democratic Party ran deep enough to trouble him about bolting to a third party, he became the permanent chairman of the Dixiecrats.

Meanwhile, a young marine veteran in Hot Springs was positioning himself to challenge the state's Democratic machine. Sidney McMath, who led what has come to be known as the "GI Revolt" in Garland County in 1946, would defy Laney's political ascendancy and offer an alternative position on race. He began in Hot Springs by confronting the corrupt Leo McLaughlin political machine in local elections, winning the office of prosecuting attorney, and thus positioning himself for a run for the governor's office two years later. He became the Democratic Party's nominee for the governor's office in 1948, defeating Laney in an almost unprecedented run for a third term in the party primary. Even as Laney assumed the leadership of the Dixiecrat Party southwide, he would not be able to convince Arkansans to vote anything but a Democratic ticket. Indeed, McMath is credited with keeping the state safe for the Democrats while four other southern states—South Carolina, Mississippi, Alabama, and Louisiana—voted the Dixiecrat ticket. Although he was a racial progressive—according to the standards of the time—who was a strong supporter of President Harry Truman's civil rights agenda, McMath stopped short of supporting a federal antilynching law. Bowing to the states' rights arguments against it, he advocated passage of a state antilynching law. Nevertheless, he broke with precedent and appointed blacks to positions on boards and commissions that had always been the preserve of whites alone. He championed the repeal of the poll tax, and he attempted to equalize school funding.

While white politicians were engaged in a struggle for power that often only peripherally involved the issue of civil rights, African American activists seized opportunities to move forward in this period. Silas Hunt, a native of Ashdown, Arkansas, became a pioneer in the integration of higher education in the state in 1948. He had excelled as a student at Booker T. Washington High School in Texarkana, serving as president of the student council and graduating as class salutatorian. He attended Arkansas Agricultural, Mechanical and Normal College in Pine Bluff (now the University of Arkansas at Pine Bluff) until he was drafted in 1942. While serving with the construction engineers during the Battle of the Bulge, he suffered wounds that would shorten his life. But he survived the war, returned to Pine Bluff, and finished his degree in English in 1947. Coincidentally, he became acquainted, possibly before he left for the war, with a young woman graduate of the college destined to blaze a trail in Oklahoma civil rights history. Ada Sipuel had completed her education and in 1946 applied for admission to the University of Oklahoma School of Law. When they denied her admission, she took her case to the US Supreme Court, winning an important concession in 1948 when the nation's highest court ordered the state to provide her with a legal education equal to that offered to white students. When the state of Oklahoma hastily created a separate law school, one which could not possibly offer the same level of education, she again took her case to the Supreme Court, finally winning admittance in 1949.

Even as Ada Sipuel was in the midst of her struggle with the state of Oklahoma, Silas Hunt was completing his studies at AM&N. While there he made the acquaintance of Wiley Branton, a fellow student who was also destined to become an important civil rights figure in Arkansas. His key introduction, however, was to Harold Flowers, who had already established himself as a force to be reckoned with. Upon approaching graduation, Hunt began the process of applying to law schools, including the University of Arkansas School of Law in Fayetteville. On February 2, 1948, Hunt, Flowers, Branton, and an AM&N photographer, Geleve Grice, drove from Pine Bluff to Fayetteville with a single purpose in mind. They had watched with interest as the Sipuel case was making its way through the court system, and they had read with enthusiasm the announcement made on January 30 that the University of Arkansas would admit qualified black applicants. University officials, particularly the law school's dean, Robert Leflar, had observed the Supreme Court decisions in cases involving other southern states—such as the Sipuel case in Oklahoma—and understood that segregation at the graduate and professional school level was being successfully challenged. Leflar believed that such segregation was indefensible and worked to convince the board of trustees, an effort that resulted in the stunning announcement on January 30, 1948. When Hunt and his cohort appeared at the law school, Leflar reviewed his application personally and admitted him immediately. Although Hunt's classes were held in a basement room separate from white students, three to five white students elected to attend classes in the basement with him. He was not allowed to eat in the all-white cafeteria and was assigned a special study area in the library. He endured some harassment while on campus and according to George Haley, who later graduated from the law school, an automobile attempted to run Hunt down on the edge of campus.

Tragically, Silas Hunt was unable to complete his studies because of illness. He developed tuberculosis and was hospitalized at the Veterans Hospital in Springfield, Missouri, where he died on April 22, 1949. It was widely believed that his illness was complicated by wounds he suffered at the Battle of the Bulge. Jackie L. Shropshire, a graduate of Little Rock's Dunbar High School, entered the university's law school in the fall of 1948 and became the first African American to graduate in 1951. George Haley, brother to *Roots* author Alex Haley, was soon to follow.

Another civil rights pioneer, Edith Mae Irby, also made her appearance in Arkansas in 1948 when she integrated the University of Arkansas Medical School. Irby arrived in Little Rock on the day she was scheduled to register with little more than the funds she thought sufficient to pay her tuition and registration. Perhaps this was unwise, the hubris of the young, but she was fired by the determination to study medicine, a goal that originated with the death of an older sister when both were children. Edith Mae had nursed her sister, who was suffering from typhoid fever, and it left a lasting impression. Her sister's sickness and death had painfully revealed to her that African Americans too often had insufficient medical care, and she wanted to remedy that situation. The experience also left her with an insatiable desire to understand disease, a desire she began to fulfill in her high school studies. However, further disruption intervened when her father died after being thrown from a horse—another reminder of the inadequate medical facilities available to African Americans. The planter for whom he worked evicted the family, and they moved to Hot Springs to live with her maternal grandmother where Edith was eventually able to earn a high school diploma. Her mother found employment as a domestic in the city's hotels, and though she helped as much as she was able, Edith had to work her way through college. She graduated Knoxville College (a black private college in Tennessee) in 1947, returned to her home in Hot Springs, and applied to twelve medical colleges, including Arkansas's medical school, knowing it would be difficult to gain admission but hoping to stay in Arkansas for her medical school education. In order to increase her chances of success, she enrolled in two classes at the University of Chicago that summer. It was there that she learned she had been accepted into Arkansas's medical college from a *Time* magazine reporter who wanted her reaction.

Irby and her family were excited about the opportunity, and the black community in Hot Springs raised funds to help pay her tuition. Housing had been lined up for her in Little Rock, and she intended to find a job to help defray her living expenses. When she reached Little Rock, however, she discovered she was just shy of the amount necessary to register. Having been told by friends that if she needed help she should contact Daisy Bates,

Irby found her at the *State Press*, secured the necessary funds, and paid her registration fees just in time to meet the deadline. Bates, however, went even further. Ascertaining that Irby's financial situation was fragile, Bates collected funds from various NAACP chapters around the state to support Irby's education. This began Irby's association with that organization, one that was deepened when she married James B. Jones, a professor at the University of Arkansas Mechanical and Normal College in Pine Bluff, a dedicated member of the local chapter of the NAACP. Like Silas Hunt, Edith Mae Irby initially endured semi-segregated conditions although not in the classroom but in the library and cafeteria where black staff members set her table elegantly and decorated it with flowers. She successfully completed her medical school education and returned to Hot Springs to open a practice in 1952.

By the time the United States Supreme Court issued the *Brown v. Board of Education* decision in May 1954, Arkansas's African American population had already achieved certain successes in promoting integration of higher education in the state. The *Brown* decision, however, raised the stakes considerably. Token integration in professional and graduate schools had hardly registered as a problem for white southerners, but desegregating the public school system proved to be far more controversial. Like southerners elsewhere, segregationists in Arkansas resisted in a variety of ways over the decades that followed the decision, and they enjoyed the support of local and state officials in orchestrating plans to thwart integration. Orval Faubus launched efforts to thwart integration, but even after his methods failed, only token integration occurred in the 1960s, largely because of so-called integration plans that were truly meant to maintain segregation. Indeed, according to a ruling of the Eighth Circuit Court of Appeals rendered in 1985, "The Executive and Legislative Branches of [Arkansas] State government set their faces like flint against the law."

The first reaction of white Arkansans to the *Brown* decision, however, was surprise. Even President Dwight Eisenhower, who had appointed Earl Warren as chief justice of the Supreme Court, was caught off guard by the decision and later declared privately that his selection of Warren to head the court had been the "biggest damn fool mistake I ever made." Eisenhower was justified in being taken aback. Warren, as a former conservative governor of California, had the right credentials from the Republican Party's point of view for appointment to the Supreme Court. He had served as California's attorney general when Franklin Roosevelt issued his executive order to intern Japanese Americans in 1942 and had played the lead role in orchestrating it. He must have seemed an unlikely risk to conservatives attached to the status quo. Instead, believing fervently that the 1896 *Plessy v. Ferguson* decision was wrong, he carefully lobbied, cajoled, and persuaded the other justices to issue a unanimous decision overturning the "separate but equal" doctrine and thus promoting integration of the country's schools.

In the months immediately following the *Brown* decision, it appeared that integration would occur without causing great difficulty in Arkansas. Schools in Fayetteville and Charleston, which both had small black populations, integrated without controversy in the fall of 1954. But this proved to be the lull before the storm. To complicate things, African Americans in Arkansas were not united in the approach to be taken. The cooperation of certain black elites in Arkansas with the NAACP in the suit Sue Morris brought against the Little Rock School Board in 1942 obscured a struggle between the old black elites and the more activist agenda of younger African Americans. To some extent, this struggle reflected the influence of the old black aristocracy on the local chapter of the NAACP, an influence that discouraged an aggressive challenge of the white power structure. Therefore, when L. C. and Daisy Bates became actively involved in the attempt to bring desegregation to Little Rock, they did not have the full support of the city's black aristocracy. As historian Calvin Smith has observed, even L. C. Bates had voiced reservations about integration and was, instead, an advocate of equality of opportunity for blacks. When he became convinced by early 1952 that separate facilities would never be equalized, he began writing strongly worded editorials in support of the NAACP's challenge to segregation in public education. He was pleased with the *Brown* decision in 1954, but warned his readers that even though the state's officials had reacted mildly to the decision, "things are going to be serious." A calm, quiet, dignified man, he was a master of understatement.

Bates was not alone among those who worked for change but feared the worst. Harry Ashmore, who was in charge of the editorial page of the *Arkansas Gazette*, coauthored a report predicting that integration would be an explosive issue. Ashmore had been commissioned by the Ford Foundation in 1953 to study the implications of the effects of the dual education system. The report, issued the day before the *Brown* decision, found that black children were greatly disadvantaged by the underfunded black schools and that southern states could not afford to provide an adequate education to either race by maintaining the dual system. Ashmore understood the forces arrayed against integration and played a role in organizing the Arkansas Council on Human Relations (ACHR) in Little Rock in 1955. It was loosely affiliated with the Southern Regional Council in Atlanta, Georgia, from which it received some funds and a good deal of advice. An interracial organization, the ACHR worked to promote peaceful integration but, as the Ford Foundation report suggested, they would be fighting an uphill battle.

Regardless of the cautionary note sounded in the report, the ACHR

Arkansas Council on Human Relations: Loosely affiliated with the Southern Regional Council in Atlanta, Georgia, the Arkansas Council on Human Relations was organized in 1955 in Little Rock in order to promote peaceful integration.

pursued efforts to foster cooperation and conciliation between the races. In March 1956, they sponsored a workshop at Camp Aldersgate near Little Rock and brought people from around the state together to participate in discussions about how the organization could promote peaceful integration on the local level. Two speakers from Fisk University served as the official consultants. Unknown to them, the state police set up surveillance outside the camp and recorded the license plate numbers of all those who reported for the meeting. Still, the ACHR stayed the course. By early 1957 they were laying plans to sponsor a "brotherhood" week, when black and white ministers would meet and work together to ease tensions and encourage observance of the law. They teamed a black with a white minister who were to speak on the topic "A Christian Looks at Race Relations Today" at a church or to a church group that extended them an invitation. Some organizers of the ACHR were disappointed by the failure of some church leaders to participate. Fred Darragh, a white businessman in Little Rock, who served as the first executive director of the ACHR, was outspoken in his criticisms of the timidity of many white ministers who refused to participate for fear of offending their congregations. Darragh's criticisms revealed the depth of the struggle ACHR members faced in their efforts to organize and promote peaceful integration.

African American activists and the ACHR would find no support from the state's governor, Orval Faubus. In retrospect, the statements Faubus made

Hoxie desegregation controversy: Originated in Hoxie, a town in northeastern Arkansas, when the school board voted to desegregate. Rabid segregationists raised a storm of protest, and though they were unsuccessful in their efforts to keep the Hoxie schools from becoming desegregated, a potent new organization emerged to fight desegregation.

during his first run for office in 1954 should have served as fair warning. He had suggested that desegregation might be delayed and even outlined a strategy that might be pursued to guarantee it. However, once in office Faubus appointed blacks to the State Democratic Committee, something that would have been unthinkable just a few years earlier. Because of this, many people throughout the state regarded Faubus as a racial progressive, but in this case appearances proved to be deceiving. Faubus attempted to steer a middle path on the desegregation issue when he could, such as his success in avoiding a role in the school desegregation controversy in Hoxie in 1955, a small town of only 1,855 people in east Arkansas.

The Hoxie desegregation controversy foreshadowed the 1956 election and a dramatic shift to the right on Faubus's part. Yet when the Hoxie School Board decided to integrate, they had little reason to fear controversy. After all,

Fayetteville and Charleston had integrated without incident the year before, and Hoxie was similar to them in racial demographics: overwhelmingly white. The Hoxie school term began on July 11, in keeping with a "split term," common in some agricultural communities that permitted a break in the fall so that children could participate in the cotton harvest. No incidents occurred on that day and things seemed to be proceeding according to plan. Although some segregationists were beginning to raise objections, a controversy only broke open after *Life* magazine decided to do a pictorial feature demonstrating peaceful integration in the South. They chose Hoxie, Arkansas, as their prime example. When the issue appeared on the newsstands on July 25, images of black and white children arm-in-arm aroused a segment of the white population. White agitators, mostly from elsewhere, flooded into Hoxie to protest. A small group of the most ardent among them launched a challenge to the school board, but the board refused to back down. When Governor Faubus declined to intervene to protect them against the crowds of hostile whites, the board was left virtually defenseless. They took their case to the federal courts, arguing that the protestors were trespassing on school property and disrupting the otherwise successful integration effort. Federal judge Thomas C. Trimble issued a restraining order against the segregationists and the Eighth Circuit Court of Appeals later backed his decision. The Hoxie schools remained integrated.

Despite the success of the efforts to integrate Hoxie schools, a potent new organization was coalescing behind the scenes during the Hoxie crisis. The White Citizens Council, organized initially in the state of Mississippi in 1954 to fight the *Brown* decision, had sprouted roots in Arkansas. State legislator James D. Johnson, who had played a small role in the segregationists' stand in Hoxie, was a prominent organizer. He began giving speeches around the state to rally anti-integrationists, and believing Faubus to be vulnerable on the issue, he mounted a challenge to him in the 1956 Democratic primary. Faubus found it necessary to shore up support among those most opposed to desegregation, especially east Arkansas planters, and was able to cast himself as a more reputable segregationist than his opponent. Although Johnson was unsuccessful in dislodging the governor, he forced Faubus to move to the right on the segregation issue.

Orval Faubus was not alone among Arkansas politicians in opposing integration. He found support not only in the state legislature but also with Arkansas's congressional delegation. Even as civil rights activists filed a suit concerning the failure to integrate the schools, Arkansas's entire congressional delegation signed on to the "Southern Manifesto," a document challenging the *Brown* decision. South Carolina's Strom Thurmond, the standard bearer for the Dixiecrats in 1948, wrote the initial draft, and it was almost certainly intended to serve as a rallying point for segregationists. It declared the Supreme Court's actions to be an abuse of power, among other things, but its principle objective was to prevent or, at the very least, delay integration. Arkansas's J. William Fulbright contributed to a revision of the document, supposedly in order to tone down its rhetoric, but Richard Russell of Georgia actually authored the final draft. In any case, with the state's congressional delegation signing on to the document, Faubus must have believed he had not only the rationale but also the backing of a significant lobby in Congress.

Meanwhile, black activists were developing plans to integrate Little Rock schools. Frustrated that no movement toward integration followed a 1955 decision of the Supreme Court to proceed with desegregation with "all deliberate speed," the NAACP lined up a group of thirty-three black students, working through their parents, to file a suit that became known as *Aaron v. Cooper* (Aaron the name of the first child listed on the suit; Cooper being William G. Cooper, president of the Little Rock School Board). Their efforts and their suit were undermined by the actions of Little Rock's white school superintendent Virgil Blossom and the Little Rock School Board, which presented an integration plan that was far different from what the black activists promoted. It provided for only modest integration of Central High School, a school in a working-class neighborhood. Yet Daisy Bates and a small group of African American activists decided to work with Blossom, and they carefully selected nine students—who became known as the "Little Rock Nine"—to make the move into Central High School in the fall of 1957: Minnijean Brown, Elizabeth Eckford, Ernest Green, Thelma Mothershed, Melba Pattillo, Gloria Ray, Terrance Roberts, Jefferson Thomas, and Carlotta Walls.

Aaron v. Cooper:
A suit filed by the parents of thirty-three black students in Little Rock after the Supreme Court issued its "all deliberate speed" decision in 1955, a follow-up to the *Brown* decision in 1954.

Little Rock Nine:
The nine black students who integrated Central High School in Little Rock in 1957.

Even as Bates was preparing the children for entry into Central High, Faubus took another step away from racial progressivism and mortgaged his political future to the extreme segregationists in order to secure approval of an ambitious twenty-two-million-dollar legislative package. To gain the support of east Arkansas planters for a package that included increases in benefits to the elderly and higher teacher salaries, Faubus acquiesced to four bills designed to delay desegregation, something that was not so very far from measures he hinted might be necessary in his first run for the governor's office in the race against Cherry. These measures, if Faubus had attempted to enforce them, would have provided financial aid to schools attempting to resist integration, changed school attendance laws in a manner designed to make sure that certain whites did not have to attend school with

Students and soldiers at Central High School, Little Rock. *Larry Obstinik Photo Archives, Special Collections Division, University of Arkansas Libraries, Fayetteville.*

blacks, required the NAACP to publish its membership lists, and established a state sovereignty commission with the express purpose of studying how to effectively block federal integration efforts. When Faubus failed to enforce the four measures, pressure from the extreme segregationists mounted.

In August 1957, as the fall term of school approached, two important developments occurred. First, federal judge John E. Miller ruled against the plaintiffs in *Aaron v. Cooper*, arguing that the plan for integration outlined by the school board was on track to take place. Under those circumstances, there was no reason to issue a court order mandating integration. This had the effect, however, of giving the Blossom plan for desegregating Central High greater visibility and, in a larger sense, established that the state could not ignore its responsibility to enforce the *Brown* decision. The governor must have realized that he could no longer obfuscate on the issue. The second development came from another direction entirely and placed additional pressure on Faubus. With the integration of Central High looming, the segregationists prepared to draw a line in the sand. They invited Governor Marvin Griffin of Georgia to speak to the Little Rock White Citizens Council; after the speech, he met with Faubus and convinced the governor to intervene.

According to Faubus biographer Roy Reed, the governor had his own objections to the Blossom plan. He was offended by the fact that Little Rock's integration would begin in a working-class school. A new school, Hall High, had been opened for upper-middle-class white children. Faubus, who came from a hill-country family of very modest means, was an outsider to the Little Rock society and business elite, and he felt snubbed by them. Whatever his motivations, after failing to convince the FBI that violence would occur if the desegregation plan was implemented, he called out the National Guard and state troopers and ordered them to prevent the "Little Rock Nine" from integrating Central High. So successful had Faubus been in straddling the issue that a woman who had worked with the Arkansas Council on Human Relations in Fayetteville to prepare the state for peaceful integration awoke that Monday morning to scenes of uniformed men surrounding the school and believed that the governor had called the military out to protect the black children and ensure peaceful integration. She was shocked to discover the truth and she, like many others, felt betrayed. To segregationists, however, Faubus was a hero.

The most iconic image captured on television cameras that September 4 morning featured Elizabeth Eckford walking stalwartly toward the front door of Central High, a crowd of hostile young people surrounding her. One female student followed her, apparently screaming invective, but Eckford soldiered on. She walked alone because she had not received an important message that morning; instead of meeting at the school as was originally planned, she was meant to go instead to Daisy Bates's home where the Little Rock Nine were to gather. From there the students were to convoy together. Bates had decided on this change of plan upon receiving word of the crowds gathered before the school. But Eckford, who had already taken the bus to Central High, could not be reached and thus she made her solitary walk in vain. Once turned away from the door by grim-faced National Guardsmen, she had no option other than to walk back through the hostile crowd and wait for a bus to take her to safety. The other eight students were later also turned away, and the school remained closed to the Little Rock Nine for nearly three weeks.

When federal district judge Ronald Davies ordered integration to pro- ceed on September 20, the stage was set for yet another ugly confrontation. In response to the judge's order, Faubus removed the National Guard but this merely left the Little Rock Nine vulnerable to a large crowd of angry and unruly whites who stood ready to defy the court order. The nine students appeared on September 23 and were ushered in through a back door while some in the crowd pounced on four black newspapermen, beating them severely. On September 24, 1957, responding to a request by the mayor of Little Rock, President Eisenhower sent the 101st Airborne Division into Little Rock and nationalized the Arkansas National Guard in order to enforce integration. Meanwhile, Harry Ashmore's strongly worded editorials led the *Gazette* into a period of struggle with segregationist forces in Arkansas that garnered him a Pulitzer Prize in 1958. The paper itself also received a Pulitzer that year, for public service for reporting on the crisis and the confrontation with Faubus.

The Little Rock Nine had gained entry into Central High, but they endured a difficult school year (1957–1958), so difficult, in fact, that one of their number, Minnijean Brown, was suspended in February 1958 for calling a student "white trash" for having struck her. On February 20, the school board petitioned the federal court to delay and desist from integration. Judge Harold J. Lemley granted the postponement in April, a decision that was immediately appealed by the same parties that had initiated the *Aaron v. Cooper* suit. The Eighth Circuit reversed his decision in August. This left all sides of the issue on tinder hooks as the fall 1958 school year was upon them. The school board delayed the beginning of classes to await the outcome of the inevitable appeal to the US Supreme Court. When that body ruled in *Cooper v. Aaron* that integration must proceed on schedule, Orval Faubus took the unprecedented step of simply closing the schools. As historian Sondra Gordy has demonstrated, the "lost year" created hardships for Little Rock's high school students and teachers alike. Still under contract, teachers sat in empty classrooms and walked eerily vacated hallways; students either attended private schools, some of them hastily created, or left the city altogether to continue their education. The closing of the schools was, of course, most difficult for the poorest students, particularly black students who had fewer options available to them.

It was high tide for segregationists as Dale Alford, an ophthalmologist and an extremist race-baiter, successfully waged a write-in campaign against Congressman Brooks Hays in the fall 1958 congressional elections. Hays, a moderate, had attempted to mediate by bringing Faubus and Eisenhower together to end the crisis. Segregationists also launched an attack against Harry Ashmore and the ACHR, labeling them agents of communism. In 1958 the Arkansas attorney general's office launched an investigation of the council and used Ashmore's association with it as evidence of its subversive character. A hearing was held before a special education committee of the Arkansas Legislative Council in December 1958, with Attorney General Bruce Bennett conducting the interrogation of various witnesses. Daisy Bates and the NAACP were identified as being in league with communists and communist front organizations. The report, laced with innuendo, circumstantial evidence, and unsubstantiated accusations, concluded that communists and fellow travelers were responsible for the racial unrest in Arkansas. The report also implied that until the interference of the communists and their dupes, African Americans in Arkansas had been content with their segregated status. The report's authors were either unfamiliar with the half-century struggle mounted by blacks in Arkansas on various fronts or had simply chosen to ignore it.

The Bennett report was only one part of a war against the NAACP and integrationist forces. It was also in 1958 that the legislature passed Act 10, which required state employees to report all memberships to any organizations over the previous five years. Introduced as an anticommunist bill, it was actually designed to identify and intimidate members of the NAACP. The threat was made all the more potent with the passage of Act 115, which made it illegal for state employees to belong to the NAACP. Although both acts were eventually ruled unconstitutional, they created problems for professors in colleges and universities within the state. James B. Jones, Edith Mae Irby's husband, faced expulsion from his position at the University of Arkansas, Pine Bluff, under these circumstances, but he avoided it when Irby elected to accept an internship in internal medicine in Houston and the family moved there. At the University of Arkansas, meanwhile, a group of professors defied the act on grounds of academic freedom and refused to report their associations. Professor John McKenney was fired, and when the university failed to reinstate him upon appeal, the American Association of University Professors (AAUP) placed the university on its censure list, a censure that was not lifted until 1968.

Although concerned about the attack on civil liberties represented in Acts 10 and 115, it was the firing of forty-four teachers on May 5, 1959, that prompted some moderate whites to assert themselves. A small group of prominent white women, the Women's Emergency Committee (WEC), had been working behind the scenes from the first days of the crisis and had created an impressive political organization, compiling lists of voters and working to encourage moderate businessmen and civic leaders to become involved in the struggle. Whether in response to the WEC or because Little Rock was beginning to feel the results of the controversy in terms of lost business and industrial opportunities, the Little Rock Chamber of Commerce voted in March 1959 to reopen the schools and integrate on a limited basis. The vote was overwhelming: 819 to 245. Their opinion, though important, had no influence on the governor or the legislature, however. In any case, the chamber attempted to avoid the label of "integrationists" by

Women's Emergency Committee: A small group of prominent white women who worked behind the scenes to peacefully integrate Central High School and end the integration crisis.

speaking in support of a new private high school that had been created solely to provide a segregated facility for white children.

Urging only limited integration was as far as the businessmen and civic leaders would go until the segregationists finally overstepped themselves and fired the forty-four teachers and administrators on May 5. The board's actions "shamed" some of them into creating a new organization called Stop this Outrageous Purge (STOP). Officially, they kept their distance from the WEC, although that organization supplied woman power in the form of campaign workers in a "recall" of the segregationist school board members. Those who supported the segregationists on the school board formed their own organization, which they called the Committee to Retain Our Segregated Schools (CROSS). Despite the imagery of their acronym, which was obviously intended to appeal to the religious sensibilities of the Little Rock electorate, voters removed the segregationists on the board and replaced them with three moderates.

Stop this Outrageous Purge: An organization formed by white business and civic leaders in Little Rock after the segregationists successfully fired white school board members favorable to integration.

The tide had turned. The businessmen and civic leaders who formed STOP would no longer tolerate the notoriety that accompanied segregationist efforts to prevent integration. Once the United States Supreme Court declared the school-closing law unconstitutional on June 18, 1959, the stage was set for the next episode in the integration of Central High. The new school board subsequently laid plans to integrate both Central and Hall high schools. The integration of Hall High School, located in a wealthier section of Little Rock, was in response to accusations that working-class children attending Central High were to bear the brunt of integration. In other words, as Faubus biographer and respected journalist Roy Reed has pointed out, it was simply a "nod to class antagonisms." Little Rock schools reopened in the fall of 1959, integrated, but it was truly only token integration. Only six black children were admitted to the two high schools, three to Central and three to Hall.

The period between 1945 and 1960 was one of considerable turmoil and change in Arkansas. The social, economic, and political winds that swept across the state gave it a different face and a new posture, but many of the state's citizens remained undereducated and often impoverished. The Central High crisis continued to taint the state's image, and more subtle strategies for maintaining segregation emerged. The legacy of ill-paid agricultural jobs lived on in the Delta in the form of low-wage, low-skill employment in factories, factories that proved all too likely to be moving south in the pursuit of even lower-wage workers. Not much would change in the Delta in the years ahead, but a burst of economic activity in the northwest section of the state augered well for that area. In fact, certain families and entities in northwest Arkansas would soon overshadow the planters of the Delta in terms of wealth. Meanwhile, Little Rock would itself experience an economic revival, and certain individuals and companies there began to enjoy wealth and success. In the end, however, economic development did not move deeply into the fabric of Arkansas, and the next decades would see more of the same.

14 ✕ Arkansas in the Sunbelt South, 1960–1992

FOR MOST OF the twentieth century, Arkansas policy makers promoted industrial development, believing that it would foster economic growth and prosperity. They did so without much success until after World War II, and the decades of the 1960s and 1970s were particularly propitious. Historian Ben F. Johnson points out that "while manufacturing production increased by nearly 50 percent in the United States between 1967 and 1980, it soared by over 300 percent in Arkansas." These manufacturing enterprises were attracted to Arkansas because of its nonunion stance and the opportunity to pay low wages. While these jobs provided much-needed income to many Arkansans, wages were so low that some of those who held full-time jobs in manufacturing plants found themselves eligible for food stamp assistance. Many communities were so eager to secure manufacturing industries that they reduced or eliminated taxes they would be subject to, thus the revenue generated by the plants was minimal.

American manufacturers were themselves facing a crisis as they endured stiff competition from some of the country's own Cold War allies. Indeed, the United States had expended enormous sums to revive the Japanese and Germany economies, for example, and by 1970, they were posing a significant challenge to US manufacturers. Meanwhile, the nation began to shift to a service economy—banking, finance, health services, and so forth—and in the direction of high tech, turning away from the old manufacturing economy. In other words, just as Arkansas was finally able to register a manufacturing sector, the country was going in a different direction. This coincided with a related development: the Sunbelt South, a phenomenon that witnessed the growth of high tech and the service-sector businesses in warmer climates; that is, generally below the 33rd parallel. Unfortunately, Arkansas, with an undereducated population, was not well positioned to participate in this new economy. Although some significant service-sector companies would emerge in the state, particularly Walmart, Inc., no appreciable high-tech industry developed, and Arkansas is generally regarded by those who study the

Sunbelt South: Refers to the region below the 33rd parallel where high-tech and service-sector industries developed in the post–World War II era.

Sunbelt South as developing relatively too late and too little. The agricultural sector continued to thrive, however, especially in the 1970s as escalating crop prices made the decade "the state's most prosperous in the twentieth century." The 1980s would witness a sharp reversal of this agricultural prosperity, and the development of Arkansas's service-sector economy would soon begin to eclipse the state's farmers. This complex mix of economic factors would have long-term consequences—both politically and economically—and permeate all aspects of Arkansas's development.

Underlying Political, Demographic, and Economic Trends

The Voting Rights Act of 1965 served as a catalyst for significant political changes in the decades that followed its passage. The Democrats of the late nineteenth century had consolidated their power by disfranchising black voters, but after 1965, Democrats began to speak to issues that represented the interests of African Americans. As southern Democrats adopted more moderate positions on race, they no longer represented a buffer between the more liberal national Democratic Party and the ultra-Christian conservatism of much of the rural South. In this context, rural Arkansans, like their counterparts in other southern states, were increasingly drawn to the new Republican ideology, dominated as it was by both fiscal and social conservatism. Many Arkansas citizens wanted a well-ordered world but one in which they were free to pursue their interests unfettered by governmental interference. Although such desires—order and freedom—are often in conflict, their negotiation within the rural South demonstrates that they can be compatible. Many rural southerners appreciate a world ordered by Old Testament principles, but they want to be free of government interference in their affairs, free to purchase and carry guns, for example. Arkansas was late in reorienting itself to the Republican Party, however, and if the historians of the Sunbelt are accurate in their assessment of the reasons for the new affinity of southerners for the GOP, then Arkansas's exceptionalism is understandable. According to their analysis, a major factor in the rise of the Republican Party in the South was a wave of immigration connected to the rise of the service-sector and high-tech industries. While Arkansas was to participate in this new economy, its early response was relatively anemic. Some immigration occurred, however, particularly in northern and western Arkansas as midwesterners moved into retirement communities like Cherokee Village and Bella Vista, both creations of entrepreneur John A. Cooper. Traditionally wedded to the Republican Party, they eventually helped solidify the party in northwestern Arkansas. Another set of migrants landed in central Arkansas, particularly around Little Rock, and assumed positions with the new jobs opening up in the service-sector economy. Often upwardly mobile and conservative in political philosophy, they settled in the suburbs springing up in Pulaski County.

Meanwhile, delta planters, as elsewhere in the country, found themselves at a crossroads. As their economic woes deepened in the 1980s, they began to turn away from the Democratic Party. Although they were dependent upon federal subsidy programs, they wanted as little regulation as possible and were receptive to politicians who espoused a states' rights position. Republicans on the national level began to preach this message, stealing the thunder of the southern states' rights tradition exemplified by the Dixiecrats. National Democrats continued to support federal regulations, such as environmental initiatives designed to address the groundwater pollution problems created by the extensive use of pesticides, and pesticides were something planters were as dependent upon as they were upon agricultural federal subsidies. Arkansas Democrats running for senate and congressional seats understood the importance of these subsidies to their constituents, but found it increasingly difficult to negotiate the contradiction between the states' rights position that appealed to their constituents and their need for continued federal farm subsidies. To complicate matters further, farmers and planters soon became pawns in the Cold War against the Soviet Union. In response to the Soviet Union's invasion of Afghanistan in 1979, President Jimmy Carter imposed an embargo on the sale of American-produced wheat to the Soviets. Although wheat was not one of the most important crops produced in Arkansas, it was a significant secondary crop, and farmers, through the state's Farm Bureau Federation, protested against it. President Ronald Reagan lifted the embargo in April 1981, but the damage had been done. The Soviet Union had turned to other wheat producers and though they eventually began buying American wheat, other factors contributed to a devastating farm crisis that deepened in the 1980s.

The problems confronting agriculturalists in this era are complex and varied, depending on location and farm commodity, but they can be summarized as follows: The high prices for agricultural products in the 1970s led to higher land values and, in the super optimism then operating, many farmers and planters overextended themselves. The tight money policies enforced by the Reagan administration in the 1980s, together with historically high interest rates, resulted in a crash in farm prices and an increase in farm foreclosures. Like farmers elsewhere, Arkansas's planters and farmers became even more dependent upon government subsidies, and continued to send Democrats to Congress who could be counted on to support a generous farm program. Nevertheless, though it was the tight money policies of a Republican president that accounted in part for their difficulties, prosperous farmers—and other Arkansas voters—began to support Republican presidential candidates.

A significant demographic shift constituted another major factor underlying the erosion of the southern wing of the Democratic Party. A century earlier, the Delta region was experiencing unprecedented growth because of the extension of the railroad network, the emergence of the lumber industry, and the expansion of the plantation system. Planters had always exercised considerable power and influence within the Arkansas political system, and their position was solidified as the plantation system expanded. By the late twentieth century, the ground had literally been cut from beneath them. Railroads were becoming obsolete and the state and interstate highway systems had worked a different result on the towns of Arkansas. While the arrival of railroads had created many new towns and encouraged the growth of the population, the expansion of the highway system encouraged a depopulation of eastern and southern Arkansas. The demographic changes that accompanied the transformation of plantation agriculture in the 1950s slowed, but blacks particularly continued their almost-century-long exodus from delta counties (see chart). The efforts to attract smokestack industries to save small delta towns had only modest success, in part because some planters could not quite bring themselves to support industrial development. A few well-situated towns convinced manufacturers to locate factories there, but their prosperity was fragile. The reliance on low-skill enterprises revealed the profound inadequacies in an educational system that had prepared the citizenry for little else but agricultural labor, and those industries, which paid little or no taxes to local government and low wages to its workers, proved to be of dubious benefit to the areas within which they settled. What benefit they bestowed proved all too transitory as many of them moved southward in search of even lower-wage labor, and most small towns found themselves on a treadmill, ever in search of yet another low-wage, low-skill factory to employ the remnants of its population. Indeed, Arkansas's plantation area was facing an uncertain future, and four of its counties have had the dubious distinction of being among the one hundred poorest in the nation: Chicot, Lee, Monroe, and Phillips counties.

PLACE	1940 WHITE	1990 WHITE	1940 BLACK	1990 BLACK
North/NW	296,140	483,724	2,809	3,036
West Central	288,667	431,909	23,601	22,741
Southwest	252,636	244,781	125,162	80,551
Eastern	522,127	531,776	287,924	175,384
Little Rock Area	112,877	252,554	43,182	92,200

Population by Race

While the old plantation counties struggled to maintain their population and save their towns, the northwestern part of the state experienced an unprecedented boom. This was in large part the result of the vast expansion of the service-sector economy in that region of the state. The most important leader in that expansion was Walmart, Inc. From a small storefront in Rogers, opened as a Walmart, Sam Walton developed his business into a retail phenomenon, and over the next several decades his enterprise expanded rapidly, becoming a world-class economic giant and changing the very nature of the retail enterprise. As historian Brent Riffel suggests, he had already "penetrated the rural market in the 1960s, opening retail stores in small towns, and often becoming a community's central retail outlet." In the 1970s Walmart opened its first distribution center and was listed on the New York Stock Exchange. In 1972, its first year on the stock exchange, Walmart's stock split twice, signaling its strength and desirability. In 1977, it moved well beyond Arkansas as Walmart began acquiring stores in Illinois and Michigan. It also introduced different services within its stores—including a pharmacy, an automobile service center, and a jewelry division. By 1979, annual sales reached more than a billion dollars. The company continued to acquire other stores in the 1980s, and its stock continued to split, as it became a highly desirable and reliable commodity on the stock exchange. In 1984, Walmart hired a dynamic chief executive officer, David Glass, who led the company through a remarkable period of growth. Under Glass's leadership, Walmart expanded both nationwide and internationally, and soon vendors were moving into northwest Arkansas, eager to supply what was rapidly becoming the world's largest retail operation.

Service-sector economy: An economy marked by significant service-sector business operations; that is, businesses that provide goods and services to consumers.

While the rise of the chicken and trucking industries in northwest Arkansas seems to pale in comparison, these enterprises were extremely important and accounted for much of the economic expansion of the region. As Brent Riffel observes, Tyson Foods, Inc.. also marketed internationally and experienced a period of rapid expansion in the 1980s. In 1977, the company purchased a hog-producing facility in North Carolina and by 1982 made it onto the Fortune 500 list. Soon it was selling to such fast-food giants as McDonald's. When it purchased Holly Farms in 1989, it doubled its market share and stood poised to buy out other companies in the coming decade. Meanwhile, a flood of workers came to Arkansas (and wherever else Tyson operated) to find employment in processing and related plants. Although these industries largely employed low-wage, unskilled labor, Tyson also hired highly paid executives in their corporate offices. Together with executives who came to work for the billion-dollar Walmart Corporation, the presence of these immigrants spurred a boom in the construction industry as high-salaried employees warranted the construction of expensive homes that set the stage for a reassessment of property values.

The placement of both Walmart and Tyson in northwest Arkansas led to an expansion in the truck industry in the region. J. B. Hunt Trucking, Inc., founded by Jimmie Bryant (J. B.) Hunt, had been operating since the 1960s, producing poultry litter for sale to farmers. Hunt, who began driving a truck in 1953 before launching his poultry litter enterprise, began his own trucking operation in 1969. He expanded rapidly in the 1970s, but his company owed much of its phenomenal success to the deregulation of the trucking industry in 1980. Unlike most companies, which preferred to hire independent truckers who bore the transportation costs themselves, J. B. Hunt owned his own trucks and depended on a cadre of drivers willing to accept low wages in exchange for steady employment. In the 1980s, Hunt was able to secure a contract to haul for Walmart, an extremely lucrative contract that propelled Hunt into a new arena. By the 1990s, the company was worth a billion dollars. Headquartered in Rogers in northwest Arkansas, J. B. Hunt eventually became the largest publicly held trucking company in the United States and employed fifteen thousand people.

As the unemployment rate hovered close to 2 percent in northwest Arkansas by the early 1990s, the industry demand for low-wage, low-skill labor grew to exceed the available workforce. The poultry industry in particular found a ready and willing labor pool in the Hispanic communities of Texas, other southwestern states, and Mexico. As Hispanic people stepped into the job market created by that industry, they also found employment opportunities in the burgeoning construction industry. For the first time in its history, northwest Arkansas was no longer an overwhelmingly white, Anglo-Saxon, and Protestant enclave. The significant Hispanic population developed its own subculture, which included cultural, economic, and religious enterprises, but the emergence of a rabid anti-immigration movement, made up in part of the transplanted midwesterners, turned what should have been merely a cultural phenomenon into a political issue. Those who embraced the anti-immigration movement complained that the expansion of the Hispanic population placed new demands upon the larger community, particularly in relation to the need for bilingual educational, law enforcement, and legal, medical, and social services. Much of the white community responded positively to these circumstances; some church and other organizations extended assistance and services to needy families. Not all of this transpired, however, without creating antagonisms fueled by stereotypes and misunderstandings.

Even as the unemployment rate in northwest Arkansas fell below the national average and economic prosperity reigned, the population growth of Little Rock and a few smaller cities accelerated. Stimulating this growth was the development of new economic enterprises in banking and finance, information technology, communications, and medical technology. Although Arkansas would experience no Sunbelt phenomenon similar to that occurring in Florida, Texas, and California, several Arkansas entrepreneurs with a central Arkansas focus moved into the service sector—if not the high-tech economy—and signaled their ability to appreciate the prospects of the developing service economy. One individual, Witt Stephens, parlayed a job as a bond salesman into his own investment company, Stephens, Inc., and leveraged the new wealth he acquired into the creation of a number of financial and business interests that played key roles in the economic transformation of the state. These interests included some more traditional enterprises like utilities, agriculture, banking, and retail merchandising, but they also included trading in commodities. In fact, at one point Stephens, Inc., was the largest commodities trader operating outside of Wall Street.

Other companies moving into the new service sector in central Arkansas included Acxiom, Alltel Corporation, and Dillard's Department Stores. Acxiom, founded in 1969 by Charles D. Ward of Conway, was originally called Demographics. Specializing in data information that it sold to a variety of companies to assist them in direct marketing their products, it established a headquarters in Little Rock and opened offices in several cities around the globe. Although Alltel began as a small firm in 1943 selling telephone poles and cables for television stations, it merged with Mid-Continent Telephone Company in 1983 and moved into wireless phone services. While it relocated its headquarters to Ohio, Alltel maintained a regional office in Little Rock and became a major player in central Arkansas's economy. Even after the company sold to Verizon Wireless in 2008, it remained an important force in the state. Dillard's Inc., the brainchild of William Thomas Dillard, began modestly in Nashville, Arkansas, with one small store and eventually became one of the largest retail clothing and home-furnishing operations in the country. Little Rock became its headquarters in the 1960s and the company expanded rapidly in the 1970s and 1980s. As Little Rock grew in relation to the successes of enterprises like these, its suburbs expanded rapidly, suburbs settled by upwardly mobile and prosperous white-collar workers who had little connection to the rural economy that had once dominated both economically and politically within the state.

Civil Rights in Arkansas

Little Rock authorities developed new strategies to delay integration in the last four decades of the twentieth century. Ben Johnson provides a particularly astute assessment in the *Arkansas Historical Quarterly* of the desegregation crisis, which includes an analysis of what transpired in the 1960s to ensure that only token integration took place. Part of the segregationist strategy hinged on residential segregation practices dating back to the years immediately preceding the *Brown* decision. Placing it in the context of the demographic revolution accompanying and following World War II, Johnson argues that as whites and blacks from rural Arkansas moved into Little Rock, they crowded up against each other in contiguous neighborhoods with some mixed neighborhoods developing. The city went so far in 1952 as to raze a black lower- and middle-class neighborhood as part of an effort to move the city's black population to eastern districts of Little Rock where they built a public housing subdivision. They had used funds provided by the federal government to build the Joseph A. Booker subdivision near Granite Mountain in east Little Rock. The intent of the small group of liberal whites who promoted a bond issue to match the federal funds was to provide better housing for the city's poor black population and some, like Adolphine Terry, a founder of the Women's Emergency Council, were dismayed by how the funds were used to serve quite another purpose. A housing authority employee, B. Finley Vinson, testified many years later that the black subdivision was "a device to maintain segregation of races . . . There was no bones made about it." For African Americans in the lower- and middle-class neighborhood destroyed in the process, it was a disaster.

Although residential segregation predated the *Brown* decision, the practice continued and played a crucial role in the 1960s in the effort to forestall integration. The city continued to use urban renewal funds to raze black neighborhoods. The Little Rock Housing Authority, real estate operators, and mortgage lenders conspired to make certain that blacks did not purchase homes in certain white neighborhoods. As Johnson points out, one broker admitted to federal authorities that the phrase "Anyone Can Buy" was a signal to black purchasers that their applications would be welcome. If no such phrase accompanied an advertisement promoting the sale of a house, African Americans understood that their offers would not be entertained. At one point, a black realtor was almost denied his real estate license for having sold a home to a black family in a sacrosanct white neighborhood. According to Ben Johnson, he had violated a regulation of the Arkansas Real Estate Commission that "a realtor should never be instrumental in introducing into a neighborhood a character of property or occupancy, members of any race or nationality, or any individuals whose presence will clearly be detrimental to property values in that neighborhood."

The city's white leadership was largely satisfied with the progress they were making in imposing further residential segregation and in maintaining certain schools in Little Rock as white enclaves. A key component of their efforts was a "pupil assignment" scheme adopted by the legislature in 1959. Modeled after an Alabama law, it gave the school board authority to decide pupil placement on a case-by-case basis. By this means, the board successfully discouraged black children from moving into white schools. Black families were far from sanguine about the situation. In September 1964 Roosevelt and Delores Clark filed suit in federal court when their four children were denied admittance to an all-white school and directed instead to a black school. Represented by black activist attorney John Walker, who was affiliated with the NAACP Legal Defense Fund, they intended to test the constitutionality of the pupil placement law. The court eventually ruled in favor of Walker's clients in *Clark v. Board of Education of the Little Rock School District*, but Little Rock authorities knew it was vulnerable on the issue of pupil placement and dropped its use. They substituted the "freedom of choice" scheme, another way that southern cities had slowed or stopped integration. This enabled the city to use a loaded term—freedom—to hide behind the idea that everyone was free to choose, ignoring the fact that the city's long-term efforts at imposing residential segregation made integration more difficult. In fact, residential segregation imposed very real and significant constraints on African Americans who might want to send their children to the better-funded white schools. Public transit was both uneven and insufficient, and schools did not provide adequate transportation for students across school lines.

In 1966, the composition of the Little Rock School Board changed in a way that made it more receptive to pressure from black activists like John Walker and from the state's Department of Health, Education and Welfare. Both Walker and the agency were concerned about the trend toward white flight and how that might make it difficult for the city to comply with desegregation orders. It was in that year that Thomas E. Patterson became the first black member of the board; it was also in 1966 that Winslow Drummond, a member of a progressive law firm headed by former governor Sidney McMath and Judge Henry Woods, was elected to the board. The school board commissioned a group of experts to analyze the situation in Little Rock and make specific recommendations to enable it to comply with desegregation orders and develop long-range plans. The University of Oregon's Bureau of Educational Research received the contract to pursue the study and issued a report in 1967 that contained a number of suggestions. Known as the Oregon Report, it would become controversial and was eventually repudiated.

The Oregon Report's recommendation that the district abandon the neighborhood school concept and, instead, conceive of itself as a single educational park proved to become its Achilles' heel. It provided those opposed to segregation a popular cause around which to rally a wide spectrum of the white population. Some in the black community also feared a move that would undermine their neighborhoods, but it was white opposition organized around a group called the "Education First Committee" that raised a storm of protest, sometimes laden with subtle and not-so-subtle racist rhetoric. Although the recommendations of the Oregon Report had been thoroughly repudiated by the time of the school board elections in 1967, it became an issue around which the segregationists rallied. They were able to elect two outspoken opponents to replace two moderate members of the board. Even a more modest plan put forward by Superintendent Floyd Parson (known as the Parson Plan), which would have required only a slight increase in busing within the district, was labeled as a danger to neighborhood schools, and in 1968 two more moderate members of the board were replaced. As Gene Vinzant argues, "the change from 1966 to 1968 in the make-up of the Little Rock School Board and its attitude toward desegregation was dramatic." According to Vinzant, "The move toward conservatism in Little Rock reflected a national mood of stiffening white resistance to 'forced integration.' Frustrated by the willingness of the white majority to make even modest steps in the direction of integration, black activists felt they had no alternative but to turn once again to the federal courts."

In 1968, the Supreme Court's ruling in *Green v. County School Board* provided an opportunity for black activists and others who supported integration to fight back. The *Green* decision made school districts indisputably responsible for ensuring that integration took place. Although the case had not arisen in Arkansas but in eastern Virginia, its applicability to the Arkansas situation was unmistakable. Declaring the "freedom of choice" plan inadequate as a means of achieving integration, the court indicated that school districts had to eliminate all vestiges of segregation, "root and branch," a far cry from the "all deliberate speed" associated with the *Brown* decision. School boards across the South had been operating under the assumption that they merely had to refrain from deliberately and openly preventing integration. Having imposed residential segregation, they had unwittingly set the stage for the next great drama, one that would unfold in the 1970s, involving the busing of children, a phenomenon that became politically loaded and expensive. The segregationist would lose no time, and probably little sleep, in manipulating the issue of busing to further their cause.

The crucial Supreme Court decision in 1971, *Swann v. Mecklenburg Board of Education*, sanctioned busing to accomplish integration, led to widespread reaction across the nation. In Arkansas, as elsewhere, it furthered a trend begun a decade earlier: the creation of segregated private schools. Because such schools were not funded by the state, they were not subject to federal rulings. The first school created in Little Rock in the aftermath of the *Swann* decision, Pulaski Academy (1971), was located in west Little Rock. Although one of the principle founders, William F. Rector, announced that children of all races would be welcome to apply, he used a coded reference signaling that black children would find a less-than-welcoming atmosphere. Historian Ben Johnson quotes him as saying, "I even hope we'll be allowed to play 'Dixie' if we want to without having a riot about it." By that point in time, the playing of "Dixie" had been embraced by white supremacists and become a symbol of their cause. Black students understood what the song was meant to acknowledge, and its use in schools was intended to remind both black and white children of white supremacy ideology. Historian Gene Vinzant cites some telling figures: of the 878 students in Pulaski Academy in 1979, only one was black; and 97 percent of those in all the private academies combined were white. "When busing began in 1971, the 13,222 white students in the Little Rock School District had greatly outnumbered the estimated 5,400 whites in the county's private schools. By 1984, however, the number of white students in the county's private schools (8,436) significantly exceeded the number of white students in the Little Rock School District (5,265)." The statistics for the city's public schools are also telling. In 1971, the Little Rock School District was 74 percent white. By 1984, whites constituted only 30 percent of the population. Meanwhile, 78 percent of the students in the Pulaski County Special School District were white. One strategy promoted by the Little Rock School District was to implement interdistrict desegregation—between the districts in Little Rock, North Little Rock, and Pulaski County. Federal district judge Henry Woods ruled in favor of the Little Rock School District's position, the Eighth Circuit Court of Appeals agreed, but a series of delaying tactics torpedoed the efforts to implement effectively interdistrict integration.

The drama unfolding in central Arkansas sometimes obscures equally important episodes of the civil rights movement occurring elsewhere in the state. In fact, the events that transpired in Little Rock in the late 1950s resulted in the postponement of integration in other towns in Arkansas. School boards in towns like Hot Springs, which had integration plans in place at the time of the Central High crisis, decided to delay. Town leaders there were concerned as much by the threat of violence as they were by the prospect of integration. As a tourist town dependent upon a good reputation for its continued prosperity, businesspersons were fearful of the violent scenes that had occurred in Little Rock. By 1962, however, town leaders determined to introduce gradual integration and quietly implemented a plan that brought them into compliance with the *Brown* decision. Compliance, however, meant

Swann v. Mecklenburg Board of Education: A US Supreme Court decision rendered in 1971 that sanctioned the use of busing to achieve integration.

merely that they had integrated on a token basis only. Most black children continued to attend the underfunded black schools.

While Hot Springs was approaching the process of integration slowly and quietly, encountering little opposition, other towns, particularly those with heavy black populations like Earle, Arkansas, in Crittenden County, delayed until 1970 and then approached desegregation so heavy handedly that ugly confrontations occurred. No one familiar with the town's history would have been surprised that it was destined for such notoriety. During Reconstruction, it had been a center of Ku Klux Klan activity and as late as the mid-1930s it became infamous for a particularly egregious case of peonage. Using a cotton picker's strike as justification, the town marshal, Paul Peacher, arrested thirteen black men on vagrancy charges and, conspiring with the town's mayor, had them remanded to him to work off their fines. This blatant violation against peonage laws was brought to the attention of Justice Department officials, and Peacher was subsequently convicted on federal peonage charges. However, his two-year jail sentence was suspended and landowners who saw nothing wrong with his actions paid his $3,500 fine.

By 1970, the Peacher case was long forgotten and, in any case, the white power structure had learned only that the consequences of defying federal law were relatively mild. Local white authorities were determined to shape court-ordered desegregation to their liking. Nearly 80 percent of the population was African American, however, and years of black activism and their collective sense of new possibilities energized African Americans, particularly the young among them. In retrospect, the two sides were headed for a showdown. When the white school board closed the black schools and summarily fired or demoted most of the black teachers, they exhibited their traditional sense of power and authority. When they relegated the black students to separate classrooms, they violated the desegregation plan they had submitted to the Arkansas Department of Health, Education and Welfare, but that agency refused to intervene when the facts were reported to them. School authorities were revealing not only their arrogance but also their ignorance of the mood and ambitions of black youths, setting in motion forces they could not control. According to historian Michael Honey, who was then covering the story for the *Southern Patriot*, "the board's desegregation plan had resulted in the ouster of all blacks in leadership positions in the schools, and the rooting out of all symbols of black pride or heritage." In reaction, black students staged a "walk-out" on Labor Day (not a holiday in Arkansas then), and what followed was a lesson in civil disobedience on the one side, and on the other side, an example of a violent reaction reminiscent of Bull Conner's vicious tactics in Birmingham, Alabama, seven years earlier.

The day following the walkout, groups of helmeted men arrested thirty black students for "parading without a license." During a spontaneous prayer pilgrimage that evening, "about 150 people walked toward City Hall, but before they arrived they were confronted by 15 to 20 units of state troopers, city and county police, and a mob of whites. Without warning, police opened fire on the crowd. Townspeople and police charged into the fleeing marchers with clubs and tire chains, beating men, women and children to the ground." White authorities targeted leaders of the black community in subsequent arrests, including the Reverend Ezra Greer, a founder of the Crittenden County Improvement Association. The Reverend Greer and his wife were both beaten and jailed by police. In the weeks that followed this encounter, black students who refused to return to the classroom were harassed and their parents fired from their jobs and evicted from plantations. White officials were determined to minimize their compliance with federal mandates, and officials in Arkansas allowed them to carry on with business as usual.

The desegregation of schools in the state was only one front in the African American struggle in Arkansas. In 1962, the Student Nonviolent Coordinating Committee (SNCC) began organizing activities in the state, and their efforts extended well beyond integration of public education and focused instead on public facilities like eating establishments and hospitals. It also took issue with continuing impediments to black voting. SNCC, founded in 1960 by black and white college students at Howard University in Washington, DC, soon identified four southern states as needing special attention. Arkansas was one of them. After some organizing forays into the state in 1962, SNCC formerly launched its "Arkansas Project" in early 1963, and black students at Philander Smith College in Little Rock and at AM&N in Pine Bluff (now the University of Arkansas at Pine Bluff) became actively involved. The first state headquarters was located in Pine Bluff, and a great deal of activity was centered in delta towns. Its initial programs focused on integrating public facilities such as restaurants. Philander Smith students, for example, wrote "An Appeal to the Negroes of Little Rock," calling on them to boycott stores on Main Street, such as Woolworths, which refused to serve African Americans at its lunch counter. The Little Rock Chapter of the National Council of Negro Women declared support for the boycott and for a subsequent sit-in demonstration at Woolworths. In the Delta, the Arkansas Project set up field offices in three towns, Helena, Pine Bluff, and Forrest City, each town having responsibility for a three- or four-county area within its vicinity. SNCC workers in those towns opened "freedom centers," where local blacks could gather and discuss the specific problems that concerned

Student Nonviolent Coordinating Committee: An organization founded by black students at Howard University in Washington, DC, in 1960. In 1962, they sent organizers into Arkansas to promote integration of public facilities and, eventually, voting rights.

them. They offered tutoring programs in black history, English, and math, but they also schooled African Americans in how to attempt to integrate a public facility or to register to vote. The white response was predictable. Local law enforcement officers harassed and sometimes beat SNCC workers, often arresting them on trumped-up charges.

February 1965 was a particularly active month for SNCC workers in Pine Bluff, and their activities captured considerable attention. Comedian Dick Gregory, along with William Hansen, a white SNCC field secretary who founded the Arkansas Project, were sentenced to six months in jail and fined five hundred dollars for attempting to integrate a segregated truck stop, a decision they later successfully appealed. Shots were fired at Reverend Benjamin Grinnage, a black SNCC worker (who later became the director of the Arkansas Project), while he was demonstrating at a local eating establishment. Thirty-nine blacks were arrested during that demonstration. Crowds of whites described by reporters as "professional segregationists" taunted black demonstrators at another eating establishment in Pine Bluff. Authorities arrested fifteen blacks and a state trooper roughed up SNCC worker James Jones, who as a student at AM&N College, had joined SNCC in 1963. Just two years later Jones would have another very personal confrontation. When his wife went into labor in December 1965, the Jefferson County Hospital denied her admission to the better-equipped white section of Jefferson County Hospital.

Although these incidents were connected to attempts to integrate public facilities, feelings ran just as high over black efforts to vote. For Faubus and other southern politicians, the voting rights issue was particularly problematic. The governor's realization of the potential power of the black vote likely accounted for his decision to begin distancing himself from the extreme segregationists. Yet Faubus was distinctly uncomfortable with SNCC's activities in the Delta, in part because his white constituents and their state legislators felt particularly threatened. Given the growing likelihood of blacks recapturing the right to vote and the demographics of the Delta, the loss of white political control on the local level there was inevitable.

As the black struggle to secure voting rights appeared destined to succeed, even Faubus, who began to court the black vote, continued to appeal to white segregations. In 1965, he called William Hansen a "professional agitator," and had SNCC activities under the surveillance of the state police. SNCC workers were undaunted. From the earliest days of SNCC's Arkansas Project, voting rights were a major focus. In the fall of 1963, for example, black high school students in Pine Bluff served as SNCC volunteers and canvassed door-to-door, encouraging blacks to pay their poll taxes and register to vote. Operating from a "Freedom House," SNCC workers distributed poll tax books to black bars, restaurants, barbershops, and private homes throughout

Pine Bluff. They sent volunteers to the downtown section on Friday nights and Saturdays, which were times when they were typically crowded with shoppers, and secured scores of voters that way. Other blacks were offered an opportunity to pay their poll taxes at churches on Sunday morning. By election day, they had registered 2,876 black voters.

The Civil Rights Act of 1964 and the Voting Rights Act of 1965 followed rather than preceded the early efforts of SNCC in Arkansas and elsewhere, and these acts by Congress have to be understood in that context. The work of SNCC personnel and community volunteers drove the civil rights movement within the state and in the South as a whole and helped put pressure on Congress to end segregation and disfranchisement. However, white society in eastern Arkansas remained dedicated to racial subordination. Most delta schools finally integrated only after threats of court orders, court orders made more potent by the Civil Rights Act of 1964, which called for the withdrawal of federal funds to schools defying integration. Some delta schools refused to integrate until forced by court order and some of them only integrated in the early 1970s. Efforts to integrate public facilities, such as hospitals, were also augmented by the 1964 act, which made it illegal for businesses engaged in interstate trade to refuse to serve blacks and denied federal funds to hospitals that failed to integrate. James Jones, the SNCC worker whose wife had been denied treatment in the white section of Jefferson County Hospital, filed a complaint on that basis shortly after the incident.

By the time Congress passed the Civil Rights Act of 1965, Orval Faubus had made his peace with integration and formed alliances with some black leaders. When he decided not to run for reelection in 1966, the Democratic Party made the mistake of selecting rabid race-baiter Jim Johnson to run in his place. Winthrop Rockefeller, who had broken with Faubus and run unsuccessfully against him in 1964, elected to run again in 1966 on the Republican ticket. Arkansas voters proved that they were not willing to return to the racial extremism that marked the Central High crisis, and elected Rockefeller. Significant numbers of white Democrats crossed party lines to elect Arkansas's first Republican governor since Reconstruction. Rockefeller's governorship did not signal a new era in race relations, however. Segregationist sentiment continued to smolder, and the state legislature and Little Rock officials continued to erect barriers to integration. It could be argued that the rabid racism revealed during the Central High crisis in 1957 had merely gone underground. Nevertheless, Arkansas voters, in choosing Rockefeller, were indicating their refusal to return to the extremism of the Faubus years. Although Rockefeller would be spectacularly unsuccessful in some of the economic and education measures he promulgated, he fashioned a new progressive agenda that later Democratic governors adapted and developed.

The New Arkansas Women

An examination of the failure of the Equal Rights Amendment (ERA) in the state reveals the profound conservatism of much of the population. By the early 1970s a challenge to women's liberation was being mounted by those who saw it as endangering the family. A century earlier, the drive for women's suffrage had been a major preoccupation of women activists, but women had been voting since 1920, and despite the rhetoric of those who fought for women's right to vote, they cast their ballots much like men. The notion that enfranchised women, with their special "female" sensibilities and instincts, would transform politics was not borne out. By the end of the century, the "exceptionality" of female voters had little currency, although it was clear that electing women to office did in some cases make a difference where women's issues were concerned.

Equal Rights Amendment: An amendment meant to ensure that women had equal rights with men that was passed by Congress in 1972 but that ultimately failed to secure ratification by the states.

Yet there were relatively few women elected to high office—elsewhere or in Arkansas—despite the fact that women continued to be active politically through Democratic and Republican women's organizations and through the League of Women Voters. By the early 1970s, the National Organization of Women (NOW), which had a more activist agenda, was attracting members in Arkansas. The decisive moment came in 1972, however, when Congress acted on two fronts. It passed Title IX, a federal regulation prohibiting sex discrimination in any school receiving federal funds, and it referred an Equal Rights Amendment to the states.

Title IX was inspired by the recognition that over the course of the twentieth century women had become a permanent fixture in the workplace and that great disparities in occupational status and in income existed between male and female workers. By 1974, almost 50 percent of all women between the ages of eighteen and sixty-four were employed outside the home, and women headed almost one-sixth of America's families. Most of them were working because they were single, widowed, divorced, separated, or deserted, or married to men who earned less than five thousand dollars a year. Of those who headed their own households, the majority of them were living at poverty or subpoverty levels. Title IX was predicated on the assumption that the problem had to be addressed at the level at which women were educated. To implement Title IX, President Gerald Ford created a Commission on the Status of Women, and soon governors throughout the country appointed similar state women's commissions. Like his counterparts elsewhere, Governor Dale Bumpers created such a state commission, and commission members took upon themselves the task of ascertaining to what extent sex discrimination existed in the state's public schools and colleges. They discovered disparities in varsity sports and sex-stereotyped curriculum offerings and requirements (such as home economics for girls and shop for boys). They attributed the fact that most school administrators were male while most public schoolteachers were female to the point of view that males should be awarded administrative positions because they had families to support, ignoring the fact that many women headed their own households or that their income was as essential to the family economy as was the husband's.

A 1978 study by the Scientific Manpower Commission, a private, non-profit organization formed by major scientific societies to investigate employment trends and problems common to the sciences, confirmed what many commission members were coming to understand. The problem of disparities in income was not determined solely by the kind of employment that women undertook. Regardless of occupational category, women earned less than their male counterparts did. In fact, males without high school diplomas made more money than women with college degrees, suggesting that eliminating obstacles to higher education for women was not enough. The study concluded that although a greater number of women were entering typically male professions (becoming engineers, doctors, dentists, and so on), "women's salaries [were] lower than those of men with comparable training and experience at every age, every degree level, in every field and with every type of employer." Already by 1978, however, signs of change were on the horizon. Beginning women engineers and chemists were securing higher salaries than male counterparts at the same level precisely because there so few women in those fields, and companies and government agencies were eager to avoid violating affirmative action guidelines.

Meanwhile, the Women's Commissions broadened their agenda to include support for the Equal Rights Amendment. Within three years of its passage, thirty-five states quickly ratified the amendment, just three short of the necessary three-fourths to make it a part of the Constitution. Of the fifteen states that had not ratified it, ten were southern states: Alabama, Florida, Georgia, Louisiana, Mississippi, Missouri, North Carolina, South Carolina, Virginia, and Arkansas. Even as Women's Commission members made ratification a major part of their agenda, the opposition began to organize against it, and they operated on two fronts. First, they worked to convince legislators in states where the measure had barely passed to "rescind" their approval, something that involved those states and Congress in a bitter debate. Second, conservatives worked furiously to convince legislators in states that had not yet voted on ratification to reject it. By 1976, Arkansas was a battleground state, and Phyllis Schlafly, a conservative radio commentator and author, came to Arkansas to debate the issue with Diane Kincaid (later

Diane Blair), a political scientist at the University of Arkansas and chair of the first Governor's Commission on the Status of Women. The highly publicized debate took place in the Capitol Building on Valentine's Day (1975). The galleries were so crowded that nearly two hundred spectators, most of them women, sat on the floor or in chairs on the second-floor rotunda. Women who opposed the amendment waved banners against it while the women who supported it wore pro-ERA buttons.

Governor's Commission on the Status of Women: A commission created to evaluate the status of women in Arkansas.

The arguments made by both Schlafly and Kincaid were familiar to most of those who attended the event. Opponents to the ERA believed that many of the problems in modern society were due to the erosion of the traditional family structure, and they blamed the emancipation of women for the rising divorce rate, the increase in juvenile delinquency, and a decline in patriotism as reflected by anti–Vietnam War protests. Some believed that the Bible sanctioned the subordination of women to their husbands and that the decline in church membership was owing to feminism. Other opponents argued that a constitutional amendment was unnecessary, that the Fourteenth Amendment was protection enough, and that additional existing laws explicitly protected women against sex discrimination in employment and other areas. Some raised fears that the ERA would eliminate some protections for married women and suggested that women would be forced into the workplace whether they wished to work or not. A heated debate arose over whether women would be required to register for the draft and fight alongside men in the trenches in case of war.

Proponents of the ERA rejected the argument that the emancipation of women was responsible for an erosion of the traditional family structure. They argued that the economy of the late twentieth century required married women to contribute to the family income and those women deserved to receive "equal pay for equal work." They suggested that the Fourteenth Amendment did not provide enough protection for women and that since existing laws explicitly protecting the rights of women were statutory, they were subject to revision or elimination, and thus provided no permanent guarantee, at least not in the way that a constitutional amendment would. As to eliminating certain protections that women enjoyed, proponents of the ERA argued that laws that conferred a specific benefit to women would be extended to men and those laws that no longer benefited women were the only ones that would be dispensed with. They denied that women would be required to work, and while they admitted that women would probably have to register for the draft, they asserted that women would not qualify physically for combat (the latter was something later feminists would reject).

Diane Kincaid (Blair) debating Phyllis Schlafly. *From* Arkansas Gazette, *February 15, 1975.*

Schlafly and Kincaid covered most of these arguments in their debate, and those who heard them claimed that both made eloquent speeches, but legislators would not allow the issue to be reported out of committee. However, the conservatives were not satisfied with the apparent victory. In 1977, a national conservative group, the Eagle Forum, created an Arkansas adjunct named FLAG (family, life, America, God) to fight ratification of the ERA by the state legislature. In 1978, as the amendment was being considered in the House State Agencies Committee, Governor Bill Clinton called for the legislature to bring the amendment to a vote. Reminiscent of Governor Brough standing with his wife on the suffrage issue sixty years earlier, Clinton "met briefly with many of the ERA opponents in the governor's conference room and defended his support for the amendment. With his wife, Hillary Rodham, standing next to him, he said he regretted that the issue had become so divisive and resented the 'labeling' of ERA supporters as being against family life and religious values." Hillary Rodham, who adopted her husband's surname in 1983, had served with Diane Kincaid on the first Women's Commission. The House State Agencies Committee subsequently voted 14 to 4 against bringing the measure to the floor of the legislature. Ultimately, an insufficient number of states approved the measure and the ERA died on the vine.

The success of the opponents of the ERA in linking it with a decline in family values and a growing lack of respect for God and country largely accounted for its failure in Arkansas and in most other southern states. Arkansas legislators had been able to see beyond arguments made against the extension of suffrage to women sixty years earlier, but the opposition to the ERA was much better organized in the 1970s. The feminism of the 1970s was connected in the minds of many to the compendium of "causes" that emerged in the 1960s: agitation against the Vietnam War, the emergence of a more militant civil rights movement, the excesses of the hippie movement, and the emergence of a politically awakened religious right. Added to that was the emergence of militant feminists who were associated with lesbianism or at least with antimale bias. Although few of the feminists in Arkansas had any connection to the causes of the 1960s, and most of them had little tolerance for radical feminism, their opponents were able to capitalize on the perception that they and the amendment they fought for were a part of the disorder that seemed to threaten home and family.

New Political Economy

Although the ERA debate reflected the conservatism of the Arkansas electorate, the voters continued to elect Democrats to office far longer than voters in other southern states where a viable Republican Party began to emerge. This was delayed in Arkansas until the 1990s because of the continuing presence of moderate Democrats capable of negotiating a continuance of the fragile alliance between the Democratic Party and the essentially conservative Arkansas electorate. Ultimately, however, rural Arkansas would come to find the Republican social agenda more persuasive than that of the state's

Democratic Party, a party growing more sympathetic to women's issues and transformed by the presence of a large number of newly enfranchised black voters. As outspoken opposition to abortion rights took shape in the rest of the nation, for example, it also became a factor in the disenchantment of the rural electorate with the Democratic Party in Arkansas. Although few state legislators of either party would venture a pro-choice opinion, the polarization of the two national parties on that issue made it easier for Republican candidates for Congress, for governor and, ultimately, for senator, to score points on the issue and capture a significant number of Arkansas voters. Meanwhile, black voters first showed their power by helping elect Republican Winthrop Rockefeller in 1966, but they proved loyal only to the man, not his party. Once Rockefeller was out of the picture and moderate Democrats arrived on the scene, blacks turned to them and, incidentally, helped transform the Democratic Party into something that many of the state's white rural voters found increasingly unattractive.

As political scientists Diane Blair and Jay Barth have argued, three successive Democratic governors helped maintain the Democratic Party in Arkansas: Dale Leon Bumpers, David Hampton Pryor, and William "Bill" Jefferson Clinton. Characterizing them as the "big three," Blair and Barth see them as moderate and progressive rather than truly liberal in orientation, and this helped make them palatable to both the increasingly Republican-leaning suburban voters and the socially conservative rural electorate. The marriage of the religious right and the Republican Party played a factor in reshaping the party of Lincoln to incorporate both those with racist leanings and Christian conservative elements in their political discourse. This newly emerging force on the Republican right had little currency in Arkansas for a while and most voters were attracted by the personalities and policies of the "big three." While they called for improvements in education and health services, these governors also practiced fiscal restraint and promoted policies designed to maximize efficiency and economy. Given the troubling economy nationwide during this period, voters showed their appreciation for their attention to both the needs of the state's citizens and the necessity of closely managing the state's finances. Although the "big three" concept has considerable merit, certain historical forces also shaped the programs and policies outlined by Bumpers, Pryor, and Clinton. Arkansas's place in the national economy as a second-tier "Sunbelt" South state, limited the degree of economic growth in the state in the 1970s and 1980s. Yet its integration into the national economy made it more vulnerable to larger economic forces over which the state had little control. If, as historians of the Sunbelt South argue, the conservatism of these areas was tied to the growth of suburbs peopled by upwardly mobile young professionals or by Republican-leaning retirees,

Arkansas was underachieving. The three Democratic governors steered a course through a number of conflicting demands and opportunities.

The continuity of Democratic administrations was interrupted briefly by the election of Republican Frank White in 1980. Like most twentieth-century governors of the state, Clinton had found it necessary during his first term to confront a seemingly intractable problem, the state's road and highway system, and, like some of his predecessors, he was to learn that in sponsoring measures to finance road building and repair, he would incur serious political liability. With the support of the trucking industry and the Highway Commission, who lobbied intensively for his program, he convinced the legislature to enact a series of fee increases, principally in title transfer and vehicle registration fees, which significantly raised revenue for highway construction and repair. Clinton would discover in 1980 when running for reelection just how much the fee increases angered Arkansas voters.

The anger of the electorate over the increase in license tags was only a part of the problem confronting Clinton in the 1980 election. A serious economic recession continued to plague the nation and the state, a series of natural disasters darkened the mood further, and then there was the Cuban refugee fiasco. When President Jimmy Carter opened America's doors to refugees escaping Cuba in the spring of 1980, he inadvertently precipitated a political liability for Governor Clinton. Carter ordered some of the Cuban refugees sent to Fort Chaffee near Fort Smith, but when they attempted to leave the facility and were turned back into the confines of the fort, two or three thousand of them rioted. Some Arkansas pundits suggested that the close relationship between Carter and Clinton was responsible for situating the refugees in Arkansas, and the governor's leadership was questioned. In fact, the relationship between Clinton and Carter had cooled, but that factor was not fully appreciated by most Arkansas voters. In any case, his Republican opponent in the fall 1980 elections used the refrain "car tags and Cubans" to defeat Clinton.

The election of the second Republican of the twentieth century to the governor's office coincided with Ronald Reagan's election to the presidency, and Frank White happened to have much more in common with Reagan than he did with Arkansas's previous Republican governor, Winthrop Rockefeller. Reagan, particularly, owed his election to the emergence of a coalition of old and new conservatives. As historian Eric Foner suggests, this coalition consisted of "Sunbelt suburbanites and working-class ethnics; anti-government crusaders and advocates of a more aggressive foreign policy; libertarians who believed in freeing the individual from restraint and the Christian Right, which sought to restore what they considered traditional moral values." Although Reagan proved much more adept at appealing to this diverse con-

Frank White "Banana" cartoon, George Fisher, *Comic Relief.* This cartoon originally appeared in the *Arkansas Gazette,* May 3, 1981.

stituency than did Frank White, White embraced Reagan's "trickle down" economic theory. Although it turns out that the nation's wealthiest citizens and corporations failed to deliver on this promise, using their newfound wealth to purchase luxuries and generating few new jobs, the idea of low taxes, always popular in Arkansas, had resonance country wide and became firmly planted in the nation's political economy.

Frank White's tenure in the governor's office coincided with another severe economic recession, one influenced by Reagan's embrace of supply side (trickle-down) economics but also by yet another international incident, this time a US-imposed embargo on the sale of wheat to the Soviet Union after it invaded Afghanistan. However, this recession was much shorter lived and was quickly followed by a long period of economic expansion, an expansion accompanied by a relaxation of governmental regulations that had some significant consequences. "By the 1990s the richest 1 percent of Americans owned 40 percent of the nation's wealth, twice their share twenty years earlier."

The two issues that generated the greatest controversy during Frank White's administration were creation science and utility regulation. The issue over creation science emerged when certain legislators introduced a bill, which became Act 590, to require the teaching of creation science along with evolution in the state's schools. Although he did not originate it, White promised to sign it if it passed, and when he did so, a firestorm of criticism was leveled against him. The controversy ended after the law was overturned by the federal district court and the state declined to appeal the decision. Frank

White's long association with the utility companies was clearly a factor in the second controversy to rock his administration. He wasted no time pursuing the interests of the utility industry, firing three leaders of the Arkansas Energy Department on inauguration day. He later abolished the Energy Department, combining it with the Arkansas Industrial Development Commission, thus potentially crippling utility regulation. He also allowed Arkansas Power and Light (AP&L) executives to meet with potential appointees to the Public Service Commission, which made it appear he was giving them a veto power over such appointments. When AP&L instituted a staggering $104 million rate increase, many believed that the governor had permitted it. The controversies accompanying White's administration greatly weakened him, but perhaps more fundamental to his defeat in 1982 was his failure to build a coalition capable of maintaining his political life. His support of a small group of powerful entities in the state could not long sustain him in elective office. Clinton was to serve in office from the time he defeated White in 1982 until his election to the presidency a decade later, and maintained the "big three" paradigm of relatively moderate democrats in the governor's post.

Cultural Renaissance

Arkansas has struggled with a self-image issue for generations but certain events in the 1980s and early 1990s led to a cultural renaissance. The process began in 1982 with Tom Dillard, who was then director of the Department of Arkansas Natural and Cultural Heritage (now the Department of Arkansas Heritage). An energetic and dynamic leader, Dillard joined a cohort of like-minded individuals who sought to promote historic preservation and history education. The project was given new life in 1986 during the state's sesquicentennial when the legislature provided a $400,000 grant. Many communities around the state participated by taking part in town and country celebrations, and the *Arkansas Democrat* published sketches of 150 prominent Arkansans after the sesquicentennial commission created a "Project Pride" initiative. Arkansas Power and Light Company commissioned a song, "Arkansas You Run Deep in Me" and even the United States Postal Service contributed by authorizing a commemorative stamp featuring the Old State House in Little Rock. While the publications of books on Arkansas history, culture, geography, and natural history had been greatly augmented by the creation of the University of Arkansas Press in 1982, the sesquicentennial commission inspired the county and local societies to create and publish their own histories. The renewed interest in Arkansas history led to the creation of the

Cultural renaissance in Arkansas: Refers to a resurgence of interest in the state's history and culture.

Arkansas History Education Coalition dedicated to reviving the teaching of the state's history in the Arkansas school system.

One particularly important cultural phenomenon that preoccupied certain state agencies and universities began a decade earlier and was reflected in the passage of federal laws while David Pryor was in the governor's office. In January 1975, President Gerald Ford signed into law the Indian Self Determination and Educational Assistance Acts, which acknowledged the right of Native Americans to self-determination and provided assistance for education. In 1978 the Indian Religious Freedom Act put an official end to the suppression of Native American religious practices. These acts did not directly impact many Native Americans in the state because most of Arkansas's Native American population had been removed in the antebellum period and were living in Oklahoma long before these acts were passed. However, subsequent legislation affected the way that Arkansas agencies and institutions dealt with artifacts recovered from archeological sites, particularly the American Graves Protection and Repatriation Act of 1990. As historian John Kirk observes, the act "permitted Indian tribes to reclaim artifacts and skeletal remains from museums and other federally funded Institutions." But as Jerome C. Rose, Thomas J. Green, and Victoria D. Green, point out, other results of the legislation included an increase in the inventory and analysis of skeletal remains curated in museums and other institutions, as well as improvements in the handling and storage of all human remains in those institutions. Perhaps most importantly, the act led to a great increase in collaboration among Indians, archeologists, and biological anthropologists concerning the excavation, study, and repatriation of not only skeletal remains but of all archeological materials. This collaboration has been especially fruitful in Arkansas. Virtually all archeological investigations include consultation, and often more extensive collaboration, between Indians and archeologists. Caddos, Osages, Quapaws, and Tunicas have repatriated many ancestral remains from state institutions. In some cases, skeletal remains and associated funerary goods have been reburied at specifically designated cemeteries in Arkansas; in other cases, repatriated artifacts that cannot be associated with skeletal remains have found new educational uses in tribal museums and cultural centers, or are available for scholarly research at Arkansas institutions that continue to curate these materials but now on behalf of the descendant communities.

The period between 1970 and 1992 was marked by a remarkable degree of change in Arkansas. By the early 1990s, in fact, the state was much more integrated into the national and international economy and thus subject to the vagaries of forces it was in no position to control. Although companies like Walmart placed Arkansas in the forefront of business innovation, and other enterprises in the state achieved success in the new service-oriented economy, Arkansas did not emerge as one of the Sunbelt states, but that proved to be a blessing in disguise. The next two decades would witness a number of significant challenges accompanying the globalization of the American economy, challenges that brought near ruin to many of the Sunbelt states. Arkansas's more diverse economy and conservative fiscal policy shielded it from some of the worst effects of the recession that struck in the early twenty-first century. The state also benefited by the discovery of natural gas reserves, but problems would soon emerge in connection with the "Fayetteville Shale," and state officials would find themselves facing some tough decisions involving how to balance the environmental and economic implications.

15 ╳ The Burden of Arkansas History, 1992–2012

A YEAR AFTER the US Supreme Court delivered the *Brown v. Board of Education* decision in 1954, C. Vann Woodward, an imminent southern historian and native-born Arkansan, published the *Burden of Southern History*, a book of essays that examined a number of vexing issues confronting the South. Echoing an argument he made in his *The Strange Career of Jim Crow,* published the same year, he ruminated over the implications of the South's segregated system. According to Woodward, segregation was a "state way" rather than a "folk way," originating after the Civil War when ex-Confederates sought to maintain the Democratic Party's power at the expense of African Americans and poor whites. Convinced that the marriage of white supremacy and the Democratic Party hamstrung both the southern Democratic Party and many of its citizens, Woodward believed that with legal barriers eliminated, the South would transform into an integrated society. His hopes and expectations faltered, however, as a violent struggle over integration erupted not only in the South but also in the North, and it became apparent that while many whites across the country clung tenaciously to the old status quo in race relations, many blacks embraced separatism in place of integration. This was as true in the North as it was in the South, an irony that hardly escaped Woodward's notice. Irony, in fact, was another theme that preoccupied Woodward in *The Burden of Southern History* and irony, as it turns out, had a special place in the history of Arkansas.

State way: Refers to a system of customs sanctioned or created by statute.

Folk way: Refers to the customs and practices of folk.

In later editions of *Burden,* Woodward made clear his disappointment with the failure of the *Brown* decision to bring about a fully integrated society. In Arkansas, like elsewhere in the South, state-based obstacles to integration remained in place—and new ones were erected—but a day of reckoning was approaching. After a decision by the Eighth Circuit Court of Appeals in 1985 citing the state's complicity in the continuation of segregation and after a Settlement Agreement reached by contending parties in 1989, Arkansas began to attempt to unravel the damage it had done. From the mid-1990s on, the state expended $50 to $70 million annually in this effort. Ironically,

Settlement Agreement: Refers to a compromise between the Little Rock School District, the North Little Rock School District, and the Pulaski County Special School District that outlined how to fund court-mandated integration.

the cost of this remedy outweighed the expense of the dual education system in place before the *Brown* decision.

By the early twenty-first century, while the state and its citizens grappled with its civil rights legacy, it also struggled with the vestiges of its colonial economy, another issue confronting the South that preoccupied Woodward. To some extent, the state's historic reliance on cheap farm labor, together with extractive industries that sent the profits of Arkansas-based enterprises to out-of-state entities, depended upon the impoverishment of African Americans and poor whites. This reflected the strength of the planter class, largely located along the eastern border fronting the Mississippi River. Bankers and merchants in Little Rock and other towns, who furnished and catered to these planters, played their role in perpetuating this system, but beginning in the New South era of the late nineteenth century, new generations of entrepreneurs and politicians began to speak a different language and focus on other forms of economic development. Remaining wedded to the principle of cheap labor and fully capitalist in their orientation, they hoped to industrialize Arkansas, but they realized few tangible results until after World War II when the plantation system itself began to mechanize and underwent a scientific revolution. Still, efforts to attract industry to Arkansas achieved only marginal success, largely because the state's poor infrastructure and poorly educated population failed to attract a large response from out-of-state manufacturers. The reliance on cheap labor, which involved the continuing impoverishment of a significant segment of the population, included a poorly educated population, which, in turn, undermined efforts to industrialize and, later, to attract knowledge-based industries. As the rest of the South began to embrace the new Sunbelt industries, Arkansas, still hamstrung by its infrastructure and educational inadequacies, failed to participate significantly.

Knowledge-based industry: An industry that relies on a highly skilled workforce to master the complexities of the science-based and technology-based world evolving in the late twentieth century.

By the early twenty-first century, however, a reversal of fortunes seemed to be on the horizon for Arkansas. Ironically, Arkansas, peculiarly insulated by its historic nemesis—the colonial (extractive) nature of its economy—was shielded from the worst of the economic recession facing the country, as knowledge-based industries took the brunt of the economic collapse. In this context, Arkansas positioned itself to step into the void left by failed enterprises elsewhere in the South and embrace the leaner and chastened knowledge-based economy.

Confronting the Education Dilemma

The civil rights movement remains an unfinished revolution in Arkansas as elsewhere. In central Arkansas, the focus of much of the state's attention, white flight to the suburbs and high enrollments of white students in a growing number of private schools undermined the state's efforts to accomplish the goals outlined by its 1989 Settlement Agreement. There were some successes, however. The creation of magnet schools had, according to Gene Vinzant, "apparently brought white flight almost to a standstill, especially at the elementary level. The magnet schools were particularly successful in keeping the enrollment near the target of 50 percent white and 50 percent black." The incentive schools, however, were overwhelmingly black, and the achievement gap between black and white students had not appreciably narrowed. The school district was still busing 14,000 students a day in 1997, but by 2007, as John Kirk puts it, the Little Rock School District went from "being a twenty-five-percent black minority district in 1957 . . . [to] . . . a twenty-four-percent white minority district in 2007. In effect there were no white students left to integrate." Although a number of schools in the district had become overwhelmingly black, the state, the school district, and many black officials favored "unitary status" as it relieved them from the burdensome requirements imposed by the court, requirements that most had come to believe were unworkable. This fact led federal judge Bill Wilson to rule in 2007 that the Little Rock School District was "unitary" (that is, no longer segregated), a ruling later ratified by the Eighth Circuit Court of Appeals.

Unitary status: A term applied to a ruling in the Little Rock desegregation case that characterized Little Rock School District as desegregated.

While the state expended from $50 to $70 million per year for well over a decade to comply with the desegregation orders in Little Rock, other school districts in Arkansas suffered from funding shortfalls. Some perceived a connection between the two but others took a different lesson. They recognized that the state only expended such enormous sums because it was forced to do so by the federal courts, and they likely understood that the money spent on attempting to achieve integration in Little Rock would not necessarily have been spread out across the state to improve education generally without a court order to do so. At issue was the state's school funding formula. Schools were typically funded in Arkansas by a combination of local, state, and federal dollars. Although the federal contribution was important, more significant—and more within Arkansas's control—was that contributed on the state and local level. On the local level, citizens voted a certain number of tax mills to be allocated for support of public education. On the state level, the contribution to each school district was predicated on the amount provided to those districts the previous year. But demographic changes within Arkansas had resulted in a built-in problem. The state was allocating to each school district the same amount it had disbursed the year before, regardless of whether the number of children in each district had changed. There was no mechanism in place to correct for changes in enrollment, and some growing districts objected to the funds allocated to shrinking districts. The catch phrase became "phantom students," and it had a powerful resonance with the public and, it turns out, with the courts.

In 1981 an important court case resulted when the Alma School District, along with ten others, filed suit against the State Department of Education alleging that Arkansas was not complying with the state constitution's guarantee of equal protection and "its requirement that the state provide a general, suitable, and efficient system of education." They cited the "phantom student" phenomenon and won at the lower court level (*Alma v. Dupree*) in 1981. The Arkansas Supreme Court upheld this decision in *Dupree v. Alma* in 1983.

***Dupree v. Alma*:** A case arising out of Alma, Arkansas, where the Arkansas Supreme Court ruled that the state's funding formula for public education was unconstitutional.

Governor Bill Clinton, who had recently been reelected to the governorship, was faced with the unenviable task of devising a plan to honor the court's ruling. He was either going to have to deprive some school districts of funds they desperately needed—the school districts shrinking the most were often already the poorest districts—or raise taxes to provide equal funds to all schools. He successfully pressed the state legislature to raise taxes in order to provide increased state funding to schools throughout Arkansas.

Although the increased funding appeared to address the issue of the funds allocated by the state, it was only a beginning. But a more fundamental problem existed. Given that schools were funded partially by local property taxes, considerable disparity continued to exist. In districts where property values were low, the amount collected might contribute only $1,000 to $2,000 per student. Meanwhile, districts with higher property values could generate $5,000 or more. To complicate matters, property taxes for schools were figured according to the millage rate assigned for the purpose. For example, local communities voted on the millage to be devoted to schools, but voters in some areas approved far less than 25 mills, a figure that came to be understood as the minimum amount necessary to generate sufficient funds from local resources. New litigants from Lake View in Phillips County filed suit in 1992, alleging that the funding formula remained unconstitutional, and two years later, chancery court judge Annabelle Imber agreed with them. The state legislature, according to her ruling, had two years to remedy the situation.

The first attempt to solve the problem involved two steps. First, the legislature passed three acts in 1995—Acts 916, 917, and 1194—which, taken together, addressed the local contribution to schools and revised the state funding formula, raising the state's contribution to public schools. Act 916 authorized a 10 percent surcharge to school districts that failed to raise their base millage available to support schools to a minimum of 25 mills. Act 917 required that all school districts raise their base millage available to education to 25 and also authorized a study that would analyze education standards and explore the question of what actually constituted an adequate education. Act 1194 provided for grants for new programs to begin to address the question of adequacy. Since local property taxes were the province of local taxpayers and governments, some critics claimed that Acts 916 and 917 violated the constitution, but members of the legislature anticipated such a charge and voted to place a constitutional amendment before the voters that would establish 25 mills as the minimum. On November 5, 1996, voters passed Amendment 74, effectively validating Acts 916 and 917.

The battle over school funding was far from over, however. Lake View litigants returned to court, dissatisfied with the failure of the legislature to fully equalize funding. In April 1997, the legislature passed Acts 1307 and 1361. The first essentially repealed the existing school funding formula and outlined how other millages (presumably passed for other purposes and underutilized) could be employed to raise the minimum number of mills allotted to support public education to the minimum 25 mills. Finally, it provided grants and various forms of financial aid to schools and outlined "what a general, suitable, and efficient system of education should include." Still, the Lake View litigants were dissatisfied. The state had not provided for a comprehensive funding system that remedied the basic inequity created by the great disparities in property values across the state. From May 1997 through 2005, the litigants and the state sparred, filing amended complaints and responses over the constitutionality of the 1994 and 1997 acts (as well as over attorney's fees). In 2002 the Arkansas Supreme Court again ruled that the state had failed to provide an adequate and equitable system of education. Arkansas officials made efforts to comply, but in 2005 the court again held that they had failed. After further remedies were implemented, the court finally ruled in 2007 that the legislature "had taken the required and necessary legislative steps to assure that the school children of this state are provided an adequate education and a substantially equal education opportunity."

At the heart of this struggle over equity and adequacy was the desire to improve education in Arkansas. Enter the charter school movement, a movement dating back to 1988 when a professor at the University of Massachusetts first gave expression to the charter school idea. The concept was to focus

Charter school movement:
Semiprivate schools that receive some public funding, and that focus on student outcomes rather than issues like teacher salaries.

narrowly on student outcomes rather than on issues like teacher salaries and certification, but as it developed, it increasingly became apparent that many of those in favor of charter schools were essentially repudiating the public education system. They believed that public education was a dismal failure and could not be redeemed. From their point of view, parents who wished to provide their children with a high-quality public education had the right to demand better, and the charter schools offered the best opportunity to do so. Speaking the language of "choice" and the "freedom to choose," they emphasized the role of the parents. Not all charter school advocates were motivated by hostility to public education, however, but focused on addressing the educational deficiencies of the state's poorest children.

Regardless of motivation, by the early 1990s, Minnesota and California soon opened charter schools, allocating some public funds for their operation, and the movement soon expanded to include a total of forty-one states and the District of Columbia. By the early twenty-first century, charter schools became a part of the education debate in Arkansas, and considerable controversy attended this issue: Some argued that charter schools did not simply augment public education but, in fact, undermined it. State funds were allocated to charter schools—though at a lower amount than for public schools—and smaller districts faced a serious potential risk: consolidation. The state had established that in order for a public school to be viable— and avoid consolidation—it had to enroll a minimum of 350 students. If a school fell below that number for two years in a row, it became subject to consolidation. If the state approved the establishment of a charter school in a small district and that district was forced into consolidation, the state could be subject to a lawsuit, something advocates of public education had demonstrated a willingness to pursue. On the other hand, the proponents of charter schools believed they were offering a viable alternative to parents who wanted to afford their children the best possible education. But what about the children of parents either indifferent to their children's education or unable to devote more time to it because they were so heavily engaged in the struggle to make a living? For those children, the best hope remained with the public school system.

Another troubling issue involving the charter schools was the allegation that they contributed to the problem of resegregation. It is an allegation that has arisen elsewhere across the country and that has pitted the Little Rock School District against the charter school movement. The fact that the state partially funds the charter schools may become an issue if it can be established that those schools promote resegregation. While there may be no constitutional right to attend integrated schools, actions by the state that contribute to segregated schools are another matter. The Eighth Circuit's 1985 ruling chronicled the state's role in perpetuating segregated schools, establishing a precedent that the state would ignore at its peril.

Despite the many legitimate criticisms aimed at the state's public education system, Arkansas's efforts to improve its system of public education received high marks in *Education Week*'s 2012 Quality Counts report, reflecting improvements that apparently have little to do with the existence of charter schools. Arkansas ranked number five, moving up from number six in the 2011 report. While the nation as a whole received a "C" grade, Arkansas earned a B-, bested only by Maryland, New York, Massachusetts, and Virginia. The state ranked first in the country for the linkages it established from its kindergarten through twelfth-grade programs and second in terms of its efforts to improve its core of teachers. All of these items speak to Arkansas's dedication to the principle of providing a high-quality public education, but a telling difference exists between the rankings for improvement and those for performance. That student performance lags behind improvements in standards, assessment, and accountability is perhaps no surprise. In a range of performance-related indices, from student achievement to graduation rates, Arkansas earns only a D and ranks at thirty-fourth in the nation. Other negative marks reflect long-standing deficiencies that recent improvements can hardly be expected to overcome. For example, in the "chance for success" ratio, Arkansas ranked forty-fourth, but this measure included the educational levels of parents and family income. In terms of the number of adults with at least a two-year college degree, Arkansas ranks at fifty. This latter measure is particularly disappointing because Arkansas, based on proximity to institutions that offer at least a two-year degree, ranks highly in terms of access to higher education. The apparent success of the Arkansas lottery, launched in 2009, in sending a greater number of Arkansas high school graduates to college bodes well for the future, but it is too soon to forecast the long-term implications. By the fall of 2011, more Arkansas high school graduates than ever before were entering college, but nearly 50 percent of them required remedial courses in math, reading, and English. The lottery scholarships expose the continuing problems in the state's educational system and puts further pressure on Arkansas officials to remedy the situation. Just as urgent is the need to generate opportunities within Arkansas for this new college-educated population. The scholarships may relieve many families of the burden of educating their children—or see them remain without college educations—but opportunities

Education Week's **Quality Counts report:** A report issued by *Education Week* in 2012, which lauded the state for its efforts to improve education but continued to find problems in certain areas.

must exist within the state if those new college graduates are to be expected to remain in the state.

From Colonial to Global Political Economy

The debate over public education in Arkansas is intimately connected to the state's economic future but that future depends on moving beyond some aspects of the state's past. Yet again, historian C. Vann Woodward has something instructive to contribute. In *Origins of the New South*, published in 1951, he focused attention on the "colonial" nature of the southern economy, one that relied on extractive industries that worked more to the benefit of the extractors—planters, lumber companies, and railroad barons—and to northern industrialists who sometimes extracted and almost always processed the raw materials elsewhere. This failure to control the profits from its own resources plagued the state for most of its history, and its inability to participate in the southern Sunbelt phenomenon in the 1970s and 1980s seemed yet another example of Arkansas's failure to promote meaningful economic growth. The key feature of this new economy was knowledge-based industries, particularly in service areas and technology. Arkansas's under-educated population and inferior infrastructure inhibited its membership in the Sunbelt fraternity. Instead, its agricultural economy, despite some set-backs, thrived in the 1970s and 1980s, and, its manufacturing sector grew, largely by attracting industries to its nonunion, low-wage opportunities. An astute observer, however, might have noticed that it was also in the 1970s and 1980s that certain Arkansas-born giants of capitalism—Walmart, Stephens, Inc., Tyson Foods, J. B. Hunt, and Murphy Oil—were laying the groundwork for growth and development. In the early years of the twenty-first century, with the national economy faltering and the Sunbelt South crashing with it, Arkansas began to position itself to modernize its economy and become the new Sunbelt phenomenon.

Even as Arkansas began to embrace the new global economy, vestiges of the old colonial economic model remained and, indeed, emerged in new forms. An essay in C. Vann Woodward's *Burden of Southern History* focused on the many ironies that run through the South's history, and one of the most potent ironies of the early twenty-first century involved the ability of Arkansas and three western states, those that maintained a greater semblance of the colonial economy, to better withstand the economic crisis that virtually crippled the nation and the world. Woodward focused his analysis on the South's colonial economy but had he turned his glance westward, he might have recognized a similar phenomenon there. Although Arkansas, North Dakota, Montana, and Wyoming suffered during the historic economic calamity of the early twenty-first century, they managed to endure precisely because they had failed to participate fully in the overheated economic expansion. They shared conservative fiscal policies and largely colonial (extractive) economies, but some of the particulars of their situations differed. In two states, Arkansas and North Dakota, new discoveries of natural gas and oil, respectively—exceptionally lucrative extractive industries—shored up their economies. In Arkansas the Fayetteville Shale, a natural gas field, allowed the state to better withstand the shortfall in regular tax collections.

However much the exploitation of this resource benefited the state, this extractive industry, much like those of the past, entailed a certain environmental cost. Some concerns were raised about the "coincidence" of earthquakes in the Fayetteville Shale area of central Arkansas, perhaps connected to "fracking," the method used to extract the deposits of natural gas. In fracking, large quantities of water mixed with chemicals are injected into the earth's crust to produce small fractures. Workers then pump the water back out and extract the gas that is made accessible in the process. Not only have observers raised questions about the seismological abnormalities that sometimes develop in areas where fracking takes place, environmentalists have been concerned about the chemicals in the waste water entering the groundwater system. While companies have been reticent to divulge the kind of chemicals and their quantities used in the process, many others have denied a connection between fracking and increased seismic activity. Concerns of residents and officials, however, have led some states to impose regulations and some countries have banned fracking altogether. In Arkansas the state's Oil and Gas Commission voted in July 2011 to close one well operating in central Arkansas using the fracking technology and imposed a moratorium on new drilling operations employing the method. The decision came in the wake of two days of testimony from residents of the region alarmed by increased seismic activity, including a 4.7-magnitude earthquake in February 2011.

Fracking: A process of injecting water mixed with chemicals into the earth in order to extract trapped deposits of oil or natural gas.

While the discovery of lucrative natural gas deposits in Arkansas resulted in significant revenue for the state, a new kind of colonial model taking shape in agricultural areas provided little new revenue. In the early twenty-first century, the rise in the value of agricultural land attracted investors looking for a safe haven in an era when the value of home and commercial property plummeted. Investment companies seeking to diversify the portfolios of jittery clients purchased millions of acres of agricultural land across the country. The profits generated by the sale of agricultural commodities produced on land held by out-of-state investors do not accrue to the benefit of many Arkansans and does not enhance tax revenues of local and state government.

The phenomenon also introduces a potential instability in the value of such land. Agricultural land values are subject to the price of the commodities produced on them, and agricultural prices have historically fluctuated for a variety of reasons. Natural disasters, changes in government support policies, or new competitors from abroad can send the prices for agricultural commodities and thus land values on a downward spiral. If short-term investors, made nervous by declining dividends, begin to dispose of their shares of agricultural lands, an economic collapse of unpredictable proportions may occur in the agricultural sector. Whether they sell their shares when the going gets rough or hold on to them, these portfolio planters are likely to have little interest in supporting the schools and roads in local communities and no impulse to concern themselves with the environmental consequences of the use of chemicals in the farming enterprise.

Throughout this period of economic adjustment, Arkansas maintained, for the most part, an attachment to moderate political candidates who espoused a largely conservative economic agenda. These politicians recognized the importance of the agricultural sector and other extractive industries to Arkansas at the same time they attempted to move the state into manufacturing and even further, toward the new knowledge-based industries that would make Arkansas into a new Sunbelt phenomenon. This was true of all three governors who served between 1992 to 2012, beginning with Jim Guy Tucker, who took over the office when Bill Clinton assumed the presidency.

Jim Guy Tucker came to the governorship with substantial experience in public service and a particular interest in knowledge-based industries. An attorney, he began his political career in 1970 when he won the office of prosecuting attorney for the Sixth Judicial District. He moved quickly into the state's attorney generalship in 1972, where he served two terms. He won election to the US Congress, representing the Second Congressional District in 1976. A failed attempt to win the Senate seat being vacated by John McClellan, which he lost to David Pryor, seemed to derail Tucker's political career in 1978, and he returned to the practice of law. This was an important and formative detour for Tucker. He began to engage in a number of business enterprises, including a cable company he founded with his wife—clearly a knowledge-based industry. His business interests, moreover, included an international component that placed him squarely in concert with the new global economy. However, Tucker never lost his taste for political office. He won the lieutenant governorship in 1990, just in time to step into the governor's office vacated when Clinton won the presidency. While in office he presided over a restructuring of the juvenile justice system, an interest of his connected to his days as a prosecuting attorney. He faced challenges arising out of the Lake View suit, which required additional funds to be allocated to education and rather than raise taxes, he cut the budgets of a number of state agencies. He failed in an attempt to convince the voters to pass a 3.5-billion-dollar bond issue to support the maintenance and expansion of the state's highway system. Ironically, Tucker's governorship was cut short when he was convicted of a white-collar crime connected to an attempt to expand his cable business. He became ensnared in Whitewater investigators looking into allegations made against Bill and Hillary Clinton regarding a failed real estate venture in Arkansas. In a completely unconnected matter,

Lake View suit:
A suit arising out of Phillips County alleging that the state's funding formula for public education remained unconstitutional.

Tucker had apparently conspired to purchase a Texas cable company that Whitewater prosecutors alleged had been fraudulently declared bankrupt in order to avoid the payment of corporate income taxes. Tucker resigned on May 29, 1996, the day after his conviction, leaving the office to his lieutenant governor, Republican Mike Huckabee.

Although a Republican who presented himself as a social conservative, Huckabee proved to be fairly moderate, and, significantly, he promoted economic development that helped position Arkansas to embrace the new knowledge-based industries. He proved capable of securing the governor's office in his own right when he won reelection in 1998. Huckabee's brand of Republicanism, moreover, closely resembled that espoused by Frank White. Like White, he was both fiscally and socially conservative. The first Baptist minister to occupy the office since James P. Eagle (1889–1893), Huckabee, like Eagle, had also served as president of the Southern Baptist Convention. A fundamentalist Christian, he appealed to like-minded voters but also took positions on certain issues that made him acceptable to the suburban middle class and the traditional Republican voter in the northwest part of the state: fiscal conservatism. He created a commission to investigate the size of the state government, and after that commission made its report, he called for a dramatic reduction in the number of state agencies. Presenting a moderate persona while espousing socially conservative positions, he began to successfully negotiate the political arena in Arkansas.

One of his first acts as governor was to launch a campaign to convince voters to endorse a bond issue to improve the state's deteriorating highway system, something his predecessor in office, Jim Guy Tucker, had attempted but failed to accomplish. The repair and expansion of the highway system was important to ordinary citizens as well as a number of well-connected business interests. J. B. Hunt Trucking, Tyson Inc., Dillard's Department Stores, and Walmart, for example, stood to gain from the expansion of the highway system and, indeed, one key component of the state's effort to participate in the Sunbelt economic phenomenon involved the modernization of such infrastructure. In pursuing support for the bond issue, Huckabee exemplified the personal style and charisma that had made certain Democrats so successful in the past. He toured the state by bus and successfully convinced the Arkansas electorate to support the issue. Exuding what some of his counterparts referred to as "compassionate conservatism," he went to the airwaves to successfully pitch his ARkids first program, which expanded healthcare to 200,000 children in the state. He used funds from the Tobacco Settlement (1998) to fund the program. In the area of education, he also struck a moderately progressive note and promoted policies crucial to moving Arkansas forward economically. With an unprecedented teacher shortage predicted in the early twenty-first century, he promised a dramatic raise in teacher salaries. With neighboring states paying higher salaries, the drain on the best and brightest teachers had begun to worry state officials.

In his third and final term in office, Huckabee faced a challenge that had plagued his predecessors in office and shadowed his governorship: education funding. When the court ruled in *Lake View v. Huckabee* in 2002 that the state's funding formula was inadequate, Huckabee was faced with the problem of how to raise sufficient funds in order to satisfy the court order. He raised the issue of the consolidation of small school districts into larger ones, thereby eliminating administrative and building costs and saving, potentially, millions of dollars. But he faced a serious backlash from small communities and many legislators who represented them. Although the legislature refused to force consolidation on the scale that Huckabee recommended, they did devise a formula that established the minimum number of students a school district had to have in order to remain viable economically: 350.

Despite the controversy that arose over the consolidation issue, Mike Huckabee was a popular governor. However, Arkansas voters, like voters elsewhere, had passed term limit amendments in 1992 and 1998, the first aimed at legislators and the second at executive offices, including that of the governor. When his second full term expired in 2006, Huckabee stepped aside, leaving the governor's office open to challenge from an experienced and well-liked Democratic legislator, Mike Beebe. Beebe, like his predecessors, emphasized the development of knowledge-based industries and sponsored measures designed to improve the educational system in order to facilitate that development.

Mike Beebe had first been elected to the legislature in 1982—the same year he was designated the state's most outstanding trial lawyer—and immediately became involved in negotiations in the debate over public education arising out of the Alma suit over school funding. He later helped fashion legislation aimed at remedying the flaws identified by the federal court in the Little Rock desegregation cases. A term as attorney general (2002–2006) provided him with the opportunity to address these issues in an executive position. Both as a legislator and as attorney general, he earned a reputation as a hard-working and practical politician, focused on achieving results but not at the expense of his principles. Raised by a single parent, Beebe grew up under trying economic circumstances and developed a deeply felt empathy for those in similar circumstances. Though a fiscal conservative in many respects, he advocated the elimination of the sales tax on groceries, a burden that fell heavily on the working poor. Similarly, he supported a minimum wage, obviously directed at those at the bottom rung of the economic ladder. Finally, a fervent believer in the value of education and in the importance of early childhood development, he supported a progressive pre-kindergarten program that would benefit all children but particularly those at the lowest end of the economic spectrum.

Skills Beebe developed during his two decades in the general assembly gave him the ability to work closely with the legislature in achieving his goals as governor, particularly in regard to reducing the tax on groceries and establishing an impressive pre-kindergarten program. At the same time, he came into office just as the worst economic crisis since the Great Depression hit the state and the nation. He trimmed the state budget, called a moratorium on raises for state employees, and instituted other cost-saving and fiscally conservative measures without sacrificing the pre-kindergarten program or the reduction in sales taxes on groceries. In other words, he maintained a fidelity to his campaign goals, goals that were far from mere rhetoric; at the same time he guided the state through a severe recession. He also recognized an opportunity to step into the void left by other states that were more devastated by the economic collapse. His strategic economic goals involved a multifaceted approach to economic development. Realizing that most of the state's population was too undereducated to step immediately into knowledge-based industries, he emphasized a continuation of efforts to promote traditional manufacturing in the state at the same time he endorsed the growth of high-tech and service-sector-related enterprises. From the time of taking office to 2012, Governor Beebe enjoyed enviable approval ratings, largely on the basis of his success in steering the state through the recession and the fact that he delivered on his campaign promise to lower grocery taxes. His style of leadership compared favorably to that of Dale Bumpers and David Pryor in that he exuded a moderate demeanor while championing progressive measures and conservative fiscal policies. It differed from that of his immediate predecessors, particularly Bill Clinton and Mike Huckabee, in that he preferred to keep a relatively low profile and work behind the scenes to accomplish his goals.

A factor of no little importance enabled Beebe to achieve remarkable success in securing his goals. He was able to capitalize on the power accruing to the governor's office in the face of term limits upon legislators. Three factors contributed to the increasing power of the governor in this context. First, although the governor's terms were also limited, the governor's office, unlike that of legislators, is a full-time position with a full-time, professional staff. Second, to complicate matters, legislative sessions are characteristically short, providing newly elected legislators with only a short time to master the processes at work in the general assembly. The legislature meets in regular session in one 60-day period in odd number years, although sessions can be extended when two-thirds of the body votes to extend the session. Governors have frequently called special sessions in even numbered years but the sessions are typically focused narrowly on designated issues. Given that legislators are paid a very small salary, they must maintain their regular livelihoods, and thus they are part-time legislators and, given the brevity of legislative sessions, they have little opportunity to master the intricacies of the legislative process. Before term limits, experienced legislators acquired greater power and authority within the general assembly and provided continuity across time, allowing new legislators to gain a mastery of the processes.

The term limits phenomenon is a national one, and scholarly studies have revealed a number of interesting consequences. First, the accrual of power to the governor's office is an obvious result. Second, term limits require lobbyists to expend more time educating legislators, thus potentially limiting the influence of special interests. Third, the Republican Party in Arkansas has enjoyed significant success, particularly in the 2010 election. Before that election, Arkansas had a higher proportion of Democrats in its general assembly than any other state with the exception of Massachusetts, Rhode Island, and Hawaii. Democrats held 72 of 100 seats in the Arkansas house and 27 of 35 seats in the state senate. In 2010, capitalizing on a poor economy nationwide and Tea Party appeal, the Republicans made significant inroads into Democratic political dominance, claiming 45 of 100 seats in the house and 15 of 35 seats in the senate. As of early 2012, the Republicans seem poised to capture control of the general assembly in the 2012 elections, and Democrats seemed ill-prepared to offer much resistance. On the other hand, some promises of term limits have not been fulfilled. Although promoted as a method of securing citizen legislators, term limits have tended to result in the election of men and women who have had political experience at the local level as mayors, county judges, or city councilmen. And it appears that imposition of term limits did not result in a significant increase in women and minorities in the legislature.

Arkansas's 1992 amendment imposing term limits on legislators included one aimed at the state's US senators and congressmen. It was later ruled unconstitutional. Though states have established the authority to impose term limits on state officers, their efforts to limit the number of terms of its congressional delegates to the United States Congress failed a constitutional test when the Supreme Court ruled in 1995 that states lacked the authority to impose limits on federal offices. In fact, even without term limits, Arkansas has had unusual turnover in its congressional delegation over the last twenty years, turnover that reflects a significant demographic shift in the state.

The rise of northwest Arkansas, the growth of Little Rock, and the decline of the Delta have had enormous implications for the state both economically and politically. By the year 2000 the Walton family, situated in northwest Arkansas and operating the phenomenally successful Walmart retail chain, was estimated to be worth $108 billion, making them among the wealthiest in the world. The Stephens family, owner of Stephens, Inc., based in Little Rock, an investment banking establishment, had wealth estimated at $3.8 billion. Both appeared at the top of a list of the one hundred wealthiest families in Arkansas. At the same time, only two delta planters appeared on the list, and their wealth ranked at seventy-fourth and eighty-fourth, respectively. Had a similar list been published one hundred years earlier, it would have been dominated by delta planters.

Strikingly, while most of the wealthiest Arkansans have achieved this distinction outside of agricultural enterprises (the Tyson Corporation is the only "agricultural" entity at the top of the list), nearly three-quarters of the gross state product is farm generated, and over 40 percent of the value of the state's manufacturing output is derived from the processing of agricultural products. One hundred years ago the poorest Arkansans often worked for the wealthiest; today, those who continue to work the land for a living have little to do with the "new" economy's top movers and shakers. The paternalism that, however imperfectly, operated to make the circumstances of the poor of immediate relevance to the wealthy, has little direct counterpart in today's Arkansas, although some parallels remain. For example, Walmart, Tyson, and other successful corporations employ large numbers of people in low-skill, low-wage jobs. Since the tremendous profits generated by these corporations are absorbed primarily by upper echelon, managerial, and skilled personnel, the result is a tendency toward bipolarization into a two-class society sep-arated by ever-increasing disparities in earnings as well as small prospects for advancement. This trend, which the nation as a whole has experienced, represents a second challenge to Arkansans hoping to build a future in which such disparities will be reduced.

The business orientation of the state's economic dynamos might augur a renewed interest in promoting roads and education, but the natural conserva-tism of business groups, particularly where taxes are concerned, leaves open the question of how to finance such improvements. And while the wealthiest Arkansans have enjoyed a decade of unparalleled prosperity, the middle class in Arkansas, as elsewhere, has not kept pace. The state's poor gained ground in the 1990s, relative to the poor in other areas of the country, but much of the rural population remains mired in a pervasive poverty and Arkansas's per capita income is well below the national average. Moreover, what seems indisputable is that the fastest-growing sectors of the American economy in the twenty-first century demand a more highly educated workforce than the state's educational infrastructure has so far proved capable of providing. This raises the question of whether Arkansas can build upon what progress it has recently made in generating high-tech employment opportunities. The major challenge facing Arkansas in the twenty-first century, therefore, will be finding solutions to the problems that have so far prevented the state from developing a truly first-rate educational system.

Arkansas's Cultural Heritage

Although C. Vann Woodward has contributed much to the understanding of southern (and Arkansas) history, there was one area in which he was deafeningly silent. He had little to say about the South's cultural legacy. He was virtually mute about the intellectuals, writers, and artists of the South, a disappointing omission. If the South—and Arkansas—had something unique to offer the nation, it certainly manifested itself in that arena. While Woodward focused his attention on the economic and political sphere, a vibrant cultural legacy was left unsung. His omission was shared by news outlets that focused attention on crises like the Little Rock fiasco in 1957. Television cameras captured the violence and insults aimed at defenseless black children and broadcast these images to the world, making the state notorious. Despite this unfortunate—and not entirely undeserved—portrayal, others in Arkansas were contributing something far more positive to American life and, indeed, to world culture. Few outside the state appreciated the role that Arkansas musicians played in the evolution of American popular music and even fewer understood the cross fertilization that occurred between black and white, between delta and mountain musicians. Perhaps because Arkansas was situated between the South and the West—indeed, some refer to Arkansas as a part of the Southwest rather than the South—the state has served as an entrepôt for the blending of different sounds. Here was an area in which black and white Arkansans crossed racial lines freely in the interest of pursuing an authentic American art form.

The sounds emanating from the Delta and the sounds coming out of the mountains of Arkansas were never truly isolated from each other, but they initially developed more or less separately. Each had their origins in musical traditions from outside the state and, initially, outside the nation. The ballads sung by Arkansas's mountain musicians were carried over from Appalachia and had a distinct connection to the British Isles, although by the early twentieth century a unique American flavor could be discerned. Elements of minstrelsy and even blues forms had crept into some mountain music, and whites used instruments that had African origins. The Delta blues had African origins, of course, reflected in its use of percussive guitar accompaniments and falsetto vocal stylings. The slave experience in America also left a profound imprint on black music. Finding themselves in "another kind of slavery," as some historians refer to the post-emancipation sharecropping arrangement, black musicians carried African/slave music into another evolutionary stage. The blues is a sound that dates back to the late nineteenth and early twentieth century, and both the music and the lyrics speak to the sense of desperation that accompanied the black experience in an era of racial segregation and legal disfranchisement. While many blues singers sang songs about poverty and imprisonment, many others favored party music and devoted little time to songs that contained elements of social commentary whether implicit or explicit. Like white mountain musicians, many black bluesmen and blueswomen sang simple ballads about lost love, something common to the experience of all humans, black or white, American or otherwise.

Another important influence on both mountain and blues music was the gospel sound. Although the white and black communities of Arkansas shared a deep religiosity and a Protestant orientation, they were very different in the way they experienced church services and expressed themselves musically. Harkening back to African traditions, blacks engaged in the "call and response" pattern during the preacher's sermon. Similarly, the cadence and emotionalism of their music owed much to Africa but had been greatly influenced by their years of bondage. The work songs sung by slaves established a rhythm and beat calculated to create a pace that made the work seem to go more quickly and certainly more tolerably. Most whites, like most blacks in Arkansas, were of the Methodist or Baptist denominations, but there were differences between black and white church services and singing styles, differences that may have been more the result of differences in class rather than differences in race. Upper-class white Baptists and Methodists were typically less enthusiastic and more restrained. Some whites belonged to Pentecostal denominations that elicited emotional responses from their members but had no tradition of "call and response," and their gospel songs had no connection to either Africa or the slave experience. Some few, in fact, foreswore musical instruments entirely and allowed singing from approved hymnals only. Others embraced instrumentation and did not require their congregants to sing only hymns sanctioned by some church authority. However blacks and whites expressed their religion, their music was important and, indeed, the first music many young southerners of either race ever heard or sung was religious music. It ran deep in them and greatly influenced their secular music. John Hancock, a black Southern Tenant Farmers Union troubadour who penned union lyrics in the mid-1930s, understood the importance of religion in rural Arkansas, so he sang his songs to religious tunes precisely because they were familiar to, and reverberated psychologically with, both black and white sharecroppers and tenants.

The best-known black gospel singer of Arkansas origins is Sister Rosetta Tharpe, who was born in Cotton Plant in 1921, into a gospel singing family. Rosetta was touring professionally when she was six years old, performing both gospel and secular music. As folklorist Robert Cochran has observed, "Few artists covered such a range of styles—Tharpe performed with blues musicians (Muddy Waters), jazz artists (Cab Calloway and Lucky Millinder), and other gospel groups (The Caravans, the Dixie Hummingbirds, the James Cleveland Singers)." The number and character of the musical venues she performed in were as wide as her repertoire. While she appeared at the Newport Folk Festival, the Apollo Theater, the Cotton Club, and Carnegie Hall, she also performed in churches and a variety of nightclubs, small and large. Johnny Cash recalled that she was playing at an out-of-the-way night-club in Chicago when he was there to perform at Soldier's Field. She sang a rendition of "This Train" that reduced him to tears, but her performance was likely a mix of blues and gospel tunes, something she was famous for. One music critic credited her with having created pop gospel.

Rosetta's journey to national prominence began in Arkansas in an era when much of the state was relatively isolated and rural. But a singular new invention would pull them into a new world of music. Beginning in the 1920s, people could hear both secular and religious music on battery-operated radios and phonographs. After electrical power was extended into rural areas, radios were among the first items purchased, and indeed, the medium played an important role in the evolution of American popular music in the 1950s. Until then, families gathered around fireplaces, in their living rooms, or on their front porches—often with neighbors in attendance—and sang their songs with or without instrumentation. In the days before electricity, even those with battery-operated radios (which had a short life and were not always reliable) entertained themselves by family sing-alongs. Levon Helm, who was raised near Elaine, Arkansas, in Phillips County, remarked that "we were a musical family." Helm would grow up to play professionally with Ronnie Hawkins and the Hawks before becoming drummer for The Band, which gained fame first playing backup for Bob Dylan. Helm remembered that his mother "sang in a clear alto voice," and he said of his father, "All of us kids remember sitting on his lap in the evenings while he relaxed in his chair. He'd sing to us . . . [and] knew so many songs he was like a fountain of music." If not singing themselves, the Helm family listened to the radio. "We'd have to buy a battery two and a half feet long and maybe eight inches thick . . . I remember my dad pulling our tractor right up to the window of the house one night when the battery was down, and he plugged the radio into the tractor battery so we wouldn't lose the *Grand Ole Opry, The Shadow,* the *Creaking Door, Amos 'n' Andy*—those were the shows you couldn't miss."

Live religious music might be heard at home or in churches, but townspeople likely got their live secular music in music halls, or, depending on the sensibilities of the individuals involved, in honkytonks and juke joints. Country folk who did not travel to town often relied on country honkytonks, tucked into deep woods or down isolated roads. They might also enjoy traveling shows. Helm reported that "going to music shows was high-level entertainment for our family. They'd set up tents at the edge of Marvell and have a stage, folding chairs, and refreshments." Sometimes the Helm family heard the F. S. Walcott Rabbits Foot Minstrels from Mississippi, who would "set up with the back of a big truck as their stage." Later, Helm's Canadian band-mates, seeking vicariously to immerse themselves in the culture Helm grew up with, would perform a song called "W. S. Walcott Medicine Show." The show that made the most lasting impression on Helm, however, was the "first show I remember . . . Bill Monroe and his Blue Grass Boys on a summer evening in 1946, when I was six years old. Boy, this really tattooed my brain. I've never forgotten it: Bill had a real good five-piece band." The Helm family had heard Monroe on the *Grand Ole Opry* and were thrilled to see him in person. "Here he was in the flesh," said Helm. While Helm himself would grow up to be a rock musician, this earliest influence was something very different. "They took that old hillbilly music, sped it up, and basically invented what is now known as bluegrass music."

Although Helm remembered his first hearing of Bill Monroe as a formative experience, he would be more heavily influenced by various African American musics, such as the blues programming emanating from nearby Helena. The pure blues sound of Helena became known to the world in the 1940s, principally because of the "King Biscuit Time" show at radio station KFFA, which featured the blues harmonica of Sonny Boy Williamson. It also served as a showcase for local talent all over the Delta—of Arkansas, Mississippi, Louisiana. Young and old blues singers alike would be allowed to sing live on the radio for fifteen to thirty minutes, receiving no pay for their services. Instead they would be allowed to plug an upcoming performance. (This phenomenon was not peculiar to the Delta or to blues, however, as white country musicians like Frankie Kelley were making the same kinds of arrangements with radio stations in Fayetteville and elsewhere.) Some of the most famous bluesmen of the 1930s and 1940s called Helena home and helped create a unique Arkansas blues sound: Williamson, Howlin' Wolf, Little Walter, and Robert Nighthawk. KFFA was heard as far away as Chicago, and the ongoing migration of blacks out of the Delta, which began in the post–World War I era, brought even more delta blues north to Chicago and Detroit. There the Arkansas bluesmen put their electric guitars to work in a louder and more muscular fashion and contributed to the direction that Chicago blues was taking. William "Big Bill" Broonzy, who was born in 1893 in Mississippi but raised on a farm near Pine Bluff, is one of the best known of the Chicago transplants. He had an innovative guitar style that made him a favorite of Chicago audiences. He would go on to tour Europe, England, Africa, South America, and Australia.

Some Arkansas blues people stayed closer to home, however, like Robert Junior Lockwood, who would heavily influence the evolving Memphis blues. Lockwood was the stepson of blues great Robert Johnson, who passed on his Mississippi blues sound to the youth. Thus, Arkansas delta bluesmen influenced bluesmen in Louisiana, Mississippi, and Tennessee—not to mention those of Chicago and Harlem—and, in turn, were influenced by them. While roughhewn blues may have been black Arkansans most important musical export, smoother sounds would also emerge—such as the "jump" of Louis Jordan, who learned to play clarinet from his father in Brinkley, and, later, the urbane sound of Al Green, a native of Forrest City.

Although the radio was one place where segregation was hard to maintain, some radio stations were reluctant at first to play "race records"; that is, music recorded by blacks. Record companies actually had white singers record black songs, which were then deemed suitable for white radio audiences. There were a few black radio stations in various locations around the country, including WDIA in Memphis, which Arkansas delta people could easily hear. Some white radio stations were eager to broadcast the black sound, and many businesses, particularly those catering to a black trade, were more than willing to advertise shows like "King Biscuit Time." By the end of the 1950s, rhythm-and-blues singers—principally black artists who had mixed blues with rock-and-roll—were readily played on white radio stations, although country blues was a sound that never achieved a wide audience there. Some whites did have an opportunity to hear delta blues over their radio stations, and the minstrel shows that traveled the South included black musicians, but Levon Helm recalled that the audiences were segregated in the Walcott Rabbits Foot Minstrel shows. "The audience was split down the middle by an aisle. On the left were the black to light-skinned folks, while the light-skinned to people with red hair sat on the right."

Whether the rest of America was ready for delta blues, many young white musicians found inspiration in the sounds coming out of Helena, West Memphis, and North Little Rock. Those from sharecropping backgrounds had already had considerable exposure to black music from their personal association with black musicians. Billy Lee Riley grew up in various communities in northeastern Arkansas where his father worked as a painter or at any other job he could secure. While a small child living near Osceola, two black friends took him "around to the black section of town, [where we would] sit around for hours and listen to that music coming out of the juke joints and maybe watch guitar players sitting on the side of the street." Riley would later become one of Sun Studio's rockabilly players—rockabilly was a blend of fast blues and country, an early form of rock-and-roll. He learned to play the guitar from a white boy and two black friends but "the one I remember above them all was an old fella called Lightening Leon, who would play a harmonica and sing." Riley even cut a blues album using the name Lightening Leon as his own. Arkansas bluesmen also inspired young whites living worlds away from the Delta. Sonny Boy Williamson, for instance, became a favorite of a number of the stars of the "British Invasion," which in the mid-1960s introduced many American teenagers to their own nation's rich musical heritage.

Not all white musicians who were influenced by black musicians went the way of rock-and-roll or rock. Early in his career it was almost impossible to identify the style of music played by Charlie Rich. Rich, who was born in Colt, Arkansas, in 1932 and raised in Benton, Arkansas, credited a black blues-singing sharecropper named C.J. as having a major influence on his musical style. He was also attracted to jazz music from an early age, but he grew up listening to the *Grand Ole Opry* and his first big hit was "Lonely Weekends," a pure country music sound. When two songs he recorded went to the top of the country chart and then to the top of the pop chart in the early 1970s, he became a solid fixture in the music world. Although they were crossover hits, "Behind Closed Doors" and "Most Beautiful Girl in the World" made him a country music giant.

Like Billy Lee Riley, Rich was initially under contract at Sun Studios in Memphis, Tennessee. Sam Phillips, who ran Sun Records, discovered and recorded artists like Elvis Presley, Carl Perkins, Jerry Lee Lewis, and other rockabilly/rock-and-roll singers. Coming out of that mix of white country, black blues, and bluegrass, the musicians who passed through Sun Studios often took their styles in different directions. Another Sun Studio recording artist from Arkansas, Johnny Cash, would, like Charlie Rich, become a country music star. Cash was born in Kingsland, Arkansas, in 1932, but moved as a small child when his family secured a place at Dyess Colony, the ill-fated FSA community in Mississippi County. It was a hardscrabble existence, and he had a lot of opportunity to hear local blues. Osceola and the clubs that Billy Lee Riley remembers were very close at hand. West Memphis, Arkansas, in nearby Crittenden County, was a mecca for bluesmen, and young whites like Cash from the surrounding area were drawn to the exotic sounds and scenes of road houses, bars, and brothels there. But Cash grew up listening to the *Grand Ole Opry* and to radio stations broadcasting from the Mexican border, which were airing hymns and ballads sung by the Carter Family. Cash himself showed musical talent early, singing gospel in church. However, his first hit recordings were blues-inspired songs like "Folsom Prison Blues" and "Rock Island Line." The latter was a prison song made famous by Leadbelly recordings but first discovered by musicologist John Lomax when he was doing field recordings at Arkansas prisons in 1934. His driver at the time was Huddie Leadbelly, who heard the song and later recorded it. Cash's most famous songs, however, became country music standards, songs like "I Walk the Line" and "A Boy Named Sue."

Many of the young blues and country singers of Arkansas got their start with cheap guitars sold by Sears and Roebuck, but not all of them passed through Sun Studios on their way to fame and glory. Glen Campbell, born in Delight, Arkansas, in 1938, was given a cheap guitar by his father when he was only four years old, and by the time he was fourteen, he had dropped out of school, moved to New Mexico, and was playing professionally with his uncle Dick Bill's band. He was destined to have a string of hit records and became a popular music star. His sound was a blending of country and pop, but he never forgot his Arkansas roots, calling one of his thirty-seven Capitol albums, *Arkansas*.

For every Arkansas musician who gained fame and fortune, there were dozens who remained obscure, sometimes quite contentedly so. Many young men and women held down ordinary jobs during the day and played their music in the evenings and on weekends, with or without an audience. Others, like Emma Dusenberry, endured a sparse obscurity living in poverty. She was born in Georgia in 1862 but came to Arkansas when she was ten years old. She lived in a variety of locations in both the Delta and the mountains and sang Anglo-American ballads. Folk archivists discovered her in the 1930s. Folk music collectors Alan Lomax from Texas and Vance Randolph from Fayetteville paid her visits and made field recordings of her songs. One hundred and sixteen of her songs are on deposit in the National Folk Music Archives and copies of all the field recordings are at the University of Arkansas Special Collections Division. She had a brief moment of fame in

1936 when she was taken to Little Rock to sing at the Arkansas centennial of statehood but then returned to Mena to live in the poverty to which she was accustomed.

The music tradition in Arkansas remains very much alive at the beginning of the twenty-first century, and towns like Helena and Mountain View have dedicated themselves to preserving the rich musical heritage of the state. Mountain View celebrates and seeks to preserve white mountain music, holding festivals and entertaining tourists from around the country and the world. Visitors are treated to special shows that feature local artists, but many of them appreciate the opportunity to hear ordinary pickers and singers sitting around the square playing for tips—or just playing. Helena sponsors the King Biscuit Festival every fall, attracting blues musicians from around the world. The harmonica, Sonny Boy Williamson's signature instrument, is especially featured. A host of young new songwriters, singers, and musicians have emerged in the last few decades and seem destined to perpetuate the tradition.

While C. Vann Woodward barely observed the contribution of musicians, artists, and writers in southern—or Arkansas—culture, they left an enduring legacy that continues to resonate into the twenty-first century. From black (classical) composer William Grant Still to popular musicians like Lucinda Williams, from poets like John Gould Fletcher to Miller Williams, from architects like Edward Durrell Stone to E. Fay Jones, from artists like Edward Washburn to Larry Alexander, and from writers like Charles Portis of *True Grit* fame to Donald Harrington, who created the imaginary and compelling world of Staymore, Arkansas, have contributed to the South's cultural legacy.

Conclusion

Does C. Vann Woodward's *Burden of Southern History* continue to have relevance in today's Arkansas? Given the changes that have occurred—and have not occurred—since the book's publication in 1954, the answer is not obvious. Woodward's expectations concerning the emergence of a truly integrated society after *Brown v. Board of Education* foundered on the realities of a South and a nation more riven by racism than he imagined, a fact he began to reckon with in later editions of the book. However, as anyone who lived through the era would attest, considerable change has occurred, and as students of history might suggest, one should not expect centuries of racism and discrimination to disappear in a few short decades. While nothing good can come of the failure to complete the unfinished revolution begun by the *Brown* decision, Arkansas's uneven integration into the global economy worked to its advantage during the early twenty-first century. Ironically, the continuation of vestiges of the colonial economy shielded the state from the worst aspects of a global economic meltdown. In any case, with a population only partly prepared to step into the new knowledge-based global economy, the best path toward economic expansion seems to be a continuation of a mixed economy: agriculture, manufacturing, and knowledge-based industries. Given the international economic collapse labeled the Great Recession that began in 2007 and lasted until, arguably, 2012, the best choice seems to be the only choice for Arkansas.

SUGGESTED READING

Chapter 1: A Land "Inferior to None"

The best source on the geography, geology, and climate of Arkansas is Thomas L. Foti and Gerald Hanson's *Arkansas and the Land* (University of Arkansas Press, 1992). See also Foti's, *Arkansas, Its Land and People* (Arkansas Department of Education, 1976). A good brief account is Foti's entry "Geography and Geology" in the *Encyclopedia of Arkansas History and Culture* (Online at http://encyclopediaofarkansas.net). A new book by Brooks Blevins in his series on the Ozarks provides very useful information: *A History of the Ozarks, Vol. 1: The Old Ozarks* (University of Illinois Press, 2018).

Chapter 2: Ancient Native Americans

A good place to begin reading about Arkansas Indians is the Race & Ethnicity/ Native American section of the *Encyclopedia of Arkansas History and Culture* (http:// encyclopediaofarkansas.net/) and the Indians of Arkansas website hosted by the Arkansas Archeological Survey (http://arkarcheology.uark.edu/indiansofarkansas/ index.html).

Authoritative summaries of American Indian archaeology and ethnology in Arkansas and the mid-South are provided in several chapters of *The Handbook of North American Indians*, Volume 13 (Plains) and Volume 14 (Southeast), edited by William C. Sturtevant (Smithsonian Institution Press, 2001 and 2004). The eastern part of the state is given detailed coverage in Dan F. and Phyllis A. Morse's *Archaeology of the Central Mississippi Valley* (University of Alabama Press, 2009). A collection of articles in *Arkansas Archaeology: Essays in Honor of Dan and Phyllis Morse*, edited by Robert C. Mainfort Jr. and Marvin D. Jeter (University of Arkansas Press, 1999), provides examples of recent research on archeology across the state.

Discovery of the decorated Paleoindian bison skull is related in *Bison Hunting at Cooper Site: Where Lightning Bolts Drew Thundering Herds*, by Leland C. Bement (University of Oklahoma Press, 1999). A detailed analysis of the Dalton-era Sloan site in eastern Arkansas, perhaps the oldest cemetery in the Western Hemisphere, is found in Dan F. Morse's *Sloan: A Paleoindian Dalton Cemetery in Arkansas* (University of Arkansas Press, 2018).

A report on Middle Archaic foodways along the Ouachita River appears in "Reconstructing Ancient Foodways at the Jones Mill Site (3HS28): Hot Spring County, Arkansas," by Mary Beth Trubitt, Kathryn Parker, and Lucretia Kelly in the *Caddo Archeology Journal* 21:43–70. Good summaries of the origins of agriculture in the mid-South are provided in Gayle Fritz's essay, "Native Farming Systems and Ecosystems in the Mississippi River Valley," in *Imperfect Balance: Landscape Transformations in the Precolumbian Americas*, edited by David L. Lentz (Columbia University Press, 2000), and in several contributions found in Bruce Smith's edited volume, *Rivers of Change: Essays on Early Agriculture in Eastern North America* (Smithsonian Institution Press, 1992). Some of the most recent studies of early domestication of native species in Arkansas and the mid-South are detailed by Natalie G. Mueller and coauthors in "Growing the Lost Crops of Eastern North America's Original Agricultural System," *Nature Plants* 3 (2017), 17092:1–5.

The most accessible work on the Poverty Point site is Jon L. Gibson's *The Ancient Mounds of Poverty Point: Place of Rings* (University Press of Florida, 2000). The impact of global climate changes on the Poverty Point culture is discussed by Tristram R. Kidder in "Climate Change and the Archaic to Woodland Transition (3000–2500 Cal B.P.) in the Mississippi River Basin," *American Antiquity* 71(2):195–231.

Excavations at Woodland sites along the Buffalo River are summarized by George Sabo III and Randall L. Guendling in *Archeological Investigations at 3MR80-Area D in the Rush Development Area, Buffalo National River, Arkansas, Vol. I and II* (Southwest Cultural Resources Center Professional Papers No. 38 and 50. Santa Fe, 1990, 1992). Information on Hopewell ceremonialism at the Helena Mounds is provided by James A. Ford in *Hopewell Culture Burial Mounds Near Helena, Arkansas* (Anthropological Papers of the American Museum of Natural History, Vol. 50, Part 1. New York, 1963). Martha Rolingson summarizes long-term research at the Toltec Mounds site and the Plum Bayou culture in *Toltec Mounds: Archeology of the Mound-and-Plaza Complex* (University of Arkansas Press, 2012). Additional information on the Woodland period in Arkansas and the mid-South is provided in various chapters of *The Woodland Southeast*, edited by David G. Anderson and Robert C. Mainfort Jr. (University of Alabama Press, 2002).

A handsomely illustrated volume on Mississippian pottery from eastern Arkansas is *Gifts of the Great River: Arkansas Effigy Pottery from the Edwin Curtiss Collection*, by John H. House (Peabody Museum Press, 2003). Studies of the Parkin and Nodena communities in northeast Arkansas include *Parkin: The 1978–1979 Archeological Investigations of a Cross County, Arkansas Site* by Phyllis A. Morse (Arkansas Archeological Survey Research Series No. 13. Fayetteville, 1981); *Nodena: An Account of 90 Years of Archeological Investigation in Southeast Mississippi County, Arkansas*, edited by Dan F. Morse (Arkansas Archeological Survey Research Series No. 30. Fayetteville, rev. 2008), and *Archeological Investigations at Upper Nodena: 1973 Field Season*, edited by Robert C. Mainfort Jr. (Arkansas Archeological Survey Research Series No. 64. Fayetteville, 2010). The current research program at Parkin is detailed by Robbie Ethridge and Jeffrey M. Mitchem in "The Interior South at the Time of Spanish Exploration," in *Native and Spanish New Worlds: Sixteenth-Century*

Entradas in the American Southwest and Southeast, edited by Clay Mathers, Jeffrey M. Mitchem, and Charles M. Haecker (University of Arizona Press, 2013). Information on the development of Caddoan traditions is provided in *Caddo Connections: Cultural Interactions within and beyond the Caddo World,* by Jeffrey S. Girard, Timothy K. Perttula, and Mary Beth Trubitt (Rowman & Littlefield, 2013). Recent research on the Plaquemine Tradition is summarized in *Plaquemine Archaeology,* edited by Mark A. Rees and Patrick C. Livingood (University of Alabama Press, 2007).

Studies of Mississippian mortuary practices, including James A. Brown's examination of the Spiro site, are found in *Mississippian Mortuary Practices: Beyond Hierarchy and the Representationist Perspective,* edited by Lynne P. Sullivan and Robert C. Mainfort Jr. (University Press of Florida, 2010), and *The Archaeology of the Caddo,* edited by Timothy K. Perttula and Chester P. Walker (University of Nebraska Press, 2012). Mississippian sacred art and associated religious beliefs are examined in the lavishly illustrated volume *Hero, Hawk, and Open Hand: American Indian Art of the Ancient Midwest and South,* edited by Richard F. Townsend (The Art Institute of Chicago and Yale University Press, 2004), and additional information from the most recent studies is found in *Ancient Objects and Sacred Realms: Interpretations of Mississippian Iconography,* edited by F. Kent Reilly III and James F. Garber (University of Texas Press, 2007), and *Visualizing the Sacred: Cosmic Visions, Regionalism, and the Art of the Mississippian World,* edited by George E. Lankford, F. Kent Reilly III, and James F. Garber (University of Texas Press, 2011).

Chapter 3: First Encounters: European Explorers Meet Arkansas Indians

An excellent and very readable book on the sixteenth-century explorations of Hernando de Soto across the Southeast is Charles Hudson's *Knights of Spain, Warriors of the Sun* (University of Georgia Press, 1997). A series of papers focusing on the expedition as it approached and crossed the Mississippi River into present-day Arkansas is provided in *The Expedition of Hernando de Soto West of the Mississippi, 1541–1543,* edited by Gloria A. Young and Michael P. Hoffman (University of Arkansas Press, 1993). The four extant accounts of the Soto expedition are available in modern English translations in *The De Soto Chronicles: The Expedition of Hernando de Soto to North America in 1539–1543,* 2 vols., edited by Lawrence A. Clayton, Vernon James Knight Jr., and Edward C. Moore (University of Alabama Press, 1993). An important series of essays providing critical evaluation of the Soto accounts is found in *The Hernando de Soto Expedition: History, Historiography, and "Discovery" in the Southeast,* edited by Patricia Galloway (University of Nebraska Press, 1997).

Disruptions affecting Southeastern Indians during the protohistoric and early historic period are given thorough consideration in *The Transformation of the Southeastern Indians, 1540–1760,* edited by Robbie Ethridge and Charles Hudson (University Press of Mississippi, 2002), and *Mapping the Mississippian Shatter Zone: The Colonial Indian Salve Trade and Regional Instability in the American South,* edited by Robbie Ethridge and Sheri M. Shuck-Hall (University of Nebraska Press, 2009).

Native Americans participating in Arkansas's colonial era history are identified in *Arkansas before the Americans,* edited by Hester A. Davis (Arkansas Archeological Survey Research Series No. 40, 1991), and *Cultural Encounters in the Early South: Indians and Europeans in Arkansas,* compiled by Jeannie M. Whayne (University of Arkansas Press, 1995). An introduction to the historic Indians of Arkansas that includes a brief review of their encounters with early Spanish and French explorers is provided in *Paths of Our Children: The Historic Indians of Arkansas,* by George Sabo III (Arkansas Archeological Survey Popular Series No. 3, revised 2001). A recently published collection that includes several essays on Arkansas Indians is *Indians of the Greater Southeast: Historical Archaeology and Ethnohistory,* edited by Bonnie G. McEwan (University Press of Florida, 2000). Kathleen DuVal's *The Native Ground: Indians and Colonists in the Heart of the Continent* (University of Pennsylvania Press, 2006) traces events from the early exploration era through the subsequent era of colonial settlement.

The standard reference on the Quapaws is W. David Baird's *The Quapaws: A History of the Downstream People* (University of Oklahoma Press, 1980). Comprehensive histories and ethnographies of the Osages, written by prominent members of the tribe, include John Joseph Mathews's *The Osages: Children of the Middle Waters* (University of Oklahoma Press, 1961) and *A History of the Osage People* by Louis F. Burns (University of Alabama Press, 2004). Other valuable sources on the Osages include *The Imperial Osages: Spanish-Indian Diplomacy in the Mississippi Valley,* by Gilbert C. Din and Abraham P. Nasatir (University of Oklahoma Press, 1983); *The Osage: An Ethnohistorical Study of Hegemony on the Prairie-Plains,* by Willard H. Rollings (University of Missouri Press, 1992). The impact of European contact on Caddo Indians is examined in *"The Caddo Nation": Archaeological and Historical Perspectives,* by Timothy K. Perttula. Caddo histories penned by prominent tribal members include *Hasinai: A Traditional History of the Caddo Confederacy,* by Vynola Beaver Newkumet and Howard L. Meredith (Texas A&M University Press, 1988), and *Caddo Indians: Where We Come From,* by Cecile Elkins Carter (University of Oklahoma Press, 1995). Important new additions to the historical literature on Caddo Indians are represented by F. Todd Smith's *The Caddo Indians: Tribes at the Convergence of Empires, 1542–1854* (Texas A&M University Press, 1995), and *The Caddos, the Wichitas, and the United States, 1846–1901* (Texas A&M University Press, 1996). See also *The Caddo Chiefdoms: Caddo Economics and Politics, 700–1835,* by David LaVere (University of Nebraska Press, 1998), and *From Dominance to Disappearance: The Indians of Texas and the Near Southwest, 1786–1859,* by F. Todd Smith (University of Nebraska Press, 2005). A general review of the culture and history of the Tunica-Biloxi people is available in Jeffrey P. Brain's *The Tunica-Biloxi* (Chelsea House, 1990), and Tristram R. Kidder provides a review of the Koroas in "The Koroa Indians of the Mississippi Valley," *Mississippi Archaeologist* 23(2):1–42. Modern efforts to preserve ancient traditions among groups tracing their ancestry back to Arkansas and surrounding states are treated in *Dancing on Common Ground: Tribal Cultures and Alliances on the Southern Plains,* by Howard L. Meredith (University Press of Kansas, 1995).

Chapter 4: Indians and Colonists in the Arkansas Country, 1686–1803

Three books by Morris S. Arnold provide an essential introduction to Arkansas colonial history. *Unequal Laws Unto a Savage Race: European Legal Traditions in Arkansas, 1686–1836* (University of Arkansas Press, 1985) provides a treatment of the French and Spanish legal systems in colonial Arkansas and also includes a great deal of social history along with an extended discussion of the various locations of Arkansas Post in the seventeenth and eighteenth centuries. Arnold's *Colonial Arkansas, 1686–1804: A Social and Cultural History* (University of Arkansas Press, 1991) furnishes a discussion of various aspects of the social and cultural history of seventeenth- and eighteenth-century Arkansas, including the sites of colonial European settlements, architecture, the social structure of the European population, the state of science and religion, the military, and the legal system. There is some attention given to European and Indian relations as well. The *Rumble of a Distant Drum: The Quapaws and Old World Newcomers, 1673–1804* (University of Arkansas Press, 2000) examines a wide range of relations between Quapaws and Europeans in colonial Arkansas, including intermarriage, trade, and military alliances. There is also a discussion of attempts by French and Spanish officials to apply European law to the Indians of the region and to convert them to Christianity. Morris S. Arnold and Gail K. Arnold, *The Arkansas Post of Louisiana* (University of Arkansas Press, 2017) furnishes a compact, illustrated introduction to and synopsis of the history of Arkansas Post.

Several new studies of different aspects of Arkansas's colonial history have been published over the last decade and offer some additional insights. Kathleen DuVal, *The Native Ground: Indians and Colonists in the Heart of the Continent* (University of Pennsylvania Press, 2006), is an essential treatment of colonial efforts in mid-America, including Arkansas. Wendy St. John, "The Chickasaw-Quapaw Alliance in the Revolutionary Era," *Arkansas Historical Quarterly* 68 (Autumn 2000): 272–82. Sonia Toudji, "The Happiest Consequences: Sexual Unions and Frontier Survival at Arkansas Post" (*Arkansas Historical Quarterly 70* [Spring 2011]: 45–56), argues that marriages and other conjugal arrangements between Frenchmen and Quapaws were common in colonial Arkansas. Also useful are Kathleen DuVal, "Indian Intermarriage and Métissage in Colonial Louisiana," *William and Mary Quarterly*, 3d Series, 65 (April 2008): 207–304; John H. House, "Wallace Bottom: A Colonial-Era Archaeological Site in the Menard Locality, Eastern Arkansas," *Southeastern Archaeology* 21 (Winter 2002): 257–68; and George E. Lankford, "Town Making in the Southeastern Ozarks," *Independence County Chronicle* 31 (October 1989–January 1990): 1–19. Joseph Patrick Key, "The Calumet and the Cross: Religious Encounters in the Lower Mississippi Valley," *Arkansas Historical Quarterly* 61 (Summer 2000): 152–68. Also useful are Ann Dubuisson, "François Sarazin, Interpreter at Arkansas Post during the Chickasaw Wars," *Arkansas Historical Quarterly* 71 (Autumn 2012): 243–63. Newer relevant contributions are Joseph Patrick Key, "The Calumet and the Cross: Religious Encounters in the Lower Mississippi Valley," *Arkansas Historical Quarterly* 61 (Summer 2002): 152–68; Linda C. Jones, "Nicolas Foucault and the Quapaws," *Arkansas Historical Quarterly* 75 (Spring 2016): 4–26; and Morris S. Arnold, "The

Métis People of Eighteenth- and Nineteenth-Century Arkansas," *Louisiana History* 57 (Summer 2016): 261–96.

Earlier treatments of the colonial era, somewhat dated but still useful if used with caution, can be found in two articles by Stanley Faye: "The Arkansas Post of Louisiana: French Domination," *Louisiana Historical Quarterly 16* (July 1943): 633–721, and "The Arkansas Post of Louisiana: Spanish Domination," *Louisiana Historical Quarterly 17* (July 1944): 629–716. Faye's main virtue is that he was the first to exploit in a professional way the various European archival materials that bear on colonial Arkansas history. Gilbert C. Din's "Arkansas Post in the American Revolution" (*Arkansas Historical Quarterly* 40 [Spring 1981]: 3–30) provides an important description of the battle fought at Arkansas Post in the American Revolution and the events that led up to and followed it.

Colonial European contact with Arkansas's native peoples is treated in several useful sources. Samuel Dorris Dickinson's "Quapaw Indian Dances" (*Pulaski County Historical Review* 32 [Fall 1984]: 42–50) furnishes a revealing description and discussion of Quapaw dances that draw on various early sources. Din's "Between a Rock and a Hard Place: The Indian Trade in Spanish Arkansas" in *Cultural Encounters in the Early South: Indians and Europeans in Arkansas,* edited by Jeannie M. Whayne (University of Arkansas Press, 1995) discusses the Indian trade at and around Arkansas Post in the Spanish colonial period. Din and Abraham P. Nasatir's *The Imperial Osages: Spanish-Indian Diplomacy in the Mississippi Valley* (University of Oklahoma Press, 1983) examines relations between the Osage tribe and the Spanish government during Louisiana's colonial period, including a great deal of important information about Arkansas Post. George Sabo's "Inconsistent Kin: French-Quapaw Relations at Arkansas Post" in *Arkansas Before the Americans,* edited by Hester A. Davis (Arkansas Archeological Survey Research Series No. 40, 1991) provides an important discussion, from an anthropological perspective, of various events involving Europeans and Quapaws that occurred in Arkansas Post during the French period. Sabo's "Rituals of Encounters: Interpreting Native American Views of European Explorers" in *Cultural Encounters in the Early South: Indians and Europeans in Arkansas,* edited by Jeannie M. Whayne (University of Arkansas Press, 1995), is an excellent article that reconstructs Indian ideas about European newcomers and how the Europeans were incorporated into the Quapaws' world and worldview.

Chapter 5: The Turbulent Path to Statehood: Arkansas Territory, 1803–1836

Although the historical literature on the territorial period in Arkansas is not abundant, there are a number of sources that provide a basic framework and a foundation for understanding the era. S. Charles Bolton's two books, *Territorial Ambition: Land and Society in Arkansas, 1800–1840* (University of Arkansas Press, 1993) and *Arkansas, 1800–1860: Remote and Restless* (University of Arkansas Press, 1998), should be a starting point for historians, students, and general readers. For a book that spans the years from 1836 through 1874, see J. W. Looney's *Distinguishing the Righteous from the Roguish: The Arkansas Supreme Court, 1836–1874* (University of

Arkansas Press, 2016). A vast scholarship on the history of slavery exists, but very few historians have included much analysis of the Arkansas experience in their broader general studies. One exception is Ira Berlin, *Many Thousands Gone: The First Two Centuries of Slavery in North America* (Belknap Press of Harvard University Press, 1998). Orville W. Taylor's *Negro Slavery in Arkansas* (1958, Reprint, University of Arkansas Press, 2000) remains the standard work on slavery in Arkansas. Donald P. McNeilly's *The Old South Frontier: Cotton Plantations and the Formation of Arkansas Society, 1819–1861* (University of Arkansas Press, 2000) provides an impressive overview of the development of plantations and the evolution of Arkansas society. For an account that focuses on kinship and gender issues, see Carolyn Earle Billingsley, *Communities of Kinship: Antebellum Families and the Settlement of the Cotton Frontier* (University of Georgia Press, 2004). For an unusually perceptive look at free black settlers in Arkansas in the antebellum period, see Billy D. Higgins, *A Stranger and a Sojourner: Peter Caulder, Free Black Frontiersman in Antebellum Arkansas* (University of Arkansas Press, 2004).

While Morris S. Arnold's work focuses on the colonial era, two of his three books provide essential background for understanding how conditions existing prior to the Louisiana Purchase set the stage for what was to follow: *Colonial Arkansas, 1686–1804: A Social and Cultural History* (University of Arkansas Press, 1991) and *Rumble of a Distant Drum: The Quapaws and Old World Newcomers, 1673–1804* (University of Arkansas Press, 2000). Arnold's *Unequal Laws Unto a Savage Race: European Legal Traditions in Arkansas, 1686–1836* actually extends beyond the colonial into the territorial era and demonstrates just how European legal traditions evolved. Lonnie J. White's *Politics on the Southwestern Frontier: Arkansas Territory, 1819–1838* (Memphis State University Press, 1964) is also an essential source.

While Bolton and Arnold give considerable and often subtle treatment to Native American history within Arkansas, other important works have focused on Native American history exclusively. Daniel Usner, in a broader study on Native Americans in the lower Mississippi River valley, devoted some attention specifically to Arkansas in *American Indians in the Lower Mississippi Valley: Social and Economic Histories* (University of Nebraska Press, 1998). Kathleen DuVal's *The Native Ground: Indians and Colonists in the Heart of the Continent* (University of Pennsylvania Press, 2006) provides a thought-provoking analysis of Native Americans, particularly the Quapaw. W. David Baird's *The Quapaw Indians: A History of the Downstream People* (University of Oklahoma Press, 1980) is the basic book on the history of the Quapaws. Two important books on the Osages take different approaches to understanding them: Gilbert Din's *The Imperial Osages: Spanish-Indian Diplomacy in the Mississippi Valley* (University of Oklahoma Press, 1983) and Willard H. Rollings's *The Osage: An Ethnohistorical Study of Hegemony on the Prairie-Plains* (University of Missouri Press, 1992). For a more recent study by Rollings, see his *Unaffected by the Gospel: Osage Resistance to the Christian Invasion, 1673–1906: A Cultural Victory* (University of New Mexico Press, 2004). For another view on the Osages, consult John Joseph Mathews, *The Osages: Children of the Middle Waters* (University of Oklahoma Press, 1961). Two basic texts on the Caddo experience are Herbert Eugene Bolton's *The Hasinais:*

Southern Caddoans as Seen by the Earliest Europeans (University of Oklahoma Press, 1987) and E. Todd Smith's *The Caddo Indians: Tribes at the Convergence of Empires, 1542–1854* (Texas A&M University Press, 1995). While there are many important works on the Cherokee experience, the most useful for the Arkansas experience is Stanley Hoig's *The Cherokees and Their Chiefs: In the Wake of Empire* (University of Arkansas Press, 1998). Finally, a volume that combines articles on Europeans and Native Americans is that edited by Jeannie M. Whayne, *Cultural Encounters in the Early South: Indians and Europeans in Arkansas* (University of Arkansas Press, 1995). George Sabo's book on the historic Indians of Arkansas is foundational reading: George Sabo III, *Paths of Our Children: Historic Indians of Arkansas,* rev. ed. (Arkansas Archeological Survey, 2001).

The drama of the New Madrid earthquakes has encouraged considerable study, including books by Jay Feldman, *When the River Ran Backwards: Empire, Intrigue, Murder, and the New Madrid Earthquakes* (Free Press, 2005), and Norma Hayes Bagnall's *On Shaky Ground: The New Madrid Earthquakes of 1811–1812 (*University of Missouri Press, 1996). An important new book by Conevery Bolton Valencius, *The Lost History of the New Madrid Earthquakes* (University of Chicago Press, 2013), has re-enlivened the field. For earlier works on the earthquakes, see James Lal Penick Jr.'s *The New Madrid Earthquakes* (University of Missouri Press, 1981, revised edition). For the Geological Survey's point of view, see *The New Madrid Earthquakes: An Engineering-Geologic Interpretation of Relict Liquefaction Features,* written by Stephen F. Obermeier and edited by David P. Russ and Anthony J. Crone (Department of Interior, 1989). An important new book on the topic is one by Conevery Bolton Valencius, *The Lost History of the New Madrid Earthquakes* (University of Chicago Press, 2015).

The implications of the Louisiana Purchase have received a great deal of attention in the scholarly literature, and among the newest and most relevant works for Arkansas is Stephen Aron's *American Confluence: The Missouri Frontier from Borderland to Border States* (Indiana University Press, 2006). Another important work is Peter J. Kastor's *The Nation's Crucible: The Louisiana Purchase and the Creation of America* (Yale University Press, 2004). For the movement of planters from the older South to Arkansas after the purchase, see James David Miller's *South by Southwest: Planter Immigration and Identity in the Slave South* (University of Virginia Press, 2002).

The expedition of William Dunbar and George Hunter has yet to produce a book-length study, but their journals have been reproduced and are a valuable source of information. For Dunbar, *Forgotten Expedition: The Louisiana Purchase Journals of Dunbar and Hunter,* Trey Berry, Pam Beasley, and Jeanne Clements, eds. (Louisiana State University Press, 2006), and *Life, Letters and Papers of William Dunbar, 1749–1810,* Mrs. Dunbar Rowland, ed. (Press of the Mississippi Historical Society, 1930). For Hunter, see *The Western Journals of Dr. George Hunter, 1796–1805* (American Philosophical Society, 1963), edited by John Francis McDermott. For a fascinating account of views of Arkansas by travelers, see Brooks Blevins, *Arkansas/Arkansaw: How Bear Hunters, Hillbillies, & Good Ol' Boys Defined a State* (University of Arkansas Press, 2009). Other accounts of early visitors to Arkansas territory can be found in Savoie Lottinville, ed., *A Journal of Travels into the Arkansas Territory during the Year*

1819 by Thomas Nuttall (University of Arkansas Press, 1999) and, for a later view, see George Featherstonhaugh's *1835 Geological Report of the Examination made in 1834 of the Elevated Country Between the Missouri and Red Rivers* (US Army Corps of Engineers, 1835) and Featherstonhaugh's *Excursion Through the Slave States, from Washington on the Potomac, to the Frontier of Mexico; with Sketches of Popular Manners and Geological Notice*s (Harper and Brothers, 1844). For an interesting biography of Featherstonhaugh, see Edmund Berkeley and Dorothy Smith Berkeley, *George William Featherstonhaugh: The First U.S. Government Geologist* (University of Alabama Press, 1988). Henry R. Schoolcraft's journal, which is an account of his tour of Missouri and Arkansas in 1818 and 1819, has been edited by Hugh Park and published as *Schoolcraft in the Ozarks* (Press-Argus Printers, 1955). Schoolcraft's account was also reedited and published as *Rude Pursuits and Rugged Peaks: Schoolcraft's Ozark Journal, 1818–1819* with an introduction by Milton D. Rafferty (University of Arkansas Press, 1996). *Arkansas, Arkansas: Writers and Writings from the Delta to the Ozarks, 1541–1960* (University of Arkansas Press, 1999), edited by John Caldwell Guilds, provides insightful commentary on the early traveler accounts. For letters and correspondence between officials during the territorial era, consult the *Territorial Papers of the United States* published by the Government Printing Office. An edited volume of essays by Patrick Williams, S. Charles Bolton, and Jeannie Whayne, *A Whole Country in Commotion: The Louisiana Purchase and the American South* (University of Arkansas Press, 2005), contains much useful information on the Arkansas experience.

For a particularly astute account of life in Arkansas and Missouri in the antebellum period, see Conevery Bolton Valencius, *The Health of the Country: How American Settlers Understood Themselves and Their Land* (Basic Books, 2002). Brooks Blevins' new series on the Ozarks includes an opening volume of importance: *A History of the Ozarks, Vol. 1: The Old Ozarks* (University of Illinois Press, 2018).

Chapter 6: "The Rights and Rank to Which We Are Entitled": Arkansas in the Early Statehood Period

A good general survey of the state's history is Michael Dougan's *Arkansas Odyssey: The Saga of Arkansas from Prehistoric Times to the Present* (Rose Publishing, 1994). Another interesting account is Bob Lancaster's *The Jungles of Arkansas: A Personal History of the Wonder State* (University of Arkansas Press, 1989). A good overview of the territorial and early statehood periods is Charles Bolton's *Territorial Ambition: Land and Society in Arkansas, 1800–1840* (University of Arkansas Press, 1993). Bolton's more recent *Arkansas, 1800–1860: Remote and Restless* (University of Arkansas Press, 1998) expands on the previous volume and covers the period up to the Civil War. Lonnie J. White's *Politics on the Southwestern Frontier: Arkansas Territory, 1819–1836* (Memphis State University Press, 1964) is an excellent source for examining the political developments of the territorial period. D. A. Stokes's "The First State Elections in 1836" in the *Arkansas Historical Quarterly* 20 (Summer 1961) is also helpful.

The state's early history as chronicled in its leading newspaper can be found in Margaret Ross's *Arkansas Gazette: The Early Years, 1819–1866* (Arkansas Gazette

Foundation, 1969). A good collection of primary sources can be found in *A Documentary History of Arkansas*, Fred Williams, Charles Bolton, Carl Moneyhon, and LeRoy Williams, eds. (University of Arkansas Press, 1984). On the men who led the state during this period, see *The Governors of Arkansas: Essays in Political Biography*, 2nd edition, edited by Timothy P. Donovan, Willard B. Gatewood, and Jeannie M. Whayne (University of Arkansas Press, 1995). Inaugural addresses of the state's chief executives can be found in *Dreams of Power and the Power of Dreams: The Inaugural Addresses of the Governors of Arkansas*, edited by Marvin DeBoer (University of Arkansas Press, 1988).

For brief sketches of governors and other major figures in the state's history, see Nancy A. Williams, ed., *Arkansas Biography: A Collection of Notable Lives* (University of Arkansas Press, 2000). Walter L. Brown's definitive biography, *A Life of Albert Pike* (University of Arkansas Press, 1997), not only sheds light on one of the major figures of antebellum Arkansas but also provides a good overview of the state's early history, including the early political parties and the Mexican War. Another major figure in antebellum Arkansas is examined in William W. Hughes's *Archibald Yell* (University of Arkansas Press, 1988). U. M. Rose's "Chester Ashley" in *Publications of the Arkansas Historical Association*, Vol. 3 (1911), is a good brief account of a powerful political leader in the territorial and early statehood period.

Ted Worley's "The Control of the Real Estate Bank of Arkansas," in the *Mississippi Valley Historical Review* 37 (December 1950), helps unravel the banking fiasco. William Oates Ragdale's *They Sought a Land: A Settlement in the Arkansas River Valley, 1840–1870* (University of Arkansas Press, 1997) is also useful. A revealing diary of an Arkansas woman in the early statehood period is "The Private Journal of Mary Ann Owen Sims," edited by Clifford Dale Whitman, in the *Arkansas Historical Quarterly* 35 (Summer and Fall 1976).

On the two major religious denominations in the antebellum period, see E. Glenn Hinson's *A History of Baptists in Arkansas, 1818–1978*, Walter N. Vernon's *Methodism in Arkansas, 1816–1976* (Joint Committee for the History of Arkansas Methodism, 1976), and, more recently, Nancy Britton's *Two Centuries of Methodism in Arkansas, 1800–2000* (August House, 2000).

On various aspects of Arkansas society and culture in the antebellum period, see Walter Moffatt's "Arkansas Schools, 1819–1840" in the *Arkansas Historical Quarterly* 12 (Spring 1953) and "Transportation in Arkansas, 1819–1840" in the *Arkansas Historical Quarterly* 15 (Fall 1956). An excellent recent study is Carolyn Billingsley's *Communities of Kinship: Antebellum Families and the Settlement of the Cotton Frontier* (University of Georgia Press, 2004). Robert B. Walz's "Migration into Arkansas, 1820–1880: Incentives and Means of Travel" in the *Arkansas Historical Quarterly* 17 (Winter 1958) is also a good source. On the development of Arkansas's image, see Brooks Blevins's *Arkansas/Arkansaw: How Bear Hunters, Hillbillies, & Good Ol' Boys Defined a State* (University of Arkansas Press, 2009). For a good example of Southwestern humor from one of its best practitioners, see *Cavorting on the Devil's Fork: The Pete Whetstone Letters of C.F.M. Noland*, Leonard Williams and George Lankford, eds. (Arkansas Classics, 2006).

Priscilla McArthur's *Arkansas in the Gold Rush* (August House, 1986) is a good account of this exciting period in the state's history. On the Mountain Meadows massacre, the standard account is Juanita Brooks's *The Mountain Meadows Massacre* (University of Oklahoma Press, 1991). A more recent interpretation can be found in "An Awful Tale of Blood," in David Bigler's *Forgotten Kingdom: The Mormon Theocracy in the American West, 1847–1896* (Arthur H. Clark, 1998).

Chapter 7: Prosperity and Peril: Arkansas in the Late Antebellum Period

Ted Worley's "Pope County One Hundred Years Ago" in the *Arkansas Historical Quarterly* 13 (Summer 1954) provides a good examination of an Arkansas county that was, in many ways, typical of the state as a whole. A good description of the early history of Mississippi County can be found in the first chapter of Jeannie Whayne's *Delta Empire: Lee Wilson and the Transformation of Agriculture in the New South* (Louisiana State University Press, 2011). On the history of some of the state's most famous structures, see *Sentinels of History: Reflections on Arkansas Properties on the National Register of Historic Places*, Mark Christ and Cathryn Slater, eds. (University of Arkansas Press, 2000). Swannee Bennett and William B. Worthen's *Arkansas Made: A Survey of the Decorative, Mechanical, and Fine Arts Produced in Arkansas, 1819–1970*, 2 vols. (University of Arkansas Press, 1991) provides a unique perspective.

On river travel, see Mattie Brown's "River Transportation in Arkansas, 1819–1890" in the *Arkansas Historical Quarterly* 1 (December 1942). On steamboats three good sources are Carl D. Lane's *American Paddle Steamboats* (Coward-McCann, 1943), Louis C. Hunter's, *Steamboats on the Western Rivers: An Economic and Technological History* (Dover, 1977; originally Harvard University Press, 1949), and Herbert Quick and Edward Quick's *Mississippi Steamboatin': A History of Steamboating on the Mississippi and Its Tributaries* (Henry Holt and Company, 1926). See also Edith McCall's *Henry Miller Shreve and the Navigation of America's Inland Waterways* (Louisiana State University Press, 1984). A good Arkansas perspective is Duane Huddleston, Sammie Rose, and Pat Wood's *Steamboats and Ferries on White River: A Heritage Revisited* (University of Central Arkansas, 1995).

A good description of a cotton-growing operation in the antebellum era can be found in U. B. Phillip's *American Negro Slavery: A Survey of the Supply, Employment and Control of Negro Labor As Determined by the Plantation Regime* (Louisiana State University Press, 1966). Eugene Genovese's *Roll, Jordan, Roll: The World the Slaves Made* (Random House, 1974; Vintage Books, 1976) remains one of the best books on American slavery. On slave religion, Albert Raboteau's *Slave Religion: The "Invisible Institution" in the Antebellum South, 1740–1870* (Oxford University Press, 1978) is an excellent source. The standard account of the institution in Arkansas is Orville Taylor's *Negro Slavery in Arkansas* (Duke University Press, 1958; recently reissued in paperback by the University of Arkansas Press, 2000). Several excellent recent interpretations of slavery in Arkansas can be found in the spring 1999 issue of the *Arkansas Historical Quarterly*, which is completely devoted to the topic. Of special interest are Carl Moneyhon's "The Slave Family in Arkansas" and Gary Battershell's

"The Socioeconomic Role of Slavery in the Arkansas Upcountry." *The American Slave: A Composite Autobiography*, 19 vols. (Westport, Connecticut, 1972), is also a valuable source.

On the events leading up to secession, see James Woods's *Rebellion and Realignment: Arkansas's Road to Secession* (University of Arkansas Press, 1987) and James J. Gigantino III, ed., *Slavery and Secession in Arkansas: A Documentary History* (University of Arkansas Press, 2015). Also valuable is Jack Scroggs, "Arkansas in the Secession Crisis," in the *Arkansas Historical Quarterly* 12 (Autumn 1953). On the politics of the 1850s, see Elsie M. Lewis's unpublished doctoral dissertation, "From Nationalism to Disunion: A Short Study of the Secession Movement in Arkansas, 1850–1861" (University of Chicago, 1947), and also her article, "Robert Ward Johnson: Militant Spokesman for the Old South-West," in the *Arkansas Historical Quarterly* 13 (Spring 1954). See also Michael B. Dougan's "A Look at the 'Family' in Arkansas Politics, 1858–1865" in the *Arkansas Historical Quarterly* 29 (Summer 1970). The diary of prominent Camden Whig John Brown, in the collections of the Arkansas History Commission, is an interesting and insightful contemporary account of the period.

Chapter 8: "Between the Hawk & Buzzard": The Civil War in Arkansas

The Arkansas Historical Quarterly is a treasure trove of excellent scholarly writing on the Civil War in Arkansas. A very good review of twenty-first-century scholarship on the war in Arkansas is Buck T. Foster and Christopher R. Mortenson's "Guns, Trumpets, and More: Recent Scholarship on the Civil War in Arkansas" in the *Quarterly* 77, no. 2 (Summer 2018). On the Civil War era, an early twentieth-century account with a decidedly pro-Confederate, anti-Republican slant is David Y. Thomas's *Arkansas in the Civil War and Reconstruction, 1861–1874* (United Daughters of the Confederacy, 1926). On the war itself, there is John L. Ferguson's *Arkansas and the Civil War* (Pioneer Press, 1965). The best military overview is *With Fire and Sword: Arkansas 1861–1874* by Thomas A. DeBlack (University of Arkansas Press, 2003). For a study of antiwar society in north Arkansas in the early days of the Civil War, see James Johnston, *Mountain Feds: Arkansas Unionists and the Peace Society* (Butler Center for Arkansas Studies, 2018). A recent synthesis of the Civil War and Reconstruction in the state is Thomas A. DeBlack's *With Fire and Sword: Arkansas, 1861–1874* (University of Arkansas Press, 2003). On the tumultuous affairs in the Indian Territory, see Mary Jane Warde's, *When the Wolf Came: The Civil War and Indian Territory* (University of Arkansas Press, 2013). On the legacy of the war, see Mark K. Christ, ed., *Competing Memories: The Legacy of Arkansas Civil War* (Butler Center Books, 2016).

Another good source is *Civil War Arkansas: Beyond Battles and Leaders* (University of Arkansas Press, 2000), edited by Anne Bailey and Daniel Sutherland. Five scholars examine Arkansas's experience in the war's first year in *The Die Is Cast: Arkansas Goes to War, 1861*, Mark Christ, ed. (Butler Center Books, 2010). See also *Rugged and Sublime: The Civil War in Arkansas*, Mark Christ, ed. (University of Arkansas Press, 1994).

On Arkansas Unionism and resistance to Confederate authority, see Ted Worley's

"The Arkansas Peace Society of 1861: A Study in Mountain Unionism" in the *Journal of Southern History* 24 (November 1958) and Carl Moneyhon's "Disloyalty and Class Consciousness in Southwestern Arkansas, 1862–1865" in Bailey and Sutherland, *Civil War Arkansas: Beyond Battles and Leaders*. See also Frank Arey, "The Skirmish at McGrew's Mill," in the *Clark County Historical Journal* (2000). The hard choices the war posed for American Indians are examined in Laurence M. Hauptman's *Between Two Fires: American Indians in the Civil War* (Free Press, 1995). The controversial battle of Poison Spring and the wider issue of the Confederate reaction to black Union soldiers in Arkansas are explored in Gregory J. W. Urwin's article, "'We Cannot Treat Negroes . . . as Prisoners of War': Racial Atrocities and Reprisals in Civil War Arkansas," in *Civil War History* 42 (1996).

On the economics of the Civil War and Reconstruction periods, see Carl Moneyhon, *The Impact of the Civil War and Reconstruction on Arkansas: Persistence in the Midst of Ruin* (Louisiana State University Press, 1994). On the political aspects of the war and its effect on Arkansas society, see Michael B. Dougan's *Confederate Arkansas: The People and Politics of a Frontier State in Wartime* (University of Alabama Press, 1976). Robert R. Mackey's "Bushwhackers, Provosts, and Tories: The Guerrilla War in Arkansas," in *Guerrillas, Unionists, and Violence on the Confederate Home Front* (University of Arkansas Press, 1999), edited by Daniel Sutherland, provides a good account of that aspect of the war as does Sutherland's "Guerrillas: The Real War in Arkansas," in the aforementioned *Civil War Arkansas: Beyond Battles and Leaders*. Arkansas also figures prominently in Robert L. Kerby's *Kirby Smith's Confederacy: The Trans-Mississippi South, 1863–1865* (Columbia University Press, 1972).

A first-rate account of the biggest and most important battle in Arkansas is William L. Shea and Earl J. Hess's *Pea Ridge: Civil War Campaign in the West* (University of North Carolina Press, 1992). For a concise treatment of the battles of Pea Ridge and Prairie Grove, see Shea's *War in the West: Pea Ridge and Prairie Grove* (McWhiney Foundation Press, 1998). A fuller discussion of the Prairie Grove campaign is Shea's excellent recent study, *Fields of Blood: The Prairie Grove Campaign* (University of North Carolina Press, 2009). A good first-person account of the effects of the Civil War on northwest Arkansas is William Baxter's *Pea Ridge and Prairie Grove* (originally published in Cincinnati by Poe and Hitchcock in 1864; republished in paperback by the University of Arkansas Press in 2000). A good local history of the fighting in White County is Scott H. Akridge and Emmett E. Powers, *A Severe and Bloody Fight: The Battle of Whitney's Lane and Military Occupation of White County, Arkansas, May and June, 1862* (White County Historical Museum, 1996). A good history of Fayetteville is Charles Y. Alison's *A Brief History of Fayetteville, Arkansas* (The History Press, 2017). On the decisive year of 1863, see Mark K. Christ's *Civil War Arkansas, 1863: The Battle for a State* (University of Oklahoma Press, 2010). The photographic legacy of the war in Arkansas is found in Bobby Roberts and Carl Moneyhon's *Portraits of Conflict: A Photographic History of Arkansas in the Civil War* (University of Arkansas Press, 1987). *The War of the Rebellion: A Compilation of the Official Records of the Union and Confederate Armies* (Government Printing Office, 1880–1901), a multivolume series, is an invaluable source, now available on CD-ROM.

There are numerous biographies of the war's major figures, including Diane Neal and Thomas W. Kremm's *The Lion of the South: General Thomas C. Hindman* (Mercer University Press, 1993). On the same topic, see Bobby L. Roberts's "Thomas C. Hindman, Jr.: Secessionist and Confederate General" (Master's thesis, University of Arkansas, 1972). One of the state's most accomplished commanders is chronicled in Craig L. Symonds's *Stonewall of the West: Patrick Cleburne and the Civil War* (University Press of Kansas, 1997). A more controversial figure is the subject of Arthur B. Carter's *The Tarnished Cavalier: Major General Earl Van Dorn, C.S.A.* (University of Tennessee Press, 1999). Another pivotal figure in the Trans-Mississippi is the subject of Albert Castel's *General Sterling Price and the Civil War in the West* (Louisiana State University Press, 1968). William H. Burnside's *The Honorable Powell Clayton* (University of Central Arkansas Press, 1991) examines the career of a major Union leader in the war and postwar eras. The story of Arkansas soldiers who fought east of the Mississippi River is found in James Willis's massive *Arkansas Confederates in the Western Theater* (Morningside Press, 1998). The Spence Family Collection at the Old State House Museum provides a fascinating glimpse into the lives of two Arkansas soldiers. The family's Civil War letters are available in edited form in *Getting Used to Being Shot At: The Spence Family Civil War Letters*, Mark K. Christ, ed. (University of Arkansas Press, 2002). A good contemporary account of the war in central Arkansas by a female observer is "An Arkansas Lady in the Civil War: Reminiscences of Susan Fletcher," edited by Mary P. Fletcher in the *Arkansas Historical Quarterly* 2 (December 1943). The "Diary of Susan Cook" in the *Phillips County Historical Quarterly* 4–6 (December 1965–March 1968) provides an extensive look at a delta woman's view of the conflict.

Chapter 9: "A Harnessed Revolution": Reconstruction in Arkansas

The best recent overview of Reconstruction on the national level is Eric Foner's *Reconstruction: America's Unfinished Revolution, 1863–1877* (Harper and Row, 1988). See also Richard N. Current's *Those Terrible Carpetbaggers* (New York: Oxford University Press, 1988). On Reconstruction in Arkansas, the standard Dunning school interpretation is Thomas Staples, *Reconstruction in Arkansas, 1862–1874* (Longmans, Green & Company, 1923). Another perspective is George H. Thompson's *Arkansas and Reconstruction: The Influence of Geography, Economics, and Personality* (National University Publications, 1976). A good overview is Martha A. Ellenburg's unpublished doctoral dissertation, "Reconstruction in Arkansas" (University of Missouri, 1967). See also Orval Driggs's "The Issues of the Powell Clayton Regime, 1868–1871" in the *Arkansas Historical Quarterly* 8 (Spring 1949). A good examination of various aspects of the Reconstruction period in the state can be found in *A Confused and Confusing Affair: Arkansas and Reconstruction*, Mark Christ, ed. (Butler Center Books, 2018). For a classic account of life in the post–Civil War Ozarks, see John Quincy Wolf's *Life in the Leatherwoods*, edited by Gene Hyde and Brooks Blevins (University of Arkansas Press, 2000).

An excellent account of the activities of the Freedmen's Bureau in the state is

Randy Finley's *From Slavery to Uncertain Freedom: The Freedmen's Bureau in Arkansas, 1865–1869* (University of Arkansas Press, 1996). On the constitutional convention of 1868, two good sources are "The Arkansas Constitutional Convention of 1868: A Case Study in the Politics of Reconstruction," by Richard L. Hume in the *Journal of Southern History* 39 (May 1973), and "The Negro Delegates in the Arkansas Constitutional Convention of 1868: A Group Profile," by Joseph M. St. Hilaire in the *Arkansas Historical Quarterly* 33 (Spring 1974). A good examination of the controversial election of 1868 is Michael P. Kelley's "Partisan or Protector: Powell Clayton and the 1868 Presidential Election" in the *Ozark Historical Quarterly* 3 (Spring 1974).

The Ku Klux Klan and the militia wars are covered in Allen W. Trelease's *White Terror: The Ku Klux Klan Conspiracy and Southern Reconstruction* (Louisiana State University Press, 1971). Another good source is Otis Singletary's *Negro Militia and Reconstruction* (University of Texas Press, 1957). The D. P. Upham letters in the Special Collections Department of the University of Arkansas at Little Rock library provide a valuable first-hand account of this turbulent era from a "carpetbagger's" perspective. See also Charles Rector's "D. P. Upham, Woodruff County Carpetbagger," in the *Arkansas Historical Quarterly* 59 (Spring 2000). The life of an infamous Reconstruction outlaw is chronicled in Barry Crouch and Donaly Bryce's *Cullen Montgomery Baker, Reconstruction Desperado* (Louisiana State University Press, 1997). For an interesting look at the extraordinary career of Joseph Corbin and the founding of one of the state's historically black colleges and second oldest public institution of higher learning, see *Joseph Carter Corbin: Educator Extraordinaire and Founder of the University of Arkansas at Pine Bluff* by Gladys Turner Finney (Butler Center Books, 2017).

A valuable primary source from one of the era's major figures is Powell Clayton's own account, *The Aftermath of the Civil War, in Arkansas* (Neal Publishing Company, 1915). A contemporary account of Reconstruction in the state and the Brooks-Baxter War in particular is John M. Harrell's *The Brooks and Baxter War: A History of the Reconstruction Period in Arkansas* (Slawson Printing Company, 1893). See also Earl F. Woodward's "The Brooks and Baxter War in Arkansas, 1872–1874" in the *Arkansas Historical Quarterly* 30 (Winter 1971). An interesting account of corruption in the Federal District Court for the Western District of Arkansas is Frances Mitchell Ross's "'Getting Up Business' in the Western District of Arkansas, 1871–1874: What Style Leadership?" (unpublished manuscript). A fascinating local study is Kenneth C. Barnes's *Who Killed John Clayton? Political Violence and the Emergence of the New South, 1861–1893* (Duke University Press, 1998).

General References for Chapters 10 through 15

There are a number of standard works that provide essential background information for most of the time period covered in chapters 10 through 15. They include *The Governors of Arkansas: Essays in Political Biography*, 2nd edition (University of Arkansas Press, 1995), edited by Timothy P. Donovan, Willard B. Gatewood Jr., and Jeannie M. Whayne, which is an essential source for material on the state's governors. Diane D. Blair's *Arkansas Politics and Government: Do the People Rule?* (University of

Nebraska Press, 1988) is the best single source on Arkansas politics generally. A new edition, published after Blair's death, is Diane D. Blair and Jay Barth, *Arkansas Politics and Government*, 2nd edition (University of Nebraska Press, 2005). *The Arkansas Delta: Land of Paradox*, edited by Jeannie M. Whayne and Willard B. Gatewood, is an important source that ranges across social, economic, military, and political history (University of Arkansas Press, 1995). Carl Moneyhon's book, *Arkansas and the New South, 1874–1929* (University of Arkansas Press, 1997), which focuses on the period between 1874 and 1929, provides valuable insight into the evolution of Arkansas society in that time frame. John Gould Fletcher's *Arkansas* (University of North Carolina Press, 1947) remains the standard work in the field. The two volumes under one title edited by David Y. Thomas, *Arkansas and Its People: A History, 1541–1930*, provide a crucial source of information (American Historical Society, 1930). Michael B. Dougan's *Arkansas Odyssey: The Saga of Arkansas from Prehistoric Times to the Present* (Rose Publishing, 1994) is an excellent single-source volume for the state's history. Dougan's *Arkansas History: An Annotated Bibliography*, which he compiled with Tom W. Dillard and Timothy G. Nutt (Greenwood Press, 1995), is an excellent source book. A book edited by Janine Parry and Richard P. Want, *Readings in Arkansas Politics and Government* (University of Arkansas Press, 2009) is a very useful source, particularly on Arkansas political history. For a new book on World War I in Arkansas, see Michael D. Polston and Guy Lancaster, eds., *To Can the Kaiser: Arkansas and the Great War* (Butler Center Books, 2015).

Three books by journalists, Harry S. Ashmore's *Arkansas: A Bicentennial History* (Norton, 1978), Bob Lancaster's *The Jungles of Arkansas: A Personal History of the Wonder State* (University of Arkansas Press, 1989), and Leland Duval's *Arkansas: Colony and State* (Rose Publishing Company, 1973), contain a good deal of very useful information. C. J. Brown's *Cattle on a Thousand Hills: A History of the Cattle Industry in Arkansas* is an essential source for reading on that industry (University of Arkansas Press, 1996). Two works that stand as excellent sources of information about specific individuals or about the state's historic landmarks are as follows: *Arkansas Biography: A Collection of Notable Lives*, Nancy A. Williams, editor, and Jeannie M. Whayne, associate editor (University of Arkansas Press, 2000); and *Sentinels of History: Reflections on the National Register of Historic Places*, edited by Mark K. Christ and Cathryn H. Slater (University of Arkansas Press, 2000). For a particularly moving account of growing up in the Arkansas delta, see Margaret Bolsterli, *Born in the Delta: Reflections on the Making of a Southern White Sensibility* (University of Tennessee Press, 1991), and for a history of her family's farm, see *During the Wind and Rain: The Jones Family Farm in the Arkansas Delta, 1848–2006* (University of Arkansas Press, 2008). Whayne's book, *A New Plantation South: Land, Labor, and Federal Favor in Twentieth-Century Arkansas* (University Press of Virginia, 1996), provides a scholarly overview of the evolution of a plantation system in northeastern Arkansas and her *Delta Empire: Lee Wilson and the Transformation of Agriculture in the New South* (Louisiana State University Press, 2011) uses the story of the 50,000-acre Lee Wilson plantation to examine the transition from slavery in the antebellum period to tenancy in the post–Civil War era to neo-plantations in the post–World War II period and to portfolio-plantations of the early twenty-first century.

Three crucial books by Brooks Blevins are essential reading on an otherwise under-studied region: *Hill Folks: A History of Arkansas Ozarkers and Their Image* (2002), *Arkansas/Arkansaw: How Bear Hunters, Hillbillies, & Good Ol' Boys Defined a State* (2009), and *Ghost of the Ozarks: Murder and Memory in the Upland South* (2012) all published by the University of Arkansas Press. A new book by this noted author, *A History of the Ozarks*, Vol. 1, is his most recent contribution to the literature (University of Illinois Press, 2018).

For an important study of the judiciary in the late nineteenth and early twentieth century that includes an analysis of Arkansas jurist Jacob Trieber, see Brent J. Aucoin, *A Rift in the Clouds: Race and the Southern Federal Judiciary, 1900–1910* (University of Arkansas Press, 2007). An important new book on the federal judiciary in Arkansas is *United States District Courts and Judges of Arkansas, 1836–1960* by Frances Mitchell Ross (University of Arkansas Press, 2016).

The study of religion in Arkansas has resulted in a number of monographs. For Methodist history, see Rev. James A. Anderson, Centennial History of Arkansas, *Methodism . . . A History of the Methodist Episcopal Church, South, in the State of Arkansas, 1815–1935* (L. B. White Printing Company, 1935) and Nancy Britton's two volumes, the first on the Methodist Church in Batesville and the second on the church in the entire state: *The First 100 Years of the First Methodist Church in Batesville* (August House, 1968) and *Two Centuries of Methodism in Arkansas, 1800–2000* (August House, 2000). For the Baptist Church, see Glenn E. Hinson, *A History of Baptists in Arkansas, 1818–1978* (Arkansas State Convention, 1979). For the Christian Church and the Disciples of Christ, see Lester G. McAllister, *Arkansas Disciples: A History of the Christian Church* (Disciples of Christ) in Arkansas (n.p., 1984), and David Edwin Harrell's *A Social History of the Disciples of Christ* (Disciples of Christ Historical Society, 1966–1973). For a new book on the formation and evolution of the Church of God and Christ, see Calvin White Jr., *Race, Religion, and Respectability: The Church of God and Christ and Its Rise to Respectability* (University of Arkansas Press, 2012). For Presbyterian history, see Thomas H. Campbell, *Cumberland Presbyterians (1812–1884): A People of Faith* (Arkansas Synod of Cumberland Presbyterian Church, 1985) and C. B. Moore et al., *The History of Presbyterianism in Arkansas, 1828–1902* (Press of the Arkansas Democrat Co., 1902). For the Episcopal Church, see Margaret S. White, *Already to Harvest: The Episcopal Church in Arkansas, 1838–1971* (Episcopal Diocese of Arkansas at the University Press of Sewanee, 1957). For Roman Catholics, see James M. Woods, *Mission and Memory, A History of the Catholic Church in Arkansas* (Diocese of Little Rock, 1993) and an important new book by Kenneth Barnes, *Anti-Catholicism in Arkansas: How Politicians, the Press, the Klan, and Religious Leaders Imagined an Enemy, 1910–1960* (University of Arkansas Press, 2016). For the Jewish experience in Arkansas, see Carolyn Gray LeMaster, *A Corner of the Tapestry: A History of the Jewish Experience in Arkansas, 1820s-1990s* (University of Arkansas Press, 1994). An important study of African Americans and religion that focuses on the Delta generally but includes analysis of Arkansas, see John M. Giggie, *After Redemption: Jim Crow and the Transformation of African American Religion in the Delta, 1875–1915* (Oxford University Press, 2008).

For the development of agriculture and the lumber industry in the state, see Stephen Strausberg, *A Century of Research: Centennial History of the Arkansas Agricultural Experiment Station, 1888–1988* (University of Arkansas Press, 1989), Gary Zellar and Nancy Wyatt, *History of the Bumpers College: Evolution of Education in the Agricultural, Food and Life Sciences in Arkansas* (Arkansas Experiment Station Special Report 194, 1999), George W. Balogh, *Entrepreneurs in the Lumber Industry: Arkansas, 1881–1963* (Garland Publishing, 1995), and Kenneth L. Smith, *Sawmill: The Story of Cutting the Last Great Virgin Forest East of the Rockies* (University of Arkansas Press, 1986). An excellent new book by Mildred Diane Gleason is *Dardanelle and the Bottoms: Environmental, Agriculture, and the Economy in an Arkansas River Valley Community, 1819–1970* (University of Arkansas Press, 2017).

For books on education and on the development of colleges in Arkansas, see the following: Thomas A. DeBlack, *A Century Forward: The Centennial History of Arkansas Tech University* (Walworth Publishing Company, 2016); Brooks Blevins, *Lyon College, 1872–2002: The Perseverance and Promise of an Arkansas College* (University of Arkansas Press, 2003); Richard Ostrander, *Head, Heart, and Hand: John Brown University and Modern Evangelical Higher Education* (University of Arkansas Press, 2003); C. Calvin Smith and Linda Walls Joshua, *Educating the Masses: The Unfolding History of Black School Administrators in Arkansas, 1900–2000* (University of Arkansas Press, 2003); and James F. Willis, *Southern Arkansas University: The Mulerider School's Centennial History, 1909–2009* (Southern Arkansas University Foundation, 2009). For a different look at education, see Thomas C. Kennedy, *A History of Southland College: The Society of Friends and Black Education in Arkansas* (University of Arkansas Press, 2009).

For studies of women in Arkansas history, three relatively recent books provide essential reading: Cherisse Jones-Branch and Gary T. Edwards, *Arkansas Women: Their Lives and Times* (University of Georgia Press, 2018); Elizabeth Griffin Hill, *Faithful to Our Tasks: Arkansas's Women and the Great War* (Butler Center Books, 2015); and Bernadette Cahill, *Arkansas Women and the Right to Vote: The Little Rock Campaigns, 1868–1920* (Butler Center Books, 2015). See also *The Afterlife of Leslie Stringfellow: A Nineteenth-Century Southern Family's Experiences with Spiritualism* (Fullcourte Press, 2005). Although studies of the slave interviews conducted by the Works Progress Administration in the late 1930s might seem more appropriate for a different section of "suggested readings," in fact, they provide much useful information about those telling the stories and their lives after slavery, particularly in the 1930s. This is one of the many virtues of *Bearing Witness: Memories of Arkansas Slavery, Narratives from the 1930s WPA Collections*, George Lankford, ed. (University of Arkansas Press, 2003). For books on lynching in Arkansas, see Kimberly Harper's *White Man's Heaven: The Lynching and Expulsion of Blacks in the Southern Ozarks, 1894–1909* (University of Arkansas Press, 2010) and Guy Lancaster's *Bullets and Fire: Lynching and Authority in Arkansas, 1840–1950* (University of Arkansas Press, 2018).

For a provocative study of gay and lesbian history in Arkansas, see Brock Thompson, *The Un-Natural State: Arkansas and the Queer South* (University of Arkansas Press, 2010). For a richly entertaining account of a variety of Arkansas stories and people, see Tom Dillard, *Statesmen, Scoundrels, and Eccentrics: A Gallery of Amazing Arkansans* (University of Arkansas Press, 2010). Ben Johnson III's excellent monograph, *Arkansas in Modern America: 1930–1999* (University of Arkansas Press, 2000), is the basic text covering the period between 1930 and 1999.

For significant books on architecture, see *Architects of Little Rock, 1833–1950* by Charles Witsell and Gordon Wittenberg (University of Arkansas Press, 2014), and *Buildings of Arkansas*, edited by Cyrus A. Sutherland (University of Virginia Press, 2018).

Archeological publications provide much insight into the nature of the landscape and native populations. *The Lower Mississippi Valley Expeditions of Clarence Bloomfield Moore*, edited by Dan F. Morse and Phyllis A. Morse (University of Alabama Press, 1998), includes Moore's venture into eastern Arkansas. See also *Arkansas Archeology: Essays in Honor of Dan and Phyllis Morse*, Robert C. Mainfort Jr. and Marvin D. Jeter (University of Arkansas Press, 2000). Leslie Stewart-Abernathy's *Ghost Boats on the Mississippi: Discovering Our Working Past* (Arkansas Archeological Survey, 2002), provides considerable insight into river traffic along the Mississippi River.

Chapter 10: Arkansas in the New South, 1880–1900

Only a few works have focused specifically on the period between 1880 and 1900, and they include a diary edited by Margaret Bolsterli, *Vinegar Pie and Chicken Bread: A Woman's Diary of Life in the Rural South* (University of Arkansas Press, 1981), an excellent source for women's history. Waddy William Moore's *Arkansas in the Gilded Age: 1874–1900* (Rose Publishing Company, 1976) provides an excellent overview of the state in this era, while John William Graves, *Town and Country: Race Relations in an Urban-Rural Context, Arkansas, 1865–1905* (University of Arkansas Press, 1990) offers a superb treatment of the issue of race. Fon Louise Gordon's book, *Caste and Class: The Black Experience in Arkansas, 1880–1920* (University of Georgia Press, 1995), provides an interesting analysis that is as relevant for the next chapter as it is for this one. A particularly entertaining account of life in the Ozarks is *Life in the Leatherwoods: John Quincy Wolf*, edited by Gene Hyde and Brooks Blevins (University of Arkansas Press, 2000). Carl Moneyhon's *Arkansas and the New South, 1874–1929* (University of Arkansas Press, 1997), which covers the period through 1929, is a must-read for anyone wishing to understand Arkansas in the late nineteenth century. For a fascinating account of populist activism in the Ozarks, see J. Blake Perkins, *Hillbilly Hellraisers: Federal Power and Populist Defiance in the Ozarks* (University of Illinois Press, 2017).

Judge Isaac Parker has been the subject of numerous treatments. Two recent studies provide new insights: Roger Tuller's *"Let No Guilty Man Escape": A Judicial Biography of "Hanging Judge" Isaac C. Parker* (University of Oklahoma Press, 2001) and Michael J. Brodhead, *Isaac C. Parker: Federal Justice on the Frontier* (University of Oklahoma Press, 2003).

Kenneth Barnes has published two important and thought-provoking books on Arkansas topics: *Who Killed John Clayton? Political Violence and the Emergence of the New South, 1861–1893* (Duke University Press, 1998) and *Journey of Hope: The Back-to-Africa Movement in Arkansas in the Late 1800s* (University of North Carolina Press, 2004).

Chapter 11: A Light in the Darkness: Limits of Progressive Reform, 1900–1932

The Progressive Era has received far more attention than has the Gilded Age in Arkansas. Several important studies of governors have appeared, beginning with Raymond Arsenault's *Wild Ass of the Ozarks: Jeff Davis and the Social Bases of Southern Politics* (University of Tennessee Press, 1984). The two most important progressive governors have had books published on them. Calvin R. Ledbetter Jr. in *Carpenter from Conway: George Washington Donaghey as Governor of Arkansas, 1909–1913* (University of Arkansas Press, 1993) details the history and administration of Governor Donaghey, arguably the most progressive governor of the period. Foy Lisenby's book on *Charles Hillman Brough: A Biography* (University of Arkansas Press, 1996) gives that progressive governor equal time. For a study of one of the state's most notable senators, see Cecil Edward Weller Jr., *Joe T. Robinson: Always a Loyal Democrat* (University of Arkansas Press, 1998). Richard L. Niswonger, *Arkansas Democratic Politics, 1896–1920* (University of Arkansas Press, 1990), provides an excellent overview of the state's political history in this era. To understand labor issues, see James R. Green, *Grass Roots Socialism: Radical Movements in the Southwest, 1895–1943* (Louisiana State University Press, 1978). *History of the Organization and Operations of the Board of Directors, St. Francis Levee District of Arkansas, 1893–1945* (St. Francis Levee District, n.d.), provides a wealth of information on that entity. Two major disasters that hit the state in this period have received ample attention. The 1927 flood has been covered by Pete Daniel in *Deep'n as It Come: The 1927 Mississippi River Flood* (University of Arkansas Press, reprint, 1996; original edition published by Oxford University Press, 1977) and by John Barry, *Rising Tide: The Great Mississippi Flood of 1927 and How it Changed America* (Simon and Schuster, 1997). For the impact of the drought of 1930-1931 on Arkansas, see Nan Elizabeth Woodruff's *As Rare as Rain: Federal Relief in the Great Southern Draught of 1930–31* (University of Illinois Press, 1985).

For books that cover one of the darkest episodes in Arkansas history, see Grif Stockley, *Blood in Their Eyes: The Elaine Race Massacres of 1919* (University of Arkansas Press, 2001), and Robert Whitaker, *On the Laps of Gods: The Red Summer of 1919 and the Struggle for Justice That Remade a Nation* (Random House, 2008). For a larger study of the history of the Mississippi delta with a special emphasis on the Arkansas story, see Nan Woodruff, *American Congo: The African American Freedom Struggle in the Delta* (Harvard University Press, 2003). A new book edited by Guy Lancaster brings some important new scholarship to the study of this tragic event:

The Elaine Massacre and Arkansas: A Century of Atrocity and Resistance, 1819–1919 (University of Arkansas Press, 2018).

Ben Johnson has contributed much to the understanding of Arkansas history, but his book on prohibition is a foundational book on that particular topic: Ben F. Johnson, *John Barleycorn Must Die: The War against Drink in Arkansas* (University of Arkansas Press, 2005).

Among the many virtues of Steven Hahn's Pulitzer Prize–winning book on the black struggle from slavery to 1920 is attention to the subject in Arkansas: Steven Hahn, *A Nation under Our Feet: Black Political Struggles in the Rural South from Slavery to the Great Migration* (Belknap Press of Harvard University Press, 2003). Mary Rolinson's study of the University Negro Improvement Association also includes attention to the Arkansas story: Mary G. Rolinson, *Grassroots Garvism: The Universal Negro Improvement Association in the Rural South, 1920–1927* (University of North Carolina Press, 2007).

Chapter 12: Darker Forces on the Horizon: The Great Depression and World War II, 1932–1945

The period covering the Great Depression has received even more attention than the Progressive Era. Several publications transcend the time period, but have most relevance within it. Dorothy Stuck and Nan Snow's *Roberta: A Most Remarkable Fulbright* (University of Arkansas Press, 1997) is not only good women's history, it provides a keen analysis of social and political forces at work. Ben F. Johnson III's *Fierce Solitude: A Life of John Gould Fletcher* (University of Arkansas Press, 1994) provides far more than a biography of a literary and historical figure.

A number of important books have been published on the Great Depression's impact on farmers. H. L. Mitchell's autobiography, *Mean Things Happening in This Land: The Life and Times of H. L. Mitchell, Cofounder of the Southern Tenant Farmers Union* (Allanheld, Osmun, 1979), provides crucial information about the founding of the Southern Tenant Farmers Union, and no fewer than four books focus on the STFU: David Eugene Conrad, *The Forgotten Farmer: The Story of Sharecroppers in the New Deal* (University of Illinois Press, 1965); Paul E. Mertz, *New Deal Policy and Southern Rural Poverty* (Louisiana State University Press, 1978); Donald H. Grubbs, *Cry from the Cotton: The Southern Tenant Farmers' Union and the New Deal* (University of Arkansas Press, 2000, reprint; originally published by University of North Carolina Press, 1971); and Howard Kester's *Revolt among the Sharecroppers* (University of Tennessee Press, reprint, 1997; originally published New York: Covici, Friede, 1936). For an examination of a radical college in Arkansas that had ties to the STFU, see William H. Cobb, *Radical Education in the Rural South: Commonwealth College, 1922–1940* (Wayne State University Press, 2000). Some failed tenants and sharecroppers found their way to Resettlement or Farm Security Administration communities, but as Donald Holley explains, most who found places in such communities were failed farm owners rather than tenants. See Holley's *Uncle Sam's Farmers: The*

New Deal Communities in the Lower Mississippi Valley (University of Illinois Press, 1975). Holley's more recent book, *The Second Great Emancipation: The Mechanical Cotton Picker, Black Migration, and How They Shaped the Modern South* (University of Arkansas Press, 2000), extends beyond the period covered in this chapter but introduces the experiments with the mechanical cotton harvester that intensified in the 1930s. Two excellent books placing cotton cultivation into larger context are Charles S. Aiken's *The Cotton Plantation South since the Civil War* (Johns Hopkins University Press, 1998) and Gene Dattel's *Cotton and Race in the Making of America: The Human Cost of Economic Power* (Ivan R. Dee, 2009). Although Jarod Roll's book focuses on the Missouri Bootheel, it is instructive for those interested in the struggle of tenants and sharecroppers in this era: Jarod Roll, *Spirit of Rebellion: Labor and Religion in the New Cotton South* (University of Illinois Press, 2010).

For a look at the Ozarks in this period, see Brooks Blevins, *Hill Folk: A History of the Arkansas Ozarkers and Their Image* (University of North Carolina Press, 2002); Milton R. Rafferty, *The Ozarks: Land and Life* (University of Arkansas Press, 2001); and Lynn Morrow and Linda Myers-Phinney, *Shepherd of the Hills: Tourism Transforms the Ozarks, 1880s-1930s* (University of Arkansas Press, 1999). For an examination of south Arkansas, see John G. Ragsdale, *As We Were in South Arkansas* (August House, 1995).

David Malone's *Hattie and Huey: An Arkansas Tour* (University of Arkansas Press, 1989) provides an interesting treatment of Hattie Caraway and Huey Long. Stephen Wilson's *Harvey Couch: An Entrepreneur Brings Electricity to Arkansas* (August House, 1986) focuses on that important political and economic force in the state. For an interesting treatment of two Arkansans who became famous radio personalities, see Randal L. Hall, *Lum and Abner: Rural America and the Golden Age of Radio* (University Press of Kentucky, 2007). For the development of the Arkansas State Police, see Michael Lindsey, *The Big Hat Law: Arkansas and Its State Police, 1935–2000* (Butler Center Books, 2008).

Several books about Arkansas's experience in World War II have been published, including C. Calvin Smith's *War and Wartime Changes* (University of Arkansas Press, 1986), which offers a valuable overview and analysis. For a look at those who served in the war, see *Unsung Valor: A GI's Story of World War II* by A. Cleveland Harrison (University Press of Mississippi, 2000). For an account of the experience of Arkansans in the Aleutians, see Donald M. Goldstein and Katherine V. Dillon, *The Williwaw War: The Arkansas National Guard in the Aleutians during World War II* (University of Arkansas Press, 1992). A particularly poignant account of the experience of Arkansans in World War II can be found in Nan Snow, *Letters Home* (Phoenix International, 2001). For an autobiography of an Arkansas's World War II veteran who became governor of the state, see Sidney S. McMath, *Promises Kept: A Memoir* (University of Arkansas Press, 2003).

No book-length study of the Japanese internment camps in Arkansas exists, but a fine recent study that includes analysis of the Arkansas camps can be found in Brian Masaru Hayashi, *Democratizing the Enemy: The Japanese American Internment* (Princeton University Press, 2004). Books by Grif Stockley and John Kirk focusing on civil rights and race relations (noted below) have some very useful information covering the World War II and immediate postwar period.

Chapter 13: From World War to New Era, 1945–1960

Many of the books published on this period focus on the Central High crisis or on figures connected to it in one way or another. A notable exception is the excellent book on J. William Fulbright by Randall S. Woods, *Fulbright: A Biography* (Cambridge University Press, 1995). Of the books that focus on Central High, some important recent books have contributed significantly to a fuller understanding of that experience and its long-term implications. Elizabeth Jacoway and C. Fred Williams edited *Understanding the Little Rock Crisis: An Exercise in Remembrance and Reconciliation* (University of Arkansas Press, 1999). Elizabeth Jacoway's memoir, *Turn Away Thy Son: Little Rock, the Crisis That Shocked the World* (Free Press, 2007), provides a particularly interesting look at the Little Rock white elite during the crisis. For an important biography of Daisy Bates, see Grif Stockley, *Daisy Bates: Civil Rights Crusader from Arkansas* (University Press of Mississippi, 2005). Pete Daniel's award-winning account of the South in the 1950s includes a close analysis of the Central High crisis, *Lost Revolutions: The South in the 1950s* (University of North Carolina Press, 2000). For a study of an important Arkansas African American civil rights leader, see Judith L. Kilpatrick, *There When We Needed Him: Wiley Austin Branton, Civil Rights Warrior* (University of Arkansas Press, 2007). Will Counts, ed., *A Life Is More Than a Moment: The Desegregation of Little Rock's Central High* (Indiana University Press, 1999), includes some riveting essays by Arkansas journalists Ernest Dumas and Robert McCord. For an insightful study by a sociologist, see Johnny F. Williams, *African American Religion and the Civil Rights Movement in Arkansas* (University Press of Mississippi, 2008). Beth Roy, *Bitters in the Honey: Tales of Hope and Disappointment across Divides of Race and Time* (University of Arkansas Press, 1999), draws on oral history to focus on the experience of white students during the Central High crisis.

For accounts from among the Little Rock nine, see Melba Patillo Beals, *Warriors Don't Cry: A Searing Memoir of the Battle to Integrate Little Rock's Central High* (Pocket Books, 1994), Terrence Roberts, *Lessons from Little Rock* (Butler Center Books, 2009), and Carlotta Walls LaNier with Lisa Frazier Page, *A Mighty Long Way: My Journey to Justice at Little Rock Central High School* (One World/Ballantine Books, 2009).

A welcome new addition to the literature of desegregation in Little Rock is one edited by Laverne Bell-Tolliver, *The First Twenty-Five: An Oral History of the Desegregation of Little Rock's Public Junior High Schools* (University of Arkansas Press, 2017).

For an important overview of race relations in Arkansas, see Grif Stockley, *Ruled by Race: Black/White Relations in Arkansas from Slavery to the Present* (University of Arkansas Press, 2008). John Kirk has contributed several important books to the subject of civil rights in Arkansas: *Race, Community, and Crisis: Little Rock, Arkansas, and the Civil Rights Struggle, 1940–1970* (University Press of Florida, 2002); *Redefining the Color Line: Black Activism in Little Rock, Arkansas, 1940–1970* (University of

Arkansas Press, 2007); *Beyond Little Rock: The Origins and Legacies of the Central High Crisis* (University of Arkansas Press, 2007); and an edited volume, *An Epitaph for Little Rock: A Fiftieth Anniversary Retrospective on the Central High Crisis* (University of Arkansas Press, 2008). His most recent contribution includes essays coedited with Jennifer Wallach: *Arsnick: The Student Nonviolent Coordinating Committee in Arkansas* (University of Arkansas Press, 2011), a very important contribution to the literature on civil rights in the state.

Jeff Woods larger study of civil rights and anticommunism includes an insightful analysis of the activities of Arkansas's segregationists. See Jeff Woods, *Black Struggle, Red Scare: Segregation and Anti-Communism in the South, 1948–1968* (Louisiana State University Press, 2004). For a different look at African American life in this period, see Robert Cochran, *A Photographer of Note: Arkansas Artist Geleve Grice* (University of Arkansas Press, 2003).

Anyone interested in the history of the Central High crisis should begin with the accounts by those on the inside. Daisy Bates's *The Long Shadow of Little Rock* (University of Arkansas Press, 1986) tells the story from the African American perspective. Elizabeth Huckaby's *Crisis at Central High, Little Rock, 1957–58* (Louisiana State University Press, 1980) provides a sympathetic teacher's perspective. The account by Sara Alderman Murphy, edited by her son, Patrick C. Murphy III, *Breaking the Silence: Little Rock's Women's Emergency Committee to Open Our Schools, 1958–1963* (University of Arkansas Press, 1997), provides a glimpse into the workings of the Women's Emergency Committee. See Roy Reed's *Faubus: The Life and Times of an American Prodigal* (University of Arkansas Press, 1997) for a keen analysis of Faubus's contribution to the crisis. For a book that focuses on the "lost year," see Sondra Gordy, *Finding the Lost Year: What Happened When Little Rock Closed Its Public Schools* (University of Arkansas Press, 2009). Two books illuminate Brooks Hays's perspective: *James T. Baker, Brooks Hays* (Mercer University Press, 1989) and Hays's own *Politics Is My Parish* (Louisiana State University Press, 1981). David Chappell's *Inside Agitators: White Southerners in the Civil Rights Movement* (Johns Hopkins University Press, 1994) provides a comparative perspective. For a fresh look at the legal history of the Little Rock crisis, see Tony A. Freyer, *Little Rock on Trial: Cooper v. Aaron and School Desegregation* (University Press of Kansas, 2007). For an examination of the role of the interposition position, see Frances Lisa Baer, *Resistance to Public School Desegregation: Little Rock, Arkansas, and Beyond* (LFB Scholarly Publishing, 2008). For an important new book on the crisis, see Karen Anderson, *Little Rock: Race and Resistance at Central High School* (Princeton University Press, 2010).

Chapter 14: Arkansas in the Sunbelt South, 1960–1992

The political history of this period has received some noteworthy attention from scholars. See especially Cathy Kunzinger Urwin's *Agenda for Reform: Winthrop Rockefeller as Governor of Arkansas, 1967–71* (University of Arkansas Press, 1991), John L. Ward's *The Arkansas Rockefeller* (Louisiana State University Press, 1978), and Ward's *Winthrop Rockefeller, Philanthropist: A Life of Change* (University of Arkansas

Press, 2004). Diane D. Blair's *Arkansas Politics and Government: Do the People Rule?* (University of Nebraska Press, 1988) is essential reading, and a revision published after Blair's untimely death, is equally useful: Diane D. Blair and Jay Barth, *Arkansas Politics and Government*, 2nd edition (University of Nebraska Press, 2005). Roy Reed's biography of Faubus, *Faubus: The Life and Times of an American Prodigal* (University of Arkansas Press, 1997) includes an intriguing examination of the governor's last years. A book that focuses on the 1970 gubernatorial elections in four southern states includes special focus on Arkansas, Randy Sanders, *Mighty Peculiar Elections: The New South Gubernatorial Campaigns of 1970 and the Changing Politics of Race* (University Press of Florida, 2002). A couple of insightful political autobiographies include Dale Bumpers, *The Best Lawyer in a One Lawyer Town* (Random House, 2003) and David Pryor and Don Harrell, *A Pryor Commitment: The Autobiography of David Pryor* (Butler Center Books, 2008).

A few "business histories" have been published that provide essential background information on some of the most important corporations in the state. They include *Wal-Mart: A History of Sam Walton's Retail Phenomenon* (Twayne, 1994), as well as Walton's autobiography, *Made in America* (Doubleday, 1992). Marvin Schwartz's *Tyson: From Farm to Market* (University of Arkansas Press, 1992) provides useful information. A study by Lu Ann Jones on the role of women in farming includes a treatment of the poultry industry, providing insight into their experience in supplying poultry to Tysons: Lu Ann Jones, *Mama Learned Us to Work: Farm Women in the New South* (University of North Carolina Press, 2002). For the trucking industry, see Marvin Schwartz's *J. B. Hunt: The Long Haul to Success* (University of Arkansas Press, 1992). Leon J. Rosenberg's *Dillard's: The First Fifty Years* (University of Arkansas Press, 1988) is also useful. William H. Bowen, *The Boy from Altheimer: From the Depression to the Boardroom* (University of Arkansas Press, 2006), is an autobiography of a highly successful Little Rock attorney with many important business and professional connections. For a study of the last days of the *Arkansas Gazette*, see Roy Reed, ed., *Looking Back at the* Arkansas Gazette: *An Oral History* (University of Arkansas Press, 2009). An important new chapter in this controversy—and more—is that by Jerry McConnell, *The Improbable Life of the* Arkansas Democrat: *An Oral History* (University of Arkansas Press, 2016).

Another less well-known topic, conservation, has received little attention, but Neil Compton's *The Battle for the Buffalo River: A Twentieth-Century Conservation Crisis in the Ozarks* (University of Arkansas Press, 1992) provides an interesting treatment of the saga leading to the establishment of the Buffalo River as a national river. Another book-length study of the conservation issue is S. Charles Bolton's *Twenty-Five Years Later: A History of the McClellan-Kerr Arkansas River Navigation System in Arkansas* (US Army Corps of Engineers, 1995).

While no scholarly books on industrialization have been published, several books on the South's experience with industrialization provide considerable insight and have resonance with the Arkansas story. James C. Cobb's foundational work on the topic includes *Industrialization and Southern Society, 1877–1984* (University of Kentucky Press, 1984; reprint, Dorsey Press, 1988), and Philip Scranton, ed., *The*

Second Wave: Southern Industrialization from the 1940s to the 1970s (University of Georgia Press, 2001).

Chapter 15: The Burden of Arkansas History, 1992–2012

Some of the best work done on Arkansas history in this period has focused on the state's political and economic giants. See Bethany Morton, *To Serve God and Wal-Mart: The Making of Christian Free Enterprise* (Harvard University Press, 2009), and Shane Hamilton, *Trucking Country: The Road to America's Wal-Mart Economy* (Princeton University Press, 2008). For a study of an important jurist from Arkansas who practiced in this period, see Polly J. Price, *Judge Richard S. Arnold: A Legacy of Justice on the Federal Bench* (Prometheus Books, 2009). Much of the information on the Little Rock desegregation case and the Alma and Lake View education funding cases came from primary documents, especially from two interviews conducted by the author with Governor Mike Beebe. Another important source for the desegregation case was Gene Vinzant's doctoral dissertation, "Little Rock's Long Crisis: Schools and Race in Little Rock, Arkansas, 1863–2009," produced at the University of Arkansas in 2009.

While there are a number of books on folk music and blues, see Robert Cochran's excellent *Our Own Sweet Sounds: A Celebration of Popular Music in Arkansas* (University of Arkansas Press, 1996) for an overview of the Arkansas experience. See also his *Singing in Zion: Music and Song in the Life of an Arkansas Family* (University of Arkansas Press, 1999). Levon Helm's *This Wheel's on Fire: Levon Helm and the Story of the Band* (W. Morrow, 1993) and Johnny Cash's *Cash: The Autobiography* (Harper, 1997) are very good sources. For a book that includes interviews with Arkansas bluesmen, see *Goin' Back to Sweet Memphis: Conversations with Blues,* Fred J. Hay, ed. (University of Georgia Press, 2005). For a book focusing on Rosetta Tharpe, see Gayle F. Ward, *Shout, Sister, Shout! The Untold Story of Rock-and-Roll Trailblazer Sister Rosetta Tharpe* (Beacon Press, 2007). Two new books are also important: *Encyclopedia of Arkansas Music,* edited by Ali Welky and Mike Keckhaver (University of Arkansas Press, 2013) and John M. Alexander's *The Man in Song: A Discographic Biography of Johnny Cash* (University of Arkansas Press, 2018).

For information on globalization and the modern economy, I have relied on primary sources such as newspaper articles. One important scholarly study on globalization in the South provided some crucial context: *Globalization and the American South,* James C. Cobb and William Stueck, eds. (University of Georgia Press, 2005).

INDEX

Aaron v. Cooper, 322, 323, 325
"A Boy Named Sue" (Cash), 376
Abenaki (Delaware) Indians, 58
Above World symbolism, 31, 50
acorns, 22–23
acreage restriction program, 272–273, 311
Acrocanthrosaurus atokensis, West Gulf
    Coast Plain, 10
Act 916, 359
Act 917, 359
Act 1194, 359
Act 1307, 359
Acxiom, 335
Adams, John Quincy, 91, 93
Adkins, Homer, 280, 281, 282, 283, 287, 289,
    292, 301
adzes (stone), 20
African Americans: Arkansas State
    Press, 293, 313, 318; "Black and Tan"
    Convention, 195–96; Back to Africa,
    229, 230, 258; black aristocracy, 229–30,
    242, 319; blacks and mulattoes in colo-
    nial era, 68–71; Civil Rights Act of 1964,
    343; Civil Rights Activism and World
    War II; 291–94; Civil Rights Activism,
    1945–1960, 313–27; civil rights legacy,
    356; civil rights movement, 358; Civil
    Rights unfinished, 357; Civil Rights,
    1960–1992, 335–43; Colored Teachers
    Association, 237; convict leasing, 245;
    disfranchisement, 215, 227–31, 243, 293,
    314, 315, 342–43; educational systems,
    211, 251; Elaine Race Riot, 256–58;
    Executive Order 8802, 291; First Kansas
    Colored Infantry, 179, 180; freed-
    men, 180, 186, 190–94, 195, 200, 211,
    211; Little Rock Classroom Teachers
    Association, 292, 293; migration pat-
    terns, 229, 230; military service, 291;
    militiamen, 201–2; Mosaic Templars,
    229, 230, 235; musical heritage, 371,
    373; ninth street in Little Rock, 229,
    293; Pine Bluff attack, 176–77; political

development, 197, 211–12, 230, 242–43;
    progressive era, 242–43; prohibition,
    246–47; residential segregation, 336;
    Second Kansas Colored Infantry, 181;
    sharecropping, 190–91, 221; slavery,
    100–102, 131–36; Southern Tenant
    Farmers Union (STFU), State Press, 293,
    313, 318; teaching profession, 212, 236,
    237, 252; Union League, 197; unionists,
    201; voting rights, 330, 341, 342–43;
    Voting Rights act of 1965, 330; Women's
    club movement, 236; World War II war
    effort, 291
African Methodist Episcopal Church,
    212, 232
Afro/creole dialect, 68
Agricultural Adjustment Administration
    (AAA), 272–73, 274, 275, 277, 280, 308
Agricultural Wheel, 223–26, 274
agriculture, 56–57, 59, 65, 68, 69, 70,
    76; acreage restriction program,
    272–73, 311; agricultural fields (Native
    Americans), 33; agricultural reorga-
    nization, 221–23; archaic period, 21;
    Caddo Indians, 47–48; chemicals and
    fertilizers, 307; contract labor system,
    221; depression, 266; drought condi-
    tions, 15, 192, 224, 255, 265–66; eco-
    nomic crisis, 266, 272–73, 287; Farm
    Security Administration (Resettlement
    Administration), 275–76; fracking,
    363–64; grain embargo, 331; wheat
    embargo, 351; colonial period, 56, 68,
    97; Korean War, 309; labor shortages,
    287; labor surplus, 308, 309; mechani-
    zation, 287, 308–9; Memphis Cotton
    Carnival, 312; Mexican Nationals
    (bracero program), 312; Mississippi
    period, 21, 28, 32; neo-plantation, 310,
    311, 312, 313; plant domestication, 21,
    23–24, 32; plantation agriculture, 97,
    127, 130–33, 257, 258–59, 260, 264,
    265, 269, 276, 299, 303–4, 305, 309,

Arkansas Education Commission, 250
Arkansas Education Department, 311
Arkansas Farm Bureau Federation, 331
Arkansas Farmers Alliance, 225
Arkansas Federation of Women's Clubs, 253
Arkansas Gazette, 78, 89, 91–92, 94, 102–3,
    105, 146, 147, 152, 153, 192, 302, 314,
    319, 325, 347, 351, 387–88; criticizes
    constitutional convention of 1868,
    195–96; endorses John Bell in presi-
    dential election of 1860, 146; first edi-
    tion published, 89; on Lincoln's election
    as president, 147
Arkansas Highlands, 7
Arkansas Highway Department, 306
Arkansas Historical Quarterly, 103, 336
Arkansas History Education Coalition, 353
Arkansas Indians, 7. See also Native
    Americans
Arkansas Industrial Development
    Commission, 302, 352
Arkansas Industrial University (University
    of Arkansas at Fayetteville), 211
Arkansas Ladies Journal, 234, 238
Arkansas land subdivision and boundary
    changes, 83
Arkansas Louisiana Gas Company, 305
Arkansas National Guard: Central High
    Crisis, 325; Korean War, 309; World
    War II, 296, 297
Arkansas Natural and Cultural Heritage,
    352
Arkansas Negro Democratic Association
    (ANDA), 262, 292
Arkansas Peace Society, 154
Arkansas Plan (AP&L's), 278
Arkansas Plan (Ben Laney's), 300
Arkansas Post, 7, 82, 88, 89, 99, 109; aban-
    doned, 54; alcohol at, 75–77; American
    Revolution battle at, 75; architecture,
    58, 79; Arkansas Gazette at, 78; billiard
    parlors, 64; blacks at, 68–71; cabarets,
    63, 76; branch of Bank of Arkansas at,
    109; church, 58, 61–63, 65–66; Civil
    War battle at, 169–70; class structure,
    64–65; commandant, 60 comman-
    dant, duties of, 60–61; cotton gin; 58;
    dancing; 65; destroyed in Civil War,
    79; established, 53; farmers at, 56–57,
    59, 65, 68, 69, 70, 76; free blacks at,
    69; gambling, 64; garrison, 55–56, 59,
    77; government, 60–61; gristmills, 58;
    hunters, 58; Jews at, 63; locations, 54;

56–58; medals, 64; merchants and trad-
    ers at, 53, 54, 55, 57, 58, 59, 60, 65, 66,
    75; mission, 54; population, 57–58, 68;
    post office, 79; sawmill, 58; slaves at, 65,
    66–71; surrendered to Americans, 78;
    territorial capital, 79; women at, 65–68
Arkansas Post National Memorial, 56, 79
Arkansas Power & Light Co., 278, 301, 352
Arkansas Prohibition Alliance, 235
Arkansas Project (SNCC), 341, 342
Arkansas Pure Food and Drug, 244
Arkansas Real Estate Commission, 336
Arkansas: Remote and Restless, 1800–1860,
    102, 114
Arkansas Resources and Development
    Commission (ARDC), 300, 301
Arkansas River, 53, 54, 55, 60, 66, 70, 74,
    76, 85, 95, 97, 102, 130, 132, 152, 161,
    165; Mississippi Alluvial Valley/Delta
    region, 12; Native American villages,
    41, 50–51; Soto expedition, 36–38
Arkansas River Valley: geological history
    and characteristics, 5, 7–10; mound
    building cultures, 27; Native American
    communities, 28, 40, 50
Arkansas Roads Scandal, 254–55
Arkansas State Board of Health, 252
Arkansas State Council of Defense, 256
Arkansas State Gazette and Democrat, 140
Arkansas State Press, 293, 313, 318
Arkansas (steamboat), 130
Arkansas Teachers Association, 249, 250,
    292
Arkansas Territory, 87
Arkansas Times, 103–4
Arkansas Traveler, 112; lithographic print,
    113
Arkansas Woman's Chronicle, 234, 238
Arkansian (Fayetteville newspaper), 148
arm bands (shell bead), 27
armor, Spanish, 33
Army and Navy General Hospital, 288
artifact styles: Archaic period, 23;
    Mississippi period, 28; Woodland
    period, 25
artisan, 128
Ashley, Harriet, photograph of, 137
Ashley, Chester, 119, 120; death of, 138
Ashley County, 200, 201
Ashmore, Harry, 319, 325
Atlatl, 28, 25
Austin, Stephen F., 90, 118
Autiamque province, 36

Blanchard Springs Cavern, 6
Blease, Gov. Cole (SC), 245
Blossom Plan, 322, 323, 324
Blossom, Virgil, 322
blues music, 371, 372, 373, 374, 375–76, 377
Blunt, James, 165; at Battle of Prairie Grove, 166–67
Blytheville, 288, 307
Benaim Israel, 233
boats (Soto expedition), 39
body ornamentation (Native Americans): Archaic period, 23; Caddo Indians, 48; Osage Indians, 44–45; paint, 45; Quapaw Indians, 42; Tunica Indians, 50–51
Bolton, Charles, 82, 102, 104, 114, 115, 129, 132
Bond, Scott, 215
bone artifacts (Native American prehistory): Archaic period, 22; Mississippi period, 28; Paleoindian period, 18; Woodland period, 25
Bone Dry Law, 248–49
bone, 17
Booker, J. R., 292
Booneville, 253
boreal, 14
boreal forests, 14
Borland, Solon, 120, 140; appointed to Senate, 138; commands militia in expedition to seize federal installation at Fort Smith, 152; in Mexican War, 120; resigns from the US Senate, 141
Boss, Steve, 10
Bossu, Jean-Bernard, 63
Boston Mountains, 157, 158, 165
Boston Plateau (Boston Mountains), 5–6
bottles (pottery), 48
bottomland forest: West Gulf Coastal Plains, 10
bottomlands: Arkansas River Valley, 9; West Gulf Coast Plains, 10
Bougy, Joseph, 68
bowie knife, 128–29
Bowie, James, 118
bowls (pottery), 48
bows and arrows (Native American): Caddo Indians, 48; Woodland period, 21, 25, 32
bracelets (beaded and woven), 22, 27, 45
Bracero Program, 286, 310–11, 312
Bradley County, 200, 201
Branton, Wiley, 316

Breckenridge, John, 144, 146, 149; receives majority of Arkansas votes for president in 1860, 147
Brindletails, 204, 206
Brinkley, 236, 374
British, 75, 120, 256, 283, 296, 375
Britt, Maurice (Footsie), 294
Brooks v. Baxter, 207
Brooks, Ida Jo, 204, 326
Brooks, Joseph, 204–5, 206, 208, 209, 236; declared legal governor, 207; painting of, 204
Brooks, Mary Burt, 238
Brooks-Baxter War, 206–209, 210
Broonzy, William (Big Bill), 374
Brough, Anne, 247
Brough, Charles Hillman, 248, 398
Brown v. Board of Education, 292, 302, 318–19, 321, 322, 323, 336, 338, 339–40, 348, 355–56
Brown, John (abolitionist), 144
Brown, John (Camden resident), 147, 168, 185; condemns Hindman's actions, 163
Brown, Minniejean, 322, 325
buffalo hair, hides and robes, 36, 42, 45
buffalo horns, 42
Buffalo hunting, 60; Caddo Indians, 48; Osage Indians, 44; Quapaw Indians, 42; Soto expedition, 36, Tunica Indians, 50
Buffalo meat, 60, 65
Buffalo River, 6, 26, 216
Buffalo tallow, 60, 65
Bull Shoals, Mississippi Alluvial Valley/ Delta Region, 12
Bumpers, Dale, 344, 349, 367
Burden of Southern History (Woodward), 355, 362, 377
Bureau of Agricultural Economics, 285
Burgess School tax segregation bill, 244
burial sites and practices (Native American prehistory): Dalton culture, 20; Mississippi period, 31; Woodland period, 26–27
Bush, John E., 229, 230
busing, 338–39
butterflies, Arkansas River Valley, 9

Cabanne de valeur, Quapaw temple, 74
Cabarets, 63, 76
Cabell, William, 170
Cache River, Mississippi Alluvial Valley/ Delta Region, 12

chickens, Quapaw Indians, 41

Chicot County, 66, 132, 133, 136, 140, 182, 185, 192, 193, 196; in Civil War, 182

chiefs and chiefdoms (Native American): Mississippi period, 21, 51; Soto expedition, 37, 40

child-rearing (Native Americans): Osage Indians, 45; Quapaw Indians, 42

Children of the Middle Waters (Osage), 43

Choctaw Indians, 56, 58, 70, 76, 85, 96, 100, 155, 156, 183

Christian Right, 350

Chugate province, 38

Church of Divine Christ, 232

Church of God in Christ, 232

Churchill, Thomas, 220; Confederate commander at Arkansas Post, 169–70; elected governor, 214

civil right movement: late-twentieth century, 335–43; post-World War II, 313–327; resegregation, 360–61; Women, 348; Student Non-Violent Coordinating Committee (SNCC), 341–343; Unfinished, 357; World War II, 291–94

Civil Rights Act of 1866, 194

Civil Rights Act of 1964, 343

civil rights legacy, 356

Civil War, 153–86, Civil War Battles in Arkansas, 176

Civil Works Administration, 276

Civilian Conversation Corps, 277–278, 280

clan, 41

clans (Native American): Caddo Indians 47; Osage Indians 43–44; Quapaw Indians, 41

Clarendon, 161, 174

Clark County, 87, 163

Clark v. Board of Education of the Little Rock School District, 336

Clark, William, 96

Clarke, James, 231, 239

Clarksville: Arkansas River Valley, 10

clay soils, 13

Clayton, Powell, 175, 202, 203, 204, 205, 207, 209, 210, 213; Arkansas Bureau of Immigration, 219; assassination attempt on, 200; at Battle of Pine Bluff, 177; brother to William, 217; declares martial law, 201; elected by legislature to US Senate, 203; elected governor, 197; ends martial law, 202; organizes state militia, 200; photo of, 199

Clayton, William, 217

Cleburne, Patrick, 154

climate, 14–15; climate patterns, 15

climate change, 14, 33; animal extinctions, 14, 19; Archaic period, 21; Ice Age, 14; impacts on sixteenth-century Native Americans, 51; Little Ice Age, 33

Clinton, Hillary, 372

Clinton, William Jefferson, 348, 349,350, 352, 364–65, 367

cloth, mulberry (Tunica), 51

cloth, mulberry (Tunica), 51

clothing (Native American): Archaic period, 22; Caddo Indians, 48; Osage Indians, 44–45; Paleoindian period, 18; Quapaw Indians, 42; Tunica Indians, 51

coal deposits, 9

Cochran, Robert, 372

coins (sixteenth century Spanish), 34

Coligua (province and river), 36

colonial economy, 356, 362–63, 375

Colorado: Arkansas River headwaters, 12

Colt, 375

columns (geological), 6

Committee on Negro Organizations (CNO), 291–92

Committee on Public Information, 256

Committee to Retain Our Segregated Schools (CROSS), 327

Commonwealth College, 274

Communist Party, 274

Concordia, English trading post, 68, 75

Congo region, 69

Congress of Industrial Organizations (CIO), 313

Congressional (Radical) Reconstruction, 195, 207

conquistadores, Spanish 34, 39

conservation of the environment, 243

Conservatives (Democrats, Post-Civil War) 189, 194, 196, 197, 203, 208, 209, 210, 211, 212, 214

contrabands, 163, 176

Convict leasing, 243, 245

Conway County, 10, 200, 201

Conway, 250, 277, 335

Conway, Elias, 92, 145, 164; elected governor, 141

Conway, Henry, 91, 92, 93, 141; duel with Robert Crittenden, 92, 112

Cossenonpoint, Quapaw chief, 72–73

Conway, James, 92, 141; death of, 138; elected first state governor, 107

Delta Pine & Land Company, 274–75
Democratic Party, 81, 105, 106, 108, 119, 120, 142, 145, 146, 147, 153, 201, 207, 208, 209, 210, 211, 212, 214; 1860 national convention in Charleston, South Carolina, 143–44; 1860 national convention in Baltimore, Maryland, 144; and agriculture, 238; Bailey's "merit" approach, 281; Baxter declines Democratic nomination in 1874; bolters, 226, challenges to, 238–39, 330–31; challenges to Family hegemony, 142; Civil War, 219; courting the black vote, 212; disfranchisement, 228; dissension within, 138; Dixiecrats, 315; dominance in early statehood period, 107; Dynasty (the Family) dominated, 145; Elias Conway receives nomination for governor, 141; emergence of, 81; evolution of, 348–49, 355; Family (Dynasty), 92, 119, 145; Ku Klux Klan, 200; newspapers, 130; Northern wing, 146; political infighting in mid-twentieth century, 245–46; political strength, 231; Sidney McMath secures nomination, 315; Southern wing, 146; split with national Democratic Party, 330; Union Labor Party pressure, 225; white primary challenge, 226
Democratic press, 226
demographic shifts, 312, 332, 334, 335
Department of Arkansas Heritage, 352
Department of Finance and Administration, 302
Department of Health, Education and Welfare, 337
Department of Public Welfare, 281
Desha County, 12, 56
DeValls Bluff, 182, 184
Devil's Den, 277
diamonds, West Gulf Coastal Plains, 10
Diana fritillary butterfly, Arkansas River Valley, 9
Dillard, Tom, 352
Dillard, William Thomas, 335
Dillard's Department Stores, 335, 365
Dillion, Katherine V., 296–97
dinosaurs, West Gulf Coastal Plain, 10
Disciples of Christ, 116, 231, 332
disfranchisement, 227–29
District of Louisiana, 82
disturbed soils (Native American), 23

Ditch Bayou, Battle of, 182
Dixie Hummingbirds, 372
Dixiecrats, 315, 321, 331
Dodd, David, 178
dog racing, 272
dogs (Native American): Paleoindian period, 18; Quapaw Indians, 42
dogs (Spanish), 33
Donaghey, George Washington, 244–45
Donation Law of 1840, 113–14
Dougan, Michael, 118, 177, 206
Douglas, Paul Page Jr., 295–96
Douglas, Stephen, 146, 147
Dorsey, Stephen, 207
Dred Scott v. Sandford, 143, 147
Drew, Thomas, 119, 138
Drew County, 201
dried meat, 28
drilled wolf canine, 27
Driver, William, 272
Drought conditions, 15, 33, 39; from 1930 to 1931, 265–66
Drummond, Winslow, 337
drums (Native American): Caddo, 45
duck hunting, Mississippi Alluvial Valley/Delta region, 13
dugout canoes, 22
Dunbar High School, 293, 317
Dunbar-Hunter expedition, 82–85
Dunbar, William, 7, 82
DuBreuil, Jacobo, 70
Du Poisson, Father, 62
Dupree v. Alma, 358
Dusenberry, Emma, 376–77
DuVal, Kathleen, 84
dwellings (Native American): Archaic period, 22–23; Caddo Indians, 46–47; Dalton culture, 20, Mississippi period, 30; Osage Indians, 43; Paleoindian period, 18; Quapaw Indians, 41; Tunica Indians, 50; Woodland period, 25
Dwight Mission, 97
Dyess Colony, 76, 277, 282, 376; photograph of Dyess resettled family, 277
Dyess, William R., 276
Dylan, Bob, 372
Dynasty, the. *See* Family, the

Eagle (steamboat), 130
Eagle Forum, 347–48
Eagle, James B., 214, 226, 231, 365

ear spools (cooper), 27
earrings (Native American): Osage Indians, 45; Tunica Indians, 51
Earle, 340–41
early childhood education, 367
Earth People, 41, 43
earthquakes, 263
East, Clay, 273
Eckford, Elizabeth, 322, 324
economic development: changes in post-World War II period, 300; industrial development, 302–4; Stephens, W. R. (Whit), 304–5; Walmart, 304–5
economy, 131–32, 136–37
Écore à Fabri, 59
Écores Rouges, 56, 58, 67
Education First Committee, 338
Education funding formula, 357–59
Education Week's Quality Counts report, 361
education: and African American access to education in early post-Civil War era, 189; and African Americans in the progressive era, 251; and *Alma v. Dupree* (and *Dupree v. Alma*), 358, 366–67; and Arkansas Education Department, 311; and Arkansas State Teachers Association, 236–37; Mike Beebe, 366–67; and the "big three" 349; and bilingual education, 334; and Ida Jo Brooks, 236–37, 249; and *Brown v. Board of Education*, 292, 302, 318–19, 321–22, 355; and busing, 338–39; and Central High Crisis, 323–27; and Charleston integration, 319; Charter Schools, 359–61; *Clark v. Board of Education of the Little Rock School District*, 337; and connection to low-wage jobs, 310; and constitution of 1868, 209; and George Washington Donaghey, 244; and dual education system, 356; and Education First Committee, 338; and *Education Week's Quality Counts* report, 361; and Equal Rights Amendment (women), 344, 345–48 Fayetteville integration, 319; and Freedmen's Bureau, 191; and Junius Marion Futrell's conflict with the Federal Emergency Relief Administration, 271–72; and the GI bill, 309; and higher education in antebellum era, 117; and history education, 352–53; and Indian Education Assistance Act, 353; and integration of higher education, 315–18; and the integration of Hoxie, 320–21; and Mike Huckabee, 366; Hunt, Silas, 315–17, 318; Edith Mae Irby (Jones), 317–18; and Lake View suit, 358–59, 365, 366; and *Lake View v. Huckabee*, 366; and Little Rock integration, 319–27; and Little Rock School District in early twenty-first century, 357; and Sue Morris suit, 292–93, 319; and Oregon's Bureau of Educational Research, 337–38; and the Parson Plan, 338; and Harvey Parnell, 266; and private education in antebellum era, 117; and progressive era reforms, 241, 249–52; and public education in antebellum period, 116; and pupil-placement, 337; and Quapaw Indians, 99; and Reconstruction, 211; and resegregation, 360; "Right to Work" law, 301; and school funding, 358–59; and segregation of black and white school taxes, 243–244; and Settlement Agreement, 357; and Ada Sipuel, 316; and Charlotte Stephens, 236; and Student-Nonviolent Coordinating Committee, 341–43; and support of black and white women, 236; and *Swan v. Mecklenburg Board of Education*, 338, 339; and teacher institutes, 237; and Winthrop Rockefeller, 343; and women,115, 249, 345; and World War II, 287
Eisenhower, Dwight, 318, 306–7, 325
El Dorado, 10, 288
Elaine Race Riot, 256, 257–59
Elaine Twelve, 258, 261, 292; image of 260
Elaine, 257, 372
Elders, elder councils (Native American): Quapaw Indians, 41
Election Law of 1891, 227
elk and elk hunting, 14, 17, 19, 44
Elkhorn Tavern, 158 159, 160. *See also* Pea Ridge
Emancipation Proclamation, 162, 168
Energy Department, 352
Engagés, 55, 70
England, Arkansas (riot), 266
English traders, 51
Englishmen, 53, 54, 70, 71
entrada (Hernando de Soto), 51
Episcopalians, 116
Equal Rights Amendment (women), 344, 345–48
escarpment, 6

Eureka Springs: Salem and Springfield Plateaus, 5
Europe, 17
European exploration and colonization: Spanish (Hernando de Soto) exploration, 33–40
Ex Parte Garland, 210
Executive Order 8802, 291

F. S. Walcott Rabbits Foot Minstrels, 373
faceted glass bead, 34
Family, Life, America, God (FLAG), 347–48
Family, the (Dynasty, the), 92, 93, 94, 102, 103, 107, 119, 138, 141, 142, 143, 145, 146, 148, 153, 163
Fancher, Alexander, 123
farm agents, 266
Farm Labor Crisis, 285
Farm Security Administration, 275–76, 282, 288–89
Farmers and Household Union of America, 257, 258, 274
Farmers Union, 250
farming/farm land: Arkansas River Valley, 9; Mississippi Alluvial Valley/Delta region, 12; West Gulf Coastal Plain, 10
Farmsteads (Native American), 30, 38, 46
Faubus, Orval, on cotton and synthetic fabrics, 311; integration, 299, 302, 318, 320, 321, 322, 323–25, 327, 342, 343; SNCC, 342
Faulkner, Sandford, 112, 113
Fayetteville, 157, 165; apportionment battle in 1836, 104; Arkansas Council on Human Relations (ACHR), 324; Bank of Arkansas branch, 109, 110; Civil War, 157, 165, 166, 167, 170, 171; as commercial center in antebellum era, 129–30; education, 117, 211; Fayetteville Arkansian, 148; integration, 319, 321; Silas Hunt and the integration of the Law School at the University of Arkansas, 316; Springfield Plateau, 5; Vance Randolph, 376; David Walker and secession, 150
feathers (Native American): Quapaw Indians, 42; Tunica Indians, 51
Featherstonhaugh, George, 111
Federal Emergency Relief Administration (FERA), 271, 272, 276, 279, 280
Fifteenth Amendment, 292
Fihliol, Jean, 59

Finley, Randy, 191, 211
Finney, Albert, 97
fire (Native American): Caddo Indians, 45–46; Tunica Indians, 50
fired-clay pottery (Native American): Caddo Indians, 48; Mississippi period, 28; Woodland period, 21, 25, 32
First Arkansas Infantry Regiment (African Descent), 172
first fruits ceremony (Caddo), 47
First Kansas Colored Infantry, 179–80
first state capital building, 110, 111
fish and fishing (Native American), 17; Archaic period, 22–23; Mississippi period, 28, 32; Quapaw Indians, 42; Woodland period, 26
fish hooks (bone), 22
Fishback amendment, 220
Fishback, William, Bureau of Immigration supporter, 119; chosen by legislature to be US Senator, 188; denied Senate seat by US Senate, 188; repudiation of "unjust" debt, 220; elected governor, 227
Five Civilized Tribes, 155, 156
Fixed Infantry Regiment of Louisiana, 61
Flanagin, Harris, 163–64, 208; elected governor, 164
Fletcher, John Gould, 377
floods: 1543, 39; 1866, 192; 1882, 224; from 1912 to 1913, 253; 1927, 253, 262–66; Arkansas Post, 89; bane to travel, 12; disaster, 13; flood control, 13; formative phenomena, 12; hindrance to agriculture, 56–57; hindrance to French, 58; hindrance to settlement, 53; Mississippi River, 12–13; periodic, 26; Quapaw Indians, 56, 98; rice fields and attracting migrating ducks, 13
Florida, 36, 62, 103, 131, 220, 262, 335, 345
flotilla (Spanish), 39
Flowers, Harold, 291, 294, 316
flowstone, 6
folk way, 355
Foner, Eric, 198, 202, 212, 213, 350
food-getting and storage practices (Native American): Archaic period, 22–24; Caddo Indians, 47–48; Dalton culture, 20; Mississippi period, 28, 30, 32; Osage Indians, 44; Paleoindian period, 18; Quapaw Indians, 42; Tunica Indians, 50–51; Woodland period, 25–26
Ford Foundation, 319
Ford, Gerald, 344, 353

gourds, 23; Quapaw Indians, 42

Governor's Commission on the Status of Women, 344–45, 346, 348

Grady, Henry, 215, 218

grain, grain processing and storage, 6, 22, 24–25, 30

Grand Chapter Order of the Eastern Star of Arkansas, 235

Grand Ole Opry, 373, 375, 376

Grand Prairie, 53, 60; Mississippi Alluvial Valley/Delta region, 13

granaries (Native American), 38

Grant County, 216

Grant, Ulysses, supports Elisha Baxter in Brooks-Baxter War, 209; wins Arkansas electoral votes in presidential election of 1868, 201; wins Arkansas electoral votes in presidential election of 1872, 206

grave offerings (Native American): Dalton culture, 20; Mississippi period, 31; Woodland period, 27

Graves, John, 228, 230

Graysonia, 216

Great Depression, 269–83

Great Lakes, 51

Green Corn ceremony (Quapaw), 42

Green County, 200, 201

Green v. County School Board, 338

Green, Ernest, 322

Green, Thomas J., 353

Green, Victoria D., 353

Greer, Ezra, 341

Gregory, Dick, 342

Grey, William, 196

Grice, Geleve, 316

Griffin, Marvin, 324

grinding stones, 22

Grinnage, Benjamin, 342

Guachoya, 37

guardian spirits (Quapaw), 41

Guasco province, 38

Gudetonguay, Quapaw chief, 73–74

guerrilla warfare, 163, 182–83

Gulf Coast, 37, 55

Gulf Coastal Plain: Native American communities, 28–51

Gulf of Mexico, 54; Geologic history and characteristics, 3, 12–13

habitants, 76

Hacanac Indians, 38

Hadley, Ozra, 204

hairstyles (Native American): Caddo Indians, 48; Osage Indians, 44–45; Quapaw Indians, 42; Tunica Indians, 51

Haley, Alex, 317

Haley, George, 316, 317

Hall High School, 327

hamlets (Native American prehistory): Mississippi period, 21; Woodland period, 32

Hancock, John, 372

handle (wood, antler), 18

Hansen, William, 342

hardwood forests (oak and hickory): Arkansas River Valley, 9; Crowley's Ridge, 14; Ouachita Mountains, 7; Ozark Mountains, 6

Harlem Renaissance, 229

harness bell (brass), 34

harpoon heads (bone), 22

Harrelson Road Act, 255

Harrington, Donald, 377

Harrison, 123, 295; Springfield Plateau, 5

harvest ceremonies (Native American): Caddo Indians, 47; Quapaw Indians, 42

Hasinai Indians, 45

Havana, Cuba, 60

Hawkins, Ronnie, 372

Hawks, The (band), 372

Hays, Brooks, 266, 280, 325

Hays, George, 246

headdresses (Quapaw), 42

Heckaton, 98–99

Helena Mound site, 27

Helena, 12, 13, 130, 142, 154, 161, 165, 174, 175, 182, 184, 232, 233; as commercial center, 130; Civil War battle at, 172–73; Crowley's Ridge, 13; Elaine race Riot, 257; Helena Mound site, 27; Mississippi Alluvial Plain/Delta region, 12; music, 373, 374, 375, 377; occupied by Federal forces, 163; secession stronghold, 149; SNCC, 341–42

Helm, Levon, 372–74

hematite, 18

Hempstead County, 87

Hendrix, James R., 295

Henriques, Josue, Jr., 63

herbs, 50

Herron, Francis, wins Medal of Honor at battle of Pea Ridge, 166; leads Union forces to Prairie Grove, 166

Hesper (steamboat), 200

Hibbler, Myles, 292
hickory nuts, 23
hide clothing, 18
hide coverings, 18
hide working (Native American), 18, 42, 44, 48
hides and furs (Native American), 28, 42
highland region, 5
Highway Commission, 302
highways. *See* road and highway system
hill-country culture, 6
Hindman, Thomas, 142, 146 148, 153, 164, 166; advocates secession, 148–49; at Battle of Prairie Grove, 165–67; backs Henry Rector for governor in 1860, 144–45; elected to Congress, 143; made commander of the Military District of the Trans-Mississippi, 162; photo of, 164
hoe blades (stone), 25, 28
hogs (Soto expedition), 33
Holly Farms, 333
Holmes, Theophilus, 164–65, 168, 169, 171, 174; at Battle of Helena, 172–73; declares martial law, 168
Holocene epoch, 18–20, 32
Honey, Michael, 340
hookworm, 253
Hoop Spur, Arkansas, 258
Hoover, Herbert, 262, 267
Hope, 288
Hopefield, 59
Hopewell culture, 26
Hopkins, Harry, 271
horse racing track, 272
horses: Quapaw Indians, 42; Soto expedition, 33, 36, 38
Hot Springs County, 200
Hot Springs National Park, 7
Hot Springs, 83, 117, 118; Army and Navy General Hospital, 288; divorce center, 290, Edith Mae Irby (Jones), 317, 318; horse racing track, 272; integration, 339, 340; Mosaic Templar's hospital, 230; Charles "Lucky" Luciano residence, 281; Sidney McMath, 315; stage-coach service, 117; SNCC, 341; state government temporarily removed to in 1862, 160
hot springs, Ouachita Mountains, 7
house construction: Caddo Indians, 47–48; Osage Indians, 44; Quapaw Indians, 41; Tunica Indians, 50

House of Death (Caddo), 48
House State Agencies Committee, 348
Houston, Sam, 118
Howard County, 10
Howard University, 341
Howard, Oliver O., 191
Howlin' Wolf, 374
Hoxie desegregation controversy, 320–21
Huckabee, Mike, 365–66, 367
Hughes, Simon P., 214, 218–19
human bone fragments, 20
humid subtropical climate, 15
Hunt, Silas, 315–17, 318
Hunter, George, 7, 36
hunter-gatherer lifestyles (Native American prehistory): Archaic period, 22–23; Paleoindian period, 18–19
hunters, 64–65, 66, 74
hunting practices (Native American): Archaic period, 22–23; Caddo Indians, 48; Dalton culture, 19; Mississippi period, 32; Osage Indians, 44; Paleoindian period, 18; Quapaw Indians, 42; Tunica Indians, 50; Woodland period, 25–26
hunting, 56, 57, 59–60
Huntington, 218

I-30, 306
I-40, 306–7
I-430, 307
I-540, 307
I-55, 307
Ice Age, 14, 17–19, 32; landscapes, 17–18
Illinois country, 54, 59
Illinois Indians, 58
Illinois River, 166
image of state, 111–13
Imber, Annabelle, 358
Immigration Convention, 219
Inca Empire, 34
Indian Religious Freedom Act, 353
Indian Self Determination and Educational Assistance Act, 353
Indian Territory, 100, 117, 155, 156, 217–18
industrial revolution, 241
industrialization, 302–4
influenza, 39
Initiative, 244
interdistrict desegregation, 339
International Harvester, 308
Interstate highway system, 306–7

milling basins, 22
Mine workers, 218
mining, 218, 238
Minstrels, 206
Mississippi Alluvial Plain: geologic history and characteristics 5, 10–14
Mississippi County, 200, 201, 216, 262, 276, 282
Mississippi period, 21, 23, 27, 32; agriculture, 28, 30, 32; architecture, 28; dwellings, 30; Mississippian tradition, 28–30, 33; mound and earthwork construction, 30–32; political organization, 21, 29–30; religious beliefs and practices, 30–31; settlement patterns, 21, 28, 30–32; social organization, 21; subsistence economy, 21, 28, 32; technology, 28; trade and exchange, 28–29, 32
Mississippi River Valley: Mississippi period, 28; Native American communities, 28, 40, 50–51; Soto expedition, 33–34, 36–37, 39–40; 51
Mississippi River, 13, 53, 56, 57, 58, 59, 75, 86, 88, 132, 136, 161, 171, 172, 173, 262, 356: 1543 flood, 39; 1912–1913 flood, 253; 1927 flood, 13, 253, 262–65; Native American villages, 41, 50
Mississippi, 53, 56, 262, 275, 345
Mississippian culture area, 39
Mississippian tradition, 28–30, 32, 40, 51
Mississippian villages, 38
Missouri Compromise, 88, 106, 139–40
Missouri Territory, 82, 85, 86, 87, 88
Missouri River, 43
Missouri: Paleoindian hunting and butchering sites, 18; Mississippi Alluvial Plain/Delta region, 12; Osage settlement, 43–51; Salem Plateau, 5; Springfield Plateau, 5
Missouri, Kansas, and Texas Coal Company, 218
Mitchell, H. L., 273, 274
Mobile, 55, 68
Moccasins, 44
Moneyhon, Carl, 134, 190, 193, 198, 233
Monroe County, 332
Monroe, Bill, 373
Monroe, James, 88, 91, 97
Monroe, Louisiana, 59
Monsanto, Isaac, 63
Montcharvaux, Jean-François Tisserant de, 65

Morrilton, 10, 95, 294; Arkansas River Valley, 10
Morris, Sue, 292–93, 319
Morton Sosna, 269
mortuary programs (Native American), 20, 27, 30–31
mortuary structures (Native American), 27
Mosaic Templars of America, 229, 230, 235
Moscoso de Alvarado, Luis, 37–38
Mothershed, Thelma, 322
Mound and earthwork construction (Native American): Archaic period, 24–32; Mississippi period, 21, 30–32; Woodland period, 21, 27
Mound Pond, 27
Mount Magazine: Arkansas River Valley, 9; highest point in Arkansas, 9
Mount Nebo: Arkansas River Valley, 9
Mountain Home: Salem Plateau, 5
Mountain Meadows Massacre, 123–26
Mountain View, 6, 377
mountainous terrain (Soto expedition), 36
Muddy Waters, 372
mumps, 39, 155
Murfreesboro: in Civil War, 177; West Gulf Coastal Plain, 10
Murphy Oil, 362
Murphy, Isaac, 189, 194, 195, 205, 213; elected governor, 188; votes against secession, 152

NAACP Legal Defense Fund, 336
Nady, 53
Naguatex province, 38
Napoleon, 130
Narvaez expedition to Florida, 36
Nashville (Arkansas), West Gulf Coastal Plain, 10
Natchez Indians, 40, 50, 62
Natchez Rebellion of 1729, 50
Natchitoches Indians, 45
Natchitoches, 60, 67
National Agricultural Wheel, 226
National American Woman Suffrage Association (NAWSA), 238, 246–47
National Association for the Advancement of Colored People (NAACP): and *Aaron v. Cooper*, 322; and accusations of communist affiliation with, 325-326; and L.C. Bates on the *Brown v. Board of Education* decision, 322; and challenge to White Primary, 261–62; and

the Elaine Race Riot, 258; and funds
for Edith Mae Irby (Jones), 318; and
the formation of Little Rock chapter,
242-3; and Sue Morris suit against the
Little Rock School Board, 292-293; and
John M. Robinson, 261-262; and *Smith
v. Allwright*, 292; 318; and struggle
between old and young African
American activists in Arkansas, 319;
and threatened publication of black
membership in, 323; and activist John
Walker, 337

National Association of Colored Women's
Clubs, 236

National Council of Negro Women, 341

National Farmers Alliance, 225, 226

National Folk Music Archives, 376

National Organization of Women (NOW),
344

National Woman Suffrage Association, 238

National Woman's Party, 247

Native American prehistory, 17–32: agriculture, 12, 28, 32; Archaic period, 19–25,
32; architecture, 28, 30, 32; burial practices, 20, 26–27, 31; Caddoan tradition,
28, 32–33; cemeteries, 20, 31; clothing
and personal ornaments, 18, 22, 27; cultural boundaries, 23, 25, 28, 39; Dalton
culture, 19–20; dwellings, 18, 22–23, 25,
30; European exploration and colonization, 32; Hopewell culture, 26; hunting
and fishing, 18–19, 22–23, 25–26, 32;
migration patterns, 17; Mississippi
period, 20–21, 27–32; Mississippian
tradition, 28–30, 32–33; mound and
earthwork construction, 21, 24, 26–27,
30, 31, 32; Paleoindian period, 17–18,
32; Plaquemine tradition, 28, 32–33;
plant domestication, 21, 23–24; Plum
Bayou culture, 27; political organization, 21, 29–30, 32; population levels,
18–19, 23, 28; religious beliefs and
practices, 18, 26–27, 30–31; settlement
patterns, 18, 20–21, 23, 25–28, 30–32;
social identity and organization, 18, 20,
23–24, 25–27, 28–32; status and rank,
26–27, 30, 32; subsistence economies,
18–26, 28, 32; technology, 18–19,
21–22, 25, 28, 32; trade and exchange,
21–22, 24, 26, 28–29; Upper Paleolithic
ancestors, 18; Woodland period, 20,
25–27, 32

Native Americans: Arkansas tribes (his-

toric), 40–51; colonial era, 55–58, 62,
64, 68 70, 71–78; European exploration
and colonization, 33–39; prehistory,
17–32; removal, 95–100; territorial
era, 91

native ground, 84

natural gas, 9

Neches River, 45

necklaces and neckbands (beaded and
woven), 22, 27, 45

needles (antler and ivory), 18, 22

neo-plantation system, 310–11 313

nets (woven fiber), 18, 22

nettle weed fiber, 45

New Deal, 269, 280

New Gascony, 208

New Madrid Act, 86

New Madrid Certificates, 86, 90, 101

New Madrid Earthquake, 85–86, 101, 262

New Madrid, 82, 85

New Orleans, 66

New York, 281

Newberry, Farrar, 95

Newport, 236, 288

Newton County, 6

Newton, Robert, 205, 207

Nighthawk, Robert, 374

Nightriders (whitecappers), 257, 273

Nine Street, Little Rock, 229

Nineteenth Amendment (federal constitution), 247

Nineteenth Amendment (state constitution), 271

Ninety-day divorce law, 290

Nodena community (Native American), 30

Noland, Charles F. M., 105

non-local raw materials (Native American
prehistory): Mississippi period, 28;
Woodland period, 26

nonutilitarian artifacts, Native American
prehistory: Mississippi period, 28–30;
Woodland period, 25–26

normal school for African American, 211

North Carolina, 220, 345

North Little Rock, 286, 288, 339, 356, 375

Northwest Arkansas Times, 282

Northwest Arkansas, 312–13; landscape, 5–7

Norwood, C. M., 226

Norwood, Hal, 280

novaculite, 7

nut storage, 6

nuts and nut gathering (Native American):
Archaic period, 22–23; Caddo Indians,

48; Osage Indians, 44; Quapaw Indians, 42; Soto expedition, 34; Tunica Indians, 50; Woodland period, 25

Nuttall, Thomas, 7, 9, 96

oak and hickory woodlands, 14

oak, hickory, and southern pine woodlands, 15

Oberlin, 230

Obsitnik, Larry, 323

Oden, Robert, 91

Ohio River: Crowley's Ridge, 13; Hopewell people, 26

oil (animal): Quapaw Indians, 42

Oil and Gas Commission, 363

oil and gas deposits: Arkansas River Valley, 9; West Gulf Coastal Plain, 10

Oklahoma, 60, 66, 74; Ada Sipuel, 316; Arkansas River, 12; Arkansas's western boundary, 88, 100; Cherokee Indians, 97; Choctaw Indians, 96; Flood of 1927, 262; geography, 5, 7, 9, 12; I-40, 306; Indian archeological sites, 18, 30, 31; Kingfisher, 305; Native American communities, 31; Native American Removal to, 353; Osage Indians, 74; Paleoindian hunting and butchering sites, 18; Quapaw Indians, 100; STFU, 273; Springfield Plateau, 5; Three Forks area, 96, Wichita (Panis) Indians, 66–67

Old Southwest, 110, 130, 131, 133, 136

Old Style (Julian) calendar, 34

Old World diseases, 39

Old World newcomers, 41

Omaha Indians, 41

Ord, E. O. C., 190, 197; commander of the Fourth Military District in Reconstruction, 195

Oregon Report, 337–38

O'Reilly, Alexandro, 63, 72

Origins of the New South (Woodward), 362

Ortiz, Juan, 36

Osage Indians, 40, 41, 43–45, 51, 58, 59, 74–75, 95; child-raising and family organization, 44–45; clothing and personal adornment, 44–45; division of labor, 44; Dunbar-Hunter expedition, 82, 85; language, 41; origin story, 43; Osage Trader, 46; repatriation of archeological materials, 353; settlement pattern, 43; social organization, 43–44; subsistence economy, 44; trade net-

works, 45; traders, 46; Wakondah, 41; warfare, 44; wars with Cherokee, 95, 96; child-raising and family organization, 44–45

Osage Orange, 48

Osceola, 304, 375, 376

Osotuoy (Quapaw village), 41

Ossuary (Native American), 31

Ouachita Mountain, 5, 7, 8, 9, 28, 36, 38, 216, 277; communities, 216; designated as national forest, 243; geologic history and characteristics, 5, 7, 10; Native American communities, 28; Soto expedition, 36, 38

Ouachita National Forest, 243

Ouachita Post, 59, 70

Ouachita River, 59, 83, 84, 85, 87, 130, 132, 136, 176, 184; geologic history and characteristics, 7; Native American communities, 28, 30, 40, 45, 50–51; Soto expedition, 38

overseer, 132

Ozark blind salamander, 6

Ozark Highlands: Osage, 51; Quapaw, 51; rock shelters, 22, 23; Southwest Trail, 86

Ozark Mountains: archeological sites, 23; Civilian Conservation Corps, 277–78; geologic feature and characteristics, 5–9; Ozark Mountain Rock Shelter, 8; Sawmill (Smith), 217; KKK, 259; Spanish explorations, 36; Works Progress Administration, 277–78

Ozark Plateau, 127

Ozark, 10, 170

Pacaha, 34–36, 40

paint (Native American): Osage Indians, 44; Quapaw Indians, 42

Paleoindian period, 17

Paleoindians, 17–18, 32: clothing, 18; hunting lifestyle, 18; migrations, 17, religious beliefs, 18; settlement pattern, 18, social organization, 18, technology, 18

paleontologists, 10

Palisema, 36

Pangea, 3

Panis Indians (Wichitas), 66

panpipe (Native American), 27

Paragould, 216, 295

Paramore, J. W., 216

Parker, Isaac, 217–18

Parkin community (Native American), 27

Plaquemine Indians: Soto expedition, 39–40, 51
plateau, 5
platform mounds (Native American): Woodland period, 27; Mississippi period, 21, 30–32; Tunica Indians, 50
platters (pottery), 48
Plazas (Native American), 30–31, 41, 50
Pleistocene epoch, 17
Pleistocene to Holocene transition, 19–20
Plessy v. Ferguson, 251, 318
pneumonia, 155
Pocahontas, 157
Poinsett County, 273, 274
Pointe Coupée, 70
Poison Spring, Battle of, 179–80
Poke Bayou (Batesville), 86
Poland, 283
Poll Tax, 227–28, 243, 314
Ponca Indians, 41
Pope County, 112, 127–28, 131
Pope, John, 93, 94, 95, 135; and Indian relations, 99; and Ten Sections controversy, 94; appointed territorial governor, 93
populist challenge, 231
Populist Party, 226
Porter, David, 169
Portis, Charles, 377
Portuguese language, 39
Pottery vessels (Native American): Caddo Indian, 48; Mississippi period, 28; Woodland period, 21, 25
Potts, Kirkbride, 123
Poverty Point culture and site, 24
power centers (Native American), 27
Prairie County, 224
Prairie D'Ane, 179
Prairie Grove, Battle of, 165–67
prairies/grasslands: Ice Age, 15, 17; Mississippi Alluvial Valley/Delta region, 13; West Gulf Coastal Plain, 10
prairie, 5
precipitation, 14
preemption certificates, 101
preemption laws, 114
pre-kindergarten program, 367
Prentiss, Benjamin, 172
Presbyterians, 116, 117, 231
Presley, Elvis, 375
Price, Sterling, 156, 157, 176, 184; at Battle of Helena, 173; at Battle of Jenkins' Ferry, 181; at Battle of Pea Ridge, 158–59; at Battle of Poison Springs, 179–80;

at Battle of Wilson's Creek, 156; in Camden Expedition, 179–80; in Little Rock campaign, 174–75; leads Missouri raid in 1864, 183
priests (Native American): Caddo Indians, 47; Mississippi Period, 21, 28, 32; Quapaw Indians, 42; Tunica Indians, 50
Princeton, 181; early educational center, 117; in Civil War, 176
Prisoners of War (POW), 286–87, 309
pro-choice, 349
Progressive Era, 236, 267, 271
Progressive Farmers and Household Union of America, 257–58
Progressivism, 241–42, 247
Prohibition Party, 235, 247
prohibition, 76, 77, 234–35, 239, 243, 245, 246, 247–49; 272
Project Pride, 352
prostitution, 66
Protestant Churches and racial subordination, 232
protestants, 63, 64
Pryor, David, 349, 353, 364, 367
public health, 244, 252–53
Pulaski Academy, 339
Pulaski County Special School District, 339
Pulaski County: and Brooks-Baxter conflict, 185, 207; and the Civil War, 175; created, 87; and demographic shifts, 312, 331; and Augustus Garland, 210; interdistrict desegregation, 339; and Settlement Agreement, 356 in Sixth Judicial District, 280; ties to the southeast, 105
pumpkins (Native American): Caddo Indians, 45; Osage Indians, 44
pupil placement law, 337
Pythian Sisters, 235

Quality Counts Report, 361
Quapaw Indians, 53, 54, 55, 58, 62, 64, 68, 70, 71, 72, 75, 77, 91, 97, 98–100; and alcohol, 75–76; alliances, 42; attack Chickasaws, 56; build road, 77; calumet ceremony, 43; clothing and personal adornment, 42; division of labor, 42; establishments of communities near confluence of Arkansas and Mississippi rivers, 40; gunsmith of, 74; intermarriage with English, 71; intermarriage with French, 64; 71–72; interpreter of,

74; law of, 72–74; language, 41; origin story, 41; paintings by, 56; population, 58; presents to, 64, 74; religion, 62–63, 77; Robe of the Three Villages, 57; small pox decimates, 58; social organization, 41; subsistence economy, 42; and Queen Anne's War, 55; repatriation of archeological materials, 353; trade networks, 42–43; warfare, 42

quartz crystal, 7

Quigualtam, 37, 39

Quiguate province, 56

Quipana province, 36

Quitamaya province, 36

Quizquiz province, 34

rabbits, 18

Raboteau, Albert, 135

race records, 374

Radical Republicans, 194, 196, 212

radio, 372

radiocarbon dating, 18

rafts (Soto expedition), 34

railroad, 10, 136, 198–99, 207, 211, 214, 238, 332, 362; agricultural expansion, 221; and Agricultural Wheel, 223, 224; and Cairo and Fulton Railroad, 136, 218; and Civil War destruction of, 182, 183; and first tracks laid, 118; connection to state debt, 219; and larger market, 216; and northern investors, 216; and during Reconstruction, 198–99, 207, 211, 214, 220; and regulations on, 243, 274; and relation to mining industry, 218; and relation to timber industry, 216; resentment against, 224; and W. R. Stephens' investment in, 304; and stimulant to economy, 216

rainfall averages, 15

Randolph County, 200

Randolph, Vance, 276

rationing (WWII), 284

Ray, Gloria, 322

readmission to Union, 197

Reagan, Ronald, 350–51

Real Estate Bank Estate Bank of Arkansas, 199; created, 109; problems with 109–10; failure of, 110

Reconstruction, 187–214

Reconstruction Finance Corporation (RFC), 267, 272, 304

Rector Anti Trust Act, 243

Rector, Henry, 144–46, 163; and arsenal crisis, 149–50; elected governor, 145; inaugurated as governor, 148; orders militia to seize federal installation at Fort Smith, 152; removes state government from Little Rock to Hot Springs, 160; response to Lincoln's call for troops, 151; returns state government to Little Rock, 162; threatens to secede from the Confederacy, 160

Rector, William F., 339

Red Cross, 253, 255, 285, 289

red ochre, 18

Red River Expedition 178–182. *See also* Camden Expedition

Red River Valley: Caddo Indians, 45–49; Native American communities, 28, 30, 40, 45, 51; Soto expedition, 38

Red River, 59, 66, 67, 77, 82, 87, 88, 98, 100, 117, 130, 136, 174, 178, 182; West Gulf Coastal Plain, 10

Red River, 87, 88, 95, 130, 132, 136

Reed, Roy, 324, 327

Reed's Bridge, Battle of, 174

Reeves, Bass, 218

Referendum, 244

Religion, 115–16, 231–34

religious beliefs and practices (African Americans), 232

religious beliefs and practices (Native Americans): Caddo Indians, 47–48; Mississippi period, 30–31; Osage Indians, 43–44; Paleoindian period, 18; Quapaw Indians, 41–43; Tunica Indians, 50; Woodland period, 26–27

Remmel, H. L., 219

reptiles, 17

Republican Party, 142, 144, 157, 195, 198, 201, 203, 206, 207, 208, 209, 210, 211, 212, 213, 214; accomplishments of in Reconstruction, 211; Agricultural Wheel and Union Labor Party, 219; Black and Tan faction, 259, black suffrage, 197; Joseph Brooks and the insurgent wing of, 204–205; Brooks Baxter War, 206; challenge from former Confederate Democrats, 189, 203, 209; Powell Clayton's leadership of, 197, 198; Samuel Curtis as, 157; divisions on the race question, 259; hatred of, 213; KKK undermines, 202; Lily White faction of, 259; radical element within, 194; recent reorientation to, 330, 348, 368; religious right's relationship to, 349; H. L. Remmel's leadership of, 219; Winthrop Rockefeller and, 302, 343, 349, 350; Jacob Trieber's association with, 232; Union Labor Party's connection to, 226; Frank White and, 350–52

Repudiation of Debt, 219–20

resegregation, 360

Resettlement Administration, 276

rice cultivation: Mississippi Alluvial Valley/Delta region, 13

Rich, Charlie, 375

Riffell, Brent, 333

Right to Work Law, 300–301

Riley, Billy Lee, 375, 376

Rison v. Farr, 189

road and highway system: and the Alexander Road Improvement Act, 254; and the Arkansas roads scandal, 254–55; and the CCC, 277; and Clinton administration, 350; economic impacts, 350; and the Harrelson Road Act, 255; highway bonds, 281, 301; and Huckabee administration, 365–66; interestate highway system, 306–7; and McMath administration, 301; military roads, 86, 90, 117, 171; and Parnell administration, 266; road construction, 77, 225; Southwest Trail, 86, 90, 101, 115, 119, 129, 130; and Tucker administration , 365; World War II, 301

Roane, John Seldon, 120; elected governor, 138; in Mexican War, 120

Robert Thompson (steamboat), 130

Roberts, Terrance, 322

Robinson v. Holman, 362

Robinson, John M., 261–62

Robinson, John, 292

Robinson, Joseph T., 245, 246, 272, 280, 281, 288

rock art (Native American), 25

rock paintings (Native American), 9, 25

rock shelters (Native American), 6, 22, 24

rockabilly, 375

Rockefeller Sanitary Commission, 253

Rockefeller, Winthrop, 302, 343, 349, 350

Rocky Mountains, 15

Rodham, Hillary, 348

Rogers: Springfield Plateau, 5

Rooksbery, W. A., 282

Roosevelt, Franklin Delano, 270, 275, 283

roots (edible), 22: Caddo Indians, 48; Quapaw Indians, 42; Tunica Indians, 50

Roots, Logan, 219

Rose, Jerome C., 353

Rose, U. M., 208, 220

Ross, John, 155, 156; enters Cherokees into alliance with the Confederacy, 156

Rousseau, Pierre, 68

Rural Electrification Administration (REA), 278–79

Russell, Richard, 322

Russell, William, 89

Russellville, 123, 296; Arkansas River Valley, 10

Rust, John D. and Mack, 287

sacred fire (Native American), Caddo Indians, 46; Tunica Indians, 50

Salem Plateau, 5–6

Saline County, 105

salt-making activities (Native Americans): Caddo Indians, 48; Mississippi period, 28; Soto expedition, 36; Tunica Indians, 51

sandstone: bluffs, 6; Ouachita Mountains, 7

Sango nation, 69

Saracen, a French-Quapaw métis, 75, 98, 100

sauropods, 10

scalawags, 196, 206

scalp locks (Osage), 44

Schlafly, Phyllis, 345–46, 347; photograph of, 347

Schoolcraft, Henry Rowe, 6

Scientific Manpower Commission, 345

Scott, 27

Scott, Andrew, W., 88–89

scrappers, blunt-end, 18

Scroggs, Jack B., 103, 105

Searcy County, 6, 154

Searcy, 154, 236

Sears and Roebuck, 376

secession convention: first, 150–51; second, 152

scientific agriculture, 307

Second Congressional District, 364

Second Great Awakening, 115

Second Kansas Colored Infantry, 181

Second Reconstruction Act, 195

sectionalism, 101–2

seeds (Native American): Archaic period, 22–23; Caddo Indians, 48; Quapaw Indians, 42; Tunica Indians, 50 segregation of school taxes, 243–44

segregation, 211–12, 215, 229–30, 231, 236, 239, 242, 243–44, 248, 256, 287, 313–14, 316, 318, 319, 321–22, 323, 324, 325

Selma (Drew County, Arkansas), 263

Seminarians, 62

Seminole Indians, 155, 156

Sequoyah (George Guess), 97

service-sector economy, 330–331, 333, 335

Settlement Agreement, 355–57

settlement patterns (Native American Prehistory): Archaic period, 21, 23, 32; Mississippi period, 21, 28, 30–32; Woodland period, 21, 25–27

settlements (Native American): Caddo Indians, 46–47; Osage Indians, 43; Quapaw Indians, 41; Soto expedition, 34–36; Tunica Indians, 50–51

Seven Years' War, 56, 72, 75

Sevier, Ambrose, 92, 94, 99, 103, 118, 146; appointed minister to Mexico, 138; chosen to be one of state's first US Senators, 107; death of, 138; duel with Robert Newton, 112; reputation harmed by involvement with state banks, 110

Sevier, County, 200, 201

Shadow, The (tv show), 373

shale: Ouachita Mountains, 7

Sharecroppers Union (Alabama), 273

sharecropping (tenancy), 190–91, 212, 222, 265, 308, 309, 312–13

Sharp County, 200

Sharp, Floyd, 282

Shaw, Isaac, 274

Shea, William, 158, 167

shell artifacts (Native American prehistory): Archaic period, 22; beads, 22, 27; bracelets, 22; Mississippi period, 28; necklaces, 22, 27; Woodland period, 25, 27

shellfish, 17: Archaic period, 22; fossil remains, 3, 10; West Gulf Coastal Plain, 10

Sheppard-Towner Act, 253

Sheridan, 181

Sherman, William Tecumseh, 170

Shinn, Joseph H., 237

Shreve, Henry, 130

shrines (Native American prehistory): Mississippi period, 21, 30–31; Woodland period, 27

Shropshire, Jackie L., 317

Shumaker, 288

Siberia, 17

silver, 36

sinew thread, 18, 22

Sipuel, Ada, 316

Sixth Judicial District, 364

Sky People, 41, 43

slavery, 100–102, 131–136; in colonial era, 66–71; laws regulating, 133; miscegenation, 135; Mississippi Alluvial Valley/Delta region, 13; treatment of slaves, 133–34; slave resistance, 134, 135; slave religion, 134, 135; slave-master relations, 135–36

Sloan site, 20

Smackover, 10

smallpox, 39, 58, 253, 263, 264

Smith v. Allwright, 292

Smith, Calvin, 289–91

Smith, Edmund Kirby, 169

Smith, Ken, 217

smoking pipes (stone), 25

snails, 6

snowfall averages, 15

social organization and hierarchies (Native American): Caddo Indians, 47–48; Mississippi period, 29–30; Osage Indians 44–45; Quapaw Indians, 41; Tunica Indians, 50; Woodland period, 27

Socialist party, 273

soils: Buffalo River, 26; Mississippi Alluvial Valley/Delta region, 12–13; Salem Plateau, 5; Springfield Plateau, 5; West Gulf Coastal Plain, 10

soldiers (Soto expedition), 33

Soto expedition accounts, 39; Native American cultural identities, 39; native guides and interpreters, 39; travel routes and place names, 35, 39

Soto, Hernando de, 27, 33–37, 39–40, 233: death and burial, 37; "son of the sun," 37

South America, 34

South Carolina, 220, 345

southeastern Arkansas: Mississippi Alluvial Plain, 10; Native American communities, 28, 50

southeastern Indians, 27, 33

Southern Baptist Convention, 365

Southern Cotton Oil Mill, 313

Southern Historical Association, 269

Southern Manifesto, 321–22

Southern Memorial Association, 235